Causal Learning

Causal Learning

Edited by **David R. Shanks** and **Douglas L. Medin**

Department of Psychology
University College London
London, England

Department of Psychology
Northwestern University
Evanston, Illinois

Keith J. Holyoak

Department of Psychology
University of California, Los Angeles
Los Angeles, California

THE PSYCHOLOGY OF
LEARNING AND MOTIVATION, VOLUME 34
Advances in Research and Theory

ACADEMIC PRESS

San Diego   London   Boston   New York
Sydney   Tokyo   Toronto

Find Us on the Web! http://www.apnet.com

This book is printed on acid-free paper. ∞

Copyright © 1996 by ACADEMIC PRESS, INC.

All Rights Reserved.
No part of this publication may be reproduced or transmitted in any form or by any
means, electronic or mechanical, including photocopy, recording, or any information
storage and retrieval system, without permission in writing from the publisher.

Academic Press, Inc.
A Division of Harcourt Brace & Company
525 B Street, Suite 1900, San Diego, California 92101-4495

United Kingdom Edition published by
Academic Press Limited
24-28 Oval Road, London NW1 7DX

International Standard Serial Number: 0079-7421

International Standard Book Number: 0-12-543334-4

PRINTED IN THE UNITED STATES OF AMERICA
96   97   98   99   00   01   BB   9   8   7   6   5   4   3   2   1

CONTENTS

CAUSATION AND ASSOCIATION

Edward A. Wasserman, Shu-Fang Kao, Linda J. Van Hamme, Masayoshi Katagiri, and Michael E. Young

DISTINGUISHING ASSOCIATIVE AND PROBABILISTIC CONTRAST THEORIES OF HUMAN CONTINGENCY JUDGMENT

David R. Shanks, Francisco J. Lopez, Richard J. Darby, and Anthony Dickinson

A CAUSAL-POWER THEORY OF FOCAL SETS

Patricia W. Cheng, Jooyong Park, Aaron S. Yarlas, and Keith J. Holyoak

CONTRIBUTORS

Numbers in parentheses indicate the pages on which the authors' contributions begin.

A. G. Baker (1), Department of Psychology, McGill University, Montréal, Québec H3A 1B1, Canada

Jerome R. Busemeyer (358), Psychological Sciences, Purdue University, West Lafayette, Indiana 47906

Eunhee Byun (358), Psychological Sciences, Purdue University, West Lafayette, Indiana 47906

Patricia W. Cheng (313), Department of Psychology, University of California, Los Angeles, Los Angeles, California 90095

Richard J. Darby (265), Department of Psychology, University College London, London WC1E 6BT, England

Anthony Dickinson (265), Department of Experimental Psychology, University of Cambridge, Cambridge CB2 3EB, England

Keith J. Holyoak (313), Department of Psychology, University of California, Los Angeles, Los Angeles, California 90095

Shu-Fang Kao (208), Department of Elementary Education, National Hsinchu Teachers College, Hsinchu City, Taiwan, Republic of China

Masoyoshi Katagiri (208), Department of Psychology, Utsunomiya University, Utsunomiya 321, Japan

Francisco J. Lopez (265), Departamento de Psicología Básica, Psicobiología, y Metodología, Universidad de Malaga, Malaga-29071, Spain

Helena Matute (133), Departamento de Psicología Básica, Universidad de Duesto, E-48080 Bilbao, Spain

Mark A. McDaniel (358), Psychology Department, University of New Mexico, Albuquerque, New Mexico 87131

Ralph R. Miller (133), Department of Psychology, State University of New York–Binghamton, Binghamton, New York 13902

Robin A. Murphy (1), Department of Psychology, McGill University, Montréal, Québec H3A 1B1, Canada

Jooyong Park (313), Department of Psychology, University of California, Los Angeles, Los Angeles, California 90095

Judea Pearl (393), Computer Science Department, University of California, Los Angeles, Los Angeles, California 90024

David R. Shanks (265), Department of Psychology, University College London, London WC1E 6BT, England

Barbara A. Spellman (167), Department of Psychology, University of Texas at Austin, Austin, Texas 78712

Frédéric Vallée-Tourangeau (1), Division of Psychology, University of Hertfordshire, Hertfordshire AL10 9AB, United Kingdom

Linda J. Van Hamme (208), Saint Joseph's Indian School, Chamberlain, South Dakota 57325

Michael R. Waldmann (47), Max Planck Institute for Psychological Research, D-80802 Munich, Germany

Edward A. Wasserman (208), Department of Psychology, University of Iowa, Iowa City, Iowa 52242

Douglas A. Williams (89), Psychology Department, University of Winnipeg, Winnipeg, Manitoba R3B 2E9, Canada

Aaron S. Yarlas (313), Department of Psychology, University of California, Los Angeles, Los Angeles, California 90095

Michael E. Young (208), Department of Psychology, University of Iowa, Iowa City, Iowa 52242

PREFACE

This special volume of *The Psychology of Learning and Motivation* series is devoted to the issue of causal learning. The past few years have seen a major surge of interest in the topic of how people acquire knowledge of cause–effect relations in their environment. Several intellectual influences seem to have played an important role in these developments. A number of researchers have obtained evidence of striking parallels between phenomena observed in studies of causal induction in people and classical conditioning in laboratory animals. For over two decades, the most prominent account of many conditioning phenomena has been the Rescorla–Wagner learning model. The recent discovery of parallels between animal conditioning and human causal learning has greatly broadened the potential scope of the Rescorla–Wagner model. Concurrently, recognition of the formal correspondence between the model and the delta rule used to implement learning in some connectionist networks has sparked additional interest. The apparent relevance of the Rescorla–Wagner and other models of animal conditioning to human casual learning has contributed to increased interaction between these research fields.

At the same time, other work on causal induction has been influenced by treatments in the philosophical and artificial intelligence literatures. Such work has emphasized models based on statistical relations between causes and their effects, theories based on general conceptions of causal power, and structural analyses of causal networks. Research based on these approaches has uncovered various phenomena in causal induction that are not readily handled by existing models derived from the conditioning literature. In addition, it has been suggested that certain conditioning phenomena long recognized as problematic for the Rescorla–Wagner model can be understood in terms of models of causal induction.

These alternative theoretical approaches have sparked vigorous debate in the psychological literature. The goal of this special volume is to provide a forum in which different approaches to causal learning are brought together, thereby advancing mutual understanding and contributing to new theoretical integrations. To help achieve this goal the series editor, Douglas Medin, invited two researchers in this area, David Shanks and Keith Holyoak, to serve as guest co-editors. (The names of the guest editors for the volume were ordered by a coin toss.) The three of us identified a number of researchers who have made important contributions to the study of human causal learning. Because of space limitations we had to be highly selective in our invitations. Our aim was not to produce some sort of encyclopedia of causal learning, but rather to provide a selection of exemplary papers that illustrate major approaches to the topic.

The experimental paradigms and theoretical ideas discussed in this volume reflect interactions between several diverse domains. These include work on animal and human contingency learning, between statistical and power-based conceptions of causality, and between psychological and artificial intelligence research on causal inference. We hope that readers with interests in causal learning will find this volume to be a useful point of entry into the field, revealing both the common ground and the controversies that have generated considerable intellectual excitement.

David R. Shanks
Keith J. Holyoak
Douglas L. Medin

ASSOCIATIVE AND NORMATIVE MODELS OF CAUSAL INDUCTION: REACTING TO VERSUS UNDERSTANDING CAUSE

A. G. Baker
Robin A. Murphy
Frédéric Vallée-Tourangeau

I. Two Models for Causal Reasoning

We intend to discuss two views of causal judgment that are roughly analogous to a distinction between being able to react appropriately to causes and being able to understand them. The associationist view is identified with the British Empiricists. It claims that our judgments of cause come from certain empirical cues to causality, which include: (1) regular succession (the effect follows the cause); (2) temporal contiguity; and (3) spatial contiguity (Hume, 1739/1960). These principles were maintained more or less unchanged in the traditional North American associative theories of animal learning and in other connectionist theories (e.g., Gluck & Bower, 1988; Hull, 1943; Rescorla & Wagner, 1972; Spence 1936). Associations between events are strengthened when the events are contiguous and are weakened when an event occurs by itself. These models have the advantage that they are computationally simple and they impose a low memory load on the organism because experience is stored as a small number of associative strengths. They have the disadvantage that information about past events is lost in the computation. In other words, these models do not have episodic memory.

1

The second class of models do involve episodic memory and in their various instantiations seem to incorporate two themes. One theme is an elaboration of the Humean tradition, which relies on empirical cues to causality; it might be traced back to the work of some modern philosophers from the positivist tradition or to Rescorla's (1968) work in conditioning. Mere contiguity is not enough to confirm causal status; rather, the reasoner must consider what happens in the absence of the cause, as well (e.g., Mackie, 1974). Furthermore, the relationship may be probabilistic rather than deterministic. In other words, the covariation of (or correlation between) cause and effect is another empirical cue to causality (e.g., Suppes, 1970). Knowledge of covariation in itself does not imply an understanding of cause. Beyond these expanded empirical cues to causality that exist in the world Kant (1781/1965) argued that another crucial feature for determining causal status was generative transmission. The idea was that a cause seems to impart its effect. As part of the causal process people and possibly other animals have models of cause that actually entail understanding or representing the causal relationship. This process is sometimes called causal power (see Cheng, Park, Yarlas, & Holyoak, this volume, Ch. 8).

We will refer to this second class of models as normative models. They claim that humans and other animals compute the covariation between cause and effect and then use this information as part of a causal model or schema (e.g., Cheng & Novick, 1992; Holyoak, Koh, & Nisbett, 1989; Waldmann & Holyoak, 1992). A contingency table showing the four types of event in a binary cause–effect scenario is shown in Fig. 1. The four events are the four possible conjunctions of the presence and absence of the cause and effect. The entries in the table represent the frequency of each of the conjunctions. For example, A represents the number of times the cause and the effect occur together. Logically each of the four event types has equal status as evidence for the existence of a contingency or causal relationship. The accepted normative statistic that represents the covariation between binary causes and effects is the one-way contingency between cause and effect called Δp (e.g., Allan, 1980). Δp captures the essence of event covariation and is defined as the difference between the conditional probability of an effect given the presence of a cause and the conditional probability of an effect in the absence of a cause: $\Delta p = p(\text{Effect}|\text{Cause}) - p(\text{Effect}|\text{No Cause})$. In terms of event frequencies from Fig. 1, $\Delta p = A/(A + B) - C/(C + D)$.

An example of a normative model that relies on Δp comes from Cheng and Novick (1992). When there is more than one possible cause people calculate Δp for the individual causes but also calculate conditional tests that are the equivalent of interaction contrasts and post hoc tests in an anlaysis of variance. For example, two possible causes (X and Y) may both

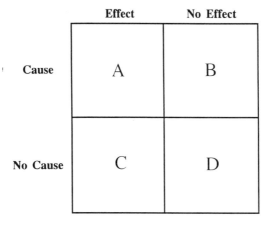

$$\Delta p = [A/(A + B)] - [C/(C + D)]$$
$$V = A\beta_O/(A\beta_O + B\beta_{NoO}) - C\beta_O/(C\beta_O + D\beta_{NoO})$$

Fig. 1. A 2×2 contingency matrix representing the four possible event conjunctions that are required to calculate the conditional relationship between an event and an outcome. The entries (A, B, C, D) are the frequency of each conjunction. Δp is the formula for the one-way contingency of the effect given that cause (Allan, 1980). V is the asymptotic associative strength with unequal βs according to the Rescorla–Wagner model (Wasserman et al., 1993).

be correlated with an effect or outcome. This may occur because they both have causal status or because the two potential causes are themselves correlated. To determine if Cause Y has causal status independent of Cause X one must calculate two Δps based on the presence of Cause X ($\Delta p_{Y|X}$) and the absence of Cause X ($\Delta p_{Y|no\,X}$). If either or both of these terms are not equal to zero then this is evidence for the causal status of Y. These tests of causal independence are very critical and allow this normative model to explain certain apparent departures from Δp. These departures include situations in which the presence of a strong causal feature results in discounting, blocking, or overshadowing of estimates of weaker features (e.g., Baker, Mercier, Vallée-Tourangeau, Frank, & Pan, 1993; Chapman & Robbins, 1990; Kamin, 1969; Shanks & Dickinson, 1987; Wagner, Logan, Haberlandt, & Price, 1968). We have called the fundamental assumptions behind these models retrospective processing: subjects store the information about their experience and then do a normative calculation at the point of decision making (e.g., Baker & Mercier, 1989). This process shares a number of properties with comparator models of animal conditioning (e.g., Miller & Schachtman, 1985).

An important decision that a retrospective normative model must make is the choice of domain in which to do the normative calculation. For example, if animals experience uncorrelated presentation of tones and electric shocks in a Skinner box (Rescorla, 1968) the normative contingency

Δp between the tone and shock is zero because the conditional probability of shock in the presence and the absence of the tones is equal. This, however, is true if the animal's experience only in the conditioning chamber is considered in the calculation of Δp. If some experience from outside the box is included in the calculation of Δp then the conditional probability of the US in the absence of the CS [p(shock|no tone)] will be reduced because the animal experiences neither tones nor shocks outside the box. Therefore Δp becomes positive. Thus the temporal frame that is chosen (Baker & Mercier, 1989) can explain the empirical results in which experience with uncorrelated events sometimes produces no conditioning (Rescorla, 1968) and at other times generates excitatory conditioning (Benedict & Ayres, 1972; Quinsey, 1971).

Cheng and Novick's (1992) idea of a focal set over which events are integrated is very similar to this notion of a temporal frame. The focal set over which contrasts are chosen is critical for calculating Δp and this choice may account for a number of situations in which human causal reasoning appears to depart from the normative. Thus the notion of focal sets is a very powerful theoretical tool. Nevertheless, without an explicit set of rules for their formation and use, focal sets can render theories using them virtually untestable (compare Shanks, 1993, with Melz et al., 1993). One of the crucial concerns for normative modelers is to try to develop principled rather than ad hoc methods for deriving these crucial constraining rules (see Cheng et al., this volume, Ch. 8; Waldmann, this volume, Ch. 2).

In summary then, covariation information is incorporated with other information into causal models that are used to reason about these data. These models have the advantage that, within the computational limits of the organism, they are normative. They allow organisms to maintain an accurate representation of the world and to reason retrospectively about their experience (cf. Baker & Mercier, 1989). They also often allow the organism to retain episodic memories. A disadvantage is that they are often computationally intensive and much of this computation must be done at the time of the decision.

Associative models and those that involve causal models or schema are appropriate to overlapping but not identical domains of information processing. Simple associative ideas can be used in many situations in which contiguity is important but in which mental models might be unlikely, unnecessary, or unavailable. These situations would range from classical conditioning to causal reasoning. Associative models postulate that at some important level information processing in all of these domains is similar, whereas causal models are appropriate only to their prescribed domain because they include domain-specific information (but see Waldmann, this volume, Ch. 2). It is important to mention that in other domains, such as categorization, other formally similar mental models may play an analogous role. Nevertheless, mental models can be used in situations in which associative networks are difficult to apply. For example, because associations are formed on a trial-by-trial basis the organism must receive this experience in order for the associations to develop. However, judgments of cause can be readily elicited with absolutely no dissonance on the part of the subjects if the covariation information is given to them in the form of propositions or in the form of contingency tables (e.g., Baker, Berbrier, & Vallée-Tourangeau, 1989; Cheng & Novick 1990). It is difficult to see how this sort of information could be incorporated into the output layer of an associative network, if networks were the sole explanation of causal judgments. Because the domains of these explanations do not overlap perfectly it is difficult to understand why it might be assumed that they are mutually exclusive. Yet this is the conclusion drawn by scientists who argue that only one of these models is correct. We argue that this is unfortunate and that if an evolutionary perspective is taken, the two classes of models may actually complement one another.

A. AN EVOLUTIONARY PERSPECTIVE

Very few modern scientists would argue that humans and other organisms do not have a great deal in common. For example, it is said that chimpanzees and humans share about 98% of their DNA (Lewontin, 1990). Organisms are made up of systems and each of these systems is subject to natural selection. It is not controversial to argue that the rat and human circulatory systems have much in common. In some circles, however, it is much more controversial to argue that rat and human minds have a great deal in common (see also Miller & Matute, this volume, Ch. 4).

Certainly some abilities must be unique. After all, each species has its own unique adaptations. What may be ignored in the argument that reasoning is unique to humans and therefore not open to a comparative analysis is that humans may not have a single unitary reasoning system. They may have several cognitive systems that have evolved to process different forms of information or perhaps even the same information in different ways. According to evolutionary theory these systems are seen as adaptations to specific selective pressures that they face. Speech and logical thinking may be specific adaptations or may reflect the output of several more general adaptations (Donald, 1991). They involve complex information processing including metacognition, which may include normative components.

But there are other systems that process causal and other covariation information. We must decide when to be nervous or anxious. We must make decisions about when to love, like, or hate a person. If we become ill following a meal we must "decide" which food caused that illness. To make any of these decisions we must somehow process our social or our dietary experience and come up with an answer. Certainly, the process by which this latter decision is made might have more in common with classical conditioning than with philosophical reasoning. It seems odd to us that anyone would argue that the mind that created *Hamlet* was the same mind that developed an aversion to tainted food.

Moreover, it is now commonly argued that rats and other animals have several different neural systems that may each be responsible for different types of learning (Sherry & Schacter, 1987; Squire, 1992). For instance, McDonald and White (1993) argue that in the rat brain the striatum is involved in reinforced stimulus–response learning, that the amygdala mediates learning about events with affective properties, and that the hippocampus represents spatial relationships. It has been argued that instrumental and classical conditioning may involve different anatomical structures (smooth vs. striped muscles) and different associative structures (e.g., Skinner, 1935, 1938). Although the clear distinction between these processes has been rejected, nearly all possible forms of "association" exist in conditioning. These range from simple S–R associations to complex hierarchical "associations" that resemble metacognitions in that a representation of an event comes to signal the existence and present status of an association between two other events (Colwill & Rescorla, 1986; Holland, 1989). Williams (1995, also this volume, Ch. 3) has argued that similar associative structures exist in human learning. Classical cognitive psychologists have returned to the doctrine of separate faculties and have argued that the mind is modular (Fodor, 1983).

Many different probably independent systems in humans and animals must be sensitive to covariation and causal information. If this is so it seems likely that covariation information is processed separately by the several different systems. It also seems reasonable to wonder if the form of the information processing in these separate systems might vary depending on the economic constraints of the system. Why then do many scientists seem to argue that causal reasoning has one structure or the other but not both? Most certainly Western science and philosophy are extremely adversarial, but there lurks a justification from the philosophy of science, namely parsimony. "**2:** economy in the use of means to an end; especially economy of explanation of conformity with Occam's razor" (Merriam-Webster's Tenth New Collegiate Dictionary, 1994). It is considered bad science and philosophy to explain things with two principles when one will do.

We believe that scientists are correct in appealing to parsimony but there are at least two relevant definitions of parsimony. Scientists may often be guided by the wrong one. Another, and primary, definition of parsimony is similar but has a different nuance: "**1:** the quality of being careful with money or resources: thrift" (Merriam-Webster's Tenth New Collegiate Dictionary, 1994). While it may seem useful to describe philosophical systems parsimoniously using a minimum number of principles, there is no reason that cognitive systems should have evolved the minimum possible number of solutions to solve problems of cognition. The aim of psychology is to understand and explain the behavior and cognitions of organisms and not necessarily to develop philosophical systems or to conform to a philosophical ideal. Since cognitive systems have evolved through a process of natural selection, we might expect that strategies for solving problems might not be ideal (Clark, 1989) or that they may be redundant (e.g., Izard, 1993).

Thus, when applying the principle of parsimony, the scientist might better ask the question: "Is this the most efficient solution to this particular problem in terms of the subject's expenditure of resources?" rather than "Can we reduce the number of ideas necessary to explain the system?" It then becomes a question of economics whether one omnibus computational system, which solves all the problems but has more power than is needed for many of the individual applications, is better than a number of individual systems, which are efficiently tailored to handle each problem but which may contain many redundancies. Sometimes evolutionary systems may meet neither criterion for parsimony.

II. Some Empirical Work

Much of our work on human causality and covariation judgments has been motivated by Rescorla and Wagner's associative model (1972). This is ironic because our earliest research in animal learning was directed at pointing out the limitations of the model (e.g., Baker, 1974; Baker & Mackintosh, 1977; Baker & Mercier, 1989; Baker, Mercier, Gabel, & Baker, 1981). Nonetheless, the Rescorla–Wagner model has provided a powerful heuristic and has generated some unexpected and counterintuitive predictions that were initially confirmed (e.g., Baker et al., 1993; Vallée-Tourangeau, Baker, & Mercier, 1994; Wasserman, Elek, Chatlosh, & Baker, 1993). We began our research on human causality judgments with the intention of rapidly eliminating the model from contention. It has, however, proved to be remarkably robust.

We now describe the Rescorla–Wagner model as we have used it and describe some of our published research, which was generated by it and generally supports it. We then dicuss some previously unpublished research that shows some of the limitations of this instantiation of associative ideas. We discuss the strengths and weaknesses of a normative approach to these data as exemplified by the work of Cheng and Novick (1992) and Waldmann and Holyoak (1992).

A. THE RESCORLA–WAGNER MODEL

Rescorla and Wagner (1972) specified how the strength of associations between events develops, over time, on the basis of contiguity alone. Figure 2 shows the simple associative network that this theory represents. This version represents two explicit cues as the input nodes and the outcome as a single output node. A third input node, which represents the context, is present on all training trials. The associative strength of A and B and of the context are calculated with a series of equations of the form:

$$\Delta V_i = \alpha_i \beta_{outcome}(\lambda - \Sigma V)$$

where ΔV_i is the change in associative strength of the cues (A, B, or Context), λ is the maximum associative strength that the outcome will

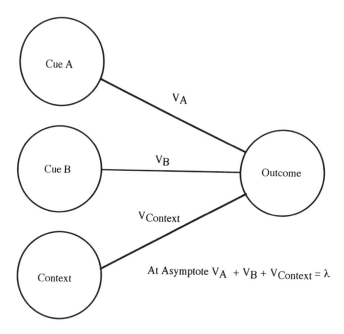

Fig. 2.   Associative model of events and associations formed between causes and an outcome according to the Rescorla–Wagner (1972) model. Training includes two cues (A and B) and a context. V_i refers to the associative strength between the cue and the outcome from the Rescorla–Wagner model.

support (which equals 1 when the outcome is present and 0 when it is absent); α_i is a learning rate parameter that is unique to each cue and roughly represents the salience or associability of that cue, and $\beta_{outcome}$ is a learning rate parameter for the outcome variables. ΣV is the sum of the associative strengths of all cues present on a given trial. When all cues are present, $\Sigma V = (V_A + V_B + V_{Context})$. Thus, a change in associative strength (ΔV_i) is calculated for each predictor that is present on a learning trial. If a cue is not present its associative strength is unaffected.

The changes in associative strength of one cue depend on the sum of the associative strength of all cues present $(V_A + V_B + V_{context})$. Because of this, if one cue acquires associative strength, then any other cue will be less likely to acquire strength because at asymptote the sum of all associative strengths will equal λ: $(V_A + V_B + V_{Context}) = \lambda)$. This leads to what has been called cue competition: if one cue acquires the associative strength, other cues will not. This property of the model is most commonly invoked when there are two cues or explicit causes, but it is important even when there is a single explicit cue.

B. LEARNING ABOUT A SINGLE CUE

When an organism is introduced to a new learning situation, none of the cues will have developed associative strength, in which case the discrepancy between λ and ΣV will be large and the resulting changes in associative strength will be large. Later on as an organism gains experience with the contingency between the predictor variables and the outcome, the sum of the associative strengths of the predictors will approach λ and little further associative strength will be gained. This is to say that when asked to learn about a contingency (Δp) between a cause and effect subjects will show a learning curve. Their initial estimates will be near zero and they will gradually approach λ. Several researchers (Shanks, 1985, 1987; Shanks, Lopez, Darby, & Dickinson, this volume, Ch. 7) have presented evidence that human contingency judgments show a learning curve over time, although in some of our reported work we have failed to observe a learning curve (Baker et al., 1989). A simplified normative view of contingency estimates might predict that individual subjects should not show a learning curve. Even though early on in training there should be a great deal of variablity in estimates because the subjects have a relatively small reservoir of experience, the mean of these estimates should still equal Δp. Normative models can account for learning curves though, if it is assumed that the subjects start with an initial zero bias. With a Bayesian perspective it need only be argued that it takes considerable evidence to overcome this prior knowledge.

Although the Rescorla–Wagner model predicts a learning curve before the asymptote for learning has been reached, at asymptote V_{cue} can approach Δp (Chapman & Robbins, 1990). Wasserman and his colleagues have carried out extensive parametric analyses of subject's accuracy in judging different contingencies between pressing a button and a light flash using a scale of -100 to 100 (Wasserman, Chatlosh, & Neunaber, 1983; Wasserman et al., 1993). Subjects are told to use 100 for a perfect positive relationship between pressing the button and the flash ($\Delta p = 1$; although the subjects are not told about Δp) and -100 for a perfect negative relationship between pressing and the flash ($\Delta p = -1$). In order to produce the contingencies the session is divided into time bins and each bin is coded as containing a response if one or more button pushes have occurred within it, and as no response if there have been no pushes. The light flash outcome occurs at the end of some bins. The occurrence of the light is based on its conditional probability following a bin that includes a response [p(light| response)] and by its conditional probability following a bin without a response [p(light|no response)]. This allows for Δps ranging from -1 to $+1$ because Δp is equal to the difference between these two probabilities. A single Δp value might represent very different total outcome densities (number of flashes) because the frequency of outcomes that make up these conditional probabilities can vary. For example, the $\Delta p = .5$ contingency that is created by combining p(light|response) $= 1$ and p(light|no response) $= .5$ has a higher outcome density than the $\Delta p = .5$ contingency made by combining p(light|response) $= .5$ and p(light|no response) $= 0$.

Wasserman et al. (1993) studied university undergraduates' estimates following exposure to 60 bins of each of 25 contingencies representing 9 different Δps ranging in steps of .25 from -1 to 1. These contingencies are shown in Table I, which shows the nine Δp values and an estimate of the outcome density of each contingency. The contingencies were generated by combining two conditional probabilities from the list (0, .25, .5, .75, 1), one as the p(light|response) and the other as p(light|no response) producing nine different Δps. Outcome density was estimated by taking the mean of the two conditional outcome probabilities from the formula for Δp. This experiment allowed us to closely monitor the subjects' abilities to estimate normatively identical contingencies (contingencies with the same Δp) that varied in outcome density.

The subjects' mean estimates of the nine contingencies for the two relevant experiments (Wasserman et al., 1993, Experiments 1 and 3) are included in Table I and are plotted in Fig. 3A. The regression line between these estimates and Δp is also plotted. These mean estimates are highly correlated with Δp ($r = .97$). Furthermore, the estimates are symmetrical about zero and there is very little evidence of any systematic bias at any contingency. This is a remarkably good performance and is certainly consis-

TABLE I

CALCULATED CONDITIONAL PROBABILITIES[a]

	Contingency								
Density	−1.0	−.75	−.50	−.25	0.0	+.25	+.50	+.75	+1.0
0					(0–0)				
					−.08				
					.00				
.125				(0–.25)		(.25–0)			
				−.41		.14			
				−.29		.29			
.25			(0–.5)		(.25–.25)		(.5–0)		
			−.59		−.05		.37		
			−.50		.00		.50		
.375		(0–.75)		(.25–.50)		(.50–.25)		(.75–0)	
		−.67		−.18		.14		.65	
		−.67		−.21		.21		.67	
.5	(0–1)		(.25–.75)		(.50–.50)		(.75–.25)		(1–0)
	−.79		−.40		−.03		.35		.88
	−.80		−.38		.00		.38		.80
.625		(.25–1)		(.50–.75)		(.75–.5)		(1–.25)	
		−.55		−.15		.15		.51	
		−.51		−.17		.17		.51	
.75			(.5–1)		(.75–.75)		(1–.5)		
			−.32		.05		.33		
			−.30		.00		.30		
.875				(.75–1)		(1–.75)			
				−.09		.11			
				−.13		.13			
1					(1–1)				
					−.01				
					.00				

[a] Outcome density estimate = [p(light|press) + p(light|no press)]/2. Below the probabilities are the mean obtained causal ratings from Experiments 1 and 3 (Wasserman et al., 1993) and below those are the Rescorla–Wagner predictions.

tent with the argument that subjects are sensitive to Δp and as such that they may use this statistic to make judgments in more complex situations.

These data do not allow us to eliminate the alternative position that the estimates are generated by an associative system using the Rescorla–Wagner model, because at asymptote the associative strength of a single cue (V_{cue}) approaches Δp (Chapman & Robbins, 1990). This happens because the model predicts that the associative strength of a single cue is established from a competition between that cue and the experimental

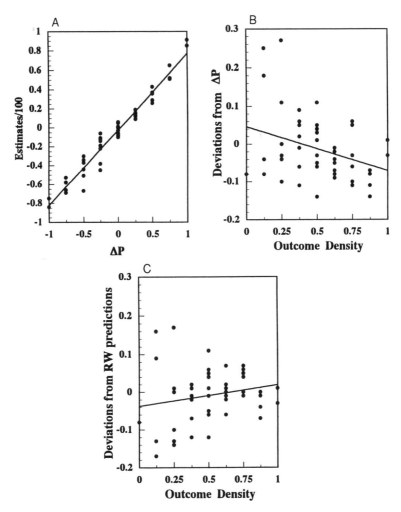

Fig. 3.   (A) Mean subject estimates of the contingency between responding and the outcome in Experiments 1 and 3 of Wasserman et al. (1993) as a function of the actual Δp contingency. (B) Deviations of the estimates from the Δp regression equation as a function of the outcome density for each contingency. (C) Deviations of the subjects' estimates from the Rescorla–Wagner model predictions as a function of outcome density.

context. Because there is a limit to the associative strength available (λ), the context and the cue compete for this associative strength.

When there is a perfect positive correlation between the cue and the outcome, the cue acquires all the associative strength because there are never any trials on which the context occurs by itself and is paired with an outcome. There are, however, many trials on which the context occurs by itself and on which there is no outcome, so the context extinguishes. With imperfect correlations more and more context → outcome pairings occur and the context acquires some associative strength at the expense of the discrete cue. With a zero correlation between cue and outcome, the associative strength of the context becomes positive and that of the cue approaches zero. When the correlation between cue and outcome is negative, fewer and fewer cue → outcome pairings occur. But there will be many more context → outcome pairings causing the context to become excitatory. On trials when there is no outcome, λ is assumed to be zero because the absence of an event cannot directly support associative strength. Because the context will be excitatory it will have a positive associative strength ($V_{context} > 0$), so the linear operator $[(\lambda - \Sigma V) = \lambda - (V_{context} + V_{cue})]$ will be negative and V_{cue} will become negative (inhibitory). Thus, this model, which is based solely on temporal contiguity, is sensitive to the correlation between cause and effect and hence can behave normatively. However, it is important to stress that it does not calculate correlations but rather accumulates associative strength.

We have no quarrel with these assumptions concerning the context and this mechanism for the generation of associative strengths. However, another assumption presumed by Chapman and Robbins is less traditional. In order to demonstrate that at asymptote $\Delta p = V_{cue}$ they assume that the learning rate parameters for the presence and the absence of the outcome are equal ($\beta_{outcome} = \beta_{no\ outcome}$). However, the tradition from animal learning assumes that $\beta_{outcome}$ is greater than $\beta_{no\ outcome}$. With this assumption V_{cue} no longer approaches $\Delta p = [A/(A + B) - C/(C + D)]$ at asymptote but rather approaches

$$V_{cue} = [A\ \beta_{outcome}/(A\ \beta_{outcome} + B\ \beta_{no\ outcome}) \\ - C\ \beta_{outcome}/(C\ \beta_{outcome} + D\ \beta_{no\ outcome})]$$

(Wagner & Rescorla, 1972; Wasserman et al., 1993).

Because Δp was so highly correlated with people's contingency estimates, it would seem folly to reject it and argue that this modified version of V_{cue} provides a better predictor of these estimates. However, in spite of the high correlation between Δp and the estimates, Wasserman et al. (1993, their Fig. 5 and our Table I) showed that there is a fan-shaped relationship between outcome density and the estimates. For any negative or positive contingency the estimates of low outcome density Δps differ more from zero (their absolute values are greater) than the higher density versions of the same contingencies. Here we provide a new analysis of this effect. The fan-shaped relationship is represented in Fig. 3B. In this panel we plot the deviations of the estimates from their own regression on Δp. In order to capture the fact that the estimates for low density negative contingencies are more negative and the estimates of low density positive contingencies are more positive we use the complements of these deviations for the negative values of Δp (their signs are reversed). The slope of the resulting regression line is negative and the moderate ($r = -.33$) correlation is reliable. Thus, even though there is a correlation of about .97 between the means and Δp there is reliable bias in estimates.

The third value shown for each contingency in Table I is the value of V_{cue} for that contingency and density assuming unequal βs. These values are corrected for the range of the estimates by multiplying them by the slope of the regression line between estimates and Δp (.8). They show an outcome density bias that is similar to that found in the subjects' estimates. Wasserman et al. (1993) showed that the subjects' estimates and the Rescorla–Wagner predictions are highly correlated ($r = .99$). To assess the fit of the model we calculated the deviation between the mean estimates and the model and then plotted them against outcome density. In this case the correlation was now modestly positive ($r = .20$) but did not differ reliably from zero. This indicates that the model provides a modestly better fit than Δp. This is quite remarkable when one considers the excellent fit between the estimates and Δp.

Nonetheless, Figure 3C indicates that even V_{cue} does not provide a perfect fit of the data. The deviations are larger for low density correlations than for high density ones. This relationship among the means is also reliable. The absolute value of the deviations is negatively correlated with outcome density ($r = -.52$). Thus there is a relationship between the variance of V_{cue} as a predictor of the outcome and outcome density; nevertheless, V_{cue} is not reliably biased. On the other hand, the relationship between Δp and the estimates is biased. Although the relationship between Δp and estimates is biased and that between V_{cue} and estimates is not, it should also be mentioned that the asymptotic formula for V_{cue} represents a weighted version of Δp. Moreover, subjects ascribe different importance to the various cells of the contingency table (Kao & Wasserman, 1993; Wasserman, Dorner, & Kao, 1990). Could the estimates not be generated from a biased cognitive calculation of Δp and not by the associative mechanism implied by V_{cue}? There are two arguments against this. First, a biased Δp is not normative. Second, in Experiments 2 and 3 of Wasserman et al. (1993) subjects were asked to estimate the conditional probabilities that make up Δp, and although these estimates were biased they did not show the bias that was implied by the pattern of the estimates of Δp.

In conclusion it can be argued that V_{cue} provides an account of the contingency estimates that is very close to the normative statistic Δp. The subjects' estimates are also very close to normative. If this type of information processing is adaptive it is appropriate that both human estimates and any model of them closely approach the normative ideal. However, the subjects' estimates do show a modest departure from Δp; the Rescorla–Wagner model mirrors this bias.

C. COMPETITION BETWEEN TWO DISCRETE CUES

The Rescorla–Wagner model was originally developed to account for experiments in which two discrete cues were each paired in compound with one outcome (e.g., Kamin, 1969; Wagner et al., 1968). The experiments reported here are roughly modeled after the experiment by Wagner et al. (1968) in which two groups of animals were exposed to two compounds consisting of one of two tones (T_1 or T_2) and a common light (L). Half of the trials were followed by an outcome (food or shock in different experiments). Thus, the light was paired with the outcome on half of the trials in both groups. The difference between the groups was in the correlation between the tones and the outcomes. In the correlated group all the T_1L compound trials and none of the T_2L trials were paired with the outcome. In the uncorrelated group half of each type of compound trial was paired with the outcome. On the crucial test the light was presented alone. In the group in which T_1 was not highly correlated with the outcome the light controlled strong conditioning, whereas in the group in which T_1 was perfectly correlated with the outcome the light generated very little conditioned behavior. Although conventionally the term blocking is restricted to another experiment by Kamin (1969), the presence of a highly correlated predictor (T_1) may be said to have blocked conditioning to the light.

The Rescorla–Wagner model accounts for this blocking. In the correlated group T_1 is always paired with the outcome so it can acquire only positive increments in associative strength. The light is also paired with the outcome on the T_1L compound trials but is extinguished on the T_2L trials, so it receives both increments and decrements in associative strength. Over the course of conditioning the associative strength of T_1 becomes quite high and the associative strength of the light becomes low. At asymptote T_1 has acquired much of the available associative strength for those T_1L compound trials and thus the linear operator ($\lambda - \Sigma V$) is very small, so little is learned about the light on future trials. The light was present on all trials and thus overshadowed the experimental context; the context was not included in this explanation but it will be in subsequent ones.

A simplistic normative view cannot handle this phenomenon because the blocked cue has the same unconditional contingency with the outcome in each treatment and therefore should control the same amount of conditioned behavior. However, it acquires differing amounts of conditioning. Waldmann and Holyoak (1992; Melz et al., 1993) have pointed out that this may not be the correct normative interpretation of this phenomenon. Each cue's overall Δp is not the critical factor in determining its informativeness; rather, the subject should be sensitive to two Δps conditional on the presence and the absence of the other cue. This is equivalent to arguing that there are several focal sets available based on the presence and absence of the various cues. A Δp can be calculated within each focal set. In some cue competition experiments these conditional Δps will be lower or higher than the overall Δp for a given cue or they will be undefined. They are undefined when certain cells of the contingency table are missing. When these conditional Δps are low or when they are undefined, this should lead to lower estimates and blocking.

In the correlated group, the light is always present on T_1 trials (this is the T_1 focal set). It is also always paired with the outcome on these trials. However, the light is never absent on any T_1 trials, so the subjects cannot calculate p(Outcome|No Light) in the presence of T_1. Δp_{light} given T_1 is thus undefined and the subjects must guess. When subjects have incomplete information they often choose a low value for Δp particularly when they have a highly correlated factor as an alternative (T_1). The picture is more complex in the control group. Δp for L given either T_1 or T_2 is still undefined because there are no trials on which L is absent. The contingencies for both T_1 and T_2 given L are both zero because the probability of an outcome in the presence or absence of either of them is equal (at 50%). This leaves two cues with zero conditional Δps and one cue with an undefined Δp. However, there is another focal set available. If the experimental context is added, it then becomes an enabling factor (see Cheng & Novick, 1991) that is present on both the compound trials and the intervals between trials. This allows the subjects to establish a focal set based on the context. Within this focal set the light is sometimes present and sometimes absent, so a Δp can be calculated for it. This Δp equals .5 because the probability of an outcome given L is .5 and the probability of an outcome given its absence is 0. Thus, the light is now a moderate positive causal factor and both tones still have Δps equal to zero based on the light.

The above analysis shows that blocking may be a "normative" phenomenon. Furthermore, the Rescorla–Wagner model predicts blocking. Therefore, just as with estimates of single contingencies, it can be seen as a good approximation of the normative. However, as with single cues, when multiple cues are considered, the Rescorla–Wagner model sometimes departs from the normative. We (Baker et al., 1993; Vallée-Tourangeau et al., 1994) have studied a number of this model's predictions using a preparation that was adapted from one first described by Shanks and his colleagues (e.g., Dickinson, Shanks, & Evenden, 1984).

Subjects played a computer video game in which they estimated the causal effectiveness of two predictors of how safe a tank was from exploding. The experiments all involved 40 trials and on each trial a tank traveled through a minefield. The subjects assessed the ability of various camouflaging colors (this is the blocked causal factor and is analogous to the light in Wagner et al., 1968) to hide the tanks from the mines. Camouflaging could make the tank either less visible or easier to see. Thus, the camouflage might make the tank more or less safe. In addition, the mines themselves could vary in effectiveness. The mines might destroy an uncamouflaged tank every time or they might never do so. Any contingency from $+1$ to -1 could be programmed. For example, in a moderate outcome density Δp equal to .5 contingency, the tank would be safe on 75% of the trials in which it was camouflaged, but would be safe on only 25% of the trials in which it was not camouflaged.

A spotter plane served as the second predictor and was the blocking stimulus (T_1) in these experiments. It could be an ally of the tank (spotting the mines and making the tank safer), it could be an ally of the mines, or it could have no effect at all. Thus, the plane could also have a contingency with safety varying from $+1$ to -1. For example, the Δp equal to 0 plane might be paired with the Δp equal to .5 camouflage just described. In this treatment the plane would occur on half of the safe and half of the unsafe camouflage trials. It would also appear on half of the safe and unsafe trials in which the camouflage did not occur.

Table II shows the contingencies and relevant conditional probabilities for the treatments we describe here. Although the original experiments included treatments involving a negative camouflage contingency, we will discuss only those using positive and zero contingencies. The camouflage as the blocked stimulus was either moderately positively correlated with the safety ($\Delta p = .5$) or uncorrelated with safety ($\Delta p = 0$). We used two $\Delta p = .5$ contingencies, which differed in outcome density. In the more dense version the two conditional probabilities were p(Safety|Camouflage) $= .75$ and p(Safety|no Camouflage) $= .25$. We will refer to this contingency as $\Delta p = .5$. In the less dense contingency, outcomes occurred only in the presence of the camouflage. The conditional probabilities were p(Safety|Camouflage) $= .5$ and p(Safety|no Camouflage) $= 0$. We called this contingency PR.5 because it is analogous to the partial reinforcement contingency for the light used by Wagner et al. (1968).

There were three plane contingencies: $\Delta p = 1$, 0, or -1. Thus, we were able to investigate the effects of perfect positive and negative predictors (the planes) on modest and zero predictors (the camouflage). Each treat-

TABLE II

CONDITIONAL PROBABILITIES FOR CAMOUFLAGE AND PLANE CONTINGENCIES

	Camouflage			Plane			Contingencies for tests of conditional independence of camouflage[a]	
Treatment	$p(O|E)$[b]	$p(O|\text{no E})$	Δp	$p(O|E)$	$p(O|\text{no E})$	Δp	$\Delta p_{C|P}$	$\Delta p_{C|\text{nop}}$
.5/0	.75	.25	.5	.5	.5	0	.5	.5
PR.5/0	.5	0	.5	.5	.5	0	.5	.5
.5/1	.75	.25	.5	1	0	1	0	0
PR.5/1	.5	0	.5	1	0	1	undefined	0
.5/−1	.75	.25	.5	0	1	−1	0	0
PR.5/−1	.5	0	.5	0	1	−1	0	undefined
0/0	.5	.5	0	.5	.5	0	0	0
0/1	.5	.5	0	1	0	1	0	0

[a] Tests of conditional independence for camouflage given presence and absence of plane. From Waldmann and Holyoak (1992).

[b] Outcome, O; event, E; camouflage, C; plane, P; partial reinforcement, PR.

ment pairs one of the three camouflage contingencies with one of the three plane contingencies. For example, treatment (PR.5/1) represents a treatment in which the partial reinforcement camouflage contingency is paired with the perfect plane. When compared with estimates of the PR.5/0 contingency, this would answer the question of whether a perfect positive plane will reduce or block subjects' estimates of the PR.5 contingency.

The subjects' estimates of the camouflage contingencies are shown in Fig. 4. Some of the treatments were carried out in several experiments but all of them were procedurally identical. When this was done we report the overall mean. All critical comparisons were carried out within individual experiments and all are statistically reliable. The two left-hand columns show estimates of the two moderate ($\Delta p = .5$) contingencies in the presence of the zero contingency plane. These contingencies are judged as moderately positive and, in spite of the differing outcome densities, equivalent. These two contingencies are discriminated from the control 0/0 contingency shown in the seventh column.

The third and fourth columns show that the presence of a perfect positive plane will block judgments of both modest camouflage contingencies. The Rescorla–Wagner model predicts that this occurs because the plane acquires all of the associative strength. The normative approach also predicts this basic finding. The conditional tests for camouflage contingency in the

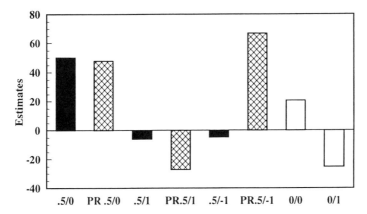

Fig. 4. The mean estimates of the causal relationship between camouflage and safety (outcome) in eight different treatments taken from Baker et al. (1993). The treatment designations refer to the contingency of the camouflage and the contingency of the accompanying plane. For example, .5/0 means the camouflage was presented with a .5 contingency and the plane had a zero contingency. PR, partial reinforcement.

presence and absence of the plane are shown in the two right-hand columns of Table II. This prediction is clear-cut for the .5/1 contingency but is not as obvious for the PR.5/1 contingency because one of the conditional Δps is undefined. With this contingency half of the camouflage occurrences are paired with safety and none of the trials in which the camouflage is absent is paired with safety. Therefore, the perfect plane occurs only on the safe camouflage trials. Thus, in the presence of the plane the Δp for the camouflage is undefined because the camouflage is present on all plane trials and there are no camouflage-absent but plane-present trials to test the likelihood of safety in the absence of camouflage. In the absence of the plane there are no outcomes but the camouflage is present on only a proportion of these plane-absent trials, so Δp is defined and is zero. If the subjects attend to trials on which there are no planes to assess the camouflage contingency then blocking is predicted (see Cheng et al., this volume, Ch. 8, for a justification of this assumption).

Estimates of the camouflage when both moderate positive contingencies were paired with a perfect negative predictor are represented in the fifth and sixth columns of Fig. 4. The estimates for these contingencies differed greatly. The estimates were reduced by the plane in the .5/−1 treatment but they were reliably enhanced in the PR.5/−1 treatment. The first of these results is an asymptotic prediction of the Rescorla–Wagner model. With this treatment, all of the unsafe crossings are paired with the plane. This causes the plane to develop strong negative associative strength. This negative associative strength blocks loss of associative strength by the context on the no outcome trials. The plane-absent context-present trials are all paired with safety, and even though on 75% of them the camouflage is also present and reinforced, as the system approaches asymptote $V_{context}$ approaches λ, V_{plane} approaches $-\lambda$ and $V_{camouflage}$ approaches 0.

The model can also predict the increased estimates of the camouflage which follow the PR.5/−1 treatment, although this is only a transient prediction. Again, there will be blocking of camouflage estimates at asymptote because $V_{context}$ will approach λ. However, early in training, excitation will accrue to the camouflage and the perfect negative plane will partially protect this excitation from extinction. In the control group (PR.5/0) the uncorrelated plane will initially compete with the camouflage for excitation, thus slowing down conditioning. Therefore, early on in training the camouflage will initially be more excitatory in the PR.5/−1 group than in the PR.5/0 group, but at asymptote blocking will occur.

The conditional independence tests of the normative model from Table II also predict blocking in the .5/−1 treatment because both conditional $\Delta ps = 0$. The predictions are not so clear for the PR.5/−1 condition. The conditional Δp for the camouflage in the presence of the plane is zero, since the plane is a perfect predictor, but the conditional Δp for the camouflage in the absence of the plane is not defined because there are only camouflage-present plane-absent trials. Each of these camouflage trials is paired with the outcome. If the focal set for the camouflage in the absence of the plane is then revised to include extra trial experience in which neither camouflaging nor outcomes occur, the conditional Δp for the camouflage would be positive and might even be very high. With these assumptions the enhanced estimates of the camouflage contingency generated by the PR.5/−1 treatment might be represented as normative.

A final result shown in Fig. 4 is that the perfect plane reduces estimates of a zero contingency camouflage. At asymptote this finding is expected by neither the associative nor the normative model. However, prior to asymptote the associative model does predict blocking in the 0/1 treatment. With a zero correlation the context will ultimately garner all the associative strength and the cue will have none; but early in training, because the cue is reinforced in compound with the context, the cue will gain some associative strength that will later be lost. During the 0/1 treatment the plane blocks the acquisition of this initial associative strength.

The four instances of blocking described above and the one example of enhanced responding are predicted by the Rescorla–Wagner model. In comparison, only two of the examples of blocking (treatments .5/1 and .5/−1) are straightforward normative predictions. Two others are also predicted by the normative model but they require resolving the problem of undefined conditional tests and perhaps changing the focal set by adding outside experience (treatments PR.5/1 and PR.5/−1). Finally, the blocking result involving the zero contingency is not normative from any perspective. Thus, our associative model appears to provide a more straightforward account of the results than the normative model. However, two important predictions of the associative model were preasymptotic. At asymptote the model predicts that the mean estimates of the two zero contingency treatments will be equal and it predicts that the enhanced responding following the partial reinforcement treatment will ultimately be lost and blocking will occur.

D.　Asymptotic Learning Experiments

In order to further test these asymptotic and preasymptotic predictions of the Rescorla–Wagner model, we carried out three unpublished experiments designed to ensure that the subjects had reached asymptote before we asked for their final estimates. Our experiments have typically involved exposing the subjects to 40 training trials. In various acquisition experiments subjects usually appear to reach an asymptotic level of prediction within 20 trials (Baker et al., 1989; Shanks, 1987). Furthermore, we usually get reliable blocking at both 20 and 40 trials (Baker et al., 1993). These results would suggest that with our 40-trial procedure we might already be close to asymptote. Nevertheless, we chose to use 120 training trials for these three experiments.

The first experiment investigated the stability of the enhanced responding found in the PR.5/−1 treatment described above. The subjects in this experiment were exposed to three contingencies, each involving the $\Delta p =$ PR.5 camouflage contingency paired with either a perfect positive, zero, or perfect negative plane contingency (treatments PR.5/1, PR.5/0, and PR.5/−1). In the second experiment, subjects received the same three treatments except that the camouflage contingency was our $\Delta p = .5$ contingency in which the conditional probability of an outcome in the presence and absence of the camouflage was .75 and .25, respectively (treatments .5/1, .5/0 and .5/−1). Both the normative and the associative models expect blocking in both treatments and expect this blocking to be stable. The final experiment involved investigating the stability of the blocking of a zero camouflage contingency by a positive plane contingency. In addition to the two appropriate treatments for this comparison (treatments 0/0 and 0/1) we included a treatment in which the camouflage was moderately correlated with the outcome and was paired with a zero contingency plane (treatment .5/0). This treatment was included to ensure that the subjects were able to discriminate the zero contingency from the modest positive contingency. Subjects were asked to estimate the contingency of the camouflage and the plane after 20, 40, and 120 trials.

The mean estimates of the camouflage following 40 and 120 trials are shown in Fig. 5. Figure 5A shows the result of the partial reinforcement contingency experiment. After 40 trials we replicated the basic results of our previous experiments. The perfect plane reduced or blocked estimates, whereas the negative plane enhanced them. The important result of this experiment was that the estimates were much the same after 120 trials. Contrary to the predictions of the Rescorla–Wagner model the enhanced

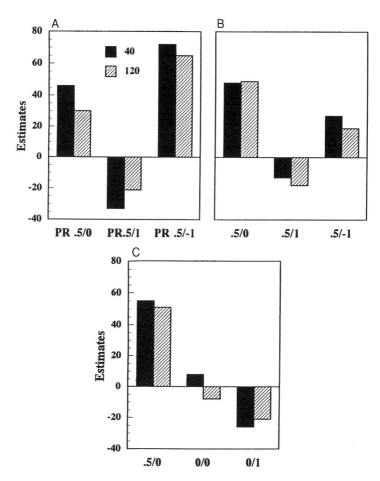

Fig. 5.   The mean subject estimates of the causal relationship between the camouflage and safety (outcome) following 40 and 120 training trials for the asymptotic learning experiments.

estimates to the PR.5/−1 camouflage were still present and showed no evidence of being transient. Figure 5B shows the results of the second experiment in which we found reliable blocking with both a perfect positive and negative plane. As expected by both models this blocking was robust.

The final experiment, shown in Fig. 5C, involved blocking the zero camouflage contingency with the perfect plane. Again, at 40 trials we replicated our previous results. The camouflage was estimated to be modestly positive (at 20 trials it was even more positive) when it was presented in conjunction with a zero plane. The estimates were reliably lower when the camouflage was paired with a positive plane. The subjects also reliably discriminated between the positive camouflage contingency and the zero contingency (treatments 0/0 vs. .5/0). The blocking of a zero contingency was not stable, however. Although the estimates in the 0/1 group stayed relatively constant, the estimates in the 0/0 group declined until they were close to those of the 0/1 treatment and no longer differed reliably from them. This result is in principle consistent with the associative prediction of initial excitation in the 0/0 treatment compared to the 0/1 treatment. This initial excitation will eventually decline as the context acquires associative strength. This decline in estimates, however, took more trials than would be expected by the model using our original parameters.

In conclusion it seems that our results at 40 trials are well predicted by the associative model, which we have used here. In addition, the prediction concerning the transience of the blocking of a zero contingency was at least partially confirmed. The prediction that the enhanced responding in the PR.5/−1 treatment would be transient was clearly not met here. It is possible that our experiments may not have been carried out for a sufficient number of trials to reach asymptote, but this is unlikely. Our subjects report that the 120-trials treatment is very long and, as we mentioned before, asymptote seems to be reached very rapidly in single-cue experiments. We suggest that a better conclusion is that the associative model is inadequate or at least incomplete.

The Rescorla–Wagner model predicts blocking in the PR.5/−1 treatment because of what happens on the trials in which the plane and the context are both present and the camouflage is not. Recall that the plane develops negative associative strength during this treatment. The asymptote for conditioning (λ) is zero because none of these context-plus-plane trials is paired with an outcome and the associative strength of the plane (V_{plane}) is negative. Although V_{context} will be positive, as long as its absolute value is not greater than that of the plane the linear operator $[\lambda - (V_{\text{plane}} + V_{\text{Context}})]$ will be greater than zero. Thus, on these no-outcome trials the context will show positive increments in associative strength. This "excitatory conditioning" to the context is what allows it to ultimately block conditioning to the camouflage. We did not find this expected blocking. This prediction that excitatory conditioning will accrue when a strong inhibitor is extinguished in the presence of a neutral or mildly excitatory cue is one of the most surprising predictions of the Rescorla–Wagner model. It is ironic to note that of our earliest empirical contributions (Baker, 1974) showed that this prediction was not confirmed in fear conditioning in rats. The successes of the Rescorla–Wagner model in predicting causal judgments have shown many parallels with conditioning. So does this failure.

As we have mentioned one of the main advantages of the associative account is its economic parsimony. We also mentioned that a realistic account of information processing might involve both types of system. It is certainly possible that when faced with an unknown contingency, subjects use an associative mechanism to estimate the contingency. Once an initial estimate is made they shift their attention from this process and are resistant to changing estimates. And if something comes along to goad them into assessing events again they may continue with the associative calculation or they may use a retrospective normative system. This notion, that subjects may switch attention away from a cue if they have already developed an expectation based on it, has been anticipated by at least one associative model of conditioning (Pearce & Hall, 1980). Baker and Baker (1985) have discussed this apparent inertia to change in a review of Pavlovian inhibitory conditioning.

E.   ONE CAUSE TWO EFFECTS VERSUS TWO CAUSES ONE EFFECT

We used a scenario in which there were two possible causes and one possible effect in each of the preceding blocking experiments. Baker and Mazmanian (1989) reported an experiment in which they asked whether they would find blocking when they had one cause and two possible effects. Waldmann and Holyoak (1992) have pointed out that this is potentially a very important question.

Waldmann and Holyoak (1992; Waldmann, this volume, Ch. 2) argued that associative systems that are sensitive to covariation will have difficultly in coding the semantic relationship that is involved in having a causal model. Associative systems are sensitive to the covariation that is involved in a causal relationship but they do not understand that causal relationship. When organisms have causal models their reasoning has several properties. First, they are more likely to learn the link between causes and effects than that between effects and causes. Second, causal models imply that it is more likely that causes will compete for control of effects than that effects will compete for causes. Waldmann and Holyoak (1992) reported three experiments that tested their claim that they would find blocking with two causes and one effect but not with one cause and two effects. They argued that because the two procedures were logically symmetrical, an associative net that does not include causal models would predict blocking in both cases.

Baker and Mazmanian (1989) used a procedure in which one cause (pressing a computer space bar) could produce two effects. Pressing the space bar could color the center of either a square or a circle, which were always present on the video screen. This operant procedure was based on the procedure for our single-cue experiments (Wasserman et al., 1993). The session was divided into 1-s bins and at the end of each response or no-response bin the circle and/or the square might be colored depending on the Δps for each response–outcome relationship. The design was very similar to our blocking experiments. Coloring the square was the potential "blocking" stimulus and coloring the circle was the potential "blocked" stimulus. Both perfect positive and negative relationships between pressing the space bar and the square becoming colored were paired with moderate positive and negative relationships between pressing the space bar and the circle becoming colored. Using the terminology from our blocking experiments these treatments would be called: .5/1, .5/0, .5/−1, −.5/1, −.5/0, and −.5/−1. The two schedules were run concurrently. Pushing the space bar might be paired with either, both, or neither stimulus changing color. Baker and Mazmanian asked the question whether a strong effect would reduce learning about a weaker one. Like Waldmann and Holyoak (1992), Baker and Mazmanian found that a strong effect or outcome did not block or reduce judgments of the concurrent second effect. In fact, the strong contingencies modestly enhanced estimates. This finding of enhanced responding in a potential cue competition situation is not unusual in animal conditioning. For example, the presence of a strong flavor will sometimes potentiate or strengthen aversions to a concurrent odor (Durlach & Rescorla, 1980).

This failure to find blocking greatly strengthens Waldmann's and Holyoak's case for the reality of this empirical phenomenon because their empirical evidence was weak. In their first experiment the comparison cue was rated very close to the top of the 10-point scale by all subjects; thus, there must have been very little variance in these ratings. This ceiling effect makes it likely that an individual comparison of this cue with the blocked cue would be statistically reliable. Regardless, the presence of a ceiling effect weakens the null comparison between these two cues and reduces confidence in the interaction between the two-cause and one-cause scenarios. Contrary to their expectations, in the second experiment they found equivalent blocking in the one-cause two-effect and the two-cause one-effect treatments. In the third experiment they got the expected result of no blocking. They did argue that the unexpected blocking in the second experiment was due to competing causal models but they made no direct test of this. Unless we are very careful, the notion of causal models could approach tautology.

What we find particularly interesting here is not the truth of the phenomenon, because we know from animal learning that sometimes cue competition is found and sometimes it is not. Baker and Mazmanian (1989) suggested that the failure to find blocking in the one-cause two-effect case was predicted by the principles embodied in the Rescorla–Wagner model. Yet Waldmann and Holyoak implied that their results ruled out associative models. Why this contradiction? We would like to argue here that many of the properties of causal models, at least in terms of the behavior they generate, are also the properties of associative models. For instance, Fig. 6 shows parts of an associative net that are relevant to the two-cause and one-cause scenarios.

Blocking occurs in the two-cause one-effect case because two predictors are connected to one outcome and they come to share the associative strength that that outcome can support (λ). The sum of the associative strengths of the causes will be limited by λ. In the case of two effects the single cause is connected to each effect by a single bond. Each of these bonds is limited by the separate asymptotic parameter for that effect λ_1 and λ_2. Thus, two output nodes (here, effects) will not compete with one another. Of course, other causes may compete with the single cause for each of the output variables.

The preceding describes the associative principles for one- or two-cause learning. Waldmann and Holyoak also point out that it is important to consider the difference between learning from cause to effect and effect to cause in a single causal relationship. They point out that to do this there must be two associative nets, one with the cause and the other with the effect, as the input nodes. However, we argue here that a single net including causes and effects as both input and output variables would also work. Either structure is less parsimonious than having a simple net with cause on the input level and effects as outputs. This is true, but we have argued that the brain is massively redundant and this traditional use of parsimony is not necessarily appropriate for analyzing evolved systems. There is also considerable evidence from animal associative systems that all of the events in a learning preparation get associated with one another (e.g., Rescorla, 1987). This is consistent with either the idea of multiple networks or the structure we propose.

Superficially it would seem that because these cause–effect and effect–cause connections are identical formally, the associations should also be identical; yet, there are important differences in the strength and other features of these two forms of reasoning. Interestingly, there are abundant

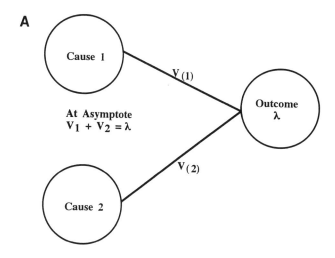

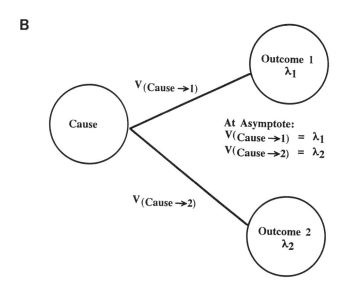

Fig. 6.   A model of the associations assumed to form during learning when either two causes predict one outcome (A) or one cause predicts two outcomes (B).

associative mechanisms that might produce these differences. For example, in some connections the output variable would be the effect and in others the cause would be the output. These two events would certainly have different learning rate parameters associated with them (βs) they also might be expected to be able to support different levels of association (λs). Similar arguments can be made about them as input variables. Furthermore, the cause usually precedes the effect, so in effect $\rightarrow$ cause learning the animal will have only a memory trace of the "reinforcer" available at the time of association. Sometimes backward pairing produces inhibition rather than excitation in conditioning (Moscovitch & LoLordo, 1968). Certainly these differences in temporal order will influence the strength and ease of learning of the two types of associations.

Another property of causal models is that they bias the subject. The subject incorporates true causal information rather easily, sometimes at the expense of other competing covariation information (e.g., Shultz, 1982). This is also true of simple associative systems. For instance, animals are prepared to form associations between flavor and illness but not between audiovisual cues and illness (e.g., Garcia & Koelling, 1966). We do not wish to argue here that all examples of "causal models" follow simple associative principles. Rather, we wish to argue that the functional principles used to derive these models are important and that a wide range of information processing systems have evolved to meet the objectives of a causal mental model. The mechanisms of some of these systems foster a true understanding of cause, whereas others are imitations that merely mimic causal models.

THE CONTEXT AND FOCAL SETS

We have emphasized how important focal sets are for the normative theory. Similarly the experimental context is very important in conditioning theory. Like the focal set, the context gives information about the events that occur within it. Bouton (1993) has provided many important and elegant demonstrations of the role of the context in conditioning. He has reported asymmetries in the contextual control of excitatory conditioning and extinction. For example, he and several others have found that excitatory conditioning transfers easily from one physical context to another, whereas extinction does not do so as readily (Bouton & King, 1983; Bouton & Nelson, 1994; Bouton & Peck, 1989; Lovibond, Preston, & Mackintosh, 1984).

We wondered whether human covariance estimates would show similar asymmetries in context specificity between cues whose values have been enhanced and those that had had their values reduced. In collaboration with two undergraduates (Angela Bissonette and Michael Chuah), we designed an experiment to investigate the context specificity of stimuli that had undergone increases in proportions of pairings with the outcome versus those that had undergone decreases in proportions of pairings. The design of the experiment is shown in Table III. The scenario involved four vehicle types (four cues) on two planets (two contexts or focal sets). The subjects were required to use a scale ranging from 0 to 100 to assess the safety of each type of vehicle during each of the four seasons on the two planets. One planet was a red field on the computer screen and the other a green field. The experiment was divided into two phases, each lasting two seasons (or estimation periods). The first phase was an initial training phase in which two vehicle types were established as positive (safe) and two were established as negative (dangerous). In the second phase one positive cue became negative and one negative cue became positive.

In the initial phase, which lasted for the first two seasons, all four vehicles (referred to by letters A, B, C, D) were presented on both planets. Two of the vehicles (A+, B+) were safe on both planets (they made it safely across the planets on 75% of the trials) the other two vehicles (C−, D−) were dangerous (they made it across 25% of the time). For ease of exposition we will use the term negative to refer to the dangerous 25% safety condition and positive to refer to the 75% safety condition. For the final phase of the experiment only two vehicles were presented on each planet (these planets are referred to as the reversal context). On one planet, one vehicle that had previously been safe remained safe (A+A+) and the second vehicle that had previously been safe had its contingency reversed to unsafe (B+B−). On the other planet one vehicle that had originally been unsafe remained unsafe (C − C−) and the second vehicle that had been unsafe became safe (D−D+). Following each season the subjects rated the safety of all four vehicles on each planet. The table shows the last of these rating

TABLE III

DESIGN OF THE CONTEXT SPECIFICITY EXPERIMENT[a]

Phase (season)	Red planet (Context I)	Green planet (Context II)
Original training	A+, B+, C−, D−	A+, B+, C−, D−
Reversal training	A+, B−	C−, D+
Test	A?, B?, C?, D?	A?, B?, C?, D?

[a] (+) refers to the cue signaling a high probability of the outcome 75%, (−) refers to a low probability of the outcome 25%. Each letter refers to a different vehicle. In the original training two cues were safe 75% of the time (A+, B+) and two cues were dangerous (C−, D−). In the reversal training two cues remained the same (A+, C−) and two were reversed, either from safe to dangerous (B−) or from dangerous to safe (D+). All four vehicles were tested in both contexts.

periods and labels this as the test. On this test each cue was tested in both contexts. It was tested in the reversal context in which it had received its second phase training. It was also tested in the other context in which it had not been trained in the second phase, although it had been trained in this context in the initial phase of the experiment. We call this the transfer context because this is the context to which we wished to see if its phase two training would transfer.

This design allowed us to ask questions concerning the context specificity of changes in estimates of a cue that had had its proportion of pairings increased $(D-D+)$ and of a cue that had had its pairings reduced $(B+B-)$. For each of cues D and B the transfer context had been previously paired with its original value, which is the opposite of the phase two value. Thus, the critical question was whether or not the cue would retain the original value that had been established in that context or whether it would show the new phase two value that had been achieved in the reversal context. It will be recalled that Bouton's research suggests that the extinguished cue $B+B-$ will not maintain the changed value in the transfer context. This preparation allows us to answer questions that could not easily be answered in Bouton's animal research. Before extinction can be carried out in conditioning there must be excitatory training. Thus, it is easy to carry out treatments analogous to $A+A+$ and $B+B-$ but it is not so easy to carry out symmetrical treatments analogous to $C-C-$ and $D-D+$. Therefore, it is not easy to know if the context specificity of extinguished stimuli occurs because extinction involves inhibition (negative values) or because the extinguished stimuli have held two motivationally significant values (have had their value switched). It was possible to answer this question in our experiment. We could ask whether positive or negative estimates that have previously had the opposite value are context specific. We could also determine whether any lack of specificity occurred because the extinguished stimulus had undergone a contingency change and not because of its value at testing time.

The data from the two training phases of the experiment indicated that the subjects could discriminate the safe from the unsafe contingencies. In the first phase in which all four cues were trained in both contexts, mean ratings were around 25 for the two unsafe stimuli $(C-C-$ and $D-D+)$ and around 75 for the safe stimuli $(A+A+$ and $B+B-)$. Similarly, in the second phase of the experiment the subjects maintained their estimates of both control stimuli $(A+A+$ and $C-C-)$ and changed their estimates of the reversed stimuli $(B+B-$ and $D-D+)$.

The subjects' mean final test estimates for the four vehicles in both the second phase reversal context and the other (transfer) context are shown

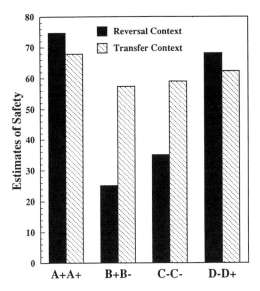

Fig. 7. Mean subject estimates of the probability of safety from explosion (outcome) for each of the four vehicles (A, B, C, D) during the test in either the second phase Reversal context or the Transfer context. (+) refers to a 75% probability of safety; (−) is a 25% probability of safety. The second phase involved a change in safety probability for two of the vehicles (B+B− and D−D+) and no change for the other vehicles (A+A+ and C−C−).

in Fig. 7. On the test the subjects maintained their estimates of the contingencies in the reversal context. Estimates of the A+A+ and D−D+ vehicles were around 75 and estimates of both the B+B− and C−C− vehicles were around 25. The crucial data in this experiment involve the estimates made in the transfer context. The subjects had received no additional training in these contexts, so the critical question was whether the estimates of the two reversed cues (B+B− and D−D+) would remain at their initial training value or switch to the new value, which had been established in the reversal context. The estimates from the B+B− extinction treatment and the A+A+ excitatory control are similar to Bouton's findings from conditioning. Estimates of the positive contingency were maintained positive, but estimates of the switched-to-negative contingency remained positive in the transfer context even though this stimulus had been extinguished in the reversal context. Estimates of the other two contingencies made in the transfer context were also all positive even though the C−C− vehicle had never been positive in either context. Unlike Bouton's interpretation of his conditioning results, this suggests that the context specificity of estimates of negative contingencies may be a general property of these contingencies and not a direct consequence of changing their contingency from positive to negative (i.e., of extinction).

These results show an asymmetry for contextual control of positive and negative stimuli. Estimates of positive stimuli are maintained in both contexts but those of negative stimuli did not survive the context switch. This apparent lack of context specificity of negative stimuli is not a simple artifact of experimental design. Each context was paired with an equal number of safe and unsafe experiences, each had one vehicle change and one stay the same, and the design was symmetrical (i.e., the positive treatments are formally the same as the negative ones). Nonetheless, this is only an initial pilot study and many important questions remain to be answered. What would happen if the switch was to a third context or focal set? What would happen if the training was not balanced in each context with the result that the various transfer contexts themselves would have different meanings? Finally, various control questions need to be asked. Because none of the estimates differed in the transfer context, is it possible that the estimates that we report in this experiment are equivalent to initial estimates when nothing is known about the vehicles?

The contingencies in this experiment were balanced, yet there was an asymmetry in estimates. Therefore, a simple normative perspective would neither explain this experiment nor suggest carrying it out. We do not wish to leave the impression that there is not a normative explanation of this finding. The subjects were given no new experience with the test vehicles in the transfer context, so they may have been unsure of whether the safety of the vehicles had changed. In the absence of any information they may have guessed. With a positive bias favoring safety, this solution would have produced our present results. It should also be mentioned that causal power theory proposed by Cheng et al. (this volume, Ch. 8) predicts asymmetries between positive and negative causes. Positive cues are assessed in the absence of other alternative cues and negative ones are best assessed in the presence of other positive cues. It is not clear how this analysis would help us here because both contexts have the same causal status. Nonetheless, it could predict a general bias whereby negative stimuli are best assessed in the, possibly excitatory, context in which they were established, whereas positive stimuli are less constrained. It is not clear how the increase in estimates for the $C-C-$ treatment would be handled by these ideas.

The Rescorla–Wagner model does not predict this asymmetry either. Responding to a cue is based on the cue's associative strength and that of the context. However, because of the symmetry of experience in the two contexts, each context should have equal associative strength. Therefore, if a cue has associative strength that is appropriate to generate a given estimate in one context, it should also generate the same estimate in the other context. The lack of symmetry between excitatory conditioning and extinction found by Bouton has led him to begin thinking about the role of the context in disambiguating information. He has suggested that the physical context may be important in "gating" inhibitory associations between conditional and unconditional stimuli. That is, to get activation of an inhibitory CS–US association, it is necessary to have the joint presence of the conditional stimulus and the appropriate context. This notion explains why inhibitory associations might be more sensitive to context switches than excitatory associations. He has extended these ideas into the temporal domain, suggesting that elapsed time also represents a context shift and that extinction and some forms of inhibitory learning show less temporal stability through a mechanism similar to that found in a switch of physical context (Bouton, 1993).

This analysis is obviously relevant to our results. We do not wish to debate its merits here because we have not yet collected any appropriate data to assess it. What we are interested in is how having a specified associative model such as the Rescorla–Wagner model is useful even when it fails because it specifies exactly which aspects of the data require a new model. The context defines some focal sets and an associative perspective is beginning to generate some rules for how these focal sets may actually work in selecting experience to be analyzed.

III. Some Concluding Comments

This volume primarily concerns causal induction but most of the research we have discussed concerns learning about covariation. We now bring some of our ideas together.

The first question one may ask is what is causal induction? We have argued that organisms may behave in a normative manner when exposed to causal relationships, and beyond that they may understand them. Humans and other organisms must reason about cause in a wide number of cognitive arenas. For example, we have spent considerable time reasoning about what causes human causal judgments. Physicists used to wonder why billiard balls do what they do. "Ordinary people" may wonder why their lawn has turned brown. At the same time, perhaps deeper down in the brain, "ordinary" people and cognitive psychologists must decide whether to perspire or not in a potentially anxiety-provoking situation. A flatworm must decide whether to contract when presented with a light that has been regularly paired with shock (McConnell, 1966).

This latter case is particularly informative. The flatworm is sensitive to the causal texture of its universe (Tolman & Brunswik, 1935) but it certainly is unlikely to have a causal model. The flatworm is probably "thinking" about the light but the real cause of the shock is not the light; rather, it is the computer that presents the shock or perhaps it is the intentional stance of the scientist who designed the experiment (e.g., Einhorn & Hogarth, 1986). Yet, the behavior of the flatworm is normative. It is behaving in a way that is consistent with the causal texture of its environment. In some sense it has induced the cause. At the level of its behavior and according to this simple test it is acting *as if* it has a causal model.

This is not a semantic distinction because we have been comparing an associative model with a normative model. There are two senses in which subjects may be normative. Just as the flatworm has done they may behave or act normatively. Alternatively they may possess cognitive processes in which normative calculations are actually carried out. Organisms may compute Δp and the interaction contrasts or tests of conditional independence. The proponents of the "normative" view sometimes take this latter strong view. For example, Melz et al. (1993) state subjects will

(a) identify as initial conditionalizing cues those that are noticeably associated with the effect; (b) compute contingencies for each target factor, conditional on the absence of as many conditionalizing cues as possible, thus dynamically revising the set of conditionalizing cues in the process and then (c) use the computed conditional contingencies and/ or unconditional contingencies to produce causal assessments for the cues. (p. 1405)

However, at other times they take a weaker line. For example, Cheng and Novick (1992) state that their theory is specified at only Marr's (1982) computational level. They also describe how animals are "sensitive to contingencies" and offer no mechanism for this sensitivity. This level of analysis is similar to Skinner's (e.g., 1950) model for psychological research in which he said it was appropriate to specify the relationship between input and output variables but to ignore intervening variables (in Marr's terms, algorithms). These empirical rules are similar to the traditional physical laws. Contemporary research on Herrnstein's (1970) matching law provides an example of this strategy from animal learning.

Normative models imply a veridical representation of the world. Δp is a normative statistical description of covariation. As well, if our notion of the causal structure of the world is correct, then mental models of cause including the notion of generative transmission are also normative or veridical representations of the world. The notion that a billiard ball moves because a cue transfers momentum to it and then that this first ball transfers its momentum to a second ball is more normative and veridical than some model whereby the second ball attracts the other objects. In order to develop a normative approach its proponents must provide an analysis of what is normative in the world. They must describe the ideal representation to which cognitive systems might aspire. For example, analysis of the physical structure of blocking in terms of conditional contrasts and thus relabeling the blocking result as "normative" is an important contribution not the least because it suggests that the cognitive process involved might actually be a useful adaptation (Waldmann & Holyoak, 1992; see also Pearl, this volume, Ch. 10). Nevertheless this provides a certain problem for those who wish to interpret this work. First of all, if an accurate representation of the world is thought to be the ideal in terms of adaptive functioning, then all theories that try to represent cause regardless of what their mechanism might be should aspire to that ideal, if the organism is to be adaptive. There are also unlimited possible versions of each type of model and only a finite amount of data. Thus, for any combination of results it is likely that an associative or any other type of model might be generated that would explain it. Any normatively correct result can obviously be generated by a mechanism that applies normative principles, but it is also the "ideal" of all classes of models. This is why much research is aimed at demonstrating normative errors. Such departures from the normative presumably illustrate the properties of the mechanism that the scientist proposes but they also are not the "ideal" of other classes of models. This argument obviously does not apply to the work of Cheng and her colleagues and Waldmann in this volume (Ch. 8 and Ch. 2, respectively) because they study the properties of mental models by artificially varying them and then studying their effects on behavior.

Leaving aside this persistent but not insurmountable problem for normative research we are still left with the problem of the level of analysis of normative theories. Considering only the simpler notion of sensitivity to covariation it is possible that minds may do the actual computation. That is, Δp may be an algorithm of the mind. Alternatively, these tests may represent a description of a state of affairs in the world that the normative group may expect human behavior to meet. In a personal communication Holyoak has suggested to us that the latter, computational, level is closer to their intentions. This leaves the question open as to what the cognitive algorithm might be.

Following Marr's analysis we propose that the Rescorla–Wagner model is one possible algorithm that outlines one way in which cognitive systems may do the computation. At the computational level this model often approximates the normative model, so its output might be mistaken for the output of a competing algorithm that calculates contrasts and implements causal models. For example, at asymptote this model approaches Δp and also many of the conditional contrasts from the probabilistic contrast model (Cheng et al., this volume, Ch. 8). The model is sensitive to contingency but does not calculate it. Also, the Rescorla–Wagner model generates blocking and overshadowing and these phenomena may be normative. But sometimes the Rescorla–Wagner model deviates from the normative. For instance, it predicts learning curves. It also predicts that at asymptote, judgments of contingencies of differing densities will deviate from Δp. This is what we found. We also found that the predictions of the model mapped onto the subjects' estimates better than did their own estimates of the individual conditional probabilities that are necessary to calculate Δp. As well, our own experiments on cue competition have shown that before asymptote the Rescorla–Wagner model predicts the results of a wide range of blocking manipulations that are not easily explained by conditional independence tests. In this article we have also mentioned that these predictions may break down at asymptote.

Again, we do not wish to be identified with the claim that any of the above results cannot be explained by a normative approach. The normative model can predict nearly any result. Subjects first gather data. They then decide on a focal set. They then calculate contrasts. They then decide upon which cue to base conditional tests. This represents another change of focal sets or more precisely maintaining at least three simultaneous focal sets for the calculation of the conditional test. These focal sets include the omnibus focal set and the sets for the presence and absence of the conditionalizing cue. Both subordinate sets must be maintained because interactions must be assessed. Furthermore, the organism cannot know a priori whether the subordinate cue is inhibitory or excitatory. This is Simpson's paradox (see Spellman, this volume, Ch. 5; Waldmann, this volume, Ch. 2). Cheng et al. (this volume, Ch. 8) argue that the conditional test in the presence of the conditionalizing cue is critical for assessing negative cues and the test done in the absence of the conditionalizing cues is critical for assessing positive cues. Depending on the results of the conditional tests subjects may reconsider the focal set. If some of the tests are undefined they might also switch focal sets. Alternatively, because evidence is missing and thus they cannot do an appropriate calculation, they may use some heuristic or merely guess. Once this covariance information has been analyzed, or perhaps in parallel with this process, the subjects apply causal models (see Waldmann, this volume, Ch. 2). Clearly, in the abstract, this general class of models has a great number of degrees of freedom to describe results.

We do not wish to appear critical of the normative model as a cognitive algorithm because we have for many years been arguing that many of the properties of conditioning require an explicit calculation of covariation (e.g., Baker, 1976; however, see Papini & Bitterman, 1990). Some cognitive systems may use a normative algorithm, still others may use an associative algorithm. We do wish to take issue with any possible claim that the two theories are mutually exclusive even within individual judgment systems such as classical fear conditioning in rats or human causality judgments. Some proponents of the normative model seem to hold the position that minds are uniform both within and between species. Once a few principles have been discovered they may be applied willy-nilly. For example, Cheng and Novick (1992) muse

> It seems reasonable to expect that a model of processing limitations should apply across many different types of tasks rather than being specific to inference tasks. Although our model does not specify the algorithm whereby contrasts are computed, abundant evidence shows that people and other animals are indeed sensitive to probabilities and changes in probabilities. (p. 368)

This one quotation shows that, at least at that time: they were not specifying their model as an algorithm; they seem to think that one normative mechanism is appropriate to a wide range of systems both within and between species; and, finally, they might not wish to distinguish between sensitivity to a cause and understanding a cause. Waldmann and Holyoak (1992) end a section in which they describe how causal models may be applied to conditioning by asking, "Is it possible that lower-order associative learning should be reduced to higher order causal induction rather than vice versa?" (Waldmann and Holyoak, 1992, p. 234). Do they mean all learned behavior follows these rules? Do only some systems follow these rules and other systems other rules? If so, which systems and what rules?

Even in "lower order associative learning" in rats it is now believed that some logically identical relationships may generate radically different information structures. For example, Holland (1985) has argued that simultaneous feature negative discriminations (A+, AB−) produce conditioned inhibition and that successive discriminations of this logical structure generate occasion setting. Conditioned inhibition can be represented theoretically by negative associative strengths, whereas occasion setting involves hierarchical associations. In a hierarchical association, one event signals the status of another association. In negative occasion setting the negative occasion setter, a light, may signal that the rule tone leads to food is not in force. Even within a single simple system more than one type of algorithm seems to be running simultaneously. This makes economic sense. Of course, the set of normative algorithms could simultaneously represent both occasion setting and conditioned inhibition but as we argued earlier this may represent overzealous use of Occam's razor.

A. What Is Normative?

Many researchers have argued that Δp is the normative model for judgments of covariation (e.g., Allan, 1980; Chapman & Robbins, 1990). However, others (e.g., Cheng and Novick, 1992; Spellman, this volume, Ch. 5; Wald-mann and Holyoak, 1992) have pointed out quite correctly that once there is more than one potential cause, Δp must be calculated conditional on the presence and the absence of the other causes. Researchers in related areas have argued that Bayes theorem is an appropriate normative model of cognition (cf. Tversky & Kahneman, 1974). Gigerenzer and Murray (1987) have argued that the fundamental tenets of signal detection theory might make a more appropriate model for causal judgments because this theory incorporates the costs and benefits of the decisions. It may be argued that these different views may be special cases of one another or that they are defined over different domains. It is also clear that given particular problems any of them might be "normative" at any given time. Deciding what might be "normative" is not simple and much of the present discussion oversimpli-fies this issue.

For example, we have mentioned that economic concerns are crucial for the evolution of cognitive systems. Signal detection theory represents the cost of false positives and negatives and the benefits of true positives and negatives. These factors bias thresholds for action. If the cost of a mistake was high then it might take a very high Δp to generate a response. An ideal system that includes economic constraints might have a normative covariance module. Some systems that judge causes may need to be exqui-sitely sensitive to covariation. But others do not. There may be cases in which covariation calculations are not necessary. A tainted food source is a case in point. The flavor aversion system may behave normatively without a normative calculation because only novel food sources are likely to pro-duce illness and it might be adaptive to avoid even a potentially tainted source.

In an economic system the norm is to optimize resource allocation. The statistical ideal might involve calculating Δp or doing some other calculation. In a philosophical sense the ideal might be an accurate mental model of cause. Nonetheless, if either of these ideals costs the organism more than it gains by having them, they are not normative.

B. ONE FINAL POINT

In some of the other chapters, a reader of this book will discover that causal models influence behavior in a manner that cannot be described by at least one simple associative model (e.g., Cheng et al., this volume, Ch. 8; Waldmann, this volume, Ch. 2). Furthermore, people behave in a way that is consistent with calculations of conditional tests and calculations of Δp (e.g., Spellman, this volume, Ch. 5). However, elsewhere Shanks et al. (this volume, Ch. 7) have argued persuasively that there is an important aspect of causal induction that cannot be easily accounted for by the normative approach. Finally, our research has shown that neither approach alone can account for even the rather narrow range of tasks that we have used. Rather than arguing that we have "refuted" one class of models or the other or resigning ourselves to feelings of despair, we are more sanguine. We have argued that the cognitive system is modular and that some modules use one mechanism, some use the other, and some may use both. There may, of course, be more than two mechanisms. We argue that from an evolutionary perspective this is as it should be.

This leaves us with a problem involving the issue of testability. It has been argued that without an explicit set of rules the notion of focal sets can become virtually untestable (Shanks, 1993). But we are now not only arguing that the scientist may choose from among many sets of possible rules, but the scientist also has the freedom to choose an associative model to explain the data. Even within the associative systems some may be like the Rescorla–Wagner model but there are many other possible alternatives. Within normative systems, focal sets may be selected by the rules that Cheng et al. (this volume, Ch. 8) suggest, but there is no principled reason why within another system another set of rules might not apply. As well, the output of the systems may have been shaped or constrained by economic selective pressures. If that is not enough, different mechanisms may generate similar behavior. We have already mentioned how systems that are sensitive to cause yet do not understand it may mimic in their behavior systems that truly understand cause. There are many other examples. In this volume Cheng et al. and Waldmann (Ch. 8 and Ch. 2, respectively) have clearly demonstrated that the existence of a causal model may influence what a human learns and the decisions that are made about this learning. However, lower systems act the same way. For instance, an ill rat will associate a flavor rather than an audiovisual cue with the illness. This system is acting *as if* it has a causal model that knows that bad food has toxins and that flavor may provide a means of identifying that bad food.

What systems have true causal reasoning and which ones only react to causes? We can intuitively narrow down the alternatives. Clearly, highly verbal human behavior such as scientific reasoning involves much data accumulation and mental computation and involves causal models, as does much other human behavior. Furthermore, although conditioning systems in other animals react to cause, many of them do not have causal models or accurate representations of covariation (see Dickinson & Shanks, 1995). However, even in the absence of positive tests we can never know that these models do not exist in these simple systems. With these two extremes in mind it becomes of interest to ask questions about intermediate systems. Following this analysis it is of most interest to find animal systems that show as many normative characteristics as possible (Dickinson & Shanks, 1995). Conversely, in humans it is of interest to find systems, and preferably those involving linguistic input, that behave as if they represent cause in an associative manner. This strategy is important because it helps answer questions about the adaptiveness of the different mechanisms. Although it has long been assumed that representing the causal structure of the environment is adaptive, there is precious little objective evidence that this is true. For example, people surely can reason about causes using normative models in some situations, but what is the evidence that this is truly adaptive and not an epiphenomenon? If other systems such as instrumental behavior have converged on this process, then this is evidence that such a cognitive structure is of adaptive significance.

Much of this volume concentrates on causal reasoning in humans. Some research suggests that it is normative and other research suggests that it is associative. What sort of tasks generate associative mechanisms and which normative? At least one variable may be the method of data presentation. In our experiments we have used preparations in which the important contingencies are probabilistic. In these we have generated data that is mostly consistent with an associative framework. Furthermore, we have replicated much of our work in a preparation in which no causal scenario is appropriate. In this preparation we asked subjects to estimate the relationships between geometric figures. Surely this should minimize the contribution of models of cause to the cognitive analysis. Much of the computational burden in these tasks lies in calculating the covariation and subjects have difficulty accurately verbalizing how they make decisions. At the other end of the spectrum are experiments in which the subjects are given the covariance information precalculated as propositions (e.g., Cheng & Novick, 1990). These experiments clearly provide evidence for normative Δp calculations, conditional tests, and causal reasoning. Thus, an associative learning mechanism may more naturally govern causal intuitions when data acquisition is temporally extended and difficult, whereas normative rules of reasoning may figure more prominently when the data is presented precategorized or the acquisition process is very simple.

In many experiments, however, the relationships between cause and effect are deterministic (not probabilistic). An example of a deterministic type of task would be a conditioned inhibition task in which a single cause is always followed by the effect and a compound of that cause and the inhibitory cause is never followed by the effect. In order to represent the contingencies in these tasks the subjects need not calculate $\Delta p;$ rather, they must remember the trial types. Subjects can simply remember the trial types and this gives them data to reason with that is already in a near propositional form. Indeed, Williams (this volume, Ch. 3) has run into this very phenomenon in some of his early experiments on learning about negative causes. Rather than requiring complex calculations, these tasks merely require an accurate memory of the individual types of events. Such tasks are thus in principle very amenable to the development of causal models (e.g., Waldmann, this volume, Ch. 2). However, most researchers who use this type of preparation require their subjects to learn several contingencies at the same time (e.g., Chapman & Robbins, 1990). Thus, even though these procedures still reduce to event-memory tasks and require no covariation calculations, the memory load may sometimes be heavy and the subjects may learn them using associative accumulators. We suggest here that when considering human contingency tasks, those with a high memory load or requiring complex calculations on input may be solved by associative accumulators because these are very good at condensing data. On the other hand, tasks that have lighter computational or memory load seem to be an ideal substrate for a causal model. Finally, the output of the associative accumulator might provide estimates of probabilistic contrasts, which are then acted upon by causal models.

At most we have outlined a few rules of thumb and some evolutionary principles for a true comparative study of how organisms represent causal information. We have not, however, provided an outline of an integrated theory. There was a long tradition of omnibus theories in behaviorist psychology (Hull, 1943) and they have fallen out of favor for good reasons. Students of psychology as early as Pavlov argued that simple associative theories could not handle the complex learning shown by humans and they tried to rectify this by adding a second signal system to their omnibus models (see Luria, 1961). We have also argued that certain normative psychologists treat their principles as an omnibus explanation of a very wide range of behavior, as well. We and others who are true associationists can also be accused of treating the Rescorla–Wagner model as a universal explanation in spite of its obvious failings (Miller, Barnet, & Grahame, 1995). It is a truism that omnibus theories misrepresent the modularity of the mind. Some systems of the mind are sensitive to causes and others understand them.

References

Allan, L. J. (1980). A note on measurement of contingency between two binary variables in judgment tasks. *Bulletin of the Psychonomic Society, 15,* 147–149.

Baker, A. G. (1974). Conditioned inhibition is not the symmetrical opposite of conditioned excitation: A test of the Rescorla-Wagner model. *Learning and Motivation, 5,* 369–379.

Baker, A. G. (1976). Learned irrelevance and learned helplessness: Rats learn that stimuli, reinforcers, and responses are uncorrelated. *Journal of Experimental Psychology: Animal Behavior Processes, 2,* 130–141.

Baker, A. G., & Baker, P. A. (1985). Does inhibition differ from excitation: Proactive interference, contextual conditioning and extinction. In R. R. Miller & N. E. Spear (Eds.), *Information processing in animals: Conditioned inhibition* (pp. 151–183). Hillsdale, NJ: Erlbaum.

Baker, A. G., Berbrier, M. W., & Vallée-Tourangeau, F. (1989). Judgments of a 2 × 2 contingency table: Sequential processing and the learning curve. *Quarterly Journal of Experimental Psychology, 41B,* 65–97.

Baker, A. G., & Mackintosh, N. J. (1977). Excitatory and inhibitory conditioning following uncorrelated presentations of CS and UCS. *Animal Learning and Behavior, 5,* 315–319.

Baker, A. G., & Mazmanian, D. (1989). Selective associations in causality judgments II: A strong causal relationship may facilitate judgments of a weaker one. In *Proceedings of the Eleventh Annual Conference of the Cognitive Science Society* (pp. 538–545). Hillsdale, NJ: Erlbaum.

Baker, A. G., & Mercier, P. (1989). Attention, retrospective processing and cognitive representations. In S. B. Klein & R. R. Mowrer (Eds.), *Contemporary learning theories: Pavlovian conditioning and the status of traditional learning theory* (pp. 85–116). Hillsdale, NJ: Erlbaum.

Baker, A. G., Mercier, P., Gabel, J., & Baker, P. A. (1981). Exposure to the US causes interference with future conditioning: An associative deficit or an analogue to learned helplessness? *Journal of Experimental Psychology: Animal Behavior Processes, 7,* 109–128.

Baker, A. G., Mercier, P., Vallée-Tourangeau, F., Frank, R., & Pan, M. (1993). Selective associations and causality judgments: The presence of a strong causal factor may reduce judgments of a weaker one. *Journal of Experimental Psychology: Learning, Memory, and Cognition, 19,* 414–432.

Benedict, J. O., & Ayres, J. J. B. (1972). Factors affecting conditioning in the truly random control procedure in the rat. *Journal of Comparative and Physiological Psychology, 78,* 323–330.

Bouton, M. E. (1993). Context, time, and memory retrieval in the interference paradigms of Pavlovian conditioning. *Psychological Bulletin, 114,* 80–99.

Bouton, M. E., & King, D. A. (1983). Contextual control of the extinction of conditioned fear: Tests for the associative value of the context. *Journal of Experimental Psychology: Animal Behavior Processes, 9,* 248–265.

Bouton, M. E., & Nelson, J. B. (1994). Context-specificity of target versus feature inhibition in a feature-negative discrimination. *Journal of Experimental Psychology: Animal Behavior Processes, 20,* 51–65.

Bouton, M. E., & Peck, C. A. (1989). Context effects on conditioning, extinction, and reinstatement in an appetitive conditioning preparation. *Animal Learning and Behavior, 17,* 188–198.

Chapman, G. B., & Robbins, S. J. (1990). Cue interaction in human contingency judgment. *Memory & Cognition, 18,* 537–545.

Cheng, P. W., & Novick, L. R. (1990). A probabilistic contrast model of causal induction. *Journal of Personality and Social Psychology, 58,* 545–567.

Cheng, P. W., & Novick, L. R. (1991). Causes versus enabling conditions. *Cognition, 40,* 83–120.

Cheng, P. W., & Novick, L. R. (1992). Covariation in natural causal induction. *Psychological Review, 99,* 365–382.

Clark, A. (1989). *Microcognition.* Cambridge, MA: MIT Press.

Colwill, R. M., & Rescorla, R. A. (1986). Associative structures in instrumental learning. In G. H. Bower (Ed.), *The psychology of learning and motivation* (Vol. 20, pp. 55–104). Orlando, FL: Academic Press.

Dickinson, A., & Shanks, D. (1995). Instrumental action and causal attribution. In D. Sperber, D. Premack, & A. J. Premack (Eds.), *Causal cognition: A multidisciplinary debate* (p. 5–25). Oxford: Clarendon Press.

Dickinson, A., Shanks, D., & Evenden, J. (1984). Judgment of act-outcome contingency: The role of selective attribution. *Quarterly Journal of Experimental Psychology, 36A,* 29–50.

Donald, M. (1991). *Origins of the modern mind.* Cambridge, MA: Harvard University Press.

Durlach, P. J., & Rescorla, R. A. (1980). Potentiation rather than overshadowing in flavor aversion learning: An analysis in terms of within-compound associations. *Journal of Experimental Psychology: Animal Behavior Process, 6,* 175–187.

Einhorn, H. J., & Hogarth, R. M. (1986). Judging probable cause. *Psychological Bulletin, 99,* 3–19.

Fodor, J. A. (1983). *The modularity of mind.* Cambridge, MA: MIT Press.

Garcia, J., & Koelling, R. A. (1966). Relation of cue to consequence in avoidance learning. *Psychonomic Science, 4,* 123–124.

Gigerenzer, G., & Murray, D. J. (1987). *Cognition as intuitive statistics.* Hillsdale, NJ: Erlbaum.

Gluck, M. A., & Bower, G. H. (1988). From conditioning to category learning. *Journal of Experimental Psychology: General, 17,* 227–247.

Herrnstein, R. J. (1970). On the law of effect. *Journal of the Experimental Analysis of Behavior, 13,* 243–266.

Holland, P. C. (1985). The nature of conditioned inhibition in serial and simultaneous feature negative discriminations. In R. R. Miller & N. E. Spear (Eds.), *Information processing in animals: Conditioned inhibition* (pp. 267–297). Hillsdale, NJ: Erlbaum.

Holland, P. C. (1990). Forms of memory in Pavlovian conditioning. In J. L. McGaugh, N. M. Weinberger, & G. Lynch (Eds.), *Brain organization and memory: Cells, systems and circuits* (pp. 78–105). Oxford: Oxford University Press.

Holyoak, K. J., Koh, K., & Nisbett, R. E. (1989). A theory of conditioning: Inductive learning within rule-based default hierarchies. *Psychological Review, 96,* 315–340.

Hull, C. L. (1943). *Principles of behavior.* New York: Appleton-Century-Crofts.

Hume, D. (1960). *A treatise of human nature.* Oxford: Clarendon Press. (Original work published 1739)

Izard, C. E. (1993). Four systems for emotion activation: Cognitive and noncognitive processes. *Psychological Review, 100,* 68–90.

Kamin, L. J. (1969). Selective association and conditioning. In N. J. Mackintosh & W. K. Honig (Eds.), *Fundamental issues in associative learning* (pp. 42–64). Halifax, NS: Dalhousie University Press.

Kant, I. (1965). *Critique of pure reason.* New York: Macmillan. (Original work published 1781)

Kao, S. F., & Wasserman, E. A. (1993). Assessment of an information integration account of contingency judgment with an examination of subjective cell importance and method of information presentation. *Journal of Experimental Psychology: Learning, Memory, and Cognition, 19,* 1363–1386.

Lewontin, L. C. (1990). The evolution of cognition. In D. N. Osherson & E. E. Smith (Eds.), *Thinking: An invitation to cognitive science* (pp. 229–246). Cambridge, MA: MIT Press.

Lovibond, P. F., Preston, G. C., & Mackintosh, N. J. (1984). Context specificity of conditioning, extinction, and latent inhibition. *Journal of Experimental Psychology: Animal Behavior Processes, 10,* 360–375.

Luria, A. R. (1961). *The role of speech in the regulation of normal and abnormal behavior,* New York: Liveright.

Mackie, J. L. (1974). *The cement of the universe.* Oxford: Clarendon Press.

Marr, D. (1982). *Vision.* San Francisco: Freeman.

McConnell, J. V. (1966). Comparative physiology: Learning in invertebrates. *Annual Review of Physiology, 28,* 107–136.

McDonald, R. J., & White, N. M. (1993). A triple dissociation of memory systems: Hippocampus, Amygdala and Dorsal Striatum. *Behavioral Neuroscience, 107,* 3–22.

Melz, E. R., Cheng, P. W., Holyoak, K. J., & Waldmann, M. R. (1993). Cue competition in human categorization: Contingency or the Rescorla-Wagner learning rule? Comments on Shanks (1991). *Journal of Experimental Psychology: Learning, Memory, and Cognition, 19,* 1398–1410.

Merriam-Webster's Collegiate Dictionary (10th ed.). (1994). Springfield, MA: Merriam-Webster.

Miller, R. R., Barnet, R. C., & Grahame, N. J. (1995). Assessment of the Rescorla-Wagner model. *Psychological Bulletin, 117,* 363–386.

Miller, R. R., & Schachtman, T. R. (1985). The several roles of context at the time of retrieval. In P. D. Balsam & A. Tomie (Eds.), *Context and learning* (pp. 167–194). Hillsdale, NJ: Erlbaum.

Moscovitch, A., & LoLordo, V. M. (1968). Role of safety in the Pavlovian backward fear conditioning procedure. *Journal of Comparative and Physiological Psychology, 66,* 673–678.

Papini, M. R., & Bitterman, M. E. (1990). The role of contingency in classical contingency. *Psychological Review, 97,* 396–403.

Pearce, J. M., & Hall, G. (1980). Model for Pavlovian learning: Variations in the effectiveness of conditioned but not unconditioned stimuli. *Psychological Review, 87,* 532–552.

Quinsey, V. J. (1971). Conditioned suppression with no CS-US contingency in the rat. *Canadian Journal of Psychology, 25,* 1–5.

Rescorla, R. A. (1968). Probability of shock in the presence and absence of CS in fear conditioning. *Journal of Comparative and Physiological Psychology, 66,* 1–5.

Rescorla, R. A. (1987). A Pavlovian analysis of goal-directed behavior *American Psychologist, 42,* 119–129.

Rescorla, R. A., & Wagner, A. R. (1972). A theory of Pavlovian conditioning: Variations in the effectiveness of reinforcement and non-reinforcement. In A. H. Black & W. F. Prokasy (Eds.), *Classical conditioning II: Current research and theory* (pp. 64–99). New York: Appleton-Century-Crofts.

Shanks, D. R. (1985). Continuous monitoring of human contingency judgment across trials. *Memory & Cognition, 13,* 158–167.

Shanks, D. R. (1987). Acquisition functions in causality judgment. *Learning and Motivation, 18,* 147–166.

Shanks, D. R. (1993). Associative versus contingency accounts of category learning: Reply to Melz, Cheng, Holyoak, and Waldmann (1993). *Journal of Experimental Psychology: Learning, Memory, and Cognition, 19,* 1411–1423.

Shanks, D. R., & Dickinson, A. (1987). Associative accounts of causality judgment. In G. H. Bower (Ed.), *The psychology of learning and motivation* (Vol. 21, pp. 229–261). San Diego, CA: Academic Press.

Sherry, D. F., & Schacter, D. L. (1987). The evolution of multiple memory systems. *Psychological Review, 94,* 439–454.

Shultz, T. R. (1982). Rules of causal attribution. *Monographs of the Society for Research in Child Development, 47*(1, Serial No. 194).

Skinner, B. F. (1935). Two types of conditioned reflex and a pseudo type. *Journal of General Psychology, 12,* 66–77.

Skinner, B. F. (1938). *The behavior of organisms: An experimental analysis.* New York: Appleton-Century-Crofts.

Skinner, B. F. (1950). Are theories of learning necessary? *Psychological Review, 57,* 193–216.

Spence, K. W. (1936). The nature of discrimination learning in animals. *Psychological Review, 43,* 427–449.

Squire, L. R. (1992). Memory and the hippocampus: A synthesis from findings with rats, monkeys, and humans. *Psychological Review, 99,* 195–231.

Suppes, P. (1970). *A probabilistic theory of causality.* Amsterdam: North-Holland.

Tolman, E. C., & Brunswik, E. (1935). The organism and the causal texture of the environment. *Psychological Review, 42,* 43–77.

Tversky, A., & Kahneman, D. (1974). Judgment under uncertainty: Heuristics and biases. *Science, 185,* 1124–1131.

Vallée-Tourangeau, F., Baker, A. G., & Mercier, P. (1994). Discounting in causality and covariation judgements. *Quarterly Journal of Experimental Psychology, 47B,* 151–171.

Wagner, A. R., Logan, F. A., Haberlandt, K., & Price, T. (1968). Stimulus selection in animal discrimination learning. *Journal of Experimental Psychology, 76,* 171–180.

Wagner, A. R., & Rescorla, R. A. (1972). Inhibition of Pavlovian conditioning: Application of a theory. In R. A. Boakes & M. S. Halliday (Eds.), *Inhibition and learning.* London: Academic Press.

Waldmann, M. R., & Holyoak, K. J. (1992). Predictive and diagnostic learning within causal models: Asymmetries in cue competition. *Journal of Experimental Psychology: General, 121,* 222–236.

Wasserman, E. A., Chatlosh, D. L., & Neunaber, D. J. (1983). Factors affecting judgments of response-outcome contingencies under free-operant procedures. *Learning and Motivation, 14,* 406–432.

Wasserman, E. A., Dorner, W. W., & Kao, S. F. (1990). Contributions of specific cell information to judgments of interevent contingency. *Journal of Experimental Psychology: Learning, Memory, and Cognition, 16,* 509–521.

Wasserman, E. A., Elek, S. M., Chatlosh, D. L., & Baker, A. G. (1993). Rating causal relations: Role of probability judgments of response outcome contingency. *Journal of Experimental Psychology: Learning, Memory, and Cognition, 19,* 174–188.

Williams, D. A. (1995). Forms of inhibition in animal and human learning. *Journal of Experimental Psychology: Animal Behavior Processes, 21,* 129–142.

KNOWLEDGE-BASED CAUSAL INDUCTION

Michael R. Waldmann

I. Introduction

Our ability to acquire causal knowledge is central for our survival. Causal knowledge allows us to predict future events and to plan actions to achieve goals. The importance of causal knowledge is the reason why this topic has attracted many philosophers and psychologists in the past. Philosophical analyses tend to focus on the ontological characteristics of causality, whereas psychological theories are primarily interested in the processes of acquiring and representing causal knowledge. Despite this apparent division of labor, the two approaches are strongly connected. For example, David Hume, one of the forefathers of modern views on causality, claimed that everything we possibly know about the causal texture in the world is based on associations between perceived events (Hume, 1739/1978; 1748/1977). This view has proven extremely influential. It still dominates modern psychological thinking on causality. However, many of Hume's insights, which have been preserved in modern *philosophical* analyses, have actually been lost in current *psychological* theories that tried to reconcile Hume's view with modern psychological learning theories.

II. The Associative View

A. Hume's Heritage

David Hume has influenced modern thinking about causality more than other philosophers (see Mackie, 1974). Hume may be viewed as the forefather of modern psychological theories that try to reduce causal knowledge to associative links (see Shanks, 1993; Shanks & Dickinson, 1987; Wasserman, 1990; Young, 1995). Hume postulated three types of associations: (1) resemblance; (2) spatiotemporal contiguity; and (3) cause–effect relations. Thus, he clearly differentiated between associations that are based on spatiotemporally contiguous single events, and those based on cause and effect. Causal associations are accompanied by the impression of a "necessary connexion." One of Hume's main interests was the question of what this impression is based on. The traditional answer that forms the background of Hume's theory postulated that causal impressions are based on the observation of *causal powers* that are transmitted from causes to effects. By contrast, Hume, being an Empiricist, assumed that all our reasoning is based on the observation of singular separated events. This ontological framework made it impossible for him to find anything like causal processes or powers. Instead he concluded that the impression of a necessary connection between causes and effects is actually a *cognitive illusion* based on an associative relation (i.e., "habit," "custom") that is caused by *repeated* observations of paired events. According to Hume (1739/1978), causal impressions are formed when the following three constraints are met:

(1) The cause and effect must be contiguous in space and time.
(2) The cause must be prior to the effect.
(3) There must be a constant union betwixt the cause and effect. "Tis chiefly this quality, that constitutes the relation." (p. 173)

Hume, particularly in his later work (Hume, 1748/1977), did not deny that causal powers may exist in the world. However, he insisted that we are unable to observe causal powers directly. Our causal impressions are based on the strength of associative links. Like his modern successors (see Wasserman, 1993), Hume thought that the importance of causal knowledge for our survival is the reason why causal impressions are based on low-level mechanical processes rather than higher order reasoning:

It is more comfortable to the ordinary wisdom of nature to secure so necessary an act of mind, by some instinct or mechanical tendency, which may be infallible in its operations, may discover itself at the first appearance of life and thought, and may be independent of all the laboured deductions of the understanding. (Hume, 1748/1977, p. 37)

B. FROM STIMULUS–RESPONSE LEARNING TO CAUSAL INDUCTION

Even though Hume's philosophy may be viewed as a predecessor of modern learning theories, the adoption of Hume's theory of causal induction is a relatively late achievement, and did not occur without costs. The traditional, behavioristically oriented learning theories viewed learning as the acquisition of associative links between stimuli and response (e.g., Pavlov, 1927), or behavior and outcomes (e.g., Thorndike, 1911). In the past 20 years, a new cognitive view of associative learning emerged that bears much more resemblance to Hume's view than to traditional reflex-oriented theories. This approach can be traced back to Tolman and Brunswik's (1935) work in which they argued that the primary goal of learning is the discovery of the causal texture of the world. Mackintosh (1983) summarizes the modern view:

> The suggestion, then, is that as a result of conditioning animals acquire knowledge about their environment which maps the relationship between events occurring in that environment. The function of conditioning, it has been suggested, is precisely to enable animals to discover the causal structure of their world. . . . (p. 11)

According to this view, Pavlov's dogs learned to predict food on the basis of the tone cue, rather than simply strengthening a reflex between the cue and the salivating response. However, in the process of translating Hume's causes and effects into the behaviorist language of stimuli and responses, some of Hume's insights were lost. Most notably, Hume's conceptual distinction between causes and effects that is reflected in his temporal priority assumption was dropped when the cue–outcome terminology of early reflex psychology was preserved. Unlike Hume, modern psychological theories of associative learning typically describe learning as the acquisition of associative links between *cues* and *outcomes* rather than causes and effects.[1] Most saliently, associative theories still use the terms "conditioned stimuli" (CS) and "unconditioned stimuli" (US) when describing human and animal causal learning.

The reduction of causes and effects to cues and outcomes is motivated by the behaviorist background assumptions of psychological associationism. The organism is conceived of as responding to the actual stimuli regardless of what type of events these stimuli actually represent. Cues play a double causal role. On one hand, they represent events in the outside world. These events may be causes or effects. On the other hand cues *cause* responses, sometimes via the representation of intermediate steps. The associative

---

[1] In order to clarify the difference between causal-model theory and associative theories, a generic paradigmatic case of associative learning theory is discussed here. This chapter focuses on associative theories of human causal induction, not on associative learning in general. In this area, the Rescorla–Wagner theory currently dominates (Rescorla & Wagner, 1972), and will therefore primarily be discussed. However, some alternative associative theories that have been proposed in the context of human causal induction will also be discussed briefly.

links between cues and outcomes reflect the strength of this *internal* causal effectiveness of cues. Typically the strength of associative weights is conceived of as representing the organism's assessment of the strength of causal relations between causes and effects. However, whether or not the internal causal relation between cues and outcomes reflects causal relations between actual causes and effects rather than other types of event relations is simply a matter of coincidence.

This reductionism to a nonrepresentational theory of learning (see also Gallistel, 1990) about causal relations is already apparent in Tolman and Brunswik's (1935) theory. Object perception, for example, is described as based on the causal relation between the distal stimulus, the object, and the proximal stimulus, the cue. The cue is the effect of the object. However, this causal relationship is lost when the authors switch from the description of the outside world to their psychological theory of object perception. This process is described as involving a process of cue integration irrespective of the causal role of the events corresponding to the cues.

Sometimes it has been implicitly assumed that cues (CS) typically code causes and outcomes (US) code effects (e.g., Van Hamme, Kao, & Wasserman, 1993; Esmoris-Arranz, Miller, & Matute, 1995), so that "CS" is just a shorthand for "cause," and "US" for "effect." However, this correspondence holds only for learning situations in which the organism is presented with causes as the learning input, when it generates a prediction parallel to the unfolding of the causal processes in the world, and then compares its prediction with the observed effects. Not all learning is stimulus bound in this sense. Learning situations may be constructed in which the information processing system responds to effect cues, and tries to figure out the causes of these effects (e.g., Waldmann & Holyoak, 1992). In this situation the internal causes of the response, the cues, correspond to effects in the outside world. Thus, the causal relations expressed by the associative links that trigger the response do not reflect the causal relations of the corresponding events in the world.

In summary, associative learning theories view causal induction as a data-driven process in which causes and effects are represented as cues and outcomes. Learning involves the acquisition of associative links between cues and outcomes. The primary role of these links is the elicitation of outcome representations. These links may reflect causal relations between causes and effects in situations in which cues actually represent causes. However, this correspondence is not a consequence of associative weights actually *representing* causal relations; it is rather a fortuitous coincidence of a restricted set of learning situations.

III. Causal-Model Theory

The majority of theories of causal induction focus on bottom-up processes of knowledge acquisition (e.g., Anderson, 1990; Cheng, 1993; Shanks & Dickinson, 1987). Typically the potential impact of domain-specific knowledge on the learning process is acknowledged but it is argued that learning can be studied separately from knowledge influencing the learning process. Associative theories, for example, may accommodate knowledge influences by assuming that in some learning situations the learning process starts with associative weights that have been transferred from previous learning occasions (see Alloy & Tabachnik, 1984; Choi, McDaniel, & Busemeyer, 1993). Similarly, the probabilistic contrast theory (Cheng, 1993; see also Cheng, Park, Yarlas, & Holyoak, this volume, Ch. 8) focuses on data-driven processes that generate causal knowledge as the output of the processing of statistical contingency information. The acquired knowledge may then be the basis of further learning. Thus, both research paradigms assume that causal knowledge is primarily acquired by means of bottom-up processes. This knowledge may then later affect learning, but bottom-up acquisition of causal knowledge and top-down influences are viewed as two processes that can be studied separately and independent of each other.

By contrast, causal-model theory (Waldmann & Holyoak, 1992; Waldmann, Holyoak, & Fratianne, 1995) assumes that the acquisition of causal knowledge is characterized by an interaction of data-driven and knowledge-driven processes (see also Wisniewski & Medin, 1994, for a similar view). This view is compatible with many findings that demonstrate the impact of *domain-specific* knowledge on learning (see Murphy & Medin, 1985). However, causal-model theory pursues the more ambitious goal of demonstrating that knowledge also influences learning in situations in which no prior domain-specific knowledge is available. It is assumed that in these situations more *abstract* kinds of knowledge are activated. Causal-model theory generally claims that causal induction is guided by knowledge. Causal models provide the basis for the interpretation of the learning input. The "tight coupling" (Wisniewski & Medin, 1994) between the learning input and top-down interpretations is the reason why knowledge and learning cannot be studied separately. The assumption of a necessary interaction between experience and abstract knowledge in the process of knowledge acquisition can be traced back to Kant's (1781/1950) philosophy. Kant postulated in his criticism of Empiricist philosophies that knowledge is possible only when the sensory input is interpreted by a priori categories of knowledge. Even though causal-model theory does not subscribe to Kant's particular view on causality (see Mackie's, 1974, critical review), its general tenet that the learning input interacts with interpretative processes is in the spirit of Kant's epistemology.

Causal models provide the basis for the flexible interpretation of the learning input. Unlike in associative theories, the learning cues can be assigned flexibly to represent causes or effects in the causal representation of the learning situation. Causal-model theory postulates that causal induction attempts to arrive at adequate *representations* of the world regardless of the order in which information about the constituents of these representations is acquired.

A.   Causal Directionality

One of the most important examples of abstract causal knowledge that may affect the processing of the learning input is knowledge about causal directionality. We know that the causal arrow is directed from causes to their effects and not the other way around. This fundamental property of causal relations is of the utmost pragmatic importance as it provides the basis for our ability to reach goals. Effects can be achieved by manipulating causes but causes cannot be accomplished by manipulating their effects. Thus, it is extremely important to be able to distinguish between causes and effects.

Accounting for causal asymmetry presents a problem for many philosophical theories of causality. Bromberger (1966) criticized Hempel's (1965) seminal theory of deductive-nomological explanation using the example of a flagpole: We can explain the length of a shadow cast by a flagpole by premises that include a statement about the length of the flagpole, the elevation of the sun, and the laws of the propagation of light. But, equally, we can derive the height of the flagpole from the length of the shadow, the elevation of the sun, and the laws of the propagation of light. Both are perfect examples of deductive-nomological explanations. Therefore, this scheme does not account for the fundamental property of causal asymmetry. Similarly, theories characterizing causes as necessary and/or sufficient conditions of their effects fail in this regard, since it is equally true that effects are necessary and/or sufficient conditions of their causes (Mackie, 1974; von Wright, 1971).

Probabilistic theories of causality represent a more recent approach (Eells, 1991; Salmon, 1971; Suppes, 1970). Roughly, it has been proposed that *causes alter the probabilities of their effects.* This idea has been adopted by psychologists who propose that causal induction involves the acquisition of knowledge about *contingencies* between causes and effects (Cheng & Novick, 1992; Cheng et al., this volume, Ch. 8; Jenkins & Ward, 1965; Pearl, this volume, Ch. 10; Wasserman, Chatlosh, & Neunaber, 1983). Formally, an (unconditional) contingency (Δp) can be defined as the difference between the conditional probability of a target effect E given the presence of a potential causal factor C and its probability given the absence of the factor (~C), that is,

$$\Delta p = p(E|C) - p(E|\sim C). \tag{1}$$

This formula allows for the representation of positive, excitatory causes ($\Delta p > 0$) and negative, inhibitory causes ($\Delta p < 0$). Contingencies per se also do not account for causal asymmetry. The problem arises from the fact that statistical correlations are symmetric. When a cause raises the probability of its effect, the reverse is typically also true, namely that the effect raises the probability of its cause.

Finally, associative accounts also fail to reflect the priority of causes. In most theories, associative weights are directed from cues to outcomes regardless of whether the cues represent causes or effects (see Waldmann & Holyoak, 1992).

In order to account for causal directionality, philosophical theories have typically followed Hume's lead and have included additional assumptions in their definitions of causality. Like Hume, many theorists added a criterion of temporal precedence as a basic characteristic of causal relations: causes temporally precede their effects (see Eells, 1991; Suppes, 1970). Psychologists who postulate that causal induction involves learning about statistical contingencies have also embraced this additional background assumption (Cheng & Novick, 1992; Einhorn & Hogarth, 1986).

Another frequently discussed criterion of causal directionality emphasizes the fact that the active manipulation of causes produces their effects but not the other way around (see Mackie, 1974; von Wright, 1971). Our ability to actively *intervene* in the processes taking place in the world allows us to impose a causal structure on the pattern of observed event covariations. The importance of our actions for our understanding of causality has also been elaborated by Piaget (1930).

A statistical method to distinguish between causes and effects has been proposed by the philosopher Reichenbach (1956, see also Pearl, 1988, this volume, Ch. 10; Salmon, 1984). In situations with multiple causes and multiple effects a typical statistical pattern emerges. Multiple correlated effects are rendered conditionally independent once their common cause is held fixed, but multiple causes cannot be rendered conditionally independent by holding fixed their common effect. A famous example involves a group of actors who suffer from a stomach disease after having dined together. Even though there is a small chance that this is a coincidence, the more plausible hypothesis is that food poisoning is the common cause of their illnesses. Conditional on the common cause of food poisoning, the individual illnesses are independent. As Reichenbach points out in his *principle of the common cause,* coincidences, may be explained by a common cause but not by a common effect. According to Reichenbach, this typical statistical pattern is a characteristic feature of the physical world. Philosophical theories that model causality as the transmission of energy (Fair, 1979), conserved quantities (Dowe, 1992), or information (Salmon, 1984) derive this feature from the fundamental physical fact that the paths of multiple causes converging on a common effect meet, whereas multiple effects emerging from a common cause are reached on independent paths.

Finally, it has been proposed that causal directionality is based on the coherence of a postulated new causal relation with our general world knowledge (Kitcher, 1989). Postulating the flagpole as the cause of the shadow rather than the reverse certainly fits better with our prior knowledge about characteristics of physical objects.

Background assumptions about differences between causes and effects have often been implicitly invoked in psychological experiments even though they have rarely been explicitly acknowledged. The experiments of Wasserman and his colleagues may suffice as one example (see Wasserman, 1990). In a typical set of experiments, Wasserman et al. (1983) presented the participants in their experiments with the task of periodically pressing a key and subsequently observing the state of a light. Wassserman et al. found that the ratings of the causal effectiveness of the key pressing corresponded surprisingly well with the objective contingencies. This is a task in which no specific knowledge about the event relations was available. However, abstract knowledge may have helped to assign causal roles to the events so that the proper cause–effect contingencies could be computed. First, the causes (key pressing) occurred *temporally prior* to the effects (temporal priority criterion). The participants were requested to actively manipulate these causes by pressing keys (intervention criterion). The rating instructions suggested the causal roles of the events (instruction-based assignment), and, finally, interpreting key presses as causes and lights as effects is certainly more consistent with our world knowledge than other assumptions (coherence criterion). This is an example of how several of the criteria of causal directionality may converge.

Causal-model theory is based on the assumption that causal induction cannot solely be based on the processing of statistical information. Additional top-down assumptions, for example, about causal directionality, have to guide the processing of the learning input. In the next sections, a number of empirical studies are reported that show how abstract knowledge interacts with the processing of the learning input. The next section presents experiments that investigated the ease of acquiring different category structures; it is shown that prior assumptions about patterns of causal directionality influence the learning of otherwise identical learning inputs. Section

IIIC focuses on one of the most important assumptions of current associative learning theories. The majority of these theories postulate cue competition. Experiments are presented that show that cue competition in fact interacts with the causal role of the cues. These results are a further demonstration of the impact of assumptions about causal directionality. In Section IIID a different example of the interaction between knowledge and learning is presented. It is shown that the way statistical contingencies between a putative cause and an effect are computed is influenced by background assumptions about the causal relevance of additional, potential cofactors This background knowledge has to be in place at the outset of the induction process in order to guide the acquisition of new knowledge. Section IIIE discusses the place of causal–model theory within the debate between theorists that view causal induction as based on the processing of statistical covariations and theorists who focus instead on causal mechanisms. A reconciliation between these two apparently different stances is offered. Section IIIF, finally, shows that not only prior assumptions about the causal role of the learning cues but also the order in which the learning input is presented may affect the causal representation of a learning situation.

B. CAUSAL MODELS AND THE LEARNING OF CATEGORY STRUCTURES

In order to test causal-model theory against associationist theories of categorization, Waldmann et al. (1995) designed a learning task in which participants received identical cues and had to learn identical outcomes, while the causal roles of the cues were varied. Standard associationist theories of categorization that model learning as the acquisition of associative weights between cues and outcomes would treat these tasks identically regardless of the causal status of the cues and the outcomes (e.g., Gluck & Bower, 1988a; Shanks, 1991; Shanks & Lopez, in press). By contrast, causal-model theory claims that participants should be sensitive to the causal roles of the cues and the outcomes, and to the different structural implications of the causal models that are used to interpret the learning input (see also Eddy, 1982; Tversky & Kahneman, 1980).

Figure 1 depicts the two causal models that were used in the experiments of Waldmann et al. (1995). Both models consist of four elements but the causal directions connecting these elements entail distinct covariational patterns. Figure 1A shows a *common-cause* structure in which a common cause simultaneously produces three effects. Figure 1B shows a *common-effect* structure in which three causes independently produce a single effect. A key difference between these two structures is that common-cause structures imply a spurious correlation among their effects. Even though the

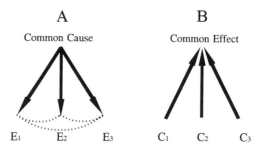

Fig. 1. Common-cause structure (A) with multiple independent effects (E_1, E_2, E_3) versus common-effect structure (B) with independent causes (C_1, C_2, C_3). Only the common-cause structure formally implies a spurious correlation (dotted curves) among effects. From Waldmann et al. (1995). Copyright © 1995 by the American Psychological Association. Reprinted with permission.

effects do not affect each other, they tend to covary as the status of the common cause varies. In contrast, a common-effect structure does *not* imply a correlation among its causes. It is possible that several causes may interact, but in such cases the underlying causal model has to be augmented to account for these interactions. The need to modify the causal model by adding explicit configural features would be expected to increase the difficulty of learning (Dawes, 1988). In general, causal-model theory predicts that learning difficulty should be dependent on the fit between the structural implications of the causal models activated during learning and the structure of the learning input.

Figure 2 displays an example of the learning materials of Experiment 4 of Waldmann et al. (1995). The cards showed stones in the middle surrounded by three colored iron compounds. The task was to judge whether the stone in the middle of the dish was a magnet or not.

All participants saw the same pictures with the stones and the iron compounds. However, we used two different instructions, which manipulated the direction of the causal arrow connecting stones and compounds. In the *common-cause* context, participants were told that scientists had discovered that some of these stones are either strong or weak magnets. In order to find out more about these stones, the scientists put the stones in dishes along with iron compounds. They found out that stones that are magnetic change the orientation of some of the iron compounds placed in the dish. Strong magnets turn the magnetized compounds so that their ends point to the stone, weak magnets turn the magnetized compounds so that their sides face the stone. If the stones are not magnetic, the iron compounds just stay in a random orientation. The participants' task was to learn to judge whether a stone was a magnet or not, basing their decisions on the

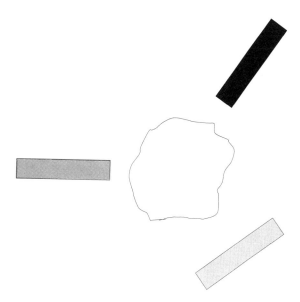

Fig. 2.   Example of the learning material from Waldmann et al.'s (1995) Experiment 4. A potential magnet surrounded by iron compounds (compounds were blue, red, and green in the original set of learning items). From Waldmann et al. (1995). Copyright © 1995 by the American Psychological Association. Reprinted with permission.

orientation of the surrounding compounds. No prior information was given about which of the different compounds were actually affected by the magnets. Participants were presented with individual cases one after the other, they had to decide whether they believed the stone displayed on the index card represented a magnet or not, and subsequently were informed whether they were correct or not. Thus, no feedback about whether the magnet was strong or weak was provided.

In the common-effect conditions, the same material was used but in the initial instructions the direction of the causal connections between stones and compounds was reversed. In these conditions participants were told that scientists had discovered that some of the iron compounds emit strong or weak magnetic waves that may magnetize the stones and turn them into strong or weak magnets. The intensity of the magnetic waves was based on the orientation of these compounds: compounds pointing to the stone emit strong magnetic waves, whereas compounds facing the stones emit weak magnetic waves. Again, the participants' task was to learn to judge whether a stone was a magnet or not by using information about the orientation of the compounds surrounding the stone. Except for the different initial instructions the learning procedure was identical across the two causal conditions.

In both causal situations the same entities are causally linked, only the direction of the causal arrow differs. In the common-cause instruction participants were confronted with a varying common cause, a strong or a weak magnet. This variation suggests that the affected compounds point to the stone when the cause is strong, and that their sides face the stone when it is weak. Thus, the common-cause model with a cause varying between a strong and a weak state should sensitize participants to a within-category correlation between the orientations of the affected compounds. These compounds should all be expected to either point to the stone (indicating a strong magnet) or face the stone (indicating a weak magnet). By contrast, the common-effect model with a varying effect does not structurally imply a within-category correlation between the causes. Here, it is more natural to assume three independent causes converging on a joint effect. We expected that the common-effect instruction should sensitize participants to category structures that exhibit independent cue-to-category correlations.

To test these predictions, we presented participants with either a category structure that embodies cue-to-category correlations, or a structure that contains a within-category correlation. Causal-model theory predicts that participants in the common-cause conditions should be biased to expect a within-category correlation, whereas participants in the common-effect conditions should find cue-to-category correlations more natural. Learning the within-category correlation after having received the common-effect instruction amounts to learning about a disordinal interaction among causes, which should be particularly hard to grasp. By contrast, the structure with cue-to-category correlations embodies a situation with three linear main effects within this causal condition.

More specifically, half of the participants received a linearly separable arrangement, which exhibits cue-to-category correlations. In this category structure, compounds pointing to the stones were more typical for the positive set ("yes"), and compounds parallel to the stones were more typical for the negative set ("no"). The other condition represented a non–linearly separable category structure in which the position of the individual compounds was not correlated with the categories. The only way to distinguish the two sets was by noticing the within-category correlation between two of the compounds. In the positive set, these two dimensions were perfectly positively correlated (i.e., both compounds either pointed to the stone or were positioned parallel to the stone); in the negative set they were negatively correlated (i.e., one of the two compounds pointed to the stone, the other compound was parallel to the stone). The non–linearly separable structure corresponded to an Exclusive-Or (XOR) structure with an additional irrelevant feature.

Figure 3 displays the results of Experiment 4 (Waldmann et al., 1995). The mean number of errors until participants reached the learning criterion was used as an indicator of learning difficulty. Within the common-cause condition the non–linearly separable structure with the within-category correlation was easier to learn than the linearly separable structure with the cue-to-category correlations, whereas the opposite was true within the common-effect conditions. The interaction between causal condition and category structure proved highly reliable. The results support the view that participants are sensitive to the underlying causal structure of the task domain. Since across the two causal conditions participants saw identical cues and had to learn to associate them with identical outcomes, these results cannot be explained by standard associationist theories that would generally assign the learning cues (compounds) to the input level and the outcomes (magnets) to the output level of an associationist network.

1. Configural Cues and the Learning of Causal Categories

A further problem for associationist theories such as the Rescorla–Wagner theory is the fact that the non–linearly separable structure proved learnable. It is a well-known fact that this theory is restricted to linearly separable

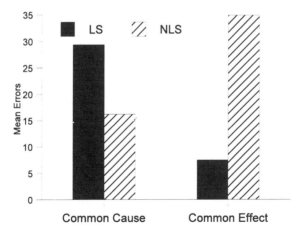

Fig. 3.   Mean errors obtained in the linearly separable (LS) and the non–linearly separable (NLS) common-cause and common-effect conditions (Experiment 4 from Waldmann et al., 1995). The NLS conditions embody a within-category correlation, the LS conditions embody cue-to-category correlations.

tasks (Minsky & Papert, 1969). As a consequence, more complex theories have been suggested in which configural cues (Gluck & Bower, 1988b; Rescorla, 1973) or hidden layers (Kruschke, 1992; Rumelhart, Hinton, & Williams, 1986) are added to code interactions. However, even though these theories predict that nonlinear tasks are learnable they still do not account for the fact that the participants proved sensitive to the causal status of the cues. All these theories have in common that they try to associate cues with outcomes regardless of the causal structure connecting these events.

The configural-cue model in which cues coding conjunctions of elements are added to the input layer of an associationist network along with the elemental cues has an additional problem: the number of cues grows exponentially with the number of elemental input cues. Gluck and Bower (1988b) therefore suggested restricting configural cues to pairwise conjunctions. An obvious drawback of this restriction is that such a network is unable to handle problems for which the correct decision requires learning an interaction among three (or more) cues. Note that networks with hidden layers will also not necessarily learn all higher order interactions. If the number of hidden units is too small, the network might be able to learn a two-way interaction but not some higher order interaction (see Kruschke, 1992). One problem with many such learning networks, therefore, is that the complexity of the learning problem has to be anticipated in advance in order to pick the appropriate size of the network.

Waldmann and Holyoak (1990) expected that within a common-cause context with a varying cause a *three-way correlation* should be learned fairly easily because it falls out of a linear model with a common cause independently affecting three effects. In contrast, in a common-effect context with a varying effect a three-way interaction of three causes should be particularly difficult to grasp.

Waldmann and Holyoak (1990, Experiment 3) conducted an experiment in which participants received four cues that were characterized either as causes of a common effect or as effects of a common cause. Three of these cues were perfectly correlated within the positive set to which participants had to learn to respond with "yes." The experiment yielded two major results. First, the three-way interaction was clearly learnable, which refutes Gluck and Bower's (1988b) restrictive assumption on configural cues. Second, despite the fact that learning cues, response, and learning feedback were equated across the two causal conditions, a clear learning advantage for the common-cause condition was obtained (errors: $M = 43.1$ vs $M = 76.0$). Again, participants proved sensitive to the different structural implications derived from differential patterns of causal directionality.

C. Causal Models and Asymmetries of Cue Competition

Since Kamin (1969) discovered the phenomenon of *blocking* in animal learning, *cue competition* has been a basic phenomenon that all associative learning theories are trying to capture. In the classic blocking paradigm, animals are first (Phase 1) trained to associate an initial conditioned stimulus CS_1 with an unconditioned stimulus US. In Phase 2 of the learning procedure, a second cue CS_2 is redundantly paired with the initial cue CS_1. Kamin's crucial finding was that, in spite of being perfectly correlated with the outcome, the later redundant cue CS_2 did not seem to acquire any associative strength as compared to a control group, which did not receive any Phase 1 training.

Rescorla and Wagner's theory (1972) views blocking as the result of a failure to acquire associative strength. According to this rule learning is error driven. In blocking experiments, animals learn to predict the outcome using the initially acquired predictive cue CS_1. Since this cue still allows perfect predictions in Phase 2, no further learning occurs. In particular, the associative weight of CS_2 stays at its initial value of zero.

Waldmann and Holyoak (1992) modified the blocking paradigm in order to test causal-model theory against the Rescorla–Wagner and similar theories. As pointed out by Reichenbach (1956), one crucial characteristic of causal relations in the physical world is the fact that multiple independent causes of a common effect potentially interact, whereas multiple independent effects of a common cause are conditionally independent. Waldmann and Holyoak asked whether our learning is sensitive to this fundamental physical feature.

In a set of experiments, Waldmann and Holyoak (1992) employed a two-phase blocking design. In Phase 1 a predictive cue (P cue) was established as the sole deterministic predictor of an outcome (along with other nonpredictive cues). In Phase 2 this P cue was paired with a second, redundant predictor (R cue) as predictive of the outcome. The P and the R cues either always occurred together or were both absent. Two conditions were compared in which the causal status of the cues was manipulated by means of different initial instructions. Otherwise the two conditions presented exactly the same learning experiences. Thus, the interaction of blocking with the manipulation of the causal assumptions about the learning cues could be tested by comparing the results of these two groups. In the *predictive learning conditions* the cues were characterized as potential causes of a common effect. In Experiments 1 and 2 (Waldmann & Holyoak, 1992), for example, the cues were descriptions of the appearance of fictitious persons (e.g., "pale skin, stiff posture, normal perspiration"), and in the predictive condition these cues were described as potential causes of an emotional response of observers of these persons. The crucial dependent measure in this condition was ratings of whether each of the cues represented an independent *cause* of the effect.

The Rescorla–Wagner rule predicts complete blocking of the R cue because it is redundantly paired with the P cue that was already established as perfectly predictive in Phase 1. A number of previous studies have demonstrated blocking with this kind of learning task (e.g., G. B. Chapman, 1991; G. B. Chapman & Robbins, 1990; Shanks, 1985).

Causal-model theory makes a similar prediction. Following recent developments of statistical relevance theory, Waldmann and Holyoak (1992) proposed that in situations with multiple causes converging on a common effect, *conditional contingencies* should be computed (see Cartwright, 1983; Cheng, 1993; Cheng & Novick, 1992; Eells, 1991; Melz, Chenz, Holyoak, & Waldmann, 1993; Salmon, 1980; Spellman, this volume, Ch. 5). Conditional contingencies (Δp_{K_i}) assess the contingencies between two events C and E conditional upon alternative causal factors K_i being kept constant, that is, as

$$\Delta p_{K_i} = p \ (E|C.K_1.K_2. \ldots K_n) - p(E|{\sim}C.K_1.K_2. \ldots K_n). \qquad (2)$$

An isolated period denotes an "and," and each K_i a choice between the presence or the absence of the factor. The computation of conditional contingencies is necessary to distinguish between true causal and spurious correlations. For example, suppose we want to test the hypothesis that smoking (C) causes lung cancer (E). Furthermore, we assume that smoking is correlated with alcohol consumption, which may also be a cause of lung cancer. In order to test the hypothesis, we should assess the conditional contingencies between smoking and lung cancer in the subpopulation of alcoholics (K_1) and people who do not drink alcohol (${\sim}K_1$). If we then discover that smoking equally leads to lung cancer in both subpopulations, we may conclude that smoking is an independent cause of this disease.

A typical feature of the blocking design is the fact that conditional contingencies between the R cue and the effect cannot be computed in the absence of the P cue that has been established as an individual cause in Phase 1. The R cue is never presented alone without the P cue. Thus, causal-model theory predicts that the participants of the learning experiment should be uncertain as to whether the R cue represents a genuine cause or not. However, in contrast to the predictions of the Rescorla–Wagner theory, blocking is expected to be partial: Rather than concluding that the R cue is not a cause, participants should be uncertain, since they are simply not given crucial information, which is necessary to arrive at a definite assessment of the causal status of the R cue. The results of the experiments showed indeed that blocking was partial, as the ratings for the

R cue were substantially lower than those for the P cue, but higher than those for other cues that were uncorrelated with the effect (see also G. B. Chapman & Robbins, 1990).

In a second condition, the *diagnostic learning condition,* the very same cues of the predictive conditions were redefined as potential effects of a common cause. The participants were told that the persons' features represent potential effects of a new disease caused by a virus. Thus, in this condition the participants were confronted with a common-cause situation.

Causal-model theory claims that the participants honor the cause–effect direction regardless of the order of presentation of the components of the common-cause model. Since there is only one cause in common-cause situations, the conditional contingency rule (Eq. 2) reduces to unconditional contingencies (Eq. 1) between the single cause and the effects. Because both the P cue and the R cue are deterministic effects of the common cause (the virus), no blocking was predicted in the diagnostic condition. In the diagnostic condition of Experiment 1 (Waldmann & Holyoak, 1992) the participants were asked to rate the degree to which they thought each of the cues represented an independent *effect* of the cause. As predicted, no cue competition was found in this condition.

It is interesting to note that the Rescorla–Wagner theory also has a built-in asymmetry between cues and outcomes (see Van Hamme et al., 1993). According to this learning rule, cues compete for the prediction of a common outcome but different outcomes of a single cue do not compete. Thus, the Rescorla–Wagner rule also predicts competition among causes but not among effects *when* the learning situation is set up the right way: when the causes are presented temporally prior to the effects, the Rescorla–Wagner theory reflects the real-world asymmetry between causes and effects. The asymmetry of cues and outcomes has been firmly established in a number of experiments with animals and humans that have demonstrated competition among causes (or cues) but not effects (or outcomes) (Baker & Mazmanian, 1989; Baker, Murphy, & Vallée-Tourangeau, this volume, Ch. 1; Matute, Arcediano, & Miller, 1996, Experiments 1, 2; Van Hamme et al., 1993). All these studies have in common that the causes were presented either prior to or simultaneous with the effects so that the Rescorla–Wagner rule happens to yield the correct predictions.

The Rescorla–Wagner rule, however, makes the wrong predictions when in the learning situation the cues represent effects and the outcomes causes. In these situations this theory predicts competition among the effects but not among the causes, a pattern contrary to that of physical causal relations in the real world. In order to test causal-model theory against standard associationist theories that model learning as the association between cues and outcomes, Waldmann and Holyoak (1992) used a diagnostic learning situation in which the effects were presented first (as cues) and the feedback about the outcome (the causes of the effects) was given after the participants' diagnostic response. Since the cues and the outcomes were identical in both the predictive and the diagnostic conditions, standard associationist theories predict equal amounts of cue competition in both conditions.

Waldmann and Holyoak's (1992) finding that no cue competition occurred in the diagnostic condition provoked a number of critical responses. Van Hamme et al. (1993) argued that the Rescorla–Wagner rule actually predicts the right pattern when cues are mapped to causes and outcomes to effects. This suggestion, however, faces the problem that it is unclear how the participants of the experiments mastered the diagnostic learning situation in which the effects were presented prior to the causes. It is not clear how an associative network in which the causes represent the input and the effects the output could generate a diagnostic response on the basis of effect cues as the input for their decisions.

Shanks and Lopez (in press) therefore proposed a more complex theory for diagnostic learning. They argued that the participants may run two associative networks in parallel, one that is directed from causes to effects, and one that is directed from effects to causes. The latter network is then responsible for diagnostic learning and the diagnostic inferences from effects to causes. Since in Experiment 1 of Waldmann and Holyoak (1992) participants were requested to give cause–effect ratings in the diagnostic learning conditions, this model appears to explain the observed absence of cue competition.

This theory, however, runs into problems when Experiment 3 of Waldmann and Holyoak (1992) is considered. In this experiment not only the cues and outcomes were held constant; in addition, the test question was identical in both the predictive and the diagnostic learning conditions. Thus, differences in the ratings can be attributed only to the different causal models underlying cues and outcomes. In both learning conditions the participants were asked to rate how "predictive" each individual cue is for the outcome. Therefore, in the diagnostic condition the participants were requested to give a *diagnostic* effect–cause rating. Since in this condition the learning as well as the test question is directed along the effect-to-cause direction, the theory of Shanks and Lopez (in press), along with standard associationist theories, predicts cue competition in the diagnostic condition.

Causal-model theory (Waldmann & Holyoak, 1992) predicts that the participants form causal models in the cause–effect direction but are able to access these representations in both the predictive cause–effect and the diagnostic effect–cause direction. Normatively this implies that the diagnostic inferences should be sensitive to whether a specific effect is caused by only one or by several competing causes. For example, a symptom, such as fever, may be a deterministic effect of a disease. It may nevertheless be a bad diagnostic cue, simply because there are many alternative causes of this symptom. Thus, ratings of whether fever is an effect of the disease should be high, whereas low ratings should be expected when the test question requests an assessment of how predictive it is for the disease.

Waldmann and Holyoak's (1992) Experiments 2 and 3 present a pattern consistent with this prediction. No cue competition was observed in the diagnostic condition with learning materials in which no alternative causes of the state of the effects were given (signal buttons of an alarm; Experiment 3). This finding refutes standard associative theories, including Shanks and Lopez's suggestion. However, reduced ratings for the R cue were obtained when the R cue represented a symptom ("underweight") with many alternative potential causes. Since in Experiment 1 the participants were able to learn that this symptom is an effect of the new disease, the lowering of the ratings with the diagnostic test question in Experiment 2 seems to reflect participants' sensitivity to the difference between predictive (cause–effect) and diagnostic (effect–cause) inferences.

1. Competition among Causes in Predictive and Diagnostic Learning

As additional evidence for the assumptions of causal-model theory, Waldmann (1996) designed an experiment ($N = 56$) that directly addresses the question of whether participants are sensitive to the fact that the predictiveness of effect cues is dependent on the presence of alternative causes. A number of critics have pointed out that Waldmann and Holyoak (1992) provided only indirect evidence for this sensitivity since the conclusions were based on a cross-experiment comparison. The more recent experiment may also serve to clarify a misunderstanding. Shanks and Lopez (in press) assert that Waldmann and Holyoak (1992) claim that cue competition in diagnostic learning is dependent on whether the cues are concrete or abstract. What we actually claimed was that people will be sensitive to whether an effect is caused by one or several causes, regardless of whether the effect is concrete or abstract. The more recent experiment used fairly abstract materials and demonstrated sensitivity to the structure of the underlying causal model with identical types of material. Finally, an additional goal of this experiment was to replicate the finding of the absence of a blocking effect in a diagnostic learning task with diagnostic test questions with more abstract kinds of learning materials. Matute et al. (1996, Footnote 1), for example, doubt the validity of the results of Waldmann and Holyoak's (1992) Experiment 3.

In the learning phases in all conditions, participants received information about the presence or absence of different substances in animals' blood,

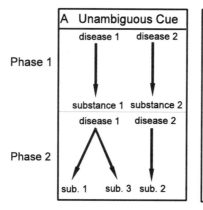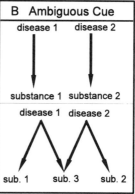

Fig. 4. The two learning phases of the two diagnostic learning conditions, unambiguous (A) and ambiguous (B) cue conditions. The cues (substances) represent potential effects of the causes (diseases) to be diagnosed.

and then they had to judge whether the animal had contracted one of two new blood diseases or not. After each decision feedback was given. The substances were all abstractly numbered and not further characterized (e.g., "Substance 1: Yes; Substance 2: No").

Figure 4 displays the causal structure of the learning domain presented in the *diagnostic* conditions. In these conditions, the substances were characterized as effects of the diseases. Participants were told that new blood diseases had been discovered that produce new types of substances in the blood. In both conditions, the unambiguous and the ambiguous cue condition, participants learned in Phase 1 that substance 1 is caused by disease 1, and substance 2 is caused by disease 2. In Phase 2, however, the two conditions differed. In the *unambiguous cue condition* (A), substance 3 is paired only with substance 1. Participants learned that disease 1 causes substance 1 as well as substance 3.

One of the crucial test questions asked the participants to rate how *predictive* substance 3 is for disease 1. The participants were told that they should imagine being confronted with new animals, and having received information about the presence of only one substance. Their task was to rate how well knowledge about the presence of the respective substance would enable them to predict the existence of the diseases. Associative learning theories, such as the Rescorla–Wagner theory, predict blocking in the unambiguous cue condition (also Shanks & Lopez, in press). The effects are mapped to the input level as the learning and the test questions are directed from effects to causes. Causal-model theory predicts absence of blocking because the symptom is an effect of the disease and because there are no alternative competing explanations.

In the *ambiguous cue condition* (B), substance 3 is caused by either disease 1 or disease 2. Again, associative theories, including Shanks and Lopez's (in press) proposal, predict complete blocking of the redundant cue. Causal-model theory predicts that participants should be sensitive to the fact that there are multiple explanations for the presence of substance 3. Therefore they should lower their diagnostic ratings in this condition.

The participants rated the predictive cues, substance 1 and 2, high both after Phase 1 as well as after Phase 2. Figure 5 displays the results of Phase 2. The most important result involves the redundant cue in the diagnostic conditions (Fig. 5A). In the unambiguous cue condition, the redundant cue

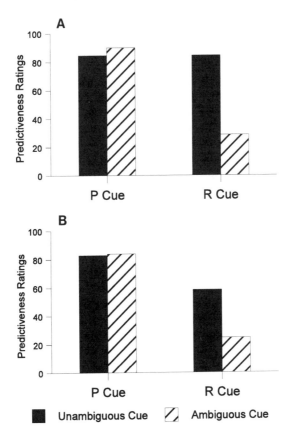

Fig. 5. Mean "predictiveness" ratings from the diagnostic (A) and predictive (B) learning conditions in Phase 2.

yielded high ratings. As in earlier experiments, no sign of blocking can be seen here. As a matter of fact, *all* participants gave identical ratings to the predictive and the redundant cue in this condition. This finding refutes standard associative learning theories. In the ambiguous cue condition the ratings are clearly lowered. The participants were apparently sensitive to the fact that there are competing theories explaining the presence of the redundant effect cue. These two results jointly support causal-model theory.[2]

As a further test of participants' sensitivity to causal directionality, a predictive version of the tank was also investigated. The structure was identical to the one outlined in Fig. 4 except for the fact that the direction of the causal arrows was reversed. In the *predictive conditions* the substances were redefined as potential causes of the new blood diseases. Participants in these conditions were told that some food items appear to contain substances that may cause new blood diseases. The *same* learning exemplars were used as in the diagnostic conditions. The participants received information about the presence or absence of the substances, and then had to judge whether the animal had contracted one of the two diseases or not. Thus, in Phase 1, participants learned that substance 1 causes disease 1, and substance 2 causes disease 2. In Phase 2, substance 3 was redundantly paired only with substance 1 to produce disease 1 (*unambiguous cue condition*), or, in the *ambiguous cue condition,* it was paired with either substance 1 to produce disease 1 or substance 2 to produce disease 2.

Assuming that Phase 1 training was asymptotic, associative learning theories generally predict complete blocking of the redundant cue in both conditions. Causal-model theory also predicts a reduction of the ratings for the redundant cue. However, blocking should be only partial in the unambiguous cue condition. Participants simply do not receive sufficient information to assess the causal status of the redundant cue. Therefore, they should be merely uncertain about whether it is a cause, not certain that it is not a cause. In the ambiguous cue condition, they also receive incomplete information. However, unlike in the unambiguous cue condition, participants see that each disease can also be absent in the presence of the redundant cue. Therefore, in the ambiguous cue condition, they

---

[2] Van Hamme et al.'s (1993) claim that the Rescorla–Wagner rule explains Waldmann and Holyoak's (1992) results has sometimes been interpreted as the implicit suggestion to generally map causes to the cue level and effects to the output level even when effects are presented first (see, e.g., Matute et al., 1996). It should be noted, however, that this account is also refuted by the results of the experiment, as it would not explain why ratings for the redundant cue were reduced in the ambiguous-cue condition. In both the unambiguous and the ambiguous-cue condition the cause-to-effect contingency of the redundant cue was maximal ($\Delta p = 1$) so that no differences should be expected.

should be more certain that it is not a cause than in the unambiguous cue condition.

Figure 5 (B) displays the means of the Phase 2 ratings in the predictive conditions. For both the ambiguous and the unambiguous cue condition, the redundant cue (R cue) yielded significantly lower ratings than the predictive cue (P cue), which can be interpreted as evidence for blocking in the predictive context. However, blocking was only partial as predicted by causal-model theory. The predicted difference between the ambiguous and unambiguous cue condition was also obtained.[3]

2. The Role of the Structure of the Causal Model

Causal-model theory has sometimes been paraphrased as predicting competition among causes but not among effects (Matute et al., 1996). This summarization is incomplete. Waldmann and Holyoak (1992) predicted cue competition in blocking situations when the cues represented potential independent *causes of a common effect,* and the absence of cue competition when the cues represented potential independent *effects of a common cause.* Of course, other causal models are possible and may yield different results. For example, a blocking task could be set up in which the R cue represents a cause of the P cue, which in turn is linked to the effect. This situation instantiates a *causal chain,* and no blocking of the R cue should be expected. Williams, Sagness, and McPhee (1994) have demonstrated that different types of pretraining may indeed influence whether participants view cues as independent or connected (see also Williams, this volume, Ch. 3).

To account for causal chains, the conditional contingency rule (Eq. 2) has to be modified (see Cartwright, 1989; Eells, 1991). Potential cofactors (K) should be kept constant only when they are *not* causal intermediates between the target cause and the target effect. Causal intermediates also screen off the relation between the primary cause and the effect so that

---

[3] Associative theories may explain a difference between the ambiguous and the unambiguous cue conditions as a consequence of preasymptotic training of the P cue in Phase 1. However, it is unlikely that this account is correct. First, it does not explain the complete absence of blocking in the diagnostic condition. Furthermore, participants had to learn to associate only three simple patterns (either substance 1 or 2 present, or both substances absent) with three responses. This is an extremely easy task and was typically mastered within a couple of trials. Then this account would predict an increase of the ratings of the P cue with increasing training which was not observed (see also Waldmann & Holyoak, 1992). Finally, Waldmann (1996) presents an additional experiment with predictive learning instructions in which the amount of Phase 1 training was varied between either two or ten presentations of each learning exemplar. The Rescorla–Wagner theory predicts an increase of the size of the blocking effect and a decrease of the difference between the ratings of the ambiguous and the unambiguous redundant cue proportional to the amount of Phase 1 training. Causal-model theory predicts no difference. The results clearly supported causal-model theory.

holding them fixed would misrepresent the true causal relations. This is a further example of how prior causal knowledge affects how the statistical relations of the learning input should be processed.

3. Evidence for Effect Competition?

Lack of control over the underlying causal structure may lead to apparent refutations of causal-model theory. Shanks and Lopez (in press) present one experiment in which they claim to have found evidence for effect competition (see also Shanks, Lopez, Darby, & Dickinson, this volume, Ch. 7). Shanks and Lopez (in press, Experiment 3) compared two conditions. The "noncontingent" condition presented the following causal structure: cause 1 → AB, cause 1 → B, no cause → C. In the "contingent" condition a different learning structure was used: cause 2 → DE, cause 2 → F, no cause → E. The letters A to F represent effects. These patterns were trained in the diagnostic direction in which the effect cues were presented first.

Standard associative theories that map these effect cues on the input layer predict effect competition. Despite being presented an equal number of times along with the target causes (i.e., diseases), effect A from the noncontingent condition should be rated lower than effect D from the contingent condition. In both conditions, the unconditional contingencies between the cause and the target effect were kept constant so that *prima facie* causal-model theory predicts no difference. Shanks and Lopez discovered a small difference in association ratings between the two conditions, which was interpreted as evidence against causal-model theory.

One problem with this experiment is that the instructions and the cues (symptoms labeled with letters) did not clearly specify the underlying causal model so that it is unclear how the learning input was actually interpreted (see also Waldmann & Holyoak, in press, for a more detailed critique of this study). In this regard, the experiment is similar to previous studies, which, however, never claimed to study causal induction (G. B. Chapman, 1991; Gluck & Bower, 1988a; Shanks, 1991). As pointed out by Waldmann and Holyoak (1992; Footnote 1), not all symptoms of a disease are effects. They may be causes (e.g., puncture wounds indicating blood poisoning), intermediate causes of a causal chain, or part of a complex causal network representing a syndrome.

A second problem is that the learning input points to different underlying causal models. Assuming that the symptoms were actually interpreted as effects as intended by Shanks and Lopez (in press), the noncontingent structure is an instantiation of a simple common-cause model (see Fig. 1A) in which cause 1 deterministically produces symptom B, and weakly produces symptom A. By contrast, the contingent structure is incompatible with a simple common-cause model. This structure exhibits a situation in which a single cause has disjunctive effects. The disease (i.e., cause 2) causes either the symptom complex DE, or the symptom F, but no other combinations of D, E, and F are ever observed. As a consequence, the initial model would have to be modified to account for the peculiar interaction of the effects. Waldmann et al. (1995) predict greater learning difficulty for the condition with the mismatch between the initially plausible common-cause model and the learning input, which was indeed obtained by Shanks and Lopez (see Waldmann & Holyoak, in press).

Very little is known about the revision processes activated when the initial causal model is incompatible with the learning input (but see Ahn & Mooney, 1995; Waldmann et al., 1995). It is readily apparent, however, that the Rescorla–Wagner model, originally not having been intended to model complex *causal* induction tasks, lacks the flexibility to reconfigure itself in light of evidence incompatible with the implicit causal structure of the learning model.

Esmoris-Arranz et al. (1995) present a study in which they tried to demonstrate effect competition in an animal learning experiment (see also Miller & Matute, this volume, Ch. 4). Assuming that the rats who partici-pated in the experiments actually interpreted the CS as causes and the US as effects, Esmoris-Arranz et al. compared two causal structures. In the experimental condition, the rats learned that a cause A produces an effect S in Phase 1, and in Phase 2 this cause A produces effect S along with a second effect X. In the control condition Phase 2 was identical, but A and S were unpaired during Phase 1. In the test phase rats were presented with the single cues S and X. The most important result involves test cue X that has been paired with A an equal amount of times in the two conditions. Responding to test cue X indicated lower associative weights in the experi-mental condition than in the control condition. This finding was interpreted by Esmoris-Arranz et al. as evidence for cue competition among the effects S and X.

Again this is a peculiar causal situation when taken at face value. In the experimental condition cause A consistently causes effect S, but it changes its causal power from not producing X during Phase 1 to deterministically producing X in Phase 2. In the control condition, cause A changes from being ineffective to being a deterministic cause of both S and X in Phase 2. It is unclear whether a cause like the one presented in the experimental condition exists in the physical world.

However, even when the unrealistic nature of the presented causal situa-tion is ignored, the results of this experiment do not present unambiguous evidence for effect competition against contingency accounts. K. J. Holyoak (personal communication) offers a contingency analysis that is consistent with the assumptions of causal-model theory. This analysis assumes that test cue X is implicitly coded as the complex event X and not-S, as the cues S and X have been consistently paired in Phase 2 of the training phase. Thus, in the test situation the rats in the two conditions are actually trying to infer how likely this complex new event (X and not-S) is caused by the unobserved cause A. Although the contingency of A and X is constant across the two conditions, the likelihood that A is producing the absence of S (not-S) seems higher in the control than in the experimental condition. In the control condition, A is paired with the absence of S during Phase 1, whereas A and the absence of S are never combined in the experimental condition. Hence the complex cue X and not-S is less likely to have been caused by A in the experimental than in the control condition, which is in line with the results of the experiment.

Matute et al. (1996) present a different set of experiments in which they tried to provide evidence for effect competition with human participants. They argued (in contrast to the Rescorla–Wagner and many other associative learning theories) that cue competition is a function of the test question that probes the knowledge base, and not a characteristic of the learning rule. In their Experiment 3 they found that the participants tended to rate the relationship of a cause and a specific effect lower when this effect was paired with a stronger as opposed to a weaker second effect (but see Baker & Mazmanian, 1989). The contingency between the cause and the target effect was kept constant across the two conditions. Therefore, this experiment appears to provide *prima facie* evidence for effect competition.

However, this finding crucially depended on the test question. When the participants were asked whether the target effect was an effect of the cause or whether the cause produced this effect, then no effect competition was found (Experiment 2). However, when the test question asked how "indicative" the effect was, then participants tended to give an assessment of the diagnostic validity of the target effect *relative* to the strength of the other collateral effect. It certainly is reasonable that in some circumstances a relative assessment of the diagnostic validity of an effect will be given (as when a physician is about to decide which diagnostic test to conduct). According to causal-model theory, this finding is a further demonstration that the participants are able to flexibly access their knowledge base. People are apparently not only able to access causal knowledge in the predictive and the diagnostic directions, they are also able to compare different causal strengths. An associative learning theory could also account for these data when the assumption is added that in some test situations the responses are based on a choice rule that compares the different associative weights obtained during learning.

Matute et al.'s equivocation of cause and effect competition blurs one of the most fundamental differences between causes and effects, the distinction between *spurious* causes and *collateral* effects. Whether or not a cause is real or spurious may be of the utmost pragmatic importance. It would make little sense to tamper with a barometer when the goal is to influence the weather. By contrast, a redundant, albeit weak effect can be produced regardless of whether there are alternative, maybe stronger effects. The pattern of results Matute et al. (1996) present is consistent with the notion that participants are indeed sensitive to this crucial distinction between spurious or interacting causes and collateral, mutually supporting effects (also Baker & Mazmanian, 1989; Rescorla, 1991, 1993, 1995; Van Hamme et al., 1993; Waldmann & Holyoak, 1992). When the participants were requested to assess *causal* relations, they always proved sensitive to potential competitions among causes but never compared collateral effects, or causes with effects. They were sensitive to the fundamental difference between converging causes and diverging effects. For Matute et al. this pattern of results is simply a result of the semantics of the test question, but this explanation begs the question of *why* participants understand the causal test questions the way they do.

D. CAUSAL MODELS AND THE ASSESSMENT OF CONTINGENCIES

Causal directionality is only one aspect of abstract prior causal knowledge influencing the interpretation of the learning input. A further problem of purely bottom-up theories of causality is a consequence of the fact that contingencies between two events may be affected by other causal factors. One solution for this problem, the *conditional contingency* approach, has already been mentioned. According to this theory, contingencies should not be computed over the universal set of events but over subsets of events. However, Cartwright (1983) points out that this method yields correct results only when the subsets are properly selected (see also Cheng, 1993). Conditionalizing on the wrong variables may lead to erroneous contingency estimates. An instance of this problem is known in the philosophical and statistical literature as Simpson's paradox (see Cartwright, 1983; Eells, 1991; Pearl, this volume, Ch. 10; Simpson, 1951).

Simpson's paradox describes the fact that a given contingency between two events that holds in a given population can disappear or even be reversed in all subpopulations, when the population is partitioned in certain ways. Waldmann and Hagmayer (1995) present an experiment that demonstrates Simpson's paradox (see also Spellman, this volume, Ch. 5). Participants were told that importers of tropical fruit are trying to improve the quality of the fruit by irradiating them. However, so far it is unknown whether the irradiation has a positive, a negative, or no effect on the quality of the fruit. Participants' task in this experiment was to assess the strength of the causal relation between the irradiation of tropical fruit and the quality of fruit using a rating scale ranging from −10 to +10. To assess the efficacy of irradiation, participants received information about the quality of samples of fruit that either had or had not been irradiated. The participants were handed a list, which contained information about 80 samples of fruit. Each sample was represented on one line, and for each sample participants could see whether or not the sample had been irradiated ("yes" or "no"), and whether the quality of this sample was "good" or "bad." In one of the conditions, the condition with the *causally relevant* variable, participants were told that there are two types of fruit, Taringes and Mamones. Additionally it was pointed out that it was expected that irradiation affects these two types of fruit differently. Furthermore, information was added to the list that indicated that one of the two pages showed Taringes, and the other page Mamones.

Table I displays how the cases were distributed. The table displays the proportion of fruit that were of good quality after they were irradiated, and the proportion of fruit that were of good quality without being irradiated. For example, within subgroup A (e.g., Mamones) 36 fruit samples were presented that were irradiated. Forty-four percent of these samples (i.e., 16 out of 36) had good quality after irradiation. As can be seen in Table I, the arrangement of the cases resulted in a reversal of the sign of the contingencies within as opposed to across the grouping variable. Disregarding the grouping variable yields a positive contingency between irradiation and quality of fruit. By contrast, the contingency within each of the subgroups is negative. For half of the participants, the mapping between irradiation and quality of fruit was switched so that these participants saw a symmetric situation with a negative overall contingency, and positive contingencies within the subgroups. The sign of their ratings was reversed in order to make the two subgroups comparable.

TABLE I

CONTINGENCIES AND RELATIVE
FREQUENCIES OF FRUIT WITH
GOOD QUALITY

	A	B	Total
Irradiation	16/36 (.44)	0/4 (.00)	16/40 (.40)
No irradiation	3/4 (.75)	5/36 (.14)	8/40 (.20)
Contingency	−.31	−.14	+.20

Even though the task for all participants was to assess the overall efficacy of irradiation, it was expected that participants in the condition with the causally relevant grouping variable would assess the causal impact of irradiation separately for each subgroup (Mamones and Taringes), and disregard the total distribution of the cases. Since the contingencies within each subgroup are negative, participants should get the overall impression that irradiation *lowers* the quality of fruit.

This example may lead to the methodological suggestion that it is always a good idea to partition into subsets of events, and compute conditional contingencies in which potential cofactors are kept constant. However, this strategy may also lead to false assessments. The reason why the analysis should be based on the fruit level in the condition with two fruit types is that the fruits are *causally relevant* for the effect under investigation. If, by contrast, it had been shown that the contingencies reverse when the fruits were partitioned on the basis of their position on the test list, this would not count as evidence for a negative causal influence of irradiation. In this situation, one should disregard the groupings, and, based on the total distribution, conclude that irradiation *raises* the quality of fruit. Only partitions by causally relevant variables are relevant for evaluating causal laws (Cartwright, 1983). If causally irrelevant variables also mattered, almost any contingency could be obtained by choosing the right partition of the event space.

In order to test whether participants are sensitive to this crucial distinction between causally relevant and causally irrelevant partitioning variables, a second condition with a *causally irrelevant* variable was included in which participants were told that, due to the large number of tests, the samples of fruit were assigned to different investigators, A and B. Otherwise this condition presented the same learning input, the same assignment of the cases to the two groups, and the same rating instructions as the condition with the causally relevant grouping variable. It was expected that participants in the condition with the causally irrelevant variable would ignore the groups and rely on the total proportions. Thus, they should arrive at the conclusion that irradiation *raises* the quality of fruit. Their ratings should indeed be similar to the ones obtained in an additional control condition in which no grouping information was provided.

Table II shows that participants indeed were sensitive to the distinction between causally relevant and causally irrelevant grouping variables. The ratings in the control condition without a grouping category and in the condition with the irrelevant grouping variable were positive, and statistically indistinguishable from each other. Thus, participants in these two conditions believed that irradiation *raises* the quality of fruit. This finding indicates that the participants based their assessments on the total distribu-

TABLE II

MEAN RATINGS OF THE CAUSAL
RELATION BETWEEN IRRADIATION AND
QUALITY OF FRUIT

Relevant	Irrelevant	Control
−4.33	5.17	4.75

tion of cases, while disregarding subgroups. By contrast, participants in the condition with the causally relevant grouping variable thought that the cause prevents the effect. These participants concluded that irradiation *lowers* the quality of fruit. Thus, despite the fact that participants in the three conditions received identical learning inputs and identical rating instructions, their assumptions about the causal relevance of an additional grouping variable dramatically influenced their assessment of the relation between a putative cause and an effect.

This example clearly demonstrates that causal induction is crucially dependent on prior causal knowledge. New causal relations may be induced using contingency estimates based on the analysis of the structure of the learning input. However, the contingencies only reflect *causal* relations when the observations are partitioned on the basis of causally relevant rather than irrelevant variables. The causal relevance of *these* partitioning variables has to be established prior to the new induction task. Thus, Simpson's paradox exemplifies the basic assumption of causal-model theory that the processing of the learning input is based on prior assumptions about general properties of the causal situation.

Simpson's paradox is an interesting example of how specific knowledge interacts with abstract causal strategies. It is true that knowledge about the causal relevance of the partitioning variable is domain specific (e.g., the fact that type of fruit is causally relevant). However, unlike in previous research on transfer of specific knowledge (e.g., L. J. Chapman & Chapman, 1967, 1969; Pazzani, 1991), this type of knowledge does not directly bias estimates about the strength of the causal relation between the target cause and the target effect. In order to obtain the correct results, abstract knowledge has to be activated that conditional contingencies based on causally relevant subgroups should be computed. Interestingly, the dramatic reversals obtained in situations exemplifying Simpson's paradox are not due to selective processing of individual cases or knowledge-driven distortions of the contingency estimates. They rather are a natural consequence of unbiased processing of differentially grouped cases.

E. Causal Models and Causal Mechanisms

The main focus of this article is on the comparison between associative theories of causal induction and causal-model theory. However, since Hume's critical assessment of causal power theories, one of the main debates within the field of causal processing relates to the question of whether causal induction is based on the observation of statistical relations or on the observation of causal mechanisms or continuous causal processes (see Ahn, Kalish, Medin, & Gelman, 1995; Cheng, 1993; Salmon, 1984).

According to causal-model theory, these two positions need not be exclusive. Causal-model theory claims that, in general, statistical input information and prior assumptions about causal processes interact. According to this view, assumptions about causal mechanisms may guide the way the statistical input is processed. Often the mechanisms connecting a cause and an effect are unknown or only partly known. In addition, causal processes cannot be observed directly but have to be inferred on the basis of prior theoretical assumptions and the structure of the observational input (see Cartwright, 1989; Cheng, 1993; Cheng et al., this volume, Ch. 8). Thus, even though causality may not be reducible to mere covariational patterns, statistical relations are a potent way to measure causal processes. Knowledge about causal directionality is one important example of a physical feature that may crucially influence the way the learning input is interpreted (Waldmann & Holyoak, 1992; Waldmann et al., 1995). However, more domain-specific knowledge about causal processes may also play a role.

Waldmann (1991) used a learning paradigm analogous to cue compounding tasks from animal learning paradigms. In one of the experiments ($N = 96$) the participants learned, for example, that drinking a blue liquid causes a heart rate of $+3$ in animals. Subsequently, the participants learned that drinking a yellow liquid causes a heart rate of $+7$. The crucial test question was what would happen when both liquids were mixed and drunk altogether.

In animal learning experiments on cue compounding a typical finding is that two separately trained cues are *additively* integrated when presented in a compound (Couvillon & Bitterman, 1982; Kehoe & Graham, 1988; Weiss, 1972). This finding fits with the *additivity bias* inherent in many associative learning theories (including the Rescorla–Wagner theory).

The participants in the experiment, however, proved sensitive to an additional hint that characterized the causal mechanisms that mediate between causes and effect. In one condition, it was mentioned that the heart rate is affected by the *taste* of the liquids, whereas the other condition characterized the liquids as drugs that could have different *strengths.* Taste is an example of an *intensive* physical quantity, whereas the strength of a drug represents an *extensive* quantity. Intensive quantities are dependent on proportions and therefore do not necessarily vary with the absolute amount of the substance, whereas extensive quantities vary with amount (see also Reed & Evans, 1987; Wiser & Carey, 1983). Despite the fact that no further domain-related information was given (e.g., about the particular kind of taste), the participants activated general integration rules that were sensitive to this fundamental physical distinction. Generally, significantly more participants computed a weighted *average* of the two causal influences in the taste condition than in the strength condition. Only in the strength condition did an *adding*-type integration turn out to be the dominant rule.

This finding is only one example of how physical knowledge affects the way the learning input is treated. This knowledge may be more concrete than knowledge about causal directionality, but it nevertheless is fairly abstract, as the participants were provided with information about only the general physical characteristics of the causes (intensive vs extensive quantities).

Another example of knowledge-driven processing is prior assumptions about the typical temporal lag between causes and effects. When causes produce their effects with a lag, a naive contingency learning mechanism may never be able to detect the contingency between the distant events. There may also be cases in which a cause produces a dynamic pattern (see Eells, 1991). For example, a drug may be harmful in the short run but cure a disease in the long run.

Gallistel (1990) has pointed out a related problem with associative contingency learning mechanisms. Frequently these theories postulate a trial clock, which determines when a trial starts and when it ends. It can be shown, however, that depending on the size of the trial window, almost every contingency estimate may ensue. A small trial window may, for example, divide a specific CS into three events and represent the following brief temporal lag as the subsequent event (US). This example shows that prior assumptions about what constitutes a potential cause and what constitutes an effect are crucial for obtaining appropriate statistical evidence.

F. CAUSAL MODELS AND THE ROLE OF LEARNING ORDER

The major goal of the experiments on causal directionality was to demonstrate that the participants of the experiments use their abstract knowledge about the asymmetry of causes and effects when interpreting the learning input. In order to test causal-model theory against associative accounts the experiments kept cues and outcomes constant. This strategy led to a design in which common-effect models were presented in a learning order that corresponds to predictive reasoning (from causes to effects), whereas the common-cause models were presented in the diagnostic order (from effects to causes). The results clearly show that the participants honored the cause–effect direction regardless of the order in which the constituents of the causal models were presented.

However, it is unlikely that learning order generally has no impact on the mental models that are constructed during learning. The competence participants exhibit in simple causal situations may well break down when confronted with more complex situations. For example, the difficulty of predictive and diagnostic learning probably differs. Bindra, Clarke, and Shultz (1980) have presented experiments that show that children have greater difficulties with diagnostic as compared to predictive inferences. Diagnostic inferences typically involve a retrospective updating or modification of an already-formed mental model. This may be more difficult to accomplish than successively augmenting a causal representation parallel or isomorphic to the unfolding of the causal structure in the observed real world, as happens in predictive learning.

In order to investigate whether learning order affects the kind of information that is acquired, Ulf-D. Reips and I conducted a number of experiments in which the participants learned about fictitious diseases (Waldmann & Reips, 1996). A prototypical example of the causal building blocks used in these experiments is depicted in Figure 4 (Phase 2 of the ambiguous cue condition) in which an M-structure with two diseases and three symptoms is shown. Each disease deterministically causes two symptoms. One of these symptoms is ambiguous, as it is caused by either disease. The other symptom is unique. It is produced by only one of the diseases.

Unlike in the previous reported experiments in which the direction of the causal arrow was varied across conditions, the causal structures were kept constant across the learning conditions in this set of studies. Thus, in all conditions the symptoms represented effects and the diseases causes.

Two basic learning conditions were compared. The participants acquired the information about the diseases either in the *predictive* direction, or in the *diagnostic* direction. In the predictive learning condition the participants were presented with information about the disease of a patient, and they had to learn to predict what (two) symptoms this patient probably would exhibit. Each patient was affected by only one of the diseases. In the diagnostic learning condition, the participants received information about the (two) symptoms of each patient first, and had to learn to diagnose the patient's disease. The crucial question was whether these two modes of acquiring knowledge about identical causal structures would lead to different representations. Besides its theoretical relevance, this question is also practically significant. Medical knowledge, for example, is typically presented in textbooks in the predictive direction regardless of the fact that later this knowledge frequently has to be used in the diagnostic direction.

In one set of experiments we varied the *base rates* of the diseases. One of the diseases of the M-structure was presented three times as often as the other (see also Medin & Edelson, 1988). The participants were trained in either the predictive or the diagnostic direction and then all participants were asked questions about the diagnostic validity of each individual symptom. The most important question involved the ambiguous symptom. Since it is caused by either disease, it would be appropriate to choose the more frequent disease when only information about the presence of this symptom is available.

We predicted that base rate appreciation should be higher after diagnostic than after predictive training. According to contingency theories, predictive learning involves estimating the probability of the effects conditional on the presence and on the absence of the causes. As long as the relevant conditional probabilities are kept constant this estimate is indpendent of whether the causes are frequent or rare (see also Cheng & Novick, 1991). Thus, it was expected that these frequencies should be disregarded in predictive learning. Causal-model theory additionally predicts the asymmetry of learning conditions as a consequence of knowledge about causal directionality. Causes are events that are often actively set in order to achieve effects. For example, when planning psychological experiments it is recommended to establish equal cell sizes. Thus, the observed frequency of the causes is often not representative of the natural frequency of these events in the world, and should therefore not be accepted at face value (see also Gigerenzer, Hell, & Blank, 1988). Even though the cover stories used in our experiments emphasize that participants are going to see unselected samples of patients, there may be a tendency to later disregard this information. This tendency may be stronger when the learning task is complex so that it becomes more difficult to keep in mind additional information that is relevant only for the transfer task. By contrast, diagnostic inferences are based on the observation of effects that cannot be directly manipulated. Thus, the frequency of the causes responsible for the observed effects is generally more representative. Furthermore, diagnostic learning involves the appreciation of base rates. Since the participants in the diagnostic training condition received direct feedback about the disease causing the observed symptoms, the importance of the use of base rates may be experienced more directly (see also Gluck & Bower, 1988a; Griffin & Tversky, 1992; Holyoak & Spellman, 1993; Klayman & Brown, 1993; Koehler, in press; Medin & Edelson, 1988).

In one of the experiments ($N = 32$), six diseases and nine symptoms (three M-structures) were presented either in the predictive or in the diagnostic learning direction. Within each M-structure one disease was presented three times as often as the other. After the learning phase, the participants were told that they should assume that they were confronted with new patients, and that they knew about the presence of only one of the symptoms of these patients. Their task was to rate the probability of the diseases on a scale from 0 ("very unlikely") to 100 ("very likely"). The most important results involve the ratings of the ambiguous symptoms. Figure 6A displays the mean ratings of the probability that the frequent and the rare diseases were present (collapsed over the three ambiguous symptoms). The results exhibit an interaction. After diagnostic training, the participants proved sensitive to the different base rates of the diseases. They gave higher ratings to the more frequent diseases than to the rare diseases. Base rates were, however, neglected after predictive training. There were no significant

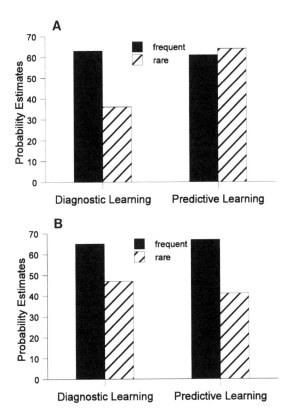

Fig. 6. Mean ratings of the probabilities of the rare and the frequent diseases conditional on the ambiguous symptom after the complex (A; three M-structures) and the simple (B; one M-structure) learning tasks.

differences between the ratings in this training condition. This neglect was not the result of a failure to encode frequencies, as the participants in both conditions turned out to be fairly good at remembering the different frequencies of the disease. Thus, the learning order seemed to affect the tendency to *use* base rates rather than the encoding.

In a second experiment, a situation with only one M-structure (two diseases, three symptoms) was presented ($N = 24$). As can be seen in Figure 6B, this reduction in complexity led to base rate appreciation after both learning situations. Thus, the results in the first experiment were not caused by a general deficit of participants' competence. It rather reflected a performance factor. The competence could be exhibited only in relatively simple learning situations. When the complexity of the learning structure was increased, additional, performance factors came into play, which led to a tendency to neglect base rate information after predictive training. The pattern of results exemplified in these two experiments has been replicated in a number of additional experiments. These findings clearly show that, at least with more complex causal situations, learning order may affect the way mental models are formed and accessed.

IV. Conclusion

The comparison between causal-model theory and associative accounts of causal induction highlighted a number of important differences between these two approaches. Causal-model theory postulates a rigorous separation between the learning input and mental representations. This characteristic allows for the flexible assignment of the learning input to elements of the resulting mental models. By contrast, most associative learning theories (e.g., the Rescorla–Wagner theory) work in the tradition of stimulus–response theories in which learning cues play the double causal role of representing events and eliciting responses. It has been shown that this inflexibility may lead to clear misrepresentations of objective causal relations. Most saliently, associative theories that code the learning cues as CS and the outcomes as US are unable to capture the structural characteristics of diagnostic learning situations in which effects are presented as cues. The Rescorla–Wagner theory correctly captures the asymmetry between causes and effects only when the learning situation is fortuitously presented in a way that corresponds to the implicit structural characteristics of this theory.

A second major tenet of causal-model theory postulates the necessity of an interaction between top-down assumptions and the processing of the learning input. Here, causal-model theory represents a reconciliation between theories focusing on statistical covariation learning and theories focusing on causal, mechanical processes. Causal-model theory is consistent with Cartwright's (1989) philosophical analyses of causality. Cartwright views causes as entities that embody an intrinsic dispositional *capacity* to produce effects. For example, smoking has the capacity to produce lung cancer. Due to additional causal factors, this capacity may not materialize in all contexts but it may still manifest itself in probabilistic relationships. Thus, covariation is one of the most potent ways to *measure* causal capacities. Like other measuring instruments it needs to be read properly. Covariation does not directly define causality. In this article a number of studies have been presented that demonstrated how identical learning inputs may be processed differently depending on participants' background assumptions about the causal processes to be observed.

Causal directionality is one of the most important features of causal relations that determine the way statistical relations are interpreted. It is a physical fact that multiple causes of a common effect potentially interact, whereas multiple effects of a common cause are rendered conditionally independent when the common cause is held constant (Reichenbach, 1956). Knowing that causes enable us to produce effects, and that redundant causes as opposed to redundant effects may be spurious, is highly relevant for planning our actions. Associative theories imply that participants are unaware of these fundamental distinctions. However, a number of studies have been presented in this chapter that show that participants are indeed sensitive to causal directionality and the asymmetry of causes and effects (see also Waldmann & Holyoak, 1990, 1992; Waldmann et al., 1995).

Assumptions about causal directionality are only one example of how prior knowledge may guide the induction process. Taking into account alternative causal factors is another important method of measuring causal capacities. In many situations, simple unconditional contingencies do not correctly reflect the underlying causal relations. When alternative causal factors are present, conditional contingencies should be computed that hold these factors constant (Cartwright, 1989; Cheng, 1993; Cheng & Novick, 1992; Melz et al., 1993). However, even this recommendation leads to correct results only when the right background conditions hold. A cofactor should be taken into account only when it is expected to be *causally relevant* (Waldmann & Hagmayer, 1995). Furthermore, causal factors should not be used as conditioning variables when they constitute intermediates in a causal chain linking the target cause and the target effect (Cartwright, 1989), or when they represent collateral side effects (Eells, 1991). In these cases, holding the cofactors fixed distorts the statistical relations between the target cause and the target effect, and prevents the causal factor from displaying its causal significance in the form of the relevant conditional probabilities. These are examples of how prior assumptions about the causal model underlying the observed events may dramatically alter the way statistical information should be processed. Other examples of effects of prior knowledge include assumptions about the integration of causal influences (Waldmann, 1991), about the temporal lag between causes and effects (Anderson, 1990), about the mathematical function relating continuous causes and effects (Zelazo & Shultz, 1989), and about the segmentation of the event stream into potential causes and effects (Gallistel, 1990). Without prior knowledge that is already available at the outset of the induction process new causal knowledge cannot properly be acquired.

Acknowledgments

I would like to thank P. Cheng, D. Medin, A. Merin, U.-D. Reips, and D. Shanks for helpful comments. I particularly thank Keith Holyoak for many stimulating discussions.

References

Ahn, W., Kalish, C. W., Medin, D. L., & Gelman, S. A. (1995). The role of covariation versus mechanism information in causal attribution. *Cognition, 54,* 299–352.

Ahn, W., & Mooney, R. J. (1995). Biases in refinement of existing knowledge. In J. D. Moore & J. F. Lehman, (Eds.), *Proceedings of the Seventeenth Annual Conference of the Cognitive Science Society* (pp. 437–442). Hillsdale, NJ: Erlbaum.

Alloy, L. B., & Tabachnik, N. (1984). Assessment of covariation by humans and animals: The joint influence of prior expectations and current situational information. *Psychological Review, 91,* 112–149.

Anderson, J. R. (1990). *The adaptive character of thought.* Hillsdale, NJ: Erlbaum.

Baker, A. G., & Mazmanian, D. (1989). Selective associations in causality judgments II: A strong relationship may facilitate judgments of a weaker one. In *Proceedings of the Eleventh Annual Conference of the Cognitive Science Society* (pp. 538–545). Hillsdale, NJ: Erlbaum.

Bindra, D., Clarke, K. A., & Shultz, T. R. (1980). Understanding predictive relations of necessity and sufficiency in formally equivalent "causal" and "logical" problems. *Journal of Experimental Psychology: General, 109,* 422–443.

Bromberger, S. (1966). Why-questions. In R. Colodny (Ed.), *Mind and cosmos* (pp. 86–114). Pittsburgh: University of Pittsburgh Press.

Cartwright, N. (1983). *How the laws of physics lie. Essay 1.* Oxford: Clarendon Press.

Cartwright, N. (1989). *Nature's capacities and their measurement.* Oxford: Clarendon Press.

Chapman, G. B. (1991). Trial order affects cue interaction in contingency judgment. *Journal of Experimental Psychology: Learning, Memory, and Cognition, 17,* 837–854.

Chapman, G. B., & Robbins, S. J. (1990). Cue interaction in human contingency judgment. *Memory & Cognition, 18,* 537–545.

Chapman, L. J., & Chapman, J. P. (1967). Genesis of popular but erroneous psychodiagnostic observations. *Journal of Abnormal Psychology, 72,* 193–204.

Chapman, L. J., & Chapman, J. P. (1969). Illusory correlation as an obstacle to the use of valid diagnostic signs. *Journal of Abnormal Psychology, 74,* 271–280.

Cheng, P. W. (1993). Separating causal laws from causal facts: Pressing the limits of statistical relevance. In D. L. Medin (Ed.), *The psychology of learning and motivation* (Vol. 30, pp. 215–264). San Diego, CA: Academic Press.

Cheng, P. W., & Novick, L. R. (1991). Causes versus enabling conditions. *Cognition, 40*, 83–120.

Cheng, P. W., & Novick, L. R. (1992). Covariation in natural causal induction. *Psychological Review, 99*, 365–382.

Choi, S., McDaniel, M. A., & Busemeyer, J. R. (1993). Incorporating prior biases in network models of conceptual rule learning. *Memory & Cognition, 21*, 413–423.

Couvillon, P. A., & Bitterman, M. E. (1982). Compound conditioning in honeybees. *Journal of Comparative and Physiological Psychology, 96*, 192–199.

Dawes, R. M. (1988). *Rational choice in an uncertain world.* San Diego, CA: Harcourt Brace Jovanovich.

Dowe, P. (1992). Process causality and asymmetry. *Erkenntnis, 37*, 179–196.

Eddy, D. M. (1982). Probabilistic reasoning in clinical medicine: Problems and opportunities. In D. Kahneman, P. Slovic, & A. Tversky (Eds.), *Judgment under uncertainty: Heuristics and biases* (pp. 249–267). New York: Cambridge University Press.

Eells, E. (1991). *Probabilistic causality.* Cambridge, UK: Cambridge University Press.

Einhorn, H. J., & Hogarth, R. M. (1986). Judging probable cause. *Psychological Bulletin, 99*, 3–19.

Esmoris-Arranz, F. J., Miller, R. R., & Matute, H. (1995). *Blocking of antecedent and subsequent events: Implications for cue competition in causality judgment.* Manuscript submitted for publication.

Fair, D. (1979). Causation and the flow of energy. *Erkenntnis, 14*, 219–250.

Gallistel, C. R. (1990). *The organization of learning.* Cambridge, MA: MIT Press.

Gigerenzer, G., Hell, W., & Blank, H. (1988). Presentation and content: The use of base rates as a continuous variable. *Journal of Experimental Psychology: Human Perception and Performance, 14*, 513–525.

Gluck, M. A., & Bower, G. H. (1988a). From conditioning to category learning: An adaptive network model. *Journal of Experimental Psychology: General, 117*, 227–247.

Gluck, M. A., & Bower, G. H. (1988b). Evaluating an adaptive network model of human learning. *Journal of Memory and Language, 27*, 166–195.

Griffin, D., & Tversky, A. (1992). The weighing of evidence and the determinants of confidence. *Cognitive Psychology, 24*, 411–435.

Hempel, C. G. (1965). *Aspects of scientific explanation.* New York: Free Press.

Holyoak, K. J., & Spellman, B. A. (1993). Thinking. *Annual Review of Psychology, 44*, 265–315.

Hume, D. (1977). *An enquiry concerning human understanding.* Indianapolis, IN: Hackett Publishing Company. (Original work published 1748).

Hume, D. (1978). *A treatise of human nature.* Oxford: Clarendon Press. (Original work published 1739).

Jenkins, H. M., & Ward, W. C. (1965). Judgment of contingency between responses and outcomes. *Psychological Monographs, 79* (Whole volume X).

Kamin, L. J. (1969). Predictability, surprise, attention, and conditioning. In B. A. Campbell & R. M. Church (Eds.), *Punishment and aversive behavior* (pp. 276–296). New York: Appleton-Century-Crofts.

Kant, I. (1950). *Critique of pure reason* (N. K. Smith, Trans.). London: Macmillan. (Original work published 1781).

Kehoe, E. J., & Graham, P. (1988). Summation and configuration: Stimulus compounding and negative patterning in the rabbit. *Journal of Experimental Psychology: Animal Behavior Processes, 14*, 320–333.

Kitcher, P. (1989). Explanatory unification and the causal structure of the world. In P. Kitcher & W. C. Salmon (Eds.), *Minnesota studies in the philosophy of science* (Vol. 13, pp. 410–505). Minneapolis: University of Minnesota Press.

Klayman, J., & Brown, K. (1993). Debias the environment instead of the judge: An alternative approach to reducing error in diagnostic (and other) judgment. *Cognition, 49,* 97–122.

Koehler, J. J. (in press). The base rate fallacy reconsidered: Descriptive, normative and methodological challenges. *Behavioral and Brain Sciences.*

Kruschke, J. K. (1992). ALCOVE: An exemplar-based connectionist model of category learning. *Psychological Review, 99,* 22–44.

Mackie, J. L. (1974). *The cement of the universe. A study of causation.* Oxford: Clarendon Press.

Mackintosh, N. J. (1983). *Conditioning and associative learning.* Oxford: Clarendon Press.

Matute, H., Arcediano F., & Miller, R. R. (1996). Test question modulates cue competition between causes and between effects. *Journal of Experimental Psychology: Learning, Memory, and Cognition, 22,* 182–196.

Medin, D. L., & Edelson, S. M. (1988). Problem structure and the use of base-rate information from experience. *Journal of Experimental Psychology: General, 117,* 68–85.

Melz, E. R., Cheng, P. W., Holyoak, K. J., & Waldmann, M. R. (1993). Cue competition in human categorization: Contingency or the Rescorla-Wagner learning rule? Comments on Shanks (1991). *Journal of Experimental Psychology: Learning, Memory, and Cognition, 19,* 1398–1410.

Minsky, M., & Papert, S. (1969). *Perceptrons: An introduction to computational geometry.* Cambridge, MA: MIT Press.

Murphy, G. L., & Medin, D. L. (1985). The role of theories in conceptual coherence. *Psychological Review, 92,* 289–316.

Pavlov, I. P. (1927). *Conditioned reflexes.* London: Oxford University Press.

Pazzani, M. J. (1991). Influence of prior knowledge on concept acquisition: Experimental and computational results. *Journal of Experimental Psychology: Learning, Memory, and Cognition, 17,* 416–432.

Pearl, J. (1988). *Probabilistic reasoning in intelligent systems: Networks of plausible inference.* San Mateo, CA: Morgan Kaufmann.

Piaget, J. (1930). *The child's conception of physical causality.* London: Routledge & Kegan Paul.

Reed, S. K., & Evans, A. C. (1987). Learning functional relations: A theoretical and instructional analysis. *Journal of Experimental Psychology: General, 116,* 106–118.

Reichenbach, H. (1956). *The direction of time.* Berkeley & Los Angeles: University of California Press.

Rescorla, R. A. (1973). Evidence for the "unique stimulus" account of configural conditioning. *Journal of Comparative and Physiological Psychology, 85,* 331–338.

Rescorla, R. A. (1991). Associations of multiple outcomes with an instrumental response. *Journal of Experimental Psychology: Animal Behavior Processes, 17,* 465–474.

Rescorla, R. A. (1993). Preservation of response-outcome associations through extinction. *Animal Learning and Behavior, 21,* 238–245.

Rescorla, R. A. (1995). Full preservation of a response-outcome association through training with a second outcome. *The Quarterly Journal of Experimental Psychology, 48B,* 252–261.

Rescorla, R. A., & Wagner, A. R. (1972). A theory of Pavlovian conditioning: Variations in the effectiveness of reinforcement and nonreinforcement. In A. H. Black & W. F. Prokasy (Eds.), *Classical conditioning II. Current research and theory* (pp. 64–99). New York: Appleton-Century-Crofts.

Rumelhart, D. E., Hinton, G. E., & Williams, R. J. (1986). Learning internal representations by error propagation. In D. E. Rumelhart, J. L. McClelland, & The PDP Research Group

(Eds.), *Parallel distributed processing: Explorations in the microstructure of cognition* (Vol. 1, pp. 318–362). Cambridge, MA: MIT Press.

Salmon, W. C. (1971). *Statistical explanation and statistical relevance.* Pittsburgh: University of Pittsburgh Press.

Salmon, W. C. (1980). Probabilistic causality. *Pacific Philosophical Quarterly, 61,* 50–74.

Salmon, W. C. (1984). *Scientific explanation and the causal structure of the world.* Princeton, NJ: Princeton University Press.

Shanks, D. R. (1985). Forward and backward blocking in human contingency judgment. *Quarterly Journal of Experimental Psychology, 37B,* 1–21.

Shanks, D. R. (1991). Categorization by a connectionist network. *Journal of Experimental Psychology: Learning, Memory, and Cognition, 17,* 433–443.

Shanks, D. R. (1993). Human instrumental learning: A critical review of data and theory. *British Journal of Psychology, 84,* 319–354.

Shanks, D. R., & Dickinson, A (1987). Associative accounts of causality judgment. In G. H. Bower (Ed.), *The psychology of learning and motivation: Advances in research and theory* (Vol. 21, pp. 229–261). New York: Academic Press.

Shanks, D. R., & Lopez, F. J. (in press). Causal order does not affect cue selection in human associative learning. *Memory & Cognition.*

Simpson, E. H. (1951). The interpretation of interaction in contingency tables. *Journal of the Royal Statistical Society, Series, B, 13,* 238–241.

Suppes, P. (1970). *A probabilistic theory of causality.* Amsterdam: North-Holland.

Thorndike, E. L. (1911). *Animal intelligence: Experimental studies.* New York: Macmillan.

Tolman, E. C., & Brunswik, E. (1935). The organism and the causal texture of the environment. *Psychological Review, 42,* 43–77.

Tversky, A., & Kahneman, D. (1980). Causal schemas in judgments under uncertainty. In M. Fishbein (Ed.), *Progress in social psychology* (pp. 49–72). Hillsdale, NJ: Erlbaum.

Van Hamme, L. J., Kao, S. F., & Wasserman, E. A. (1993). Judging intervent relations: From cause to effect and from effect to cause. *Memory & Cognition, 21,* 802–808.

von Wright, G. H. (1971). *Explanation and understanding.* Ithaca, NY: Cornell University Press.

Waldmann, M. R. (1991, November 23–25). *Cue-compounding versus cue-decompounding of complex causes.* Paper presented at the 32nd annual meeting of the Psychonomic Society, San Francisco.

Waldmann, M. R. (1996). *Competition among causes in predictive and diagnostic learning.* Manuscript in preparation.

Waldmann, M. R., & Hagmayer, Y. (1995). When a cause simultaneously produces and prevents an effect. In J. D. Moore & J. F. Lehman (Eds.), *Proceedings of the Seventeenth Annual Conference of the Cognitive Science Society* (pp. 425–430). Hillsdale, NJ: Erlbaum.

Waldmann, M. R., & Holyoak, K. J. (1990). Can causal induction be reduced to associative learning? In *Proceedings of the Twelfth Annual Conference of the Cognitive Science Society* (pp. 190–197). Hillsdale, NJ: Erlbaum.

Waldmann, M. R., & Holyoak, K. J. (1992). Predictive and diagnostic learning within causal models: Asymmetries in cue competition. *Journal of Experimental Psychology: General, 121,* 222–236.

Waldmann, M. R., & Holyoak, K. J. (in press). Determining whether causal order affects cue selection in human contingency learning: Comments on Shanks and Lopez (in press). *Memory & Cognition.*

Waldmann, M. R., Holyoak, K. J., & Fratianne, A. (1995). Causal models and the acquisition of category structure. *Journal of Experimental Psychology: General, 124,* 181–206.

Waldmann, M. R., & Reips, U.-D. (1996). *Base rate appreciation after predictive and diagnostic learning.* Manuscript in preparation.

Wasserman, E. A. (1990). Detecting response-outcome relations: Toward an understanding of the causal texture of the environment. In G. H. Bower (Ed.), *The psychology of learning and motivation* (Vol. 26, pp. 27–82). San Diego, CA: Academic Press.

Wasserman, E. A. (1993). Comparative cognition: Beginning the second century of the study of animal intelligence. *Psychological Bulletin, 113,* 211–228.

Wasserman, E. A., Chatlosh, D. L., & Neunaber, D. J. (1983). Perception of causal relations in humans: Factors affecting judgments of response-outcome contingencies under free-operant procedures. *Learning and Motivation, 14,* 406–432.

Weiss, S. J. (1972). Stimulus compounding in free-operant and classical conditioning: A review and analysis. *Psychological Bulletin, 78,* 189–208.

Williams, D. A., Sagness, K. E., & McPhee, J. E. (1994). Configural and elemental strategies in predictive learning. *Journal of Experimental Psychology: Learning, Memory, and Cognition, 20,* 694–709.

Wiser, M., & Carey, S. (1983). When heat and temperature were one. In D. Gentner & A. Stevens (Eds.), *Mental models* (pp. 267–297). Hillsdale, NJ: Erlbaum.

Wisniewski, E. J., & Medin, D. L. (1994). On the interaction of theory and data in concept learning. *Cognitive Science, 18,* 221–281.

Young, M. E. (1995). On the origin of personal causal theories. *Psychonomic Bulletin & Review, 2,* 83–104.

Zelazo, P. D., & Shultz, T. R. (1989). Concepts of potency and resistance in causal prediction. *Child Development, 60,* 1307–1315.

A COMPARATIVE ANALYSIS OF NEGATIVE CONTINGENCY LEARNING IN HUMANS AND NONHUMANS

Douglas A. Williams

I. Introduction

Learning about the causal structure of their surroundings allows organisms to anticipate future events, and, if called upon, to respond adaptively. A field mouse learns that foraging in a sheltered location allows it to avoid predation by a hawk. A teacher learns that an icy glare will silence a talkative student in the back of the classroom. Both of these examples involve the learning of a negative interevent contingency. The occurrence of one event (a negatively predictive cue) is reliably followed by a reduction in the probability of another event (the consequence). Returning to our examples, the sheltered location and the icy glare serve as cues for a reduction in predation or chatter. It is natural to ask whether the learning in the preceding examples, and that seen when two events are positively contingent, can be attributed to a common underlying process: Is there a general learning process responsible for the behavior of both the field mouse and the lecturer, or are animal and human behavior specialized products of evolution that are more dissimilar than similar?

Although specialists with interests in animal learning have always believed that behavior is not entirely species specific, early comparisons of the adaptive behavior of humans and nonhumans were more anecdotal

TABLE I

Experiment Design for Expectancy
Violation Mechanism[a]

Stage 1	Stage 2	Test
PC → market rise	PNC → no market rise	N ?
C → no market rise	RC → no market rise	R ?

[a] After Chapman and Robbins (1990, Experiment 2).

than theoretically telling. Little was known about the process by which any organism detected interevent contingencies. However, a number of researchers have commented on some unexpected similarities in the contingency detection mechanisms of humans and other animals (e.g., Allan, 1993; Shanks, 1993b; Shanks & Dickinson, 1987; Wasserman, 1990b; Young, 1995). For illustration, consider the conditions under which humans and animals divine that two events are negatively related—the topic of the present chapter. *Expectancy violation*[1] is the term that best describes the conditions that produce negative contingency learning in both humans and nonhumans: A cue becomes negatively contingent when its presentation is correlated with a decrease in the probability of some consequence. Negative contingency learning is a two-stage process. First, subjects must appreciate that one cue signals the consequence, and second, they must appreciate that when this positive cue appears in the presence of the negative cue, the otherwise predictable consequence is less likely.

Chapman and Robbins (1990, Experiment 2) were the first researchers to provide evidence for the expectancy violation mechanism in human negative contingency learning. They asked subjects to predict whether the overall value of a fictional stock market would rise (consequence) or not rise (no consequence) on the basis of whether the value of particular stocks had risen (cue present) or not (cue absent). The design of their experiment is shown in Table I. Using a within-subject procedure, they varied whether subjects expected a market rise in the presence of two cues in Stage 1: Stock P (positive) always signaled a market rise, while Stock C (constant feature or context) did not. Stock C was actually present on every trial in the experiment; however, when presented independently of Stock P in Stage 1, the market did not rise. In Stage 2, subjects were shown that when Stock N (negative) occurred in the company of Stocks P and C, the overall value of the stock market did not rise as it had on the PC trials in Stage

---

[1] The term *expectancy violation* is reserved for describing the surprising *non*occurrence of the consequence; it will not be used to refer to the surprising occurrence of the consequence.

1. That is, the presence of Stock N canceled the usual effect of Stock P, a negation or inhibition effect. Consistent with the expectancy violation principle, Stock N was rated as negatively predictive at the end of Stage 2.

Most important for comparison purposes are the contingency ratings of another cue, Stock R (redundant), which appeared in compound in Stage 2 with the nonpredictive Stock C. The RC trials, like the PNC trials, were associated with no market rise. However, Stock R was rated by subjects as being neutral rather than negative at the termination of Stage 2. This critical finding is predicted by the expectancy violation principle. Subjects were not expecting a market rise in the presence of Stock C, and when none occurred, there was no reason to attribute the absence of a market rise to the inhibitory effect of Stock R. Stock R might appear to be a negative cue because it was not followed by a market rise, but unlike the PNC trials, the absence of a market rise on RC trials was not unexpected (pseudo-negation rather than true negation). In summary, although neither Stock N nor Stock R was followed by a rising market, only Stock N provided nonredundant information about the absence of an otherwise likely event.

These data are formally analogous to those reported by Rescorla (1979) in conditioned suppression with rats. In Rescorla's experiment, a tone conditioned stimulus (CS) was reinforced with a shock unconditioned stimulus (US) in one group; in the other group the tone was not followed by shock. Next, both groups received compound presentations of the tone and a light, which were not reinforced. At issue in this experiment was whether the light would become preferentially inhibitory in the group for which the tone was excitatory. In this group, the light had appeared when shock was expected but no shock was received (negation). In a subsequent test, the rats of this group did not respond fearfully when the light was presented with another auditory CS that had been separately reinforced with shock. This transfer effect to another excitatory CS was not observed in the remaining group: Although the light had always been followed by "no shock" in the past, it did not exhibit the capacity to inhibit the fear evoked by a separately reinforced CS. This null result makes sense because the light had not originally appeared in conjunction with a fear-evoking tone. Thus, the light's inhibitory properties depended on it providing information about the omission of an otherwise likely US.

Correspondences in human and animal data have encouraged a number of researchers to articulate the view that a single learning mechanism might explain the adaptive behavior of humans and other animals (e.g., Allan, 1993; Shanks & Dickinson, 1987). Associative, rule-based learning, and temporal coding currently provide the most viable accounts of the learning of interevent contingencies (Shanks, 1993b). Until the interest in connectionist modeling (McClelland & Rumelhart, 1986; Rumelhart & McClelland, 1986), associative models were well on their way to being cast as a minor player in human cognitive psychology. Associative models encode the causal structure of the environment in a network of learned connections between mental representations of cues and consequences. Learning consists of modifications of the weights of associative connections, so that consequences become positively associated with antecedent cues that reliably precede them. Negative contingency learning is modeled by the development of inhibitory connections that regulate the behavior of the network. Predictable absences cause the formation of negative cue-to-consequence associations, which allow the organism to learn that in some instances a positive cue will not be followed by its usual consequence. The idea that association formation is the mechanism behind the development of conditioned reflexive behavior has always been well received. What is new, however, is the suggestion that associative models can be regarded as powerful vehicles for understanding behavior in general. This includes seemingly complex forms of learning such as human contingency judgments.

This revival of associationism in human learning occurred, paradoxically, during a period in which modern research was showing that Pavlovian and instrumental conditioning were more richly determined processes than previously thought. Perhaps the key finding was Rescorla's (1968, 1969a) discovery of the sensitivity of conditioned responding to the contingency between the CS and US (see Section II). The rule-like character of conditioning, combined with a paucity of alternative mechanisms, suggested to some that contingency learning may reflect the application of unconscious, statistical rules by animals to predict future events. For example, animals may withhold a learned response when the probability of the occurrence of the US is lower in the presence of the CS than in its absence, or $\Delta p = p(\text{US/CS}) - p(\text{US/no CS}) < 0$. This suggestion in the conditioning literature fitted nicely with contemporary depictions of humans as intuitive scientists (Kelley, 1973) or intuitive statisticians (Peterson & Beach, 1967). Subsequent developments in animal and human learning revealed that contingency learning is not well described by the Δp rule (see Section IV). Departures of the real mechanism from this statistical norm, however, did not lead to a wholesale abandonment of the rule-based approach. Instead, some researchers were encouraged to explore whether the experimental data were better described by other types of statistical rules (e.g., Allan & Jenkins, 1980; Cheng & Novick, 1992; Holyoak, Koh, & Nisbett, 1989; Wasserman, Chatlosh, & Neunaber, 1983).

Associative and rule-based accounts have been criticized for being too far removed from actual perception (e.g., Gallistel, 1990). If so, theories that assume that temporal relationships are directly perceived might provide a better fit to the data. Much of the recent work in animal learning on temporal models was stimulated by Honig (1981; see also Miller & Barnet, 1993). He suggested that animals encode the locations of events in the temporal stream. When discriminable events repeat themselves in a fixed sequence, such as a response always being followed 2 s later by a food pellet, the animal learns about the sequence of the events and their durations (i.e., response, 2-s interval, food). Honig speculated that temporal information might be stored in long-term memory in the form of a map. Unlike a typical road map, which contains spatial information, this temporal map would be the subject's recollection of the occurrence of events in the flow of real time. Of particular relevance to the present review is the claim of Janssen, Farley, and Hearst (1995) that pigeons, and by extension humans, are able to directly apprehend both "contiguity" and "noncontiguity," the latter term referring to the learning that two events are temporally isolated from one another (negatively related).

The purpose of the present article is: (1) to summarize the major points of correspondence in human and animal negative contingency learning; and (2) to ask whether associative, rule-based, or temporal mechanisms can explain the totality of the data. Before considering these issues, I describe the paradigms used to study negative contingency learning in humans and nonhumans, and introduce data that are consistent with the possibility of a single mechanism.

II. Paradigms of Study

Pavlov (1927) was the first to systematically explore negative contingency learning in animals. He used a conditioned inhibition paradigm in which one CS, P, was always followed by the US except when it was accompanied by another CS, N (i.e., P+, PN−, where "+" is the US and "−" is "no US"). Studies in appetitive conditioning demonstrated that dogs quickly learned to differentiate the reinforced and nonreinforced trials. In addition, Pavlov showed that if N was presented in combination with a transfer CS that had been separately paired with food on other trials (i.e., T+, where T = transfer), the responding normally evoked by T would be attenuated. This result, now known as *summation,* suggested to Pavlov that his dogs had learned that N signaled food omission.

Progress on the study of negative contingency learning was slowed by Skinner (1938), who pointed out, quite correctly, that discriminative performance in the conditioned inhibition paradigm could emerge for reasons other than the dogs having learned that N predicted a diminished rate of US occurrence. If P and PN can be differentiated perceptually, the latter compound stimulus may simply be less of a behavioral "excitor" than the former. How then does this perceptual differentiation explain summation? One possibility that occurred to Skinner is that subjects might have confused the only two stimulus composites in the experiment, namely PN and TN, and this could explain the low levels of responding to TN. In his own experiments, Pavlov had demonstrated that a novel stimulus would disrupt responding to a well-trained CS (external inhibition). Thus, negative summation might be a special case of external inhibition in which N drew attention away from P.

It was in the late 1960s, with the publication of an influential paper by Rescorla (1969a), that empirical grounds for negative contingency learning were established to nearly everyone's satisfaction. Rescorla urged researchers to conduct a second test, the *retardation* test, in an effort to show that reduced responding during the summation test was due to inhibition. In the retardation test, N is individually paired with the US until it evokes a conditioned response. Slow acquisition of the conditioned response compared to control levels would show that N was not a stimulus that simply possessed a low or zero level of excitation. There is no reason on this account to predict slower acquisition to N than to a control stimulus that also had never been previously associated with the US. Likewise, if N had merely acquired the ability to command the subject's attention, it should not be slow to evoke a conditioned response when paired with the US.

In an early experiment using the two-test strategy, Rescorla (1969b) examined whether the magnitude of retardation and summation would be related to the magnitude of the negative contingency. Background apparatus cues played the role of the positive cue. In Experiment 1, he divided the session into 2-min intervals. A background shock US was presented to the rats of the low probability group every 10th interval on average. Rats of the high probability group received a shock every 4th interval on average. Any background USs scheduled during the presentation of the 2-min tone, the negative CS, or during the following 2-min period were omitted. He found that the greater the magnitude of the negative contingency between the tone and shock, the greater the number of CS–US pairings it would subsequently take for the CS to evoke a conditioned fear response (retardation effect): The group that received the higher rate of background USs were slower to acquire a fear response to the tone than the group that had received the lower rate of background USs. Experiment 2 confirmed these findings using a wider range of negative contingencies and a summation test.

Further impetus for the two-test strategy came a few years later when researchers in two independent laboratories (Reiss & Wagner, 1972; Rescorla, 1971) showed that repeated nonreinforced presentations of the CS cause it to lose salience, but this effect called *latent inhibition* does not give the preexposed CS the ability to inhibit responding in a summation test. Subsequent findings in the conditioning literature provided further evidence for the learning of negative CS–US relations. They include the observation of Rescorla (1979), described in the introduction of this article, that negative summation depends on N being nonreinforced in compound with an excitor. Baker (1977) reports a similar effect. Some researchers also observed the development of a new response when the CS and US were negatively correlated. Wasserman, Franklin, and Hearst (1974) found that pigeons approached an illuminated keylight CS that was positively correlated with food. A new response, withdrawal, emerged in response to a keylight CS that was negatively correlated with food. In the approach–withdrawal procedure, the periodic presentation of food has an activational effect on the subject. This establishes a behavioral baseline of activity that can be modulated by signals for food omission. Performance of the withdrawal response depends on the presence of food in the situation. The withdrawal response evoked by a negatively correlated CS will disappear if food is withheld in the absence of the CS (Bottjer, 1982; Kaplan & Hearst, 1985).

Unlike animals, humans are able to say whether or not a cue signals a reduction in the probability of the consequence (negatively contingent). Thus, most researchers have simply asked human subjects to rate whether a particular cue is negatively correlated with the consequence. Neunaber and Wasserman (1986) had subjects tap a telegraph key and then indicate whether their tapping had affected the illumination of a lamp. A tapping response could occur during each 1-s sampling interval at the subject's discretion. Subjects were exposed to various programmed contingencies by varying the probability of the consequence (C) in the presence and absence of a response (R), $\Delta p = p(C/R) - p(C/\text{no } R)$. Experiment 1 included four positive ($\Delta p = 0.8, 0.6, 0.4, 0.2$), four negative ($\Delta p = -0.8, -0.6, -0.4, -0.2$), and five zero contingency problems. At the end of each problem, subjects were asked to rate the degree to which tapping affected the illumination of the lamp using a scale that ranged from -100 (prevents the light from illuminating) to $+100$ (causes the light to illuminate). Ratings of the contingency were strongly related to the nominal contingency and were symmetrical around zero.

The ratings procedure, like the approach–withdrawal measure in conditioning experiments, is a direct measure of negative contingency learning. Direct measurement of negative contingency using ratings scales has many advantages but also one important disadvantage. It is not particularly surprising that, when told about the possible existence of negative relations, subjects correctly discriminate negative and positive contingencies. Good psychological practice would have the experimenter provide as few clues as possible to the subject about the hypotheses under study. Neunaber and Wasserman were concerned about demand characteristics and asked another group of subjects to simply rate their degree of control over the illumination of the lamp from 0 (no control) to +100 (complete control). Subjects given this unidirectional scale were also sensitive to negative relations between tapping and lamp illumination. However, ratings of control tended to underestimate the actual negative contingency. As the negative contingency became more extreme, ratings of control approached +100, but not as quickly as they should have based on the magnitude of the unsigned Δp. In Experiment 2, subjects using the unidirectional scale were given more elaborate instructions in which they were informed that high ratings of control might be used to describe either highly positive or highly negative contingencies. Such cause–prevent information did eliminate the tendency to underestimate negative contingencies on the unidirectional scale. However, the unidirectional ratings were still less well correlated with the actual Δp than the bidirectional ratings because subjects were reluctant to give ratings that neared zero.

Results like these suggest that making strong claims about cognitive mechanisms based on the absolute value of the verbal judgment is a delicate matter (see Shanks, 1993a, 1993b). Neunaber and Wasserman (1986) found that unidirectional ratings were more likely to correlate with simpler, non-Δp strategies than were bidirectional ratings. One might conclude on this basis that subjects had multiple strategies at their disposal (e.g., Arkes & Harkness, 1983), and cause–prevent instructions encouraged the use of the more sophisticated Δp strategy. Alternatively, these correlations between strategies and scaled ratings may have more to do with the psychometric qualities of the particular rating instrument than with the actual mechanism underlying human contingency learning. Thus, although these experiments demonstrate a sensitivity of the reflective judgments of humans to the magnitude of the negative contingency, they provide no strong basis for adjudication among different theories.

Another way to avoid giving subjects clues that interevent relations may be negative as well as positive is to use a transfer test. Rather than asking subjects to *rate* whether a cue is negatively contingent, the experiment can focus on whether the negative cue *functions* as a negative cue should in a summation test. Using this approach, experiments from my laboratory have confirmed the findings of Neunaber and Wasserman (1986). Our subjects were not directly instructed that some cues might be negative, nor was this implied by other clues in the experiment such as a -100 to $+100$ ratings scale. Using a modified version of the stock market task described previously (Chapman & Robbins, 1990),[2] I showed that a negatively contingent cue

---

[2] In this variation, the cues were traded stocks (not traded = no cue) and a change in market value was the consequence (no change = no consequence).

will have an inhibitory effect in a summation test (e.g., Williams, 1995). In these experiments, Stock N was established as a signal for no change in the stock market by compounding it with Stock P, which always signaled a market change in the absence of N. Stock N also appeared in the absence of Stock P and was followed by no change in the stock market. When Stock N was subsequently compounded with Stock T, which had been positively correlated with a market change, subjects did not believe that TN would be followed by a market change like Stock T had. To further strengthen the foundation for the analogy, Williams and Docking (1995) demonstrated that N's summation with T was dependent on P being positive during the original learning stage. This conceptual replication of Rescorla's (1979) findings in rats suggests that expectancy violation is an important component of the mechanism that detects negative relationships in humans. Parallels of this sort provide a basis for suspecting a common mechanism in human and animal negative contingency learning.

III. Points of Correspondence

Although the data in the previous section provide clear evidence of parallels in human and nonhuman behavior, the parallels only hint at similar mechanisms. In most human experiments the critical data are judgments about interevent relations. Judgments are expressions of the subject's declarative knowledge, whether the judgments are numerical ratings (Neunaber & Wasserman, 1986) or predictions of what will happen in a transfer test (e.g., Williams, 1995). In nonhuman experiments, the probability of a conditioned response is the usual measure, an implicit test of learning as measured by a change in performance. Nissen and Bullemer (1987), among others (Hayes & Broadbent, 1988; Willingham, Nissen, & Bullemer, 1989), have provided evidence of dissociations between verbal reports (explicit learning) and performance (implicit learning) in humans. In their experiment, a light appeared in one of four horizontally arranged locations on a computer screen. The subject's task was to press the button located beneath the visible stimulus. When asked about the sequence of the light stimuli, amnesic subjects and normal subjects that were simply unaware could not report the order of the stimuli. They also denied having learned anything at all during the task. However, evidence of learning without awareness could be found in decreasing reaction times to the next stimulus in the sequence. Subjects could not say what stimulus would appear next, but anticipatory learning was evidenced by faster reaction times over trials.

If the distinction between explicit and implicit learning is a valid one (cf. Shanks & St. John, 1994), the parallels in cognitive processing noted in Section II could reflect a common sensitivity of two different learning systems, explicit (human data) and implicit (animal data), to negative inter-event relations. A detailed examination of the two learning systems might reveal profound differences in the properties of the mechanisms. However, dissociations between animal and human learning have been harder to come by than this hypothesis might suggest. This section reviews some of the shared properties of the mechanisms that detect negative contingencies in animals and humans.

A. Blocking and Overshadowing

The contingency detection mechanisms of humans and animals share many properties, most fundamental of these being the selective nature of the learning. The best known instance is Kamin's (1968, 1969) blocking effect. If Cue A signals the consequence in Stage 1, and Cues A and B are then compounded with each other and followed by the consequence in Stage 2, Cue A will block Cue B's association with the consequence. The blocking of a cue-to-consequence relation suggests that multiple cues compete to act as signals for the consequence. Most intriguing is that precisely the same cue-competition effects are obtained whether the subjects are rats or people. Animal and human blocking are both unidirectional: multiple consequences do not compete with each other to be signaled by a single cue (Rescorla, 1991; Van Hamme, Kao, & Wasserman, 1993; Waldmann & Holyoak, 1992), but multiple cues do compete to signal a single consequence (Dickinson, Shanks, & Evenden, 1984; Kamin, 1969). The competition between multiple cues suggests that temporal contiguity, or joint occur-rence, is not sufficient for the learning of a cue-to-consequence relation. The cue must provide new information about the occurrence of the consequence.

Of particular interest to the present review is the observation that a strongly conditioned negative cue can block or overshadow learning to a weaker one. Baker, Mercier, Vallée-Tourangeau, Frank, and Pan (1993; Baker, Murphy, & Vallée-Tourangeau, this volume, Ch. 1) systematically examined this problem in human contingency learning in an important series of experiments. Guided by associative analyses, they began by con-ducting experiments that were analogous to those conduced in instrumental conditioning with rats (Wagner, Logan, Haberlandt, & Price, 1968). In the experiments of Wagner et al. (1968), a light occurred in compound with one of two tones with equal probability (LT_1 and LT_2). In the overshadow-ing group, the LT_1 compound always signaled the availability of response-contingent food and the LT_2 compound always signaled that food was unavailable. In the control group, the two compounds were reinforced on a 50% basis. The important comparison was the degree of control exerted by the light when presented alone in the two groups. Wagner et al. (1968)

reasoned that if absolute validity, or simple contiguity, is critical for learning, both groups should respond at moderate levels to the light because it was reinforced with food, on average, every second trial. Contrary to the contiguity hypothesis, however, the rats of the control group responded more in the presence of the light than did the rats in the overshadowing group. This demonstrates that whether rats associate a discriminative cue with food reinforcement depends on the relative validity of the cue, not its absolute validity. In the overshadowing group, T_1 was perfectly correlated with the presence of food, so its strong association with food selectively overshadowed conditioning of the light. All of the cues in the control group were equally predictive, and thus, all of them acquired some control over responding.

In the experiments of Baker et al. (1993), subjects played a video game in which the objective was to safely guide a tank through a minefield (consequence). Their success at this task was correlated with the presence or absence of a plane (Cue A) and whether the tank was camouflage painted or not (Cue B). Experiments 1 and 2 demonstrated that a moderately positive paint/safety contingency, $\Delta p = .5$, was underestimated if a more valid predictor of safety was present, for example, if the plane/safety contingency was equal to either 1.0 or .8. These results are analogous to those reported by Wagner et al. (1968; for related human findings, Wasserman, 1990a).

In their Experiment 3, Baker et al. (1993) asked whether this selective learning could also be demonstrated using strong and weak negative contingencies. In this experiment, camouflaging the tank reduced the likelihood of the tank successfully traversing the minefield. In the overshadowing and control groups, there was a moderately negative camouflage/safety contingency, $\Delta p = .5$. The groups differed on the magnitude of the accompanying contingency between the plane and safety. In the overshadowing group, the presence of the plane always signaled the absence of a safe trip, $\Delta p = -1.0$, whereas in the control group, there was no relationship between the presence of the plane and safety, $\Delta p = 0$. The major finding was that subjects' estimates of the relation between camouflaging and safety were influenced by the value of the accompanying contingency. When the painted tank failed to cross the minefield safely, subjects in the control group attributed this outcome to the moderately negative paint/safety contingency; however, subjects in the overshadowing group selectively attributed the outcome to the presence of the plane. Ratings of the paint/safety contingency were close to the objective contingency, $\Delta p = -.5$, in the control group but were near 0 in the overshadowing group. Earlier, Suiter and LoLordo (1971) demonstrated in rats that when the absence of an electric shock was signaled by a compound of light and tone, the tone failed to signal "no shock" if, in a prior stage, the light had been shown to signal the absence of shock.

B. FORMS OF NEGATIVE CONTINGENCY LEARNING

Humans and animals are quick to detect negative correlations between events occurring in the same context. This learning, which can be symbolized as P+, PN− if there is a perfect negative contingency, can take at least two forms. First, subjects may learn that N provides information about the absence of a consequence that would otherwise occur (elemental or linear strategy). Second, subjects may learn that PN signals the absence of the consequence (configural or nonlinear strategy). Whether a linear or a nonlinear strategy is adopted can be influenced by, among other things, the number of negative exemplars.

In a typical summation experiment in animal learning, the subject is shown that P signals the consequence (P+) except when it is accompanied by the negative cue (PN−). Later, the subject is presented with the transfer compound, TN, which contains the negative cue and a transfer cue that had been individually paired with the consequence (T+). To withhold responding on TN trials, the animal must recognize that N is the same cue that previously appeared with P. In animal learning, transfer is rarely complete (e.g., Rescorla, 1982). One interpretation of this finding is that PN is perceived to some extent as a composite (i.e., a configural stimulus, Rescorla, 1972, 1973). On PN− trials, three distinct cues are present: P, N, and the PN configural cue (e.g., Gluck, 1991; Gluck, Bower, & Hee, 1989; Holyoak et al., 1989). The latter two cues, N and PN, share whatever inhibitory tendencies are necessary to suppress the response tendencies evoked by P. Negative summation on TN test trials can then be attributed to the inhibitory properties that N has acquired on its own. Incomplete transfer is explained by the absence of the PN integral stimulus. Note that unlike the earlier proposal of Skinner (1938), this particular configural analysis does not deny the existence of inhibition as a process.

Other animal data also support the elemental/configural distinction. In a little-known but important experiment, Strub and Barske (1977) compared the level of negative transfer on two types of summation trials, TN and TNP. The TNP triplet was of interest because two of the three elements, T and P, had separate associations with food reinforcement. Surprisingly, when the P stimulus was added to TN to create the triplet, the rats responded as little to TNP as to TN. Responding was also much lower on both of these trials than on T trials. An elemental theory cannot explain this finding because there are more excitatory elements on a TNP trial (T and P) than on a TN trial (T), and both trials contain a single negative element. Stated differently, the N element might have carried enough inhibition to cancel the effect of either T or P, but not both. Responding on TNP trials should have been equal to that seen on either T or P trials. The data are especially problematic because T and P were also shown to sum positively in a separate test (TP > T or P individually). However, the similar levels of responding to TN and TNP can be explained once the presence of configural cues is recognized. When P is added to TN, the coalescent PN cue is now present. Hence, the strong negative summation on the TNP trial can be attributed to the additional inhibitory influence of the configural cue.

Experiments from my laboratory also provide strong evidence for two distinct forms of coding in human contingency learning. Williams (1995) and Williams and Docking (1995) found that negative summation in contingency judgment is especially strong if, in addition to PN− trials, the subject is exposed concurrently to N− trials. Our working hypothesis in these experiments was that multiple examples should favor a linear strategy over a nonlinear strategy. If N provides consistent information about the nonoccurrence of the consequence in a number of instances, it makes sense to believe that N is generally negative rather than to attribute the lack of the consequence to the peculiar combination of cues present on that trial.

Table II shows the trial configurations and frequencies that Williams (1995) used in Experiment 2b. In that experiment, subjects were asked to predict on a trial-by-trial basis the deterministic relation between cues (traded stocks) and a consequence (change in the overall value of the stock market). To control trial frequency, it was necessary to include two negative cues in this experiment. The target cue is labeled simply as N in Table II. The control cue is identified by subscript (N_C). In the single groups, subjects received a single example that N was associated with no change in market value. In the single/combination group, N was presented only in compound with a known positive stock (PN−). In the single/alone group, N was presented only alone (N−). In the double group, N was presented both in compound (PN−) and alone (N−); thus, there were two examples that N was a negative cue. The critical data were obtained in the following summation test. Each subject indicated (yes/no) whether they believed each of TN, TU, N, and U (unknown) would be followed by a market change. Stock U was a control cue that subjects knew was a possible cue, but one that had never been previously seen.

The results of the summation test can be seen in Fig. 1. As can be seen in the figure, there was only a hint of transfer in the single groups (TN < TU). About 40% of the subjects in each of the single groups believed that TN would be followed by a market change. This is close to the base rate for unsystematic guessing and is similar to the level of summation transfer observed by other experimenters with a single PN exemplar (e.g., O'Boyle &

TABLE II

TRIAL CONFIGURATIONS AND FREQUENCIES FOR EXPERIMENT 2b[a]

	Learning stage		
	Block 1	Block 2	Test stage
Single/alone			
	P → consequence (5)[b]	P → consequence (10)	U → ?
	T → consequence (5)	T → consequence (10)	N → ?
		N → no consequence (10)	TU → ?
		PN_C → no consequence (10)	TN → ?
		PT → consequence (10)	
Single/combination			
	P → consequence (5)	P → consequence (10)	U → ?
	T → consequence (5)	T → consequence (10)	N → ?
		N_C → no consequence (10)	TU → ?
		PN → no consequence (10)	TN → ?
		PT → consequence (10)	
Double/combination and alone			
	P → consequence (5)	P → consequence (10)	U → ?
	T → consequence (5)	T → consequence (10)	N → ?
		N_C → no consequence (10)	TU → ?
		PN → consequence (5)	TN → ?
		N → no consequence (5)	
		PT → consequence (10)	

[a] From Williams (1995).
[b] Event frequencies are shown in parentheses.

Bouton, 1996; Tassoni, 1995). On the other hand, virtually all of the subjects of the double group believed that TN would be followed by "no consequence."

Before one accepts the notion that two exemplars facilitated inhibitory control by the N element, several alternative accounts need to be ruled out. For example, the data cannot be explained by assuming that subjects merely learned to associate N with "no consequence" after being shown the N− trials. Both the single/alone and double groups knew that N would be followed by "no consequence" (see shaded bars of Fig. 1), but strong transfer was seen only in the double group. Also arguing strongly against this account is the finding of Williams and Docking (1995, Experiment 1) that N does not have an inhibitory effect in a summation test when it appears in a discrimination in which P is not positive (C+, P−, PN−, N−).

At first blush, these findings are also at odds with the expectancy violation principle because on N− trials there is no explicit P to signal the possible occurrence of the consequence, and thus, the absence of the consequence should not have been especially surprising on the N− trials. One might

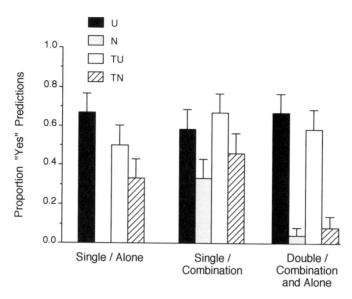

Fig. 1. The proportion of subjects that predicted the occurrence of the consequence ("yes") in the summation test of Experiment 2b of Williams (1995). In the single/alone group, the negative (N) cue was presented by itself in the absence of the consequence. In the single/combination group, N signaled that a specific positive cue would not be followed by its usual consequence. In the double/combination and alone group, N appeared both alone and in combination with a positive cue and the consequence did not occur. The data shown in the figure are the subjects' responses during test trials with U (unknown), N, TU (T = transfer), and TN.

attempt to reconcile this finding with the expectancy violation principle by noting that contextual cues are present on all trials. With contextual cues included, the trials of the discrimination can be symbolized as PC+, PNC−, and NC−, where C stands for contextual cues. Because contextual cues are paired with the consequence on some trials, N might provide information about the absence of the consequence on NC− trials, as well as on PNC− trials. In addition, subjects are instructed about the possible occurrence of the consequence, and this alone might cause them to believe that N had prevented the occurrence of the consequence on N− trials (e.g., Tassoni, 1995). These attempts at reconciliation, however, fall short of a complete account. The magnitude of expectancy violation should be greater if N appears in combination with P than if it appears in compound and with less predictive contextual cues. Note, trial frequency was equated in this experiment by replacing half of the PN− trials with N− trials; hence, the absence of P on half of the negative trials in the double group should have reduced the overall level of expectancy violation.

However, a quite plausible account based on expectancy violation is available if one provides for configural and elemental forms of cue encoding. A summation test measures the ability of the N element to inhibit any positive cue; that is, it measures elemental learning. Thus, the extra N− trials could simply have encouraged a change from configural to elemental encoding. The configural coding hypothesis was tested further in Experiments 3–5 (Williams, 1995). In Experiments 3 and 4, a double group was given a postlearning N+ treatment following mastery of the original discrimination (Stage 1: P+, PN−, N−; Stage 2: N+). These N+ trials abolished the summation effect and the original discrimination: After seeing the N+ trials, subjects no longer believed that N would inhibit either T (Experiment 3) or P (Experiment 4) any more than would an unknown cue. These findings are consistent with those in animal learning demonstrating that reinforcement of a conditioned inhibitory stimulus following discrimination learning undermines transfer and performance of the original discrimination (e.g., DeVito & Fowler, 1986).

Of special importance to the coding hypothesis was the finding in Experiment 5 that postlearning N+ trials had absolutely no detrimental impact on retention of the single/combination discrimination (P+, PN−). Figure 2 displays the results of Experiments 4 and 5, and allows a comparison of the very different effects of the reversal manipulation (N+) on retention of the double discrimination of Experiment 4 (A: PN judgments are different in the intact and reversed conditions) and the single discrimination of Experiment 5 (B: PN judgments are similar in the intact and reversed conditions). The retention effect in Experiment 5 is surprising in the context of Experiment 4, but is entirely consistent with the notion that the PN configural cue had acquired the lion's share of the available inhibition in the single/combination group. Retention of the original discrimination despite the contradictory N+ trials eliminates the possibility of poor learning of the single/combination discrimination. The original discrimination was solved by the PN configuration becoming negative instead of the N element. Shanks, Lopez, Darby, and Dickinson (this volume, Ch. 7) also report an experiment in which a reversal manipulation failed to affect the original discrimination in humans. Pearce and Wilson (1991) report a similar result in Pavlovian inhibitory conditioning with rats.

In humans, whether a linear (elemental) or nonlinear (configural) method is used appears to be under the control of the subject; that is, the strategy used can be influenced by either past experience in similar situations, mere suggestion, or the demands of the task. Williams, Sagness, and McPhee (1994, Experiment 4) exposed groups of college students to contingency problems that either did or did not have an elemental solution in order to determine the effect of prior learning on later contingency judgments.

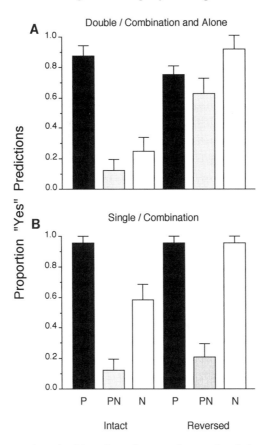

Fig. 2. The proportion of subjects in each group that predicted the occurrence of the consequence ("yes") in the retention tests of Experiments 4 (A) and 5 (B) of Williams (1995). In the double/combination and alone group, subjects received two concurrent discriminations in which each of the negative (N) cues appeared alone and in combination with their own positive (P) cues. Both trials were followed by no consequence. Next, one of the two negative cues was associated with the consequence (reversed or N+); the other was left intact. In the single/combination group, each of two negative cues signaled that its own positive cue would not be followed by the consequence. One negative cue was then reversed by association with the consequence. The data shown in the figure are the subjects' responses during a retention test of the intact or reversed discriminations.

Subjects in the configure group learned that separate presentations of either X or Y did not signal the consequence, but XY did (X−, Y−, XY+). The purpose of this training was to show the subjects that XY was a unique cue with its own special properties. Later, when tested on a blocking problem (A+, AB+), these subjects did not show the standard blocking effect.

There was no discounting of the added B element when it appeared in conjunction with A, as might be expected if the subjects were viewing the compound as "AB" rather than as A and B. Subjects in other groups that had previously experienced contingency problems that could be solved elementally, however, did show a robust blocking effect. Another experiment suggested that task instructions that emphasized the correct identification of elemental roles could also influence whether contingency ratings followed a linear or nonlinear strategy. It is important to recognize that facilitation of elemental processing in these experiments was caused by the subject's history of problem solving or by suggestion and not by the specific treatment of the A and AB cues. These findings are not inconsistent with Waldmann's (this volume, Ch. 2; Waldmann & Holyoak, 1992) contention that contingency judgments are influenced by subjects' prior experience.

This raises an interesting question: Do similarities in animal and human contingency learning flow out of the tendency of organisms to use either a linear or a nonlinear strategy? If so, past experience with linear or nonlinear problems should affect the later performance of animals as it does that of humans. Although no experiments have been conducted in negative contingency learning that address this question, there are related animal studies. For example, Alvarado and Rudy (1992) trained rats in a water-escape task to swim to a hidden platform that was located in the area of one of two stimulus cards. In Stage 1, for all subjects, the platform was located in the area of the black card (A+) and not the white card (B−). The critical manipulation occurred in Stage 2. The nonlinear group learned that the previously incorrect white card now signaled the correct location of the platform in a white/horizontal (B+/C−) discrimination. The control group was exposed to a vertical/horizontal (D+/C−) discrimination that was orthogonal to the original black/white (A+/B−) problem. In Stage 3, both groups were exposed to a nonlinearly solvable problem in which horizontal was correct (C+) and black (A−) was incorrect. Upon introduction of the new problem, performance in the control group deteriorated to chance on all three problems. However, rats that had previously experienced a nonlinear problem had no difficulty incorporating this new incompatible trial into their existing repertoire. The results of the experiments of Alvarado and Rudy (1992) show that rats are also capable of using either a linear or a nonlinear strategy, and most important, they also demonstrate that which strategy is used depends on prior knowledge.

In closing this section, it is important to mention another possible connection between the human and animal domains. In a serial feature negative discrimination, an animal learns that P is not followed by the consequence when preceded by a negative feature stimulus (N precedes P−, and "no N" precedes P+). The capacity of the feature to modulate responding to the P cue does not appear to be attributable to either the PN or the N cues signaling the nonoccurrence of the consequence. Instead, the negative feature is thought to "set the occasion" for nonreinforcement (e.g., Holland, 1984, 1985). For example, the feature may inhibit retrieval of a particular CS–US association. The human analogue of this finding can be seen in the distinction between a cause and an enabling condition (e.g., Einhorn & Hogarth, 1986). A match will light in the presence of oxygen, but not in the absence of oxygen. Oxygen is not causal, it is an enabling condition that allows another cause, striking a match, to produce an effect.

C. Retrospective Expectancy Violations

One finding in animal learning that is attracting much interest is the observation that negative summation is attenuated when the positive CS, P, is extinguished (deflated) after mastery of the original discrimination (i.e., P+, PN−, then P−). Using a fear-conditioning procedure, Hallam, Matzel, Sloat, and Miller (1990) first trained water-deprived rats to lick a tube for water reinforcement. The tube was then removed for the next two stages of the experiment. In the conditioning stage, P was consistently reinforced with the shock US, and the simultaneous compound of P and N was reinforced on a 25% basis. T was then reinforced with shock on separate trials in a different chamber for use in a later summation test. This conditioning stage was followed by an extinction stage. In the experimental group, P was repeatedly presented in the absence of shock for 48 trials. The control group did not receive P during this stage; they sat in the conditioning chamber in the absence of any CSs and the US. The rats were then returned to the test chamber and, with water reinforcement available, test trials were presented while the rats were licking the tube. Hallam et al. (1990) found that in the control group, suppression of the licking response by the fear-evoking T was inhibited in the presence of N; however, this negative summation effect was greatly attenuated in the experimental group. In another experiment, extinction of P was shown to decrease the magnitude of the retardation effect observed in a test in which N was repeatedly paired with shock. However, one must be cautious about making too much of these results. Hallam et al. (1990) did not show that attenuated inhibition was specific to the extinction of P, rather than just any positive CS. A number of other researchers have found contrary results (e.g., Rescorla, 1982; Williams, Travis, & Overmier, 1986); the reasons for the discrepancies are unclear.

Nonetheless, the findings of Hallam et al. (1990) are consistent with better controlled studies showing that if P is a context, rather than a discrete CS, N's inhibition is attenuated (e.g., Kasprow, Schachtman, & Miller,

1987; Miller, Hallam, Hong, & Dufore, 1991; Schachtman, Brown, Gordon, Catterson, & Miller, 1987). If the original relation between P and the consequence no longer holds, N may lose its negative properties even though it is absent at this time. In this case, P no longer signals a dangerous US, so N no longer signals safety. That N's ability to signal safety might depend on the continued association of P with the shock makes intuitive sense. A negative cue should not continue to negate a relation that no longer exists. The real surprise is that a conditioning mechanism could be this sophisticated. That is, the real mechanism is able to update, or retrospectively adjust, the value of an absent cue to bring it in line with the cue's overall correlation with the consequence.

I have recently tested whether a block of P− deflation trials following a P+, PN−, N− discrimination will also reduce the perception that N is a negative cue in contingency judgment (Williams & Docking, 1995). In these experiments, subjects judged whether a fictitious "widget press" machine was operating (consequence) or not (no consequence) on the basis of the cue lamps located on the face of the machine. Table III contains the trial

TABLE III

TRIAL TYPES AND THEIR FREQUENCY OF OCCURRENCE
IN EXPERIMENT 4[a]

Learning	Revaluation	Test
Deflated		
P → consequence (3)[b]	P → no consequence (9)	P ?
C → consequence (3)	C → consequence (3)	C ?
T → consequence (10)		T ?
A → consequence (10)		PN ?
PN → no consequence (10)		N ?
N → no consequence (10)		U ?
TA → consequence (10)		TN ?
		TU ?
Intact		
P → consequence (3)	P → consequence (3)	P ?
C → consequence (3)	C → no consequence (9)	C ?
T → consequence (10)		T ?
A → consequence (10)		PN ?
PN → no consequence (10)		N ?
N → no consequence (10)		U ?
TA → consequence (10)		TN ?
		TU ?

[a] From Williams and Docking (1995).
[b] Event frequencies are shown in parentheses.

types and their frequency of occurrence in various stages of Experiment
4. In the learning stage, subjects of both groups were exposed to a common
negative contingency (T+, C+, P+, PN−, N−, where C = control). The
important manipulation occurred in the revaluation stage. During that
stage, the deflated group was shown that P, which had earlier appeared
with N, no longer signaled an operating machine. In the intact group, P
continued to signal an operating machine. In its place, the control cue, C,
was subjected to the deflation treatment.

The results of this experiment are shown in Fig. 3. At the termination
of the experiment, subjects in the deflated group no longer believed that
P was positive (left-most bars). Subjects in the intact group believed that
P was still positive, but that C no longer signaled the consequence as it
had in Stage 1. Subjects in both groups remembered the original T+, PN−,
and N− trials; there was no evidence of differential forgetting. However,
on summation trials, the negative cue was significantly more effective in
canceling the transfer cue, T, in the intact group than in the deflated group.
Additionally, there was significant transfer only in the intact group (TN <
TU). It is interesting to note that our deflation effect was selective, a finding
of some theoretical significance. Cheng et al. (this volume, Ch. 8) describe
an extinction method in human negative contingency learning, which they
call "indirect," that is similar to the finding in this experiment. Like Hallam
et al. (1990), we also found no evidence of a deflation effect unless a

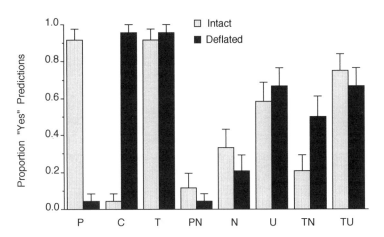

Fig. 3. Predictions in a summation test after deflation of either the positive cue that had
appeared with the negative cue (deflated, C+, P+, PN−, N−, then P−) or the control cue
(intact, C+, P+, PN−, N−, then C−). Results are taken from Williams and Docking (in
press, Experiment 4), where P is positive, C is control, T is transfer, N is negative, and U
is unknown.

reasonably high proportion of all the P trials throughout the experiment were P− trials rather than P+ trials.

Deflation of negative contingency learning is just one of many potential types of retrospective cue interactions (see Wasserman, Kao, Van Hamme, & Katagiri, this volume, Ch. 6). For example, the conditioned inhibition trials can be administered in a backward order rather than in a forward or concurrent order. In a backward inhibition experiment, both the experimental and control groups receive PN− trials in Stage 1. Next, the experimental group receives P+ trials and controls do not. There has been much interest in the question of whether negative contingency learning can be supported in a backward trial order (i.e., PN− then P+), and if so, whether a backward trial order supports the same degree of learning as a forward trial order (i.e., P+ then PN−).

Chapman (1991), in a series of carefully designed experiments, was the first to demonstrate backward inhibition in humans (see also Williams & Docking, 1995), that is, negative contingency learning can develop in a PN− then P+ trial order. In her experiments, subjects read medical charts that listed the symptoms (cues) presented by various fictional patients. After examining the charted symptoms, subjects made a diagnosis of whether the patient suffered from a disease called "morolis" (consequence). In Experiment 4 of Chapman (1991), the P_F (positive forward) and P_C (positive control) symptoms were diagnostic of morolis in Stage 1. Symptom P_C continued to predict morolis in subsequent stages. In Stage 2, symptom N_F (negative forward) appeared in compound with symptom P_F and the disease was unexpectedly absent. Subjects also learned that compound $P_B N_B$ (positive backward, negative backward) did not predict morolis. In the last stage, Stage 3, patients with only symptom P_B presented themselves for the first time and each had the disease morolis. In response to new information that symptom P_B was positively predictive of morolis, subjects began to rate symptom N_B as negative, although it never appeared in Stage 3. Subjects reasoned that symptom N_B must have been canceling the diagnosticity of symptom P_B in the prior stage. Although N_B was rated negatively in the backward trial order, these negative ratings were much less extreme than those of the corresponding cue, N_F, that had appeared in the forward trial order.

As far as I am aware, there are no experiments showing backward negative contingency learning in animals. Repeated attempts in one laboratory to uncover reliable learning in PN− then P+ backward trial order have been unsuccessful (e.g., Miller, Hallam, & Grahame, 1990). The failure to demonstrate backward inhibition in animals is problematic for the hypothesis that animal and human contingency learning are products of the same cognitive process. On the other hand, the dependency of negative contingency learning on the continued association of P and the US does indicate a retrospective inhibitory learning process in animals. Retrospective learning effects have also been observed in excitatory conditioning in rats in the recovery-from-overshadowing paradigm (AB+ then A−). Kaufman and Bolles (1981) found that suppression of general activity by a shock-associated B was increased if, after the compound conditioning, A's interfering association with the US was extinguished (see also Matzel, Schachtman, & Miller, 1985; Matzel, Shuster, & Miller, 1987). Thus, backward PN− then P+ learning in animals could be a parameter-sensitive phenomenon that has yet to be well documented. It should be noted that experiments in Pavlovian conditioning differ in many ways from the paradigms used to investigate human contingency learning. One important difference is that conditioning is a relatively slow process and the various stages of the experiment may be separated by several days or weeks. The data in a human contingency judgment experiment are collected in a single sitting. Thus, the original learning trials, having occurred recently, are more likely to be given the same weight as the revaluation trials.

IV. Mechanisms

One way to begin to evaluate various theories is to ask whether any of the mechanisms considered in the introduction of this article are, in principle, incapable of explaining the documented facts about negative contingency learning. Suggested mechanisms are always open to modification; therefore, it is often hard to determine the point at which a mechanism should be rejected outright. The predictions of the theory may not match observations because the mechanism is incomplete or wrong in a single important detail.

A. TEMPORAL CODING

Of the three classes of mechanisms considered in the introduction, associative, rule-based, and temporal contiguity, it is the last class that is in most urgent need of modification. It is worthwhile spending some time evaluating the temporal isolation hypothesis of negative contingency learning in animals (Janssen et al., 1995), because it strikes at the heart of traditional accounts. The temporal isolation hypothesis holds that temporally distant events should be perceived as disconnected from each other, and hence, negatively contingent. If the negative cue stands in a different place in the temporal stream of events than does the consequence, this learning should be incompatible with its opposite—positive contingency learning—and both summation and retardation effects would be expected.

Consistent with the temporal isolation hypothesis are recent experiments that disclose that animals learn more about interevent relations than is evident in standard tests of conditioned responding. Matzel, Held, and Miller (1988), in a provocative experiment, first taught rats that a 5-s clicker would be followed immediately by a 5-s tone. In Stage 2, the rats were shown that shock would occur for the entire duration of the tone, the second CS of the chain. Simultaneous pairings support little excitatory conditioning, so the rats did not respond fearfully when later presented with the tone. However, when tested with the clicker, the rats appeared to assimilate the temporal relations in Stages 1 and 2 into a single representation of the flow of time to produce the expectation that clicker would terminate with shock.

The notion that rats learn about the intervals of time separating events in a conditioning experiment, however, is not well connected with what is most fundamental about the conditions that produce negative contingency learning in animals. A negatively contingent cue conveys information about a reduction in the probability of the consequence. It negates the information provided by a positively correlated cue. Thus, the temporal isolation hypothesis is a poor model of negative contingency learning, because "not being related" and "being negatively related" are two very different things. In a P+, PN− discrimination, a multitude of events are absent in the moment following the presentation of N, not just the US signaled by P. However, N does not come to signal "nothingness."

This point is nicely demonstrated in an experiment described by Colwill (1991). She established N_F as a signal for the omission of food, and N_S as a signal for the omission of liquid sucrose. For example, the rat might learn that nose poking, a response that normally earned pellets, would not be reinforced in the presence of a light, and handle pulling, a response that normally earned sucrose, would not be reinforced in the presence of noise. The two negative stimuli were then tested for transfer with different responses that were associated with either food or sucrose reinforcement. She found that N_F selectively depressed a second response that earned food, and N_S selectively depressed a second response that earned sucrose. N_F and N_S came to signal the absence of a particular reinforcer, although neither stimulus had occurred at a time in which either food or sucrose reinforcement was available. Kruse, Overmier, Konz, and Rokke (1983) report a similar selective effect of an inhibitory CS on response latency.

A number of other observations also support tbe view that N signals a reduction in the probability of an expected event. In Pavlov's (1927) "method of contrasts," P+ and N− trials are intermixed and separated by relatively long intertrial intervals. The result is differential inhibition, which suggests an effect of temporal isolation. However, differential conditioning is effective in producing conditioned inhibition only if the context (C) becomes excitatory during training (Miller et al., 1991). Subjects perceive the discrimination as PC+, NC− and not P+, N−. In addition, it is not altogether clear from the temporal isolation hypothesis that a latent inhibition treatment should not produce conditioned inhibition (see Section II). If subjects are preexposed to the CS well in advance of the introduction of the US, the CS and the US are temporally isolated and should become negatively related. One might deal with latent inhibition by saying that if the CS and US are too distant, their negative relation will not be perceived. However, this post hoc accommodation begs the question of what it means to say that two events are temporally isolated. Lastly, the temporal isolation hypothesis cannot explain why N is capable of showing an inhibition effect in summation and retardation tests when PN is followed by the US with a nonzero frequency (e.g., Hallam et al., 1990; Kasprow et al., 1987); the probability of the US in the presence of PN, $p(US/PN) = .25$, may be less than P, $p(US|P) = 1.0$, but not zero. In this case, N is not reliably temporally isolated from the US, but it provides information about a partial reduction in the probability of the US.

It is always possible that some instances of negative contingency learning are the result of temporal isolation, although most instances are not. Temporal isolation and expectancy violation could be separate mechanisms with a common effect. A natural prediction of the temporal isolation hypothesis is that negative contingency learning should be stronger the farther apart that two events stand in the temporal stream. For example, a CS that is presented in the middle of a long intertrial interval should become strongly inhibitory, especially if the USs are spaced at predictable intervals (the explicitly unpaired procedure). On the other hand, these conditions should not be favorable for the expectancy violation mechanism because the absence of the US in the middle of the intertrial interval is not surprising. It also follows that if the intertrial interval is decreased (Droungas & LoLordo, 1994), or if the CS is moved closer to the US within an intertrial interval of fixed duration (Kleiman & Fowler, 1984), negative contingency learning should weaken because of a decrease in the temporal isolation of the CS and US.

Predictions such as these have been confirmed in animal learning (e.g., Janssen et al., 1995). However, the data are open to alternative interpretations. When the CS is moved closer toward the US, it also becomes more contiguous with the US. It may also become associated with local contextual cues that, in turn, are associated with the US (CS-context learning). If so, the CS may acquire excitatory tendencies that mask its own inhibition. The inhibition may not be weak at all. Indeed, Droungas and LoLordo (1994) concluded that their findings were most likely due to a masking effect. In sum, even the more limited claim that negative contingency learning can arise through temporal isolation, in addition to expectancy violation, remains open to question in animal learning.

Of course, no one would dispute the more general claim that temporal contiguity is an integral part of the contingency detection mechanism in animals. The question is how temporal information is transformed into knowledge that enables animals to predict the occurrence and nonoccurrence of another event. Is temporal contiguity a mere catalyst for the formation of excitatory or inhibitory associations, or do subjects record all of the interevent temporal relations in an experiment and use these as primitives for higher order computations of contingency? Gallistel (1990), in his book *The Organization of Learning,* describes a conditioning model based on the latter premise. His model is not open to the same criticisms as the temporal isolation hypothesis. It distinguishes cues that signal a reduction in the probability of the consequence from cues that are merely temporally isolated from one another. It also deals with Shanks' (1993b) concerns that models giving a primary role to temporal contiguity are usually poorly specified and have little to say about the cue-interaction effects (Section IIA). In many ways, Gallistel's alternative account is not unlike statistical rule-based accounts, discussed in the next few paragraphs, inasmuch as it can be likened to a time-series analysis and does not predict any effect of varying the order of trials (see Section IIIC).

With the exception of Wasserman (1990a) and Anderson and Sheu (1995), few experimenters have attempted to systematically apply a temporally based model to human contingency judgments. In his review, Young (1995) laments the fact that most human studies have used either discrete trials or summary information, which leave no room for an evaluation of temporal models like the one described by Gallistel (1990). In summary, more data is needed to evaluate whether temporal coding is the process by which humans and animals learn negative relationships.

B. ASSOCIATIVE

Associative and rule-based theories have enjoyed the most popularity as accounts of animal and human contingency learning. Most associative and rule-based theories have been substantially revised to accommodate new findings about the contingency detection mechanism. Because these theories are moving rather than stationary targets, it is more informative to trace the paths of change than to make strong claims about which of these two competing perspectives is a better representative of the true mechanism.

The Rescorla–Wagner model (e.g., Rescorla & Wagner, 1972; Wagner & Rescorla, 1972) is most closely identified with the associative approach.

This remarkable model was originally developed as a parsimonious account of cue interactions in animal learning (Section IIIA). The model's predictions about animal conditioning have been shown to be wrong in many instances (for review, see Miller, Barnet, & Grahame, 1995), and these mistaken claims are well enumerated in textbook discussions (e.g., Domjan, 1993). However, the theory remains highly cited. Its graceful account of the selective nature of the conditioning mechanism captures what is most striking about the process of Pavlovian conditioning.

The essence of the theory is that animals learn to identify which of the stimulus elements in a complex environment are correlated with reinforcement and nonreinforcement. During a conditioning episode, the animal is presented with one or more CSs (input events), and the US may occur or not occur (output event). Over many such trials, the animal gradually learns the roles of the various CSs—those that signal US presence, those that signal US absence, and those that signal neither US presence nor absence. The role of an individual CS is represented in its signed connection strength with the US (i.e., positive, negative, zero). Connection strengths are adjusted to minimize error using the least mean squares (LMS) rule. This psychological process is formalized in the following equation:

$$V_i = \alpha\beta \ (\lambda - V_{total}) \tag{1}$$

In Equation 1, V_i is the weight change in the connection between CS_i and the US on a given trial. The quantities, α and β are learning parameters for CS_i and the US, respectively, and they are constants varying between 0 and 1. If the CSs are equally salient, α can be set at 1 when the CS is present and 0 when the CS is absent; the US is usually coded as either 0 (absent) or 1 (present). The purpose of the algorithm is to bring the subject's expectation of the US, based on the CSs present on the current trial ($V_{total} = V_1 + V_2 \ldots V_N$), into agreement with the actual US (present: $\lambda = 1$; absent: $\lambda = 0$). The Rescorla–Wagner model differs from the model of Bush and Mosteller (1951), from which it is derived, in the quantity V_{total}. The subject uses the aggregate of all of the currently present CSs to generate an expectation. Thus, if the US is well predicted by CS_A ($V_A = 1$) at the time at which it is compounded with the CS_B, the latter CS will acquire no associative strength because the US is not surprising ($\lambda - V_{total} = 1 - 1 = 0$). Blocking of negative contingency learning is also predicted by this algorithm (e.g., Baker et al., 1993; Suiter & LoLordo, 1971).

According to the model, a P+, PN− discrimination is solved by P becoming positively associated with the US to the level of 1λ, and N becoming negatively associated with the US to the level of -1λ. When P and N elements occur in combination, the negative association cancels the positive association, and the net effect is 0λ. If the absence of the US is not surprising on PN trials, the model correctly predicts that N should not acquire negative associative strength (P− then PN−, and thus, $V_{total} = 0$ when N is presented for the first time). N should also suppress the US expectation evoked by a separately trained excitor, T, because responding on compound trials is assumed to be monotonically related to the summed associative strengths of the individual CSs. These successful predictions about cue interactions have encouraged generalization of the model, with minor modifications, to the human contingency judgment domain (e.g., Gluck & Bower, 1988).

The Rescorla–Wagner learning rule, in its original form, does not provide anything close to a complete account of negative contingency learning in either humans or nonhumans. First, the model does not remember which cues have appeared together as stimulus configurations. As a consequence, the model cannot learn problems that are not linearly separable (Minsky & Papert, 1969). For example, the model predicts that subjects should not be able to learn a negative patterning problem, A+, B+, AB− (Rescorla, 1972, 1973). Also, if one replaces the P with T in a summation test, the model predicts that P and T should be interchangeable. Transfer should be complete (T > TN and TN = PN). The aforementioned findings can be explained at the informal level if it is assumed that subjects are sensitive to the unique cue generated when P and N are presented together (see Section IIIB; Saavedra, 1975). One problem with this unique cue solution is that α values for configural and component stimuli are usually not specified (see Pearce, 1994). In addition, when predictions are formally derived by dividing attention among the configural and component stimuli, there are circumstances in which no set of parameter values yields a correct prediction (e.g., Pearce & Redhead, 1993; Redhead & Pearce, 1995a, 1995b).

For these reasons, Pearce (1987, 1994) has taken the extreme view that none of the learning displayed by animals is elemental. He argues that the constituents of the compound do not enter into individual associations with the predicted US, nor are the representations of these elemental cues activated on a compound trial. Instead, negative transfer (Section II), blocking (Section IIIA), and other elemental-like effects are explained by the generalization of excitation, inhibition, or both, from one stimulus configuration to another. Pearce's configural mechanism can readily master a discrimination between the reinforced and nonreinforced trials of a P+, PN− discrimination. P becomes associated with the US, and this excitatory learning generalizes to some extent to PN, because of the perceptual similarity of PN and P. Over trials, the PN compound will acquire enough of its own inhibition to counteract the generalized excitation from P. Because

TN and PN share the feature N, there should be generalization of inhibition from the original PN to the transfer compound, TN.

Pearce's model also predicts the low levels of responding that Strub and Barske (1977) observed on the TNP trial in their stimulus compound test (Section IIIB). The TNP trial, although novel, bears a strong resemblance to the nonreinforced PN trial of the original discrimination. Other findings in the experiment of Strub and Barske, however, are better explained by an elemental theory. Pearce's configural theory cannot explain the positive summation of two excitatory elements, P and T. I also argue in Section IIIB that animals do not always learn the same problems in the same way. A problem may be solved elementally or configurally, depending on the conditions prevailing at the time of learning or sometime in the past (Alvarado & Rudy, 1992, Section IIIB). These data suggest that animals have multiple coding strategies at their disposal. If so, the impressive list of successful predictions of the Pearce model (e.g., Pearce & Redhead, 1993; Redhead & Pearce, 1995a, 1995b) is best interpreted as evidence that configural learning is more general in animals than one might have anticipated, and perhaps, that pigeons solve visual discrimination problems on a purely configural basis. The results do not imply that elemental learning never occurs.

Nonetheless, the direction of change is clear. Associative models based on the Rescorla–Wagner learning rule must begin to pay more attention to how inputs are represented (e.g., Gluck & Myers, 1993) and to consider how prior bias might be incorporated into associative networks (e.g., Choi, McDaniel, & Busemeyer, 1993). One possibility is that subjects treat configural and elemental cues as if they are separate physical dimensions, like the dimensions of color and shape in object categorization. A connectionist model that learns to attend to stimulus dimensions that are relevant to the task at hand, such as the one described by Kruschke (1992), might explain the results.

A second problem with the original implementation of the Rescorla–Wagner model is its failure to predict learning when the trials are presented in a backward order (Section IIIC). Associative accounts of the cue-interaction effects in animal learning emphasize the importance of expectancy violation at the point of learning. A cue becomes negatively valued when it announces that a positive cue is less likely to be followed by the consequence. Thus, the model cannot explain why N is perceived as negative when it appears in the presence of a cue that is initially neutral and is only positive thereafter (i.e., P−, PN−, N− then P+; Williams & Docking, 1995). In humans, although learning in a backward trial order is often weaker than in a forward trial order (Chapman, 1991), it is often not negligible (e.g., Williams et al., 1994).

An accommodation of these facts by an associative model was not arrived at quickly, so it came as a surprise that a simple change in the model's treatment of absent stimuli could account for these troublesome data. This accommodation is based on the finding that humans and nonhumans can use the explicit absence of an expected cue as a stimulus (e.g., Hearst, 1991; Jenkins & Sainsbury, 1969; Newman, Wolfe, & Hearst, 1980). One spectacular instance of the use of absent cues by animals was reported by Weiss (1969). In the positive group, rats could earn food reinforcement during the presentation of A and during the presentation of B, but not in the absence of both A and B (intertrial interval). Later, when tested for stimulus additivity, there was a positive summation effect with more responses to the AB compound than to either A or B alone. The data of primary interest are from the negative group. Like the positive group, this group was also trained to expect food for lever pressing in the presence of the individual A and B cues; however, responding was not reinforced when both A and B were present (i.e., A+, B+, AB−). Weiss then tested the hypothesis that rats learned this problem by noticing the missing B on A+ trials and the missing A on B+ trials. During an additivity test for absent cues, the rats responded more frequently during an empty intertrial interval (missing A and B) than to either A (missing B) or B (missing A). Surprisingly, the magnitude of the summation effect was equivalent in the positive and negative groups. This suggests that stimulus absence in the negative group was just as powerful a cue as stimulus presence was in the positive group. It is important to note that summation in the negative group was obtained under somewhat artificial circumstances; the rats had never been exposed to a stimulus-free period in the conditioning apparatus before the additivity test. In most other situations, the presence of a cue would be more noticeable than its absence.

In the original implementation of the LMS rule by Rescorla and Wagner, the absence of a strongly expected cue (informative absence or missing cue) and the absence of a potential cue (uninformative absence) are treated the same. The model assumes that V_i changes only on trials in which CS_i is present, that is, when α has a positive value. When CS_i is absent, α is assumed to be 0, whether CS_i's absence is surprising or not. Based on the finding that subjects pay attention to missing cues, Tassoni (1995) and Van Hamme and Wasserman (1994; Wasserman et al., this volume, Ch. 6; see also Markman, 1989) have suggested that informative absences should be coded as negative α values (maximum $\alpha = -1$). In a P+, PN− discrimination, N is correlated with P, but not perfectly. When P is presented alone on the reinforced P+ trial, N's absence is a notable event. The expected N is not present. Of course, there are an infinite number of other cues that are absent on P trials, but these cues are not strongly expected and the absence of these potential cues should not be informative (all αs = 0).

For the sake of consistency, this method of information coding is applied in kind to the predicted event. If the consequence is highly probable, the absence of the consequence should be perceived as a "negative instance" rather than as "nothing," and it should be coded as -1λ rather than 0λ. This alteration changes the asymptote for negative contingency learning: Because P is associated with the consequence to the level of 1λ, and the training signal on negative trials is -1λ, the negative cue must carry a level of association strength of -2λ ($-2\lambda + 1\lambda = -1\lambda$). In human learning, subjects are instructed of the binary nature of the consequence and the data are usually modeled with equal weights, 1λ and -1λ, respectively). This equal weight assumption is consistent with binary representation, although it is not strictly correct to say that the absence of the consequence is a highly probable event.

When absent stimuli are coded in this way, the LMS rule is suddenly able to accommodate a wider range of phenomena (see Wasserman et al., this volume, Ch. 6). Chapman's finding of learning in a backward trial order (PN$-$ then P+) is a case in point. In Stage 1, P and N predict the absence of the consequence and each should acquire a small measure of negative associative strength (-1λ divided by 2 cues = $-.5\lambda$ each). In Stage 2, the absence of N on P+ trials should be surprising. Thus, N should acquire additional negative associative strength because its absence is correlated with the sudden occurrence of consequence [$\lambda - V_N = 1\lambda - (-.5\lambda) = 1.5\lambda$]. The terminal associative strength of N will be influenced by the degree to which the subject notices the absent N, at asymptote, ($-\alpha \cdot 1.5\lambda$) $+ -.5\lambda$. The revised model also handles the retroactive deflation of negative contingency learning, which is seen when P is not followed by the consequence after a block of intermixed P+ and PN$-$ trials (e.g., Hallam et al., 1990; Williams & Docking, 1995). In human experiments, one can ask for judgments after every trial. This has allowed the predicted changes in the associative strengths of missing cues to be directly measured on a trial-by-trial basis (Van Hamme & Wasserman, 1994).

The coding scheme is also recommended by experiments focusing on the perception of the consequence by human subjects. If the subject knows that the target event is binary, a series of nonreinforced N trials should cause N to accrue negative associative strength (i.e., -1λ). This prediction was recently confirmed by Tassoni (1995). It will be interesting to see whether the notion of "negative" coding will continue to be well received; it produces the required computational effects, and it has a high level of psychological appeal. One's enthusiasm for the revised model, however, should be tempered by the recognition that what counts as a missing cue is yet to be specified (see Cheng et al., this volume, Ch. 8).

One long-standing problem of the LMS approach that has yet to be fully reconciled with the experimental data is the assumption that organisms have access to only the updated strength of the cue-to-consequence association (Miller & Matzel, 1988; Miller & Schachtman, 1985). The current status of the target cue is stored in memory, but the subject does not retain any memory of where the cue stood on previous trials. The means by which the cue has acquired its associative status is unimportant; all important is the cue's terminal associative strength. This assumption of path independence is simply untenable, although the magnitude of the problem is somewhat less in configural cue versions of the Rescorla–Wagner model. For example, when a CS–US association is extinguished, the positive association does not disappear, rather it becomes latent (e.g., Bouton, 1994; Rescorla, 1989). Cheng and Holyoak (1995) suggest that in this case the model is too parsimonious—it is more simplistic than simple. I find myself in strong agreement with this criticism. This is certainly an important area for future theory development.

Another faulty prediction of the Rescorla–Wagner model is that presentations of N in the absence of the consequence should diminish negative contingency learning (Zimmer-Hart & Rescorla, 1974; see Cheng et al., this volume, Ch. 8). The Rescorla–Wagner model predicts that a block of N− trials following a P+, PN− discrimination should cause the negative associative strength of N to extinguish. This prediction is based on the assumption that $V_N = -1\lambda$ should move toward the training signal, 0λ (or from -2λ to -1λ with information coding). This faulty prediction is probably best handled by abandoning the assumption that positive and negative associations are symmetrical (for review see Williams, Overmier, & Lo-Lordo, 1992; see Cheng et al., this volume, Ch. 8, for similar concerns). In animal learning, conditioned inhibition is increasingly being described as a modulatory process. A negative cue may raise the threshold for activation of the US representation (e.g., Rescorla, 1979), rather than cause negative activation of the US representation (e.g., Van Hamme & Wasserman, 1994; Wagner & Rescorla, 1972).

In summary, it is surprising that a simple model like the one proposed by Rescorla and Wagner (1972)—with a few assumptions about the coding of cues—can explain such a wide variety of facts about human and nonhuman negative contingency learning. Other defects of the model, however, are not so easily corrected (the nonsensical prediction that inhibition should extinguish). The Rescorla–Wagner model, perhaps because of its ease of implementation in a connectionist form, has received more than its share of attention. Of course, the success of the associative approach does not fall entirely on the shoulders of the Rescorla–Wagner model. There are other associative models (for review, LoLordo & Fairless, 1985), although one would hardly know this from reading the human contingency judgment literature. One of these was mentioned in this discussion (Pearce, 1987). Most try, with varying degrees of success, to avoid repeating the mistaken predictions of the Rescorla–Wagner model (e.g., Wagner & Larew, 1985).

C. Rule-Based

The major theme of the present article is that humans and nonhumans appear to acquire knowledge about negative interevent relations in similar ways. As we have just seen, a number of researchers have extended associative models of classical conditioning to explain higher level judgments of causality and contingency. In the last part of this section, I turn this hypothesis on its head and ask whether classical conditioning can be regarded as a primitive form of rule-based learning.

Interest in the rule-based approach to classical conditioning can be traced to the experiments of Rescorla (1967, 1968). He showed that a statistical measure of contingency, Δp, was a useful empirical description of the conditions under which individual CS–US relations are learned. On a conditioning trial, the CS and the US may both occur (A), the CS may occur without the US (B), the US may occur without the CS (C), or both events may be absent (D). The mathematical relation between the CS and US can be represented in a 2×2 contingency table (see Fig. 4). The statistical

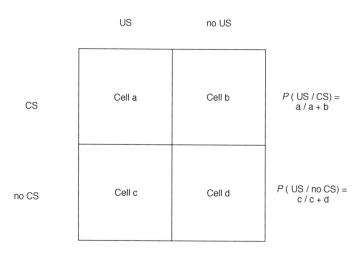

Fig. 4.   A 2×2 contingency table.

dependence of the target on the presence of the cue is Δp, where Δp, $= a/(a + b) - c/(c + d)$ or $p(\text{US/CS}) - p(\text{US/no CS})$.

A unique prediction of the Δp rule is that random presentations of two events should produce learned irrelevance. A cue is irrelevant if subjects learn that it provides no useful information about the consequence (Baker & Mackintosh, 1976, 1977; Matzel, Schachtman, & Miller, 1988). In animal learning, if the CS and US are presented on independent schedules, there should be approximately equal frequencies in the four cells of the contingency table. If the CS is then correlated with the US, either negatively or positively, learning should be exceedingly slow because the new correlated trials are diluted by the old uncorrelated ones. The Rescorla–Wagner model does not predict learned irrelevance. The theory predicts that an uncorrelated cue will have zero associative strength ($V_C = 0$) and should be neutral.

The Δp approach also assumes that learning is updated as trials accumulate in the four cells of the contingency table. Cue absence is represented directly in the contingency matrix, and thus, Δp models predict retroactive learning (Section IIIC). This central assumption has recently found its way into associative theories. However, Δp models are perhaps too normative. They predict no effect of trial order. This prediction is inconsistent with the finding that learning is usually much stronger in a forward trial order than in a backward trial order (Chapman, 1991). The Δp rule can be reconciled with the data by introducing the complicating assumption that subjects do not weigh each and every trial equally (see Williams & Docking, 1995). However, this involves adopting the assumption of associative models that contingency learning is not normative. Even so, models like these remain underspecified with respect to which trials are included in the subject's evaluation of contingency.

The most serious challenge to Δp models has been to provide a workable psychological mechanism for cue interactions (Section IIIA). A comparison of the probability of the consequence in the presence and absence of the predictive cue produces a judgment that is isolated from judgments about other cues: The unconditional Δp strategy does not predict blocking. Because negative contingency learning is caused by the interaction of a positive and a negative cue, this cue-interaction effect also cannot be explained by the Δp rule (Chapman & Robbins, 1990).

As Cheng (e.g., Cheng & Holyoak, 1995; Cheng et al., this volume, Ch. 8; Cheng & Novick, 1992) shows in her analysis of human causal judgment, the problem that cue interactions pose for a Δp model is partly an illusion. When there are alternative cues that can act independently of the evaluated cue, it is reasonable to evaluate the effect of the cue after separating out the effect of the alternative cues (conditional Δp rather than unconditional Δp). This is what good scientists do. They assess the influence of the experimental factor, holding other factors constant (e.g., $p(US/P$ and N$) - p(US/$ P and no N$)$. Otherwise, the test is clouded by the presence of confounding variables. Spellman (this volume, Ch. 5) provides interpretations along these lines for the results of the experiments of Baker et al. (1993) described in Section IIIA. Miller and his colleagues (e.g., Miller & Matzel, 1988; Miller & Schachtman, 1985) have argued that cue interactions in animal learning, like blocking, are explained by such a mechanism (the comparator hypothesis), although their accounts cannot be characterized as fully normative.

Unfortunately, the partial correlation approach to selective learning is encumbered by indeterminacy (see Shanks, 1993a; Shanks et al., this volume, Ch. 7). If A and B are highly intercorrelated cues, and both are highly correlated with the consequence, the partial correlation of either cue with the consequence will be near zero. Thus, neither of the two alternative cues should be perceived as causal.

One might turn indeterminacy into virtue by suggesting that subjects will lack confidence in their final judgments because there are discrepancies between bivariate correlations and partial correlations. If estimates of contingency are affected by the subject's level of confidence, this might also explain the occurrence of acquisition curves (e.g., Shanks, 1987; for a discussion of this contentious point, see Fales & Wasserman, 1992). When information about interevent relations is incomplete, contradictory, or when trial frequencies are low, subjects may lower their calculated estimates of the contingency relation to minimize error in judgment (e.g., Baker, Berbrier, & Vallée-Tourangeau, 1989). The less extreme rating may not be justifiable on a purely normative basis, but it takes into account the possibility that new information may be disconfirmatory. Looking at my own data, it would not be unreasonable to assume that subjects in the double group might have been more confident that N was negative than subjects in the single groups (Williams, 1995; Section IIIB).

Indecision could very well be the *sine qua non* of the application of rules, whether these rules are conscious or unconscious. That is, a prediction based on the application of a statistical rule might always be accompanied by a feeling about the correctness of the prediction. Subjects may predict that a "blocked" cue will not be followed by the consequence, but they may also have low confidence in this prediction. If statistical rule learning is the mechanism underlying human and nonhuman behavior, it would be important to know if rats, like people, can feel uncertain about the signal value of a cue. If there are common cognitive systems, rats should indicate a high level of uncertainty about their response to a blocked cue. A finding such as this would certainly raise the level of cognitive sophistication in the rat (application of statistical rules). Cheng and her colleagues (Cheng &

Holyoak, 1995; Cheng & Novick, 1992; Melz, Cheng, Holyoak, & Wald-mann, 1993) have not taken the position that a "feeling of knowing" will necessarily accompany the application of a rule. However, level of confidence is not readily incorporated into a connection strength; hence, a finding such as this would be difficult to model associatively.

In summary, neither associative nor rule-based (contingency) models provide a thorough description of negative contingency learning. Perhaps what is most striking about the evolution of associative and rule-based theories is how closely they have moved from very different initial positions toward a common position. Notable differences between the predictions of rule-based and associative theories regarding the effects of trial order have disappeared with new assumptions about how subjects weigh trials (conditional Δp) or respond to absent cues (revised Rescorla–Wagner model).

V. Conclusions

A comparative analysis of human and nonhuman learning reveals many parallels in the cognitive process that detects negative interevent relations. There are two ways of interpreting the parallels in this article. First, evolution may have equipped the nervous system of humans and nonhumans with a primitive contingency detection mechanism. This mechanism could be associative and readily embodied in a connectionist model, not unlike that suggested by David Hume (1739/1969). Presumably, these interevent associations would be learned implicitly, with the products of the learning available for conscious report by humans. If the parallels are the result of a single mechanism (e.g., temporal coding, associative, or rule based), behavioral tests should continue to reveal similarities in the behavior of humans and nonhumans. With continued study, we should eventually learn all there is to know about the precise nature of this mechanism.

The suggestion of a single mechanism might seem fanciful to many, and it probably is, given that rats and humans are not close cousins. Anderson and Sheu (1995), for example, suggest that humans themselves possess at least two different mechanisms for judging interevent contingencies, one rule based and the other temporally based. Fales and Wasserman (1992) suggest a distinction between mechanistic learning and reasoned cognition. A second way of interpreting the parallels, then, is to attribute them to analogous learning mechanisms rather than to homologous ones (see Baker et al., this volume, Ch. 1). Faced with the problem of adapting to temporal regularities, different adaptive mechanisms might have stumbled upon similar solutions. Like the wings of birds and bats, these adaptive mechanisms are similar but not the same. In Section IIIB, for example, I suggested that multiple cues may be coded linearly, as elements, or nonlinearly, as stimulus complexes. Linear problem solving has many advantages, for example, it reduces memory load because the number of stimuli is less than the number of possible combinations of those stimuli. Linear coding also allows subjects to rapidly generalize their learning to a new situation. In other circumstances, the meaning of a cue is ambiguous unless it is clarified by referring to context (nonlinear). Thus, common pressures on two different information processing systems would be expected to produce many parallels in behavior.

Finding hard evidence that researchers are studying a behavioral analogy, rather than a behavioral homology, has not been easy. If the null hypothesis is a common mechanism, a lack of parallelism could be dismissed as being caused by task dissimilarity. It is impossible to fully equate the conditions of learning, so any observed differences could be task specific and not species specific. In looking for parallels, there is also a natural tendency to cite examples of behavioral similarities, even though the selected example may not be representative of the literature as a whole. In this article, I have tried to indicate when the results are mixed (e.g., Section IIIB). Additionally, given common selective pressures, there may simply be few qualitative differences in the learning mechanism. For example, cue interactions in animal learning result from the mechanistic blocking of the formation of associations, while a human reasoner may draw the same conclusion based on an analysis of alternative causes. Both are elemental solutions and amenable to LMS modeling.

ACKNOWLEDGMENTS

This work was supported by a grant from the Natural Sciences and Engineering Council of Canada. I thank Carla Kytaychuk, Genny Docking, Vin LoLordo, Harry Strub, and Ken Johns for helpful discussions and comments.

REFERENCES

Allan, L. G. (1993). Human contingency judgments: Rule based or associative? *Psychological Bulletin, 114,* 435–448.
Allan, L. G., & Jenkins, H. M. (1980). The judgment of contingency and the nature of the response alternatives. *Canadian Journal of Psychology, 34,* 1–11.
Alvarado, M. C., & Rudy, J. W. (1992). Some properties of configural learning: An investigation of the transverse-patterning problem. *Journal of Experimental Psychology: Animal Behavior Processes, 18,* 145–153.
Anderson, J. R., & Sheu, C.-F. (1995). Causal inference as perceptual judgments. *Memory & Cognition, 23,* 510–524.

Arkes, H. R., & Harkness, A. R. (1983). Estimates of contingency between two dichotomous variables. *Journal of Experimental Psychology: General, 112,* 117–135.

Baker, A. G. (1977). Conditioned inhibition arising from a between-session negative correlation. *Journal of Experimental Psychology: Animal Behavior Processes, 3,* 144–155.

Baker, A. G., Berbrier, M., & Vallée-Tourangeau, F. (1989). Judgments of a 2 × 2 contingency table: Sequential processing and the learning curve. *Quarterly Journal of Experimental Psychology, 41B,* 65–97.

Baker, A. G., & Mackintosh, N. J. (1976). Learned irrelevance and learned helplessness: Rats learn that stimuli, reinforcers, and responses are uncorrelated. *Journal of Experimental Psychology: Animal Behavior Processes, 2,* 130–141.

Baker, A. G., & Mackintosh, N. J. (1977). Excitatory and inhibitory conditioning following uncorrelated presentations of the CS and UCS. *Animal Learning & Behavior, 5,* 130–141.

Baker, A. G., Mercier, P., Vallée-Tourangeau, F., Frank, R., & Pan, M. (1993). Selective associations and causality judgments: Presence of a strong causal factor may reduce judgments of a weaker one. *Journal of Experimental Psychology: Learning, Memory, and Cognition, 19,* 414–432.

Bottjer, S. W. (1982). Conditioned approach and withdrawal behavior in pigeons: Effects of a novel extraneous stimulus during acquisition and extinction. *Learning and Motivation, 13,* 44–67.

Bouton, M. E. (1994). Context, ambiguity, and classical conditioning. *Current Directions in Psychological Science, 3,* 49–53.

Bush, R. R., & Mosteller, F. (1951). A mathematical model for simple learning. *Psychological Review, 58,* 313–323.

Chapman, G. B. (1991). Trial order affects cue interaction in contingency judgment. *Journal of Experimental Psychology: Learning, Memory, and Cognition, 17,* 837–854.

Chapman, G. B., & Robbins, S. J. (1990). Cue interaction in human contingency judgment. *Memory & Cognition, 18,* 537–545.

Cheng, P. W., & Holyoak, K. J. (1995). Complex adaptive systems as intuitive statisticians: Causality, contingency, and prediction. In H. L. Roitblat & J.-A. Meyer (Eds.), *Comparative approaches to cognitive science* (pp. 271–302). Cambridge, MA: MIT Press.

Cheng, P. W., & Novick, L. R. (1992). Covariation in natural causal induction. *Psychological Review, 99,* 365–382.

Choi, S., McDaniel, M. A., & Busemeyer, J. R. (1993). Incorporating prior biases in network models of conceptual rule learning. *Memory & Cognition, 21,* 413–423.

Colwill, R. M. (1991). Negative discriminative stimuli provide information about the identity of omitted response-contingent outcomes. *Animal Learning & Behavior, 19,* 326–336.

DeVito, P. L., & Fowler, H. (1986). Effects of contingency violations on the extinction of a conditioned fear inhibitor and conditioned fear excitor. *Journal of Experimental Psychology: Animal Behavior Processes, 12,* 99–115.

Dickinson, A., Shanks, D. R., & Evenden, J. (1984). Judgment of act-outcome contingency: The role of selective attribution. *Quarterly Journal of Experimental Psychology, 36A,* 29–50.

Domjan, M. J. (1993). *The principles of learning and behavior* (3rd ed.). Pacific Grove, CA: Brooks/Cole.

Droungas, A., & LoLordo, V. M. (1994). Evidence for simultaneous excitatory and inhibitory associations in the explicitly unpaired procedure. *Learning and Motivation, 25,* 1–25.

Einhorn, H. J., & Hogarth, R. M. (1986). Judging probable cause. *Psychological Bulletin, 99,* 3–19.

Fales, E., & Wasserman, E. A. (1992). Causal knowledge: What can psychology teach philosophers? *Journal of Mind and Behavior, 13,* 1–28.

Gallistel, C. R. (1990). *The organization of learning.* Cambridge, MA: MIT Press.

Gluck, M. A. (1991). Stimulus generalization and representation in adaptive network models of category learning. *Psychological Science, 2,* 50–55.

Gluck, M. A., & Bower, G. H. (1988). From conditioning to category learning: An adaptive network model. *Journal of Experimental Psychology: General, 117,* 225–244.

Gluck, M. A., Bower, G. H., & Hee, M. R. (1989). A configural-cue network model of animal and human associative learning. In *Proceedings of the Eleventh Annual Conference of the Cognitive Science Society* (pp. 323–332). Hillsdale: NJ: Erlbaum.

Gluck, M. A., & Myers, C. (1993). Hippocampal mediation of stimulus representation: A computational theory. *Hippocampus, 3,* 491–516.

Hallam, S. C., Matzel, L. D., Sloat, J. S., & Miller, R. R. (1990). Excitation and inhibition as a function of post-training extinction of the excitatory cue used in Pavlovian inhibition training. *Learning and Motivation, 21,* 59–84.

Hayes, N. A., & Broadbent, D. E. (1988). Two modes of learning interactive tasks. *Cognition, 28,* 249–276.

Hearst, E. (1991). Psychology and nothing. *American Scientist, 79,* 432–443.

Holland, P. C. (1984). Differential effects of reinforcement of an inhibitory feature after serial and simultaneous negative discrimination training. *Journal of Experimental Psychology: Animal Behavior Processes, 10,* 461–475.

Holland, P. C. (1985). The nature of conditioned inhibition in serial and simultaneous feature negative discriminations. In R. R. Miller & N. E. Spear (Eds.), *Information processing in animals: Conditioned inhibition* (pp. 267–298). Hillsdale, NJ: Erlbaum.

Holyoak, K. J., Koh, K., & Nisbett, R. E. (1989). A theory of conditioning. Inductive learning within rule-based default hierarchies. *Psychological Review, 96,* 315–340.

Honig, W. K. (1981). Working memory and the temporal map. In N. E. Spear & R. R. Miller (Eds.), *Information processing in animals: Memory mechanisms* (pp. 167–197). Hillsdale, NJ: Erlbaum.

Hume, D. (1969). *A treatise of human nature.* New York: Penguin Books. (Original work published 1739)

Janssen, M., Farley, J., & Hearst, E. (1995). Temporal location of unsignaled food deliveries: Effects on conditioned withdrawal (Inhibition) in pigeon signtracking. *Journal of Experimental Psychology: Animal Behavior Processes, 21,* 116–128.

Jenkins, H. M., & Sainsbury, R. S. (1969). The development of stimulus control through differential reinforcement. In N. J. Mackintosh & W. K. Honig (Eds.), *Fundamental issues in associative learning.* Halifax, NS: Dalhousie University Press.

Kamin, L. J. (1968). "Attention-like" processes in classical conditioning. In M. R. Jones (Ed.), *Miami symposium on the production of behavior: Aversive stimulation* (pp. 9–33). Coral Gables, FL: University of Miami Press.

Kamin, L. J. (1969). Predictability, surprise, attention, and conditioning. In B. A. Campbell & R. M. Church (Eds.), *Punishment and aversive behavior* (pp. 279–296). New York: Appleton-Century-Crofts.

Kaplan, P. S., & Hearst, E. (1985). Excitatory versus inhibitory learning: Studies of extinction, reinstatement, and interference. In P. D. Balsam & A. Tomie (Eds.), *Context and learning* (pp. 195–224). Hillsdale, NJ: Erlbaum.

Kasprow, W. J., Schachtman, T. R., & Miller, R. R. (1987). The comparator hypothesis of conditioned response generation: Manifest conditioned excitation and inhibition as a function of the relative excitatory strengths of CS and conditioning context at the time of testing. *Journal of Experimental Psychology: Animal Behavior Processes, 13,* 395–406.

Kaufman, M. A., & Bolles, R. C. (1981). A nonassociative aspect of overshadowing. *Bulletin of the Psychonomic Society, 18,* 318–320.

Kelley, H. H. (1973). The process of causal attribution. *American Psychologist, 28,* 107–128.

Kleiman, M. C., & Fowler, H. (1984). Variations in explicitly unpaired training are preferentially effective in producing conditioned inhibition. *Learning and Motivation, 15,* 127–155.

Kruschke, J. K. (1992). ALCOVE: An exemplar-based connectionist model of category learning, *Psychological Review, 99,* 22–44.

Kruse, J. M., Overmier, J. B., Konz, W. A., & Rokke, E. (1983). Pavlovian conditioned stimulus effects upon instrumental choice behavior are reinforcer specific. *Learning and Motivation, 14,* 165–181.

LoLordo, V. M., & Fairless, J. L. (1985). Pavlovian conditioned inhibition: The literature since 1969. In R. R. Miller & N. E. Spear (Eds.), *Information processing in animals: Conditioned inhibition* (pp. 1–49). Hillsdale, NJ: Erlbaum.

Markman, A. B. (1989). LMS rules and the inverse base-rate effect. Comment on Gluck and Bower (1988). *Journal of Experimental Psychology: General, 118,* 417–421.

Matzel, L. D., Held, F. P., & Miller, R. R. (1988). Information and expression of simultaneous and backward associations: Implication for contiguity theory. *Learning and Motivation, 19,* 317–344.

Matzel, L. D., Schachtman, T. R., & Miller, R. R. (1985). Recovery of a overshadowed association by extinction of the overshadowing stimulus. *Learning and Motivation, 16,* 398–412.

Matzel, L. D., Schachtman, T. R., & Miller, R. R. (1988). Learned irrelevance exceeds the sum of the CS-preexposure and US-preexposure deficits. *Journal of Experimental Psychology: Animal Behavior Processes, 14,* 311–319.

Matzel, L. D., Shuster, K., & Miller, R. R. (1987). Covariation in conditioned response strength between stimuli trained in compound. *Animal Learning & Behavior, 15,* 439–447.

McClelland, J. L., & Rumelhart, D. E. (1986). *Parallel distributed processing: Explorations in the microstructure of cognition: Vol. 2. Psychological and biological models.* Cambridge, MA: MIT Press.

Melz, E. R., Cheng, P. W., Holyoak, K. J., & Waldmann, M. R. (1993). Cue competition in human categorization: Contingency or the Rescorla-Wagner, Learning Rule? Comment on Shanks (1991). *Journal of Experimental Psychology: Learning, Memory, and Cognition, 19,* 1398–1410.

Miller, R. R., & Barnet, R. C. (1993). The role of time in elementary associations. *Current Directions in Psychological Science, 2,* 106–111.

Miller, R. R., Barnet, R. C., & Grahame, N. J. (1995). Assessment of the Rescorla-Wagner model. *Psychological Bulletin, 118,* 363–386.

Miller, R. R., Hallam, S. C., & Grahame, N. J. (1990). Inflation of comparator stimuli following CS training. *Animal Learning & Behavior, 18,* 434–443.

Miller, R. R., Hallam, S. C., Hong, J. Y., & Dufore, D. S. (1991). Associative structure of differential inhibition: Implications for models of conditioned inhibition. *Journal of Experimental Psychology: Animal Behavior Processes, 17,* 141–150.

Miller, R. R., & Matzel, L. D. (1988). The comparator hypothesis: A response rule for the expression of associations. In G. B. Bower (Ed.), *The psychology of learning and motivation* (Vol. 22, pp. 51–92). San Diego, CA: Academic Press.

Miller, R. R., & Schachtman, T. R. (1985). Conditioning context as an associative baseline: Implications for response generation and the nature of conditioned inhibition. In R. R. Miller & N. E. Spear (Eds.), *Information processing in animals: Conditioned inhibition* (pp. 51–88). Hillsdale, NJ: Erlbaum.

Minsky, M. L., & Papert, S. (1969). *Perceptrons: An introduction to computational geometry.* Cambridge, MA: MIT Press.

Neunaber, D. J., & Wasserman, E. A. (1986). The effects of unidirectional versus bidirectional rating procedures on college students' judgments of response-outcome contingency. *Learning and Motivation, 17,* 162–179.

Newman, J., Wolff, W. T., & Hearst, E. (1980). The feature-positive effect in adult human subjects. *Journal of Experimental Psychology: Human Learning and Memory, 6,* 630–650.

Nissen, M. J., & Bullemer, P. (1987). Attentional requirements of learning. Evidence from performance measures. *Cognitive Psychology, 19,* 1–32.

O'Boyle, E. A., & Bouton, M. E. (1996). Conditioned inhibition in multiple-category learning. *Quarterly Journal of Experimental Psychology, 49B,* 1–23.

Pavlov, I. P. (1927). *Conditioned reflexes.* New York: Dover.

Pearce, J. M. (1987). A model of stimulus generalization in Pavlovian conditioning. *Psychological Review, 94,* 61–73.

Pearce, J. M. (1994). Similarity and discrimination: A selective review and a connectionist model. *Psychological Review, 101,* 587–607.

Pearce, J. M., & Redhead, E. S. (1993). The influence of an irrelevant stimulus on two discriminations. *Journal of Experimental Psychology: Animal Behavior Processes, 19,* 180–190.

Pearce, J. M., & Wilson, P. N. (1991). Failure of excitatory conditioning to extinguish the influence of a conditioned inhibitor. *Journal of Experimental Psychology: Animal Behavior Processes, 17,* 519–529.

Peterson, C. R., & Beach, L. R. (1967). Man as an intuitive statistician, *Psychological Bulletin, 68,* 29–46.

Redhead, E. S., & Pearce, J. M. (1995a). Similarity and discrimination learning. *Quarterly Journal of Experimental Psychology, 48B,* 46–66.

Redhead, E. S., & Pearce, J. M. (1995b). Stimulus salience and negative patterning. *Quarterly Journal of Experimental Psychology, 48B,* 67–83.

Reiss, S., & Wagner, A. R. (1972). CS habituation produces a "latent inhibition effect" but no active "conditioned inhibition." *Learning and Motivation, 3,* 237–245.

Rescorla, R. A. (1967). Pavlovian conditioning and its proper control procedures. *Psychological Review, 64,* 114–120.

Rescorla, R. A. (1968). Probability of shock in the presence and absence of the CS in fear conditioning. *Journal of Comparative and Physiological Psychology, 66,* 1–5.

Rescorla, R. A. (1969a). Conditioned inhibition of fear resulting from negative CS-US contingencies. *Journal of Comparative and Physiological Psychology, 67,* 504–509.

Rescorla, R. A. (1969b). Pavlovian conditioned inhibition. *Psychological Bulletin, 72,* 77–94.

Rescorla, R. A. (1971). Summation and retardation tests of latent inhibition. *Journal of Comparative and Physiological Psychology, 75,* 77–81.

Rescorla, R. A. (1972). "Configural" conditioning in discrete-trial bar pressing. *Journal of Comparative and Physiological Psychology, 79,* 307–317.

Rescorla, R. A. (1973). Evidence for "unique stimulus" account of configural conditioning. *Journal of Comparative and Physiological Psychology, 85,* 331–338.

Rescorla, R. A. (1979). Conditioned inhibition and extinction. In A. Dickinson & R. A. Boakes (Eds.), *Mechanisms of learning and motivation: A memorial volume to Jerzy Konorski* (pp. 83–110). Hillsdale, NJ: Erlbaum.

Rescorla, R. A. (1982). Some consequences of associations between the excitor and the inhibitor in a conditioned inhibition paradigm. *Journal of Experimental Psychology: Animal Behavior Processes, 8,* 288–298.

Rescorla, R. A. (1989). Redundant treatments of neutral and excitatory stimuli in autoshaping. *Journal of Experimental Psychology: Animal Behavior Processes, 15,* 465–474.

Rescorla, R. A. (1991). Associations of multiple outcomes with an instrumental response. *Journal of Experimental Psychology: Animal Behavior Processes, 17,* 465–474.

Rescorla, R. A., & Wagner, A. R. (1972). A theory of Pavlovian conditioning: Variations in the effectiveness of reinforcement and nonreinforcement. In A. H. Black & W. F. Prokasy (Eds.), *Classical conditioning II: Current theory and research* (pp. 64–99). New York: Appleton-Century-Crofts.

Rumelhart, D. E., & McClelland, J. L. (1986). *Parallel distributed processing: Explorations in the microstructure of cognition: Vol. 1. Foundations.* Cambridge, MA: MIT Press.

Saavedra, M. A. (1975). Pavlovian compound conditioning in the rabbit. *Learning and Motivation, 6,* 314–326.

Schachtman, T. R., Brown, A. M., Gordon, E. L., Catterson, D. A., & Miller, R. R. (1987). Mechanisms underlying retarded emergence of conditioned responding following inhibitory training: Evidence for the comparator hypothesis. *Journal of Experimental Psychology: Animal Behavior Processes, 13,* 310–322.

Shanks, D. R. (1987). Acquisition functions in contingency judgment. *Learning and Motivation, 18,* 147–166.

Shanks, D. R. (1993a). Associative versus contingency accounts of category learning: Reply to Melz et al. (1993). *Journal of Experimental Psychology: Learning, Memory, and Cognition, 19,* 1411–1423.

Shanks, D. R. (1993b). Human instrumental learning: A critical review of data and theory. *British Journal of Psychology, 84,* 319–354.

Shanks, D. R., & Dickinson, A. (1987). Associative accounts of causality judgments. In H. Bower (Ed.), *The psychology of learning and motivation* (Vol. 21, pp. 229–261). San Diego, CA: Academic Press.

Shanks, D. R., & St. John, M. F. (1994). Characteristics of dissociable human learning systems. *Behavioral and Brain Sciences, 17,* 367–447.

Skinner, B. F. (1938). *Behavior of organisms.* New York: Appleton-Century-Crofts.

Strub, H., & Barske, B. W. (1977). A stimulus-compounding assay of conditioned inhibition and excitation. *Learning and Motivation, 8,* 414–428.

Suiter, R. D., & LoLordo, V. M. (1971). Blocking of inhibitory Pavlovian conditioning in the conditioned emotional response procedure. *Journal of Comparative and Physiological Psychology, 76,* 137–144.

Tassoni, J. T. (1995). The least mean squares network with information coding: A model of cue learning. *Journal of Experimental Psychology: Learning, Memory, and Cognition, 21,* 193–204.

Van Hamme, L. J., Kao, S., & Wasserman, E. A. (1993). Judging interevent relations: From cause to effect and from effect to cause. *Memory & Cognition, 21,* 802–808.

Van Hamme, L. J., & Wasserman, E. A. (1994). Cue competition in causality judgments: The role of nonpresentation of compound stimulus elements. *Learning and Motivation, 25,* 127–151.

Wagner, A. R., & Larew, M. B. (1985). Opponent processes and Pavlovian inhibition. In R. R. Miller & N. E. Spear (Eds.), *Information processing in animals: Conditioned inhibition* (pp. 223–266). Hillsdale, NJ: Erlbaum.

Wagner, A. R., Logan, F. A., Haberlandt, K., & Price, T. (1968). Stimulus selection in animal discrimination learning. *Journal of Experimental Psychology, 76,* 171–180.

Wagner, A. R., & Rescorla, R. A. (1972). Inhibition in Pavlovian conditioning: Application of a theory. In R. A. Boakes & M. S. Halliday (Eds.), *Inhibition and learning* (pp. 301–336). London: Academic Press.

Waldmann, M. R., & Holyoak, K. J. (1992). Predictive and diagnostic learning in cue competition. *Journal of Experimental Psychology: General, 121,* 222–236.

Wasserman, E. A. (1990a). Attributions of causality to common and distinctive elements of compound stimuli. *Psychological Science, 1,* 298–302.

Wasserman, E. A. (1990b). Detecting response-outcome relations: Toward an understanding of the causal texture of the environment. In G. H. Bower (Ed.), *The psychology of learning and motivation* (Vol. 26, pp. 27–82). New York: Academic Press.

Wasserman, E. A., Chatlosh, D. L., & Neunaber, D. J. (1983). Perception of causal relations in humans: Factors affecting judgments of response-outcome contingencies under free-operant procedures. *Learning and Motivation, 14,* 406–432.

Wasserman, E. A., Franklin, S. R., & Hearst, E. (1974). Pavlovian appetitive contingencies and approach versus withdrawal to conditioned stimuli in pigeons. *Journal of Comparative and Physiological Psychology, 86,* 616–627.

Weiss, S. J. (1969). Attentional processes along a composite stimulus continuum during free-operant summation. *Journal of Experimental Psychology, 82,* 22–27.

Williams, D. A. (1995). Forms of inhibition in animal and human learning. *Journal of Experimental Psychology: Animal Behavior Processes, 21,* 129–142.

Williams, D. A., & Docking, G. L. (1995). Associative and normative accounts of negative transfer. *Quarterly Journal of Experimental Psychology: Human Experimental Psychology, 48A,* 976–998.

Williams, D. A., Overmier, J. B., & LoLordo, V. M. (1992). A reevaluation of Rescorla's early dictums about Pavlovian conditioned inhibition. *Psychological Bulletin, 111,* 275–290.

Williams, D. A., Sagness, K. E., & McPhee, J. E. (1994). Configural and elemental strategies in predictive learning. *Journal of Experimental Psychology: Learning, Memory, and Cognition, 20,* 694–709.

Williams, D. A., Travis, G. M., & Overmier, J. B. (1986). Within-compound associations modulate the relative effectiveness of differential and Pavlovian conditioned inhibition procedures. *Journal of Experimental Psychology: Animal Behavior Processes, 12,* 351–362.

Willingham, D. B., Nissen, M. J., & Bullemer, P. (1989). On the development of procedural knowledge. *Journal of Experimental Psychology: Learning, Memory, and Cognition, 15,* 1047–1060.

Young, M. E. (1995). On the origin of personal causal theories. *Psychonomic Bulletin & Review, 2,* 83–104.

Zimmer-Hart, C. L., & Rescorla, R. A. (1974). Extinction of Pavlovian conditioned inhibition. *Journal of Comparative and Physiological Psychology, 86,* 837–845.

ANIMAL ANALOGUES OF CAUSAL JUDGMENT

Ralph R. Miller
Helena Matute

I. Introduction

Several investigators have suggested that human causal judgment and Pavlovian conditioning (which is examined primarily in experiments with animals) are governed by similar underlying processes (e.g., Allan, 1993; Alloy & Tabachnik, 1984; Shanks, 1993; Shanks & Dickinson, 1987; Wasserman, 1990b, 1993; Young, 1995). Two issues are raised here: To what degree do phenomena seen in causal judgment resemble those seen in Pavlovian conditioning, and to what degree do the processes responsible for human causal judgment also occur in animals? The first of these questions, among others, has been addressed in a number of thoughtful reviews (e.g., Allan, 1993; Shanks, 1993; Dickinson & Shanks, 1995; Wasserman, 1990b). In this chapter, we examine a few facets of the former issue, but focus on the latter one. Furthermore, we describe some experiments with animals that were inspired by the human causal judgment literature, and the results of which provide potential insight into processes underlying both human causal judgment and animal Pavlovian conditioning.

II. Are Animals Capable of Causal Judgments?

Before we go any further, one might ask whether animals possess any sense of causality. There are at least two theoretical reasons to suspect that

133

animals share with humans the ability to make causal judgments. First, humans and nonhuman animals evolved from common ancestors that likely long ago evolved the capacity for learning causal relationships. Second (and closely related), we inhabit the same world as our furry and feathered friends. Consequently, we face similar problems posed by the environment in obtaining shelter, controlling temperature, finding food, obtaining mates, avoiding predators, and so on. Even if common ancestors did not bestow upon humans and animals similar senses of causality through homology, common problems are apt to have created similar senses of causality through convergent evolution.

Logical arguments notwithstanding, empirical evidence is needed to support the contention that animals have a sense of causality. Although the issue is hardly resolved, there are some data bearing on the question. Several experiments have been conducted to test this view. For example, Killeen (1981) has reported that a pigeon in an instrumental situation can distinguish between the onset of a stimulus produced by the pigeon's own behavior and the onset of the stimulus produced by factors other than its own behavior. Killeen interprets this observation as indicative of pigeons having a sense of which event *caused* the stimulus to onset. Nevertheless, although Killeen's results are highly suggestive, one could develop an explanation of his observations in terms of chaining of responses without recourse to a sense of causation.

Consider now an animal learning a relation between exogenous events, such as in Pavlovian experiments in which a CS is paired with a US. The view that what animals learn during Pavlovian conditioning is analogous to what humans learn during causality experiments is accepted by most students of animal learning (e.g., Rescorla, 1988). However, Pavlovian conditioning may also involve the initially neutral CS acquiring biological relevance as a result of its being paired with the biologically relevant US (Pavlov, 1927). Such a stimulus substitution theory can explain a number of observations. In this framework, the CS is hypothesized to simply substitute for the US in its ability to elicit the response, both in humans and in animals, and no predictive or causal learning is necssarily involved in this process. An example of this is a cologne from a pleasant situation in our past that elicits an emotional response, or the thought of food that makes us salivate. Neither of these CSs necessarily anticipate the occurrence of the US, but CRs are evidenced. A simple (not causal) association to a US is sufficient to generate this type of responding, but would not suffice if the assessment technique evaluated, explicitly or implicitly, whether subjects actually expect the US to follow. Thus, a problem in regarding most Pavlovian and instrumental animal studies as examples of causal learning is that these experiments use stimuli of high biological relevance as outcomes

(USs), thereby allowing explanations in terms of stimulus substitution (which frequently leads to affective conditioning), as well as explanations in terms of signaling of the impending US (a characteristic of a cause). The view that conditioning embraces two different components (affective conditioning and signaling of the US) is not new. This sort of dualism was proposed by Konorski (1967), was explored by Wagner and Brandon (1989), and has also drawn the attention of students of human conditioning (e.g., Baeyens, Eelen, & van den Bergh, 1990; Levey & Martin, 1975).

However, what if animals could learn a causal relation between neutral events devoid of biological relevance, just as humans can learn the relation between fictitious allergens and fictitious allergies in a typical causal learning study? This learning could be due to neither biological relevance being acquired by the CS (because the outcome has no biological relevance), nor mechanistic acquisition of a CR (because there is no CR during training). Acquisition with outcomes of low biological relevance in a Pavlovian situation can be obtained through the use of a *sensory preconditioning procedure.* In this situation, two neutral events (e.g., a tone and a light of modest intensities) are repeatedly paired in Phase 1 (the sensory preconditioning phase, e.g., A → B) and then one of those events is paired with a biologically relevant event in Phase 2 (e.g., B → US). At test, A is presented and vigorous responding to A relative to appropriate control subjects indicates that an A–B association was formed during Phase 1. In these experiments, the critical learning can be regarded as a purely predictive relation (which may be causal, but is clearly devoid of any acquired biological relevance) between the two neutral events, such as a cause has to an effect. Only if subjects have learned that A predicts B, will they respond to A during the test phase. Thus, sensory preconditioning studies with animals seemingly share certain characteristics of the research being performed in human causal learning laboratories. For this reason, several of the studies that we chose to review in this chapter used a sensory preconditioning procedure.

III. The Problem of Prior Knowledge and the Benefit of Animal Subjects

Although explicit training on a causal task invariably involves exposure to a relationship between the putative cause and effect, many authors have noted the important role of preexperimental knowledge in causal judgment (e.g., Alloy & Tabachnick, 1984; L. J. Chapman & Chapman, 1969; Cheng, 1993; Medin, Wattenmaker, & Hampson, 1987; Pazzani, 1991). For example, Waldmann and Holyoak (1992) interpreted the results of their Experiment 2 in terms of preexperimental knowledge. In Experiment 3, they redesigned the cover story of their causal problem in order to reduce the influence of prior knowledge. Having done this, they obtained results quite different from those in Experiment 2, and attributed this difference to differences in prior knowledge between the two studies (but see Shanks & Lopez, in press). Additionally, Matute, Arcediano, and Miller (1996, Experiments A1 and A2) actually assessed prior knowledge in a causal situation by testing subjects without exposing them to any causal training. Using a situation originally developed by Van Hamme, Kao, and Wasserman (1993) to assess causal judgment following training, Matute et al. (1996) tested their subjects *without any training* and found strong opinions as to which foods (shrimp, strawberries, or peanuts) were most apt to act as causes of allergic reactions. They found bias even among three types of fictitious mushrooms as causes of allergic reactions. Moreover, subjects exhibited biases among possible effects (i.e., symptoms such as headache, fever, and rash) of an allergen consumption. Thus, we see that human subjects often enter studies of causal judgment with definite views concerning the potential causal relationships.

The influence of prior knowledge is an interesting issue in its own right, as it surely plays a major role in most causal inference outside laboratory settings. For example, it is likely that prior knowledge (specific or generalized from similar situations) plays a large role in determining whether multiple causes and multiple effects will be configured during training (Williams, Sagness, & McPhee, 1994), and if not, whether the separate elements will act competitively or synergically (see Einhorn & Hogarth, 1986; Leddo, Abelson, & Gross, 1984; Locksley & Stengor, 1984, for discussions of these opposing outcomes). However, prior knowledge is a potential confound with respect to studies designed to evaluate the impact of experimental contingencies and variables other than prior knowledge. Although careful selection of putative causes and effects presumably free of preexperimental bias can minimize the consequences of prior knowledge (e.g., Matute et al., 1996), the consequences of prior knowledge are extremely hard to avoid in studies that use humans as subjects because of the extensive preexperimental experience of all humans with causal relationships. In contrast, animals, particularly laboratory animals (which ordinarily lead less stimulating lives than free-roaming animals), are potential subjects with relatively little prior knowledge that would generalize to causal tasks in the laboratory. Of course, the role of prior knowledge in causal judgment is important and worthy of study in its own right, but is best not confused with other factors that influence causal judgment. Thus, laboratory animals are in some sense superior to humans as subjects in the study of how contingencies are transformed into causal (or at least predictive) judgments. However, this is not to suggest that the study of animal behavior will suffice to draw firm conclusions about human causal learning without additional experiments with human subjects.

IV. Problems with Verbal Assessment of Causal Judgment

Human causal judgments are ordinarily assessed through verbal reports. In a typical causal judgment task (e.g., Wasserman, 1990a), a potential cause (e.g., a fictitious allergen) and a potential effect (e.g., a fictitious allergic reaction) are presented in some contingent relationship. After observing these presentations in the guise of data from a fictitious situation (e.g., patients' records), subjects are asked to verbally rate the degree to which they believe that a causal relation exists between the putative cause and effect. Using such procedures, researchers have been able to replicate many well-known phenomena obtained in Pavlovian preparations with animals (see Allan, 1993; Shanks, 1993; Wasserman, 1990b, 1993; Young, 1995, for recent reviews). Thus, verbally assessed causal judgments in humans appear analogous in many ways to conditioned responses (CRs) in animal subjects. However, verbal assessment presents some methodological problems in that it is known to be influenced by many variables in addition to the critical ones under study. For example, Cheng and Novick (1991) report studies in which verbal assessment of causal judgment was influenced by the social status and the knowledge state of the experimenter asking the question.

A recent debate in the causal judgment literature illustrates how sensitive causal judgment data are to the specific assessment procedure. Waldmann and Holyoak (1992) studied cue competition between causes and between effects in humans. They observed that a blocking effect (such as is commonly seen in animals, e.g., Kamin, 1968) could be obtained in human subjects only if the competing events were causes of a common effect, not when they were effects of a common cause. That is, when learning about two potential causes of one effect ($C_1C_2 \rightarrow E$) had been preceded by learning of the relationship between one of these causes and the effect ($C_1 \rightarrow E$), then subjects discounted the potential causal role of the other cause (C_2). However, this blocking effect did not appear when two potential effects of one cause ($C \rightarrow E_1E_2$) had been preceded by learning of a relationship between the cause and one of the effects ($C \rightarrow E_1$). In that case, subjects did not discount E_2 as a potential effect of C. This result was replicated by Van Hamme et al. (1993). However, numerous other researchers have reported observing competition between effects (G. B. Chapman, 1991; Price & Yates, 1993; Shanks, 1991; Shanks & Lopez, in press; Waldmann & Holyoak, 1992, Experiment 2). The focus of the debate (Shanks & Lopez, in press; Van Hamme et al., 1993; Waldmann & Holyoak, 1992) was whether one or the other of these results favored associative theories or cognitive theories of causal judgment. But the conditions that yielded one or the other result were unclear.

Matute et al. (1996) analyzed these studies and found that different test questions had been used to assess causal judgments in the studies that obtained blocking of effects than in those that did not. To further examine the issue, Matute et al. (1996) manipulated whether multiple causes or multiple effects were presented to their subjects, and then used a series of different test questions to assess causal jdugment. The result was that both effects and causes competed *as a function of the wording of the test question.* For example, competition between target effect (E) and some competing effect, that was simultaneously present when E was paired with a common potential cause (C), was evident when they asked their subjects, "Is [E] indicative that [C] has occurred?" but not when they asked "Is [E] the effect of [C]?" Due to the presence of the singular cause implied by "the" in the latter question, one might have expected less, not more, competition between effects in this case, but that is not what was observed. Apparently, subjects interpreted the first question in terms of the relative diagnosticity of each of the effects (i.e., when one effect had a large diagnostic value, this competed with other effects' being viewed as good diagnostic cues), and the second question in terms of absolute diagnosticity, in which case each cause–effect association was assessed independently of the others. This suggests that slight variations in the wording of test questions in the earlier experiments were likely responsible for the contradictory results, which some researchers mistook as arising from a fundamental difference between causes and effects in their susceptibility to cue competition. Thus, the demand characteristics of a verbally stated assessment question are seen to have great impact on causal judgment. However, it seems implausible that the perception of causal relations per se, as opposed to their verbal report, is influenced by the wording of assessment questions if the questions are asked only *after* completion of causal training, which is usually the case. Thus, we see that verbal assessment often confounds intended and unintended variables, resulting in inconsistent data between experiments designed to investigate the same phenomenon but using slightly different assessment procedures.

V. Behavioral Assessment of Causal Judgment

One alternative to verbal assessment of causal judgment is (nonverbal) behavioral assessment. Behavioral assessment has several advantages. As already indicated, verbal assessment is highly dependent on the wording of the assessment question. Behavioral assessment, while certainly not free of such bias arising from the way that the behavioral question gets "asked," appears less susceptible to the vagaries of language than is verbal assessment. Additionally, organisms presumably evolved the capacity to learn causal relationships in order to predict and sometimes control outcomes. Despite people frequently talking about causality, ultimately it is human action rather than human speech that is important. Verbal tools are largely a means of influencing nonverbal behavior. Nonverbal behavior is one step closer than verbal behavior to what influences survival and reproduction. Thus, behavioral assessment is ecologically a more valid measure of causal judgment.

Although the primary justifications of behavioral assessment of causal judgment are the avoidance of the biases of language and ecological validity, an additional benefit is convergence on procedures that are readily implemented with animals. Whereas verbal assessment of causal judgment is not feasible with animal subjects, behavioral assessment of humans and animals using similar procedures is possible. This convergence of assessment techniques applicable to human and animal subjects makes possible comparisons between results from human and animal subjects with minimal confounds due to procedural differences.

VI. Different Types of Behavioral Assessment

Here, we consider different types of behavioral assessment, specifically *testing* in Pavlovian and instrumental situations. Consider first, assessment in a Pavlovian framework. Following training, the CS is presented alone at test and responding to it relative to appropriate controls can be viewed as indicative of the subject's having learned that the CS will be followed by the US.

A potential problem of using a Pavlovian situation for assessing causal judgment is that any observed Pavlovian response might reflect either (1) the CS coming to substitute for the US, or (2) the predictive value of the antecedent event, rather than the CS's causal value. We discussed the problem of stimulus substitution in Section II and pointed out how it could be circumvented by use of a sensory preconditioning procedure. However, the possibility remains that a CS might *predict* that a US will occur without being viewed as causing the US. An instrumental testing procedure for assessing causal judgment seemingly provides better grounds for rejecting this possibility (see Dickinson & Shanks, 1995). Suppose the outcome of a response in an instrumental task has positive valence for the subject. Then a subject's responding relative to that of a control subject lacking causal training can reasonably be viewed as evidence of the subject's having learned a causal relationship between the response and the effect (provided appropriate controls have been included to permit rejection of the possibility that emission of the response has become reinforcing in its own right). If a causal relationship between the response and outcome has been acquired, subjects should increase their responding (frequency and speed) if the outcome has positive valence and decrease their responding if the outcome has negative valence.

Instrumental behavior has occasionally been used for causal assessment (e.g., Chatlosh, Neunaber, & Wasserman, 1985; Matute, 1995; Shanks & Dickinson, 1991; Wasserman, 1990b). For instance, Wasserman describes several experiments in which behavioral assessment was used and the subjects' responding was found to closely reflect the prevailing contingencies, with subjects increasing their responding in conditions in which responding resulted in a positive outcome, and decreasing their responding otherwise. A noncausal association would not be expected to produce this pattern of results. A noncausal predictive association would not suffice to make a subject try to induce the antecedent event in order to obtain the subsequent event. For example, although arrival of a train almost always follows activation of the flashing red light on the railroad crossing sign, when we are anxiously waiting for a train to come we do not ask the stationmaster to turn on the flashing red light. We try to precipitate a subsequent event by making its antecedent occur only if we believe that the antecedent actually *causes* the subsequent event. Thus, with appropriate control groups, antecedent behavior or behavior that produces the antecedent event is indicative of the antecedent being viewed as a cause of the subsequent event.

The question of whether subjects exposed to Pavlovian training simply learn that a CS predicts the occurrence of a US, or learn that the CS actually causes the US, is an empirical one. If subjects worked to make the CS occur in order to obtain the US (assuming a positive valence) during a subsequent instrumental test, causal learning would be indicated. Of course, one would have to control for the possibility of the CS becoming a second-order reinforcer. This could be done by posttraining devaluation of the US (e.g., satiation or habituation) for some subjects, which is known to have little effect on second-order reinforcement (e.g., Rizley & Rescorla, 1972), but should attenuate responding based on a causal relationship in which responding determines reinforcement (e.g., Adams & Dickinson, 1981). Thus, regardless of whether Pavlovian or instrumental procedures are used in training, an instrumental test provides a somewhat clearer means of determining if causal learning per se has occurred.[1]

---

[1] Despite our acknowledging that Pavlovian assessment is ambiguous with respect to whether causal or merely predictive learning has occurred, hereafter for the sake of brevity we will refer to this learning as "causal" rather than "causal" or predictive."

Despite the seeming superiority of instrumental tasks for behavioral assessment of causal judgment, the experiments that we report later in this chapter used a Pavlovian test procedure. We did this in part because the phenomena emerging from instrumental and Pavlovian learning are empirically seen to be highly similar if not identical (see Miller & Balaz, 1981, for a review), and in part because of the distinct advantages of using Pavlovian procedures for training in causal judgment experiments (see Section VII), and our not wanting to risk generalization decrement by switching from Pavlovian training to a non-Pavlovian procedure for testing.

VII. Causal Training: Verbal, Pavlovian, and Instrumental Procedures

We have addressed various types of assessment of causal judgment in Sections IV through VI. However, the problems of assessment (testing) are not necessarily the same problems that arise with respect to training. Unlike verbal assessment, the potential problems of using a verbal format for causal training have not been systematically examined. However, it is likely that the exact wording of the verbally framed task will be found to have considerable influence on the judgment of causality, just as it does in testing. For this reason we view nonverbal training as less likely to be influenced by unintended details of presentation, thereby allowing clearer examination of covariation and other central variables of causal judgment.

Nonverbal training can be either observational (i.e., Pavlovian) or dependent on the subject's behavior (i.e., instrumental). Although use of an instrumental task in assessment obviates concerns about the antecedent being viewed only as a predictor rather than a cause, this does not imply that instrumental tasks are superior for training. Instrumental causal training poses three problems, all of which arise because the subject's own behavior is the potential cause. First, such training surrenders to the subject a degree of freedom, because the subject, rather than the experimenter, determines whether and when a response (i.e., cause) will be made. The experimenter may retain control of the contingencies given the occurrence of a response or no response, but the subject controls the frequency and timing of responses (see Gibbon, Berryman, & Thompson, 1974; Skinner, 1985).

The second problem posed by instrumental contingency training is that subjects are notoriously susceptible to biases in rating the consequences of their own behavior. Alloy and Abramson (1979) and Langer (1975) have described the tendency of human subjects to verbally overestimate the degree to which their behavior is the cause of outcomes of positive valence (i.e., illusion of control) and underestimate the degree to which their behav-

ior is the cause of outcomes of negative valence. Other authors have reported this effect as evidenced behaviorally through high response rates
when positive outcomes (positive or negative reinforcement) occur noncontingent upon the subject's behavior (e.g., Matute, 1994, 1995; Wright, 1962).
Moreover, a strong illusion of control frequently appears in experiments
designed to study phenomena other than illusion of control per se but
which use instrumental training procedures (e.g., Shanks, 1985).

The third difficulty created by the potential cause being the subject's
response is that when subjects are trying to obtain an outcome of positive
valence, they tend to respond at a high rate. Matute (in press) showed that
human subjects, exposed to a situation in which there were random aversive
noises with a potential (but actually noncontingent) escape response, responded at every opportunity unless they were told to refrain from responding on some trials. Consequently, despite outcomes being independent of
responding, they tended to occur far more frequently in the presence than
in the absence of a response. In the extreme case in which a subject's
probability of responding, $p(R)$, is 1, the subject samples no outcomes (or
their omissions) in the absence of responding. Thus, the effective contingency to which the subject is exposed is a partial reinforcement (contingent)
schedule, rather than a response-independent schedule of reinforcement.
As noted by Skinner (1985), the subject's $p(R)$ effectively modifies the
events to which the subject is exposed. Indeed, it is not uncommon for
researchers using instrumental training to discard the data from some of
their subjects because the subjects chose to perform the same response on
each trial, and thus, were not well exposed to the intended contingency
(e.g., Allan & Jenkins, 1983; Shanks, 1985). Such subjects receive little
information concerning the probability of the effect given no response. A
high response rate would not affect subjects' ratings if they were using
some metrics of contingency (e.g., Δp, provided that there were at least
some trials in which no response was made; Allan, 1980). However, a high
response rate certainly would affect ratings if subjects were using other
metrics of contingency (e.g., Δd)[2] or if their judgments were based on some
associative process such as that postulated by Rescorla and Wagner (1972;
see Allan, 1993, for elaboration).

Some researchers have circumvented this problem by telling subjects
that, to best assess the situation, they should respond on approximately
half of the training trials (see Shanks & Dickinson, 1987; Wasserman, 1990b,
for reviews). The difference in subjects' $p(R)$ prompted by differential
instructions results in significant differences in the reported causal ratings,

---

[2] Δd is (the number of trials with both a response and an outcome plus the number of trials
with neither a response nor an outcome) minus (the number of trials with either a response
or an outcome but not both).

with subjects that respond on about 50% of the trials giving more accurate judgments than subjects that respond at a greater rate (Matute, in press). This largely corrects the immediate problem, but at the expense of requiring pretraining instructions such as "To best learn the relation between events, respond only on about 50% of the trials," which creates an artificial situation quite distinct from the subject's natural tendency to make the response at every opportunity.

None of these problems arises with Pavlovian training because the potential causes are exogenous events (as opposed to the subject's behavior), which are fully under the control of the experimenter. Thus, causal training embedded within a Pavlovian task is less subject to bias than is causal training within an instrumental task. Ideally, a researcher studying causal judgment and not interested in the biases raised by using an instrumental task for training would want to train in a Pavlovian situation and (as explained in Section VI) test in an instrumental situation. Although it is possible to use different tasks for training and testing, changing tasks between training and testing poses problems concerning the transfer of knowledge from one situation to the other. Thus, in the experiments to be described later in this chapter, we used a Pavlovian situation for both training and testing. This provides a good analogy and possibly a homology to causal judgment by humans. However, with this procedure we cannot rigorously distinguish between causality and mere prediction.

VIII. Trial Order: Backward Blocking as a Discrepancy between Causal Learning in Humans and Conditioning in Animals

Pavlovian responding is highly sensitive to trial order. The order in which different types of trials occur (e.g., reinforcement and nonreinforcement of a CS) often strongly impacts behavior, which is one reason why researchers of Pavlovian learning favor associative models (e.g., Rescorla & Wagner, 1972) over contingency models (e.g., Rescorla, 1968), which ignore trial order. In causal judgment, however, trial order appears to have less consequence (e.g., G. B. Chapman, 1991; Shanks, 1985; but see Hogarth & Einhorn, 1992; Shanks, Lopez, Darby & Dickinson, this volume, Ch. 7). One of the most widely discussed differences in trial-order effects between causal and Pavlovian learning arises in blocking. Blocking is one of a number of phenomena that are collectively called cue competition. More generally, cue competition refers to degraded identification of a target cue as a cause of some outcome (or to degraded Pavlovian responding to a target cue) as a consequence of that cue being trained in the presence of another cue that is independently paired with the outcome.

"Blocking" ordinarily refers to forward blocking. In forward blocking, a nontarget cue or event is first trained as a cause of, or CS for, some outcome (i.e., A → US). Then the target cue (X), presented in compound with the previously trained nontarget cue, is paired with the outcome (AX → US). Blocking is evidenced by less causal attribution or conditioned responding to the target cue (X) than if the nontarget cue (A) had not been previously paired with the outcome. This effect, although not ubiquitous over all parameters, is well documented in both causal tasks with humans (e.g., Shanks, 1985) and Pavlovian tasks with animals (e.g., Kamin, 1968) and humans (e.g., Hinchy, Lovibond, & Ter-Horst, 1995).

However, a discrepancy arises with backward blocking. In backward blocking, the compounded target and nontarget cues are first paired with the outcome (AX → US) and then there are further pairings of the nontarget cue with the outcome (A → US); that is, trial order is reversed with respect to forward blocking. Backward blocking is evidenced by subjects discounting the causal role attributed to X relative to control subjects that did not receive the critical A → US pairings in Phase 2. Backward blocking has frequently been observed in causal judgments by humans (G. B. Chapman, 1991; Shanks, 1985; Van Hamme, 1994; Williams et al., 1994), but it is ordinarily not seen in Pavlovian conditioning with animals (e.g., Miller, Hallam, & Grahame, 1990; Schweitzer & Green, 1982). This discrepancy is potential grounds for challenging the claim that causal judgments by humans and Pavlovian conditioning with animals share common or similar underlying associative processes. Superficially, it appears that humans, but not animals, have the capacity to reevaluate causal information after it has been acquired. However, the discrepancy could just as well arise from some inherent difference between the two tasks (causality judgment vs. Pavlovian conditioning), or some nonessential procedural difference between the two tasks (see Shanks et al., this volume, Ch. 7; Wasserman et al., in press, for other views on backward blocking).

Highly notable among the procedural differences in these two traditions is that the type of events conventionally used are quite different. Whereas human causal judgment studies typically use outcomes that are innocuous to the subject (e.g., a fictitious allergy developed by a fictitious patient), animal Pavlovian experiments typically use outcomes that are of high biological relevance (e.g., footshock, food, and water). This procedural difference might be the source of the apparent discrepancy in backward blocking. One way to assess the impact of this procedural difference would be to examine backward blocking in a causal judgment task with humans using a biologically relevant outcome. Beyond the difference of assessing causal attribution as opposed to conditioned responses, would this situation differ from Pavlovian conditioning? Seemingly not. Another avenue would be to examine backward blocking in a Pavlovian conditioning task with animals using an outcome that was not biologically relevant. Of course, if we define Pavlovian conditioning as requiring the use of a biologically relevant US, this would no longer be a Pavlovian conditioning task, but a form of training closer to what occurs in the laboratory studies of causal judgment. We chose to employ this latter option (Miller & Matute, in press). As previously discussed, the sensory preconditioning procedure provides a means of examining a form of learning highly similar to Pavlovian conditioning but in the absence of a biologically relevant outcome. For this reason, we decided to see if our using a sensory preconditioning procedure would reveal in animals the backward blocking that is readily obtained in causal judgment situations with human subjects.

A. Backward Blocking within Sensory Preconditioning

In this and all subsequently described studies, the subjects were water-deprived naive adult rats, and fear-induced conditioned suppression of drinking was used for testing. Subjects were initially allowed to drink in the experimental apparatus where training would later occur. In this study, the stimuli, A, B, C, and X, were all innocuous auditory cues at modest intensities and the US was a mildly aversive footshock. Previous research in sensory preconditioning had demonstrated that $X \rightarrow B$ training followed by $B \rightarrow US$ training would support conditioned responding (i.e., suppression of drinking) to X at test (Rizley & Rescorla, 1972). Phase 1 of conventional sensory preconditioning was subdivided into Phases 1 and 2 (see Table I). These two phases constituted Phases 1 and 2 of a backward blocking procedure. Here, B was used as a surrogate US. The only purpose of Phase

TABLE I

DESIGN SUMMARY FOR BACKWARD BLOCKING WITHIN
SENSORY PRECONDITIONING

| | Treatment | | | | |
Group	Phase 1	Phase 2	Phase 3	Tests	
BB	$AX \rightarrow B^a$	$A \rightarrow B$	$B \rightarrow US$	X?	A?
CON1	$AX \rightarrow B$	$C \rightarrow B$	$B \rightarrow US$	X?	A?
CON2	$AX \rightarrow B$	No treatment	$B \rightarrow US$	X?	A?

[a] A and C, Buzzer and tone, counterbalanced; X, click train; B, white noise; US, footshock; $\rightarrow$, followed by.

3 was to give B biological relevance so that the status of the previously trained X–B association could be assessed in a subsequent test phase. The two control groups lacked the Phase 2 pairings of A and B. Instead they received either comparable exposure to B (Group CON1) or merely comparable exposure to the experimental apparatus (Group CON2). As can be seen on the left side of Fig. 1, Group Backward Blocking (BB) responded less vigorously to X than did either control group.

Thus, backward blocking was observed in rats when the competing cues during the blocking procedure (Phases 1 and 2) were of low biological relevance. A retrospective discounting of the causal role attributed to X was seen in rats exposed to a learning task that was similar to the tasks used to study causal judgment by humans (i.e., devoid of biological relevance).

In the conventional backward blocking procedure, subjects received AX → US in Phase 1 and A → US in Phase 2. Consequently, in Phase 1 both A and X ordinarily acquire biological relevance through their pairings with the US. The absence of backward blocking in this case suggests that biologically relevant cues are at least partially protected from the processes

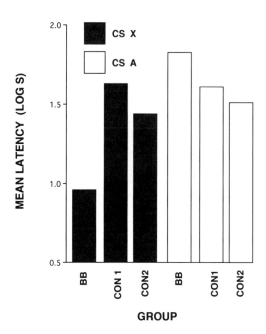

Fig. 1.   Backward blocking within sensory preconditioning. Mean time to lick for 5 cumulative seconds in the presence of the blocked stimulus X and the blocking stimulus A. The conditioned response was lick suppression; hence, the longer the time the stronger the implicit association. Adapted from Miller and Matute (in press).

that produce cue competition. This can be contrasted with the typical procedure of forward blocking (A → US followed by AX → US), in which A becomes biologically relevant during Phase 1 and then A prevents X from becoming functionally biologically relevant in Phase 2.[3] Thus, forward blocking may occur because the biological relevance acquired by X in Phase 2 is latent rather than functional. In contrast, backward blocking may not be observed in conventional conditioning preparations because X acquires functional biological relevance during the AX → US pairings of Phase 1, and the (unsuccessful) effort in Phase 2 is to eliminate (or render latent) that biological relevance. Seemingly, preventing a stimulus from gaining functional biological relevance is easier than degrading it after it has gained relevance. However, if the outcome is an innocuous stimulus such as B in the present experiment or the typical effect used in human causal judgment experiments, X never acquires biological relevance. The only associative component available to be learned is the causal (or predictive) one. The observation of backward blocking in these cases is consistent with cues of low biological relevance being highly susceptible to cue competition even after causal (or predictive) learning has occurred (in Phase 1).

B. Backward Blocking within Sensory Preconditioning as a Function of CS Intensity

We have used the expression biological relevance without discussion of what it might mean. In our terminology, a biologically relevant stimulus is one that directly impacts survival and reproduction, such as food, sex, and aversive stimulation (e.g., electric shock). Additionally, any cue of high intensity, even if it does not directly bear on survival and reproduction, is presumably of high biological relevance because intense stimulation in the natural habitat usually comes from large, potentially threatening sources, and natural selection has favored individuals who treat any intense stimulus as potentially important until proven otherwise. Thus, an intense auditory cue is presumably of higher biological relevance than is an otherwise identical auditory cue of low or moderate intensity. Empirically, higher biological relevance might be observed in terms of the stimulus eliciting a stronger orienting response. Moreover, we have assumed that initially innocuous cues that are paired with events of inherently high biological relevance (i.e., USs) can themselves acquire biological relevance. Consequently, as

---

[3] We say *functional* biological relevance because there are grounds to believe that cue competition reflects a deficit in expressing information rather than in acquiring that information (e.g., Cole et al., 1995; also see Section XI). In this view, contiguity (temporal and spatial proximity, to be more precise) is sufficient for the formation of the associations that support the acquisition of biological relevance, causality, and simple prediction. However, these associations can be either latent or functional.

discussed previously, pairing a cue with a biologically relevant event does two things. It transforms the cue into a signal (cause or predictor) for the inherently biologically relevant event with which it has been paired, and it imparts to the cue acquired biological relevance.

In the preceding experiment, we examined the hypothesis that backward blocking does not usually occur in animals because the potentially blocked stimulus gains biological relevance in Phase 1. To prevent the potentially blocked stimulus of the preceding experiment from gaining biological relevance in Phase 1, we embedded the two phases of blocking into what would ordinarily constitute Phase 1 of a sensory preconditioning procedure (see Table I). Although backward blocking was observed, use of this procedure raises the possibility that, rather than differences in biological relevance being responsible for the observed backward blocking (relative to the numerous prior failures to observe backward blocking), use of the sensory preconditioning procedure per se might have precipitated the occurrence of backward blocking.

To test this alternative, we conducted another backward blocking study (again embedded within a sensory preconditioning procedure), but this time used CSs with inherent biological relevance (Denniston, Miller, & Matute, in press, Experiment 1). Specifically, rather than using auditory cues of moderate intensity as we had in the preceding study, we used cues of higher intensity, which are presumably of high biological relevance. If the sensory preconditioning procedure itself facilitates backward blocking, we should still observe backward blocking. But if low biological relevance was responsible for the backward blocking observed in the preceding experiment, it would not be expected in the present experiment.

The procedure for this study is summarized in Table II. Two groups (BB-M and CON1-M) were treated identically to Groups BB and CON1 of the previous study, including the use of cues of moderate intensity (i.e., 10 dB above background). Two additional groups (BB-H and CON1-H) were included that were also treated similarly except that the blocked, the blocking, and the blocking control stimuli (X, A, and C, respectively) were all of high intensity (i.e., 30 dB above background). Our expectation was that blocking would be observed in Group BB-M relative to CON1-M, but would not be seen in Group BB-H relative to Group CON1-H due to the high intensity (presumably biological relevance) of X. Of course, the possibility existed that the high level of responding to X that we anticipated observing at test in Group BB-H would reflect not conditioned behavior, but unconditioned responding due to the high intensity of X. To control for this alternative interpretation, we included Group CON2-H. For this group, X was not paired with B in Phase 1, so, despite subsequent B–US

TABLE II

DESIGN SUMMARY FOR BACKWARD BLOCKING WITHIN SENSORY
PRECONDITIONING AS A FUNCTION OF CS INTENSITY

Group	Treatment				
	Phase 1	Phase 2	Phase 3	Tests	
BB-M	AX → B[a]	A → B	B → US	X?	A?
CON1-M	AX → B	C → B	B → US	X?	A?
BB-H	A'X' → B	A' → B	B → US	X'?	A'?
CON1-H	A'X' → B	C' → B	B → US	X'?	A'?
CON2-H	A'X'/B	A' → B	B → US	X'?	A'?

[a] A and C, Moderate-intensity white noise or tone, counterbalanced; A' and C', high-intensity white noise or tone, counterbalanced; X, moderate-intensity clicks; X', high-intensity clicks; B, flashing light; US, footshock; →, followed by; /, unpaired.

pairings in Phase 3, conditioned responding to X based on sensory preconditioning would not be expected.

Of focal interest is responding to the blocked stimulus (X). As can be seen on the left side of Fig. 2, blocking was seen in the moderate-intensity condition (M), but not in the high-intensity condition (H). Moreover, Group CON2-H did not respond appreciably to the blocked stimulus, indicating that the observed responding to X in Group BB-H was not unconditioned. The absence of backward blocking in Group BB-H despite the backward blocking treatment having been embedded within a sensory preconditioning procedure indicates that the occurrence of backward blocking in Group BB of the last experiment and in Group BB-M of the current experiment was not due to the use of a sensory preconditioning procedure per se, but to the low biological relevance of the cues at the time of the blocking treatment. When CSs of inherently high biological relevance were used, backward blocking was not detected. Thus, the potential of the sensory preconditioning procedure to yield backward blocking is not an inevitable consequence of the procedure, but rather stems from the procedure permitting backward blocking treatment without the blocking stimulus acquiring biological relevance in Phase 1. This condition and outcome are consistent with the backward blocking that is observed in human causal judgment studies.

Although our concern in this study was the intensity of the blocked stimulus, if we had increased its intensity without also similarly increasing the intensity of the blocking stimulus, any observed decrease in blocking might have merely reflected perceptual masking of the blocking stimulus by the blocked stimulus. Thus, we increased equally the intensity of both

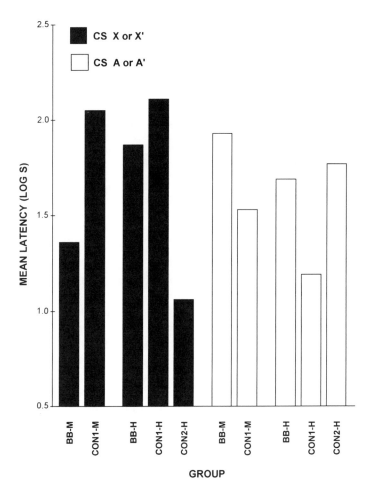

Fig. 2. Backward blocking within sensory preconditioning as a function of CS intensity. Mean time to lick for 5 cumulative seconds in the presence of the blocked stimulus X and the blocking stimulus A. The conditioned response was lick suppression; hence, the longer the time the stronger the implicit association. Adapted from Denniston, Miller, and Matute (in press).

stimuli. However, this potentially obscures which factor prevented the occurrence of blocking in this situation, the high intensity of the blocked stimulus or the high intensity of the blocking stimulus. But Hall, Mackintosh, Goodall, and dal Martello (1977) previously performed a study in which they increased the intensity of only the blocked stimulus and by so doing eliminated blocking. Although their study is open to an explanation in terms of perceptual masking, and the present experiment does not differentiate between the importance of the high intensity of the blocked stimulus and the blocking stimulus, together these two studies strongly suggest that the high intensity (i.e., high biological relevance) of the potentially blocked stimulus is what prevented blocking from occurring in the present high-intensity condition.

In this last study, we found that using CSs of inherent biological relevance (intense stimuli) eliminated the backward blocking observed when we embedded the blocking treatment within a sensory preconditioning procedure. However, we wondered if a similar loss of backward blocking could be obtained by using other forms of biologically relevant CSs. To answer this question, we performed a similar experiment (Denniston et al., in press, Experiment 2) entirely with CSs of moderate intensity, but for some groups we gave a few B $\rightarrow$ US trials prior to all other treatment (i.e., before Phase 1 in Table II). This presumably gave B biological relevance, which in turn imparted biological relevance to X (and A) during the AX $\rightarrow$ B trials of Phase 1. The result was that these initial B $\rightarrow$ US trials eliminated backward blocking compared to a number of different control groups that did not receive these initial B $\rightarrow$ US trials. Thus, the view that cues of high biological relevance are protected from cue competition is not limited to equating biological relevance to intense stimuli; moderate-intensity cues appear to acquire biological relevance through pairings with a stimulus that itself has biological relevance, and this protects them from cue competition.

C.   FORWARD BLOCKING AS A FUNCTION OF CS INTENSITY

If, as we have suggested, the occurrence of cue competition in causal judgment and Pavlovian conditioning requires that the target (i.e., blocked) cue not possess functional biological relevance at the time of cue competition treatment, this rule should apply equally to forward and backward blocking. Unlike the conventional backward blocking procedure (AX $\rightarrow$ US, A $\rightarrow$ US, test X), the forward blocking procedure (A $\rightarrow$ US, AX $\rightarrow$ US, test X) does not call for the target cue (X) acquiring biological relevance prior to the critical treatment (A $\rightarrow$ US) that is potentially going to induce degraded responding to X. Presumably, this is why forward blocking is readily obtained, not only in situations in which the outcome is biologically irrelevant (i.e., human causal judgment situations), but also in situations in which the outcome is biologically relevant (i.e., conventional Pavlovian conditioning). However, it is possible in the forward blocking procedure to endow the blocked stimulus with biological relevance prior to the blocking treatment simply by selecting as the potentially blocked cue a stimulus of inherent biological relevance (e.g., high intensity). If our hypothesis concerning the impact of biological relevance on cue competition is correct, this ought to prevent the occurrence of forward blocking in situations where it is otherwise observed.

We recently performed a study to test this prediction (Miller & Matute, in press). Again, the CSs were auditory cues and the US was a mild foot-shock. Two groups (FB-M and CON1-M) constituted, respectively, a standard forward blocking group and a control for forward blocking (see Table III). The intensity of A, C, and X in these two groups was 10 dB above background. Groups FB-H and CON1-H received identical treatment except that the cues were all 30 dB above background. If cues of high intensity are of high biological relevance and cues of high biological relevance are relatively protected against cue competition, we would expect less blocking in Group FB-H than in Group FB-M (each relative to its own control). However, as before we must consider the possibility that subjects might exhibit unconditioned suppression to a loud cue. Consequently, Group CON2-H was added to assess unconditioned responding to X when its intensity was 30 dB above background. As can be seen in Table III, Group CON2-H never had X paired with the US.

The critical finding was that forward blocking was observed in Group FB-M relative to Group CON1-M, but not in Group FB-H relative to Group CON1-H (see the left side of Fig. 3). Moreover, the low level of responding to X in Group CON2-H indicates that the responding seen in Group FB-H was not due to unconditioned responding to X. Thus, even with the forward blocking procedure, in which blocking is normally obtained (e.g., in the behavior of Group FB-M), blocking does not occur if the target

TABLE III

DESIGN SUMMARY FOR FORWARD BLOCKING AS A
FUNCTION OF CS INTENSITY

Group	Treatment		Tests	
	Phase 1	Phase 2		
FB-M	A → US[a]	AX → US	X?	A?
CON1-M	C → US	AX → US	X?	A?
FB-H	A′ → US	A′X′ → US	X′?	A′?
CON1-H	C′ → US	A′X′ → US	X′?	A′?
CON2-H	A′ → US	A′X′/US	X′?	A′?

[a] A and C, Moderate-intensity white noise and high-frequency tone, counterbalanced; A′ and C′, high-intensity white noise and high-frequency tone, counterbalanced; X, moderate-intensity low-frequency tone; X′, high-intensity low-frequency tone; US, footshock; →, followed by; /, unpaired.

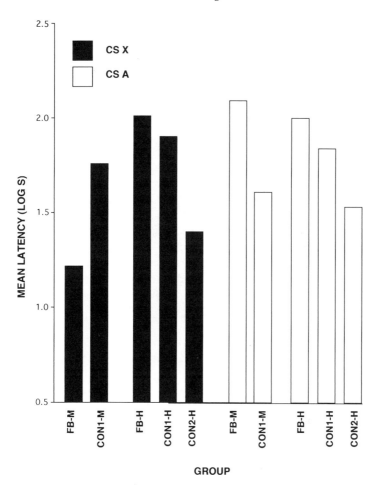

Fig. 3.   Forward blocking as a function of CS intensity. Mean time to lick for 5 cumulative seconds in the presence of the blocked stimulus X and the blocking stimulus A. The conditioned response was lick suppression; hence, the longer the time the stronger the implicit association. Adapted from Miller and Matute (in press).

cue (X) is biologically relevant at the time of blocking treatment (Group FB-H). In the present experiment, this was achieved through the use of unusually intense CSs in Group FB-H.

Van Hamme and Wasserman (1994; also see Shanks et al., this volume, Ch. 7; Wasserman et al., this volume) have suggested an alternative explanation of backward blocking in human causal judgment. However, their proposed mechanism fails to explain either the commonly seen absence of backward blocking in animals (without further assumptions that Miller & Matute, in press, have tested and found wanting) or why our manipulations of biological relevance are able to influence whether backward blocking is observed.

The findings of the three experiments that we have just described are interesting for two reasons. First, they are generally illuminating concerning the factors that determine an event's vulnerability to cue competition, a phenomenon that is still not fully understood. Apparently, cues of low biological relevance are more prone to cue competition than are cues with inherent or acquired high biological relevance. Second, these findings suggest that the presence of backward blocking in human causal judgment data and the absence of it in animal Pavlovian data are not sufficient grounds for concluding that different processes are at work in humans and animals. Rather, the apparent discrepancy appears to arise from the procedural difference of causal judgment tasks in the laboratory using outcomes (effects) of low biological relevance (i.e., allergic reactions in fictitious patients), and Pavlovian studies using outcomes (USs) of high biological relevance (i.e., footshock).

IX. Cue Competition between Effects as Well as between Causes

If we accept the possibility that Pavlovian conditioning data from animals may have a similar or common basis as causal judgment by humans, we might profitably use findings in one literature to illuminate issues in the other literature. The above instances of backward blocking in animals were instances of how animal research may benefit from looking at human causal learning experiments and examining analogous situations. Here, we present an example of an instance in which Pavlovian data from animals potentially clarifies a problem within the human causal literature.

Traditionally, cue competition has taken the form of a more valid predictor (i.e., cause or CS) of an outcome (i.e., effect or US) interfering with a less valid predictor coming to be viewed as a cause of, or CS for, the same outcome. There are numerous examples in the literature of competition between causes (e.g., Dickinson, Shanks, & Evenden, 1984) and between CSs (e.g., Kamin, 1968). However, not until 1992 (Waldmann & Holyoak, 1992; also see Waldmann, this volume, Ch. 2) did anyone clearly ask the reciprocal question: are effects as prone to compete with other simultaneously presented effects as causes are to compete with other simultaneously presented causes? In fact, other researchers had previously performed experiments that, although not explicitly designed to study competition between effects, had in practice done exactly that. G. B. Chapman (1991), Price and Yates (1993), Shanks (1991; also see Shanks & Lopez, in press) all found competition between effects, but did not emphasize that aspect of their findings. In contrast, Waldmann and Holyoak (1992, Experiments 1 and 3) and Van Hamme et al. (1993) report that, although they readily obtained competition between causes, they did not observe competition between effects. The issue of whether causes and effects are equivalent in their susceptibility to cue competition is potentially important in deciding the type of theory that can best account for cue competition. Thus, this inconsistency in the published data is disturbing.

There are, however, numerous potential reasons for this inconsistency (for discussions of these, see Esmoris-Arranz, Miller, & Matute, 1995; Matute et al., 1996; Shanks & Lopez, in press; Van Hamme et al., 1993). Potentially confounding factors include prior knowledge (compare Waldmann & Holyoak, 1992, Experiments 2 and 3, but see Shanks & Lopez, in press), order of cue presentation in training, and order of cue presentation in testing (i.e., cause before effect or effect before cause, see Matute et al., 1996; Shanks & Lopez, in press; Waldmann & Holyoak, 1992). Inversion of the "natural" order of events produced what Waldmann and Holyoak called a "diagnostic" task (in which putative effects are presented prior to the potential causes), in contrast to the conventional order of cause-before-effect in what they called a "predictive" task. In that the effect in this case becomes a signal for the cause, this may have created ambiguities in differentiating causes from effects. For this reason, we felt that the question of whether effects compete among themselves might best be answered without the inversion of events that occurred in Waldmann and Holyoak's study of competition between effects in human subjects. Consequently, we performed a study in which effects were presented as subsequent events (events occurring after causes rather than before causes, Esmoris-Arranz et al., 1995). Moreover, we felt that the effect of prior knowledge could be minimized through the use of animals as subjects and novel events as cues. Last, we wanted to equate causes and effects in terms of their biological relevance. Toward this end, we again embedded a cue competition task (specifically, forward blocking) in a sensory preconditioning procedure.

The CSs were auditory cues of moderate intensity, and the US was a mild footshock. Phase 1 of the blocking treatment consisted of our presenting subjects in Groups EXPA and EXPS with sequentially paired cues (i.e., A → S, where A and S stand for the antecedent and subsequent event, respectively; see Table IV). During this phase, control Groups CONA and CONS received unpaired presentations of A and S. In Phase 2, a target cue (X) was compounded with A and followed with S for some subjects (Groups EXPA and CONA). Thus, cue X was an antecedent event for

TABLE IV

DESIGN SUMMARY FOR BLOCKING BETWEEN CAUSES AND
BETWEEN EFFECTS

Group	Treatment			Tests	
	Phase 1	Phase 2	Phase 3		
EXPA	A → S[a]	AX → S	S → US	X?	A?
CONA	A/S	AX → S	S → US	X?	A?
EXPS	A → S	A → SX	A → US	X?	S?
CONS	A/S	A → SX	A → US	X?	S?

[a] A and S, Tone and buzzer, counterbalanced; X, clicks; US, footshock; →, followed
by; /, unpaired.

Groups EXPA and CONA. For other subjects the target cue was compounded with S and preceded by A (Groups EXPS and CONS). Thus, cue
X was a subsequent event for Groups EXPS and CONS. Then in Phase 3,
the subjects that had received AX → S in Phase 2 experienced S → US
pairings, whereas the subjects that had received A → SX in Phase 2 received
A → US pairings. Finally, conditioned responding to X was assessed. Notably, in Groups EXPS and CONS responding to X was necessarily mediated
by a backward association between X and A (i.e., with X diagnosing that
A had occurred). Prior research had shown that when such an association
is embedded within a sensory preconditioning procedure with the other
link being in the forward direction (i.e., A → US), X gains behavioral control
(at least in noncue competition situations [Matzel, Held, & Miller, 1988]).

As is evident on the left side of Fig. 4, blocking of X was observed in
both the antecedent condition (compare Groups EXPA and CONA) and
the subsequent condition (compare Groups EXPS and CONS). Blocking
in the antecedent condition consisted of blocking of an association between
a target antecedent event and a subsequent event by another antecedent
event that had a previously established association to the subsequent event.
This is equivalent to conventional blocking of one CS by another, and is
analogous to the blocking of one cause by another.

More interesting is the observed blocking of subsequent events. Blocking
in the subsequent condition consisted of blocking of an association between
an antecedent event and a target subsequent event by another subsequent
event that had its own previously established association to the antecedent
event. This is equivalent to blocking between USs and is analogous to
blocking between effects, except that the use of a sensory preconditioning
procedure avoided the problem of the potentially competing cues being

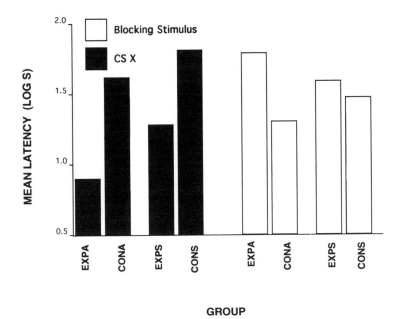

Fig. 4.   Blocking between causes and between effects. Mean time to lick for 5 cumulative seconds in the presence of the blocked stimulus X and the blocking stimulus, which was A for Groups EXPA and CONA and S for Groups EXPS and CONS. The conditioned response was lick suppression; hence, the longer the time the stronger the implicit association. Adapted from Esmoris-Arranz, Miller, and Matute (1995).

biologically relevant at the time of cue competition treatment. The experiments described in Section VIII found that blocking between antecedent events does not occur when the antecedent events are biologically relevant. Extrapolating to the present study, blocking of subsequent events presumably would not have occurred if we had used a conventional US rather than a US surrogate as the subsequent event.

Waldmann (this volume, Ch. 2) suggests that our observation of blocking between subsequent events in rats is an artifact of cue X being presented to subjects only during Phase 2, which would make subjects doubt during testing whether cue A is going to be followed by X (as in Phase 2) or not (as in Phase 1). However, this argument fails to explain the difference we obtained between the experimental and control groups (see Fig. 4). Additionally, this argument ignores that presenting the target cue only during Phase 2 is an inherent feature of the blocking design, including human (e.g., G. B. Chapman, 1991; Shanks, 1985; Waldmann & Holyoak, 1992) and animal (Kamin, 1968) instances of blocking between causes or between CSs. Experiments that modify this feature could surely be conducted, but they would no longer be instances of blocking. Additionally, our results are concordant with the data of G. B. Chapman (1991), Matute et al. (1996, Experiment 3), Price and Yates (1993), Shanks (1991), and Shanks and Lopez (in press), all of whom observed competition between effects in human subjects. We believe that Matute et al. (1996, Experiment 2), Van Hamme et al. (1993), and Waldmann and Holyoak (1992, Experiment 3) failed to obtain blocking between effects for a number of divere reasons including but not limited to their choice of assessment question. (For detailed discussions of why each of these studies might have failed to obtain blocking between effects, see Esmoris-Arranz et al., 1995; Matute et al., 1996; Shanks & Lopez, in press; Van Hamme et al., 1993).

K. J. Holyoak (personal communication) has provided an explanation for our observation of blocking between effects in terms of differences in contingency. Because we gave Group CONS unpaired exposures to A and S in Phase 1, the contingency between A and S over both Phases 1 and 2 was lower for Group CONS than for Group EXPS. However, Holyoak's hypothesis applies not only to blocking between effects, but to any instance of blocking (between causes or between effects) that gives control subjects unpaired exposures to the Phase 1 elements. Such control treatments are relatively common in studies of blocking, but other control treatments have also been used in successful demonstrations of blocking of antecedent events (e.g., Kamin, 1968). Thus, we conducted another experiment identical to the one just described for Groups EXPS and CONS, except that Group CONS was not exposed to A or S in Phase 1. Consequently, A and S had the same correlation for both groups. Yet, blocking of subsequent events was still observed.

Our observation of competition between subsequent events cannot be accounted for by traditional associative theories (e.g., Rescorla & Wagner, 1972), which assume a predictive directionally during both training and testing, and thus, do not speak to our subsequent-to-antecedent (diagnostic) testing phase. More flexible is Waldmann and Holyoak's (1992) causal-model theory in that it allows for diagnostic test conditions in which subjects can infer a potential cause given the effect. However, Waldmann and Holyoak's theory makes the wrong prediction in this case, in that it assumes that, during diagnostic inference (i.e., testing), effects always collaborate rather than compete in diagnosing the potential cause. In fact, the results of their own Experiment 2 showed that competition between effects can occur. We (Matute et al., 1996) suggested that the most parsimonious way to explain the now numerous reports of competition between effects was to assume that associations are learned noncompetitively and bidirectionally (from cause to effect and from effect to cause) and are based on simple contiguity. In this way, during subsequent testing, the activation of one of the events (cause or effect) can activate the representation of the other event (in either direction), and competition occurs when several associations are simultaneously trying to activate the representation of the same event (be it a cause or an effect). Waldmann (this volume, Ch. 2) now acknowledges that competition between effects can occur under select conditions. Additionally, he now states that this is consistent with Waldmann and Holyoak's causal-model theory. But Waldmann and Holyoak (1992, p. 226) clearly stated that "causal-model theory predicts a basic difference between the impact of redundancy for causes versus effects; causes compete, and effects collaborate." Of course, if the assumptions that competition occurs during testing rather than training, and that effects can compete in diagnostic testing, are added to Waldmann and Holyoak's (1992) view (or to any associative theory), as has been suggested by Waldmann (this volume, Ch. 2), then there would be few substantive differences between the resultant theories and our own proposal (Matute et al., 1996).

X. Temporal Priority

Distinct from the issue of trial order (previously discussed in Section VIII), there is the issue of event order within a trial. Summarizing the efforts of numerous researchers over several decades (and largely consistent with the views of the eighteenth century British empiricist philosopher David Hume, 1739/1964), causal judgment increases with contingency (i.e., an ideal cause should be both necessary and sufficient for the occurrence of the effect), contiguity (i.e., an ideal cause should have temporally and spatially high proximity to its effect), temporal priority (i.e., a cause must precede its effect), and a lack of alternative cause (i.e., no other cause that can account for the effect should be present during trials on which the target cause and effect are paired). Interestingly, if we make a list of necessary conditions for Pavlovian responding, the list is surprisingly similar. This of course is what has encouraged numerous researchers to suggest that causal judgment and Pavlovian responding arise from similar and perhaps identical underlying associative processes.

Extensive experiments have demonstrated that contingency (e.g., Allan & Jenkins, 1983; Dickinson et al., 1984; Wasserman, Chatlosh, & Neunaber, 1983) and contiguity (e.g., Shanks, Pearson, & Dickinson, 1989; Wasserman & Neunaber, 1986) are as essential to causal judgment as they are to Pavlovian responding. Moreover, in Section VIII we have described research that led us to conclude that the apparent difference in cue competition (specifically, in backward blocking) between causal judgment and Pavlovian responding was an artifact of the different procedures that are typically used rather than any fundamental difference in underlying associative processes (unless one defines Pavlovian conditioning to require that the subsequent event be biologically relevant [as Pavlov did] and defines causal judgment to exclude biologically relevant effects [as is the case in the laboratory], in which case the difference would be inherent to these two different types of learning). However, the comparability of temporal priority of causes-before-effects and CSs-before-USs has received little attention to date. Hence, we examine the issue here.

Students of causal judgment have long recognized that temporal order is essential for subjects to report a causal relationship. One might argue that Pavlovian responding is also subject to the same constraint; simultaneous and backward pairings (i.e., CS and US onset and terminate at the same time, and US prior to CS, respectively) are well known to result in weaker conditioned responding than do forward paintings (i.e., CS prior to US). However, the impaired responding observed with simultaneous and backward pairings has recently been shown to reflect a deficit in expressing acquired information rather than a lack of learning (e.g., Barnet, Arnold, & Miller, 1991; Matzel et al., 1988; Miller & Barnet, 1993). These authors have presented data indicating that subjects *learn* the CS–US association regardless of temporal order (provided that the events are temporally proximate), but that *responding* to the CS normally requires a predictive relationship (i.e., CS prior to US). Thus, Pavlovian responding (but not Pavlovian learning; see Miller & Barnet, 1993) is strongly dependent on temporal order. Moreover, Matute et al. (1996) have presented data suggesting that causal associations in humans also are bidirectional (from effect to cause as well as from cause to effect), and Arcediano, Matute, and Miller (1995), Shanks and Lopez (in press), and Waldmann and Holyoak (1992) have shown that human subjects can learn causal relations regardless of whether causes or effects are presented first.

The important point to be made here is the close correspondence between overt causal judgment and Pavlovian responding on one hand, and between the processes underlying causal and Pavlovian learning on the other hand. A causal judgment (and Pavlovian responding) is effectively a statement by the subject that if the putative cause were to occur, it would result in the occurrence of the effect. In contrast, learning refers to a link between internal event representations that must be further processed to yield a causal judgment or a conditioned response. In most circumstances, in addition to an association between the CS and US or cause and effect (and absence of cue competition), there must be an anticipatory relationship between the paired events for responding to occur. Thus, we suggest that formation of a basic link between events does not require temporal priority in either causal or Pavlovian situations, but that the element of temporal priority is necessary to allow the associative link to support either conditioned responding or causal judgment. In this framework, the requirement of temporal priority does not differentiate causal learning from Pavlovian conditioning.

XI. Conclusions

We have made three points in this chapter. First, nonverbal behavioral assessment of causal jugment is apt to be more veridical than is verbal assessment, which is compromised by the demand characteristics and ambiguities of language. Organisms presumably evolved the ability to learn cause–effect relationships in order to prepare for and sometimes influence future events in the real world, not in order to verbally describe these causal relationships.

Second, the use of nonverbal behavioral assessment invites direct comparisons between human causal judgment behavior and animal behavior in similar situations. Most of the phenomena observed to date in causal judgment tasks have clear parallels in the animal learning literature. One seeming discrepancy was the absence of backward blocking in Pavlovian tasks with animals in contrast with its presence in causal judgment by humans. However, this apparent difference between animals in Pavlovian situations and humans in causal judgment situations appears to arise from differences in the biological relevance of the outcome rather than from fundamental differences in either the way that humans and animals process causal information or the underlying associative processes (unless we defined Pavlovian and causal tasks, respectively, by whether or not they use biologically relevant outcomes). Cues of high biological relevance appear to be relatively invulnerable to cue competition compared to cues of low biological relevance (such as are ordinarily used in human causal judgment tasks), which are quite susceptible to cue competition.

Third, this convergence of findings in the causal judgment and animal learning literatures suggests that the two fields can each benefit by attending to the findings of the other. For example, we regard our observation of blocking of subsequent events in animals as supportive of the view that competition can occur between effects in causal judgment situations. Another likely finding from studies of cue competition in animals that might be profitably examined in causal judgment situations with humans is the learning-performance distinction. Historically, deficits in both causal judgment and Pavlovian responding due to cue competition (such as blocking, overshadowing, and the effect of stimulus relative validity) have been viewed as acquisition deficits. However, recent findings from the Pavlovian laboratory suggest that some or all of these deficits are due to a failure by subjects to express something that they did learn, rather than their failing to initially acquire the target relationship (e.g., for blocking, see Balaz, Gutsin, Cacheiro, & Miller, 1982; for the relative validity deficit, see Cole, Barnet, & Miller, 1995; for overshadowing, see Matzel, Schachtman, & Miller, 1985). Although a few similar effects have been reported in the human causal judgment literature, (e.g., G. B. Chapman, 1991; Shanks, 1985; Shanks & Dickinson, 1987; Van Hamme, 1994), they sometimes have been interpreted as acquisition effects (Van Hamme & Wasserman, 1994; but see Miller & Matute, in press) and sometimes as performance effects in which acquired associations are not transformed into causal judgments (Shanks & Dickinson, 1987). We might well view these nonexpressed associations as being analogous to latent Pavlovian associations. Associations can be latent for many reasons. For example, they lack consistent temporal priority of the cause (or CS) preceding the effect (or US), or, in the case of biologically irrelevant cues, a more valid competing cue may be present. For example, we might actually think that the flashing red light at the railroad crossing causes the train to come if we did not know about other causes that are associated with the arrival of trains. These other, previously known, causes of a train's motion may compete with the flashing red light in being perceived as the cause of the train's arrival. In this case, the light–train association is learned but is not transformed into a causal judgment because of the alternative causes (though it is transformed into a predictor of the train). More generally, causal judgments might simply result from those associations that have a *forward* relationship from one event to another (temporal priority) and that are *not in competition* with other associations that are active at the time the target association is tested.

ACKNOWLEDGMENTS

Support for the preparation of this chapter was provided by National Institute of Mental Health (USA) Grant 33881 and Dirección General de Investigación Científica y Tecnica (Spain) Grant PB91-0288. We thank Francisco Arcediano, Robert Cole, James Denniston, Martha Escobar, Lisa Gunther, Philippe Oberling, and Debra Rothberg for their helpful comments on an earlier draft of the manuscript.

REFERENCES

Adams, C. D., & Dickinson, A. (1981). Instrumental responding following reinforcer devaluation. *Quarterly Journal of Experimental Psychology, 33B,* 109–122.

Allan, L. G. (1980). A note on measurement of contingency between two binary variables in judgment tasks. *Bulletin of the Psychonomic Society, 15,* 147–149.

Allan, L. G. (1993). Human contingency judgments: Rule based or associative? *Psychological Bulletin, 114,* 435–448.

Allan, L. G., & Jenkins, H. M. (1983). The effect of representations of binary variables on judgment of influence. *Learning and Motivation, 14,* 381–405.

Alloy, L. B., & Abramson, L. Y. (1979). Judgment of contingency in depressed and nondepressed students: Sadder but wiser? *Journal of Experimental Psychology: General, 108,* 441–485.

Alloy, L. B., & Tabachnik, N. (1984). Assessment of covariation by humans and animals: The joint influence of prior expectations and current situational information. *Psychological Review, 91,* 112–149.

Arcediano, F., Matute, H., & Miller, R. R. (1995). *Competition between causes and between effects in predictive and diagnostic training and testing.* Manuscript submitted for publication.

Baeyens, F., Eelen, P., & van den Bergh, O. (1990). Contingency awareness in evaluative conditioning: A case for unaware affective-evaluative learning. *Cognition and Emotion, 4,* 3–18.

Balaz, M. A., Gutsin, P., Cacheiro, H., & Miller, R. R. (1982). Blocking as a retrieval failure: Reactivation of associations to a blocked stimulus. *Quarterly Journal of Experimental Psychology, 34B,* 99–113.

Barnet, R. C., Arnold, H. M., & Miller, R. R. (1991). Simultaneous conditioning demonstrated in second-order conditioning: Evidence for similar associative structure in forward and simultaneous conditioning. *Learning and Motivation, 22,* 253–268.

Chapman, G. B. (1991). Trial order affects cue interaction in contingency judgment. *Journal of Experimental Psychology: Learning, Memory, and Cognition, 17,* 837–854.

Chapman, L. J., & Chapman, J. P. (1969). Illusory correlation as an obstacle to the use of valid psychodiagnostic signs. *Journal of Abnormal Psychology, 74,* 271–280.

Chatlosh, D. L., Neunaber, D. J., & Wasserman, E. A. (1985). Response-outcome contingency: Behavioral and judgmental effects of appetitive and aversive outcomes with college students. *Learning and Motivation, 16,* 1–34.

Cheng, P. W. (1993). Separating causal laws from causal facts: Pressing the limits of statistical relevance. In D. L. Medin (Ed.), *The psychology of learning and motivation (Vol. 30,* pp. 215–264). San Diego, CA: Academic Press.

Cheng, P. W., & Novick, L. R. (1991). Causes versus enabling conditions. *Cognitive Psychology, 40,* 83–120.

Cole, R. P., Barnet, R. C., & Miller, R. R. (1995). Effect of relative stimulus validity: Learning or performance deficit? *Journal of Experimental Psychology: Animal Behavior Processes. 21,* 293–303.

Denniston, J. C., Miller, R. R., & Matute, H. (in press). Biological relevance as a determinant of cue competition. *Psychological Science.*

Dickinson, A., & Shanks, D. (1995). Instrumental action and causal representation. In D. Sperber, D. Premack, & A. J. Premack (Eds.), *Causal cognition: A multidisciplinary debate* (pp. 5–25). Oxford: Clarendon Press.

Dickinson, A., Shanks, D., & Evenden, J. (1984). Judgment of act-outcome contingency: The role of selective attribution. *Quarterly Journal of Experimental Psychology, 36A,* 29–50.

Einhorn, H. J., & Hogarth, R. M. (1986). Judging probable cause. *Psychological Bulletin, 99,* 3–19.

Esmoris-Arranz, F. J., Miller, R. R., & Matute, H. (1995). *Blocking of antecedent and subsequent events: Implications for cue competition in causality judgment.* Manuscript submitted for publication.

Gibbon, J., Berryman, R., & Thompson, R. L. (1974). Contingency spaces and measures in classical and instrumental conditioning. *Journal of the Experimental Analysis of Behavior, 21,* 585–605.

Hall, G., Mackintosh, N. J., Goodall, G., & dal Martello, M. (1977). Loss of control by a less valid or by a less salient stimulus compounded with a better predictor of reinforcement. *Learning and Motivation, 8,* 145–158.

Hinchy, J., Lovibond, P. F., & Ter-Horst, K. M. (1995). Blocking in human electrodermal conditioning. *Quarterly Journal of Experimental Psychology, 48B,* 2–12.

Hogarth, R. M., & Einhorn, H. J. (1992). Order effects in belief updating: The belief-adjustment model. *Cognitive Psychology, 24,* 1–55.

Hume, D. (1964). *Treatise of human nature* (L. A. Selby-Bigge, Ed.). London: Oxford University Press. (Original work published 1739)

Kamin, L. J. (1968). "Attention-like" processes in classical conditioning. In M. R. Jones (Ed.), *Miami symposium on the prediction of behavior: Aversive stimulation* (pp. 9–31). Miami, FL: University of Miami Press.

Killeen, P. R. (1981). Learning as causal inference. In M. L. Commons & J. A. Nevins Eds.), *Quantitative analyses of behavior: Vol. 1. Discriminative properties of reinforcement schedules* (pp. 89–112). Cambridge, MA: Ballinger.

Konorski, J. (1967). *Integrative activity of the brain.* Chicago: University of Chicago Press.

Langer, E. J. (1975). The illusion of control. *Journal of Personality and Social Psychology, 32,* 311–328.

Leddo, J., Abelson, R. P., & Gross, P. H. (1984). Conjunctive explanations: When two reasons are better than one. *Journal of Personality and Social Psychology, 47,* 933–943.

Levey, A. B., & Martin, I. (1975). Classical conditioning of human 'evaluative' responses. *Behavior Research & Therapy, 13,* 221–226.

Locksley, A., & Stengor, C. (1984). Why and how often: Causal reasoning and the incidence of judgmental biases. *Journal of Experimental Social Psychology, 20,* 470–483.

Matute, H. (1994). Learned helplessness and superstitious behavior as opposite effects of uncontrollable reinforcement in humans. *Learning and Motivation, 25,* 216–232.

Matute, H. (1995). Human reactions to uncontrollable outcomes: Further evidence for superstitions rather than helplessness. *Quarterly Journal of Experimental Psychology, 48B,* 142–157.

Matute, H. (in press). Illusion of control: Detecting response-outcome independence in analytic but not in naturalistic conditions. *Psychological Science.*

Matute, H., Arcediano, F., & Miller, R. R. (1996). Test question modulates cue competition between causes and between effects. *Journal of Experimental Psychology: Learning, Memory, and Cognition., 22,* 182–196.

Matzel, L. D., Held, F. P., & Miller, R. R. (1988). Information and expression of simultaneous and backward associations: Implications for contiguity theory. *Learning and Motivation, 19,* 317–344.

Matzel, L. D., Schachtman, T. R., & Miller, R. R. (1985). Recovery of an overshadowed association achieved by extinction of the overshadowing stimulus. *Learning and Motivation, 16,* 398–412.

Medin, D. L., Wattenmaker, W. D., & Hampson, S. E. (1987). Family resemblance, conceptual cohesiveness, and category construction. *Cognitive Psychology, 19,* 242–279.

Miller, R. R., & Balaz, M. A. (1981). Differences in adaptiveness between classically conditioned responses and instrumentally acquired responses. In N. E. Spear & R. R. Miller (Eds.), *Information processing in animals: Memory mechanisms* (pp. 49–80). Hillsdale, NJ: Erlbaum.

Miller, R. R., & Barnet, R. C. (1993). The role of time in elementary associations. *Current Directions in Psychological Science, 2,* 106–111.

Miller, R. R., Hallam, S. C., & Grahame, N. J. (1990). Inflation of comparator stimuli following CS training. *Animal Learning and Behavior, 18,* 434–443.

Miller, R. R., & Matute, H. (in press). Biological relevance in forward and backward blocking: Resolution of a discrepancy between animals and humans in contingency judgment. *Journal of Experimental Psychology: General.*

Pavlov, I. P. (1927). *Conditioned reflexes.* London: Clarendon Press.

Pazzani, M. J. (1991). Influence of prior knowledge on concept formation acquisition. *Journal of Experimental Psychology: Learning, Memory, and Cognition, 17,* 416–432.

Price, P. C., & Yates, J. F. (1993). Judgmental overshadowing: Further evidence of cue interaction in contingency judgment. *Memory & Cognition, 21,* 561–572.

Rescorla, R. A. (1968). Probability of shock in the presence and absence of CS in fear conditioning. *Journal of Comparative and Physiological Psychology, 66,* 1–5.

Rescorla, R. A. (1988). Pavlovian conditioning: It's not what you think it is. *American Psychologist, 43,* 151–160.

Rescorla, R. A., & Wagner, A. R. (1972). A theory of Pavlovian conditioning: Variations in the effectiveness of reinforcement and nonreinforcement. In A. H. Black & W. F. Prokasy (Eds.), *Classical conditioning II: Current research and theory* (pp. 64–99). New York: Appleton-Century-Crofts.

Rizley, R. C., & Rescorla, R. A. (1972). Associations in higher order conditioning and sensory preconditioning. *Journal of Comparative and Physiological Psychology, 81,* 1–11.

Schweitzer, L., & Green, L. (1982). Reevaluation of things past: A test of the "retrospective hypothesis" using a CER procedure in rats. *Pavlovian Journal of Biological Science, 17,* 62–68.

Shanks, D. R. (1985). Forward and backward blocking in human contingency judgment. *Quarterly Journal of Experimental Psychology, 37B,* 1–21.

Shanks, D. R. (1991). Categorization by a connectionist network. *Journal of Experimental Psychology: Learning, Memory, and Cognition, 17,* 433–443.

Shanks, D. R. (1993). Human instrumental learning: A critical review of data and theory. *British Journal of Psychology, 84,* 319–354.

Shanks, D. R., & Dickinson, A. (1987). Associative accounts of causality judgment. In G.H. Bower (Ed.), *The psychology of learning and motivation* (Vol. 21, pp. 229–261). San Diego, CA: Academic Press.

Shanks, D. R., & Dickinson, A. (1991). Instrumental judgment and performance under variations in action-outcome contingency and contiguity. *Memory & Cognition, 19,* 353–360.

Shanks, D. R., & Lopez, F. J. (in press). Causal order does not affect cue selection in human associative learning. *Memory & Cognition.*

Shanks, D. R., Pearson, S. M., & Dickinson, A. (1989). Temporal contiguity and the judgment of causality by human subjects. *Quarterly Journal of Experimental Psychology, 41B,* 139–159.

Skinner, E. A. (1985). Action, control judgments, and the structure of control experience. *Psychological Review, 92,* 39–58.

Van Hamme, L. J. (1994). *Associative and statistical accounts of cue competition in causality judgments.* Unpublished doctoral dissertation, University of Iowa, Iowa City.

Van Hamme, L. J., Kao, S.-F., & Wasserman, E. A. (1993). Judging interevent relations: From cause to effect and from effect to cause. *Memory & Cognition, 21,* 802–808.

Van Hamme, L. J., & Wasserman, E. A. (1994). Cue competition in causality judgments: The role of nonpresentation of compound stimulus elements. *Learning and Motivation, 25,* 127–151.

Wagner, A. R., & Brandon, S. E. (1989). Evolution of a structured connectionist model of Pavlovian conditioning (AESOP). In S. B. Klein & R. R. Mowrer (Eds.), *Contemporary learning theories: Pavlovian conditioning and the status of traditional learning theory* (pp. 149–189). Hillsdale, NJ: Erlbaum.

Waldmann, M. R., & Holyoak, K. J. (1992). Predictive and diagnostic learning within causal models: asymmetries in cue competition. *Journal of Experimental Psychology: General, 121,* 222–236.

Wasserman, E. A. (1990a). Attribution of causality to common and distinctive elements of compound stimuli. *Psychological Science, 1,* 298–302.

Wasserman, E. A. (1990b). Detecting response-outcome relations: Toward an understanding of the causal texture of the environment. In G. H. Bower (Ed.), *The psychology of learning and motivation* (Vol. 26, pp. 27–82). San Diego, CA: Academic Press.

Wasserman, E. A. (1993). Comparative cognition: Toward an understanding of cognition in behavior. *Psychological Science, 4,* 156–161.

Wasserman, E. A., Chatlosh, D. L., & Neunaber, D. J. (1983). Perception of causal relations in humans: Factors affecting judgments of response-outcome contingencies under free-operant procedures. *Learning and Motivation, 14,* 406–432.

Wasserman, E. A., & Neunaber, D. J. (1986). College students' responding to and rating of contingency relations: The role of temporal contiguity. *Journal of the Experimental Analysis of Behavior, 46,* 15–35.

Williams, D. A., Sagness, K. E., & McPhee, J. E. (1994). Configural and elemental strategies in predictive learning. *Journal of Experimental Psychology: Learning, Memory, and Cognition, 20,* 694–709.

Wright, J. C. (1962). Consistency and complexity of response sequences as a function of schedules of noncontingent reward. *Journal of Experimental Psychology, 63,* 601–609.

Young, M. E. (1995). On the origin of personal causal theories. *Psychonomic Bulletin & Review, 2,* 83–104.

CONDITIONALIZING CAUSALITY

Barbara A. Spellman

I. Introduction

When I attended my first psychology class in the mid-1970s, I learned the following two pieces of up-to-the-minute wisdom. The first was that rats were very good reasoners. In study after study, involving conditioning and extinction, rats behaved as if they were adhering to a formal statistical model of the relationship between conditioned and unconditioned stimuli. The second thing I learned was that humans were very bad reasoners. In study after study, involving many kinds of decisions, humans behaved as if they were ignoring relevant statistical information and relying instead on non-normative heuristics (see Kahneman, Slovic, & Tversky, 1982, for a collection of early papers, and Nisbett & Ross, 1980, for the classic review). I decided that if I ever went into psychology, I would like to show that humans are at least as smart as rats.

The findings that demonstrated that humans were irrational decision makers showed up starkly against a backdrop of belief that humans were good reasoners. In the preceding decade it had been fashionable to call people "intuitive statisticians" (Peterson & Beach, 1967) and to suggest that they are intuitive scientists (Kelley, 1967). In particular, Kelley's causal schema model and ANOVA model (see Kelley, 1973, for the distinction) suggested that humans were excellent causal reasoners and that such reasoning was based on the use of normative rules. But along with the attacks on human statistical reasoning came attacks on human causal reasoning (see Cheng & Novick, 1992, for a review). Some of the assailants agreed that humans did use rules but that the rules were used badly; others suggested that humans did not use normative rules at all.

A number of these latter attacks are based on findings that humans do not use the "normative" Δp contingency rule when evaluating the causal efficacy of multiple potential causes (see Allan, 1993; Shanks, 1993; Young, 1995, for recent reviews). Rather, in cases of multiple potential causes, humans show "cue-interaction effects"—systematic violations of the Δp rule supposedly due to the contingency between the other potential causes and the outcome. Such cue-interaction effects are observed in animals and have been taken as an argument that human learning of causal relations is better described by the same function that describes animals' learning of the associative strength between conditioned and unconditioned stimuli (e.g., the Rescorla–Wagner model; see Rescorla & Wagner, 1972) than by the Δp contingency rule.

This article addresses human deviations from the Δp rule and argues that they are the result of a normative process that involves the conditionalizing of causal judgments on the existence of other potential causes. Section II shows how in cases of multiple potential causes the simple Δp rule is not, in fact, normative. In that section I argue that in cases of multiple potential causes humans do what scientists do, and that is evaluate the efficacy of a target cause conditional on the constant presence and/or absence of alternative causes. I then describe two experiments that contrast unconditional and conditional causal evaluations, showing that subjects use the more sophisticated conditional rule. Section III lays out various mathematical properties of the analysis of conditional contingencies. Section IV uses the mathematical formulations to "post-dict" several experiments involving discounting (e.g., Baker, Mercier, Vallée-Tourangeau, Frank & Pan, 1993; Price & Yates, 1993) and to predict some surprising results. Section V describes the limitations of the conditional contingency analysis. Section VI shows that conditionalization is a general procedure that humans use in various kinds of causal reasoning.

II.   Conditional versus Unconditional Contingencies

Proponents of the rule-based view of causal reasoning believe that in evaluating causal efficacy, humans compute statistical functions based on the frequency of the occurrence of the cause and effect. Performance in many experiments can be characterized by a particular contingency rule called the Δp rule. That rule is often considered the normative rule for computing causal strength. Using the Δp rule, one determines the strength of the relationship between a proposed cause (C) and an effect (E) as follows:

$$\Delta p = p(E|C) - p(E|\overline{C}),$$

where $p(E|C)$ is the proportion of times the effect occurs given the presence of the proposed cause and $p(E|\overline{C})$ is the proportion of times the effect occurs given the absence of the proposed cause. The difference, Δp, is the contingency, which is bounded by -1 and 1. Positive numbers denote facilitative causes, which make the effect more likely to occur; negative numbers denote inhibitory causes, which make the effect less likely to occur.

The contingency relationship captures (at least part of) our everyday notion of the concept "cause"; for example, we say that smoking causes lung cancer in part because the probability of getting lung cancer if you smoke is greater than the probability of getting lung cancer if you do not smoke. We make this causal claim even though we know that smoking is neither necessary nor sufficient for getting lung cancer.

As a numerical example, suppose that we wish to evaluate whether a particular red liquid, advertised as a plant fertilizer, indeed causes plants to bloom. To do so we determine whether the effect (blooming) is more probable when given the liquid than when not given the liquid. We pour the liquid on 20 of our 40 plants and find that of the treated plants 15 out of 20 $[p(E|C) = .75]$ bloom and of the untreated plants only 5 out of 20 $[p(E|\overline{C}) = .25]$ bloom. The contingency (Δp) is then $.75 - .25 = .5$ and it seems that the liquid is a fairly effective fertilizer.

A. The Problem of Multiple Simultaneous Causes

What if in the above example our gardener had surreptitiously sprinkled a blue liquid (also advertised as a fertilizer) on some of our plants? Now there are two potential causes of the blooming. How can we evaluate the causal efficacy of each liquid? Under these conditions, many researchers have found that humans deviate from the Δp contingency rule (see Allan, 1993; Shanks, 1993; Young, 1995, for recent reviews). Cheng and her colleagues have suggested however, that humans do not use that rule because in circumstances involving multiple potential causes, the simple Δp rule, which computes *unconditional* contingencies, is the wrong rule to apply (Cheng, 1993; Cheng & Holyoak, 1995; Cheng, Park, Yarlas, & Holyoak, this volume, Ch. 8; Melz, Cheng, Holyoak, & Waldmann, 1993).

Many philosophers have argued that in cases of multiple causes unconditional Δp is not normative. They have suggested that if there exist multiple potential competing causes for an effect, then one needs to analyze the effect of each cause independent of the effect of the other causes; that is, for any target cause, one should assess causality conditional on both the presence and absence of other potential causes (e.g., Cartwright, 1979; Salmon, 1984). As Salmon notes: "Each of two drugs can be positively relevant to good health, but taken together, the combination may be detrimental. . ." (p. 39). And, of course, combinations may react in other ways as well. Obviously, it is not possible to know for certain that one has considered all possible alternative causes, but controlling for *known* alternative causes is a technique intentionally used by scientists to reduce the probability of errors in attribution. In fact, it seems that people know to do that in everyday attributions. For example, when I perversely suggest that drinking coffee causes lung cancer because people who drink lots of coffee tend to get lung cancer more often than those who do not, my caffeine-addicted friends and my trickery-attuned students are quick to point out that perhaps drinking coffee covaries with smoking, so it only *looks* like coffee causes lung cancer, while it is really smoking that is doing the causal work.

Continuing the gardener example, to find the causal efficacy of the red liquid we should now examine the effect of the red liquid in both the presence and absence of the blue liquid. Consider the representation of frequencies shown in Fig. 1.[1] The fraction in each cell represents the number of times a flower blooms (numerator) over the number of times that combination of liquids was given to the plants (denominator). As described previously, to find the *unconditional* contingency (Δp) for the red liquid, we look at the right-hand marginal and find the difference between the proportion of times plants bloom given the red liquid (15/20) and the proportion of times plants bloom when not given the red liquid (5/20). Therefore, Δp_{red} = .5. Now, however, suppose we wish to control for the blue liquid and find the *conditional* contingencies for the red liquid based on the constant presence or absence of the blue liquid. First, consider what happens when the blue liquid *is given* (left-hand side of contingency table). Taking the difference between the proportion of times plants bloom when given the red liquid (15/15 = 1) and the proportion of times plants bloom when not given the red liquid (5/5 = 1) yields a conditional contingency of 0. Next consider what happens when the blue liquid *is not given* (right-hand side of contingency table). Taking the difference between the proportion of times plants bloom given the red liquid (0/5 = 0) and the proportion of times plants bloom when not given the red liquid (0/15 = 0) again yields a conditional contingency of 0. So, conditional on the blue liquid, the red liquid has no effect at all! Another way to understand this result is to notice that when blue is given (left-hand side) the plants *always* bloom regardless

[1] The frequencies in the cells equal the frequencies in the ".5/1" condition of Experiment 1 of Baker et al. (1993).

Blue Liquid

	given	not given	
Red Liquid given	$\frac{15}{15}$	$\frac{0}{5}$	$\frac{15}{20}$
not given	$\frac{5}{5}$	$\frac{0}{15}$	$\frac{5}{20}$
	$\frac{20}{20}$	$\frac{0}{20}$	

Unconditional contingency (ΔP) for red liquid:

$$\frac{15}{20} - \frac{5}{20} = \frac{10}{20} = .5$$

Conditional contingency for red liquid GIVEN blue liquid:

$$\frac{15}{15} - \frac{5}{5} = 0$$

Conditional contingency for red liquid NOT GIVEN blue liquid:

$$\frac{0}{5} - \frac{0}{15} = 0$$

Fig. 1. Contingency table for example in text showing that the red liquid's conditional contingencies are not equal to its unconditional contingency. The fraction in each cell represents the number of times a flower blooms (numerator) given the number of times that the combination of liquids was poured on the plants (denominator).

of whether red is given (20/20), and when blue is not given (right-hand side) the plants *never* bloom regardless of whether red is given (0/20). Thus the red liquid has no effect on blooming. It merely seems to have an effect because of the way the application of the liquids covaries (i.e., because there are more events in the upper left and lower right corners).

Note, by the way, that there is no necessary reason that the conditional contingencies must be equal to each other. If, however, they are not equal, the predictions of a conditional contingency analysis are less clear (see Section V).

B. Humans Use Conditional Rather Than Unconditional Contingencies

I recently ran an experiment designed to evaluate whether subjects use unconditional or conditional contingencies in rating causal efficacy when information about two causes and an effect is presented on a trial-by-trial basis. Subjects were undergraduates enrolled in introductory psychology at the University of Texas. They were told to pretend that while looking through the garage of the house they had just rented, they had found some containers of variously colored liquids. The landlady said that the liquids were expensive plant-treatment liquids of differing strengths and that some were flower-growth stimulators (fertilizers) and some were flower-growth inhibitors (weed killers). She would reduce the subjects' rent if they could prove to her that they could distinguish the liquids. They could do so by observing combinations of the liquids being poured on plants and then accurately predicting whether or not the plants would produce flowers.

On each trial subjects saw a picture of a plant and two containers of liquid, one red and one blue. On some trials both containers were on the ground indicating that neither fertilizer had been used, on other trials one or both of the containers was in the air, pouring liquid onto the plant. Below the plant was the question: "Do you think the plant will produce a flower?" After subjects pressed either the "yes" or "no" key, they received feedback by seeing a picture of the same plant either with or without a flower.

Subjects made causal strength evaluations after the 40th and 80th (final) trials. For each liquid they were shown a scale with points labeled: -100, ("total flower inhibitor (never grows)"), -50, 0 ("no effect"), 50, and 100, ("total flower stimulator (always grows)") and were instructed to type in a number from -100 to 100. Accompanying text reminded subjects to use the numbers in the middle of the scale to indicate that they thought the liquids had some, but not a guaranteed, effect on the flowers.

The first three conditions of the experiment were designed so that the blue liquid had equal unconditional contingencies but unequal conditional contingencies. Figure 2 shows the frequencies of presentation of each combination of liquids and flowers for each condition along with the unconditional and conditional contingencies. As shown in Fig. 2A, in conditions 1, 2, and 3, flowers bloomed 10/20 times when the blue liquid was given and 10/20 times when the blue liquid was not given, for an unconditional contingency of 0.[2] However, due to differences in the frequencies in the cells rather than the marginals, it conditional contingency varied downward across conditions: condition 1 = .33, condition 2 = 0, and condition 3 = $-.33$.

---

[2] Note that in addition to keeping Δp constant, the number of times the subjects saw the effect in the presence of the blue liquid (i.e., the "outcome density") was also held constant across conditions. See Allan (1993) and Baker et al. (this volume, Ch. 1) for reviews of why this procedure is necessary.

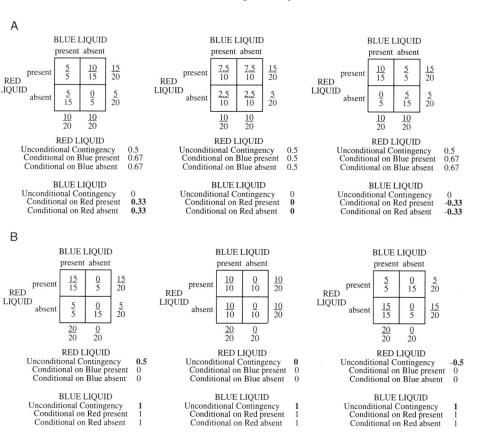

Fig. 2.   Frequencies of presentation of each combination of liquids and flowers for each condition along with unconditional and conditional contingencies. The fraction in each cell represents the number of times a flower blooms (numerator) given the number of times that the combination of liquids was poured on the plants (denominator). Subjects saw 40 trials (distributed as in this figure), then made causal strength ratings, then saw 40 more trials (from the same condition) and made ratings again. (A) Blue has equal unconditional contingencies but unequal conditional contingencies. (B) Red has unequal unconditional contingencies but equal conditional contingencies.

(For the red fertilizer, $\Delta p = .5$ in all conditions; its conditional contingency was held nearly constant: .67, .5, and .67.)

The last three conditions of the experiment were designed such that the red liquid had unequal unconditional contingencies but equal conditional contingencies. As can be seen in Fig. 2B, for the red fertilizer Δp was different in all conditions; condition 4 = .5, condition 5 = 0, and condition

6 = −.5; but its conditional contingency was 0 in all conditions.[3] (In all conditions both Δp and the conditional contingency for the blue fertilizer were 1.)

The results were in accordance with a conditional contingency analysis. As shown in Fig. 3A, for the first three conditions subjects rated the causal strength of the blue liquid higher in condition 1 ($M = 7.4$) than in condition 2 ($M = 28.4$) and higher in condition 2 than in condition 3 ($M = −61.4$), indicating that they were sensitive to the different conditional contingencies. As shown in Fig. 3B, for the second three conditions subjects rated the red liquid as not significantly different across conditions ($−29.3$, $−29.1$, $−38.8$ in conditions 4, 5, and 6, respectively), indicating that they were sensitive to the equal conditional contingencies.[4] Note that although in all conditions the actual ratings were between 26 and 39 rating-scale points lower than predicted, the trends were in accordance with the predictions of the conditional contingency theory.[5]

C.   HUMANS KNOW THEY NEED CONDITIONAL CONTINGENCIES

The fact that subjects make causal ratings in accordance with conditional rather than unconditional contingencies indicates that when people are presented with trial-by-trial information they are sensitive to the information in the cells (which gives them information about the conditional contingencies) rather than information solely in the marginals (which gives them information about the unconditional contingencies). But (1) would they be

[3] Condition 4 is the same as the ".5/1" condition from Experiment 1 of Baker et al. (1993) and Condition 6 is the same as the "−.5/1" condition from their Experiment 4. Their first number refers to the unconditional contingency for the cause analogous to the blue liquid. Subjects gave that cause a mean rating (on a −100 to 100 scale) of −6 in the ".5/1" condition and −26 in the "−.5/1" condition, suggesting that they were using conditional rather than unconditional contingencies.

[4] For the first three conditions, an omnibus F test showed an overall difference in the means for the blue liquid, $F(2, 57) = 16.92$, $p < .001$; a Newman-Keuls test revealed that all three means were significantly different from each other. For the second three conditions, for the means for the red liquid, $F(2, 57) < 1$.

[5] This underrating seems to be due to a misinterpretation of the rating scale by some of the subjects. It appears that some subjects believed that −100 (the lowest rating possible), rather than 0, meant "no effect." Evidence for this interpretation comes from two sources. First, in a later partial replication, subjects were (1) told that the liquids might be colored water and (2) given more instruction on using the scale. In the replication of condition 2, 20 subjects rated the blue fertilizer as having a mean strength of −17.7; also only 9 rather than 11 subjects gave the blue fertilizer a negative rating. In the replication of condition 6, subjects gave the red fertilizer a mean rating of −5.0; in addition, only 3 subjects (rather than 11 as in the original version), gave the red fertilizer a negative rating. Second, in a later experiment, after reading more detailed instructions, subjects were asked to "type in the number that means the liquid had no effect." Some subjects still typed in "−100" rather than 0. These problems were remedied in Spellman (in press).

sensitive to cell information when the information is presented in summary form and (2) do they actually *know* that they need that cell information?

To answer that question, I ran a study that was logically equivalent to the previous study but in which subjects were presented with contingency information in the form of summary statistics. Subjects read a story about a doctor who had treated cases of a deadly virus with neither, either, or both of two treatments: a clear one (with contingencies equivalent to the blue liquid) and a cloudy one (with contingencies equivalent to the red liquid). Subjects were given summary information about the treatments and outcomes for 80 patients (i.e., the information in Fig. 2 was doubled to reflect the total information available to subjects in the trial-by-trial study). Subjects in the six "cell-by-cell" conditions were given information about how each combination treatments performed (i.e., the information from the four cells for each condition). Subjects in the four "marginal-only" conditions were given information about how each treatment performed without regard to whether the other treatment was given or not (i.e., the information from the marginals of conditions 1–3, which are identical, and conditions 4, 5, and 6). After reading the story, subjects made three types of judgments. First, they were asked to rate the effectiveness of the treatments on a scale from −100 (labeled "always kills patients") to 100 (labeled "always saves patients") with an additional label at 0 ("no effect"). Second, they were asked to rate their confidence in their effectiveness judgments on a scale from 0 ("not at all confident") to 10 ("totally confident"). Finally, they were asked whether there was anything they would like to know that would make them more confident in their judgments.

The results from the six cell-by-cell conditions are shown on the left-hand sides of the graphs in Fig. 3C and 3D. Subjects' ratings were similar to the ratings of subjects in the trial-by-trial experiment in that for the first three conditions the ratings for the clear (analogous to the blue) treatment went down across those conditions (10.4, −9.2, −81.9), whereas for the last three conditions the ratings for the cloudy treatment (analogous to the red liquid) did not significantly differ from each other (−33.2, −19.8, −29.4). Thus, subjects must have been using a conditional contingency analysis.

The results from the marginals-only conditions are shown on the right-hand sides of the graphs in Fig. 3C and 3D. For the marginal condition in Fig. 3C (conditions 1–3), subjects' mean ratings for the blue liquid was 6.3 and for the red liquid was 59.4—very close to 0 and 50, the values for both the unconditional and conditional contingencies for condition 2, in which there are an equal number of subjects in all conditions. In the marginal conditions in Fig. 3D, the ratings for the cloudy treatment went from 9.0 to −7.6 to −32.6 across conditions. These differences are predicted by use of unconditional rather than conditional contingencies (which is the only

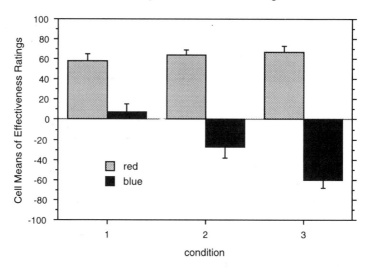

A   Blue Has Equal Unconditional Contingencies
     but Unequal Conditional Contingencies

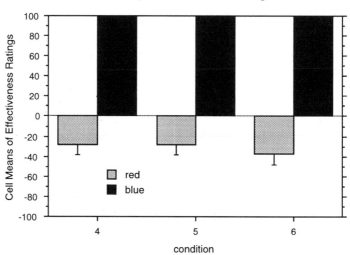

B   Red Has Unequal Unconditional Contingencies
     but Equal Conditional Contingencies

Fig. 3. (A, B) Causal strength ratings for red and blue liquids by condition. Information was presented on a trial-by-trial basis. (A) Blue liquid is relevant; (B) red liquid is relevant. (C, D) Causal strength ratings for red and blue liquids by condition. Information was presented in a summary table. (C) Clear treatment is relevant; (D) cloudy treatment is relevant.

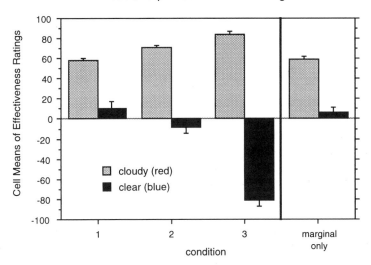

C   Blue Has Equal Unconditional Contingencies but Unequal Conditional Contingencies

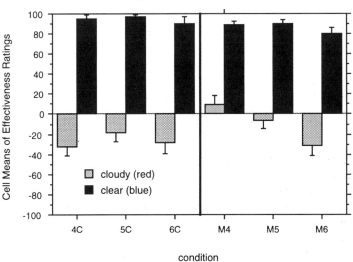

D   Red Has Unequal Unconditional Contingencies but Equal Conditional Contingencies

Fig. 3. *Continued*

information subjects have in these conditions); however, it is also predicted by the use of conditional contingencies *assuming that the cells have equal frequencies* (see Property 4 in Section III, below). It is likely that in the absence of other information, subjects guess that there are equal cell frequencies (Spellman, 1995b).

Subjects in the marginal-only condition for conditions 1–3 were much less confident of their effectiveness ratings for the clear treatment (mean = 4.4) than were subjects in the cell-by-cell conditions (mean = 6.7). For conditions 4, 5, and 6, subjects in the marginal-only conditions (mean = 6.1) were also less confident about the relevant treatment than subjects in the cell-by-cell conditions (mean = 6.3). Thus, given that their effectiveness ratings were similar to the cell-by-cell conditions but their confidence was lower, subjects may have been aware that they were making an assumption about cell frequency.

More important, in response to the open-ended question about whether there was anything they would like to know that would make them more confident in their judgments, 68% of the subjects in the marginal-only conditions said they would be more confident if given cell-by-cell information (not, of course, in those exact words). Some subjects asked to know how many patients were given each combination of treatments; others wanted to know what happened for each treatment when given alone.

III. Mathematical Properties of Contingencies with Two Potential Causes

In order to predict how people using a conditional contingency analysis will respond in cases of multiple potential causes, it is helpful to understand some of the properties of such an analysis. These properties will be used in Section IV to explain and predict some experimental findings, and in Section V to explain some limitations of a conditional contingency analysis. Consider the two-way contingency table displayed in Fig. 4. This representation will be used to illustrate some of the mathematical properties of contingencies with two potential causes.

Property 1. If the pair of conditional contingencies for one variable are equal, then the pair of conditional contingencies for the other variable must also be equal. To illustrate, if the contingency for Cause 2 conditional on the *presence* of Cause 1 is equal to the contingency for Cause 2 conditional on the *absence* of Cause 1 then:

$$\frac{a}{b} - \frac{c}{d} = \frac{e}{f} - \frac{g}{h}. \tag{1}$$

Cause 2

	present	absent
present	$\dfrac{a}{b}$	$\dfrac{c}{d}$
absent	$\dfrac{e}{f}$	$\dfrac{g}{h}$

Cause 1

Cause 1:
    Unconditional contingency: $\dfrac{a+c}{b+d} - \dfrac{e+g}{f+h}$

    Conditional contingency:
        Cause 2 present: $\dfrac{a}{b} - \dfrac{e}{f}$

        Cause 2 absent: $\dfrac{c}{d} - \dfrac{g}{h}$

Cause 2:
    Unconditional contingency: $\dfrac{a+e}{b+f} - \dfrac{c+g}{d+h}$

    Conditional contingency:
        Cause 1 present: $\dfrac{a}{b} - \dfrac{c}{d}$

        Cause 1 absent: $\dfrac{e}{f} - \dfrac{g}{h}$

Fig. 4. Abstract mathematical representation of unconditional and conditional contingencies for two causes of an effect. Fractions in each cell indicate the number of times the effect was present (numerator) given the number of times that combination of causes was present (denominator).

It is then simple to move the second and third terms of the equation to the opposite sides of the equal sign, showing that the contingencies for Cause 1 conditional on the presence and absence of Cause 2 must be equal to each other, as well:

$$\frac{a}{b} - \frac{e}{f} = \frac{c}{d} - \frac{g}{h}. \qquad (2)$$

An intuitive interpretation of this property is that if you draw a line graph of the results of a 2×2 experiment and find parallel lines (i.e., no interaction) when graphing with one variable on the x-axis, then you will also see parallel lines (i.e., still no interaction) when graphing with the other variable on the x-axis.

Property 2. The sum of the unconditional *contingencies of Cause 1 and Cause 2 is not bounded by −1 and 1, as one might expect; rather it is bounded by −2 and 2.* This property is illustrated in Fig. 5, and results from the way the two causes covary. Thus, it seems that when two causes are present, an effect can be "overpredicted."

Property 3. When Property 1 holds (i.e., the conditional contingencies are equal), the sum of the conditional *contingencies of Cause 1 and Cause 2 is bounded by −1 and 1.* To demonstrate, adding the conditional contingency for Cause 2 based on the presence of Cause 1 and the conditional contingency for Cause 1 based on the presence of Cause 2 yields:

$$\frac{a}{b} - \frac{c}{d} + \frac{a}{b} - \frac{e}{f}. \tag{3}$$

Cause 2

		present	absent	
Cause 1	present	$\dfrac{1000}{1000}$	$\dfrac{0}{1}$	$\dfrac{1000}{1001}$
	absent	$\dfrac{1}{1}$	$\dfrac{0}{1000}$	$\dfrac{1}{1001}$
		$\dfrac{1001}{1001}$	$\dfrac{0}{1001}$	

Cause 1:
  Unconditional contingency: $\dfrac{1000}{1001} - \dfrac{1}{1001} = .998$

  Conditional contingency:
  Cause 2 present: $\dfrac{1000}{1000} - \dfrac{1}{1} = 0$

  Cause 2 absent: $\dfrac{0}{1} - \dfrac{0}{1000} = 0$

Cause 2:
  Unconditional contingency: $\dfrac{1001}{1001} - \dfrac{0}{1001} = 1$

  Conditional contingency:
  Cause 1 present: $\dfrac{1000}{1000} - \dfrac{0}{1} = 1$

  Cause 1 absent: $\dfrac{1}{1} - \dfrac{0}{1000} = 1$

Fig. 5. Illustration of how the sum of unconditional contingencies is bounded by 2 and −2, whereas the sum conditional contingencies is bounded by 1 and −1.

Substituting for the last term from Equation 1 yields:

$$\frac{a}{b} - \frac{c}{d} + \frac{a}{b} - \frac{(a}{(b} - \frac{c}{d} + \frac{g)}{h)}.$$

Removing common terms yields:

$$\frac{a}{b} - \frac{g}{h}. \tag{4}$$

Each of the terms in Equation 4 is bounded by 0 and 1, therefore the sum of the conditional contingencies is bounded by -1 and 1. Under this analysis, when two causes are present an effect cannot be "overpredicted."

Note that since g/h represents the proportion of the times that the effect occurs in the absence of both causes, the result of applying Equation 4 yields a number that loosely can be thought of as the proportion of times that the presence of the effect is due to either or both of the causes (rather than to its random baseline occurrence).

More important, given Property 1, when the sum of the unconditional contingencies is greater than 1, the sum of the conditional contingencies must still be less than 1; therefore, for at least one of the causes the conditional contingency must be less than the unconditional contingency.

Property 4. When Property 1 holds (i.e., the conditional contingencies are equal), and when the number of events is the same in all cells (i.e., b = d = f = h), then the unconditional and conditional contingencies are equal. That is, if:

$$\frac{a}{b} - \frac{c}{d} = \frac{e}{f} - \frac{g}{h}$$

and

$$b = d = f = h$$

then:

$$\frac{a + e}{b + f} - \frac{c + g}{d + h} = \frac{a}{b} - \frac{c}{d}. \tag{5}$$

Therefore, when there are an equal number of events in each cell, the sums of the conditional and unconditional contingencies are not only equal, but also must be less than or equal to 1 (by Property 3).

IV. "Post-dictions" and Predictions of the Conditional
Contingency Analysis

The conditional contingency analysis leads to several interesting, testable, and nonintuitive predictions. In addition, an analysis of the stimuli from other researchers' experiments suggests that most cue-interaction effects and violations of the Δp rule can be explained by assuming that subjects are using conditional rather than unconditional contingencies in their causal judgments.

A. DISCOUNTING

The fact that subjects seem to be using conditional rather than unconditional contingencies in their causal judgments explains the "overshadowing" or "discounting" effects found by many researchers (e.g., Baker et al., 1993; Price & Yates, 1993).

In the literature, the term "discounting" is often used to refer to the finding that when subjects believe that there are two (simultaneous) potential causes of an outcome and are asked to judge the efficacy of each, the presence of a strong causal factor will reduce judgments of the efficacy of the weaker one. In the associationist literature, this effect is referred to as overshadowing (Mackintosh, 1976; Price & Yates, 1993, use the term "judgmental overshadowing"). In the human causal literature, Kelley proposed discounting with respect to his causal schema model and not his ANOVA model; that is, with respect to making causal attributions based on single events rather than after a series of events (Kelley, 1973; see Morris & Larrick, 1995). Within the causal schema framework, judgments of the efficacy of all causes (not just a weaker one) are reduced when other potential causes may be present relative to when no other potential causes are present (Kelley, 1972). That expectation has not carried over into the contingency literature; however, a conditional contingency analysis suggests that it should.

1. "Post-dictions"

Price and Yates (1993) showed discounting in an experiment in which subjects were to pretend to be physicians who were shown the medical records for 40 fictional patients. Patients were reported as either having or not having a rash and a fever, and the subjects' task was to predict whether or not each patient had the disease "chronitis" on the basis of that information. After attempting to diagnose the patients (and receiving feedback on each one), subjects were asked to make conditional probability judgments for the disease given the presence and absence of each symptom. (For example, one of the four questions that subjects would be asked was: If a patient has a rash, but you don't know whether that patient has fever, what is the probability that the patient has chronitis?)[6] Ratings were made on a scale of 0 to 100.

Price and Yates (1993) had what they called "strong rash" and "weak rash" conditions. In both conditions the probability of a patient having chronitis given that the patient had fever was .7, whereas the probability of a patient having chronitis given that the patient did not have fever was .3, so $\Delta p_{fever} = .4$. In the weak rash condition, the probability of a patient having chronitis given that the patient had a rash was .5, whereas the probability of a patient having chronitis given that the patient did not have rash was .5, so $\Delta p_{rash} = 0$. In the strong rash condition, the probability of a patient having chronitis given that the patient had a rash was .9, whereas the probability of a patient having chrontis given that the patient did not have a rash was .1, so $\Delta p_{rash} = .8$. Price and Yates found discounting: subjects rated Δp_{fever} higher in the weak rash condition (mean $\Delta p = 26.5$) than in the strong rash condition (mean $\Delta p = 1.6$). They concluded that the presence of a strong alternative causal factor reduces judgments of efficacy of a weaker causal factor.

It is important to note, however, that Price and Yates (1993) expressed the contingencies for fever and rash in terms of *unconditional* contingencies, that is, without taking into account the presence or absence of the other symptom. When the conditional contingencies are taken into account, a different picture emerges. Figure 6 depicts the frequencies with which subjects saw each combination of presence or absence of rash, fever, and chronitis. In (A), which depicts the weak rash condition, both the unconditional and conditional contingencies for fever are .4 (consistent with Property 4 from Section III). However, in (B), which depicts the strong rash condition, the unconditional and conditional contingencies for fever are not equal. The unconditional contingency is in fact .4, as reported by Price and Yates; however, the conditional contingencies for fever based on the presence and absence of the rash are only .1. Therefore, if subjects were using conditional contingencies, the rating should be lower. If contingencies are mapped linearly into the rating scale, then a rating of 10 rather than 40 would be expected for the fever in the strong rash condition; in fact, subjects gave the fever a rating of 2 (vs a rating of 26 in the weak rash

---

[6] Note that causal direction seems to be reversed in this experiment: symptoms are the result of, not the causes of, diseases. Waldmann and Holyoak (1992) have shown that subjects' beliefs about causal direction influence cue-interaction effects. Price and Yates (1993) acknowledge this problem; however, they suggest that in this case subjects may have used the symptom-to-disease causal direction because "the symptom/disease relationship is somewhat ambiguous in terms of cause and effect, especially for naive subjects" (footnote 3).

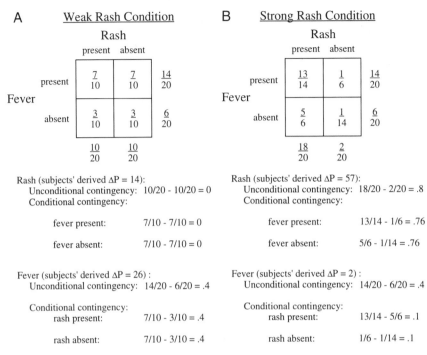

Fig. 6. The weak and strong rash conditions from Experiment 1 of Price and Yates (1993). Fractions in each cell indicate the number of times the effect (the disease "chronitis") was present given the number of times that combination of symptoms was present.

condition). Thus, subjects who based their judgments on conditional contingencies were justified in rating the fever as a worse predictor in the strong than in the weak rash condition because, conditional on their knowledge of the efficacy of the rash as a predictor, fever *is* a worse predictor in the strong than in the weak rash condition. (See Shanks, 1995, for a similar analysis but of a different dependent variable.)

A similar finding was reported by Baker et al. (1993). In their experiments, subjects played a video game in which they were to help a tank travel across a minefield. On each trial, subjects were able to push a button to "camouflage" the tank (at which they only sometimes succeeded). In addition, on some trials a plane (whether friend or enemy was unknown) flew overhead. After viewing 40 trials, and seeing various combinations of the presence and absence of camouflage, the presence and absence of the plane, and the success and failure of the tank traversing the minefield, subjects were asked to estimate, on a scale from -100 to 100, the effectiveness of the camouflage and the plane at helping the tank get through the minefield.

As part of their Experiment 1, Baker et al. (1993) contrasted what they called the ".5/0 condition" with the ".5/1 condition." In each of these conditions the first number represents the contingency for the camouflage and the second number represents the contingency for the plane. In both conditions the probability of the tank successfully traversing the minefield given that it had been camouflaged was .75, whereas the probability of the tank's success given no camouflage was .25, so $\Delta p_{\text{camouflage}} = .5$. In the ".5/0 condition," the plane had a zero contingency: the probability of success was .5 regardless of whether the plane was present, so $\Delta p_{\text{plane}} = 0$. In the ".5/1 condition," the plane showed a perfect contingency with success: when the plane was present the tank always succeeded and when it was absent the tank always failed, so $\Delta p_{\text{plane}} = 1$. Similar to Price and Yates (1993), Baker et al. found that subjects rated $\Delta p_{\text{camouflage}}$ higher in the ".5/0 condition" (mean $\Delta p = 49$), where the alternative causal factor was weak, than in the ".5/1 condition" (mean $\Delta p = -6$), where the alternative causal factor was strong.

Again, however, as in Price and Yates (1993), the contingencies for camouflage and plane were expressed as *unconditional* contingencies. And again, when the conditional contingencies are taken into account, a different picture emerges. Figure 7 depicts the frequencies with which subjects saw each combination of the presence and absence of camouflage, the presence and absence of the plane, and the success and failure of the tank traversing the minfield. In (A), which depicts the .5/0 condition (the "weak plane" condition), both the unconditional and conditional contingencies for camouflage are .5. However, in (B), which depicts the .5/1 condition (the "strong plane" condition), the unconditional and conditional contingencies for camouflage are not equal. The unconditional contingency is in fact .5, as reported by Baker et al.; however, the conditional contingencies for camouflage based on the presence and absence of the plane are 0. That is, given knowledge of whether the plane appeared or not, information about camouflage is irrelevant to predicting success. Therefore, if subjects are using conditional contingencies, a rating of 0 rather than 50 would be expected in the .5/1 condition; in fact, subjects gave the camouflage a rating of -6 (vs a rating of 49 in the .5/0 condition). Thus, subjects who based their judgments on conditional contingencies were justified in rating the camouflage as a worse predictor in the .5/1 condition than in the .5/0 condition because, conditional on their knowledge of the efficacy of the plane predictor, camouflage *is* a worse predictor in the .5/1 than in the .5/0 condition. (See Baker et al., this volume, Ch. 1; Shanks, 1993; Spellman, 1993, in press, for similar analyses.)

Thus, in both of these experiments, discounting can be explained by the subjects' using conditional rather than unconditional contingencies.

A   .5/0 Condition   B   .5/1 Condition
              Camouflage   Camouflage
           present   absent   present   absent

                    ┌─────┬─────┐   ┌─────┬─────┐
           present │ 7.5 │ 2.5 │ 10   present │ 15 │ 5 │ 20
                    │ 10 │ 10 │ 20   │ 15 │ 5 │ 20
Plane   ├─────┼─────┤   Plane   ├─────┼─────┤
           absent   │ 7.5 │ 2.5 │ 10   absent   │ 0 │ 0 │ 0
                    │ 10 │ 10 │ 20   │ 5 │ 15 │ 20
                    └─────┴─────┘   └─────┴─────┘
                     15   5   15   5
                     20   20   20   20

Plane (subjects' ΔP rating = 1):   Plane (subjects' ΔP rating = 92):
   Unconditional contingency: 10/20 - 10/20 = 0   Unconditional contingency: 20/20 - 0/20 = 1
   Conditional contingency: Conditional contingency:

      camouflage present: 7.5/10 - 7.5/10 = 0   camouflage present: 15/15 - 0/5 = 1

      camouflage absent: 2.5/10 - 2.5/10 = 0   camouflage absent: 15/15 - 0/5 = 1

Camouflage (subjects' ΔP rating = 49) :   Camouflage (subjects' ΔP rating = - 6) :
   Unconditional contingency: 15/20 - 5/20 = .5   Unconditional contingency: 15/20 - 5/20 = .5

   Conditional contingency: Conditional contingency:
      plane present: 7.5/10 - 2.5/10 = .5   plane present: 15/15 - 5/5 = 0

      plane absent: 7.5/10 - 2.5/10 = .5   plane absent: 0/5 - 0/15 = 0

Fig. 7.   The .5/1 and .5/0 conditions from Experiment 1 of Baker et al. (1993). Fractions in each cell indicate the number of times the effect (successful traversing of the minefield) was present given the number of times that combination of causes was present.

2. Predictions

Conditional contingency analysis makes the following two interesting predictions about discounting. First, it predicts that whether discounting occurs should *not* depend on the relative sizes of the unconditional contingencies of the two potential causes, but rather should depend on their covariation with each other. For example, consider the frequency tables shown in Fig. 8 and focus on the red liquid. In all of the tables the unconditional contingency for the red liquid is .33. In the Baseline Condition, the unconditional contingency for the potential competing cause, the blue liquid, is 0. In the

Fig. 8.   Example contingency tables for which a conditional contingency analysis would predict no discounting in the No Discounting Condition but discounting in the Discounting Condition (relative to the Baseline Condition). Note that in both of those conditions the unconditional contingency for the blue liquid is much higher than that in the Baseline Condition.

Baseline Condition

Blue Liquid
present   absent

Red Liquid

	present	absent	
present	$\frac{3}{9}$	$\frac{3}{9}$	$\frac{6}{18}$
absent	$\frac{0}{9}$	$\frac{0}{9}$	$\frac{0}{18}$

$\frac{3}{18}$ $\frac{3}{18}$

Red Liquid:
   Unconditional contingency: .33
   Conditional contingency:
      blue present: .33
      blue absent: .33

Blue Liquid :
   Unconditional contingency: 0
   Conditional contingency:
      red present: 0
      red absent: 0

No Discounting Condition

Blue Liquid
present   absent

Red Liquid

	present	absent	
present	$\frac{9}{9}$	$\frac{3}{9}$	$\frac{12}{18}$
absent	$\frac{6}{9}$	$\frac{0}{9}$	$\frac{6}{18}$

$\frac{15}{18}$ $\frac{3}{18}$

Red Liquid:
   Unconditional contingency: .33
   Conditional contingency:
      blue present: .33
      blue absent: .33

Blue Liquid :
   Unconditional contingency: .67
   Conditional contingency:
      red present: .67
      red absent: .67

Discounting Condition

Blue Liquid
present   absent

Red Liquid

	present	absent	
present	$\frac{12}{15}$	$\frac{0}{3}$	$\frac{12}{18}$
absent	$\frac{3}{3}$	$\frac{3}{15}$	$\frac{6}{18}$

$\frac{15}{18}$ $\frac{3}{18}$

Red Liquid:
   Unconditional contingency: .33
   Conditional contingency:
      blue present: -.20
      blue absent: -.20

Blue Liquid :
   Unconditional contingency: .67
   Conditional contingency:
      red present: .80
      red absent: .80

other two conditions, the unconditional contingencies for the blue liquid are .67. If cue-interaction effects merely depend on the contingency between the other potential causes and the outcome, then subjects in both of those latter conditions should rate the red liquid as less efficacious than do subjects in the Baseline Condition (where the competing cause has an unconditional contingency of 0). However, if subjects are using conditional contingencies, then a different pattern of results should emerge. In accordance with Property 4, in the Baseline and No Discounting Conditions the conditional and unconditional contingencies for the red liquid are equal and so there should be no discounting. In contrast, in the Discounting Condition the conditional contingency for the red liquid is less than its unconditional contingency. Thus, if subjects are using conditional contingencies, the causal efficacy ratings for the red liquid should be lower in the Discounting Condition than in the other two conditions.

Note that this experiment would maximize the chances of finding discounting between the Baseline and No Discounting Conditions (by moving the unconditional contingency for the alternative cause from 0 all the way to .67) without allowing the sum of the unconditional contingencies of the two causes (.33 and .67) to exceed 1. Once the two unconditional contingencies sum to greater than 1, the conditional contingencies must be less than the unconditional contingencies (see Property 3), and a conditional contingency analysis would therefore also predict some discounting.

B. "DOUBLE DISCOUNTING"

The conditional contingency analysis also predicts that, as in Kelley's (1972) causal schema model, there should be cases of "double discounting"; that is, that there should be times when the causal efficacy ratings of both potential causes should be lessened due to the presence of the other cause. Such a situation occurred in the ".5/.8" condition of Experiment 2 of Baker et al. (1993). Because the sum of the unconditional contingencies (.5 + .8) is greater than 1 (but given that the conditional contingencies are equal), we immediately know that (1) there must be an unequal number of events in the cells and (2) for at least one of the causes the unconditional contingency must be greater than its conditional contingency. In fact, as shown in Fig. 9, for *each* cause the conditional contingency was less than the unconditional contingency: $\Delta p_{\text{camouflage}} = .5$, whereas its conditional contingency was only .21; $\Delta p_{\text{plane}} = .8$, whereas its conditional contingency is .71. Thus, subjects should discount *both* causes, which is what Baker et al. found. On a scale from -100 to 100, subjects rated the effectiveness of the camouflage as 22 and of the plane as 65; both of those ratings are obviously closer to the conditional rather than the unconditional analysis.

Camouflage

present   absent

	present	$\frac{13.5}{14}$	$\frac{4.5}{6}$	$\frac{18}{20}$
Plane				
	absent	$\frac{1.5}{6}$	$\frac{0.5}{14}$	$\frac{2}{20}$

$\frac{15}{20}$ $\frac{5}{20}$

Plane (subjects' ΔP rating = 65):
Unconditional contingency: 18/20 - 2/20 = .8
Conditional contingency:

    camouflage present: 13.5/15 - 1.5/6 = .71

    camouflage absent: 4.5/6 - 0.5/14 = .71

Camouflage (subjects' ΔP rating = 22) :
Unconditional contingency: 15/20 - 5/20 = .5

Conditional contingency:
    plane present: 13.5/14 - 4.5 / 6 = .21

    plane absent: 1.5/6 - 0.5/14 = .21

Fig. 9.   The .5/.8 condition from Experiment 2 of Baker et al. (1993). Fractions in each cell indicate the number of times the effect (successful traversing of the minefield) was present given the number of times that combination of causes was present. Note that for both causes the conditional contingency is less than the unconditional contingency.

C.   SIMPSON'S PARADOX

Simpson's paradox (after Simpson, 1951) refers to the problem that for any given causal attribution to some cause C1, it is hypothetically possible to find another cause C2 such that the conditional contingency of C1 predicated on the presence and absence of C2 will yield a contingency for C1 that is zero or that is even *opposite* to that of C1's unconditional contingency. (See Cheng, 1993, pp. 250–252; Pearl, this volume, Ch. 10; Waldmann, this volume, Ch. 2; see Hintzman, 1980; Martin, 1981, for a discussion relevant to the interpretation of psychological data.) A favorite hypothetical example of philosophers is that of birth control pills and thrombosis (Salmon, 1984, citing Hesslow, 1976). Scientists believed that birth control pills might cause thrombosis; then later it was discovered that pregnancy was an even stronger cause of thrombosis (and, of course, birth control pills are a very high inhibitor of pregnancy). Hesslow imagined that it could have been possible that when considering the entire population of women, scientists might have found that women who took birth control pills had a lower probability of thrombosis than those who did not, suggesting that birth control pills were not a cause of thrombosis. Examining the contingency for birth control pills conditional on the absence of pregnancy, however, might have revealed that the pills did, in fact, increase the probability of thrombosis.

Subjects' sensitivity to conditional contingencies, and therefore to the covariation between causes, should lead them to be willing to judge a cause with a positive unconditional Δp as an inhibitory (i.e., negative) cause if the conditional contingencies are negative. Such results have been found in my laboratory (Spellman, 1995b). Forty different undergraduates also enrolled in introductory psychology did the same trial-by-trial task as described in Section II but with somewhat clearer instructions for the use of the 0 and -100 points on the scale. The frequency of presentation of the various conditions is shown in Fig. 10. Note that in (A) the conditional

A   Equal Condition   **B**   Unequal Condition

Blue Liquid

	present	absent	
present	$\frac{9}{10}$	$\frac{7}{10}$	$\frac{16}{20}$
absent	$\frac{3}{10}$	$\frac{1}{10}$	$\frac{4}{20}$
	$\frac{12}{20}$	$\frac{8}{20}$	

Red Liquid (A)

Blue Liquid

	present	absent	
present	$\frac{10}{15}$	$\frac{4}{5}$	$\frac{14}{20}$
absent	$\frac{0}{5}$	$\frac{2}{15}$	$\frac{2}{20}$
	$\frac{10}{20}$	$\frac{6}{20}$	

Red Liquid (B)

Red Liquid (subjects' $\Delta P = 67.3$):
Unconditional contingency: $16/20 - 4/20 = .6$
Conditional contingency:

     blue present: $9/10 - 3/10 = .6$

     blue absent: $7/10 - 1/10 = .6$

Blue Liquid (subjects' $\Delta P = 14.1$):
Unconditional contingency: $12/20 - 8/20 = .2$

Conditional contingency:
     red present: $9/10 - 7/10 = .2$

     red absent: $3/10 - 1/10 = .2$

Red Liquid (subjects' $\Delta P = 65.9$):
Unconditional contingency: $14/20 - 2/20 = .6$
Conditional contingency:

     blue present: $10/15 - 0/5 = .67$

     blue absent: $4/5 - 2/15 = .67$

Blue Liquid (subjects' $\Delta P = -35.3$) :
Unconditional contingency: $10/20 - 6/20 = .2$

Conditional contingency:
     red present: $10/15 - 4/5 = -.13$

     red absent: $0/5 - 2/15 = -.13$

Fig. 10. The trial-by-trial version of the "Simpson's Paradox" experiment from Spellman (1995b). Fractions in each cells indicate the number of times a flower blooms (numerator) given the number of times that combination of liquids was poured on the plants (denominator).

contingency equals the unconditional contingency for both liquids, whereas in (B) the conditional contingencies do not equal the unconditional contingencies. In particular, for the blue liquid, the unconditional contingency is *positive* (.2), whereas its conditional contingency is *negative* (−.13).

Subjects gave the blue liquid ratings in accordance with the conditional contingency. In the Equal Condition the blue liquid was given a positive rating of 14.1, while in the Unequal Condition subjects gave it a negative rating of −35.3. The ratings for the red liquid were similar in the two conditions (67.3 and 65.9, respectively). In addition, only 20% of subjects gave the blue liquid a negative rating in the Equal Condition, whereas 70% gave it a negative rating in the Unequal Condition.

The conditional contingency analysis and these results thus suggest the way that people will resolve Simpson's paradox is to interpret the data in accordance with the conditional rather than the unconditional information—at least in cases in which there are two *known* causally relevant factors.

That last comment raises a crucial issue: Are subjects happy to conditionalize contingencies on all other variables? For example, suppose that in the previous experiment, subjects were asked to evaluate the efficacy of the blue liquid, just as they did. Suppose however, that they never saw (or heard of) the red liquid; instead, in exactly those cases where the red liquid had been poured onto the plant, there was a decoration on the flowerpot, and in exactly those cases where the red liquid had not been poured onto the plant, there was no decoration on the flowerpot. Thus, the statistical relationships would all remain exactly the same. Would subjects now rate the efficacy of the blue liquid by its unconditional contingency or by its contingency conditional on the decoration? Results from Waldmann and Hagmayer (1995; see Waldmann, this volume, Ch. 2) suggest that subjects will conditionalize only on variables that they believe to be (from prior experience) causally relevant. So, if subjects did not believe that the decoration was causally relevant to the flower blooming, they would not conditionalize on it, and they would rate the blue liquid in accordance with its unconditional contingency. If, however, subjects were told that the decoration was the cap of a vial that released some chemical into the flowerpot, and therefore they believed that the decoration was causally relevant to blooming, they would rate the blue liquid in accordance with its conditional contingency.

V. Limitations of the Conditional Contingency Analysis

A. Information Available in All Four Cells

In order to compute both the contingency for a cause conditional on the presence of another cause and the contingency for a cause conditional on the absence of another cause, information must be available for all four cells. (If no information is available in a cell, the value in that cell would be 0/0, which is uncomputable.) Thus the present analysis is not appropriate for some designs, such as those involving blocking, in which information is missing for one or more of the cells (e.g., Chapman, 1991; Chapman & Robbins, 1990; Waldmann & Holyoak, 1992).

Cheng and Holyoak (1995) seem to be agnostic about how subjects will make causal judgments in such cases. Consider a standard blocking design illustrated in Fig. 11. When the predictive cue, P, is presented alone, the outcome always occurs (filling in f/f). The outcome never occurs in the absence of P (filling in 0/h). Later, cues P and R (redundant cue) are presented together and the outcome always occurs (filling in b/b). What is R's contingency? Conditional on the presence of P, R's contingency is 0; that is, learning about R is completely blocked. R's contingency on the absence of P cannot be computed because there is no information in the R-present/P-absent cell. R's unconditional contingency is greater than 0—how much greater depends on the relative sizes of f and h—so, if unconditional contingencies are used, R will be only partially blocked. Cheng and Holyoak suggest that in such cases of missing information, subjects may base their causal assessments on some mixture of contingencies. Individual subjects might combine the available contingency information or different subjects might use different information (leading to a multimodal distribution).

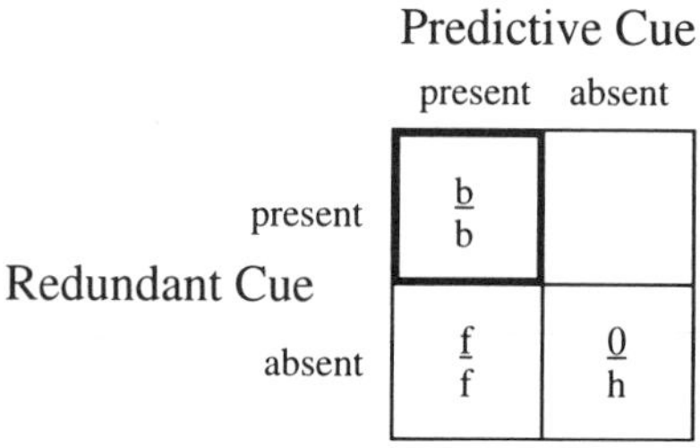

Predictive Cue

	present	absent
present	$\dfrac{b}{b}$	
absent	$\dfrac{f}{f}$	$\dfrac{0}{h}$

Redundant Cue

Redundant Cue:
Unconditional contingency: $\dfrac{b}{b} - \dfrac{f}{f+h} > 0$

Conditional contingency:
Predictive cue present: $\dfrac{b}{b} - \dfrac{f}{f} = 0$

Predictive cue absent: not computable

Fig. 11. Representation of a blocking study. Bold represents later information. After Cheng & Holyoak, 1995.

They believe that such strategies could lead to the partial blocking shown in many blocking experiments.

In a later paper, however, these researchers (Yarlas, Cheng, & Holyoak, 1995) seem committed (perhaps unnecessarily) to the idea that subjects will base causal judgments solely on the one complete conditional contingency. The effect under investigation is the extinction of conditioned inhibition, illustrated in Fig. 12A. To get conditioned inhibition, when an excitatory cue, E, is presented alone, the outcome always occurs (filling in f/f). The outcome never occurs in the absence of E (filling in 0/h). Later, when the inhibitory cue, I, is presented along with E, the outcome does not occur (filling in 0/b). Thus, I has a negative contingency: the exact value is -1 if computed conditional on the presence of E, or is between 0 and -1 (depending on the relative sizes of f and h) if computed unconditionally.

Yarlas et al. (1995) argue that the basis of conditioned inhibition is the computable conditional contingency (0/b $-$ f/f). They then discuss two methods of extinguishing conditioned inhibition, showing how such an analysis predicts their results. In the "direct" method (Fig. 12B), the inhibitory cue is later presented without the outcome. According to Yarlas et al., no extinction should occur (which is what they found); the inhibitory value of I should remain unchanged because the relevant contingency, 0/b $-$ f/f, yields an unchanged negative number. In the "indirect" method (Fig. 12C), the excitatory cue is later presented without the outcome (0/f'). According to Yarlas et al., in this case extinction should occur (which is what they found); the inhibitory value of I does change because the relevant contingency, 0/b $-$ f/(f $+$ f'), yields a smaller negative number.

Yet these results do not rule out the possibility that subjects are using the unconditional contingency or some combination of the unconditional and available conditional contingency. As shown in Fig. 12, using unconditional contingencies predicts the same pattern of responses. Also, conditional contingency predicts a contingency of -1 and unconditional contingency predicts a contingency of between 0 and -1, which is what they found. As Cheng and Holyoak (1995) earlier noted, in such cases of partial information, individual subjects may be using a mixture of strategies or different subjects could be using different strategies (but see Cheng, Park, Yarlas, & Holyoak, this volume, Ch. 8).

B. CONDITIONAL CONTINGENCIES ARE EQUAL

Except for the experiments with missing cells immediately described previously, for all of the other experiments discussed in this chapter the two conditional contingencies for the same cause were always equal. Such equality is certainly *not* a necessary property of multiple causes. Equality implies

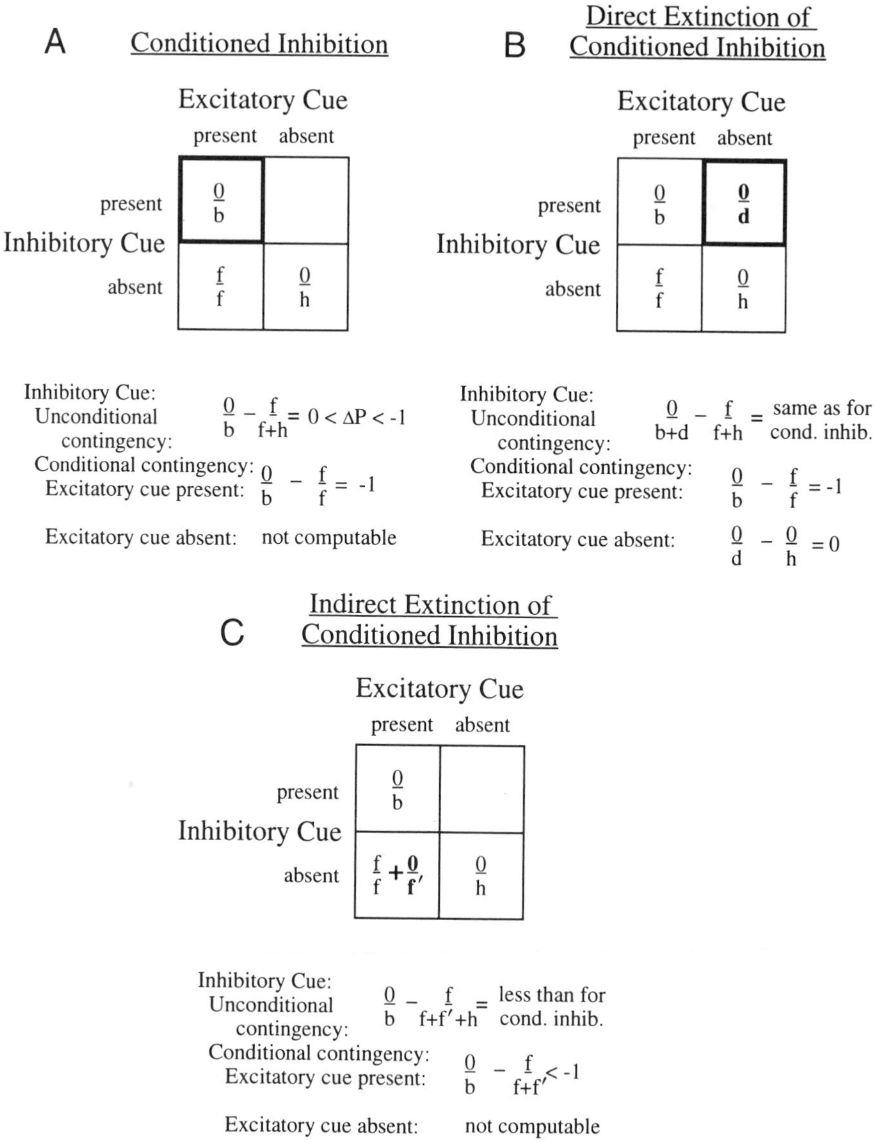

A   Conditioned Inhibition

Excitatory Cue

present absent

	present	absent
present	$\frac{0}{b}$	
absent	$\frac{f}{f}$	$\frac{0}{h}$

Inhibitory Cue

Inhibitory Cue:
Unconditional contingency: $\frac{0}{b} - \frac{f}{f+h} = 0 < \Delta P < -1$

Conditional contingency:
Excitatory cue present: $\frac{0}{b} - \frac{f}{f} = -1$

Excitatory cue absent: not computable

B   Direct Extinction of Conditioned Inhibition

Excitatory Cue

present absent

	present	absent
present	$\frac{0}{b}$	$\mathbf{\frac{0}{d}}$
absent	$\frac{f}{f}$	$\frac{0}{h}$

Inhibitory Cue

Inhibitory Cue:
Unconditional contingency: $\frac{0}{b+d} - \frac{f}{f+h} =$ same as for cond. inhib.

Conditional contingency:
Excitatory cue present: $\frac{0}{b} - \frac{f}{f} = -1$

Excitatory cue absent: $\frac{0}{d} - \frac{0}{h} = 0$

C   Indirect Extinction of Conditioned Inhibition

Excitatory Cue

present absent

	present	absent
present	$\frac{0}{b}$	
absent	$\frac{f}{f} + \mathbf{\frac{0}{f'}}$	$\frac{0}{h}$

Inhibitory Cue

Inhibitory Cue:
Unconditional contingency: $\frac{0}{b} - \frac{f}{f+f'+h} =$ less than for cond. inhib.

Conditional contingency:
Excitatory cue present: $\frac{0}{b} - \frac{f}{f+f'} < -1$

Excitatory cue absent: not computable

Fig. 12. Representation of conditioned inhibition, direct extinction of conditioned inhibition, and indirect extinction of conditioned inhibition studies. Bold represents later information.

at most two main effects and that the causes act independently; inequality implies an interaction.

When the conditional contingencies are not equal, what information is relied on? Cheng and Holyoak (1995) argue that tests based on the absence of other causes are more informative than those in which other causes are present. Fratianne and Cheng (1995) show that subjects are more confident about their causal judgments when they have information about a target cause conditional on the *absence* of alternative causes than when the information is conditional on the *presence* of alternative causes. However, it is not clear that subjects are solely relying on other-cause-absent information. In the PR.5/.4" condition of Experiment 5 of Baker et al. (1993), illustrated in Fig. 13, for each cause the conditional contingencies were not equal to each other and were not equal to the unconditional contingency. Subjects

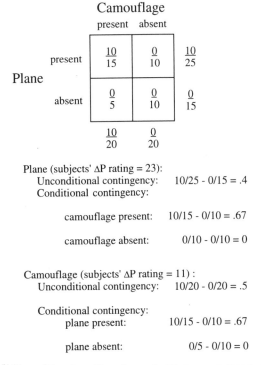

Fig. 13.   The ".5/.4" condition from Experiment 5 of Baker et al. (1993). Fractions in each cell indicate the number of times the effect (successful traversing of the minefield) was present given the number of times that combination of causes was present. Note that for each cause the conditional contingencies are not equal to each other and not equal to the unconditional contingency.

gave the causes a rating between what would be expected by a plain Δp analysis and what would be expected had they relied solely on the other-cause-absent conditional contingency.

C. DISCRETE RATHER THAN CONTINUOUS EVENTS

For all of the experiments discussed in this chapter, both the causes and the outcomes (fertilizer or not; treatment or not; bloom or not; live or die) were discrete, not continuous, events. Busemeyer, Myung, and McDaniel (1993) found evidence of discounting in predicting continuous outcomes from continuous causes. Their subjects were told the amount of two different plant-growth hormones that a plant would receive and were asked to predict how high the plant would grow. Thus, both the causes (there were five different levels of each hormone) and the effect (the plant heights ranged from 140 to 260 units) were continuous. Subjects saw all combinations of amounts of the two hormones equally frequently; the resulting height was a linear function (plus an error term) of those amounts. The researchers found that in the prediction task subjects' reliance on the amount of one hormone varied depending on how strong a predictor of height the other hormone was: They relied on a hormone less if the other hormone was a strong predictor than if it was a weak predictor. This cue-competition effect cannot be explained by the conditional contingency analysis.

VI. Conditionalizing as a General Procedure in Causal Attribution

Up until now, all of the experiments I have presented and discussed have had two things in common: first, no matter whether the information is given in trial-by-trial or summary form, subjects are aware of the outcomes of multiple trials; and, second, when multiple causes are present they are interpreted as acting simultaneously, not sequentially, in producing the effect. Neither of those conditions is necessary for the use of conditionalization. Rather, as I will illustrate below, humans seem to know that when making various kinds of causal attribution, it is necessary to conditionalize causality on the contribution of other causes. In particular, when there are two (or presumably more) candidate causes of an effect, people evaluate each of the causes (1) conditional on the presence and absence of the other causes for simultaneous causes, and (2) conditional on the presence of preceding causes for sequential causes.

A. MULTIPLE SIMULTANEOUS CAUSES

When subjects learn about multiple simultaneous causes of a single event they may conditionalize on other causes in order to make causal attributions. Consider the case of two multiple sufficient causes, for example, A shoots C in the head at the same time that B shoots C in the heart. C dies and the doctor says that either wound was sufficient to kill C. Who is the cause of C's death? It has been argued that counterfactual reasoning, that is, imagining the counterfactual situation in which if the cause does not occur then the effect does not occur, is the essence of causal reasoning (e.g., Lipe, 1991). Thus, A could make the following argument: "I am not the cause of C's death because even if I hadn't shot C, he would have died anyway." B, of course, could make the same argument as A; therefore, it seems that no one has caused C's death. In that way, multiple sufficient causes pose a problem for the counterfactual view.

Consider, in addition, the case of two multiple necessary causes. Imagine A and B again shooting C, but this time the doctor says that neither shot alone was sufficient to kill C but because of the combination he lost enough blood to die. This time A might argue that he was not the cause of C's death because C should not have died from his actions alone. B would argue the same thing and again they should both go free. Yet neither result accords with our intuitions. It seems that in the multiple sufficient case, causal judgments should be made for A conditional on what would happen if B *hadn't* acted; whereas in the multiple necessary case, causal judgments should be made for A conditional on what actually happens when B *has* acted.

To test these ideas, I (Spellman, 1993) had subjects read a story about Jessica and Amanda, who both left on their gas burner after chemistry class. Subjects read that the burners exploded simultaneously that night and that the resulting fire destroyed the chemistry building. In the multiple-sufficient-cause condition, the fire marshal declares that either explosion would have been enough to burn down the building; in the multiple-necessary-cause condition, subjects were told that neither burner explosion alone would have destroyed the building, but because of the combination of explosions acting together the building was destroyed.

Among other questions, subjects were asked to rate, on a 0 (no contribution) to 10 (major contribution) scale how much they thought each of the two girls contributed to causing the fire. Not surprisingly, every subject in the experiment attributed the same amount of causality to Jessica and Amanda. In addition, the amount of cause attributed to each girl did not differ across conditions (mean for multiple sufficient = 8.1, mean for multiple necessary = 8.3).

A few pages later, subjects read that Amanda had gone on trial for arson. In the multiple-sufficient-cause scenario, Amanda's lawyer argues that she did not cause the fire that destroyed the building because even if she had never lit her burner the building would have burned down anyway. Because her actions did not matter, Amanda was not a cause. In the multiple-necessary-cause scenario, Amanda's lawyer argues that she did not cause the fire that destroyed the building because her fire alone could not have done it. Subjects were then asked to rate on a 0 ("not at all important") to 5 ("very important") scale how important to their causal attribution each of the following was: "Considering what would have happened if Jessica's burner had not been left on?" and "Considering what would have happened if Jessica's burner had been left on, too (as actually happened)?" Note that it was predicted that subjects would prefer the information *opposite* to the information in the argument suggested by the lawyer.

The results of the final rating tasks support the hypothesis that people condition their causal attributions on the presence or absence of other potential causes and that they weight the information that shows that the potential cause does have causal strength more heavily when making those attributions. The data is most revealing when analyzed by examining which type of information each subject rated higher (rather than the actual ratings). Table I presents the numbers of subjects who rated the true or counterfactual information as more important, or who gave the same rating to both. The subjects' choice of which information was more important differed across the two conditions: In the case of multiple sufficient causes, more subjects thought it was important to consider the information conditional on the absence of the other cause; in the case of multiple necessary causes, more subjects thought it was important to consider the information conditional on the presence of the other cause. Thus, even in cases of simultaneous causes of a single event, subjects

TABLE I

SUBJECTS' RATINGS OF WHICH INFORMATION WAS MORE IMPORTANT TO
THEIR CAUSAL ATTRIBUTION ANALYZED AS FREQUENCY DATA

	Most important information		
Condition	Jessica's burner on (true)	Jessica's burner not on (counterfactual)	Equal
Multiple sufficient cause	5	11	12
Multiple necessary cause	16	3	9

are using conditional information in causal attributions and are aware of the benefits of doing so.

B. MULTIPLE SEQUENTIAL CAUSES

In the social psychology literature, there are many experiments in which subjects are asked to make causal attributions to events that together, but sequentially, cause some outcome. In some experiments, subjects make more attributions to the earliest event (e.g., Vinokur & Ajzen, 1982; Wells, Taylor, & Turtle, 1987), and in others subjects make more attributions to the last event (e.g., Kahneman & Miller, 1986; D. T. Miller and Gunasegaram, 1990). I believe that the differences across experiments are neither due to the use of some heuristic, nor to the easier mutability of some events as those authors and others have suggested; rather, I believe that the differences reflect the subjects' process of conditionalizing the effect of each of the causes on what has already occurred.

1. Attributions to the First or Last Event

D. T. Miller and Gunasegaram (1990) found that people made causal attributions to the *last* event of a sequence. They told subjects to imagine that Jones and Cooper were each to toss a coin; if the two coins came up the same (either both heads or both tails), they would each win $1000; however, if the two coins came up different, they would each receive nothing. Jones tosses a head and then Cooper tosses a tail. Almost all of the subjects said that Cooper would feel more guilt for the outcome (86%), that Jones would blame Cooper more for the outcome (92%), and that it was easier to imagine changing the outcome by imagining Cooper's toss being different rather than Jones's toss being different (89%). Although none of these questions directly asks "who was more of a cause of the outcome," all of the questions appear to measure causal attributions indirectly, and those attributions were made to the *last* event.

In another experiment in which it also seems that the first and last players contribute equally to the outcome, Vinokur and Ajzen (1982) found that people made causal attributions to the *first* event of a sequence. Their subjects read about teams of players that tried to solve 20 multiple-choice problems. Each problem had four alternative answers. The first half of the team was responsible for narrowing down the choice from four to two possible answers; the second half of the team was responsible for selecting the final correct answer from the two handed over by the first half of the team. Subjects were told the team's total number correct (either 8 or 17) and asked how much each half of the team had caused the final outcome. A control group of subjects rated the two tasks as equally difficult, but experimental subjects attributed greater causality for the total number correct to the *first* half of the team.

2. *Potential Explanations*

Several explanations have been proposed to explain the differences in attributions in these seemingly similar cases. One explanation (D. T. Miller & Gunasegaram, 1990) proposes that in cases when the causal events are independent of each other (like the coin toss), attributions are made to the last event; whereas in cases when the events are not independent because earlier events in the sequence cause (or, at least, "restrict," see Vinokur & Ajzen, 1982) later events in the sequence, attributions are made to the first event. However, such a characterization seems at best merely a description of past results rather than an explanation of those results. Another explanation involves counterfactual reasoning and proposes that the most causal event is the most mutable event. Mutability is the ease with which we can imagine alternatives to an event that will undo the outcome: "An event will be judged as causal of an outcome to the extent that mutations to that event would undo the outcome" (Wells & Gavanski, 1989, p. 161). Yet mutability fails as an explanation because it leads to seemingly plausible but actually conflicting predictions.

A third explanation, the crediting causality hypothesis (Spellman, 1993, 1995a), proposes that if there are two relevant potential causes of an effect, and the causes act in sequence, people assign causality in the following way:

1. determine the probability of the actual outcome before the first pro-posed cause occurs;
2. determine the probability of the actual outcome after the first pro-posed cause occurs but before the second proposed cause occurs (i.e., conditional on the first cause);
3. find the change in the probability of the actual outcome due to the first cause (the difference between 1 and 2);
4. find the change in probability of the outcome due to the second cause (the difference between 2 and the true outcome); and
5. assign causality based on a comparison between the values of points 3 and 4.

Consider the coin toss. Before Jones tosses, the probability of losing (the actual outcome) is .5. After Jones tosses (in fact, no matter what he tosses), the probability of losing is still .5. Therefore, the change in probability due to Jones is 0. When Cooper tosses, the probability of losing is .5, but his toss (tails) brings the probability to 1. (Analogous reasoning holds for all other tosses and possible outcomes.) Cooper contributed a .5 change in probability of the outcome. Thus, Cooper, who tossed last, will be viewed as more causal than Jones.

Now consider the multiple-choice game. The analysis here is less precise because subjects learned about a set of results (i.e., 8 or 17 correct out of 20) rather than an individual result. Before the first half of the team performs, the probability of coming up with the final correct answer (assuming a chance level, though this analysis works for all levels) is .25. After the first half goes the probability is either .5 (if their set of two includes the correct answer) or 0 (if it does not). In the former case, the second half of the team will change the probability of the outcome, but in the latter case the second half of the team cannot have any effect at all on the outcome. That latter possibility is why subjects attribute more causality to the first than to the second half of the team.

The crediting causality hypothesis rests on two assumptions: first, point 2 in the preceding list, the updating assumption, which is that the change in probability due to the second event is computed after the first event has occurred (i.e., conditionalized on the first cause); second, point 5, the assignment assumption, which is that subjects base their causal attributions on the relative extent to which each event changes the probability of the eventual outcome. In addition to providing a way to distinguish the results of the D. T. Miller and Gunasegaram (1990) and Vinokur and Ajzen (1982) experiments, the assumptions of the crediting causality hypothesis have been further tested in Spellman (1993, 1995a).

C.   Conditionalizing as a General Procedure

In this last section, I have described two experiments (chemistry lab and coin toss) in which people are asked to judge the cause of a single "one-time only" event. Kelley (1973) distinguishes the way in which people make attributions when presented with multiple repetitions of a situation (the ANOVA model) versus a single one-trial event (the causal schema model). But this distinction may be illusory. People almost never[7] make causal evaluations based solely on a one-shot event. Kelley (1972) admits that our causal schemas are induced after much learning about causality in previous situations. When we are presented with an "entirely new" scenario for which we have to make a causal attribution, we invoke what we already know (similar events, perhaps similar at a more abstract level, that have happened in the past) or what we can imagine. In each of the experiments

---

[7] This qualification of the Humean position is due to the seeming "innateness" of some causal attributions in both humans and animals (e.g., attributing stomach pains to novel food). Cheng and Novick (1992) point out that a positive contingency exists even in such cases of one-trial learning.

subjects implicitly had contingency information because they had either frequency or probability information about the potential combinations of causes and outcomes. For example, in the chemistry lab experiment, in the multiple sufficient cause condition, subjects knew that the probability of a fire given Amanda leaving her burner on is 1 and the probability of a fire given that she didn't depends on how often other causes (like Jessica) operate. The contingencies in the coin toss (and the multiple-choice game) change depending on what has already happened. For example, before Jones tosses, assuming fair coins, the probability of winning if Cooper tosses a tail is .5 and if he does not toss a tail (i.e., tosses a head) is .5. Thus, a priori, tossing a tail is not a cause of winning. But once Jones tosses a head, the probability of winning if Cooper tosses a tail is 0 and if he does not toss a tail is 1. In that case of tossing a tail, Cooper is a cause of *not* winning. Thus, one can view the situations involving single events and/or sequential causes as involving contingency, and therefore conditional contingency, analyses.

VII.   Summary

In this chapter I have argued that in the case of multiple potential causes of an effect, humans do not use the simple unconditional Δp contingency rule. Rather, like scientists, we conditionalize our judgments of causal efficacy on other potential causes. Several experiments support the use of conditional contingencies in both trial-by-trial and summary statistic presentations of information. Subjects not only use conditional information but also *know* that they need that information in making causality judgments. They also use conditionalization as a general procedure in assigning causality in cases of multiple simultaneous and multiple sequential causes when information about only a single trial is given. The use of conditional contingencies explains many cue-interaction effects, which have been used to argue that humans are not reasoning with rules but rather must be doing associative learning; in fact, those results suggest that humans are just using better rules than the experimenters expected.

What about all the other research showing that humans are poor reasoners? The data stand, of course, but interpretive angles come and go. Although there still seems to be a cottage industry in finding new heuristics (e.g., the quantity principle of Josephs, Giesler, & Silvera, 1994; the numerosity heuristic of Pelham, Sumarta, & Myaskovsky, 1994), these and other investigators in reasoning are now trying to explain, justify, and understand the limits of the data supporting the "poor reasoners" view. Some argue that the findings are limited to a very narrow set of experiments (e.g.,

Koehler, 1996, on the limitations of the base rate fallacy). Others attack the methodology of the research, showing that many "cognitive illusions" will "disappear" when experimenters ask people to reason in terms of event frequencies (at which they are good) rather than in terms of single-event probabilities (at which they are bad; see Gigerenzer, 1991, for a review). Still others argue that sometimes humans only seemed to be poor reasoners because they used different information from that on which the researchers based the "normative" result (e.g., see Cheng & Novick, 1990, on deviations from Kelley's 1967 ANOVA model).

So, might humans actually be as smart as rats? Sometimes we might expect equivalent performance. For example, simulations of the first experiment and the Simpson's paradox experiment reported in this chapter reveal that the conditional contingencies are equal to (100 times) the asymptotic values that are derived for each liquid under the Rescorla–Wagner (1972) model.[8] Thus, one would expect humans using the conditional Δp rule and rats performing according to the Rescorla–Wagner rule to perform similarly. But, more generally, it seems that the way the game is arranged, humans don't stand a chance. When humans don't perform according to the normative models we construct, we say that humans are bad; when rats don't perform according to the statistical models we construct, we say that the models are bad (e.g., see R. R. Miller, Barnet, & Grahame, 1995, for a recent review of the successes and failures of the Rescorla–Wagner model). Of course, it is possible to argue that those human "imperfections" are, in fact, "rational" because they are adaptive (e.g., Anderson, 1990; Simon, 1990). Under that view we lose the evaluative stance that has allowed us to disparage the skills of humans while lauding those of rats.

Acknowledgments

The first experiment was supported by a Summer Research Award from the University Research Institute at The University of Texas. I would like to thank Marie Barrera, Bruce Burns, Todd Key, and Tim Loving for running subjects and Tom Trainham for writing a Rescorla–Wagner model simulator. Thanks also to Patricia Cheng, Keith Holyoak, Douglas

---

[8] The simulations were run assuming: two stimuli, a context that is present on all trials, asymptotic learning of 1, and equal learning rate parameters for the presence and absence of the outcome. However, this assumption is not traditional in the animal learning literature, which instead assumes that more learning occurs on outcome-present (i.e., reinforced) trials than on outcome-absent (i.e., nonreinforced) trials (see, e.g., Baker et al., this volume, ch. 1; R. R. Miller et al., 1995). On the other hand, the same comment could be made about humans, who, in a standard 2×2 contingency matrix, tend to underutilize the B cell relative to the A cell and the D cell relative to the C cell (i.e., the outcome-absent cells relative to the outcome-present cells; e.g., Kao & Wasserman, 1993).

Medin, and David Shanks for helpful comments on an earlier draft. Requests for reprints may be addressed to Barbara A. Spellman, Department of Psychology, Mezes 330, University of Texas, Austin, TX 78712 or to spellman@psy.utexas.edu.

REFERENCES

Allan, L. G. (1993). Human contingency judgments: Rule based or associative? *Psychological Bulletin, 144*, 435–448.

Anderson, J. R. (1990). *The adaptive character of thought.* Hillsdale, NJ: Erlbaum.

Baker, A. G., Mercier, P., Vallée-Tourangeau, F., Frank, R., & Pan, M. (1993). Selective associations and causality judgments: Presence of a strong causal factor may reduce judgments of a weaker one. *Journal of Experimental Psychology: Learning, Memory, and Cognition, 19*, 414–432.

Busemeyer J. R., Myung, I. J., & McDaniel, M. A. (1993). Cue competition effects: Empirical tests of adaptive learning models. *Psychological Science, 4*, 190–195.

Cartwright, N. (1979). *How the laws of physics lie.* Oxford: Clarendon Press.

Chapman, G. B. (1991). Trial order affects cue interaction in contingency judgment. *Journal of Experimental Psychology: Learning, Memory, and Cognition, 17*, 837–854.

Chapman, G. B., & Robbins, S. J. (1990). Cue interaction in human contingency judgment. *Memory & Cognition, 18*, 537–545.

Cheng, P. W. (1993). Separating causal laws from casual facts: Pressing the limits of statistical relevance. In D. Medin (Ed.), *The psychology of learning and motivation* (Vol. 30, pp. 215–264). San Diego, CA: Academic Press.

Cheng, P. W., & Holyoak, K. J. (1995). Complex adaptive systems as intuitive statisticians: Causality, contingency, and prediction. In H. L. Roitblat & J.-A. Meyer (Eds.), *Comparative approaches to cognitive science* (pp. 271–302). Cambridge, MA: MIT Press.

Cheng, P. W., & Novick, L. R. (1990). A probabilistic contrast model of causal induction. *Journal of Personality and Social Psychology, 58*, 545–567.

Cheng, P. W., & Novick, L. R. (1992). Covariation in natural causal induction. *Psychological Review, 99*, 365–382.

Fratianne, A., & Cheng, P. W. (1995). *Assessing causal relations by dynamic hypothesis testing.* Unpublished manuscript. Department of Psychology, University of California, Los Angeles.

Gigerenzer, G. (1991). How to make cognitive illusions disappear: Beyond "Heuristics and Biases." In W. Stroebe & M. Hewstone (Eds.), *European review of social psychology* (Vol. 2, pp. 83–115). Chichester, UK: Wiley.

Hesslow, G. (1976). Two notes on the probabilistic approach to causality. *Philosophy of Science, 43*, 290–292.

Hintzman, D. L. (1980). Simpson's paradox and the analysis of memory retrieval. *Psychological Review, 87*, 398–410.

Josephs, R. A., Giesler, R. B., & Silvera, D. H. (1994). Judgment by quantity. *Journal of Experimental Psychology: General, 123*, 21–32.

Kahneman, D., & Miller, D. T. (1986). Norm theory: Comparing reality to its alternatives. *Psychological Review, 93*, 136–153.

Kahneman, D., Slovic, P., & Tversky, A. (Eds.). (1982). *Judgment under uncertainty: Heuristics and biases.* New York: Cambridge University Press.

Kao, S., & Wasserman, E. A. (1993). Assessment of an information integration account of contingency judgment with examination of subjective cell importance and method of information presentation. *Journal of Experimental Psychology: Learning, Memory, and Cognition, 19,* 1363–1386.

Kelley, H. H. (1967). Attribution theory in social psychology. *Nebraska Symposium on Motivation, 15,* 192–238.

Kelley, H. H. (1972). Causal schemata and the attribution process. In E. E. Jones, D. E. Kanouse, H. H. Kelley, R. E. Nisbett, S. Valins, & B. Weiner (Eds.), *Attribution: Perceiving the causes of behavior* (pp. 151–174). Morristown, NJ: General Learning Press.

Kelley, H. H. (1973). The processes of causal attribution. *American Psychologist, 28,* 107–128.

Koehler, J. J. (1996). The base rate fallacy reconsidered: Descriptive, normative and methodological challenges. *Behavioral and Brain Sciences, 19,* 1–17.

Lipe, M. G. (1991). Counterfactual reasoning as a framework for attribution theories. *Psychological Bulletin, 3,* 456–471.

Mackintosh, N. J. (1976). Overshadowing and stimulus intensity. *Animal Learning & Behavior, 4,* 186–192.

Martin, E. (1981). Simpson's paradox resolved: A reply to Hintzman. *Psychological Review, 88,* 372–374.

Melz, E. R., Cheng, P. W., Holyoak, K. J., & Waldmann, M. R. (1993). Cue competition in human categorization: Contingency or the Rescorla-Wagner Learning Rule? Comment on Shanks (1991). *Journal of Experimental Psychology: Learning, Memory, and Cognition, 19,* 1398–1410.

Miller, D. T., & Gunasegaram, S. (1990). Temporal order and the perceived mutability of events: Implications for blame assignment. *Journal of Personality and Social Psychology, 59,* 1111–1118.

Miller, R. R., Barnet, R. C., & Grahame, N. J. (1995). Assessment of the Rescorla-Wagner model. *Psychological Bulletin, 117,* 363–386.

Morris, M. W., & Larrick, R. P. (1995). When one cause casts doubt on another: A normative analysis of discounting in causal attribution. *Psychological Review, 102,* 331–355.

Nisbett, R. E., & Ross, L. (1980). *Human inference: Strategies and shortcomings of social judgment.* Englewood Cliffs, NJ: Prentice-Hall.

Pelham, B. W., Sumarta, T. T., & Myaskovsky, L. (1994). The easy path from many to much: The numerosity heuristic. *Cognitive Psychology, 26,* 103–134.

Peterson, C. R., & Beach, L. R. (1967). Man as an intuitive statistician. *Psychological Bulletin, 68,* 29–46.

Price, P. C., & Yates, J. F. (1993). Judgmental overshadowing: Further evidence of cue interaction in contingency judgment. *Memory & Cognition, 21,* 561–572.

Rescorla, R. A., & Wagner, A. R. (1972). A theory of Pavolvian conditioning: Variations in the effectiveness of reinforcement and non-reinforcement. In A. H. Black & W. F. Prokasy (Eds.), *Classical conditioning II: Current research and theory* (pp. 64–99). New York: Appleton-Century-Crofts.

Salmon, W. C. (1984). *Scientific explanation and the causal structure of the world.* Princeton, NJ: Princeton University Press.

Shanks, D. R. (1993). Human instrumental learning: A critical review of data and theory. *British Journal of Psychology, 84,* 319–354.

Shanks, D. R. (1995). Is human learning rational? *Quarterly Journal of Experimental Psychology, 48A,* 257–279.

Simon, H. A. (1990). Invariants of human behavior. *Annual Review of Psychology, 41,* 1–19.

Simpson, E. H. (1951). The interpretation of interaction in contingency tables. *Journal of the Royal Statistical Society, Series B, 13*(2), 238–241.

Spellman, B. A. (1993). *The construction of causal explanations.* Unpublished doctoral dissertation, University of California, Los Angeles.

Spellman, B. A. (1995a). *Crediting causality.* Unpublished manuscript. Department of Psychology, University of Texas at Austin.

Spellman, B. A. (1995b). *Resolving Simpson's paradox: Using base rates in causal reasoning.* Unpublished manuscript. Department of Psychology, University of Texas at Austin.

Spellman, B. A. (in press). Acting as intuitive scientists: Contingency judgments are made while controlling for alternative potential causes. *Psychological Science.*

Vinokur, A., & Ajzen, I. (1982). Relative importance of prior and immediate events: A causal primacy effect. *Journal of Personality and Social Psychology, 42,* 820–829.

Waldmann, M. R., & Hagmayer, Y. (1995). When a cause simultaneously produces and prevents an effect. In J. D. Moore & J. F. Lehman (Eds.), *Proceedings of the Seventeenth Annual Conference of the Cognitive Science Society* (pp. 425–430). Hillsdale, NJ: Erlbaum.

Waldmann, M. R., & Holyoak, K. J. (1992). Predictive and diagnostic learning in cue competition. *Journal of Experimental Psychology: General, 121,* 222–236.

Wells, G. L., & Gavanski, I. (1989). Mental simulation of causality. *Journal of Personality and Social Psychology, 56,* 161–169.

Wells, G. L., Taylor, B. R., & Turtle, J. W. (1987). The undoing of scenarios. *Journal of Personality and Social Psychology, 53,* 421–430.

Yarlas, A. S., Cheng, P. W., & Holyoak, K. J. (1995). Alternative approaches to causal induction: The probabilistic contrast versus the Rescorla-Wagner model. In J. D. Moore & J. F. Lehman (Eds.), *Proceedings of the Seventeenth Annual Conference of the Cognitive Science Society* (pp. 431–436). Hillsdale, NJ: Erlbaum.

Young, M. E. (1995). On the origin of personal causal theories. *Psychonomic Bulletin & Review, 2,* 83–104.

CAUSATION AND ASSOCIATION

Edward A. Wasserman
Shu-Fang Kao
Linda J. Van Hamme
Masayoshi Katagiri
Michael E. Young

[I]t may be that . . . reason, self-consciousness and self-control which seem to sever human intellect so sharply from that of all other animals are really but secondary results of the tremendous increase in the number, delicacy and complexity of associations which the human animal can form. It may be that the evolution of intellect has no breaks, that its progress is continuous from its first appearance to its present condition in adult . . . human beings. If we could prove that what we call ideational life and reasoning were not new and unexplainable species of intellectual life but only the natural consequences of an increase in the number, delicacy, and complexity of associations of the general animal sort, we should have made out an evolution of mind comparable to the evolution of living forms. (p. 286)

Bold thinkers pen bold words. When Edward Thorndike published these lines in 1911, he challenged conventional wisdom that the human animal was unique among all others in the powers of advanced cognition and judgment. But, this daring thesis of mental continuity was not new. Robert Chambers had anonymously written in 1844 that, "The difference in mind in the lower animals and in man is a difference in degree only; it is not a specific difference" (1844/1994, pp. 335–336). Charles Darwin famously reiterated that proposal in 1871 in connection with the theory of evolution by natural selection: "The difference in mind between man and the higher animals, great as it is, certainly is one of degree and not of kind" (1871/

THE PSYCHOLOGY OF LEARNING
AND MOTIVATION, VOL. 34

207

1920, p. 128). Yet, the notion that humans and other animals are intellectual kin remains controversial to this day.

What does contemporary psychological science have to say on the matter? Recent research in comparative cognition strongly suggests that nonhuman animals are capable of remarkable feats of learning, memory, and cognition (Wasserman, 1993), many of them appearing analogous to cases of advanced intelligence in human beings. More pertinent to the present volume, recent research in human cognition suggests that causal judgment may be understood as due to associative learning, a process well investigated and well documented in nonhuman animals.

This chapter reviews some of the research conducted over the past five years in our laboratory; earlier research was reviewed in a 1990 chapter for this series. The centerpiece of this program of investigation is the application of associative learning theory—specifically, Rescorla and Wagner's (1972) highly influential conditioning model—to human causality judgments. Three lines of research are highlighted in the present review: (1) comparison of associative learning theory with an information processing account of causality judgment advanced by Busemeyer (1991); (2) application of associative learning theory to subjects' trial-by-trial ratings of both constant and changing interevent contingencies; and (3) application of associative learning theory to cases in which subjects rate the causal efficacy of stimuli that are not actually presented on a given trial. The general conclusion of this work is that Rescorla and Wagner's original theory of associative learning does an excellent job in accounting for subjects' momentary ratings of both constant and changing interevent contingencies, in fact better according with subjects' data than Busemeyer's information integration theory. With one significant change, Rescorla and Wagner's theory can even account for backward blocking and backward conditioned inhibition, behavioral effects that have proven to be especially difficult for associative learning theories to explain.

I. Comparing Information Integration Theory with Associative Learning Theory

Any process account of causal judgment must be able to describe how the flow of events affects subjects' momentary ratings of target stimuli as putative causes for particular effects. Despite their very different origins, we are fortunate to have two highly specific mathematical models that can be clearly compared with one another.

A. THEORETICAL ACCOUNT 1: BUSEMEYER'S INFORMATION
   INTEGRATION MODEL

Busemeyer's (1991) account is based on the principles of the very prominent
information integration theory (Anderson, 1981, 1982). Beyond providing
a rational means of generating moment-by-moment judgments of causality,
information integration theory can incorporate the fact of unequal cell use
in people's causal judgments through *subjective weighting* of each of the
cells of a simple contingency table. Most research in this area has entailed
the factorial combination of the occurrence/nonoccurrence of a putative cause with the occurrence/nonoccurrence of a particular effect: Cell
A = cause–effect, Cell B = cause–no effect, Cell C = no cause–effect,
Cell D = no cause–no effect. It has generally been found that most subjects
use the 2 × 2 contingency information unequally when they judge interevent
relations, with use ordered Cell A > Cell B > Cell C > Cell D (e.g.,
Arkes & Harkness, 1983; Levin, Wasserman, & Kao, 1993; Wasserman,
Dorner, & Kao, 1990); unequal cell use is even more dramatic when contingency information is presented trial by trial than when it is presented in
tabled summaries (Kao & Wasserman, 1993).

Kao and Wasserman (1993) found that an information integration model
could describe 70 and 80% of individual subjects' final causal judgments
under the trial-by-trial and tabled-summary procedures, respectively. To
simplify their experimental design, Kao and Wasserman (1993) did not
measure subjects' initial estimates of interevent contingency, which is included in Busemeyer's (1991) model. If we add the initial expectancy term
to the model used by Kao and Wasserman (1993), then the information
integration process employed by nonnormative[1] strategy users to judge
interevent relations is:

$$R = \frac{W_I \cdot I + W_A \cdot A - W_B \cdot B - W_C \cdot C + W_D \cdot D}{|W_I \cdot I| + |W_A \cdot A| + |W_B \cdot B| + |W_C \cdot C| + |W_D \cdot D|} + \text{error.} \quad (1)$$

Here, the term I denotes subjects' initial expectation about the relation
between events based on their previous knowledge or experience. The

---

[1] Theoretically, normative strategy users should employ the Δp rule [A/(A + B) − C/
(C + D)] to judge interevent relations and they should not have any prior expectation of
contingency. Kao and Wasserman (1993) found that *none* of their 200 subjects used the
normative Δp rule to judge interevent contingency when information was presented trial-by-
trial. This finding is consistent with Shanks's (1987) contention that the acquisition function of
causal judgment is not correlated with Δp. Therefore, we focus here only on the nonnormative
description of subjects' judgments because the present studies involved only the trial-by-trial
information presentation procedure.

terms A, B, C, and D denote the frequencies of the four cells in the 2 × 2 contingency table. The term W_I denotes the subjective importance of the initial expectation; the terms W_A, W_B, W_C, and W_D denote the subjective importance of the four cells, respectively. And, the term R denotes the estimate of interevent contingency for nonnormative strategy users. Given that Kao and Wasserman (1993) had earlier found the information integration account to be useful in describing *final* judgments of interevent relations, the initial experiment detailed in this article examined for the first time the utility of the model in describing subjects' *momentary* judgments when they received evidence bit by bit.

The information integration approach allows different algorithms for updating R in Equation (1). In one algorithm, R is recalculated after each new piece of evidence (i.e., after every trial) and it gives equal consideration to each one. This approach will be called the *simple averaging* strategy. In a second algorithm, R is a *running average* of some number of recent trials; only these most recent trials are considered in the determination of R. This second approach is highly sensitive to recency effects; however, because of the rarity of recency in causal judgment research, it will not be considered further. In a third algorithm, a *serial averaging* strategy is used to update R; here, R is updated through a weighted averaging of the current estimate with the estimate derived from the most recent trial, that is, $R_t = w_t s + (1 - w_t)R_{t-1}$, where t is the index of the trial, w is the weighting parameter, and s is a single trial estimate of R. Thus, in serial averaging, each new piece of evidence is given the same weight (w_t) regardless of the amount of experience underlying the prior estimate of the relation (R_{t-1}). For example, when new evidence is averaged in with a weight of .10 (i.e., the new evidence accounts for 10% of the updated estimate), this weighting is independent of whether the prior estimate was derived from 1 prior trial, 10 trials, or 1000 trials. When w_t is 1/t, the serial averaging strategy reduces to the simple averaging strategy: the weight of the new evidence decreases as the sample size making up the prior estimate increases.

The serial averaging strategy is algebraically equivalent to $R_t = R_{t-1} + w_t(s - R_{t-1})$, making it identical to a simplified version of the Rescorla–Wagner model, one that does *not* deal with cue-competition effects. In the following trio of experiments, we will compare the simple averaging version of Busemeyer's model (hereafter called the "Busemeyer model") with the serial averaging strategy of the Rescorla–Wagner model.

B. THEORETICAL ACCOUNT 2: RESCORLA AND WAGNER'S ASSOCIATIVE LEARNING MODEL

Another important account of causal judgment derives from the associative learning model of Rescorla and Wagner (1972), which is based on contemporary research in animal conditioning. The ability of the Rescorla–Wagner model to account for humans' sensitivity to interevent relations has drawn many researchers' attention (for recent reviews, see Allan, 1993; Young, 1995). The model states that changes in the associative strength of a stimulus result from the outcome—either reinforcement or nonreinforcement—on each trial involving presentation of that stimulus.

Application of this model to causal judgment proceeds as follows: the effectiveness of a putative cause F (V_F) (e.g., the receipt of a fertilizer in our plant-fertilizer scenario) producing a particular outcome B (e.g., a plant's blooming) is determined by the associative strength of the compound of the putative cause and the background stimuli (V_{FX}) (e.g., the receipt of the fertilizer and water) and by the associative strength of the background stimuli alone (V_X) (e.g., the receipt of water alone or other contextual factors). Changes in the associative strengths of the putative cause (ΔV_F) and the background stimuli (ΔV_X) with the outcome are determined by the following conditions, representing information in Cells A, B, C, and D, respectively:

1. Cell A. If the presence of the compound of the putative cause (F) and the background (X) is followed by the outcome (B), then changes in the associative strengths of the respective components are represented as Equation (2a):

$$\Delta V_F = \alpha_F \cdot \beta_B(\lambda_B - V_{FX}) \text{ and } \Delta V_X = \alpha_X \cdot \beta_B(\lambda_B - V_{FX}). \quad (2a)$$

2. Cell B. If the presence of the compound of the putative cause (F) and the background (X) is *not* followed by the outcome (NB), then changes in the associative strengths of the respective components are represented as Equation (2b):

$$\Delta V_F = \alpha_F \cdot \beta_{NB}(\lambda_{NB} - V_{FX}) \text{ and } \Delta V_X = \alpha_X \cdot \beta_{NB}(\lambda_{NB} - V_{FX}). \quad (2b)$$

3. Cell C. If the presence of the background (X) alone (i.e., the absence of the putative cause F) is followed by the outcome (B), then the change in the associative strength of X, ΔV_X, is represented as Equation (2c) (the strength of F will *not* change on these trials):

$$\Delta V_X = \alpha_X \cdot \beta_B(\lambda_B - V_X). \quad (2c)$$

4. Cell D. If the presence of the background (X) alone (i.e., the absence of the putative cause F) is *not* followed by the outcome (NB), then the change in the associative strength of X, ΔV_X, is represented as Equation (2d) (the strength of F will *not* change on these trials):

$$\Delta V_X = \alpha_X \cdot \beta_{NB}(\lambda_{NB} - V_X). \quad (2d)$$

Three sets of parameters affect the magnitude of the changes. The α values are stimulus saliences associated with the component stimuli, α_F for the putative cause (F) and α_X for the background (X). The β values are learning rate parameters associated with the outcome, β_B for the occurrence of the outcome and β_{NB} for the nonoccurrence of the outcome. The λ values are the asymptotic levels of associative strength that can be supported by the outcome, λ_B for the occurrence of the outcome and λ_{NB} for the nonoccurrence of the outcome. The values of α and β are confined to the unit interval, $0 \leq \alpha, \beta \leq 1$. The value of λ is not strictly bounded, but simply shifts the scale on which associative strengths are observed. Furthermore, the Rescorla–Wagner model assumes that the relation among the associative strengths of the putative cause (F), the background (X), and the compound of the putative cause and the background (FX) is linear:

$$V_F + V_X = V_{FX}. \tag{3}$$

As most subjects unequally use the 2×2 cell information in the order Cell A > Cell B > Cell C > Cell D, we expect that the salience of the putative cause (α_F) should be relatively high and that the learning rate parameter associated with the occurrence of the outcome (β_B) should be greater than that associated with the nonoccurrence of the outcome (β_{NB}). For those subjects who do not use the cell information in the above order, the values of the α and β parameters should differ from the above inequalities.

Note that, unlike Busemeyer's model, which *explicitly* includes a weighted impact of the subject's initial expectancy on causal judgment, the Rescorla–Wagner model does not; instead, the Rescorla–Wagner model *implicitly* deals with initial expectancies by positing some prior existing strength of the putative cause with the outcome. The Rescorla–Wagner model has particular merit in explaining trial order effects like blocking (Kamin, 1969; see later discussion), because it postulates that the predictive strength of the putative cause is updated on each trial in which it is presented. The prime determining factors in Busemeyer's model are the frequencies of the four evidential cells; the sequence of information presentation should not affect the final estimate of contingency, although different sequences should materially affect approach to the final estimate.

C. EXPERIMENT 1

The first experiment that we describe in this chapter (Kao, 1993) was principally aimed at discriminating between Busemeyer's simple averaging version of information integration theory and Rescorla and Wagner's associative learning theory. Subjects were given a series of interevent contingencies to respond to and rate. Prior to, during, and after the presentation of contingency information, some subjects were asked to rate the efficacy of a putative cause in producing a particular effect; other subjects made causal ratings only before and after the receipt of all contingency information.

Very little work prior to this investigation had carefully tracked subjects' causal ratings as contingency information was received, despite the fact that the trial-by-trial receipt of information is a much more likely way for us to obtain contingency information in everyday life than is the receipt of neatly tabled summaries. Arkes and Harkness (1983, Experiment 7) conducted an experiment in which one group of subjects (the running-estimate group) was asked to estimate interevent contingency *to that point* after *every* piece of information was shown, whereas the other (the final-estimate group) was asked to estimate contingency only after the *last* piece of information was shown. They found that the two groups of subjects gave somewhat different final estimates of contingency; forcing subjects (in the running-estimate group) to update their estimates after every piece of information raised subjects' consideration of the information in Cells C and D. Unexpectedly, Arkes and Harkness also found that giving Cell D information made subjects change their estimates of interevent relations in a *negative* direction, whereas Cell D logically represents *positive* contingency information.

Shanks (1985a, 1987) also monitored subjects' contingency judgments over trials, although ratings here were measured after every five trials instead of after every single trial. He found that contingency judgments followed growth functions: when the contingency was positive, judgments increased over trials; when the contingency was negative, judgments decreased over trials; and, when the contingency was zero, judgments were close to zero over trials. Baker, Berbrier, and Vallée-Tourangeau (1989) were less successful than Shanks in plotting acquisition functions, as their subjects had essentially reached judgment asymptote within 10 trials.

The present study also monitored the *time* that subjects spent processing each piece of contingency information. This monitoring might not only disclose whether people use one type of information more than another, but also why they do so, because differential study time may be correlated with differential cell use; subjects may spend more time processing the type of information that more strongly affects their judgments. No research has investigated this issue.

1. Method

The subjects were 100 (50 male, 50 female) University of Iowa undergraduate students tested individually on a personal computer with a 14-in. color monitor. Each subject was given several different interevent contingencies to respond to and rate (Table I):

a. Noncontingent Problem Set   Thirteen different noncontingent problems were constructed, with A/B = C/D. The frequencies of the four cells in Problem 1 were all equal; this problem class was termed four-cells-identical. The frequencies of the four cells in Problems 2 to 5 were equal in pairs; this class was termed paired-cells-identical. The frequencies of the four cells in Problems 6 to 13 all differed from one another; this class was termed four-cells-different. The cell frequencies of each of the noncontingent problems summed to 24. Presentation of cell information in each problem was divided into three unbroken blocks.

b. Contingent Problem Set   Construction of the contingent problem set was based on the idea (first proposed and tested by Wasserman et al., 1990) of holding the frequencies of three cells constant and varying the fourth. The contingent problem set comprised eight different problems (Δps = .25 or −.25; see Footnote 1 for definition of this measure of contingency). Half of the eight contingent problems (Problems 14 to 17) entailed cell frequencies of 6 for three cells and 2 for the fourth; the cell frequencies of each of these problems summed to 20. The other half of the eight contingent problems (Problems 18 to 21) entailed cell frequencies of 6 for three cells and 18 for the fourth; the cell frequencies of each of these problems summed to 36. The eight contingent problems can be categorized into Cell A (Problems 14 and 18), Cell B (Problems 15 and 19), Cell C (Problems 16 and 20), and Cell D (Problems 17 and 21) classes, because only one cell was changed (increased or decreased) in each class. As in the noncontingent set, presentation of cell information in each problem was divided into three unbroken blocks.

Half of the subjects were assigned to a running-estimate condition, in which they had to update their judgments on every trial; the other half were assigned to a final-estimate condition, in which they made their judgments before the first and after the last trial of each problem. For each subject, study time for each piece of information was collected; the measure began when contingency information was presented after a brief warning tone and ended when the subject pressed the space bar to turn off that information. To better equate the two conditions, each subject in the running-estimate condition was paired with one of the same sex in the final-estimate condition; the same information-presentation sequence was given to these pairs. Subjects in the final-estimate condition had 2 s added to the time between successive pieces of contingency information;

this time was close to that taken by running-estimate subjects to make their rating.

After arriving at the laboratory and giving their informed consent, subjects were instructed on the computer screen to follow these instructions step by step:

Suppose you are employed by the American Flowering Plants Laboratory that has developed 24 experimental fertilizers, which are labeled F1 through F24, for promoting the Lanyu to bloom. The Lanyu, an exotic plant, is imported from Brazil. *It is possible that an experimental fertilizer may promote or suppress the Lanyu's blooming, or it may have no effect at all on the Lanyu's blooming.* Before being introduced to the market, each fertilizer has to be tested and evaluated for its effectiveness. To do so, each fertilizer was tested with a different group of plants. Within each group, the fertilizer was given once to some plants, but not to others. When the fertilizer was given, it was dissolved in a quantity of water; when the fertilizer was not given, the plant was provided with the same quantity of water. After 2 days, within each test group, four types of plants can be identified:

A—Plant received the fertilizer and bloomed.
B—Plant received the fertilizer, but did not bloom.
C—Plant did not receive the fertilizer, but bloomed.
D—Plant did not receive the fertilizer and did not bloom.

Now, given the test result of each plant in a group, your job is to assess the effectiveness of each tested fertilizer on the Lanyu's blooming. The evaluation procedure for each fertilizer is as follows:

1. Before being given any test results, you will be asked to give your expectation of the ability of the fertilizer to affect the Lanyu's blooming, rating its possible effectiveness on a scale of −10 to +10: A score of −10 means that you think the fertilizer may have a strong negative effect on the Lanyu's blooming. A score of 0 means that you think the fertilizer may have no effect on the Lanyu's blooming. A score of +10 means that you think the fertilizer may have a strong positive effect on the Lanyu's blooming. And, scores between −10 and +10 on the scale indicate different degrees of the fertilizer's effectiveness.

The response scale will look like this:

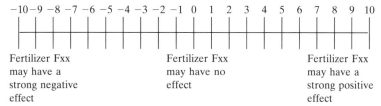

Fertilizer Fxx
may have a
strong negative
effect

Fertilizer Fxx
may have no
effect

Fertilizer Fxx
may have a
strong positive
effect

2. You will then be given a series of descriptions each indicating the state of a Lanyu plant: it either received or did not receive the fertilizer and it either bloomed or did not bloom. The left side of the screen indicates the status of a Lanyu plant before the test, whereas the right side of the screen indicates the status of the same Lanyu plant after the test.

For example:

If the plant received the fertilizer and bloomed, then you will see the left side of the screen display "Did the plant receive Fertilizer xx? YES," and the right side display "Did the plant bloom? YES." [press SPACE BAR to see what happens . . .]

If the plant received the fertilizer, but did not bloom, then you will see the left side of the screen display "Did the plant receive Fertilizer xx? YES," and the right side display "Did the plant bloom? NO." [press SPACE BAR to see what happens . . .]

If the plant did not receive the fertilizer, but bloomed, then you will see the left side of the screen display "Did the plant receive Fertilizer xx? NO," and the right side display "Did the plant bloom? YES." [press SPACE BAR to see what happens . . .]

If the plant did not receive the fertilizer and did not bloom, then you will see the left side of the screen display "Did the plant receive Fertilizer xx? NO," and the right side display "Did the plant bloom? NO." [press SPACE BAR to see what happens . . .]

The following instructions were for the running-estimate condition alone:

3. Before being given a particular description, you will hear a short tone to forewarn you to pay attention to the upcoming information.

4. After seeing a particular description, you will then update your evaluation of the effectiveness of that particular fertilizer. This means that your rating is to reflect the overall influence of all of the plants you have observed to that point—not just the last plant.

5. Note that the position of the cursor along the response scale on each trial, except on the initial guess trial, indicates your judgment from the previous trial, so that you can adjust your judgment from there (a short description of the numerical value of your earlier judgment will also appear above the scale). In addition, each time after you make a decision you can modify your decision by pressing the DEL key or confirm your decision by pressing SPACE BAR.

6. Steps 3 to 5 will be repeated until all test results of a group of plants are given.

The following instructions were for the final-estimate condition alone:

3. Before being given a particular description, you will hear a short tone to forewarn you to pay attention to the upcoming information. The presentation interval between pieces of information is 2 seconds. This step will be repeated until all test results of a group of plants are given.

4. You will then be asked to give your overall evaluation about the effectiveness of that particular tested fertilizer.

5. Note that the position of the cursor along the response scale on the last trial indicates your initial estimate so that you can adjust your judgment from there (a short description of the numerical value of your initial estimate will also appear above the scale). In addition, each time after you make a decision you can modify your decision by pressing the DEL key or confirm your decision by pressing SPACE BAR.

When making their ratings, subjects were instructed to use the left and right arrow keys to move the cursor along the response scale. Subjects were also given a practice problem with 24 trials to help familiarize them with the procedure; each type of cell information had an equal probability of being presented on each trial of this practice problem. The contingency problems were given in two sessions; each lasted about 50 min. Subjects received a 5-min break between sessions. Successive contingency problems were distinguished by displaying the descriptions of one problem in red and the next problem in green.

2. Results

a. Causal Ratings Table I shows the 21 contingency problems along with their mean initial and final estimates of causality from both the running-

Wasserman et al.

TABLE I

Problems Used in Experiments 1 and 2

Problem	A	B	C	D	Running-estimate Initial	Running-estimate Final	Final-estimate Initial	Final-estimate Final
Noncontingent problem set								
1 $\Delta p = .00$	6	6	6	6	.18	1.22	1.26	.32
2 $\Delta p = .00$	3	3	9	9	.56	.04	.94	−.06
3 $\Delta p = .00$	3	9	3	9	.56	−1.28	.72	−1.42
4 $\Delta p = .00$	9	3	9	3	.84	1.72	.80	2.72
5 $\Delta p = .00$	9	9	3	3	.84	.98	1.80	.76
6 $\Delta p = .00$	3	5	6	10	.86	.86	.36	−.36
7 $\Delta p = .00$	3	6	5	10	.32	−.62	.82	−.70
8 $\Delta p = .00$	5	3	10	6	.34	−.24	.00	.10
9 $\Delta p = .00$	5	10	3	6	.90	−.26	.44	−1.74
10 $\Delta p = .00$	6	3	10	5	.90	.84	.26	−.12
11 $\Delta p = .00$	6	10	3	5	.10	−1.06	.38	−1.10
12 $\Delta p = .00$	10	5	6	3	1.20	2.10	.38	3.04
13 $\Delta p = .00$	10	6	5	3	.40	1.72	.52	2.90
Contingent problem set								
14 $\Delta p = -.25$	2	6	6	6	.62	−1.04	.26	−2.70
15 $\Delta p = .25$	6	2	6	6	.44	1.70	1.42	3.08
16 $\Delta p = .25$	6	6	2	6	.70	1.66	.80	1.80
17 $\Delta p = -.25$	6	6	6	2	.88	.40	.46	−.58
18 $\Delta p = .25$	18	6	6	6	1.12	5.16	.42	6.08
19 $\Delta p = -.25$	6	18	6	6	.34	−3.72	1.14	−5.16
20 $\Delta p = -.25$	6	6	18	6	.86	−.82	.46	−2.24
21 $\Delta p = .25$	6	6	6	18	1.04	3.20	.48	2.28
Seriation problem set								
22 $\Delta p = .00$	6	6	6	6	1.02	1.80	.86	.68
(5, 1, 1, 5; 1, 5, 5, 1)								
23 $\Delta p = .00$	6	6	6	6	.44	.82	.40	−.28
(1, 5, 5, 1; 5, 1, 1, 5)								
24 $\Delta p = .00$	6	6	6	6	.88	.76	.64	.44
(3, 3, 3, 3; 3, 3, 3, 3)								

and final-estimate groups. Subjects' initial ratings of the relation between the receipt of a fertilizer and the plant's blooming were slightly positive across all problems and both conditions (.00 ≤ means ≤ 1.80). After being given contingency information, subjects in both the running- and final-estimate conditions incorrectly judged some noncontingent problems as "positive" and others as "negative." Subjects' judgment patterns of noncontingency were generally similar; both groups gave "positive" ratings to

Problems 1, 4, 5, 12, and 13, and "negative" ratings to Problems 3, 7, 9, and 11. Although the two groups oppositely rated the interevent relations of Problems 2, 6, 8, and 10, the mean ratings of these problems were very close to zero. As to the eight contingent problems, subjects in both conditions correctly judged the directions of these interevent relations, except that the running-estimate group incorrectly judged Problem 17 as slightly "positive."

Analyses of variance were conducted on these data to determine the reliability of any main effects and interactions. No group differences on the initial ratings were found, suggesting that subjects in the different rating groups did not have strongly disparate prior beliefs about the interevent relation between the receipt of a fertilizer and a plant's blooming. Subjects' initial causal estimates in both conditions were reliably greater than zero, indicating that before being given any contingency information, subjects had a positive bias of the relation between the receipt of a fertilizer and a plant's blooming. For the final estimates, only the main effect of problem and the interaction of condition and problem were reliable. Follow-up tests suggested that the final judgments of the two groups differed on Problems 9, 13, 14, and 15; however, in all four of these problems, the directions of contingency judged by the two groups were consistent, although the judgments of the final-estimate group were more extreme. The results suggest that, overall, the final judgments of causation did not greatly differ in the running- and final-estimate conditions.

As discussed in our earlier study (Kao & Wasserman, 1993), the absolute rating of *noncontingent* relations can be regarded as an index of judgment accuracy, because all nonzero ratings, either positive or negative, are incorrect. In that study, we found that when the frequencies of all four cells differed from one another, subjects' judgments were least accurate; when the frequencies of the four cells were identical in pairs, they were moderately accurate; and, when the frequencies of all four cells were identical, they were most accurate. To see if we could replicate these prior results and to see if subjects in the different judgment conditions exhibited different degrees of accuracy in rating noncontingency, an analysis of variance was conducted on the absolute final ratings of all 13 noncontingent problems. The analysis yielded only a significant main effect of noncontingent problem class. The nonsignificance of the condition main effect and the interaction between condition and noncontingent problem class suggest that subjects' accuracy in judging noncontingency did not differ in the running- and final-estimate groups. The mean absolute ratings of the three problem classes were ordered as in our previous work: four-cells-different (Problems 6 to 13: mean = 2.41) > paired-cells-identical (Problems 2 to 5: mean = 2.23) > four-cells-identical (Problem 1: mean = 1.81).

Although it may not be meaningful to use the absolute ratings of *contingent* relations to examine judgment accuracy, they can be used to see if different cell information generated different degrees of judgment influence. Thus, Problems 14 and 18 were those in which the frequency of Cell A differed from the other three cells; the absolute ratings of these two problems can therefore indicate the extent to which causal judgments were affected by Cell A information. Similarly, the absolute ratings of Problems 15 and 19 can measure the impact of Cell B; those of Problems 16 and 20 can measure the impact of Cell C; and, those of Problems 17 and 21 can measure the impact of Cell D. Analyses of variance suggested that the impact of Cell A (mean = 4.44) and Cell B (mean = 4.06) was greater than that of Cell C (mean = 2.54) and Cell D (mean = 2.82).

Finally, momentary changes in ratings were examined as Arkes and Harkness (1983) had done earlier. For each subject in the running-estimate condition, the judgment difference between Trial n and Trial $n + 1$ was classified into four categories depending on the type of information received on Trial $n + 1$: Cell A, Cell B, Cell C, or Cell D. Mean judgment change for each of the four types of cell information was then computed by dividing the total judgment change after each type of information by the number of times that type of information was given. Mean judgment changes after receiving information in Cells A, B, C, and D, respectively, were 1.69, −1.46, −.43, and .23 during the first session, and 1.27, −1.06, −.40, and .18 during the second. Subjects reliably increased their ratings when they received information in Cells A and D, and they reliably decreased their ratings when they received information in Cells B and C. The absolute values of the judgment changes were ordered Cell A > Cell B > Cell C > Cell D in both sessions.

b. Information Study Time   Figure 1 shows the median study time of the four types of cell information in both conditions and in both sessions.[2] The running-estimate group spent more time than the final-estimate group studying each type of cell information in both sessions. Both groups spent more time studying contingency information during the first session than during the second; they also spent more time studying information in Cells B and C than they spent studying information in Cells A and D. Analyses of variance confirmed the reliability of these results.

It was also of interest to see how information study time changed as the number of trials in a given contingency problem increased. Figure 2 displays the median information study time over trials in the noncontingent and

---

[2] The median, rather than the mean, study time of each type of cell information was calculated for each subject in each session in order to eliminate the possible effects of outlier scores with relatively small numbers of observations.

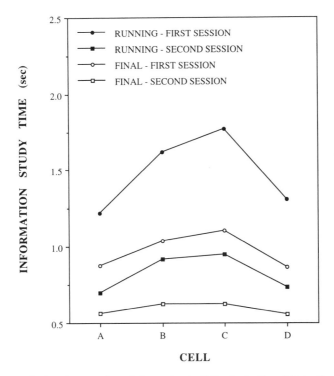

Fig. 1. Study time in seconds to information in Cells A, B, C, and D in Experiment 1. Data are separately depicted for subjects in the running- and final-estimate groups during the first and second sessions of experimental training. Data are averaged across all trials of all 21 of the contingency problems.

contingent sets for both the running- and final-estimate groups. Both groups spent more time studying the first few pieces of incoming information, particularly the very first piece, than they spent studying the later pieces of information.

3. Parameter Estimation

a. Information Integration Theory For each subject, the values of W_I, W_A, W_B, W_C, and W_D can be estimated by placing subjects' initial estimates of causation and the frequencies of the four cells into Equation (1) (Busemeyer's information integration model) and then applying the Hooke and Jeeves (HJ) parameter search method to seek the best set of parameter values; the HJ method, presented by Nash and Walker-Smith (1987) in BASIC, is a direct search process to find a set of parameters by minimizing a given mathematical function. The to-be-minimized function was a least-

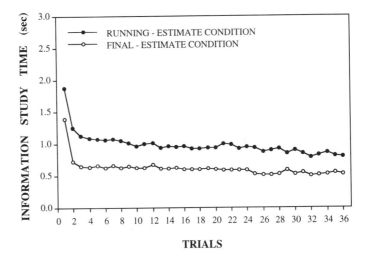

Fig. 2. Information study time in seconds over trials in Experiment 1. Data are separately shown for subjects in the running- and final-estimate groups. Data are averaged across the two sessions of training and all 21 of the contingency problems.

squares function.[3] Two constraints on the estimates of W_I, W_A, W_B, W_C, and W_D were employed: (1) when comparing the values of W_I, W_A, W_B, W_C, and W_D to one another, all of the weight parameters were constrained to sum to 1 ($W_I + W_A + W_B + W_C + W_D = 1$) for each subject; (2) when comparing the contributions of the four cells to causal judgments from subject to subject, only the cell weight parameters from Cells A, B, C, and D were constrained to sum to 1 ($W_A + W_B + W_C + W_D = 1$) for each subject.

By applying the first constraint on the parameters in Equation (1), the results revealed that the means of W_I, W_A, W_B, W_C, and W_D, respectively, were .19, .29, .22, .16, and .14 for the running-estimate group and .15, .33, .27, .14, and .11 for the final-estimate group. The ordering of weights was the same in both groups, with W_I falling between W_B and W_C. The values of W_I, W_A, W_B, W_C, and W_D all reliably differed from zero, indicating that

---

[3] A least-squares function is the sum of the squared differences between the predicted terminal ratings and the subject's terminal ratings across problems [i.e., $\sum_{i=1}^{N} (R_{pi} - R_{si})^2$], where N is the number of problems, R_p is the predicted terminal rating computed from a tested model, and R_s is a subject's terminal judgment of contingency. Here, subjects' ratings were divided by 10 to fall within the range of -1 to 1 to be comparable with the ratings predicted by the tested model.

the initial expectancy of interevent contingency and the four types of cell information all contributed to subjects' judgments.

To compare the contributions of the four cells alone to causal judgments, the second constraint on the weight parameters in Equation (1) was applied. The means of W_A, W_B, W_C, and W_D, respectively, were .36, .29, .19, and .16 for the running-estimate group, and .38, .32, .17, and .13 for the final-estimate group. The cell utilization order for both groups was the same as in all of our earlier studies (Kao & Wasserman, 1993; Levin et al., 1993; Wasserman et al., 1990).

b. Associative Learning Theory For each subject, the learning rate parameters (α_F, α_X, β_B, and β_{NB}) in Equations (2a) to (2d) of the Rescorla–Wagner model can also be estimated by applying the HJ method; subjects' initial estimates of causation were considered to be prior existing associative strengths of the target event. As in the preceding, the to-be-minimized mathematical function was a least-squares function. The means of α_F, α_X, β_B, and β_{NB}, respectively, were .40, .27, .51, and .42 for the running-estimate group, and .36, .24, .47, and .37 for the final-estimate group. Analyses of variance disclosed that the salience of the target event was greater than that of the background stimulus in both conditions. Also, the learning rate parameter associated with the occurrence of the outcome was greater than that associated with its nonoccurrence in both conditions. Logically, when α_F is relatively high, the information in Cells A and B should be much more influential than that in Cells C and D, and when β_B is greater than β_{NB}, the information in Cells A and C should be more influential than that in Cells B and D. The results of the learning-rate-parameter analyses were then consistent with the finding that subjects generally used the cell information in the order Cell A > Cell B > Cell C > Cell D.

4. Comparison of Information Integration and Associative Learning Accounts

A major goal of this experiment was to compare the utility of the simple averaging version of Busemeyer's information integration model with Rescorla and Wagner's associative learning model in describing human causality judgment. To achieve this objective, the following analyses were conducted.

a. Predictions of Final Causality Judgments If a model validly describes a subject's judgment process, then the final ratings predicted by the model should correlate highly with the subject's final judgments. So, each individual's final ratings of the 21 problems were correlated with the ratings predicted by Busemeyer's model and with those predicted by the Rescorla–Wagner model. A total of 84 of the 100 subjects' judgments (38 in the running-estimate group; 46 in the final-estimate group) reliably correlated with the ratings predicted by Busemeyer's model, and a total of 87 of the 100 subjects' judgments (42 in the running-estimate group; 45 in the final-estimate group) reliably correlated with the ratings predicted by the Rescorla–Wagner model (smallest reliable rs $>$ .433). Both models can thus describe most subjects' final causality judgments.

To see if subjects' final ratings better correlated with the scores predicted by one model than by the other and to see if both models described subjects' final ratings better in one condition than in the other, the correlation scores were converted into z scores and an analysis of variance was conducted. Subjects' final judgments slightly, but reliably, correlated better with the ratings predicted by Busemeyer's model (mean r = .683) than with those predicted by the Rescorla–Wagner model (mean r = .626), and the ratings predicted by both models correlated reliably better with subjects' final judgments in the final-estimate condition (mean r = .706) than with those in the running-estimate condition (mean r = .603).

b. Predictions of Moment-by-Moment Causality Judgments   More germane to the utility of the two models as process accounts of causality judgment is the answer to the question: are both models equally able to describe subjects' moment-by-moment ratings? To answer this question, only the data obtained from the running-estimate group were examined. As derived from the *initial* and *final* ratings *only* for each individual subject, the estimated set of initial expectancy and cell weight parameters (i.e., W_I, W_A, W_B, W_C, and W_D) was placed back into Equation (1) (Busemeyer's model), and the set of learning rate parameters (i.e., α_F, α_X, β_B, and β_{NB}) was placed back into Equations (2a to 2d) (the Rescorla–Wagner model). Then, the moment-by-moment causal judgments predicted by both Busemeyer's model and the Rescorla–Wagner model were obtained within and across problems for each subject.[4]

Figure 3 shows the running-estimate group's mean judgments over trials along with the mean trial-by-trial ratings predicted by both models for each of the 8 contingent relations, as the two models did not as clearly differ in their predicted ratings for the 13 noncontingent relations. For the first set of contingent relations (Problems 14 to 17), both models slightly overestimated the extremity of subjects' judgments over trials. For the second set of contingent relations (Problems 18 to 21), the ratings predicted by the Rescorla–Wagner model were much closer to subjects' judgments than were those predicted by Busemeyer's model; the occurrence of an early

---

[4] For this portion of the analysis, all 24 problems that subjects were given were entered into statistical tests. The three as yet-undescribed seriation problems are listed in Table I and are discussed as Experiment 2 in this chapter for purely expository purposes.

overestimation bias in Busemeyer's model was especially evident in Problems 18 to 21.[5]

To compare the fits of both models with actual judgments, the correlations between subjects' trial-by-trial ratings and the ratings predicted by the tested models for each of the problems were first calculated and analysis of variance was then conducted. Subjects' trial-by-trial ratings correlated reliably better with the ratings predicted by the Rescorla–Wagner model (mean $r = .687$) than with those predicted by Busemeyer's model (mean $r = .432$); this numerical superiority was true on *each* of the tested problems.

5. Discussion

Overall, this experiment disclosed that momentary judgments of causality did systematically change as more and more contingency information was received. Noncontingent relations were not always rated so by subjects; both positive and negative biases were observed and were largely due to differential weighting of the 2×2 cell information. Normatively equivalent contingent relations were rated differently by subjects depending on which cells in the contingency table were changed, with impact also ordered Cell A > Cell B > Cell C > Cell D.

Differential cell weighting is the centerpiece of Busemeyer's information integration theory; it is no surprise then that this theory did particularly well in describing most subjects' final causality ratings. Perhaps more surprisingly, Rescorla and Wagner's associative learning theory also did a fine job in accounting for subjects' final causality ratings; it reliably described a few more subjects' ratings than did Busemeyer's account, although its overall correlation with subjects' ratings was not quite as high. More important, the Rescorla–Wagner model outperformed the Busemeyer model in retracing the moment-by-moment changes in subjects' causality ratings.

Perhaps unrelated to either of the theories under consideration, subjects spent more time studying information in Cells B and C than they spent studying information in Cells A and D. Information in Cells A and D *confirms* the relation between fertilizer application and plant blooming, whereas information in Cells B and C *disconfirms* it. As subjects generally harbored a slight, but reliable positive belief in the effectiveness of the hypothetical fertilizers, the obtained study time results may be governed

---

[5] Recall that the simple averaging version of Busemeyer's (1991) model places every new piece of contingency information into Equation (1) and it outputs R to that point. Changes in R are at first large and then progressively decrease as more and more information is added to Equation (1). Overestimation is therefore to be expected with Δps of large absolute value and with small values of W_I. A number of ad hoc methods were used to try to reduce this overestimation bias (Kao, 1993). All met with only limited success, the Rescorla–Wagner model always outperforming the ad hoc revisions.

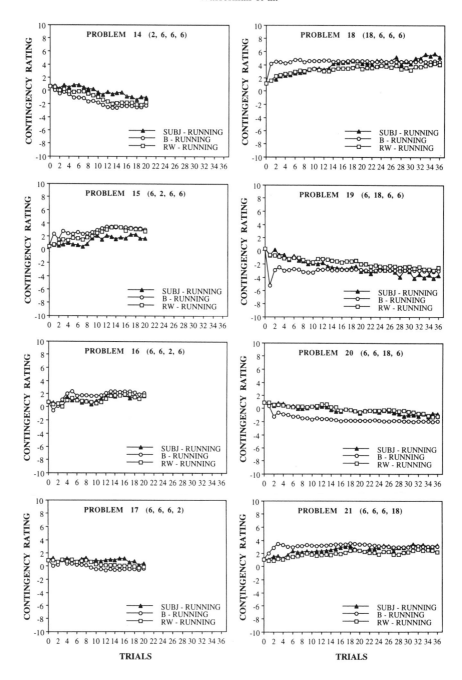

by subjects' prior expectations. Future work should explore cell study time when subjects harbor negative cause–effect beliefs. Study time was also longer for the first item or two that subjects received and it was longer for subjects who were required to rate causal relations after every piece of contingency information was received than for those who were required to do so only after the final piece of contingency information. The last result probably derives from the extra rating demands that were placed on running-estimate subjects.

II. Tracking Causal Ratings over Changing Interevent Relations

Critical to the development of Rescorla and Wagner's associative learning theory was the challenge posed by blocking (Kamin, 1969). The fact that prior training with one stimulus element (A) reduced later conditioning to another stimulus element (B) during compound stimulus (AB) training required a model of learning that took into account the precise order in which interevent information was given.

Rather little experimental attention has nevertheless been paid to sequence effects in human contingency and causal judgment (see Franson, Chatlosh, & Wasserman, in Wasserman [1990] for one of our own first investigations of the matter; see Chapman [1991] for possibly the most important study in the area; and, see Medin & Bettger [1991] for a report in the related domain of human category learning). In everyday situations, most of us have had the discomforting experience of early empirical evidence suggesting a relation between events that eventually turned out not to hold true in the long run. A new sales campaign might at first seem to be more effective than the old one; submitting papers to a new journal might initially appear to be more successful than submitting them to a familiar periodical; or testing an experimental drug might at first seem to be more therapeutic than the old drug treatment. It is precisely because of the unrepresentativeness of small data samples and our possible predispo-

---

Fig. 3. Trial-by-trial ratings of subjects in the running-estimate group of 8 of the 21 contingency problems in Experiment 1 along with those predicted by Busemeyer's information integration model and by Rescorla and Wagner's associative learning model. Problems in the left column were created by holding the contents of three cells constant at 6 and reducing the fourth to 2; problems in the right column were created by holding the contents of three cells constant at 6 and increasing the fourth to 18. In all eight problems, the absolute value of Δp was .25.

sition to form premature impressions of that evidence that we experimentalists are admonished by statisticians to wait until a large sample of data has been collected and a proper statistical analysis has been conducted before we decide whether or not a reliable relation holds between the variables of interest.

Yates and Curley (1986) reported a "primacy" effect in the contingency scores they *derived* from their subjects' conditional probability ratings (see Trolier & Hamilton, 1986, for more on this issue). However, because no one had *directly* addressed the question of primacy in contingency or causality judgments, Kao (1993) included 3 problems in her total set of 24 that did so. Both Yates and Curley (1986) and Kao (1993) used interevent relations in which the first half of the evidence subjects were given suggested one relation, but the second half of the evidence suggested exactly the opposite relation. So, overall, there was no statistical association between the pairs of binary variables in the reversed relations of either of these two studies.

A. EXPERIMENT 2

1. Method

The present investigation was an integral part of Experiment 1. All features of the experiment were the same as described earlier, except for the fact that this investigation comprised three contingency problems not described earlier.

a. Seriation Problem Set   The seriation set comprised three problems whose overall cell frequencies, like Problem 1, were 6 for all four cells; so, over the entire information sequence, there was no interevent contingency. But, unlike the noncontingent set, the presentation of cell information in each of the three seriation problems was divided into two unbroken blocks instead of three. More important, for Problem 22, the interevent contingency was .67 in Block 1 (A = D = 5 and B = C = 1), but −.67 in Block 2 (A = D = 1 and B = C = 5); for Problem 23, the interevent contingency was −.67 in Block 1 (A = D = 1 and B = C = 5), but .67 in Block 2 (A = D = 5 and B = C = 1); and, for Problem 24, the interevent contingency was .00 in both Blocks 1 and 2 (A = B = C = D = 3). If subjects exhibit primacy, then they should give "positive" final judgments to Problem 22, "negative" final judgments to Problem 23, and "zero" final judgments to Problem 24. Half of the 100 subjects were again placed in the running- and final-estimate conditions.

2. Results

a. Final Ratings   Table I shows that the final-estimate group responded "positive" to Problem 22 and "negative" to Problem 23; it also responded "positive" to Problem 24, and this rating was less than that of Problem 22. The running-estimate group responded "positive" to all three seriation problems. All of the above scores were within ±1.80 of .00 along the −10 to 10 rating scale. Analysis of variance yielded only a reliable main effect of condition, indicating that the running-estimate group gave generally higher ratings to the three seriation problems than did the final-estimate group. The nonsignificance of the problem main effect and the condition by problem interaction represents a failure to find a primacy effect (cf. Yates & Curley, 1986).

b. Trial-by-Trial Ratings Figure 4 shows the momentary ratings of the three seriation set problems for subjects in the running-estimate group along with the scores predicted by the simple averaging version of Busemeyer's information integration account and by Rescorla and Wagner's associative learning account. The fits of both models in Problem 24, where each type of cell information was *evenly* distributed to the two blocks, were similar and quite successful, as ratings stayed near zero throughout all 24 trials. Most notably, the fits of both models in Problems 22 and 23, where each type of cell information was *unevenly* distributed to the two blocks, were clearly different. The Rescorla–Wagner model described subjects' judgments very well, except for a slight deviation on the last few trials; but, Busemeyer's model dramatically overestimated subjects' judgments in the first block, although the discrepancy greatly diminished in the second.

3. Discussion

Given this failure to obtain primacy, it was important to see if the Rescorla–Wagner model would ever predict a primacy effect, not only because the model very nicely described subjects' final and moment-by-moment causal ratings, but also because it was developed largely to predict another trial-order effect—blocking. Close inspection of Problems 22 and 23 in Figure 4 discloses that the trial-by-trial ratings predicted by the Rescorla–Wagner model generated a *recency* effect, rather than primacy (for more on this prediction, see Shanks, Lopez, Darby, & Dickinson, this volume, Ch. 7; cf. Benedict & Ayres, 1972; Quinsey, 1971). As the figure shows, final associative strengths were positive in Problem 23 and negative in Problem 22, suggesting that the second-half contingency had greater impact than did the first-half contingency.

A wide range of trial-by-trial rating functions for the three seriation problems was therefore simulated to see if the Rescorla–Wagner model would generate primacy with different sets of stimulus salience and learning rate parameters; some are shown in Fig. 5. Three sets of α parameters ($\alpha_F < \alpha_X$, $\alpha_F = \alpha_X$, and $\alpha_F > \alpha_X$) and β parameters ($\beta_B < \beta_{NB}$, $\beta_B = \beta_{NB}$,

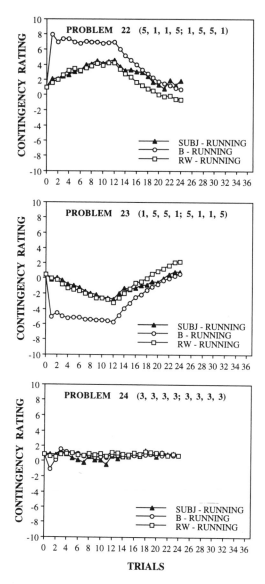

Fig. 4.   Trial-by-trial ratings of subjects in the running-estimate group of the three seriation problems in Experiment 2 along with those predicted by Busemeyer's information integration model and by Rescorla and Wagner's associative learning model. The parenthetical numbers denote the contents of Cells A, B, C, and D during the first 12 and second 12 trials of the 24-trial problems.

and $\beta_B > \beta_{NB}$) were used; the factorial combination of these sets of α and β parameters thus generated nine different cases. The value of λ was bounded within the range of -1 to 1. Although the interevent relations of the three seriation problems are different in each block, the contingency of each problem is zero at the end of the series. If primacy were to occur, then the second block of trials would not completely nullify the first. On the other hand, if recency were to hold, then the second block would not only nullify but overwhelm the first. According to the simulations in Fig. 5, the Rescorla–Wagner model *never* predicts primacy in causal judgment. The simulations suggest that the greater the value of α_F relative to that of α_X, the stronger the *recency* effect the Rescorla–Wagner model predicts. The overall pattern of results was also affected by the values of the β parameters. The greater the value of β_B relative to that of β_{NB}, the more positive the ratings; conversely, the lower the value of β_B relative to that of β_{NB}, the more negative the ratings.

Given this evidence, if primacy were to be a reliable effect in human contingency and causal judgments, then the utility of the Rescorla–Wagner model would be called into question. Because of the importance of establishing the existence or nonexistence of primacy, a second experiment into the matter was conducted.

B. Experiment 3

1. Method

The 100 subjects (50 male, 50 female) in this experiment (Katagiri, Kao, Simon, & Wasserman, 1995) were given a total of 13 different contingency problems to respond to and rate: 5 involved interevent relations that remained the same throughout the 24 trials of each problem, and 8 involved interevent relations that changed without warning at the midway point. This set of problems afforded us the opportunity to examine subjects' general sensitivity to the relations that they were given as well as the chance to see whether subjects' judgments were disproportionately influenced by the early interevent information to which they were exposed—primacy. Although Kao (1993) had found little effect of subjects making running or final estimates, we again had two different groups of subjects make causal judgments in one way or the other.

The experiment involved the 13 different problems that are shown in Table II. These 13 problems can be arranged into three different groupings in order to clarify the behavioral effects of those problems that either did or did not involve an unsignaled change in contingency at the halfway point. All of the 24-trial problems were specified by the contents of the 2×2 information matrix scheduled during the first and second halves of

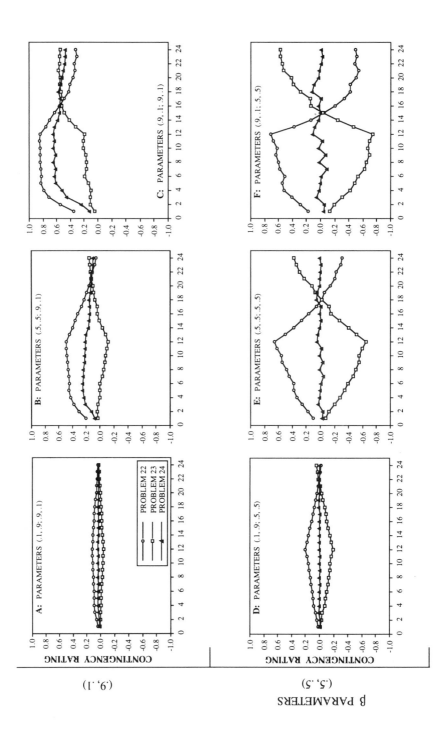

232

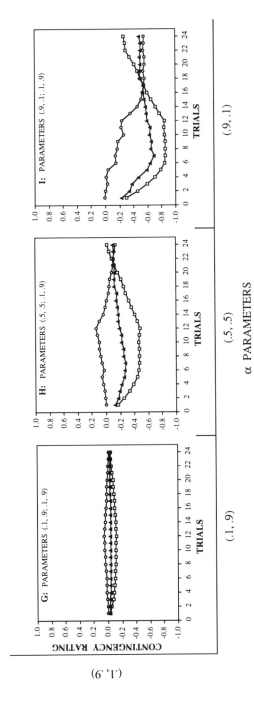

Fig. 5. Trial-by-trial ratings predicted by the Rescorla–Wagner model for the three seriation problems of Experiment 2, scaled to range from −1 to 1. The 9 panels result from the 3 × 3 combination of α and β parameters, with each parameter taking on the values of .1, .5, and .9.

TABLE II

PROBLEMS USED IN EXPERIMENT 3 AND SUBJECTS' RATINGS

Problems	Cell entries												Contingencies			Subjects' ratings			
	Block 1				Block 2				Overall							Final-estimate		Running-estimate	
	A	B	C	D	A	B	C	D	A	B	C	D	Block 1	Block 2	Overall	T0	T24	T0	T24
Problems with all contingencies constant																			
1	5	1	1	5	5	1	1	5	10	2	2	10	.667	.667	.667	1.14	6.36	.08	5.32
2	4	2	2	4	4	2	2	4	8	4	4	8	.333	.333	.333	.82	2.90	.30	4.06
3	3	3	3	3	3	3	3	3	6	6	6	6	.000	.000	.000	1.54	.24	.66	.38
4	2	4	4	2	2	4	4	2	4	8	8	4	−.333	−.333	−.333	1.22	−2.30	.50	−2.34
5	1	5	5	1	1	5	5	1	2	10	10	2	−.667	−.667	−.667	.96	−5.02	.74	−4.96
Problems with zero overall contingency																			
6	5	1	1	5	5	5	1	1	6	6	6	6	.667	−.667	.000	.66	.42	.98	−.42
7	4	2	2	4	4	4	2	2	6	6	6	6	.333	−.333	.000	1.22	.54	.58	−.12
(3)[a]	3	3	3	3	3	3	3	3	6	6	6	6	.000	.000	.000	1.54	.24	.66	.38
8	2	4	4	2	2	2	4	4	6	6	6	6	−.333	.333	.000	.22	.42	.52	.06
9	1	5	5	1	1	1	5	5	6	6	6	6	−.667	.667	.000	.30	.38	.24	1.24
Problems with contingency of |.333|																			
10	5	1	1	5	3	3	3	3	8	4	4	8	.667	.000	.333	.16	4.50	1.36	2.98
(2)	4	2	2	4	4	2	2	4	8	4	4	8	.333	.333	.333	.82	2.90	.30	4.06
11	3	3	3	3	5	1	1	5	8	4	4	8	.000	.667	.333	1.04	3.88	.42	3.14
12	1	5	5	1	3	3	3	3	4	8	8	4	−.667	.000	−.333	.96	−2.78	.82	−2.26
(4)	2	4	4	2	2	4	4	2	4	8	8	4	−.333	−.333	−.333	1.22	−2.30	.50	−2.34
13	3	3	3	3	1	5	5	1	4	8	8	4	.000	−.667	−.333	.60	−2.42	.54	−3.02

[a] ( ) indicates that the problem has already appeared above.

the problems. Individual cell entries were either 1, 2, 3, 4, or 5, with the constraint that the sum of the four cells was 12 in each half of each problem. These cell frequencies yielded Δps whose absolute values were .000, .333, or .667 in either half of the problems or over both halves of the problems. The three groupings were:

1. *Problems with the same contingency in each half.* This group included Problems 1, 2, 3, 4, and 5 entailing Δps of .667, .333, .000, −.333, and −.667, respectively;

2. *Problems with an overall Δp of .000.* This group included: Problem 3 with Δp = .000 in both halves; Problem 6 with Δp = .667 in the first half and Δp = −.667 in the second; Problem 9 with Δp = −.667 in the first half and Δp = .667 in the second; Problem 7 with Δp = .333 in the first half and Δp = −.333 in the second; and Problem 8 with Δp = −.333 in the first half and Δp = .333 in the second;

3. *Problems with an overall absolute value of Δp = .333.* Problems 2, 10, and 11 had an overall Δp = .333; Problems 4, 12, and 13 had an overall Δp = −.333. Problems 2 and 4 entailed no change in contingency; Problems 10 and 12 entailed a change from a nonzero to a zero contingency; and Problems 11 and 13 entailed a change from a zero to a nonzero contingency.

The apparatus and general procedure were the same as in Kao (1993).

2. Results

a. Comparison of Running- and Final-Estimate Conditions   Mean initial (T0) and final (T24) ratings of the 13 problems in the two estimation conditions are shown in Table II. In general, judgments sensitively reflected the overall Δp in effect, without any strong indication that initial interevent information exerted greater impact than did terminal interevent information. There was also little evidence to suggest that the running- and final-estimation procedures importantly influenced subjects' initial or final ratings.

Analysis of variance indicated that final, but not initial, judgments differed as a function of problem type. Follow-ups showed that prior to the receipt of any contingency information, ratings were similar and slightly, but reliably positive in both conditions. Final ratings generally accorded with the overall interevent contingency. Mean ratings with Δp = .667 ranged from 5.32 to 6.36; mean ratings with Δp = .333 ranged from 2.90 to 4.50; mean ratings with Δp = .000 ranged from −0.42 to 1.24; mean ratings with Δp = −.333 ranged from −3.02 to −2.26; and mean ratings with Δp = −.667 ranged from −5.02 to −4.96. Critically, there was no sign of primacy. So, for example, with Problems 3, 6, 7, 8, and 9, final ratings were neither substantially more positive in Problems 6 and 7 (entailing an initially positive contingency) nor more negative in Problems 8 and 9 (entailing an initially negative contingency) than they were in Problem 3 (entailing a noncontingent relation throughout) (see Table II). If there was any consistent tendency in these data, it was for final ratings in the running-estimate condition to show a (nonsignificant) trend toward recency, with ratings in Problems 6 and 7 more negative and ratings in Problem 9 more positive than in Problem 3 (see Table II) (also see Shanks, Lopez, Darby, & Dickinson, this volume, Ch. 7).

b. Trial-by-Trial Ratings The mean momentary causal ratings of subjects in the running-estimate condition on each of the 13 problems is shown in Fig. 6. The three panels of this figure represent the three different groupings of problems shown in Table II. Each panel of this figure and its associated analysis of variance speak to different features of the data under consideration.

Figure 6A depicts the five problems with constant contingencies throughout all 24 trials. Beginning just above zero on Trial 0 (the initial judgment prior to the receipt of any interevent information), ratings progressively diverged in clear accord with the contingencies. Figure 6B depicts the five problems with no overall contingency across all 24 trials. Ratings in the first 12 trials progressively diverged, in clear accord with the prevailing contingencies; however, ratings in the second 12 trials promptly converged, in synchrony with the changed interevent relations then in effect. Figure 6C depicts the six problems with an absolute overall Δp of .333. Ratings in the first 12 trials progressively diverged, in clear accord with the prevailing contingencies; however, ratings in the second 12 trials soon converged in the two subgroups of problems with overall Δps of .333 and $-.333$, in synchrony with the changed interevent relations then in effect. In all three cases, the reliability of these results was confirmed by problem by trial interactions. These data thus disclose that our subjects' causal ratings not only sensitively accorded with the *overall* interevent relations to which they were exposed, but they closely tracked any *momentary* changes in those relations with little measurable lag. Just how did the subjects accomplish such impressive cognitive feats?

Fig. 6. Trial-by-trial ratings of subjects in the running-estimate condition of Experiment 3 on each of the 13 contingency problems. The parenthetical numbers denote the contents of Cells A, B, C, and D during the first 12 and second 12 trials of the 24-trial problems. The three panels depict performance in the three sets of problems outlined in Table II and are discussed at greater length in the text.

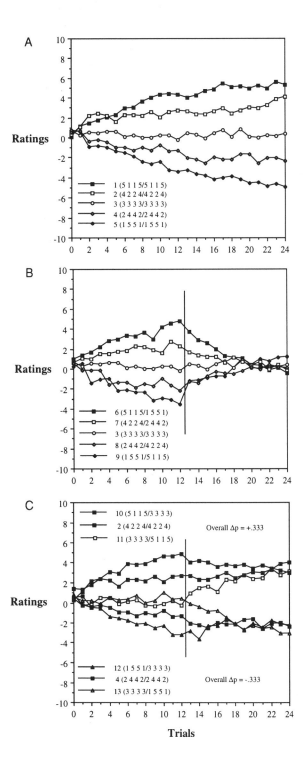

c. Predictions of Moment-by-Moment Causality Judgments   Once again, the parameter estimation and simulation procedures of Kao (1993) were used to check the fits of the simple averaging version of Busemeyer's information integration theory and Rescorla and Wagner's associative learning theory to subjects' momentary causality ratings. As in Figs. 3 and 4, graphic fits were notably better for the Rescorla–Wagner model than for the Busemeyer model. Four such fits are shown in Fig. 7. In Problems 7 and 8, contingencies whose absolute value was .333 during the first 12

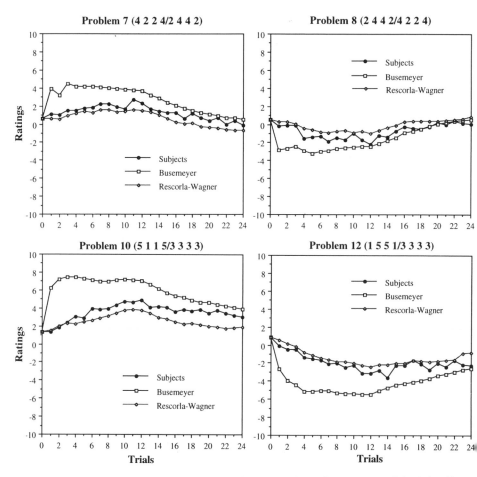

Fig. 7. Trial-by-trial ratings of subjects in the running-estimate group of 4 of the 13 contingency problems in Experiment 3 along with those predicted by Busemeyer's information integration model and by Rescorla and Wagner's associative learning model. The parenthetical numbers denote the contents of Cells A, B, C, and D during the first 12 and second 12 trials of the 24-trial problems. The text discusses these particular problems at greater length.

trials reversed during the second 12 trials, so that the final contingency was .000. The Rescorla–Wagner model closely tracked subjects' momentary ratings as they moved first upward and then downward in Problem 7, and as they moved first downward and then upward in Problem 8; Busemeyer's model overshot subjects' ratings during the first 12 trials, but it then converged on subjects' ratings during the second 12 trials. In Problems 10 and 12, contingencies whose absolute value during the first 12 trials was .667 shifted to .000 during the second 12 trials, so that the absolute value of the final contingency was .333. Here, too, the same general trends were observed.

In this experiment, Rescorla and Wagner's model again proved to provide a better account of causal ratings than did the simple averaging version of Busemeyer's information integration model. That superiority is therefore no less true of interevent relations that change without warning at the midpoint of information presentation (Figs. 4 and 7) than it is of interevent relations that remain the same throughout the course of information presentation (Fig. 3). Although primacy in contingency or causality judgment would pose a serious challenge to the Rescorla–Wagner model, we again failed to observe it, despite the use of a large number of reversed and revised interevent relations.

It might be argued that Busemeyer's model was put at a competitive disadvantage because we pitted the simple averaging version of his model against the serial averaging model of Rescorla and Wagner. Busemeyer (1991), himself, took no stance regarding the various methods of updating subjects' ratings, leaving it to other investigators to assess their relative suitability. By documenting the superiority of the Rescorla–Wagner model over a simple averaging model, we have provided evidence for a serial averaging account of human causality judgment. The Rescorla–Wagner model, however, goes well beyond any of the information integration models presented by Busemeyer (1991) by including mechanisms to explain *competitive* learning. The Rescorla–Wagner model relies on a serial averaging process for updating judgments within a domain where cues compete with one another for associative strength. It is to the competitive nature of associative learning and causal judgment that we now turn.

III. Judging the Causal Efficacy of Nonpresented Stimuli

The Rescorla–Wagner model was devised to explain the selective nature of conditioning as exemplified by blocking, overshadowing, and conditioned inhibition (Kamin, 1969; Mackintosh, 1975; Williams, this volume, Ch. 3). Rescorla and Wagner argued that a reinforcer can sustain only a limited amount of associative strength; so, simultaneously presented cues will compete with one another for the ability to predict an outcome. Rescorla and Wagner's formulation proposed that the increment in associative strength that accrues to a stimulus on a given trial is proportional to the degree to which the outcome is *un*predicted by the combined associative strengths of *all* of the stimuli present on that trial.

Many workers have recently proposed that selectional processes in human causality judgments also can be described by associative learning models like that of Rescorla and Wagner, but not by noncompetitive accounts like that of Busemeyer (1991). Several researchers have found clear evidence of blocking, overshadowing, and conditioned inhibition in human contingency judgment and causal inference (Baker, Mercier, Vallée-Tourangeau, Frank, & Pan, 1993; Chapman, 1991; Chapman & Robbins, 1990; Dickinson, Shanks, & Evenden, 1984; Gluck & Bower, 1988; Price & Yates, 1993; Shanks, 1986, 1989; Van Hamme & Wasserman, 1993; Williams, Sagness, & McPhee, 1994).

As the evidence described in this chapter suggests, associative models appear to have the greatest potential for providing a process account of how causality judgments are made. But, as it was originally formulated, the Rescorla–Wagner model does not use *all* of the covariation information in the four cells of the contingency table for *each* of the competing cues. Table III shows that the Rescorla–Wagner model directly uses only Cell A and Cell B information for each of the relevant possible causes; it does not directly or completely use Cell C or Cell D information, because cues not present on a trial are assumed not to change immediately in associative strength. The Rescorla–Wagner model uses Cell C and Cell D information in an indirect, nonimmediate way because it assumes that there is a limited

TABLE III

ORIGINAL AND REVISED RESCORLA–WAGNER MODELS

Original Rescorla–Wagner model
    Cue present–outcome present (Cell A): $\Delta V_i = \alpha_1 \beta_1 (\lambda - \Sigma V_k)$
    Cue present–outcome absent (Cell B): $\Delta V_i = \alpha_1 \beta_2 (0 - \Sigma V_k)$

Revised Rescorla–Wagner model
    Cue present–outcome present (Cell A): $\Delta V_i = \alpha_1 \beta_1 (\lambda - \Sigma V_k)$
    Cue present–outcome absent (Cell B): $\Delta V_i = \alpha_1 \beta_2 (0 - \Sigma V_k)$
    Cue absent–outcome present (Cell C): $\Delta V_i = \alpha_2 \beta_1 (\lambda - \Sigma V_k)$
    Cue absent–outcome absent (Cell D): $\Delta V_i = \alpha_2 \beta_2 (0 - \Sigma V_k)$

Note: α_1, Learning rate parameter for cue i present; α_2, learning rate parameter for cue i absent; β_1, learning rate parameter for outcome present; and β_2, learning rate parameter for outcome absent. V_ks are summed only for those cues that are *present* on a given trial.

amount of associative strength available between an outcome and all of the cues presented on a trial. On reinforced (outcome present) trials when a particular cue (N) is not presented (Cell C for cue N), any cue (P) that is presented acquires a portion of this limited amount of associative strength; this portion of the associative strength is then unavailable on later trials when P is presented, including compound-cue (NP) trials. A Cell C trial thus results in the loss of *available* associative strength, rather than in the immediate decrease in a cue's *actual* associative strength. The sequence of trial types P+ : NP+ should (as it does) produce forward blocking, in which the strength of cue N is less after the entire training sequence than it is after NP+ training only. Although the Rescorla–Wagner model readily explains forward blocking, it cannot explain backward blocking (Chapman, 1991; Shanks, 1985b), in which the reverse sequence of trial types, NP+ : P+, results in a lower strength of cue N after the entire sequence than after NP+ training only; according to the Rescorla–Wagner model, the strength of cue N should not change in the second phase because it is not presented then.

The Rescorla–Wagner model can, however, be modified so that it directly and immediately uses and appropriately weights all four types of contingency information by adding equations to reflect Cell C and Cell D information. In this revised model (Van Hamme & Wasserman, 1994; Table III), the strengths of *all* relevant cues are updated on *all* trials, even when individual cues are *not* given. A cue would become relevant after acquiring some level of positive or negative associative strength. For animals, it would be necessary to present the stimulus at least once in the experimental context; for humans, a cue could be made a potential cause with verbal instructions.

For any particular cue, there are, of course, four different types of trial, representing the four types of contingency table information (Cells A, B, C, and D). Revision of the Rescorla–Wagner model to allow the immediate updating of all of this information requires modifying the way in which the model's α and β parameters are applied. In the original version of the model (shown in Table III in a slightly different form than in Equation [2]) applied to all causal cues presented on a trial, the β_1 parameter (on outcome trials) is usually assumed to be larger than the β_2 parameter (on no outcome trials). (Cell A information is weighted more heavily than is Cell B information.) The β_2 parameter retains a nonzero value even when the outcome event is not presented. But, when the causal cue is not presented on Cell C and Cell D trials, the α_2 parameter is always reduced to zero, resulting in no change in the associative strength of the cue on that trial. (Cell C and Cell D information each carry zero weight.) An associative learning model in which the α_2 parameter *also* retains a nonzero (negative)

value when the relevant cue does not occur might better reflect the generation of conditioned responses or causal judgments. (The α_1 parameter on
cue present trials is, of course, nonzero and positive.) The combined $\alpha\beta$
values in the resulting four equations are thus equal to cell information
weightings.

This modification of the Rescorla–Wagner model allows cue and outcome
nonoccurrence to be treated in a *parallel* manner. The Rescorla–Wagner
model does not treat these two types of event consistently; it assumes
that outcome nonoccurrence is a salient event because a prior history
of cue–outcome pairings has made a cue–no outcome event unexpected.
Changes in associative strength are proportional to the difference between
actual and expected outcomes. The model implicitly assumes that cue nonoccurrence has no salience. The modified model assumes that missing input
cues—as well as missing output cues—are actively encoded as *absent*.[6] This
modification results in changes in the predictive strength of absent cues.
Outcome expectancy, however, is derived from the sum of the associative
strengths for those cues that are actually *present* on a given trial (see
Table III).

This revised Rescorla–Wagner model is able to predict effects—like
backward blocking, backward conditioned inhibition, and recovery from
overshadowing—that have been observed in studies of humans' and animals' sensitivity to interevent contingencies, but are not predicted by the
original Rescorla–Wagner model (Chapman, 1991; Miller & Matzel, 1988;
Miller & Schactman, 1985; Shanks, 1985b). All of these effects involve
the apparent *retrospective* processing of stimuli: changes in the associative

---

[6] Markman (1989) previously suggested this modification of the Rescorla–Wagner equations
in a connectionist model. Markman's model encodes the presence of a feature with an activation
level of 1 and the absence of a feature with an activation level of -1. (In most connectionist
models, a nonpresented cue is assigned an activation level of 0.) His model, therefore, assumes
that the *absolute* values of the weights attached to cue presence and cue absence are equal
($\alpha_1 = \alpha_2$ in the modified Rescorla–Wagner model shown in Table III). And, because this
connectionist model was used to simulate a categorization problem—predicting which of two
outcomes will occur given a particular set of input cues rather than predicting the occurrence
or nonoccurrence of a single outcome—the weights attached to each of the two outcomes
were also equal ($\beta_1 = \beta_2$). All four types of contingency table information were thus weighted
equally in that application of Markman's model. The four different types of information
represented by the four possible combinations of the presence and absence of the cue and
the outcome could, however, be appropriately *weighted* according to the type of contingency
table information that they represent by choosing values for the α and β parameters so that
$|\alpha_1\beta_1| > |\alpha_1\beta_2| <=> |\alpha_2\beta_1| > |\alpha_2\beta_2|$ (Cell A > Cell B <=> Cell C > Cell D). This strategy
would be preferable to that used by Markman because it would more accurately reflect the
way in which subjects actually use these four types of contingency information (Kao &
Wasserman, 1993; Levin et al., 1993; Wasserman et al., 1990). Tassoni (1995) has adopted
this strategy in his recent connectionist model of effect $\rightarrow$ cause judgment.

strength of a stimulus after a series of trials on which the stimulus is *not* presented.

Chapman (1991) and Shanks (1985b), for instance, found backward blocking in human causality judgments. Chapman (1991) also found backward conditioned inhibition; NP−:P+ training produced ratings of cue N that were lower than those produced by NP− training only. According to the Rescorla–Wagner model, the strength of cue N should not change in the second phase because it is not presented then. The revised associative model does, however, predict backward conditioned inhibition, because the second phase represents Cell C information for cue N, which is negative contingency information. Although backward blocking and backward conditioned inhibition have not been observed in animals, Kaufman and Bolles (1981) and Matzel, Schactman, and Miller (1985) have reported "retrospective" changes in responding in an animal conditioning procedure that they called "recovery from overshadowing." Rats were given the trial sequence NP+:P−. Conditioned responding to cue N was greater for subjects given the entire sequence than for subjects given only NP+ training, suggesting an increase in the response strength of cue N during the second phase. According to the original Rescorla–Wagner model, the strength of cue N should not change in the second phase, because it is not presented then. The revised Rescorla–Wagner model does predict recovery from overshadowing, however, because the second phase represents Cell D information for cue N, which is positive contingency information.

Van Hamme and Wasserman (1994) began development and assessment of the newly revised associative model by seeing if the causal ratings of a cue do immediately change when the cue is not presented, but is nevertheless rated on a particular trial. Their results supported the possibility that the judged efficacy of a potential causal factor *does* change during stimulus events in which the factor is *not* present. Rating changes were appropriately related to the specific type of contingency table information (Cells C and D) provided by the experienced events. Impetus was thus given for the exploration of an associative model of causal or contingency judgments that immediately uses and appropriately weights *all* of the contingency table information.

Because our earlier experiment (Van Hamme & Wasserman, 1994) did not involve any "retrospective" processing procedures, Experiments 4 and 5 were designed to test further our revision of the Rescorla–Wagner model (Table III) by explicitly comparing its predictions with those of the original Rescorla–Wagner formulation. Experiment 4 entailed forward and backward blocking and recovery from overshadowing procedures. Experiment 5 entailed forward and backward conditioned inhibition and comparator control procedures.

A. EXPERIMENT 4

In this experiment (Van Hamme, 1994), blocking procedures were implemented in a probabilistic rather than a deterministic manner so that information from all four cells of the contingency table could be given for all of the rated cues. Shanks (1985b) has previously demonstrated that probabilistic procedures produce strong forward and backward blocking effects. Experiment 4 extended previous work (Chapman, 1991; Shanks, 1985b; Waldmann & Holyoak, 1992) that has used blocking procedures to investigate human causality judgments by, for the first time, obtaining subjects' judgments of the causal efficacy of *all* relevant cues on *each* trial.

Both forward and backward blocking procedures were studied. A third procedure was also included, in which the first phase was identical to the backward blocking condition, but the second involved "deflation" of the comparator stimulus $(AX + : A -)$. This "recovery from overshadowing" procedure has not previously been employed in human causality judgment research. The original Rescorla–Wagner model predicts that forward blocking will occur and that neither backward blocking nor recovery from overshadowing will occur. The revised Rescorla–Wagner model predicts that both forward and backward blocking will occur, that backward blocking will be smaller than forward blocking, and that recovery from overshadowing will occur. Both the original and revised Rescorla–Wagner models predict that incremental acquisition curves will be observed; but, the predicted curves should differ substantially from one another during "retrospective" revaluation procedures.

1. Method

A total of 54 subjects were asked to rate three possible causes of one effect; the effect was an allergic reaction and the potential causes were different foods. Three different sets of foods were used and were counterbalanced across the three conditions: (1) bananas, peas, and chicken; (2) peaches, cabbage, and pork; and (3) blueberries, corn, and beef. Each subject made ratings in all three conditions (Forward Blocking [FB], Backward Blocking [BB], and Recovery from Overshadowing [ROS]). Within each condition, the three foods were designated elements X, A, and B, with the potentially blocked or overshadowed cue always designated element X and the blocking or overshadowing cue always designated element A. Element B was present on trials in which neither element X nor element A was present. Element B trials were necessary because of the probabilistic nature of the procedures. Each subject was randomly assigned to one of three conditions to counterbalance which food set was used in each condition and which food (within each set) was indicated by each stimulus element (X, A, or B).

The order of presentation of the three conditions was also counterbalanced. Table IV shows the three conditions; the number and type of trials presented are summarized in contingency tables. The allergic reaction is designated Q. The trial orders were randomly determined for each subject. The two phases of the three conditions were divided into two blocks of 12 trials. All of the computer equipment was the same as in the first three experiments described in this article.

The within-subjects design and counterbalancing of stimuli and presentation order allowed use of Phase 1 of the Backward Blocking condition (BB-1) and Phase 1 of the procedurally identical Recovery from Overshadowing condition (ROS-1) as controls to assess both forward and backward blocking. Ratings of element X were compared at the end of BB-1 and ROS-1 with ratings of element X at the end of Phase 2 in both blocking conditions (FB-2 and BB-2).

Before seeing any contingency information, the subjects were told which three foods they would be asked to assess in order to make *all* of the stimulus elements relevant causal cues at that point. On each trial, subjects saw information about the results of 1 day of a hypothetical allergy test; the information included which of the relevant foods were eaten on that day followed by information about whether or not an allergic reaction occurred. Subjects were asked to use *all* of the information that they had seen *up to that point* to estimate the extent to which eating each of the three foods affected the likelihood that the allergic reaction would occur. Subjects were also asked to make an initial estimate of each food's causal

TABLE IV

CONTINGENCY TABLE SUMMARIES OF THE NUMBER AND TYPE OF
TRIALS IN EXPERIMENT 4

		Phase 1			Phase 2	
		Q^a	No Q		Q	No Q
Forward blocking	A	10	2	AX	10	2
	B	2	10	B	2	10
	X rating $= -12.39$			X rating $= 21.76$		
Backward blocking	AX	10	2	A	10	2
	B	2	10	B	2	10
	X rating $= 68.54$			X rating $= 15.09$		
Recovery from overshadowing	AX	10	2	A	2	10
	B	2	10	B	2	10
	X rating $= 65.70$			X rating $= 58.33$		

[a] A, B, and X are possible causes; Q is the possible effect.

efficacy *before* they saw any contingency information; these initial estimates were used to assess the effectiveness of the counterbalancing procedures in eliminating differences in prior expectancies regarding the causal effectiveness of food X in the three conditions. Subjects expressed their ratings as a number from -100 to 100. The following written instructions appeared on subjects' computer screens:

Screen 1

Thank you for participating in this experiment. Your complete cooperation and attention are vital to the success of this project. You will be instructed step by step through the screens. Please follow the instructions carefully.

Screen 2

Imagine that you are an allergist who is trying to determine what causes an allergic reaction that sometimes occurs shortly after your patient eats dinner. You arrange that the patient eat particular foods at dinner over a series of evenings and then report to you whether an allergic reaction followed. The results of the allergy test series will be shown to you on a series of screens. You will see a separate screen for each day of the allergy test. On each screen, you will be told what the patient ate for dinner that day and if there was an allergic reaction. The foods being tested are: [Food A] [Food X] [Food B].

Before seeing any of the allergy test results, we would like you to make a guess about the extent to which eating each of these foods might affect the likelihood of an allergic reaction. You will be given instructions about how to make these guesses on the next screen.

Screen 3

Use the following rating scale to make your initial guesses about the extent to which eating each of the foods might affect the likelihood of an allergic reaction.

-100	-80	-60	-40	-20	0	20	40	60	80	100

Makes	Doesn't	Makes
Very	Affect	Very
Unlikely	Likelihood	Likely

that an allergic reaction will occur

Type in any number between −100 and +100 to indicate your initial guess about the extent to which eating [Food A] affects the likelihood of an allergic reaction.

Type in any number between −100 and +100 to indicate your initial guess about the extent to which eating [Food X] affects the likelihood of an allergic reaction.

Type in any number between −100 and +100 to indicate your initial guess about the extent to which eating [Food B] affects the likelihood of an allergic reaction.

Screen 4

On the following screens, you will see a description of each day of the allergy test. After seeing each day's test result, you will be asked to make new estimates for each food about the extent to which each affects the likelihood of the allergic reaction. Use the rating scale shown below to make your daily estimates. This is the same rating scale you used for your initial estimates. When you make your estimates, always consider *all* of the information you have received up to that point—*not* just the last day.

```
←-----------------------------------------------------------------→
 −100   −80   −60   −40   −20   0   20   40   60   80   100
←-----------------------------------------------------------------→
```

Makes	Doesn't	Makes
Very	Affect	Very
Unlikely	Likelihood	Likely

that an allergic reaction will occur

Screens 5 to 52

Day [   ]
Patient ate [   ]
Allergic Reaction? [   ]

Type in any number between −100 and +100 to indicate your estimate of the extent to which eating [Food A] affects the likelihood of the allergic reaction. Your previous estimate was [   ].

Type in any number between −100 and +100 to indicate your estimate of the extent to which eating [Food X] affects the likelihood of the allergic reaction. Your previous estimate was [   ].

Type in any number between −100 and +100 to indicate your estimate of the extent to which eating [Food B] affects the likelihood of the allergic reaction. Your previous estimate was [   ].

Items in brackets [ ] were completed with the appropriate information.

a. Selection of Parameters for the Associative Models   The values chosen for the revised Rescorla–Wagner model were based on the cell weights derived by Kao (1993): the α_1, α_2, β_1, and β_2 values were .70, −.40, .50, and .40, respectively. The α_2 value used for predictions of the original Rescorla–Wagner model was, of course, .00. Choosing a single set of parameters to use for all subjects was purely for the sake of simplicity, as changes in the parameters of the two models affect only the magnitude (but not the direction) of change on a trial and the number of trials to asymptote. These parameters resulted in the following absolute cell weights: Cell A = .35; Cell B = .28; Cell C = .20, and Cell D = .16. The λ parameter was set to 1.00.

2.   Results

The dependent measures were the initial and trial-by-trial estimates of the extent to which the foods represented by element X were causally related to the allergic reaction.[7]

a. Initial Ratings   Subjects' mean initial ratings of element X did not differ reliably among the three conditions: FB = 16.20; BB = 27.41; and ROS = 18.22.

b. Final Ratings   Ratings of element X at the end of each phase of the three conditions are designated: (1) Forward Blocking Phase 1 (FB-1); (2) Forward Blocking Phase 2 (FB-2); (3) Backward Blocking Phase 1 (BB-1); (4) Backward Blocking Phase 2 (BB-2); (5) Recovery from Overshadowing Phase 1 (ROS-1); and (6) Recovery from Overshadowing Phase 2 (ROS-2). Subjects' mean scores are shown in Table IV. The reliable overall analysis of variance was followed up by several strategic analyses.

The difference between (BB-1 + ROS-1)/2 (67.12) and FB-2 (21.76) was reliable, indicating forward blocking, because element X had a lower rating after the A+ : AX+ trials represented by Phases 1 and 2 of the FB condition than it had after only the AX+ trials represented by the BB-1 and ROS-1 phases. There was also a reliable difference between (BB-1 + ROS-1)/ 2 (67.12) and BB-2 (15.09), indicating backward blocking, because element X had a lower rating after the AX+ : A+ trials represented by Phase 1 and 2 of the BB condition than it had after only the AX+ trials represented

---

[7] Although subjects rated the foods represented by all three stimulus elements (X, A, and B) on every trial, analyses are reported only for the target cue, X. The reason for this selective portrayal is that the results of the other cues (A and B) do not critically differ between the rival theories being tested. A full account of the remaining results is contained in Van Hamme (1994).

by the BB-1 and ROS-1 phases. FB-2 (21.76) did not differ reliably from BB-2 (15.09), indicating that forward and backward blocking were similar in size. There was also no reliable difference between ROS-1 (65.70) and ROS-2 (58.33), indicating that recovery from overshadowing did not occur. Recovery from overshadowing would have been demonstrated if element X had been rated higher after the AX+ : A− trials represented by Phases 1 and 2 of the ROS condition than it was after only the AX+ trials represented by ROS-1. Finally, ROS-2 (58.33) differed reliably from BB-2 (15.09), showing that backward blocking was not due to forgetting. Element X was not presented in either BB-2 (A+ trials) or ROS-2 (A−trials). Had backward blocking been due to forgetting alone, the differential treatment of another cue (A) in Phase 2 should not have affected ratings of element X in that phase, and ratings of element X after BB-2 and ROS-2 should not have differed.

The forward blocking observed in this experiment is predicted by both the original and the revised Rescorla–Wagner models. The obtained backward blocking is predicted by the revised Rescorla–Wagner model, but not by the original model. The failure to observe recovery from overshadowing is predicted by the original, but not by the revised, Rescorla–Wagner model.

c. Trial-by-Trial Ratings As in the prior experiments reported in this article, the final ratings were achieved by gradual increments or decrements. The resulting learning curves better accorded with the revised associative model than with the original. As one illustration, Fig. 8A shows subjects' actual ratings of element X during the 48 trials of the BB problem along with the ratings that were predicted by the original and revised models using the selected parameters. Subjects' ratings of element X gradually decreased in Phase 2 of the Backward Blocking procedure, as predicted by the revised model; the original Rescorla–Wagner model predicts that ratings of element X should remain constant throughout BB-2, because it is not presented during that period.

To assess the fit of these two models to subjects' learning curves in all of the training conditions, correlations compared the mean trial-by-trial ratings across the 54 individual simulations predicted by the original and revised Rescorla–Wagner models to the mean trial-by-trial ratings computed across the 54 subjects. The 54 stimulations were needed because each subject received a different randomized order of information presentation. The correlation of the revised model with subjects' ratings substantially exceeded that of the original model in all three conditions (FB: RW = .181, REV = .828; BB: RW = .107, REV = .933; ROS: RW = .582, REV = .832).

The failure to observe recovery from overshadowing (an increase in ratings of element X from ROS-1 to ROS-2) may have been due to a

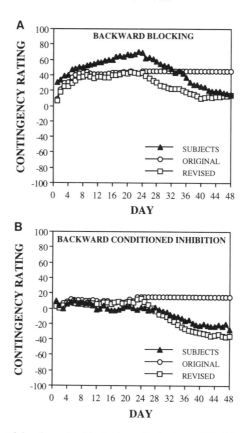

Fig. 8. Trial-by-trial ratings of subjects given the backward blocking (Experiment 4) and backward conditioned inhibition (Experiment 5) problems along with those predicted by Rescorla and Wagner's associative learning model and by the revision of their model by Van Hamme and Wasserman (1994).

"ceiling" effect for element X. A low level of baseline training (ROS-1) might be required if one is to observe an increase in ratings of element X during ROS-2. A high baseline that is sensitive to backward blocking is often not sensitive to recovery from overshadowing (R. R. Miller, personal communication, 1993).

B.   EXPERIMENT 5

Backward conditioned inhibition (Chapman, 1991) in human multiple-cue causality judgments represents a further serious challenge to associative interpretations. The original Rescorla–Wagner model predicts forward conditioned inhibition from $A+ : AX-$ training, in which element X becomes inhibitory as a result of its nonreinforced presentation in compound with element A that has previously acquired positive associative strength; it does not, however, predict conditioned inhibition when the training order is reversed (AX−:A+). Chapman (1991) found reliable backward conditioned inhibition that was smaller than forward conditioned inhibition.

Experiment 5 (Van Hamme, 1994) involved forward and backward conditioned inhibition procedures that were implemented in a probabilistic manner. It included a third condition that involved no change in the relation of the comparator stimulus with the outcome between the first and second phases (AX− : A−) as a control for forgetting in the backward conditioned inhibition condition.

The original Rescorla–Wagner model predicts that forward conditioned inhibition will occur and that backward conditioned inhibition will not occur. The revised Rescorla–Wagner model predicts that both forward and backward conditioned inhibition will occur and that the backward effect will be smaller than the forward effect. Both the original and revised models predict that gradual acquisition curves will be observed; but, they make decidedly different predictions concerning these curves during the "retrospective" revaluation phase.

1. Method

Another 54 subjects were asked to make ratings about three possible causes of one effect. The instructions were identical to those used in Experiment 4. The same foods were used and were counterbalanced in the same manner as in Experiment 4. Table V outlines the three conditions. The number

TABLE V

CONTINGENCY TABLE SUMMARIES OF THE NUMBER AND TYPE OF
TRIALS IN EXPERIMENT 5

		Phase 1			Phase 2	
		Q^a	No Q		Q	No Q
Forward conditioned inhibition	A	10	2	AX	2	10
	B	2	10	B	2	10
	X rating = −14.37			X rating = −33.98		
Backward conditioned inhibition	AX	2	10	A	10	2
	B	2	10	B	2	10
	X rating = 1.93			X rating = −27.22		
Comparator control	AX	2	10	A	2	10
	B	2	10	B	2	10
	X rating = −1.26			X rating = −9.31		

[a] A, B, and X are possible causes; Q is the possible effect.

and type of trials presented are summarized in contingency tables. Each subject made ratings in all three conditions (Forward Conditioned Inhibition [FCI], Backward Conditioned Inhibition [BCI], and Comparator Control [CON]). Within each condition, the three foods were designated elements X, A, and B, with the potentially inhibitory cue always designated element X and the comparator cue always designated element A. The order of presentation of the three conditions was also counterbalanced. The trial orders were randomly determined for each subject. The two phases of the three conditions were divided into two blocks of 12 trials.

The within-subjects procedure and complete counterbalancing of stimuli and presentation order allowed use of Phase 1 of the Backward Conditioned Inhibition condition (BCI-1) and Phase 1 of the procedurally identical Comparator Control condition (CON-1) as controls to assess both forward and backward conditioned inhibition.

2. Results

a. Initial Ratings Subjects' means initial ratings of element X did not differ reliably among the three conditions: FCI = 10.56; BCI = 14.81; and CON = 22.11.

b. Final Ratings Ratings of element X at the end of each phase of the three conditions are designated: (1) Forward Conditioned Inhibition Phase 1 (FCI-1); (2) Forward Conditioned Inhibition Phase 2 (FCI-2); (3) Backward Conditioned Inhibition Phase 1 (BCI-1); (4) Backward Conditioned Inhibition Phase 2 (BCI-2); (5) Comparator Control Phase 1 (CON-1); and (6) Comparator Control Phase 2 (CON-2). Subjects' mean scores are shown in Table V. The reliable overall analysis of variance was followed up by several strategic analyses.

The difference between (BCI-1 + CON-1)/2 (0.34) and FCI-2 (−33.98) was reliable, indicating forward conditioned inhibition, because element X had a lower rating after A+ : AX− trials represented by Phases 1 and 2 of the FCI condition than it had after only AX− trials represented by the BCI-1 and CON-1 phases. There was also a reliable difference between (BCI-1 + CON-1)/2 (0.34) and BCI-2 (−27.22), indicating backward conditioned inhibition, because element X had a lower rating after AX− : A+ trials represented by Phases 1 and 2 of the BCI condition than it had after only AX− trials represented by the BCI-1 and CON-1 phases. FCI-2 (−33.98) did not differ reliably from BCI-2 (−27.22), indicating that forward and backward conditioned inhibition were of similar size. Finally, BCI-2 (−27.22) differed reliably from CON-2 (−9.31), indicating that backward conditioned inhibition was not due to forgetting. Element X was not presented in either BCI-2 (A+ trials) or CON-2 (A− trials). If backward conditioned inhibition had been due to forgetting, then the differential treatment of another cue (A) in Phase 2 should not have affected ratings of element X and, thus, ratings of element X should not have differed after BCI-2 and CON-2.

The forward conditioned inhibition observed in this experiment is predicted by both the original and the revised Rescorla–Wagner models. The obtained backward conditioned inhibition is predicted by the revised Rescorla–Wagner model, but not by the original.

c. Trial-by-Trial Ratings   The final ratings again emerged from gradual increments or decrements. The obtained learning curves better accorded with the revised associative model than with the original. As one illustration, Fig. 8B shows subjects' actual ratings of element X during the 48 trials of the BCI problem along with the ratings that were predicted by the original and revised models using the selected parameters. Subjects' ratings of element X gradually decreased in Phase 2 of the Backward Conditioned Inhibition procedure, as predicted by the revised model; the original Rescorla–Wagner model predicts that ratings of element X should remain constant throughout BCI-2, because it is not presented during that period.

To assess the fit of these two models to subjects' learning curves in all of the training conditions, correlations compared the mean trial-by-trial ratings across the 54 individual simulations predicted by the original and revised Rescorla–Wagner models to the mean trial-by-trial ratings computed across the 54 subjects. The correlation of the revised model with subjects' ratings substantially exceeded that of the original model in two of the three conditions: the Backward Conditioned Inhibition condition (RW = −.619, REV = .938) and the Comparator Control condition (RW = −.015, REV = .382). The original model better correlated with subjects' ratings in the Forward Conditioned Inhibition condition (RW = .926, REV = .726).

3.   Discussion of Experiments 4 and 5

These two experiments provide good evidence that the revised associative model can indeed predict and explain "retrospective" revaluation effects that are unpredictable and unexplainable by the original Rescorla–Wagner model. Experiment 4 demonstrated a backward blocking effect predicted only by the revised model as well as a forward blocking effect predicted by both models. Experiment 5 demonstrated a backward conditioned inhibition effect predicted only by the revised model as well as a forward conditioned inhibition effect predicted by both models.

In prior research on "retrospective" processing effects in human contingency judgment, ratings of individual cues have been obtained only at the *end* of each phase of the experimental procedures (Chapman, 1991; Shanks, 1985b). Subjects in the present experiments rated *all* of the relevant causal cues on *each* trial, whether or not a cue was actually presented on that trial. This procedural innovation allowed us to compare subjects' trial-by-trial ratings with the trial-by-trial predictions of both associative models. The momentary comparisons were accomplished by computing correlations of the predictions of each model with subjects' trial-by-trial ratings. For the target cue (element X), the revised model was more highly correlated with subjects' mean trial-by-trial ratings than the original model in five of the six conditions (forward conditioned inhibition was the sole exception), providing further support for our modification of the Rescorla–Wagner model.

Experiment 4 did not yield a recovery from overshadowing effect that has previously been assessed and observed only in animal conditioning studies. Additional research using baselines of varying strength for the target cue will be needed to determine if this "retrospective" processing effect can be demonstrated in human contingency judgment. A lower level of baseline training than that given here might be required in order to allow an increase in ratings of the target cue during the second phase of the recovery from overshadowing procedure.

The precise trial order effects observed in Chapman's (1991) experiments—in which backward blocking was weaker than forward blocking and in which backward conditioned inhibition was weaker than forward conditioned inhibition—were not observed in the present experiments. Consistent with the present results, but inconsistent with those of Chapman, Shanks (1985b) also reported that forward and backward blocking effects did not differ in magnitude. These disparate results will necessitate further experiments elucidating whether the exact trial order effects predicted by associative models occur in human causal and contingency judgment.

There is also a need for further theoretical development of the revised Rescorla–Wagner model. Although the revised model may represent an improvement in the original, it makes some predictions that might be considered to be unusual in the traditional context of associative learning. It could be argued that changes in the associative strength of nonpresented cues should be limited to those cues whose associative history makes their absence *unexpected*. For instance, in the backward blocking condition, subjects received AX+ trials followed by A+ trials. Because X was previously presented together with A, the absence of X in the second phase is unexpected and the revised model correctly predicts that the stength of X will decrease in Phase 2. The revised model also predicts, however, that the strength of *all* other relevant cues (cues having *any* level of positive or negative associative strength) will also decrease on A+ trials. The change in associative strength is therefore not specific to cues that have previously appeared together with A.

The lack of cue specificity may not be problematic if it is considered in the larger context of integrating the positive features of various models of human and animal contingency learning. The human contingency judgment literature provides abundant support for the notion that Cell C information—in which a relevant cue is not presented and the outcome does occur—is considered important by subjects, even when no information is provided concerning which cues (if any) are present on a trial. Contingency judgment research, however, sometimes differs from Experiments 4 and 5 and from investigations of animal conditioning in one possibly important respect: subjects may be given explicit information about the presence and *absence* of a cue (Tassoni, 1995), as they were in Experiments 1, 2, and 3, where information was provided that the fertilizer was not given on Cell C and Cell D trials. In Experiments 4 and 5, on the other hand, subjects were informed only about which putative causes were *present,* not absent, on a particular trial.

Cell C trials provide information about the lack of necessity of a cue for an outcome to occur. The revised Rescorla–Wagner model attempts to add consideration of the *necessity* of a cue to the *sufficiency* information that is addressed by other associative models. Both types of information are addressed by statistical models like Busemeyer's (1991) and are required for an accurate judgment of contingency or causality. Even though the conditions in Experiments 4 and 5—in which no explicit information about the absence of a cue was given—represent a fairly realistic multiple-cue learning situation for both humans and animals, additional theoretical and empirical consideration should be given to the manner in which cues are identified as relevant in real-life situations.

If empirical research proves to demand it, then specificity of associative change could be incorporated by invoking the idea of within-compound association (see Dickinson & Burke, 1996, and Shanks et al., this volume, Ch. 7, for application of within-compound association to possible associative changes in nonpresented stimuli during "retrospective" revaluation procedures). In addition to the traditional assumption that compound stimulus training results in each of the individual elements separately forming an association with the outcome, there is considerable evidence that, at least in certain situations, associations are formed between the individual elements of the compound stimulus (Cunningham, 1981; Rescorla & Durlach, 1981; Williams, Travis, & Overmier, 1986). So, information tantamount to that in Cells C and D could arise if one or more elements of a familiar compound were given *without* the target element. Rules specifying the nature of within-compound associations might be derivable from the

Rescorla–Wagner model itself or from the more recent model of Wagner (1981).

IV. Competition among Uncorrelated Cues

Although we have not yet subjected the matter to empirical test, we did have the initial hunch that our recent revision of the Rescorla–Wagner model might be able to contend with another possible shortcoming of the original model: namely, that, at least at asymptote, it does not predict competition among statistically *independent* cues (Busemeyer, Myung, & McDaniel, 1993a, 1993b).[8] This hunch was based on our revised model's direct incorporation of Cell C and Cell D information, information that may become especially relevant when two putative causes occur alone, as they must when neither is statistically associated with the other.

Before testing the matter empirically, we decided that it would be prudent to conduct several simulations of one of the most basic of cue competition effects, overshadowing, with the kinds of *discrete* variables that are customarily used in the field of human contingency and causal judgment. Such a move is justified considering that Busemeyer et al. (1993a, 1993b) had conducted their empirical and theoretical tests of cue competition only with *continuous* input and output variables.[9] Perhaps their criticism of models like that of Rescorla and Wagner might not generalize to the kinds of judgment situations that have concerned us in this chapter.

Table VI illustrates one set of contingency information to which we applied the original Rescorla–Wagner model and our own recent revision of it. The upper left portion of the table shows the key condition, in which both stimulus A and stimulus B are equally often presented; each cue is equally correlated with the outcome ($\Delta p = 48/48 - 24/48 = 1.00 - .50 = .50$), but the two cues are completely uncorrelated with one another. This is the condition that, at asymptote, Busemeyer el al. believe should not

---

[8] Busemeyer et al. (1993a, 1993b) never directly discussed the Rescorla–Wagner model in their paired papers. Instead, they concentrated their discussion on adaptive network models that are closely related to the Rescorla–Wagner formulation. We have therefore assumed for the present discussion that Busemeyer et al. would have made similar arguments concerning the ability of the Rescorla–Wagner to predict cue competition with uncorrelated predictive stimuli.

[9] In Busemeyer et al.'s (1993a) experimental situation, the two predictive stimuli were presented on *every* trial and they assumed numerical values between 10 and 90. The predicted variable was also presented on *every* trial and it assumed numerical values between 140 and 260. Under these particular circumstances, subjects gave evidence of cue competition when the predictive stimuli were statistically uncorrelated with one another. This situation is very different from those of most studies of causal or contingency judgment, in which putative causes and their possible effects are either presented or not on any given trial.

TABLE VI

Contingencies Submitted to Simulation with the Original
Rescorla–Wagner (1972) Model and with Its Revision by
Van Hamme and Wasserman (1994)

| | Both A and B presented[a] | | Only A presented | |
	B present	B absent	B present	B absent
Uncorrelated				
A present	24+, 0−	24+, 0−	0+, 0−	48+, 0−
A absent	24+, 0−	0+, 24−	0+, 0−	24+, 24−
Correlated				
A present	48+, 0−	0+, 0−	0+, 0−	48+, 0−
A absent	0+, 0−	24+, 24−	0+, 0−	24+, 24−

[a] A and B are putative causes of an effect that either does (+) or does not (−) occur on a trial.

produce cue competition between stimulus A and stimulus B in models like that of Rescorla and Wagner. In order to assess cue competition in this two-cue condition, we included the one-cue condition shown in the upper right portion of Table VI. Here, stimulus A alone is given for the same number of trials as it is in the two-cue condition and with the same correlation with the outcome. Overshadowing would be shown if the associative strength of stimulus A were lower in the A and B condition than in the A only condition.

The conventional condition for assessing overshadowing involves the case where stimulus A and stimulus B are perfectly correlated with one another, neither cue being presented alone; this case is shown in the lower left portion of Table VI. As in the uncorrelated condition directly above it, stimulus A and stimulus B here are equally correlated with the outcome; indeed, stimulus A and stimulus B are equally correlated with the outcome in both the correlated and uncorrelated conditions. The control condition for overshadowing is shown in the lower right portion of Table VI. Here, stimulus A is presented for the same number of trials as it is in the A and B condition and with the same correlation with the outcome. In fact, we contrived the two-cue contigencies so that their appropriate one-cue controls would be equivalent for the cases of correlated and uncorrelated cues; so, the upper right and lower right contingencies in Table VI are the same. Overshadowing would again be shown if the associative strength of stimulus A were lower in the A and B condition than in the A only condition.

We conducted the simulations with the following parameters: α_1 for stimulus A and stimulus B was set at .35; α_2 was set at $-.20$ for the revised model and at .00 for the original Rescorla–Wagner model; β_1 was set at

.25; and β_2 was set at .20. Because different conventions exist in the literature for assigning salience to background stimuli, we conducted the simulations with two different values for background salience: in one case we set α_1 for the background equal to .35 (the same as for stimulus A and stimulus B), whereas in the other case we set α_1 for the background equal to .035 (an order of magnitude lower than for stimulus A or stimulus B) (see Experiment 1). Ten 96-trial simulations under the two background salience conditions were run for each of the three different contingencies shown in Table VI: A and B uncorrelated, A and B correlated, and A only.

The key results of these simulations are illustrated in Fig. 9. The depicted scores represent the *difference* in associative strength of stimulus A between the *one*-cue and *two*-cue conditions over the last 16 trials. Positive difference scores represent overshadowing of stimulus A by stimulus B; a difference

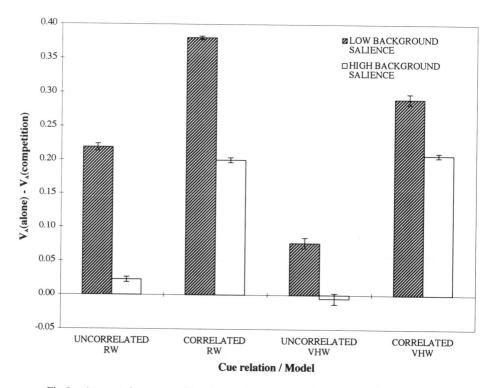

Fig. 9. Amount of cue competition observed between correlated cues and between uncorrelated cues in 96-trial stimulations of Rescorla and Wagner's (RW) associative learning model and the Van Hamme and Wasserman (VHW) (1994) revision. Competition (in this case, overshadowing) is operationalized as the decrease in associative strength of a cue when training includes an additional (uncorrelated or correlated) cue. Standard error bars are included.

score of zero represents no overshadowing of stimulus A by stimulus B; and negative difference scores represent facilitation of stimulus A by stimulus B. There are two surprises in Fig. 9. First, unlike the results expected from Busemeyer et al.'s (1993a, 1993b) anaysis of asymptotic performance, during this period of training the original Rescorla–Wagner model *does* predict overshadowing in the case of uncorrelated cues; statistically reliable overshadowing was seen under both context salience conditions, although the overshadowing effect was larger with lower context salience. The strength of overshadowing was larger still when the cues were perfectly correlated with one another. The second surprise was that the modified model made essentially the same predictions as did the original, with the size of the predicted overshadowing effects generally being smaller. With uncorrelated cues, only under the low context salience condition did the revised model predict a statistically reliable overshadowing effect; with correlated cues, the revised model predicted statistically reliable overshadowing effects under both salience conditions.

It is, of course, possible that 96 trials may be insufficient for performance to have reached asymptote. To address this possibility, we examined performance over time and determined that 800 trials provided ample opportunity for the models to reach a stable point. The results from the last 16 trials of these 10 simulations are shown in Fig. 10. The competition among correlated cues remained strong. In accord with Busemeyer et al.'s (1993a, 1993b) analysis of asymptotic performance, competition among uncorrelated cues was close to zero for both the original and the modified models. Surprisingly, both models predicted minor facilitation of stimulus A rather than competition when stimulus B was present (although the facilitation for the revised model in the low salience background condition was not statistically significant). The presence of the second cue actually overshadowed the background, an important result when the background is highly salient and is thus a strong competitor for control by stimulus A. Uncorrelated cues are therefore predicted by these two associative models to compete *early* in training, but not to do so *late* in training. It is, of course, difficult to determine whether an individual subject's performance has in fact reached asymptote. According to both versions of the Rescorla–Wagner model, any failure to provide sufficient training can result in demonstrable competition among uncorrelated cues.

We therefore conclude that our revised model does not need to repair the original Rescorla–Wagner theory to enable it ever to predict cue competition among uncorrelated cues; the original theory *already* predicts preasymptotic cue competition. The analysis of Busemeyer et al. (1993b) does correctly indicate that adaptive network models of the same general sort as that of Rescorla and Wagner may fail to show competition among uncor-

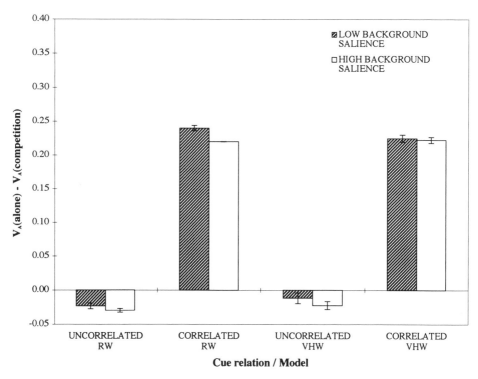

Fig. 10.   Amount of cue competition observed between correlated cues and between uncorrelated cues in 800-trial simulations of Rescorla and Wagner's (RW) associative learning
model and the Van Hamme and Wasserman (VHW) (1994) revision. Competition (in this
case, overshadowing) is operationalized as the decrease in associative strength of a cue when
training includes an additional (uncorrelated or correlated) cue. Standard error bars are included.

related cues; our simulations indicate that their analysis holds true only
when subjects' performance is at or near asymptote, and that both the
original and revised versions of the Rescorla–Wagner model actually predict asymptotic facilitation among cues in the presence of a salient background.

V.   Concluding Comments

Notwithstanding occasional empirical inconsistencies (Miller, Barnet, &
Grahame, 1995; Williams, this volume, Ch. 3) and vigorous theoretical
challenges (Busemeyer et al., 1993b; Cheng & Holyoak, 1995; Waldmann &

Holyoak, 1992), pursuit of associative theories of human causal judgment is amply justified by the considerable evidence from prior research and from the present investigations disclosing notable similarities between the factors determining animals' conditioned responses and humans' causal judgments.

Although it may be surprising to some, Edward Thorndike, whose intrepid thesis introduced the present chapter, would surely not have been surprised by this empirical state of affairs. Nor would David Hume (1739/1964), whose idea of association was central to his eighteenth-century theory of causal judgment (see Fales & Wasserman, 1992). Both Thorndike and Hume, we believe, would be truly delighted that a mechanistic theory of association can be rendered mathematically and that it appears to be the most attractive current account of causal judgment.

ACKNOWLEDGMENTS

We gratefully acknowledge the financial support of the research reported in this chapter from numerous sources: a James Van Allen Natural Science Fellowship and a research award from the Vice President for Research at the University of Iowa to Wasserman, Don Lewis dissertation awards from the Department of Psychology at the University of Iowa to Kao and Van Hamme, an American Psychological Association Division 25 dissertation award to Van Hamme, and an award from the Japanese Ministry of Education to Katagiri.

REFERENCES

Allan, L. G. (1993). Human contingency judgments: Rule based or associative? *Psychological Bulletin, 114,* 435–438.
Anderson, N. H. (1981). *Foundations of information integration theory.* New York: Academic Press.
Anderson, N. H. (1982). *Methods of information integration theory.* New York: Academic Press.
Arkes, H. R., & Harkness, A. R. (1983). Estimates of contingency between two dichotomous variables. *Journal of Experimental Psychology: General, 112,* 117–135.
Baker, A. G., Berbrier, M. W., & Vallée-Tourangeau, F. (1989). Judgments of a 2 × 2 contingency table: Sequential processing and the learning curve. *Quarterly Journal of Experimental Psychology, 41B,* 65–97.
Baker, A. G., Mercier, P., Vallée-Tourangeau, F., Frank, R., & Pan, M. (1993). Selective associations and causality judgments: Presence of a strong causal factor may reduce judgments of a weaker one. *Journal of Experimental Psychology: Learning, Memory, and Cognition, 19,* 414–432.
Benedict, J. O., & Ayres, J. J. B. (1972). Factors affecting conditioning in the truly random control procedure in the rat. *Journal of Comparative and Physiological Psychology, 78,* 323–330.
Busemeyer, J. R. (1991). Intuitive statistical estimation. In N. H. Anderson (Ed.), *Contributions to information integration theory* (Vol. 1, pp. 187–215). Hillsdale, NJ: Erlbaum.

Busemeyer, J. R., Myung, J., & McDaniel, M. A. (1993a). Cue competition effects: Empirical tests of adaptive network learning models. *Psychological Science, 4,* 190–195.

Busemeyer, J. R., Myung, J., & McDaniel, M. A. (1993b). Cue competition effects: Theoretical implications for adaptive network learning models. *Psychological Science, 4,* 196–202.

Chambers, R. (1994). *Vestiges of the natural history of creation and other evolutionary writings* (J. A. Secord, Ed.). Chicago: University of Chicago Press. (Original work published 1844)

Chapman, G. B. (1991). Trial order affects cue interaction in contingency judgment. *Journal of Experimental Psychology: Learning, Memory, and Cognition, 17,* 837–854.

Chapman, G. B., & Robbins, S. J. (1990). Cue interaction in human contingency judgment. *Memory & Cognition, 18,* 537–545.

Cheng, P. W., & Holyoak, K. J. (1995). Complex adaptive systems as intuitive statisticians: Causality, contingency, and prediction. In H. L. Roitblat & J.-A. Meyer (Eds.), *Comparative approaches to cognitive science* (pp. 271–302). Cambridge, MA: MIT Press.

Cunningham, C. L. (1981). Associations between the elements of a bivalent compound stimulus. *Journal of Experimental Psychology: Animal Behavior Processes, 7,* 425–436.

Darwin, C. (1920). *The descent of man: And selection in relation to sex* (2nd ed.). New York: Appleton. (Original work published 1871)

Dickinson, A., & Burke, J. (1996). Within-compound associations mediate the retrospective revaluation of causality judgments. *Quarterly Journal of Experimental Psychology, 49B,* 60–80.

Dickinson, A., Shanks, D., & Evenden, J. (1984). Judgment of act-outcome contingency: The role of selective attribution. *Quarterly Journal of Experimental Psychology, 36A,* 29–50.

Fales, E., & Wasserman, E. A. (1992). Causal knowledge: What can psychology teach philosophers? *Journal of Mind and Behavior, 13,* 1–27.

Gluck, M. A., & Bower, G. H. (1988). From conditioning to category learning: An adaptive network model. *Journal of Experimental Psychology: General, 117,* 227–247.

Hume, D. (1964). *Treatise of human nature* (L. A. Selby-Bigge, Ed.). London: Oxford University Press. (Original work published 1739)

Kamin, L. J. (1969). Predictability, surprise, attention, and conditioning. In B. A. Campbell & R. M. Church (Eds.), *Punishment and aversive behavior* (pp. 279–296). New York: Appleton-Century-Crofts.

Kao, S. F. (1993). *Information integration and associative learning as accounts of human contingency judgment.* Unpublished doctoral dissertation, University of Iowa, Iowa City.

Kao, S. F., & Wasserman, E. A. (1993). Assessment of an information integration account of contingency judgment with examination of subjective cell importance and method of information presentation. *Journal of Experimental Psychology: Learning, Memory, and Cognition, 19,* 1363–1386.

Katagiri, M., Kao, S.-F., Simon, A. M. & Wasserman, E. A. (1995). *Ratings of causal efficacy under constant and changing interevent contingencies.* Unpublished manuscript.

Kaufman, M. A., & Bolles, R. C. (1981). A nonassociative aspect of overshadowing. *Bulletin of the Psychonomic Society, 18,* 318–320.

Levin, I. P., Wasserman, E. A., & Kao, S. F. (1993). Multiple methods for examining biased information use in contingency judgments. *Organizational Behavior and Human Decision Processes, 55,* 228–250.

Mackintosh, N. J. (1975). A theory of attention: Variations in the associability of stimuli with reinforcement. *Psychological Review, 82,* 276–298.

Markman, A. B. (1989). LMS rules and the inverse base-rate effect: Comment on Gluck and Bower (1988). *Journal of Experimental Psychology: General, 118,* 417–421.

Matzel, L. D., Schactman, T. R., & Miller, R. R. (1985). Recovery of an overshadowed association achieved by extinction of the overshadowing stimulus. *Learning and Motivation, 16,* 398–412.

Medin, D. L., & Bettger, J. G. (1991). Sensitivity to changes in base-rate information. *American Journal of Psychology, 104,* 311–332.

Miller, R. R., Barnet, R. C., & Grahame, N. J. (1995). Assessment of the Rescorla-Wagner model. *Psychological Bulletin, 117,* 363–386.

Miller, R. R., & Matzel, L. D. (1988). The comparator hypothesis: A response rule for the expression of associations. In G. H. Bower (Ed.), *The psychology of learning and motivation* (Vol. 22, pp. 51–92). San Diego, CA: Academic Press.

Miller, R. R., & Schactman, T. R. (1985). Conditioning context as an associative baseline: Implications for response generation and the nature of conditioned inhibition. In R. R. Miller & N. E. Spear (Eds.), *Information processing in animals: Conditioned inhibition* (pp. 51–88). Hillsdale, NJ: Erlbaum.

Nash, J. C., & Walker-Smith, M. (1987). *Nonlinear parameter estimation: An integrated system in BASIC.* New York: Dekker.

Price, P. C., & Yates, J. F. (1993). Judgmental overshadowing: Further evidence of cue interaction in contingency judgment. *Memory & Cognition, 21,* 561–572.

Quinsey, V. L. (1971). Conditioned suppression with no CS-US contingency in the rat. *Canadian Journal of Psychology, 25,* 1–5.

Rescorla, R. A., & Durlach, P. J. (1981). Within-event learning in Pavlovian conditioning. In N. E. Spear & R. R. Miller (Eds.). *Information processing in animals: Memory mechanisms* (pp. 81–111). Hillsdale, NJ: Erlbaum.

Rescorla, R. A., & Wagner, A. R. (1972). A theory of Pavlovian conditioning: Variations in the effectiveness of reinforcement and nonreinforcement. In A. H. Black & W. F. Prokasy (Eds.), *Classical conditioning II: Current research and theory* (pp. 64–99). New York: Appleton-Century-Crofts.

Shanks, D. R. (1985a). Continuous monitoring of human contingency judgment across trials. *Memory & Cognition, 13,* 158–167.

Shanks, D. R. (1985b). Forward and backward blocking in human contingency judgment. *Quarterly Journal of Experimental Psychology, 37B,* 1–21.

Shanks, D. R. (1986). Selective attribution and the judgment of causality. *Learning and Motivation, 17,* 311–334.

Shanks, D. R. (1987). Acquisition functions in contingency judgment. *Learning and Motivation, 18,* 147–166.

Shanks, D. R. (1989). Selectional processes in causality judgment. *Memory & Cognition, 17,* 27–34.

Tassoni, J. T. (1995). The least mean squares network with information coding: A model of cue learning. *Journal of Experimental Psychology: Learning, Memory, and Cognition, 21,* 193–204.

Thorndike, E. L. (1911). *Animal intelligence: Experimental studies.* New York: Macmillan.

Trolier, T. K., & Hamilton, D. L. (1986). Variables influencing judgments of correlational relations. *Journal of Personality and Social Psychology, 50,* 879–888.

Van Hamme, L. J. (1994). *Associative and statistical accounts of cue competition in causality judgments.* Unpublished doctoral dissertation, University of Iowa, Iowa City.

Van Hamme, L. J., & Wasserman, E. A. (1993). Cue competition in causality judgments: The role of method of information presentation. *Bulletin of the Psychonomic Society, 31,* 457–460.

Van Hamme, L. J., & Wasserman, E. A. (1994). Cue competition in causality judgments: The role of nonpresentation of compound stimulus elements. *Learning and Motivation, 25,* 127–151.

Wagner, A. R. (1981). SOP: A model of automatic memory processing in animal behavior. In N. E. Spear & R. R. Miller (Eds.), *Information processing in animals: Memory mechanisms* (pp. 5–47). Hillsdale, NJ. Erlbaum.

Waldmann, M. R., & Holyoak, K. J. (1992). Predictive and diagnostic learning within causal models: Asymmetries in cue competition. *Journal of Experimental Psychology: General, 121,* 222–236.

Wasserman, E. A. (1990). Detecting response-outcome relations: Toward an understanding of the causal texture of the environment. In G. H. Bower (Ed.), *The psychology of learning and motivation* (Vol. 26, pp. 27–82). San Diego, CA: Academic Press.

Wasserman, E. A. (1993). Comparative cognition: Beginning the second century of the study of animal intelligence. *Psychological Bulletin, 113,* 211–228.

Wasserman, E. A., Dorner, W. W., & Kao, S. -F. (1990). Contributions of specific cell information to judgments of interevent contingency. *Journal of Experimental Psychology: Learning, Memory, and Cognition, 16,* 509–521.

Williams, D. A., Sagness, K. E., & McPhee, J. E. (1994). Configural and elemental strategies in predictive learning. *Journal of Experimental Psychology: Learning, Memory, and Cognition, 20,* 694–709.

Williams, D. A., Travis, G. M., & Overmier, J. B. (1986). Within-compound associations modulate the relative effectiveness of differential and Pavlovian conditioned inhibition procedures. *Journal of Experimental Psychology: Animal Behavior Processes, 12,* 351–362.

Yates, J. F., & Curley, S. P. (1986). Contingency judgment: Primacy effects and attention decrement. *Acta Psychologica, 62,* 293–302.

Young, M. E. (1995). On the origin of personal causal theories. *Psychonomic Bulletin & Review, 2,* 83–104.

DISTINGUISHING ASSOCIATIVE AND PROBABILISTIC CONTRAST THEORIES OF HUMAN CONTINGENCY JUDGMENT

David R. Shanks
Francisco J. Lopez
Richard J. Darby
Anthony Dickinson

I. Introduction

In an article published in 1984, Dickinson, Shanks, and Evenden suggested and provided some supporting evidence for the idea that human judgments of event contingency might be profitably analyzed from an associationist perspective, and more particularly that they might be understood in terms of the processes embodied in prevailing associationist theories of animal conditioning. With the benefit of hindsight, an associative perspective on contingency judgment does not seem especially radical. In a contingency judgment task, subjects are asked to rate the extent to which an action and outcome or a cue and outcome are related, and the parallels to (respectively) instrumental and Pavlovian conditioning procedures should be obvious.

In the years that have followed, the associative view of contingency judgment has been explored in a large number of studies and has generated a good deal of controversy (as the existence of this volume demonstrates). In this chapter, we survey some of the main aspects of this field, and in particular we review some of the progress that has occurred since our earlier evaluation of associative theory (Shanks & Dickinson, 1987) in this series. In that review, we presented a number of experiments that were consistent with an associationist account of contingency judgment, but we also noted several deeply problematic findings. We concentrate in the present chapter on reevaluating those problematic results in the light of more recent investigations.

Why has the study of contingency judgment expanded into such a large area of research interest? Doubtless there are very many reasons, but it is important to recognize three of the main ones. First, a moment's reflection reveals that many aspects of our daily lives require us to make accurate evaluations of event contingencies. In general, we perform an action because we believe that an outcome that we value or wish to avoid covaries with that action: we take exercise, for instance, because we believe that it covaries with good health, and we stop smoking because it causes lung cancer. Similarly, many of our judgments depend on accurate assessments of event covariations: a doctor makes a particular disease diagnosis because he or she has learned that certain symptoms covary with the disease. Thus, it is not hard to recognize the potential importance of laboratory studies of the mechanisms of contingency judgment.

Second, the idea that human judgments and animal conditioning may be served by similar mechanisms appears to have evoked strong reactions in many researchers, with some finding the idea highly appealing and others totally unacceptable. Those who find the idea appealing are likely to be enthusiastic about the increasing impact of associationism and connectionist theories in cognitive psychology, which has led many researchers to look more closely at the basic mechanisms of learning. Although a widespread view in psychology is that the best place to study such mechanisms is in the animal laboratory, it has been increasingly recognized that certain issues concerning elementary learning processes are more amenable for study with humans than with animals. Contingency judgment tasks represent one example in which such processes can be readily investigated (another would be studies of category learning; see Nosofsky, 1992; Shanks, 1994).

In contrast, those researchers who are unhappy with the idea that similar processes may underlie animal conditioning and human contingency judgment tend to point to the latter's more "high-level" and "cognitive" aspects, which they contrast with the relative automaticity and cognitive impenetrability of conditioning. For example, Waldmann and Holyoak (1992; see Waldmann, this volume, Ch. 2) emphasized the way in which subjects might bring complex causal theories to bear in making contingency judgments. Although we would dispute the claim that contingency judgments are always mediated by complex and high-level cognitive processes (see Section III), we hope that the present chapter will make it clear that we do not regard associative mechanisms as "dumb." On the contrary, contemporary animal learning theories have to appeal to quite rich representational structures to explain even such simple behaviors as approach to a food source (see Dickinson, 1980; Dickinson & Shanks, 1995).

The third reason why contingency judgment has become the focus of so much research interest is that it provides a very simple domain in which questions about rationality can be addressed. Dickinson et al.'s (1984) paper came against a backdrop of studies concerned not so much with explaining contingency judgment but rather with determining whether humans are capable of normatively accurate judgments (e.g., Allan & Jenkins, 1980; Jenkins & Ward, 1965; Smedslund, 1963; Wasserman, Chatlosh, & Neunaber, 1983). Like the simple decision making tasks studied by Kahneman and Tversky (1972), contingency judgment experiments seemed to be easy to analyze from a normative point of view and also seemed to some to yield clear evidence of violations of normative behavior. Although we will only briefly consider this issue in the present chapter, it is important to note that the associative view of contingency judgment has a good deal to say about normativeness (see Shanks, 1995a, 1995b).

The plan of the present chapter is as follows. We begin by briefly describing the well-known conditioning theory of Rescorla and Wagner (1972), which serves as our associationist starting point, and we contrast it with a new nonassociationist theory that has recently generated a good deal of interest (see Chapters 8 & 2, respectively, by Cheng, Park, Yarlas, & Holyoak and by Waldmann, this volume), namely Cheng and Holyoak's (1995) "probabilistic contrast" theory. We then consider three problems that seem to be particularly acute for the associationist approach (the apparent lack of convergence of judgments under different noncontingent schedules, the influence of causal models, and the existence of a phenomenon known as retrospective revaluation). We describe new results that suggest that these problems may not after all be too damaging to associationist theories. Instead, we conclude that it is the probabilistic contrast theory that has the greatest difficulty accounting for our results. Finally, we report some new results that suggest that the basic units of analysis in associationist theories, namely independent "elemental" representations of stimuli, are inadequate. We consider ways in which "configural" representations might be incorporated into associative theories of contingency judgment.

A. THE RESCORLA–WAGNER THEORY

In an influential animal conditioning experiment, Saavedra (reported by Wagner, 1969) demonstrated that the extent to which a cue and an outcome come to be associated is a function not simply of their repeated pairing but rather of the degree to which the cue is a reliable predictor of the outcome. Saavedra's experiment used a rabbit eyelid conditioning procedure. In this procedure, a brief neutral stimulus such as a light is paired with a mild shock to the eye. As a result, it becomes a conditioned stimulus (CS) capable of eliciting by itself the conditioned response of blinking. In one group (called the *contingent* group) the light was paired on some trials with another neutral stimulus, a tone, and this compound was followed by shock. On other trials the tone occurred on its own and was unreinforced. If the light is cue A and the tone cue B, and shock is the outcome (O), then the animals in this group received intermixed AB → O and B → no O trials, with shock being contingent on cue A's presence. At the end of the training phase, cue A was tested on its own, and (unsurprisingly) elicited a substantial conditioned response, indicating that it had become strongly associated with shock.

A second group of animals (the *noncontingent* group) again received AB → O trials, but for these animals trials with cue B by itself were reinforced rather than unreinforced; thus these animals received intermixed AB → O and B → O trials. Since shock could occur on trials with B alone, it is not contingent on cue A's presence. When this group was tested with cue A by itself, little conditioned responding was elicited, indicating that cue A had become only weakly (if at all) associated with the shock.

The importance of Saavedra's result (and of a number of other, similar results obtained around the same time; see Mackintosh, 1983) lies in the fact that even though cue A was paired with the outcome an equal number of times in the two groups, its association with the outcome differed. The reason is that in the contingent group, A was a good predictor of the outcome compared to cue B, whereas in the noncontingent group, A was an entirely redundant stimulus in that it provided no information that was not already conveyed by B. Thus, a process of *cue selection* appears to operate in associative learning: a cue will be selected for association with another event only if it is a good relative predictor of that event.

This sort of cue selection effect played a major role in the late 1960s in the development of formal associationist learning theories such as that of Rescorla and Wagner (1972), which is equivalent to the "delta" rule used to update the weights in many current connectionist models of human learning (e.g., Gluck & Bower, 1988; Kruschke, 1992, 1993; McClelland & Rumelhart, 1985). The Rescorla–Wagner theory is just one of a number of accounts of associative learning that were developed in response to demonstrations of selective conditioning. In one way or another, however, they all deploy the idea that learning is controlled by the relative predictive validity of a cue as assessed by an expectancy error term. An error exists whenever there is a mismatch between what is predicted to occur on a trial and what actually occurs. Attentional theories, for example, argue that the absolute (Pearce & Hall, 1980) or relative (Mackintosh, 1975) error term generated on a learning episode determines the subsequent associability of a cue with the outcome. Although the relative merits of these various theories is still a matter of dispute within the context of conditioning, we shall focus on the Rescorla–Wagner model in the present discussion. Rescorla and Wagner's (1972) theory explains Saavedra's result by assuming that there is a ceiling or limit to the amount of association strength that can be supported by any given outcome event. On each trial, the strength (V) of the target association is changed by amount dV, proportional to the error $(\lambda - \Sigma V)$:

$$dV = \alpha\beta \, (\lambda - \Sigma V), \tag{1}$$

where α is a learning rate parameter determined by the salience of the cue, β is another learning rate parameter determined by the salience of the outcome, λ is the associative strength that is required to predict fully the occurrence of the outcome, and ΣV is the sum of the associative strengths of all cues present on the current trial. It is assumed that a subject's judgment about the relationship between a cue and the outcome is monotonically related to the associative strength of that cue (V).

How does the model generate the effect observed by Saavedra? Learning will cease when the outcome is fully predicted on each trial. In the noncontingent condition, involving AB → O and B → O trials, cue B must have associative strength of λ in order that the outcome is predicted on the B → O trials. For the outcome also to be fully predicted on the AB → O trials, A must therefore have associative strength of zero. In the contingent condition, by contrast, the B → no O trials mean that B's asymptotic strength is zero. This in turn requires that A have associative strength of λ in order that the outcome is fully predicted on the AB → O trials. Hence A has associative strength of zero in the noncontingent condition and λ in the contingent one.

Another important cue selection effect is the well-known phenomenon of "blocking." This phenomenon, originally reported in animal conditioning by Kamin (1968), refers to the fact that when a compound of two cues is paired with an outcome, the amount learned about one of the cues (the target) is reduced if the other (competing) cue has been separately pre-trained as a predictor of the outcome. Under these circumstances, the competing cue is said to "block" learning about the target cue. As with Saavedra's results, the importance of blocking lies in its illustration that simple associative learning is informationally sensitive and reflects the relative predictive validity of a cue. Although the target cue is presented in temporal contiguity with the outcome—a condition traditionally thought to be sufficient for learning—the target is in fact informationally redundant in the sense that the occurrence of the outcome is fully predicted by the pretrained, competing cue.

From the point of view of human contingency judgment, cue selection effects are critical because if they can be demonstrated to occur in humans, that would encourage the claim that an associationist mechanism is responsible for generating such judgments. The idea would be that judgments are based on the strength of a mental bond or association connecting representations of the predictive event and outcome. And, indeed, it turns out that cue selection effects are easy to obtain with human subjects (see Spellman, this volume, Ch. 5). For instance, a result comparable to that obtained by Saavedra has been observed in humans. Shanks (1991) presented subjects with hypothetical medical patients who had different symptoms, and subjects had to predict which disease each patient had. When the pattern of symptom–disease pairings was analogous to Saavedra's contingent condition, in that subjects saw AB → O and B → no O trials, ratings of the contingency between symptom A and the disease were high. But when the trial types conformed to the noncontingent arrangement (AB → O, B → O), ratings were much lower. Cue-selection effects have now been observed in human contingency judgment by a number of researchers (e.g., Baker, Mercier, Vallée-Tourangeau, Frank, & Pan, 1993; Chapman, 1991; Chapman & Robbins, 1990; Price & Yates, 1993; Shanks, 1985b, 1989, 1991; Wasserman, Elek, Chatlosh, & Baker, 1993; Williams, Sagness, & McPhee, 1994; see Chapters 1, 6, 5, & 3, respectively, by Baker, Murphy, & Vallée-Tourangeau; Wasserman, Kao, Van Hamme, Katagiri, & Young; Spellman; Williams, this volume). The existence of such effects is highly encouraging for the notion that contingency judgment can be interpreted within an associationist framework of the sort provided by Rescorla and Wagner (1972).

B. The Probabilistic Contrast Model

In a challenge to this associationist approach, Cheng, Holyoak, and their colleagues have argued that cue-selection effects emerge for entirely different reasons: subjects do not increment and decrement mental associations, but instead base their judgments on the difference between the conditional probability of the outcome given the presence versus the absence of the target predictor. A large and very interesting research program is being pursued by these authors and their colleagues that challenges the enterprise of understanding human and animal learning in terms of associationist principles (Cheng, 1993; Cheng & Holyoak, 1995; Cheng & Novick, 1990, 1991, 1992; Holyoak, Koh, & Nisbett, 1989; Melz, Cheng, Holyoak, &

Waldmann, 1993; Waldmann & Holyoak, 1992). In fact, it is fair to say that the emergence of this theory has been the main theoretical development of the last decade in this field.[1]

So-called "contingency" theories take as their starting point the idea that judgments of contingency are computed via a mental version of the normative Δp equation. Subjects maintain mental records of the conditional probability of the outcome given the target cue, $p(O/C)$, and of the conditional probability of the outcome in the absence of the target cue, $p(O/-C)$, and base their judgments on the difference between these probabilities:

$$\Delta p = p(O/C) - p(O/-C). \tag{2}$$

The probabilistic contrast model (PCM) constitutes a normative generalization of the standard Δp measure to situations in which multiple predictors or cues are involved and where the background for a given target cue may not be constant. In these more complex situations, it is not just the relationship between the target cue (A) and the outcome that is taken into account but also the predictive status of other cues. Specifically, the contingency between cue A and the outcome must be computed over certain restricted *focal sets* of events. Suppose that A co-occurs with some background cue that we will designate B. Since the true predictive value may lie with B rather than with A, one focal set is formed by the set of events in which cue B is always present. Then, the contingency between A and the outcome conditional on the presence of this alternative cue is just the difference between the proportion of cases in which the outcome is present given the presence of both cues and the proportion of cases in which the outcome is present given the absence of the target cue A and the presence of the alternative cue B:

$$\Delta p = p(O/A.B) - p(O/-A.B) \tag{3}$$

Thus, Equation 3 represents a special case of Equation 2 in which the trial types over which contingency is computed are restricted to those in which the alternative cue B is present, and it should be fairly straightforward to see that Equation 3 represents a "contrast" between what happens when A is present versus when it is absent, holding B's presence constant. In

[1] It should be noted that the probabilistic contrast model was originally presented as a computational-level theory (e.g., Cheng & Novick, 1992) with no specification of how the computations might be performed in mental processing terms. In the present chapter, we are solely concerned with the algorithmic-level version of the PCM formulated by Cheng and Holyoak (1995) and Melz et al. (1993) and directly contrasted by them with the Rescorla–Wagner theory.

accordance with this simple idea, the values of Δp the equation yields for the contingent and noncontingent conditions of Saavedra's experiment differ in the right direction. In both the contingent (AB $\rightarrow$ O, B $\rightarrow$ no O) and noncontingent (AB $\rightarrow$ O, B $\rightarrow$ O) conditions, cue B is the alternative predictor and the focal set contains all trials on which B is present. Applying Equation 3, it is easy to see that $\Delta p_A = 1$ in the contingent condition and 0 in the noncontingent one.

In fact, many different contrasts can potentially be computed that have the same form as Equation 3. If the target cue covaries with many other cues, then multiple contrasts can be calculated in which different background cues are held constant. Thus, in a design involving AB $\rightarrow$ O, B $\rightarrow$ no O, AC $\rightarrow$ no O, and C $\rightarrow$ O trials, it is possible to compute one contrast for the focal set of trials in which B is present and another one for the focal set of trials in which C is present. These contrasts yield values of $\Delta p_A = 1$ in the former case and $\Delta p_A = -1$ in the latter, reflecting the fact that A predicts the outcome when it is paired with B and predicts its omission when paired with C. The PCM assumes that when multiple contrasts can be computed and the subjects have to provide a single contingency judgment, some integration process is employed to collapse the outputs of the contrasts. For our purposes we will simply assume that this integration process is monotonic such that if all of the contrasts for one cue are greater than the comparable contrasts for a second cue, then judgments will be greater for the first than for the second cue.

Cheng and Holyoak's (1995) implementation of the PCM includes several steps: (1) selecting which cues will be incorporated in the focal sets; (2) choosing the conditional contrasts to be calculated; and (3) determining how the information provided by the different conditional contrasts is integrated within a single judgment about the predictive value of the target cue. To see how this implementation works, let us consider a specific application of the model to another experiment by Shanks (1991) involving a slightly different version of Saavedra's design in which subjects saw AB $\rightarrow$ O_1, B $\rightarrow$ no O, C $\rightarrow$ O_1, DE $\rightarrow$ O_2, E $\rightarrow$ O_2, and F $\rightarrow$ no O trials, where the letters are medical symptoms and O_1 and O_2 are different diseases. With regards to the relationship between the target cue A and outcome O_1, the implementation of the model specifies that subjects will initially select cue C as a conditionalizing cue given that this cue has been consistently paired on its own with the outcome, the outcome never occurs outside the experimental trials, and subjects have no prior beliefs about the predictive values of the different cues. However, because A and C are never paired, the only meaningful contrast that can be computed for A is the contrast conditional on the absence rather than presence of cue C. According to this contrast, subjects will compute the probability of O_1 given the presence of A and the absence of C, $P(O_1/A.-C)$, which has a value of 1. In addition, subjects will compute the probability of O_1 in the absence of both A and C $[P(O_1/-A.-C)]$, which has a value of 0. Thus, cue A has a conditional contingency of $\Delta p = 1$ in the focal set in which cue C is absent.

With regards to the relationship between the target cue D and disease 2, cue E will be selected as a conditionalizing cue, as it has been consistently paired with disease 2. In this case the only conditional contrast that can be computed is one conditional on the presence of cue E (in fact, the target cue D never occurs in the absence of this conditionalizing cue). Thus, subjects will compute the probability of O_2 given the presence of the target cue D and cue E $[P(O_2/D.E)]$, which is 1, and the probability of this disease given the absence of cue D and the presence of cue E $[P(O_2/-D.E)]$, which is also 1. Therefore, cue D has a conditional contingency of $\Delta p = 0$ in the focal set in which cue E is present. Hence, it is straightforward to generate higher ratings for A than for D from the contrasts, which was the outcome observed in the subjects' ratings.

The probabilistic contrast model represents a major advance in our conception of normative theories of contingency judgment because it is readily able to explain a broad range of cue selection effects. The key idea behind the PCM is simply that the evaluation of a cue must be based on a contrast between what happens when it is present versus what happens when it is absent, all else being held constant, and this idea should require little justification in the context of a scientific methodology that emphasizes the use of controlled experiments that adopt exactly this procedure: in scientific experiments, the researcher sets up an experiment and a control condition in which everything is held constant other than the presence versus absence of the critical factor. The crucial question for our present purposes, of course, is whether we can discriminate between associative and contingency-based theories.

II. Convergence in Noncontingent Conditions

Plainly, the Rescorla–Wagner and probabilistic contrast models stand as powerful alternative descriptions of the contingency judgment mechanism, and each is able to explain the basic fact that variations in objective contingency influence subjects' judgments. Thus, more subtle methods must be developed for pitting the theories against one another, and in the present section, we consider a phenomenon that we identified in our earlier chapter (Shanks & Dickinson, 1987)—concerning contingency judgments under noncontingent conditions—which seems to present a major problem for the Rescorla–Wagner theory. Suppose that subjects are required to make contingency judgments after varying numbers of trials. Briefly, the theory predicts that when the objective contingency between a target cue or action and the outcome is zero, judgments should converge to an asymptotic value of zero (see Melz et al., 1993; Shanks, 1993). The reason for this is plain: as we saw for the noncontingent (AB → O, B → O) condition in Saavedra's study, A's asymptotic associative strength must be zero in order for the outcome to be accurately predicted on both trial types. Note that the prediction is the same even if $p(O/A)$ and $p(O/-A)$ are less than 1.

The problem with the theory is that, in contrast to this prediction, judgments in a number of experiments seem to be strongly affected (even at asymptote) by the overall probability of the outcome (Baker, Berbrier, & Vallée-Tourangeau, 1989; Shanks, 1985a, 1987). Moreover, in some of these experiments (e.g., Shanks, 1987) judgments were actually negative when the probability of the outcome was low (i.e., .25). Although such findings are at variance with the predictions of associationist theories, they are quite easily explained by contingency theory because it is reasonable to assume that subjects give different weights to the terms in the contingency equation. Evidence from a different domain (see Kao & Wasserman, 1993; Wasserman, Dorner, & Kao, 1990; Wasserman et al., this volume, Ch. 6) has shown that subjects give more weight to trials on which the target cue occurs than to trials on which it is absent. In terms of the Δp formula, this simply means adding weighting parameters a and b ($a > b$) such that:

$$\Delta p = a \cdot p(O/C) - b \cdot p(O/-C). \tag{4}$$

The important cases for our present purposes are noncontingent conditions in which $p(O/C) = p(O/-C) = p(O)$. The equation then becomes:

$$\Delta p = p(O) \cdot (a - b).$$

With different values of $p(O)$, the obtained values of Δp from this equation will converge to a common asymptote only when $a = b$. Whenever $a > b$, Δp (and hence judgments) will be an increasing function of the probability of the outcome, $p(O)$, and hence will not converge to a common asymptote. This, of course, is exactly what was observed in the experiments mentioned above (e.g., Shanks, 1987). Thus, with the simple addition of some well-motivated psychological weighting parameters, a contingency-based theory can readily account for the observed absence of convergence.

Despite the apparent difficulty the empirical results present for associative theories, it is possible that some undesirable experimental artifact is responsible for the convergence results. What might such an artifact be? The likeliest candidate is the use of a within-subjects design in all of the experiments referred to previously, which creates the possibility that judgments from one condition to another are not independent. Although Shanks (1985a) failed to support this suggestion using a rather indirect method, we decided in our first experiment to look at learning curves in a completely between-subjects design.

A. EXPERIMENT 1

In this study, subjects made judgments of contingency across 40 trials in an experiment that used a task developed by Baker et al. (1989). On each trial a tank moved across the computer screen through a minefield and was either blown up by a mine or not. On half the trials the tanks were camouflaged and were able to avoid the mines, which were color sensitive. Every five trials, subjects judged the relationship between the cue (camouflage) and the outcome (avoiding being blown up), using a scale from -100 to $+100$ (they also gave a confidence rating for each judgment, but these data are not presented here). In addition, once subjects had seen the status of the tank on a given trial they had to predict whether the tank was going to explode or not on that particular trial.

There were four groups in the experiment ($n = 20$ per group), each seeing a different combination of $p(O/C)$ and $p(O/-C)$. For one group, there was a positive but imperfect contingency of $\Delta p = .50$, resulting from values of $p(O/C)$ and $p(O/-C)$ of .75 and .25, respectively. In another condition, the contingency was $-.50$, derived from values of $p(O/C) = .25$ and $p(O/-C) = .75$. Finally, in two conditions Δp was zero. This was achieved in one case by having two quite high conditional probabilities $[p(O/C) = p(O/-C) = .75]$ and in the other case by having two low probabilities $[p(O/C) = p(O/-C) = .25]$. For the positive contingency condition, the Rescorla–Wagner theory predicts that as more and more trials are presented, an increasing but negatively accelerated learning function should appear. The reason for this is that on early trials, the discrepancy between the asymptote of learning (λ) and the combined associative strength of the cues present (ΣV) will be large and hence the increment to associative strength will be large. However, as learning proceeds, this discrepancy will get smaller and smaller (and likewise for the strength changes) until learning ceases when $\lambda = \Sigma V$. In the negative contingency condition, where the outcome is less likely in the presence than in the absence of the cue, judgments should become negative and take a form that is roughly the mirror image of the curve for positive contingencies; that is to say, judgments should drop rapidly in the first few trials and then fall more slowly before reaching a negative plateau.

As can be seen from Fig. 1, judgments started close to zero in each condition. When there was a positive contingency of $\Delta p = .50$, judgments

Shanks et al.

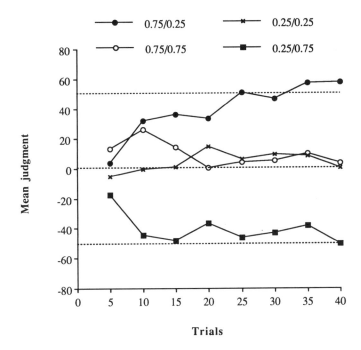

Fig. 1.   Mean judgments of contingency across 40 trials under four different cue–outcome contingencies. Judgments were made on a rating scale from −100 to +100. Each condition is designated by two numbers, the first being $p(O/C)$ and the second $p(O/-C)$. Judgments increase under the positive (.75/.25) contingency and decrease under the negative (.25/.75) contingency, in each case yielding terminal judgments close to the actual contingencies (× 100). In the noncontingent conditions (.75/.75 and .25/.25), judgments converge to zero, but when the probability of the outcome is high (in the .75/.75 condition), early judgments are erroneously positive.

increased steadily across trials toward an asymptote of around 50, and when the contingency was −.50, judgments decreased across trials. Crucially, in the noncontingent conditions judgments stayed close to zero across trials, although in the .75/.75 case there was a preasymptotic increase and then decrease during the early trials. This latter effect is important, because it replicates previous observations (e.g., Shanks, 1987) and is predicted by the Rescorla–Wagner theory, as we show later. There is no suggestion that judgments differed at asymptote in the two noncontingent conditions, and accordingly we suggest that previous failures to obtain convergence have been biased by the use of within-subjects methodologies. Of course, this conclusion would be bolstered by a single experiment in which some subjects saw a single condition and others saw all four conditions, but we feel that the present results are sufficient to reestablish confidence in the predictions of the Rescorla–Wagner theory.

B. SIMULATIONS OF EXPERIMENT 1

In a series of simulations we tried to see whether the Rescorla–Wagner theory and PCM can accurately predict the pattern of results obtained in the different groups of Experiment 1. Intuitively, it would seem unlikely that a normative theory such as the PCM could, in principle, predict the changes of judgments seen across trials as the conditional probabilities on which contrasts are computed remained constant across trials. In our experiment, each block of eight trials contained four trials with the cue and four without. Of the four trials of each type, exactly one or three were paired with the outcome, depending on whether the relevant conditional probability was .25 or .75. Thus, for each block of eight trials, Δp was *exactly* $-.5$, 0, or .5, and remained constant across trials for each eight-trial block. But while Δp was constant, judgments were not.

Although the fact that judgments in the noncontingent conditions converged suggests that differential weighting of $p(O/C)$ and $p(O/-C)$ is unnecessary, in our PCM simulations we included the two weighting parameters a and b, as specified in Equation 4. We computed the contingency judgments derived from the PCM, taking (weighted) estimations of the conditional probabilities. The predicted judgment on any given trial was simply the difference between the weighted conditional probabilities estimated up to that moment ($\times$ 100). The mean predicted judgments were compared with subjects' mean actual judgments and a sum of squared errors (SSE) was calculated between mean observed and predicted judgments across all contingency groups (8 $\times$ 4 data points). A search was made to find the values of the two free parameters a and b in the [0,1] interval, which provided the best fit to the actual judgments (i.e., which minimized SSE). The best fitting solution was obtained when $a = .93$ and $b = .85$. The parameters suggest that slightly different weights were given to $p(O/C)$ and $p(O/-C)$, in accordance with previous results. As the actual sequence of events that each subject experienced was recorded during the experiment, the theory's predictions could be computed for trial sequences identical to those presented to the subjects. The results are therefore averaged across 20 simulated subjects receiving the same sequences of events as the actual subjects. Figure 2 shows the judgments the PCM predicted under these circumstances.

Plainly, at a qualitative level the fit is not very good in that unlike the actual judgments, the predicted judgments hardly change across trials. Moreover, the model fails to predict any preasymptotic difference in ratings

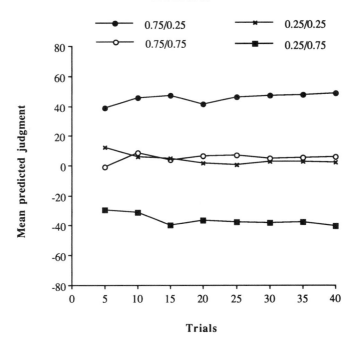

Fig. 2. Best fitting PCM predictions for the data shown in Fig. 1. The figure shows mean computed contingencies across 40 trials under 4 different contingencies: positive (.75/.25), zero (.75/.75 and .25/.25), and negative (.25/.75), where the first figure refers to $p(O/C)$ and the second to $p(O/-C)$.

for the two noncontingent conditions. Can the model be easily revised in order to improve the predictions? One possibility is that subjects start each problem with the assumption that the contingency is zero, and their estimates are then updated by a Bayesian process that incorporates such prior beliefs (see Fales & Wasserman, 1992). But although such an account would allow judgments to increase and decrease across trials under positive and negative contingencies, there is no reason to suppose that preasymptotic divergence in the two noncontingent conditions would be generated. Clearly, further explorations are needed to see if contingency theories can reproduce acquisition data.

In contrast to this poor fit, the Rescorla–Wagner theory provides a very good account of the data. Again, the results are based on 20 simulated subjects receiving trial sequences identical to those presented to the subjects. Four free parameters were included and these were constrained within the [0,1] interval. In this case one pair of parameters was for the salience (α) of the target cue (camouflage) and the background contextual cues, and the other pair was for the salience (β) of the occurrence and nonoccurrence of the outcome. The Rescorla–Wagner theory assumes that outcomes occurring in the absence of the target cue become associated with contextual cues that compete for the limited associative strength supportable by the outcome. λ was given a value of 100 in order to scale the associative strengths into the same range as subjects' judgments. Again, the mean values of the predicted judgments were calculated and compared with subjects' mean judgments. The parameters chosen were .7 and .3 for the salience (α) of the camouflage and the contextual cues, respectively, and .5 and .9 for the salience (β) of the outcome and of no outcome, respectively, Figure 3 shows the predicted judgments.

As can be seen, the associative model provides a much better fit to the results than the PCM. First, clear changes in judgments are predicted across trials. Second, the preasymptotic divergence of judgments in the noncontingent conditions is reproduced (see Rescorla, 1972; Shanks, 1985a, 1995a, for similar predictions). In the .75/.75 condition, the associative strength of

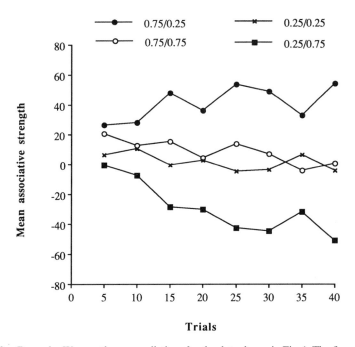

Fig. 3. Rescorla–Wagner theory predictions for the data shown in Fig. 1. The figure shows mean associative strengths across 40 trials under 4 different contingencies: positive (.75/.25), zero (.75/.75 and .25/.25), and negative (.25/.75), where the first figure refers to $p(O/C)$ and the second to $p(O/-C)$.

the target cue becomes substantially positive on early trials, just as in the subjects' judgments. In sum, the results from this experiment are much more conducive to an associative than to a contingency-based explanation. Not only did judgments converge under noncontingent conditions, but the shapes of the learning curves were much better fit by the Rescorla–Wagner theory than by the PCM.

III.   Causal Models and Causal Order

Another recent challenge to the associationist view of contingency judgment has come from some studies by Waldmann and Holyoak (1992) on the role of background causal knowledge in subjects' judgments (see also Miller & Matute, this volume, Ch. 4; Matute, Arcediano, & Miller, 1996; Waldmann, this volume, Ch. 2). In contrast to the sort of mechanism embodied in the Rescorla–Wagner theory, Waldmann and Holyoak adopt a mentalistic "causal model" approach to learning, in which "people use meaningful world knowledge, often of a highly abstract sort, to guide their learning about new domains. One major example of abstract world knowledge is knowledge about the basic characteristics of causal relations, such as the temporal precedence of causes to their effects" (Waldmann & Holyoak, 1992, p. 224). According to this account, subjects use real-world knowledge to interpret the cues and outcomes in an experiment, and in particular use knowledge about such things as causal precedence: regardless of the order in which the events are perceived, subjects know about the directionality of causation.

Having brought an interpretative causal mental model to bear on the task, subjects then determine (via Equation 3) the extent to which the cause and effect are related, with the cue being the cause and the outcome the effect. Waldmann and Holyoak noted that different predictions can be derived from the associationist and causal model theories in so-called "diagnostic" learning tasks. Suppose the subject is required to learn some cue–outcome relationship, but the appropriate causal interpretation is that the event labeled as the outcome would (in the real world) have caused the event labeled as the cue rather than vice versa. For instance, in a number of studies (e.g., Shanks, 1991), subjects have learned to predict diseases on the basis of symptoms, but, of course, in the real world it is diseases that cause symptoms rather than vice versa. This sort of "diagnostic" learning can be distinguished from "predictive" learning where the cues are the causes and the outcomes the effects.

Waldmann and Holyoak predicted that while cue selection may emerge in predictive contexts, it should not emerge in diagnostic conditions. In the noncontingent AB → O, B → O design, for example, the mental model theory assumes that the subject interprets these trial types as E_1E_2 ← cause and E_2 ← cause, where E_1 and E_2 are different effects. Despite the fact that the order in which the events are experienced is opposed to their true causal order, on this theory subjects will learn relationships from the cause to the effects, and the presence of E_2 should not alter in any way the judged causal relationship between the cause and E_1. This is because the presence of multiple effects does not change the computed value of Δp for a given cause–effect relationship. As Waldmann and Holyoak say (1992, p. 224), "People have a strong disposition to learn directed links from causes to their effects, rather than vice versa, even in situations in which they receive effect information prior to cause information," and (p. 226) "different effects, like different dependent measures obtained in an experiment, do not compete with one another, rather, each effect, as well as any interaction among the effects, provides information about the consequences of the cause."

For an associative account, however, the real-world interpretation of the events is immaterial. If the subject is required to predict outcomes from cues, then the cues represent the input to the system and the outcome represents the target to be predicted, regardless of causal order. Thus, even though cue selection in predictive situations (where the cues are interpreted as causes and the outcomes as effects) can be explained by either theory, the causal model account predicts no cue selection in diagnostic situations where the opposite interpretation is made, while the associationist theory does. Note that we use the terminology "cause–effect" (CE) and "effect–cause" (EC) for "predictive" and "diagnostic" tasks, respectively.

The crucial question, then, is whether cue selection occurs in EC tasks. Waldmann and Holyoak reported an experiment (Experiment 3), which on the face of it seems to cast doubt on the associative theory's prediction that selection will occur under such circumstances. Subjects were told to imagine they were in a bank and had to learn relationships between the state of activation of the alarm system and various buttons (CE condition) or indicator lights (EC condition). Both tasks took place across two stages and used a blocking design. In Stage 1, a predictive cue P was consistently paired with the outcome in that it was present every time the outcome was present and absent whenever the outcome was absent. Another two cues were also presented, cue C, which occurred on every trial regardless of whether the outcome was present or not, and cue U, which was uncorrelated with the outcome. During Stage 2 the same cues were again present but a target cue R was added. This redundant cue was present only on those trials in which cue P was also present. Waldmann and Holyoak reasoned that since cues P and R had each been paired with the outcome, any difference between them in terms of subjects' ratings at the end of Stage 2 would be evidence of cue selection. The relevant result was that an attenuation of the ratings of cue R occurred in the CE but not the EC context, so that, apparently, cue competition had arisen only in the former context, in accordance with the causal model theory and contradictory to an associationist analysis.

Waldmann and Holyoak's results are, on the face of it, highly problematic for associationist explanations of cue selection. Associationist accounts assume that when the subject is asked to predict an outcome, the cues represent the input and the outcome represents the output, with prediction responses being determined by unidirectional weights from the cues to the outcomes. Cue selection should emerge whenever multiple cues predict a single outcome, regardless of the possible causal order interpretation that can be put on the events. Since Waldmann and Holyoak's (1992, Experiment 3) result contradicts this prediction, our next study was undertaken in an attempt to examine their findings.

A. EXPERIMENT 2

We (Shanks & Lopez, 1996, Experiment 3) adopted a different experimental design to distinguish between the two accounts (see Table I). In this EC design, the trial types for the noncontingent cue A are $AB \to O_1$, $B \to O_1$, $C \to$ no O, and the trial types for the contingent cue D are $DE \to O_2$, $E \to$ no O, $F \to O_2$, where O_1 and O_2 refer to the outcomes and no O is no outcome. Applying the causal model contingency formula to the target cues A and D yields a value of .5 in each case:

$$\Delta p = p(E/C) - p(E/-C) = .5 - 0 = .5.$$

For instance, the $AB \to O_1$, $B \to O_1$, and $C \to$ no O trials are now interpreted as $E_A E_B \gets$ cause$_1$, $E_B \gets$ cause$_1$, and $E_C \gets$ no cause trials, from which the crucial cause$_1 \to E_A$ contingency is readily seen to be $\Delta p = .5$. The calculation is the same for the contingent cue D.

TABLE I

TRIAL TYPES IN EXPERIMENT 2

	Cues → outcomes	Target relationship
Noncontingent	$AB \to O_1$, $B \to O_1$, $C \to$ no O^a	$A \to O_1$
Contingent	$DE \to O_2$, $E \to$ no O, $F \to O_2$	$D \to O_2$

[a] A–F are symptoms; O_1 and O_2 are diseases; no O, no disease.

Thus, Waldmann and Holyoak's causal model theory predicts the absence of any difference between ratings for the contingent and noncontingent cues in this design. What about associationist theories? The addition of the extra trial type ($C \rightarrow$ no O and $F \rightarrow O_2$) compared to Saavedra's design to equate the outcome frequencies does not effect the predictions of the Rescorla–Wagner (1972) theory, since the contingent cue remains a better predictor of the outcome than the noncontingent cue, and a selection effect is again predicted (see Shanks, 1991, p. 438, for a simulation of this trial design). The inclusion of the $C \rightarrow$ no O trials does not alter the fact that cue B is able to "overshadow" cue A and prevent it (at asymptote) from acquiring any associative strength for outcome O_1. Similarly, the inclusion of the $F \rightarrow O_2$ trials does not impair cue D's ability to obtain an asymptotic associative strength of λ for outcome O_2. The experiment therefore provides a crucial test between the two theories. Note that Shanks (1991, Experiment 2) conducted an experiment with this design that yielded a significant difference in judgments for the target contingent and noncontingent cues. But although that study used an EC medical diagnosis task, the cues (symptoms) were given real names (e.g., swollen glands). Waldmann and Holyoak (1992) argued that subjects in this case may have recruited real-world knowledge of extraexperimental causal factors that would have altered the nature of the task. The present experiment therefore uses abstract cues such as "symptom A."

The cover story stated that on each trial a patient's symptoms would be described and the task was to predict the accompanying disease. The symptoms were labeled with letters (A to L) and diseases with numbers (1 to 4), and the specific letters were initially assigned at random to the trial types given in Table I. The cues appeared on the screen in a list, and for trial types containing more than one cue, the order of cues in the list was chosen at random. The subject selected a category response and typed the appropriate key, and then corrective feedback was given. After this training phase, subjects were given a questionnaire in which they had to rate on a scale from 0 to 100 how strongly cues A and D were associated with each of the outcomes.

The critical result is that contingent ratings ($M = 66.6$) were reliably higher than noncontingent ones ($M = 58.2$). Although the difference between these means is small, the results plainly show that a cue-selection effect occurs with this design. The results are at variance with the idea that subjects compute contingency in the manner prescribed by Waldmann and Holyoak's (1992) causal model theory. In contrast, the results are exactly what would be predicted by an associative account of learning such as the Rescorla–Wagner theory. One such a theory, the cues—regardless of their real-world interpretation—represent the inputs to an associative network and the outcomes represent the target outputs of the network. Cue competition is predicted, since the relative predictiveness of the target cue is greater in the contingent than in the noncontingent conditions. The results replicate prior instances of cue selection but also show that selection occurs even when the appropriate interpretation of the cues and outcomes is as effects and causes, respectively.

On the other hand, we have failed to replicate Waldmann and Holyoak's apparent finding that cue selection is absent in EC tasks. Although our design and procedure differ in many ways from those used by Waldmann and Holyoak, we believe that our result is the more convincing one because, as Shanks and Lopez (1996) argue, there are a number of methodological problems in Waldmann and Holyoak's studies. The fact that a cue-competition effect occurs even in EC tasks allows us to eliminate the causal-model hypothesis, which attributes such effects to subjects' prior beliefs. It should be noted, however, that the present results do not per se rule out the idea that subjects base their contingency judgments on conditional contingencies; they merely challenge the claim that judgments are mediated by background causal knowledge (i.e., knowledge of causal direction), which directs subjects' assignments of cues and outcomes to causes and effects. Of course, if subjects compute the conditional contingency Δp by taking the difference between $p(O/C)$ and $p(O/-C)$ rather than the difference between $p(E/C)$ and $p(E/-C)$, then the results can be explained. It is to this more generic form of the theory that we will return later. First, though, we will consider yet another experimental result, which, as Shanks and Dickinson (1987) noted, seems to be inconsistent with associative theories of contingency judgment.

IV. Retrospective Revaluation

In a blocking design, judgments of the predictive value of cue A after AB → O compound trials are reduced if cue B has independently been pretrained as a predictor of the outcome. According to the variable reinforcement rule of Rescorla and Wagner (1972), blocking occurs because pretraining endows the competing cue B with a positive associative strength so that the error term is reduced in magnitude during compound training relative to a control condition in which the competing cue has not been pretrained. The consequence of this reduction in the error term is to attenuate the size of the increments in associative strength accruing to the target cue A during compound training. On the assumption that the associative strength of a cue determines the judged strength of its relationship with the outcome, the Rescorla–Wagner rule not only provides an explanation

TABLE II

DESIGN OF A BACKWARD
BLOCKING EXPERIMENT

Stage 1	Stage 2	Test
AB → O[a]	B → O	A
CD → O	D → no O	C

[a] A and C are the target cues, B and D the competing cues. O, Outcome; no O, no outcome.

of the blocking of contingency judgments but also predicts the way in which such judgments are controlled by variations in the contingency between a putative cause and the outcome (e.g., Dickinson et al., 1984; Wasserman et al., 1993).

Although the demonstration of blocking in contingency judgments provided the original impetus for associative accounts, Shanks and Dickinson (1987) concluded with a discussion of a variation of this paradigm, which had generated the most problematic evidence for such explanations. While replicating the forward blocking observed by Dickinson et al. (1984), Shanks (1985b) reported that judgments of a target event were also affected by the status of the competing cue in a backward procedure in which the order of compound training and the training of the competing cue alone was reversed. The design of the backward procedure is illustrated in Table II. In the first stage (Shanks, 1985b, Experiment 3) subjects receive a series of episodes in which target cues, A and C, are presented in compound with two competing cues, B and D, respectively, and these compounds are paired with the outcome across a number of AB → O and CD → O episodes.[2] The Rescorla–Wagner theory anticipates that as a result of this experience, both the target and competing cues in each compound should acquire associative strength in proportion to their relative saliences (Rescorla & Wagner, 1972). In the second stage both competing cues receive further training. Cue B is paired with the outcome by itself on B → O episodes, whereas D is presented without the outcome on D → no O episodes.

This second stage should have the effect of augmenting the associative strength of B while decreasing that of D. Of prime interest, however, is the effect of this training with B and D on the associative strength of the two target cues, A and C. Given that the two competing cues and the two target events have the same relative salience (a reasonable assumption given that the stimuli and events that took the roles of the cues were

[2] This a schematic description. In Shanks's (1985b) experiment the pairing of the compound events with the outcome was probabilistic.

counterbalanced across A and C and across B and D in the Shanks, 1985b, study), A and C should have the same associative strength at the end of compound training in the first stage. Moreover, these strengths should not be affected by the training schedules of the competing cues in the second stage. As the target cues, A and C, are not presented during the second stage, they have no salience on these episodes and hence a zero α value with the result that no increments or decrements of their associative strengths should occur (see Equation 1). In contrast to this prediction, however, Shanks (1985b) observed that A was rated as less predictively effective than C. Thus, the training of B and D in the second stage retrospectively affected the attribution of predictive efficacy to A and C, a process that lies outside the scope of standard associative theories.

On the basis of this retrospective revaluation effect, Shanks and Dickinson (1987) concluded that contingency judgments are not based directly on the associative strength of the target event but rather involve the application of a comparator decision rule. A recent study by Van Hamme and Wasserman (1994), however, has produced a significant advance in our understanding of this retrospective revaluation process by demonstrating that it can occur on an episode-by-episode basis. Across a series of episodes, some of which contained an outcome and some not, their subjects received two compound cues composed of a common cue X and cues unique to each compound, A and B, to generate the compounds AX and BX. When asked to rate the predictive efficacy of each cue after every episode, not surprisingly AX → O and AX → no O episodes enhanced and reduced the ratings for A, respectively. More important, however, was the finding that these episodes also changed the rating for B, with the AX → O episodes decreasing the rating and AX → no O augmenting it. Thus, the absent cue underwent a change in contingency judgment that was opposite in sign to that for the presented cue.

Not only did Van Hamme and Wasserman (1994) demonstrate the dynamic nature of retrospective revaluation, they also suggested a formal revision to the Rescorla–Wagner equation to encompass this process (see Chapters 8 & 6, respectively, by Cheng et al. and Wasserman et al., this volume). While noting that in the original formulation the β learning rate parameter has nonzero (and potentially different) values on episodes when the outcome is present and omitted (Rescorla & Wagner, 1972), they argued that the same might be true for the α parameter for the cue. Specifically, they suggested that α for a cue has a negative value on episodes when that cue is absent. Markman (1989) and, more recently, Tassoni (1995) have made the corresponding suggestion in the case of a connectionist network governed by the delta rule learning algorithm by coding an absent cue with a negative activation of the respective input unit.

The consequences of this revised coding for retrospective revaluation can be illustrated by reconsidering the backward procedure (see Table II). On the initial B → O episodes in Stage 2 the error term in Equation 1 will be positive because the associative strength of B will be less than λ after the compound training in Stage 1, whereas the α value for A will be negative in the absence of this cue. Consequently, the associative strength of A will suffer a decrement on the B → O episodes. By contrast, the error term will be negative on D → no O episodes (as the outcome is omitted) with the result that λ is zero. This negative error will then interact with the negative α for the omitted target cue C to yield a positive increment in its associative strength. A reiteration of these processes across the episodes of Stage 2 will produce a progressive increase in the associative strength of C and a decrement in that for A, thus producing the retrospective revaluation effect. Note that in this modified Rescorla–Wagner model only the associative strengths of the cues actually presented on an episode enter into the error term.

An obvious omission in this modified application of the Rescorla–Wagner rule is any specification of the processes that determine whether or not a particular absent cue should take on a negative rather than zero α value. To complete an associative account of retrospective revaluation, we need an associative process that would endow A but not C with a negative α on B → O episodes in order to predict the retrospective effect. A number of authors (Chapman, 1991; Markman, 1989; Tassoni, 1995) have suggested that only the omission of the *expected* cue should generate a negative α (or a negative activation on its input unit in a network), and that it is the formation of within-compound associations during the first stage of training that provides the basis for this expectation in the case of A but not C. Thus, an association is formed not only between A and the outcome and between B and the outcome during the AB → O training but also between A and B themselves. Rescorla (1981) has provided evidence for the formation of such within-compound associations during a blocking procedure. As a result of this within-compound association, the presentation of B on the B → O episodes in Stage 2 should produce an expectation of A, but not C, via the within-compound association between A and B. If it is assumed that an expectation of a cue together with its omission endow the stimulus with a negative α, a selective loss of associative strength by cue A during B → O episodes is anticipated. Correspondingly, only C should have a negative α on D → no O episodes and thus acquire associative strength during these episodes.

A. Experiment 3

According to this account, therefore, retrospective revaluation depends on the formation of within-compound associations, so that manipulations that interfere with such associations should attenuate the effect. Recently, Dickinson and Burke (1996) have investigated the role of within-compound associations by varying whether or not each target cue was consistently paired with the same competing cue during compound training on the grounds that consistent pairing favors the formation of within-compound associations. In their procedure three sets of two target cues, collectively designated A and C, were trained under one of two contingencies, with the cues being foods that a hypothetical patient ate and the outcome being an allergy that ensued. Under the AB → O, B → O contingency each target A cue was compounded with one of three competing B cues and this compound was paired with the outcome for three trials in Stage 1 (see Tables II & III). Similarly, compounds of each target C and competing D cue were also paired with the outcome during the first stage of the CD → O, D → no O contingency. Then, in the second stage each of the competing B cues was paired with the outcome, whereas each competing D cue was presented alone and without the outcome. Given this design, retrospective revaluation would be manifest by higher ratings of contingency for the target C cues than for the A cues.

Because a number of different stimuli took the roles of the target and competing cues in each contingency, Dickinson and Burke were able to manipulate the association between them during the compound training in the first stage. As Table III shows, in the consistent condition each target cue was paired with the same competing cue on each of the three trials of Stage 1, thus allowing the formation of within-compound associations

TABLE III

TRIAL TYPES IN THE CONSISTENT AND VARIED CONDITIONS OF THE COMPOUND STAGE OF EXPERIMENT 3

Condition	Trial blocks		
	1	2	3
Consistent	$A_1B_1 \rightarrow O^a$	$A_1B_1 \rightarrow O$	$A_1B_1 \rightarrow O$
	$A_2B_2 \rightarrow O$	$A_2B_2 \rightarrow O$	$A_2B_2 \rightarrow O$
	$A_3B_3 \rightarrow O$	$A_3B_3 \rightarrow O$	$A_3B_3 \rightarrow O$
Varied	$A_1B_1 \rightarrow O$	$A_1B_2 \rightarrow O$	$A_1B_3 \rightarrow O$
	$A_2B_1 \rightarrow O$	$A_2B_2 \rightarrow O$	$A_2B_3 \rightarrow O$
	$A_3B_1 \rightarrow O$	$A_3B_2 \rightarrow O$	$A_3B_3 \rightarrow O$

[a] A_1–A_3 are the target cues, B_1–B_3 the competing cues; O, Outcome. In the Consistent condition, each target cue is paired three times with the same competing cue. In the Varied condition, each target cue occurs with a different competing cue on each trial.

between target A and C cues and their respective competing B and D cues. By contrast, each target cue was paired with a different competing cue on each of the three compound trials of Stage 1 in the varied condition. Within-compound associations should be minimized in this varied condition not only because each target cue is paired only once with any given competing cue but also because any association formed on this single pairing should be extinguished on trials when the competing cue is compounded with a different target cue. Thus, to the extent that retrospective revaluation depends on within-compound association, less revaluation should be observed in the varied than in the consistent condition.

Figure 4, which displays the mean difference between the ratings for the target cues on test and their initial ratings prior to training, shows that the data fulfilled this prediction. Retrospective revaluation was evident in the consistent condition in that the target A cues trained under the AB → O, B → O contingency yielded lower difference scores than the target C cues trained under the CD → O, D → no O contingency. In fact, the revaluation appears to have been complete in that training with the AB → O, B → O contingency enhanced the ratings for the target cues no more than in a

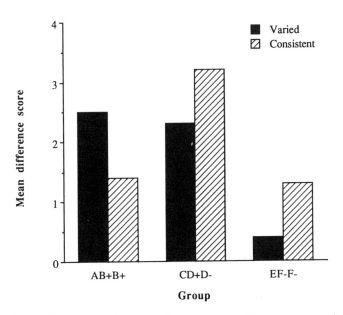

Fig. 4.   Mean difference score for the contingency ratings of the target cues trained under the backward contingencies shown in Table II, depending on whether the pairing of the competing and target cues during compound training in Stage 1 was consistent or varied. + Indicates outcome; − indicates no outcome.

control EF → no O, F → no O contingency in which the cues were never paired with the outcome. By contrast to the pattern observed in the consistent condition, no retrospective revaluation was observed with varied training. In this condition the difference scores were very similar for target cues trained under the AB → O, B → O and CD → O, D → no O contingencies and higher than those for the targets exposed under the control EF → no O, F → no O contingency.

To check that any influence of the consistency of compound training was not just a product of a general effect on selective learning, a further group of subjects was exposed to a forward condition in which training with the competing cue alone preceded compound training, thus producing B → O, AB → O, D → no O, CD → O and F → no O, EF → no O contingencies. Associative learning theories anticipate that whether or not the target and competing cues are consistently paired during compound training should have no effect on the magnitude of blocking in a forward condition. Under the B → O, AB → O contingency each pairing of a target cue with the outcome during compound training would occur in the presence of a pretrained competing cue, thus producing a reduced error term on these episodes. Moreover, the magnitude of the reduction should be the same whether or not a target cue is compounded with the same competing cue on each trial or with a different one. In accord with this expectation, comparable blocking was observed in the consistent and varied conditions. As Fig. 5 shows, in each case the difference scores were lower for the target A cues trained under the B → O, AB → O contingency than for the target C cues trained under the D → no O, CD → O contingency. The fact that the scores for the A cues did not differ from those for the control E cues suggests that pretraining the competing B cues completely blocked learning about the target cues under the B → O, AB → O contingency.

Although the dependence of retrospective revaluation on within-compound associations allows such effects to be encompassed by formal associative learning rules, such as that offered by Rescorla and Wagner (1972), what we lack at present is any account of the processes by which these associations function to control learning. As we have already noted, Markman (1989) and Tassoni (1995) have suggested that within-compound associations result in an absent but expected cue being coded by a negative activation of the respective input unit within a connectionist network, and Dickinson and Burke (1996) have revised Wagner's (1981) SOP model of conditioning to create a specific mechanism by which this might be achieved. Whatever the merits of this account, it is clear that retrospective revaluation, which we initially thought was fatal for a pure associative explanation of contingency judgment, can be encompassed by associative theory once the role of within-compound associations is recognized. Indeed,

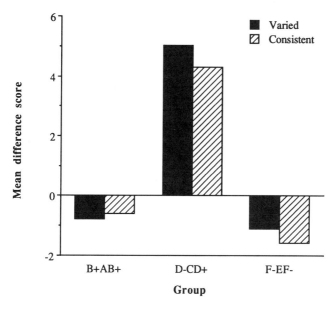

Fig. 5. Mean difference score for the contingency ratings of the target cues trained under the forward contingencies, depending on whether the pairing of the competing and target cues during compound training in Stage 2 was consistent or varied. + Indicates outcome; − indicates no outcome.

the evidence that retrospective revaluation is mediated by such association provides positive support for the operation of associative processes in contingency judgment.

V. Trial Order Effects

Returning to the contrast between associative and contingency-based theories, it is important to note that the results of the foregoing experiment are quite troublesome for the PCM. Perhaps the clearest way of distinguishing between the contingency and Rescorla–Wagner theories is in terms of their predictions concerning manipulations of the order in which different trial types are seen. Since, according to the PCM, subjects simply maintain records of the relevant conditional probabilities, changing the order in which trials are seen should have no effect: a conditional probability is the same whatever the order of the events on which it is based. Yet, in Experiment 3 the forward and backward orders were not equivalent: the manipulation of varied versus consistent pairings affected backward but not forward blocking.

The Rescorla–Wagner theory, on the other hand, predicts profound effects of trial order variations. We will elaborate the predictions of the model later, but for present purposes the main thing to note is that the model predicts what we might call "recency/density" effects, whereby the most recent and dense trial types will have the biggest impact on judgments. Apart from the results of Experiment 3, what other evidence is there for trial order effects in contingency judgment? Some fairly clear examples were reported by Chapman (1991), who noted that her results were problematic for contingency-based theories. However, the effects she obtained were quite small in absolute terms, and we therefore decided to adopt some rather more radical manipulations of trial order to test the probabilistic contrast model.

A. Experiment 4

In this experiment subjects saw trial types in which cue A was contingently related to outcome O_1 when compounded with cue B (AB $\rightarrow$ O_1, B $\rightarrow$ no O trials) in Stage 1. Then, in Stage 2, trials were presented in which A was negatively related to the same outcome when compounded with cue C (AC $\rightarrow$ no O, C $\rightarrow$ O_1). This is labeled Condition +/− to reflect the fact that the positive contingency preceded the negative one. Subjects also saw trial types in which cue D was negatively related to outcome O_2 in Stage 1 when compounded with cue E (DE $\rightarrow$ no O, E $\rightarrow$ O_2 trials), and trials in Stage 2 in which it was positively related to the outcome when compounded with cue F (DF $\rightarrow$ O_2, F $\rightarrow$ no O). In this case (Condition −/+), the negative contingency trials preceded the positive ones. At the end of Stage 2, subjects made judgments about the magnitude of the A $\rightarrow$ O_1 and D $\rightarrow$ O_2 relationships. Table IV shows the actual design used during the learning stage.

TABLE IV

Design of Experiment 4

Trial order	Stage 1	Stage 2	Test cue	Judgment
+/−[a]	AB $\rightarrow$ O_1[b]	AC $\rightarrow$ no O	A	$M = 18.2$
	B $\rightarrow$ no O	C $\rightarrow$ O_1		
−/+	DE $\rightarrow$ no O	DF $\rightarrow$ O_2	D	$M = 45.0$
	E $\rightarrow$ O_2	F $\rightarrow$ no O		

[a] In Condition +/− the contingency between the target cue and outcome is positive in Stage 1 and negative in Stage 2. In Condition −/+ the contingencies are reversed.
[b] A–F are symptoms; O_1 and O_2 are diseases; no O, no disease.

The Rescorla–Wagner theory makes a clear and simple prediction for this design, namely that there will be a strong recency effect in judgments: specifically, cue A should receive lower ratings than cue D, because at the time the judgment is made, the most recent contingency for A is negative, while that for D is positive. Figure 6 shows the predicted association strengths of cues A and D across trials under these conditions, and, as predicted, the terminal strength for A is much lower than that for D. In fact, at asymptote A's associative strength is $-\lambda$ and D's is $+\lambda$.

What does the PCM predict about this experiment? Apart from the order in which trials are seen, the evidence concerning the A $\rightarrow$ O$_1$ and D $\rightarrow$ O$_2$ relationships is identical. In each case, two obvious contrasts can be computed. For cue A, one contrast is conditional on the presence of B and another is conditional on the presence of C. Despite the fact that these contrasts yield entirely different values (i.e., $+1$ and -1, respectively), the *pair* of contrasts for A is exactly analogous to the pair for D (one conditional on the presence of E, the other conditional on the presence of F). Hence, across the whole experiment, values of Δp computed for A and D must be

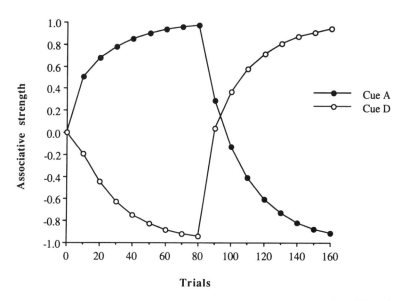

Fig. 6. Rescorla–Wagner theory predictions for the trial order manipulation of Experiment 4. In the first stage, the trial types are AB $\rightarrow$ O$_1$, B $\rightarrow$ no O, DE $\rightarrow$ no O, E$\rightarrow$ O$_2$. In the second stage the trial types are AC $\rightarrow$ no O, C $\rightarrow$ O$_1$, DF $\rightarrow$ O$_2$, F $\rightarrow$ no O. The figure shows the evolution of the A $\rightarrow$ O$_1$ and D$\rightarrow$ O$_2$ associative strengths across trials under these conditions. The parameter α was set to .2 for each cue and β was set to .2 on trials with the outcome and .1 on trials with no outcome.

identical. Because it is silent on the issue of trial order effects, a difference in judgments for A and D would appear to be outside the theory's scope.

However, a straightforward way to apply the theory would be to assume that subjects maintain a restricted temporal "window" of trials over which contingencies are computed. At the time of making their contingency judgments, perhaps subjects only include the Stage 2 trials in their window, in which case a trial order effect (greater judgments for D than for A) will be anticipated. Assuming that a trial order effect is obtained, how can we evaluate this window-based version of the PCM? Suppose that after making their judgments, subjects are presented with test trials in which Stage 1 and Stage 2 trial types are re-presented and have to make choice responses (without feedback). The key issue is whether subjects are able to remember the correct responses for the Stage 1 trial types. If we present a patient with symptom C, we will obviously expect subjects to diagnose disease O_1 with greater probability than they will for a patient with symptoms AC. Since to explain a trial order effect we have to assume that the temporal window includes only the Stage 2 trials, A will be evaluated as having a negative contingency. But if the window excludes the Stage 1 trials, then subjects should apply the negative contingency for A to the Stage 1 test trials, as well, which is to say that they should be less likely to predict O_1 on an AB than on a B trial. Thus, subjects will reverse the diagnoses they make for the Stage 1 trials: in Stage 1 itself, they learned to predict O_1 on AB but not on B trials, but after Stage 2 they should now (on the temporal window theory) more often predict O_1 on B rather than AB trials. A similar argument can be made for cue D, with the opposite change of predictions.

Note also that it does not matter whether the window contains less than all of the Stage 2 trials or whether it contains some but not all of the Stage 1 trials. If it contains some Stage 1 trials, then a trial order effect cannot be explained. So long as one trial of each type is included in the window, the conditional probabilities that can be computed are the same as if many trials are included. On the other hand, if the window contains less than all of the Stage 2 trials, the test trial results should still show a reversal. In sum, the critical prediction of the temporal window version of the PCM is that if there is a trial order effect, then subjects will make many incorrect responses on the test trials.

The learning stage consisted of 160 trials, divided into two stages of 80 trials. The stages were presented within a single series so that subjects could not distinguish them. Actually, the design shown in Table IV represents only half of the trial types: the remaining ones used additional cues and diseases to replicate the design, such that two sets of trials were included in which the trial types were as specified for Condition +/−, and two other conditions corresponding to Condition $-/+$. The program randomly selected 1 of the 8 trial types in each phase with the single restriction that 10 trials of each trial type should occur. Subjects' ratings were required at the end of the learning stage. Once the subjects had made their ratings, the test phase took place. This phase consisted of 32 trials. Each of the 16 trial types presented during the learning stage was presented twice in a random order. Subjects were not given any feedback about their responding in the test stage.

Subjects' judgments showed a substantial trial order effect, with ratings in the $-/+$ condition being significantly higher than those in the $+/-$ condition ($M = 45.0$ and 18.2, respectively). However, the main purpose of Experiment 4 was to evaluate the temporal window version of the PCM, and this requires examination of the percentage of correct diagnoses during the test stage. For those trial types originally presented within the first stage, the percentage of correct diagnoses was 71.6. For those trial types originally presented in the second stage, the percentage was 70.3. The difference was not statistically significant. Thus, subjects do not seem to have unlearned the Stage 1 trial arrangements as a result of learning new contingencies in Stage 2.

The results broken down for the different trial types are shown in Table V. Here, the figures are in terms of the percentages of O_1 predictions on the test trials involving cues A, B, and C, and of O_2 predictions for trials

TABLE V

PERCENTAGES OF DISEASE DIAGNOSES ON
THE TEST TRIALS OF EXPERIMENT 4 FOR
TRIAL TYPES THAT HAD BEEN SEEN IN
STAGE 1 AND STAGE 2

Trial Type	% Diagnoses
Stage 1	
AB[a]	48.8
B[a]	2.5
DE[b]	21.3
E[b]	78.8
Stage 2	
AC[a]	23.8
C[a]	70.0
DF[b]	48.8
F[b]	6.3

[a] Data are the percentages of diagnoses of disease O_1.
[b] Data are the percentages of diagnoses of disease O_2.

with D, E, and F. Thus, the figure of 48.8 for AB means that subjects chose disease O_1 on 48.8% of trials, whereas they chose disease O_1 only on 2.5% of B trials. Inspection of these data show that for the Stage 2 trial types, cue A had a strongly negative strength in that it dramatically reduced (from 70.0 to 23.8) the percentage of trials on which cue C was assumed to predict O_1. In contrast, cue D had a strongly positive strength in that it substantially increased (from 6.3 to 48.8) the percentage of trials on which cue F was assumed to predict O_2. On the basis of the temporal window theory, then, we should expect that these strengths will transfer to the Stage 1 trial types, but the table shows that this is most definitely not the case. Far from reducing the percentage of O_1 predictions on B trials, the addition of cue A actually leads to more disease diagnoses (48.8 vs 2.5). At the same time, far from increasing the percentage of disease O_2 diagnoses on E trials, there are actually fewer (21.3 vs 78.8) on DE trials. In fact, there is no evidence whatsoever that Stage 2 has left A and D with, respectively, generalized negative and positive strength.

This experiment provides, we suggest, clear evidence against the PCM. First, the standard version of the theory cannot explain the basic trial order effect. With unconstrained representation of the trial types, the conditional probabilities for the $A \rightarrow O_1$ and $D \rightarrow O_2$ contingencies are identical and hence judgments should be identical. Moreover, there is no mechanism in the theory whereby different contrasts might be given different weights depending on the recency of the trial types across which they are computed. The only way to create a trial order effect is to argue that the record of trial types subjects use to make their judgments does not include *any* Stage 1 trials. If such trials are excluded, then a trial order effect is indeed predicted because the $A \rightarrow O_1$ and $D \rightarrow O_2$ contrasts in Stage 2 differed. However, it is hard to see how subjects would then be able to make correct predictions for the Stage 1 trial types which, *ex hypothesi*, have been excluded from their mental record.

We argued above that the trial order results from this experiment are quite congenial to the Rescorla–Wagner theory, but actually the test trial results of the present experiment require some modification to the theory. However, before we return to the issue of associationist models, we present one further experiment that provides even stronger trial order results that the PCM cannot deal with.

B.   EXPERIMENT 5

In this experiment subjects again saw trial types in which cue A was contingently related to outcome 1 when compounded with cue B (AB $\rightarrow O_1$, B $\rightarrow$ no O trials), as well as trials in which it was negatively related to the same outcome when compounded with cue C (AC $\rightarrow$ no O, C $\rightarrow$ O$_1$). However, rather than being presented in separate blocks, these trial types were intermixed except that the positive contingency trials predominated at the start of the learning phase while the negative ones were predominant toward the end (Condition $+/-$). Subjects also saw trial types in which cue D was negatively related to outcome O$_2$ when compounded with cue E (DE $\rightarrow$ no O, E $\rightarrow$ O$_2$ trials), as well as trials in which it was positively related to the outcome when compounded with cue F (DF $\rightarrow$ O$_2$, F $\rightarrow$ no O). In this case (Condition $-/+$), the negative contingency trials predominated at the start of the experiment and the positive ones at the end. At the end of the learning stage, subjects made judgments about the magnitude of the A $\rightarrow$ O$_1$ and D $\rightarrow$ O$_2$ relationships as in the previous experiment. Table VI shows the actual design used during the learning stage.

What does the PCM predict about this experiment? Apart from the order in which trials are seen, the evidence concerning the A $\rightarrow$ O$_1$ and D $\rightarrow$ O$_2$ relationships is identical, as in the previous experiment, and hence across the whole experiment, Δp for these relationships must be identical and no trial order effect on judgments is expected. Two obvious contrasts are again computable for each cue. For cue A, the two contrasts are:

$$\Delta p_A = p(O_1/A \cdot B) - p(O_1/-A \cdot B) = 1.0 - 0 = 1.0$$

conditional on the presence of B, and

$$\Delta p_A = p(O_1/A \cdot C) - p(O_1/-A \cdot C) = 0 - 1.0 = -1.0$$

TABLE VI

DESIGN OF EXPERIMENT 5

Condition	No. of trials per Block 1 2 3 4	Trial types	Test cue	Judgment
$+/-$[a]	4 3 2 1	AB $\rightarrow$ O$_1$[b]	A	$M = 39.7$
	4 3 2 1	B $\rightarrow$ no O		
	1 2 3 4	AC $\rightarrow$ no O		
	1 2 3 4	C $\rightarrow$ O$_1$		
$-/+$[a]	4 3 2 1	DE $\rightarrow$ no O	D	$M = 52.9$
	4 3 2 1	E $\rightarrow$ O$_2$		
	1 2 3 4	DF $\rightarrow$ O$_2$		
	1 2 3 4	F $\rightarrow$ no O		

[a] In Condition $+/-$ the predominant contingency between the target cue and outcome is positive early in the experiment and negative later. In Condition $-/+$ the contingencies are reversed.
[b] A–F are symptoms; O$_1$ and O$_2$ are diseases; no O, no disease.

conditional on the presence of C. For cue D, the contrasts are:

$$\Delta p_D = p(O_2/D \cdot E) - p(O_2/-D \cdot E) = 0 - 1.0 = -1.0$$

conditional on the presence of E, and

$$\Delta p_D = p(O_2/D \cdot F) - p(O_2/-D \cdot F) = 1.0 - 0 = 1.0$$

conditional on the presence of F. Plainly, these pairs of contrasts yield identical values.

Even if contingency is computed across a limited retrospective "window" the prediction is the same. Thus, suppose that contingencies are computed across, say, the last quarter of the experiment. This block contains trial types of every sort, and the conditional probabilities across this block that figure in the relevant contrasts are the same as they are across the whole learning phase. With the gradual transition of phases that occurs in this experiment, whatever the size of the moving window subjects consider, trial types of every sort must be included. And because such probabilities are independent of sample size, it is hard to see how the theory can explain effects due to the relative density of different trial types in different blocks of the experiment. Thus, according to the PCM, there is no reason to expect different ratings in the two trial order conditions. We will turn later to the predictions of the Rescorla–Wagner theory.

The learning stage consisted of 160 trials and it was divided into four blocks of trials. During the first block of trials, four trials were presented of each of the following trial types: $AB \rightarrow O_1$, $B \rightarrow$ no O, $DE \rightarrow$ no O, $E \rightarrow O_2$; and one trial of each of the following types: $AC \rightarrow$ no O, $C \rightarrow O_1$, $DF \rightarrow O_2$, $F \rightarrow$ no O (see Table VI). During the second block of trials, three and two trials were presented of the first and second trial types, respectively. During the third block of trials, two and three trials were presented. Finally, during the fourth block of trials, one and four trials were presented of the first and second trial types, respectively. On each trial, the program randomly selected 1 of the 16 trial types within each block.

The key result is that the mean ratings in Condition $-/+$ were greater than in Condition $+/-$ ($M = 52.9$ and 39.7, respectively), and the difference was statistically significant. Clearly, a substantial trial order effect has been obtained in this study, contrary to the PCM's predictions, and we can see no obvious way in which the theory can accommodate these data. The problem really seems to lie in the basic entity represented in the PCM, namely records of conditional probabilities. Because such probabilities are independent of sample size, it is very difficult for the theory to explain effects due to the relative density of different trial types.

This concludes our consideration of contingency theory. We believe that the results we have reported thus far make a strong case against the idea that people base their contingency judgments on the outcome of conditional contrasts computed over probability estimates. Experiments 3–5 showed that such a theory cannot explain the effects of trial order on judgments, Experiment 2 showed that the theory makes an incorrect prediction about so-called "diagnostic" tasks, and Experiment 1 showed that it cannot accurately predict the shapes of learning curves, particularly the initial divergence followed by convergence of judgments under noncontingent conditions with different outcome probabilities.

VI. Configural Representations

Although to this point we have argued that the Rescorla–Wagner theory provides an excellent account of contingency judgment (assuming the sort of within-compound associations needed to account for backward blocking), we now turn to some deeper problems that require a reexamination of the representational assumptions embodied in the theory. These begin with the results of Experiments 4 and 5, because it turns out that those results are as problematic for the Rescorla–Wagner theory as for the probabilistic contrast model. Why is this? First, consider Experiment 4. In the test stage presented at the end of the experiment, subjects were able to remember the cue–outcome contingencies they had observed in Stage 1 despite the fact that in Stage 2 contradictory contingencies had been presented. As Fig. 6 shows, at the end of Stage 2 cue A is predicted to have a strongly negative associative strength (equal at asymptote to $-\lambda$), which means that subjects should have been less likely to diagnose disease 1 on AB than on B test trials. This was not what happened, however, and so the theory makes the same incorrect prediction as the PCM.

In fact, in this experiment the Rescorla–Wagner theory predicts a phenomenon known as "catastrophic forgetting" (Lewandowsky, 1991; McCloskey & Cohen, 1989; Ratcliff, 1990; Sloman & Rumelhart, 1992). As a result of learning new contingencies in Stage 2, the relationships learned in Stage 1 should be totally unlearned. Although catastrophic forgetting has mainly been studied from the point of view of so-called "back propagation" networks, it represents as much of a problem for the basic Rescorla–Wagner theory. This is hardly surprising given that the back propagation learning algorithm is fundamentally just an extension of the Rescorla–Wagner rule to networks with hidden units.[3] The design of the experiment is rather similar to the classic A-B, A-C design used to study forgetting.

[3] In a number of simulations we have conducted, multilayer feedforward connectionist networks trained with the backpropagation algorithm have been uniformly unable to account for the test trial data of Experiment 4. All manifest catastrophic interference of the Stage 1 contingencies from the Stage 2 trials.

In Experiment 5, the difficulty is with the fact that subjects were able to master the task in the first place. During the experiment, subjects were able to make correct predictions for AB $\rightarrow$ O_1, B $\rightarrow$ no O, AC $\rightarrow$ no O, and C $\rightarrow$ O_1 trial types, but a moment's reflection reveals that there is no set of associative strengths that allow this to be achieved (in the language of category learning studies, this is a nonlinear classification problem). If B has a strength of zero (allowing correct responses on the B trials) then A must have an associative strength of λ to allow correct responses on the AB trials. On the other hand, if C has an associative strength of λ (allowing correct responses on the C trials) then A must have a strength of $-\lambda$ if correct responses are to be made on the AC trials. Clearly, A cannot simultaneously have both a positive and a negative strength for the same outcome, and hence according to the Rescorla–Wagner theory the discrimination should not be solvable.

Readers familiar with the application of the theory to animal conditioning will recognize that a simple solution to these problems, one that Rescorla (1973) himself proposed, is to allow the possibility that "unique" cues are generated whenever cues are combined together. Thus, the combination of cues A and B leads to the creation of an additional unique cue X, such that the configuration is actually ABX. The existence of such unique cues allows the problematic results of Experiments 4 (the test trial results) and 5 (the fact that the discrimination was solvable) to be explained. For Experiment 5, the task becomes solvable because the discrimination is now construed as ABX $\rightarrow$ O_1, B $\rightarrow$ no O, ACY $\rightarrow$ no O, C $\rightarrow$ O_1, and correct responses to each trial type will occur because the cues at asymptote will have the following associative strengths: A = 0, B = 0, C = λ, X = λ, and Y = $-\lambda$. For Experiment 4, the test trial results can be explained if the unique cues play a role. The crucial Stage 1 trial types are ABX $\rightarrow$ O_1 and B $\rightarrow$ no O and the Stage 2 trial types are ACY $\rightarrow$ no O and C $\rightarrow$ O_1. If X is sufficiently salient to acquire a significant amount of associative strength in Stage 1, then any change in A's associative strength during Stage 2 will be insufficient to allow the original ABX $\rightarrow$ O_1, B $\rightarrow$ no O discrimination to be reversed. Hence, responding on the test trials can still be reasonably accurate.

The fact that the Experiment 5 discrimination (AB $\rightarrow$ O_1, B $\rightarrow$ no O, AC $\rightarrow$ no O, C $\rightarrow$ O_1) can be solved by the model when unique cues are incorporated reflects an important and general point about the basic Rescorla–Wagner theory, namely that like other linear models it is incapable of solving nonlinear discriminations (see Smith & Medin, 1981, pp. 141–142). If each of the elements of the stimulus is regarded as being coded by an independent binary dimension, then a discrimination is said to be linear if it is possible to construct a plane in the stimulus space that perfectly

TABLE VII

DESIGN OF EXPERIMENT 6

Stage 1	Stage 2	Test
A → O, AB → no O, AC → O[a]	B → O, DE → no O	A, AB, AC

[a] A–D are foods; O is the allergy; no O, no allergy.

partitions it into regions corresponding to the different outcomes. The contingencies programmed in Experiment 5 represent an example of a nonlinear discrimination in that no such plane exists. However, the addition of unique cues means that nonlinear discriminations can be solved, since in the limit it will always be possible to produce the correct output for each trial type if all of the predictive weight is borne by the unique cues. Gluck (1991) has explored a number of other phenomena in human associative learning tasks that the unique cue idea is able to explain.[4]

Despite its ability to account for the learning data of the present experiment, we do not believe that the unique cue hypothesis is in fact viable. One immediate difficulty is that the model predicts that cue A (and by similar calculations cue D) has an asymptotic associative strength of 0, in which case the effect of trial order on judgments is left unexplained. This failure encourages us to look at alternative conditioning theories in which compounds of stimuli have direct configural representations and in which performance is mediated by the degree of similarity between one stimulus configuration and another. In its original form, as well as in the unique cue version, the Rescorla–Wagner theory assumes that responding to a compound stimulus is simply a linear function of the associative strengths of its components. Instead, it seems that subjects can learn about whole configurations of elements.

A. EXPERIMENT 6

In our final experiment, we looked further at the issue of configural representations. In this study (see Table VII), which exploited a design used in animal conditioning experiments by Holland (1984) and Pearce and Wilson (1991), as well as in a recent human contingency judgment experiment by Williams (1995; see also Williams, this volume, Ch. 3), subjects in the first stage received A → O, AB → no O, and AC → O trials. In the second stage they received B → O and DE → no O trials, and in the test stage

[4] One such problem for the Rescorla–Wagner theory that can readily be accommodated by a unique cue version is the finding that nonreinforced presentation of an inhibitor does not attenuate its ability to function as such (see Cheng et al., this volume, Ch. 8).

A, AB, and AC trials. What can we predict about the course of learning in these circumstances? It is fairly straightforward to see that the first stage should have led cue B to have negative associative strength, since outcome O occurred on A but not AB trials. Also, the standard form of the Rescorla–Wagner theory predicts that C should have zero associative strength at asymptote. In fact, the terminal strengths at asymptote will be λ for cue A, 0 for cue C, and $-\lambda$ for cue B. In the second stage, cue B is now paired with the outcome, so its negative associative strength should become positive. Again, assuming that learning reaches asymptote, B's associative strength will reach λ. Then, in the test phase subjects should be more likely to predict the outcome on the AB test trials than on the AC ones. This is because AB has a strength of 2λ, while AC has a strength of λ.

What about the unique cue version of the theory? As Pearce and Wilson noted, the predictions of the theory when unique cues are present depend on the relative saliences of the cues. In this case, the Stage 1 trial types become functionally $A \rightarrow O$, $ABX \rightarrow$ no O, and $ACY \rightarrow O$, and the critical Stage 2 trial type remains $B \rightarrow O$. Whatever the relative saliences of the unique and actual cues, though, the total association strength of ABX for the outcome must be at least as great at the end of Stage 2 as the total associative strength of ACY. This comes about because B's associative strength increases by at least an amount λ during Stage 2, which then transfers back to the ABX compound. Thus, the combined associative strength of the ABX compound must be at least λ (AB cannot be less than 0), which equals the total associative strength of ACY, and the prediction in this case is therefore that subjects should be at least as likely to predict the outcome on the AB test trials as on the AC ones. Plainly, the one outcome that cannot be predicted by either the original or unique cue version of the theory is that subjects predict the outcome with greater probability on AC than on AB test trials. Yet, if subjects are able to remember the correct Stage 1 associations for these trials types, that is exactly what they should do. Subjects saw 15 trials of each type in the first stage and 10 trials in Stage 2. In Stage 2, filler $DE \rightarrow$ no O trials were included to ensure that the correct response varied from trial to trial. The cues were foods and the outcomes allergies, and the assignment of names to the foods and allergies was counterbalanced.

The results are shown in Fig. 7, which reveals that learning proceeded as expected in Stages 1 and 2. During the latter, a marked increase in correct responses on B trials was observed, exactly as would be expected if B's associative strength was changing markedly. The critical data are shown on the right-hand side of the figure. They indicate that subjects were more likely to predict the outcome on AC than on AB trials, exactly contrary to the Rescorla–Wagner model's predictions. Why did this result

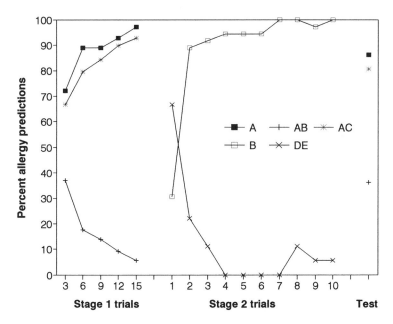

Fig. 7. Results from Experiment 6. In Stage 1 subjects received A → O, AB → no O, and AC → O trials, in Stage 2 B → O and DE → no O trials, and in the test stage A, AB and AC trials, where O is the outcome and no O is no outcome. The figure shows that during stage 1, subjects learned rapidly to make correct predictions, and during Stage 2 cue B became strongly associated with the outcome. In the test stage, subjects made many more allergy predictions on the AC than on the AB trials. This is exactly opposite to the predictions of the Rescorla–Wagner theory, even assuming that additional "unique" cues are formed by each stimulus compound.

emerge? Although the second stage B → O trials may have changed cue B's associative strength, the fact that subjects were more confident that the outcome would follow AC than AB trials in the test stage is entirely consistent with their experience of those compounds in Stage 1. The data seem to suggest that the change in the strength of element B in Stage 2 does not alter the strength of the AB compound.

The results of this experiment replicate those obtained in an animal conditioning procedure by Pearce and Wilson (1991), and Pearce and his colleagues have now reported numerous results that (like the present one) question the idea that the associative strength of a compound is a linear function of the strengths of its elements. How can the present results be reconciled with associationist theories? Briefly, Pearce's (1987, 1994; see also Kruschke, 1992) suggested solution is to retain the basic notion of increments and decrements in association strength but to modify the way in which stimuli are assumed to be represented. In a nutshell, the idea is that each stimulus (whether a single element or a compound of elements) should be represented by a single node in a network, and these nodes then become independently associated with the various outcomes. When a given stimulus is presented, it maximally activates the node that is dedicated to representing it, but also activates other units in proportion to its similarity to the stimuli that those units represent.

The consequence of this representational scheme is that revaluing one of the elements of a compound stimulus (as in Experiment 6) will have rather little impact on the associative strength of the compound itself, because the element and the compound are represented independently: from the network's point of view, the element is not part of the compound. Space limitations prevent us from going into the details of Pearce's configural theory, but Pearce and Wilson (1991) show that at a formal level, such a theory can account for the results of Experiment 6. The theory can also deal with the test trial data from Experiment 4, since the network would have distinct internal representations of the Stage 1 and Stage 2 trial types. Plainly, the continued development and analysis of associative models in which stimuli are represented in a configural manner will be an important avenue of future research.

VII. Conclusions

In this chapter we have ranged over a rather broad set of theoretical issues concerning contingency judgment, so a summary of our main conclusions is probably in order. We began by noting that one empirical result exists that appears straightaway to challenge the idea that contingency judgments can be modeled by the Rescorla–Wagner theory. This is the finding that judgments under noncontingent schedules do not always appear to converge across trials. In Experiment 1 we showed, however, that with a between-subjects design, judgments do converge in the appropriate manner and that acquisition profiles conform quite nicely to the theory's predictions. In Experiment 3 we showed that another problem for associative theory, namely retrospective revaluation of cue strength, is fairly easily understood via the formation of associations between the elements of the stimulus.

We have considered at some length Cheng and Holyoak's (1995) version of contingency theory called the probabilistic contrast model. We showed that this theory is able to provide only a poor fit to the data from Experiment 1, and in Experiment 2 we showed that interpreted in terms of causes and effects, the theory makes incorrect predictions about manipulations of contingency. In fact, Experiment 2 directly contradicted Waldmann and Holyoak's (1992) results. In Experiments 3–5, we showed that the PCM is unable to explain the effects of manipulations of trial order on judgments of contingency. Even when supplemented by a mechanism in which only a restricted window of trials are used for judgments, the theory is unable to generate the observed effects.

The basic trial order effect we obtained in Experiment 4 is easily predicted by the Rescorla–Wagner theory, but the results of the test stage of that experiment, and the results of Experiment 5, require some modification to the theory. One simple possibility is to allow for unique cues to be formed whenever cues or elements are combined. In Experiment 6, however, we showed that the unique cue hypothesis is insufficiently powerful. Instead, it seems that what is represented at the input level of an associative system is the entire configuration present on that trial: the elements from which the configuration is formed are treated quite independently.

Although the idea that stimuli are represented configurally allows the results of our experiments to be accommodated, it should be acknowledged that there are a number of problems facing this approach. First, our account of retrospective revaluation effects requires an elemental rather than a configural analysis: in an $AB \rightarrow O$, $B \rightarrow O$ design, subjects are assumed to relate what they learn in the second stage about element B to what they already know about compound AB, such that the balance of associative strengths of A and B is altered. It is hard to see how a configural analysis, whereby the compound AB is represented quite independently of its elements, would allow this to happen. Second, some recent data reported by Williams et al. (1994; see Williams, this volume, Ch. 3) raise the possibility that subjects may behave "configurally" only under certain conditions: sometimes, they may behave more in the "elemental" manner proposed by the Rescorla–Wagner theory. Williams et al. conducted a simple blocking experiment but pretrained various groups of subjects in different ways. In one condition the pretraining was designed to foster an "elemental" strategy whereby subjects would to some degree analyze each cue separately. Specifically, the pretraining phase involved exposure to intermixed $X \rightarrow O_1$ and $XY \rightarrow O_1$ trials, and although the XY configuration is paired with the outcome, there is explicit information suggesting that it is the X element of the configuration that is the important one. In a second condition, pretraining was designed to foster a "configural" strategy. Here, subjects received $XY \rightarrow O_1$, $X \rightarrow$ no O, and $Y \rightarrow$ no O trials; clearly, in this case it is the XY configuration rather than either of its elements that predicts the outcome.

After this pretraining phase, subjects then went on to the main phase of the experiment in which they received a standard blocking problem using a new set of cues. In the first stage B → O_2 and D → no O trials were presented, followed in the second stage by AB → O_2 and CD → O_2 trials. What would we expect to happen in this situation when subjects finally rate cues A and C? On the basis of the results of Experiment 3, we might expect to see that cue A is blocked and receives lower ratings than cue C, and this is exactly what happened for subjects who received the elemental pretraining. However, for those subjects given the configural pretraining, no blocking was observed, and instead A and C received equal ratings.

To explain this intriguing result, Williams et al. (1994) argued that when subjects saw the AB and CD trials, they could treat these compounds either as being composed of separable elements or as constituting configurations. In the former case, analysis will reveal that cue B is more likely than cue A to be the element most predictive of the outcome and that cue C is more likely than cue D to be predictive, and hence blocking will be observed. In contrast, if the subjects are inclined to treat the AB and CD configurations as being relatively unrelated to the B and D elements seen in the earlier stage, then they should treat them equally, since each is paired to the same extent with the outcome. In this case, no blocking would be expected.

The success of Williams et al.'s pretraining manipulations to bias the way subjects rated the cues in the blocking part of the experiment suggests that this strategic theory is correct. However, in preliminary experiments we have been unable to reverse the "configural" behavior seen in Experiment 6. Regardless of the form of pretraining given, when subjects went on to the training and test phases of that experiment, they were more likely to predict the outcome on AC than on AB trials, contrary to the "elemental" strategy. In fact, we have been unable to find any manipulation that reverses (or indeed removes) this tendency. Although our experimental procedure and materials are rather different from those of Williams et al. (1994), the results plainly suggest that there is a limit to people's ability to switch between different strategies. Further investigation of the ways in which subjects can actively modulate their strategies for judging event contingencies is clearly a priority.

A final issue that we must address is the question of whether human judgments of contingency are "rational" or not, in the restricted sense of conforming to a normative theory. Many researchers (e.g., Allan, 1980; Cheng & Holyoak, 1995; Wasserman et al. 1983) agree that the appropriate normative theory is provided by the Δp metric: contingency judgments should then be evaluated for their objective accuracy against Δp, and are assumed to be biased whenever they deviate from that statistic. On such a view, it would appear that we must be committed to the claim that contingency judgments are not normative, since we have argued at some length that they cannot be understood in terms of the computation of Δp. We have instead endorsed the Rescorla–Wagner theory, yet at the same time it is well known that the associative strengths generated by that theory are (at asymptote and subject to certain constraints) equivalent to the values of Δp (Chapman & Robbins, 1990; Cheng & Holyoak, 1995). How can we explain this apparent paradox?

It is crucial to distinguish between the claims (1) that judgments conform to the Δp rule (a notion that we generally support), and (2) that judgments are produced by an explicit mental version of the Δp rule in which subjects maintain some representations of the relevant conditional probabilities and base their judgments on the difference between these probabilities (a view that we regard as false with respect to typical contingency judgment tasks). While we argue that our results show that claim (2) cannot be correct, we would agree that, in general, and *under ideal circumstances,* contingency estimates do conform to the Δp rule and are hence perfectly rational (see Shanks, 1995a). The ideal circumstances in question would be that learning needs to have proceeded to asymptote, that the trial types need to be intermixed, and so on. Plainly, in many of our studies (e.g., Experiments 4 and 5) these requirements were not met, and this is why judgments deviated from Δp. Rather than proving that contingency judgment is non-normative, however, such results should be viewed in the same way as visual illusions: manifestations of an incorrect output from a system that fundamentally does provide a true picture of the world but that can be misled as a result of having to produce a response on the basis of insufficient evidence.

Acknowledgments

The research described here was supported in part by a project grant from the United Kingdom Biotechnology and Biological Sciences Research Council to D. R. Shanks. The support of the Economic and Social Research Council is also gratefully acknowledged. The work was part of the program of the ESRC Centre for Economic Learning and Social Evolution. We thank Keith Holyoak, Doug Medin, and Michael Waldmann for their helpful comments. Correspondence concerning this article should be addressed to David R. Shanks, Department of Psychology, University College London, Gower St., London WC1E 6BT, England. Electronic mail may be sent to: david.shanks@psychol.ucl.ac.uk.

References

Allan, L. G. (1980). A note on measurement of contingency between two binary variables in judgment tasks. *Bulletin of the Psychonomic Society, 15,* 147–149.

Allan, L. G., & Jenkins, H. M. (1980). The judgment of contingency and the nature of the response alternatives. *Canadian Journal of Psychology, 34,* 1–11.

Baker, A. G., Berbrier, M., & Vallée-Tourangeau, F. (1989). Judgments of a 2 × 2 contingency table: Sequential processing and the learning curve. *Quarterly Journal of Experimental Psychology, 41B,* 65–97.

Baker, A. G., Mercier, P., Vallée-Tourangeau, F., Frank, R., & Pan, M. (1993). Selective associations and causality judgments: Presence of a strong causal factor may reduce judgments of a weaker one. *Journal of Experimental Psychology: Learning, Memory, and Cognition, 19,* 414–432.

Chapman, G. B. (1991). Trial order affects cue interaction in contingency judgment. *Journal of Experimental Psychology: Learning, Memory and Cognition, 17,* 837–854.

Chapman, G. B., & Robbins, S. J. (1990). Cue interaction in human contingency judgment. *Memory & Cognition, 18,* 537–545.

Cheng, P. W. (1993). Separating causal laws from causal facts: Pressing the limits of statistical relevance. In D. L. Medin (Ed.), *The psychology of learning and motivation* (Vol. 30, pp. 215–264). San Diego, CA: Academic Press.

Cheng, P. W., & Holyoak, K. J. (1995). Complex adaptive systems as intuitive statisticians: Causality, contingency, and prediction. In H. L. Roitblat & J.-A. Meyer (Eds.), *Comparative approaches to cognitive science* (pp. 271–302). Cambridge, MA: MIT Press.

Cheng, P. W., & Novick, L. R. (1990). A probabilistic contrast model of causal induction. *Journal of Personality and Social Psychology, 58,* 545–567.

Cheng, P. W., & Novick, L. R. (1991). Causes versus enabling conditions. *Cognition, 40,* 83–120.

Cheng, P. W., & Novick, L. R. (1992). Covariation in natural causal induction. *Psychological Review, 99,* 365–382.

Dickinson, A. (1980). *Contemporary animal learning theory.* Cambridge, UK: Cambridge University Press.

Dickinson, A., & Burke, J. (1996). Within-compound associations mediate the retrospective revaluation of causality judgments. *Quarterly Journal of Experimental Psychology, 49B,* 60–80.

Dickinson, A., & Shanks, D. R. (1995). Instrumental action and causal representation. In D. Sperber, D. Premack, & A. J. Premack (Eds.), *Causal cognition: A multidisciplinary debate* (pp. 5–25). Oxford: Clarendon Press.

Dickinson, A., Shanks, D. R., & Evenden, J. L. (1984). Judgment of act-outcome contingency: The role of selective attribution. *Quarterly Journal of Experimental Psychology, 36A,* 29–50.

Fales, E., & Wasserman, E. A. (1992). Causal knowledge: What can psychology teach philosophers? *Journal of Mind and Behavior, 13,* 1–28.

Gluck, M. A. (1991). Stimulus generalization and representation in adaptive network models of category learning. *Psychological Science, 2,* 50–55.

Gluck, M. A., & Bower, G. H. (1988). Evaluating an adaptive network model of human learning. *Journal of Memory and Language, 27,* 166–195.

Holland, P. C. (1984). Differential effects of reinforcement of an inhibitory feature after serial and simultaneous negative discrimination training. *Journal of Experimental Psychology: Animal Behavior Processes, 10,* 461–475.

Holyoak, K. J., Koh, K., & Nisbett, R. E. (1989). A theory of conditioning: Inductive learning within rule-based default hierarchies. *Psychological Review, 96,* 315–340.

Jenkins, H. M., & Ward, W. C. (1965). Judgment of contingency between responses and outcomes. *Psychological Monographs, 79* (Whole No. 594).

Kahneman, D., & Tversky, A. (1972). Subjective probability: A judgment of representativeness. *Cognitive Psychology, 3,* 430–454.

Kamin, L. J. (1968). "Attention-like" processes in classical conditioning. In M. R. Jones (Ed.), *Miami Symposium on the Prediction of Behavior, 1967: Aversive stimulation* (pp. 9–31). Coral Gables, FL: University of Miami Press.

Kao, S.-F., & Wasserman, E. A. (1993). Assessment of an information integration account of contingency judgment with examination of subjective cell importance and method of information presentation. *Journal of Experimental Psychology: Learning, Memory, and Cognition, 19,* 1363–1386.

Kruschke, J. K. (1992). ALCOVE: An exemplar-based connectionist model of category learning. *Psychological Review, 99,* 22–44.

Kruschke, J. K. (1993). Human category learning: Implications for backpropagation models. *Connection Science, 5,* 3–36.

Lewandowsky, S. (1991). Gradual unlearning and catastrophic interference: A comparison of distributed architectures. In W. E. Hockley & S. Lewandowsky (Eds.), *Relating theory and data: Essays on human memory in honor of Bennet B. Murdock* (pp. 445–476). Hillsdale, NJ: Erlbaum.

Mackintosh, N. J. (1975). A theory of attention: Variations in the associability of stimuli with reinforcement. *Psychological Review, 82,* 276–298.

Mackintosh, N. J. (1983). *Conditioning and associative learning.* Oxford: Clarendon Press.

Markman, A. B. (1989). LMS rules and the inverse base-rate effect: Comment on Gluck and Bower (1988). *Journal of Experimental Psychology: General, 118,* 417–421.

Matute, H., Arcediano, F., & Miller, R. R. (1996). Test question modulates cue competition between causes and between effects. *Journal of Experimental Psychology: Learning, Memory, and Cognition, 22,* 182–196.

McClelland, J. L., & Rumelhart D. E. (1985). Distributed memory and the representation of general and specific information. *Journal of Experimental Psychology: General, 114,* 159–188.

McCloskey, M., & Cohen, N. J. (1989). Catastrophic interference in connectionist networks: The sequential learning problem. In G. H. Bower (Ed.), *The psychology of learning and motivation* (Vol. 24, pp. 109–165). San Diego, CA; Academic Press.

Melz, E. R., Cheng, P. W., Holyoak, K. J., & Waldmann, M. R. (1993). Cue competition in human categorization: Contingency or the Rescorla-Wagner learning rule? Comment on Shanks (1991). *Journal of Experimental Psychology: Learning, Memory, and Cognition, 19,* 1398–1410.

Nosofsky, R. M. (1992). Exemplar-based approach to relating categorization, identification, and recognition. In F. G. Ashby (Ed.), *Multidimensional models of perception and cognition* (pp. 363–393). Hillsdale, NJ: Erlbaum.

Pearce, J. M. (1987). A model for stimulus generalization in Pavlovian conditioning. *Psychological Review, 94,* 61–73.

Pearce, J. M. (1994). Similarity and discrimination: A selective review and a connectionist model. *Psychological Review, 101,* 587–607.

Pearce, J. M., & Hall, G. (1980). A model for Pavlovian conditioning: Variations in the effectiveness of conditioned but not of unconditioned stimuli. *Psychological Review, 87,* 532–552.

Pearce, J. M., & Wilson, P. N. (1991). Failure of excitatory conditioning to extinguish the influence of a conditioned inhibitor. *Journal of Experimental Psychology: Animal Behavior Processes, 17,* 519–529.

Price, P. C., & Yates, J. F. (1993). Judgmental overshadowing: Further evidence of cue interaction in contingency judgment. *Memory & Cognition, 21,* 561–572.

Ratcliff, R. (1990). Connectionist models of recognition memory: Constraints imposed by learning and forgetting functions. *Psychological Review, 97,* 285–308.

Rescorla, R. A. (1972). Informational variables in Pavlovian conditioning. In G. H. Bower (Ed.), *The psychology of learning and motivation* (Vol. 6, pp. 1–46). New York: Academic Press.

Rescorla, R. A. (1973). Evidence for a "unique stimulus" account of configural conditioning. *Journal of Comparative and Physiological Psychology, 85,* 331–338.

Rescorla, R. A. (1981). Within-signal learning in autoshaping. *Animal Learning and Behavior, 9,* 245–252.

Rescorla, R. A., & Wagner, A. R. (1972). A theory of Pavlovian conditioning: Variations in the effectiveness of reinforcement and nonreinforcement. In A. H. Black & W. F. Prokasy (Eds.), *Classical conditioning II: Current theory and research* (pp. 64–99). New York: Appleton-Century-Crofts.

Shanks, D. R. (1985a). Continuous monitoring of human contingency judgment across trials. *Memory & Cognition, 13,* 158–167.

Shanks, D. R. (1985b). Forward and backward blocking in human contingency judgement. *Quarterly Journal of Experimental Psychology, 37B,* 1–21.

Shanks, D. R. (1987). Acquisition functions in causality judgment. *Learning and Motivation, 18,* 147–166.

Shanks, D. R. (1989). Selective processes in causality judgment. *Memory & Cognition, 17,* 27–34.

Shanks, D. R. (1991). Categorization by a connectionist network. *Journal of Experimental Psychology: Learning, Memory, and Cognition, 17,* 433–443.

Shanks, D. R. (1993). Associative versus contingency accounts of category learning: Reply to Melz, Cheng, Holyoak, and Waldmann (1993). *Journal of Experimental Psychology: Learning, Memory, and Cognition, 19,* 1411–1423.

Shanks, D. R. (1994). Human associative learning. In N.J. Mackintosh (Ed.), *Animal learning and cognition* (pp. 335–374). San Diego, CA: Academic Press.

Shanks, D. R. (1995a). Is human learning rational? *Quarterly Journal of Experimental Psychology, 48A,* 257–279.

Shanks, D. R. (1995b). *The psychology of associative learning.* Cambridge, UK: Cambridge University Press.

Shanks, D. R., & Dickinson, A. (1987). Associative accounts of causality judgment. In G. H. Bower (Ed.), *The psychology of learning and motivation* (Vol. 21, pp. 229–261). San Diego, CA: Academic Press.

Shanks, D. R., & Lopez, F. J. (1996). Causal order does not affect cue selection in human associative learning. *Memory & Cognition, 24.*

Sloman, S. A., & Rumelhart, D. E. (1992). Reducing interference in distributed memories through episodic gating. In A. F. Healy, S. M. Kosslyn & R. M. Shiffrin (Eds.), *From learning processes to cognitive processes: Essays in honor of William K. Estes* (Vol. 1, pp. 227–248). Hillsdale, NJ: Erlbaum.

Smedslund, J. (1963). The concept of correlation in adults. *Scandinavian Journal of Psychology, 4,* 165–173.

Smith, E. E., & Medin, D. L. (1981). *Categories and concepts.* Cambridge, MA: Harvard University Press.

Tassoni, C. J. (1995). The least mean squares network with information coding: A model of cue learning. *Journal of Experimental Psychology: Learning, Memory, and Cognition, 21,* 193–204.

Van Hamme, L. J., & Wasserman, E. A. (1994). Cue competition in causality judgments: The role of nonpresentation of compound stimulus elements. *Learning and Motivation, 25,* 127–151.

Wagner, A. R. (1969). Stimulus selection and a "modified continuity theory." In G. H. Bower & J. T. Spence (Eds.), *The psychology of learning and motivation* (Vol. 3, pp. 1–41). New York: Academic Press.

Wagner, A. R. (1981). SOP: A model of automatic memory processing in animal behavior. In N. E. Spear & R. R. Miller (Eds.), *Information processing in animals: Memory mechanisms* (pp. 5–47). Hillsdale, NJ: Erlbaum.

Waldmann, M. R., & Holyoak, K. J. (1992). Predictive and diagnostic learning within causal models: Asymmetries in cue competition. *Journal of Experimental Psychology: General, 121*, 222–236.

Wasserman, E. A., Chatlosh, D. L., & Neunaber, D. J. (1983). Perception of causal relations in humans: Factors affecting judgments of response-outcome contingencies under free-operant procedures. *Learning and Motivation, 14*, 406–432.

Wasserman, E. A., Dorner, W. W., & Kao, S. F. (1990). Contributions of specific cell information to judgments of interevant contingency. *Journal of Experimental Psychology: Learning, Memory, and Cognition, 16*, 509–521.

Wasserman, E. A., Elek, S. M., Chatlosh, D. L., & Baker, A. G. (1993). Rating causal relations: The role of probability in judgments of response-outcome contingency. *Journal of Experimental Psychology: Learning, Memory, and Cognition, 19*, 174–188.

Williams, D. A. (1995). Forms of inhibition in animal and human learning. *Journal of Experimental Psychology: Animal Behavior Processes, 21*, 129–142.

Williams, D. A., Sagness, K. E., & McPhee, J. E. (1994). Configural and elemental strategies in predictive learning. *Journal of Experimental Psychology: Learning, Memory, and Cognition, 20*, 694–709.

A CAUSAL-POWER THEORY OF FOCAL SETS

Patricia W. Cheng
Jooyong Park
Aaron S. Yarlas
Keith J. Holyoak

I. Introduction

A. COVARIATION AND POWER VIEWS OF CAUSAL INDUCTION

Both philosophical and psychological theories of causal induction have been dominated by two basic approaches, which can be respectively traced to Hume (1739/1987) and to Kant (1781/1965). The fundamental idea underlying the Humean or *covariation* approach is that our sensory input, which is the ultimate source of all information that we have, does not explicitly include causal relations. It follows that acquired causal relations must be computed from the sensory input in some way. Our sensory input clearly yields such information as the presence and absence of a candidate cause and of the effect, and the temporal and spatial relations between the two. Treating such observable information as the input to the process of causal induction, models based on the covariation approach attempt in some way to assess covariation between a candidate cause and the effect (i.e., the extent to which the two vary together). An influential model of covariation was proposed by Jenkins and Ward (1965). Interpreting their contingency model in causal terms, the covariation between effect e and candidate cause i is defined by

$$\Delta P_i = P(e|i) - P(e|\bar{i}), \tag{1}$$

THE PSYCHOLOGY OF LEARNING
AND MOTIVATION, VOL. 34

313

where $P(e|i)$ is the probability of e given the presence of i, and $P(e|\bar{i})$ is that probability given the absence of i. If ΔP_i is noticeably positive, i is an excitatory, or facilitatory, cause; and if it is noticeably negative, i is an inhibitory, or preventive, cause. Otherwise, i is noncausal.

In the psychological literature, the Humean approach has split into several subdivisions. Statistical contingency models based on the ΔP rule have been contrasted with various types of associative models, such as contiguity learning (see Williams, this volume, Ch. 3) and discrepancy-based predictive learning, as embodied in the learning rule proposed by Rescorla and Wagner (1972; see Baker, Murphy, & Vallée-Tourangeau, this volume, Ch. 1; Miller & Matute, this volume, Ch. 4; Shanks, Lopez, Darby, & Dickinson, this volume, Ch. 7; Wasserman, Kao, Van Hamme, & Katagiri, this volume, Ch. 6). However, it is important to emphasize that all covariation models of causality face a major common theoretical hurdle: as many have noted, covariation does not equal causation (see Pearl, this volume, Ch. 10). Although ΔP may be a necessary criterion for causal induction, it is clearly insufficient, as not all predictive cues are perceived as causal. Many things follow one another regularly, yet we do not infer a causal relation between them. One song might routinely follow another in a religious ritual (and without the first song, the second song is not sung), and sunrise might occur every day after a rooster on a farm crows (and sunrise does not occur at other times during the day when the rooster does not crow). Yet we would not infer that one song causes another, or that the rooster's crowing causes the sun to rise. None of the subtypes of covariation models has provided an account of why some perceived covariations are given a causal interpretation while others are not.

This basic problem with the covariation approach has in part motivated the alternative Kantian approach to causal induction, which we will term the *power* view. According to this approach, there exists some *a priori* knowledge that serves as a framework for interpreting potentially causal information. This view has often been interpreted to mean that people do not infer that one thing is a cause of another unless they perceive or know of a specific generative source, causal mechanism, causal propensity, or causal power linking the candidate cause to the effect (e.g., Ahn & Bailenson, in press; Ahn, Kalish, Medin, & Gelman, 1995; Bullock, Gelman, & Baillargeon, 1982; Harré & Madden, 1975; Michotte, 1946/1963; Shultz, 1982; White, 1989). Causal power (the general term we will use to cover all the above variants) is the intuitive notion that one thing causes another by virtue of the power or energy that it exerts over the other (see Taylor, 1967, for a historical review; and Cartwright, 1989, for a discussion). For example, when the sun warms our back, we think of the sun as emitting energy, some of which reaches our skin, raising its temperature. According to the power view, causes are not merely followed by their effects; rather, they *produce* their effects. Sequences such as sunrise following crowing exhibit similar observable statistical relations as do causal sequences, but are missing the critical connection provided by the understanding of a causal power.

Although the Kantian view has intuitive appeal, it does not present a solution to Hume's problem of how causal relations are uncovered from the input that is available to our information processing system. It suffers from the weakness of not being computational: it does not explicitly define a mapping between the ultimate input to the causal induction process and its output. Moreover, its interpretation in terms of specific causal powers has an additional limitation: It appears to be circular, implying that people do not learn that something is causal unless they can somehow first understand that it is causal. It is not clear how the understanding of causal power, which presumably is the *output* of the process of causal induction, can itself be a necessary part of the inductive process itself.

Can the covariation and power views be reconciled in a way that provides a solution to the problem of causal induction first posed by Hume? Cheng (1993) notes that the topic of causal inference may be divided into two component issues: how an acquired causal relation is first acquired, and how prior domain-specific causal knowledge regarding superordinate kinds (whether innate or learned) influences subsequent causal judgments. When these component issues are distinguished, the two views are complementary rather than contradictory. A variant of the covariation approach termed the *probabilistic contrast model,* developed and tested by Cheng and her colleagues (Cheng, 1993; Cheng & Holyoak, 1995; Cheng & Lien, 1995; Cheng & Novick, 1990, 1991, 1992; Melz, Cheng, Holyoak, & Waldmann, 1993), has provided a basis for an integration of the two approaches with respect to the issue of the induction of causal relations. A key idea underlying this model is that people base causal judgments not on contingencies computed unconditionally over all events, but on *conditional* contingencies computed over a contextually constrained set of events termed the *focal set.* Cheng (in press) and Cheng and Novick (1995) have argued that an application of the notion of causal power can provide a theory of how people select focal sets, thereby linking the two approaches that had previously been considered to be incompatible with one another. This power theory provides an explanation of why people use conditional contrasts to estimate causal power. To distinguish the power theory of the probabilistic contrast model from other interpretations of the power view, we will refer to it as the *power PC theory.*[1]

---

[1] Neil Cheng Holyoak suggested this name for the probabilistic contrast model as interpreted by the power theory. We use "theory" in the special sense of a theory of a model, as will be explained below.

In the present chapter we review the probabilistic contrast model and its notion of focal sets, as well as the power PC explanation of why people use certain specific types of focal sets to evaluate causal relations. The power analysis generates a variety of testable predictions about people's causal judgments. We describe and discuss some experimental tests that differentiate the predictions of the power PC theory from those of the major competing account, the Rescorla–Wagner (1972) model. The latter model, originally proposed as a model of classical conditioning in animals, has more recently been applied to human causal induction (e.g., Gluck & Bower, 1988; Shanks, 1991; see Shanks et al., this volume, Ch. 7).

The central difference between the two approaches involves the distinction between the computational and algorithmic levels of cognitive analysis (Marr, 1982). Marr argues that the issues of *what* function is being computed by an information process and *why* it is computed (i.e., the goal and the constraints that motivate the process) logically precede the issue of *how* a given function is computed. He classifies the former issues as being at a computational level, and the latter as being at an algorithmic level. If the function being computed does not mirror its human counterpart, no algorithm that computes this function can be an accurate model of human behavior. The Rescorla–Wagner model is founded on an algorithm for discrepancy reduction on a trial-by-trial basis. In contrast, the power PC theory (Cheng, in press) is a computational model. As we explain, it seeks to specify the abstract function relating the input and the output of the process of causal induction given the constraints in the environment and processing system that govern this process.

We describe some recent findings from our laboratory that test discriminating predictions of the power PC theory and the Rescorla–Wagner model, using causal analogues of two well-known paradigms that have been used in studies of animal conditioning: overexpectation and extinction of conditioned inhibition. We also discuss other phenomena that discriminate between these two theories. Moreover, we provide an analysis of what function the Rescorla–Wagner algorithm actually computes in various paradigms, so that one can compare the Rescorla–Wagner model to the power PC theory at Marr's (1982) computational level. In addition, we consider the adequacy of a recently proposed modification of the Rescorla–Wagner model that attempts to remedy some of its empirical failures (Van Hamme & Wasserman, 1994). Finally, we explain how the power PC theory solves some of the fundamental problems afflicting the covariational and the power approaches to causal induction.

B. PROBABILISTIC CONTRAST MODEL

It has long been argued that contingency is a component of the normative criterion for inferring a causal link between a factor and an effect (e.g.,

Kelley, 1967; Rescorla, 1968; Salmon, 1971). Cheng and Novick (1990) proposed the probabilistic contrast model as a generalized contingency model to provide a descriptive account of the use of statistical regularity in human causal induction. The model, which applies to events describable by discrete variables, assumes that one of the initial criteria for identifying potential causes is perceived priority (causes must be perceived or understood to precede their effects). A potential cause is then evaluated by its *contrast* computed over a *focal set,* which is a contextually determined set of events that the reasoner uses as input to the covariation process. (We use the terms "contrast" and "contingency" interchangeably.) The focal set often is not the universal set of events, contrary to what had been assumed by previous contingency models in psychology. In inferring what causes a forest fire, for example, reasoners will normally restrict their focal set to ordinary terrestrial events, in which oxygen is always present, and will exclude events that the reasoner might know of that involve oxygen-free environments. (See Spellman, this volume, Ch. 5, and Waldmann, this volume, Ch. 2, for further discussion of the role of conditional contrasts in causal judgments.)

Using the events in the focal set, a *main-effect* contrast for evaluating a candidate cause i of effect e is defined as in Equation (1). The conditional probabilities in the equation are estimated by the respective relative frequency of events for which e occurs in the presence and in the absence of i.

Confidence in the assessment of a contrast is presumed to increase monotonically with the number of cases observed (Cheng & Holyoak, 1995). The increase in confidence with additional observations is therefore consistent with the general form of empirically observed learning curves, which increase in absolute value as a function of sample size to an asymptote determined by the contrast (see Shanks et al., this volume, Ch. 7). In addition, number of observations influences causal judgments by altering the denominators of the relative frequencies used to estimate the two conditional probabilities from which a contrast is computed. The latter influence explains the differentiation between a novel candidate cause and an irrelevant one, a phenomenon that has parallels in the classical conditioning literature: learned irrelevance and the effect of preexposing a stimulus (Cheng & Holyoak, 1995).

Main-effect contrasts assess the causal status of each factor considered individually. However, it is also possible for factors to combine in a nonindependent way to produce the effect, as when talent and hard work jointly produce success. Such situations involve *interactions* between factors, which according to Cheng and Novick (1990) are evaluated by interaction contrasts.

Using the concept of focal sets, the probabilistic contrast model has elucidated some psychological differentiations between causal and other similar but distinct relations, which had been problematic for the covariation approach. For example, the introduction of focal sets allows an explanation of the psychological distinction between causes and *enabling conditions.* In our example about what causes a forest fire, people might consider a lightning strike as the cause, but they will view the presence of oxygen as merely an enabling condition. Although oxygen is necessary for the fire, it is constant in the relevant focal set so that a contrast cannot be computed. In a different context, which evokes a focal set within which the presence of oxygen may vary (e.g., a special laboratory intended to be oxygen free), oxygen would be considered the cause of a fire that breaks out when oxygen leaks into that environment. Cheng and Novick (1991, 1992) defined candidate i as an enabling condition for a cause j if i is constantly present in a reasoner's current focal set but covaries with the effect in another focal set, and j no longer covaries with the effect in a focal set in which i is constantly absent. In contrast, associative learning models such as the Rescorla–Wagner model, in which inference regarding a stimulus is represented solely by a connection weight, are unable to distinguish causes from enabling conditions (Cheng & Holyoak, 1995).

C. POWER PC THEORY AND THE SELECTION OF FOCAL SETS

Cheng and Novick (1990, 1991; Novick, Fratianne, & Cheng, 1992) were silent on the issue of what determines the adoption of a focal set. To avoid circularity in their argument, however, they provided evidence for the focal set used by the participants in their experiments, independent of their causal judgments. They either manipulated the events in a focal set, independently assessed them, or both. Thus, one approach to specifying the focal sets used by reasoners is to empirically identify them.

More recently, Cheng and Holyoak (1995; also Melz *et al.,* 1993) described an algorithmic process model of causal judgments applicable to trial-by-trial learning. This process model predicts the focal sets people use for facilitatory and preventive causes. In essence, the model assumes that people prefer to assess whether a candidate is facilitatory using a focal set in which all other possible causes are constantly absent, but to assess whether a candidate is preventive using a focal set in which some facilitatory cause is constantly present but other possible causes are absent. In addition, the model specifies strategies for coping with situations in which the environment does not provide any focal set that allows clearly informative contrasts to be computed. In such cases, some mixture of contrasts based on the next best available focal sets may be employed. This process model provides an account of partial blocking (which is not explained by the Rescorla–Wagner model) and other phenomena observed in experimetns reported by Shanks (1991; see Melz *et al.,* 1993).

Cheng and Holyoak's (1995) process model has been criticized for failing to constrain the selection of focal sets (Shanks, 1993). In fact, the model licenses use of only a tiny subset of the possible partitions of events into focal sets. Nonetheless, a key theoretical issue for the probabilistic contrast model is to explain *why* certain focal sets are favored by human reasoners. An answer is provided by the power PC theory (Cheng, in press). Laws and models in science, which deal with observable properties, are often explained by theories, which posit unobservable entities. In chemistry, for example, the Kinetic Theory of Gases explains gas laws such as Boyle's Law (pressure · volume = constant) and their boundary conditions (e.g., when temperature and the number of moles of gas are held constant) by positing gases as tiny particles in a large space moving at a speed proportional to their temperature. Causal power is to covariation as the Kinetic Theory of Gases is to Boyle's Law. Whereas causal power is unobservable, covariation is defined in terms of observable events.

Cheng (in press) postulates a probabilistic concept of causal power and derives a theory of the probabilistic contrast model based on that concept. Moreover, she proposes that ordinary folk are like scientists in that they postulate a similar notion of causal power, which they use to interpret and explain their intuitive covariation model. That is, people do not simply treat observed covariations as equivalent to causal relations. Rather, they follow an intuitive version of the power PC theory: they use their observations of covariations as evidence for the operation of unobservable causal powers, with the tacit goal of estimating the magnitude of these powers. The power PC theory explains: (1) why covariation reveals causal power in some focal sets, whereas in other sets it does not; and (2) the boundary conditions under which these revelations occur.

1. Facilitatory Causes

The power PC theory assumes that the power of a facilitatory cause x to produce an effect e can be represented by p_x, the probability with which x produces e when x is present. Thus, $0 \le p_x \le 1$ for all x. To estimate p_i, the power of candidate cause i, the analysis distinguishes between i and the composite of (known and unknown) causes alternative to i, which is designated as a. Whereas $P(e|i)$, the probability of e occurring in the presence of i, can be directly estimated by observable events (the proportion of times e occurs in the presence of i), p_i is a theoretical entity that can be only indirectly estimated. Because other causes, known or unknown to the reasoner, might be present when i is present, $P(e|i)$ may not be equal to p_i. For example, the probability with which birth defects occur in the offspring of women who drink alchohol during pregnancy is not in general equal to the probability with which alchohol produces birth defects, because other causes of birth defects might be present. $P(e|i)$ and p_i are not equal if a is present and produces e in the presence of i (i.e., if $P(a|i) \cdot p_a \neq 0$).

Assuming that i and a independently produce e, Cheng (1995) derived that

$$\Delta P_i = [1 - P(a|i) \cdot p_a] \cdot p_i + [P(a|i) - P(a|\bar{i})] \cdot p_a. \tag{2}$$

Equation (2) shows how the theoretical entities p_i and p_a, along with the conditional probabilities $P(a|i)$ and $P(a|\bar{i})$, produce or explain ΔP_i, the observable contrast for i. To see what the power PC theory predicts for the estimation of the power of i, however, we rearrange this equation to put p_i on the left-hand side (LHS), obtaining

$$p_i = \frac{\Delta P_i - [P(a|i) - P(a|\bar{i})] \cdot p_a}{1 - P(a|i) \cdot p_a}. \tag{3}$$

If an alternative cause does exist (i.e., $p_a > 0$), and a does not occur independently of i (i.e., $P(a|i) \neq P(a|\bar{i})$), the numerator of the right-hand side (RHS) of Equation (3) would have both positive and negative terms in addition to ΔP_i. It follows that under these conditions, ΔP_i, is not interpretable as an estimate of p_i: it could overestimate p_i or underestimate it, depending on the values of $P(a|i)$ and $P(a|\bar{i})$. This is the situation in which covariation does *not* equal causation, and Equation (3) explains why it does not do so under these conditions.

Now, consider situations in which a does occur independently of i [i.e., $P(a|i) = P(a|\bar{i}) = P(a)$].[2] In this case, Equation (3) reduces to

$$p_i = \frac{\Delta P_i}{1 - P(a) \cdot p_a}. \tag{4}$$

Equation (4) tells us when and how well ΔP_i gives an estimate of p_i. Consider the extreme case in which $P(a) \cdot p_a \cong 0$. Note that $P(a) \cdot p_a$ yields the probability of the effect attributable to a within the focal set. This probability can be estimated by observing the frequency of the effect in the presence of a alone. (Because a occurs independently of i, the same estimate holds in the presence of i as in its absence.) Thus, this is the situation in which

---

[2] This is not the same assumption as i and a independently producing e.

the effect (almost) never occurs when the candidate is absent (e.g., when alternative causes are held constantly absent in the focal set). In this case, $p_i \cong \Delta P_i$, which means that in this optimal situation, the reasoner can interpret the contrast for i as the close estimate of the causal power of i.

It might be objected that in Equation (4) one needs to know about p_a, a theoretical entity, in order to obtain an estimate of p_i. In cases where the reasoner has prior knowledge about p_a, this knowledge can be applied. In other cases, however, it might seem that there is a problem of circularity: namely, the estimation of p_i begs the question of how p_a can be estimated. The key to this problem is that, as we mentioned, $P(a) \cdot p_a$ in the equation can be estimated by *observing* the frequency of the effect in the presence of a alone, circumventing the need to know about p_a. The power PC theory thereby circumvents the circularity that plagues formulations of causal inference based purely on conditional contrasts (e.g., Cartwright, 1989; Salmon, 1971; see Pearl, this volume, Ch. 10).

Given that reasoners have the estimation of causal power as a goal, Equations (3) and (4) explain why reasoners prefer to assess covariation in focal sets in which alternative causes are constant, as proposed by Cheng and Holyoak (1995): a occurs independently of i in these focal sets. More-over, Equation (4) explains Cheng and Holyoak's assumption that, to assess the facilitatory nature of a candidate cause, reasoners prefer focal sets in which alternative causes are constantly absent: they get the best estimate of causal power in such focal sets.

Now, consider the other extreme case of Equation (4), in which $P(a) \cdot p_a \cong 1$. Recall, that $P(a) \cdot p_a$ yields the probability of the effect attributable to a within the focal set. Thus, this is the situation in which the effect is (almost) always occurring, even when the candidate i is absent. In this case, p_i is undefined. In other words, $\Delta P_i \cong 0$ regardless of the magnitude of p_i, which means that in this situation, the reasoner can no longer interpret the contrast for i as an estimate of the causal power of i. Equation (4) explains Cheng and Holyoak's (1995) assumption that reasoners are uncertain of the causal status of a candidate with a zero contrast in such a focal set.

Between these two extreme cases, it follows from Equation (4) that as $P(a) \cdot p_a$ increases from 0 to 1, p_i is increasing larger than ΔP_i because it is equal to ΔP_i divided by an increasingly smaller number less than 1; in other words, ΔP_i is increasingly a conservative estimate of p_i. Two implica-tions follow for situations under which a occurs independently of i. First, for a reasoner whose goal is to judge whether a candidate is causal, it seems that ΔP_i, being a generally conservative estimate, should be regarded as a generally useful criterion for judging causation. A conservative criterion errs on the side of promoting simple explanations. Second, for a reasoner whose goal is not simply to judge whether a candidate is causal, but also to estimate its causal strength, Equation (4) shows that, as $P(a) \cdot p_a$ increases, a ΔP_i of the same magnitude will yield higher values of p_i, that is, higher estimates of the power of i.

2. Preventive Causes

A directly analogous analysis applies to preventive causes. Rather than raising the probability of an effect, some causes lower this probability. The power PC theory assumes that a preventive cause i has the power to stop with probability p_i an effect that would otherwise occur. Using assumptions otherwise identical to those used in the derivation of Equation (2), Cheng (in press) derived that

$$p_i = \frac{[P(a|i) - P(a|\bar{i})] \cdot p_a - \Delta P_i}{P(a|i) \cdot p_a}.$$ (5)

Equation (5) shows that, if a does not occur independently of i, ΔP_i does not provide an estimate of p_i: the numerator of the RHS of Equation (5) has both a positive term and a negative term in addition to ΔP_i. In this case, a negative contrast does not necessarily imply that i is a preventive cause. This is the direct analogue of the situation for facilitatory causes in which covariation does not equal causation.

When a occurs independently of i [i.e., $P(a|i) = P(a|\bar{i}) = P(a)$], however, Equation (5) reduces to

$$p_i = \frac{-\Delta P_i}{P(a) \cdot p_a}.$$ (6)

Let us first consider the extreme case of Equation (6) in which $P(a) \cdot p_a \cong 1$. This is the situation in which the effect (almost) always occurs in the absence of the candidate. In this case, $p_i \cong -\Delta P_i$, which means that in this optimal situation for evaluating inhibitory causes, the reasoner can interpret the contrast for i as a close estimate of $-p_i$. This result implies that if the contrast is a negative number, $-x$, then i stops the effect from occurring with a power of magnitude x. Note that this is the opposite of the optimal situation for evaluating an excitatory cause, in which alternative causes are constantly *absent*. This radical asymmetry between facilitatory and inhibitory causes, which has parallels in the conditioning literature (Baker et al., this volume, Ch. 1; Miller, Barnet, & Grahame, 1995; Williams, this volume, Ch. 3), was recognized in the process model proposed by Cheng and Holyoak (1995). The power PC theory provides an explanation for this asymmetry.

Let us now consider the other extreme case of Equation (6), in which $P(a) \cdot p_a \cong 0$. This is the situation in which the effect (almost) never occurs, even in the absence of the candidate. We see that in this case, p_i is undefined. In other words, $\Delta P_i \cong 0$ regardless of the value of p_i, which means that the reasoner cannot at all estimate p_i from ΔP_i. Recall that, in contrast, when evaluating the excitatory nature of a cause, the reasoner runs into the analogous problem when the effect is always *present*. Whereas the boundary condition for evaluating facilitatory causes stems from the axiomatic assumption that probabilities have an upper bound of 1, the boundary condition for evaluating inhibitory causes stems from the axiomatic assumption that probabilities have a lower bound of 0.

In between these two extremes, when $0 < P(a) \cdot p_a < 1$, the reasoner should regard ΔP_i as a conservative estimate of $-p_i$. Moreover, for a negative ΔP_i of the same magnitude, as $P(a) \cdot p_a$ increases, lower strengths should be inferred for i. This direction of change relative to the value of $P(a) \cdot p_a$ is opposite to that in the interpretation of a positive ΔP_i.

3. From Covariation to Causation

In summary, the power PC theory explains why covariation sometimes reveals causation, and specifies the boundary conditions under which such revelations occur. When the composite of alternative causes a does not occur independently of candidate cause i, ΔP_i does not reflect causal status. But when a does occur independently of i (e.g., when a is constant in a focal set), then to assess the excitatory nature of i, we see that, excluding the extreme case in which the effect (almost) always occurs in the focal set, ΔP_i should provide an estimate of the causal status of i. This estimate is increasingly conservative as the probability of the effect in the absence of i increases, with the focal set in which a is (almost) constantly absent giving the closest estimate of the power of i. Analogously, to assess the inhibitory nature of candidate cause i, we see that when a occurs independently of i, excluding the extreme case in which the effect (almost) never occurs in the focal set, ΔP_i should provide an estimate of the causal status of i. In this case, ΔP_i becomes an increasingly conservative estimate as the probability of the effect in the absence of i decreases, with the focal set in which a is (almost) always present and producing the effect giving the closest estimate of the power of i. As mentioned earlier, Cheng (in press) proposes that people implicitly adhere to an intuitive version of the mathematical theory, rather than the theory itself. The predictions of the power PC theory are therefore qualitative and ordinal.

Cheng's (in press) analysis implies that a reasoner whose goal is to infer causal power should attempt to obtain the best estimates of the causal powers of candidate causes from covariation in the focal sets available in the input. They should first attempt to select sets of events in which a occurs independently of i. Even among these, however, not all will allow an estimation of the causal power of i. If there is only one set that allows this estimation, there would be no conflicting information, and reasoners should adopt that as their focal set. If there is more than one available set that reveals causal power, but they are consistent in the causal power they indicate, there would still be no conflicting information. If the causal powers revealed in multiple informative sets conflict, however, reasoners would have to either withhold judgment or resolve the conflict in some way. Finally, if the information available does not allow any partitioning that renders a independent of i, or if none of the focal sets in which a occurs independently of i allows an unambiguous estimation of causal power, reasoners would have to either withhold judgment or select the next best available set (or sets) with reduced confidence if forced to make a decision.

Notice that throughout our analysis, to infer causation from covariation the reasoner need not know *what* the alternative causes are. Rather, the reasoner needs to know only that the alternatives occur independently of the candidate cause (e.g., are constant), and to observe the base rate of the effect in the relevant context, noting the extreme base rates that disallow causal inferences. Because the reasoner need not know the identity of any cause prior to making a causal induction about a candidate cause, there is no circularity in the power analysis.

Let us illustrate the case in which covariation does imply causation. One situation in which alternative causes are independent of a candidate cause is when alternative causes are constant. Suppose people observe that pressing a button on a remote control is followed by their television turning on. If they believe that alternative causes remain unchanged before, during, and after the button is pressed, the power PC theory would predict that they should come to believe from their observations that the remote device has a power to turn the set on. They will reach this conclusion even if they do not know what the alternative causes might be, and even if they have only the vaguest conception of what the underlying mechanism is (i.e., have no prior causal knowledge about the type of relation).

Once the leap from observed covariation to underlying power has been made, however, people may apply their acquired causal understanding in a top-down fashion when making causal judgments about similar cause–effect relations (Cheng & Lien, 1995). Thus, learning that remote controls can operate a television set and a driveway gate "prepares" the reasoner to accept that the covariation between pressing a remote control and the opening of a garage door is also due to a causal power.

As mentioned earlier, Cheng and Holyoak (1995) discuss the possible use of mixtures of focal sets (either by a single participant or by different participants) in experimental designs that do not provide information about any focal set sufficient to unambiguously estimate causal power (e.g., the design of Experiment 3 in Shanks, 1991; see Melz et al., 1993). It is important to recognize, however, as we just explained, that if the available information does include one and only one focal set that provides an unambiguous estimate of causal power, reasoners will base their causal judgments on that focal set alone, rather than any mixture of focal sets.

The constraints on selection of focal sets can be applied to an example used by Shanks (1993) to argue that the Cheng and Holyoak (1995) process model is underconstrained in its specification of potential focal sets. Shanks noted that in studies using an AB−, B+, AC+ design, the A cue becomes an inhibitor (as predicted by the Rescorla–Wagner model). As in other designs, trials in which no cue is presented and no effect occurs are implicitly implied. He also observed that it is possible to partition the set of events observed by participants into sets that generate a contrast for A of −1 (for the set in which B is constantly present, consisting of AB− and B+ trials), 1 (for the set in which A and C co-occur, consisting of AC+ and no cue trials), or 0 (for an entirely arbitrary partition). Because different partitions generate very different contrasts for A, Shanks argued that Cheng and Holyoak's (1995) model makes no predictions for this design.

However, Cheng and Holyoak's (1995) model does make a clear prediction for this design, and the power PC theory explains it. According to Equation (6), of the three partitions considered by Shanks, one and only one is optimal for assessing the power of candidate cause A. This is the focal set in which A is variously present or absent, while a clear facilitatory cause, B, is constantly present. This focal set, which allows the assessment of the preventive power of A, generates a contrast of −1 for A, revealing that it is a strong preventive cause. In contrast, the other two partitions do not allow an estimation of the power of A, because not all plausible alternative causes occur independently of A: in the set in which A and C co-occur, this problem is self-evident; in the arbitrary partition, A and B are perfectly correlated. The power PC theory thus explains why the design discussed by Shanks (1993) does not generate multiple focal sets; rather, the one unambiguous focal set is crucial.

In the following section, we describe some empirical tests of the power PC theory we have performed in our laboratory, using causal analogues of the two well-known paradigms of overexpectation and extinction of conditioned inhibition. We will compare how well the power PC theory and the Rescorla–Wagner model explain our results.

II.   Empirical Tests of the Power PC Theory

A.   A BOUNDARY CONDITION ON "OVEREXPECTATION" DUE TO COMBINING EXCITATORY CAUSES

1.   The Overexpectation Paradigm

A particularly interesting paradigm for testing the power PC theory is based on a design that in the animal conditioning literature is termed *overexpectation* (Kremer, 1978; Rescorla & Wagner, 1972). This paradigm involves two learning phases. In phase 1, stimuli A and B are separately established as excitors (A+ and B+). In phase 2, the combination of A and B is shown to also lead to the effect (AB+) to the same degree as did each of the individual stimuli in phase 1. Tests subsequent to phase 2 typically reveal that the excitatory power of both A and B has *decreased* relative to phase 1. The Rescorla–Wagner model predicts this result because the combined associative strengths of A and B after phase 1 "overpredict" the outcome associated with the AB compound in phase 2, leading to reduction in both weights.

From the perspective of the power PC theory, this result depends on the fact that the animal studies have used effects (e.g., shock administered at various times) that are naturally interpreted as occurring with certain rates rather than with certain probabilities (Gallistel, 1990). The distinction between rates and probabilities is important. Rates have no *a priori* upper bound (except that imposed by technology and our perceptual systems), in contrast to probabilities, which have an upper bound of 1. For example, an experimenter might define a trial to be of a certain length in time (e.g., 2 min), with a shock occurring once every trial indicating that it occurs with a probability of 1. However, it is physically possible for shocks to occur at rates higher than this artificial upper bound, and to be perceived as such up to the limit imposed by the participants' perceptual system. (Like probabilities, however, rates do have a lower bound—it is physically impossible for effects to occur at a rate slower than 0 per unit time interval.) For excitatory causes, therefore, rates do not have an analogue of the boundary condition for interpretation specified by the power PC theory, which applies to probabilities rather than to rates. The failure of the AB compound in phase 2 to increase the rate beyond that associated with each cue alone is thus normatively interpreted in terms of rates as evidence that neither cue is as potent as it had appeared in phase 1. Ironically, the application of the Rescorla–Wagner model to animal studies of overexpectation assumes trials with experimenter-defined durations, thus implicitly representing the events probabilistically (Gallistel, 1990). However, the model is not normative with respect to probabilistic events because it assumes that associative strengths are additive (unlike probabilities). But since animals actually code the events as rates rather than probabilities, and rates *are* additive, the two wrongs of the Rescorla–Wagner model in this case turn out to make a right.

There are other cases, however, in which two wrongs are just plain wrong. It should be theoretically discriminating to test discrete versions of the overexpectation paradigm, in which the pairing of the stimuli and the effect are either at ceiling level or not. Discrete trials, unlike trials with durations that are arbitrarily assumed by investigators, are naturally coded in terms of probabilities rather than rates. The power PC theory should therefore apply. As we explain, the power PC theory predicts that there should be overexpectation of the effect in the "nonceiling" case, but not in the "ceiling" case. In contrast, the Rescorla–Wagner model does not distinguish between these two cases, and predicts overexpectation in both.

2. Estimating Facilitatory Causal Power from Main-Effect Contrasts

First, consider the "ceiling" situation. Recall that in phase 1, when either stimulus A or B is present, the effect always occurs. Otherwise, the effect does not occur. The design in this phase allows the selection of focal sets in which causes alternative to a candidate are constant, and therefore independent of the candidate [i.e., focal sets to which Equation (4) applies]. With respect to the assessment of candidate A, trials on which B is absent constitute such a focal set. In this focal set, the only alternative cause is the "context," which is constant, and therefore independent of A. We also know that the probability of the effect produced by the context [i.e., $P(a) \cdot p_a$ in Equation (4)] does not approximate 1. In fact, it is 0, as inferred from the nonoccurrence of the effect when the context alone is present. (Because the context is independent of A in this focal set, this probability is also inferred to be 0 when both A and the context are present.) Under these conditions, Equation (4) tells us that the contrast for A, which equals 1, provides a good estimate of its causal power. The same inferences apply to stimulus B in this phase.

Recall that in phase 2 in the ceiling situation, when the compound stimulus AB is present, the effect occurs with the same frequency as when either A or B is present in the earlier phase. That is, it always occurs. When neither A nor B is present, the effect is absent. Accumulating information from both phases allows the selection of a second type of focal set in which causes alternative to a candidate are constant. With respect to the assessment of candidate A, this additional focal set consists of trials on which B and the context are always present. In this focal set, the contrast for A, $P(e|A\ B\ C) - P(e|\overline{A}\ B\ C)$ (where C is the context), is 0: both component conditional probabilities equal 1. According to the power PC theory, however, this contrast is uninterpretable as an estimate of causal power: $P(a)\cdot p_a$ in Equation (4) equals 1 in this focal set. The same reasoning applies to stimulus B, for which the analogous conditional contrast is likewise 0 and likewise uninterpretable. Therefore, despite the fact that the contrast for each stimulus changes from 1 in the focal set used in phase 1 to 0 in the focal set available in phase 2, there is no conflict in the interpretation according to causal power. Accordingly, the power PC theory predicts that people will not change their causal assessment of either A or B in this situation during phase 2; that is, "overexpectation" will not occur.

Now, consider a "nonceiling" situation. The only difference in design between this case and the previous one is that in those stimulus contexts in which the effect occurs, rather than always occurring, it occurs with a constant probability that is clearly greater than 0 and less than 1. It follows that in phase 1 of a nonceiling situation, the contrast for either A or B conditional on the absence of the other is clearly between 0 and 1. These contrasts should be good estimates of causal power, because the only alternative cause in these focal sets is the context, which does not produce the effect. A and B therefore should each have excitatory causal powers of a value clearly less than 1. Now, in phase 2, as in the ceiling situation, the contrast for either stimulus conditional on the presence of the other is 0. Contrary to those in the ceiling situation, however, these contrasts should provide an estimate of causal power: $P(a)\cdot p_a$ in Equation (4) is clearly less than 1 in these focal sets (as the probability of the effect produced by alternative cause A or B is clearly less than 1). Therefore, a conflict appears between the causal powers inferred in the two phases.

For a reasoner who assumes that causal powers remain stable, there are three ways of resolving this conflict: the reasoner (1) trusts the observations in both phases, and infers an interaction between the two causes; (2) trusts the observations presented in phase 1 and doubts those in phase 2; or (3) trusts the observations in phase 2 but doubts those in phase 1. A reasoner taking either of the first two options should not revise the causal powers of A or B estimated in phase 1, because this reasoner does not doubt the observations in that phase. A reasoner taking the second option, for example, might hypothesize that the proportion of cases in phase 2 for which the AB combination is paired with the effect is higher than they originally estimated, thereby obtaining consistent estimates of causal power in the two phases. A reasoner taking the third option (i.e., doubting the observations in phase 1), however, should lower the previous estimates of the causal power of both A and B. Such a reasoner could resolve the conflict by hypothesizing that the proportion of cases in phase 1 for which A or B produced the effect is lower than originally estimated. Such a modification would result in lower estimates of causal power for A or B, which would be consistent across the two phases. Accordingly, the power PC theory predicts that overexpectation will occur in this situation if the experimental procedure encourages participants to trust the observations in phase 2 but doubt those in phase 1.

In sum, the power PC theory predicts a possible reduction in the perceived causal power of A and B during phase 2 of the overexpectation paradigm using discrete trials when the effect occurs with a nonceiling probability in the presence of A, B, or their combination, but no such reduction when the effect occurs with a probability of 1 in these stimulus contexts. We are not aware of any alternative theory that makes this prediction.

3. An Experimental Test of "Overexpectation" Using Discrete Trials

As far as we know, no previous study has examined the overexpectation paradigm with humans performing a causal induction task; nor has any study with any species investigated whether and when overexpectation is obtained when the effect is coded in term of probabilities rather than rates. Recently, Park and Cheng (1995) have performed such a study to test the predicted boundary condition on overexpectation derived from the power PC theory. Two separate experiments were performed, identical in design except for the theoretically crucial distinction between whether the critical stimulus contexts produce the effect sometimes (Nonceiling experiment) or always (Ceiling experiment). Participants were presented with a cover story in which they were asked to infer how likely it is that various newly discovered (fictitious) proteins called "endomins," which were said to sometimes be produced by the body, caused hypertension in people who have those endomins. Trials therefore consisted of people, who are discrete entities.

Because the two experiments were identical in design and procedure with the exception of certain conditional probabilities of hypertension given types of endomins, we will describe both experiments together. There were two groups of participants: an Experimental group designed to yield "overexpectation" according to the Rescorla–Wagner model, and a Control group. None of the participants had been exposed to probability theory.

They were presented with two successive learning phases. On each learning trial participants saw a "hospital record" listing information about the presence or absence of three endomins in an individual patient. They indicated whether or not they thought the patient had hypertension, after which they were informed whether the patient indeed had hypertension.

In the elemental phase, the patients displayed four types of endomin patterns: endomin R only, S only, T only, or no endomins. In the subsequent compound phase the patients displayed three types of patterns: R and S together, T only, or no endomins. In the Experimental group of the Non-Ceiling experiment, the proportion of patients with hypertension in phase 1 was .75 for endomin R and for endomin S, and .92 for endomin T. Endomin T, the stimulus with a higher proportion, was added to the standard overexpectation paradigm described earlier to provide a comparison for confirming that a probability of .75 was perceptibly below a (near) ceiling level. In the corresponding phase 2, the proportion was .75 for the R and S combination and .92 for T. Patients with no endomins never had the disease. The sole difference for the Control group was that in phase 1 patients who had endomin R alone did not have the disease.

The design for the Ceiling experiment was identical to that of the Nonceiling experiment except that the proportion of patients with the disease was 1 whenever it was nonzero in the Nonceiling experiment. See Table I for a summary of the design of these two experiments.

TABLE I

PROPORTION OF PATIENTS WITH DISEASE IN EACH PHASE FOR EACH CONDITION IN "OVEREXPECTATION" EXPERIMENTS[a]

| | Elemental phase | | Compound phase | |
	Experimental group	Control group	Experimental group	Control group
Nonceiling experiment				
R	.75	.00	—[b]	—
S	.75	.75	—	—
T	.92	.92	.92	.92
R&S	—	—	.75	.75
None	.00	.00	.00	.00
Ceiling experiment				
R	1.0	.00	—	—
S	1.0	1.0	—	—
T	1.0	1.0	1.0	1.0
R&S	—	—	1.0	1.0
None	.00	.00	.00	.00

[a] Experimental designs used by Park and Cheng (1995). Each proportion of patients is out of a total of 24.

[b] —: No information was presented about patients with this configuration of endomins.

To measure the participants' causal judgments, they were given a response sheet that listed patterns of endomins (the three individual endomins, the combination of R and S, and no endomins). For each pattern, participants were asked, "Out of 100 patients with this pattern of endomins, how many do you think have hypertension?"

Recall that for the discrete-trial version of the overexpectation paradigm, the power PC theory predicts overexpectation (a reduction in the perceived strengths of the individual stimuli in phase 2) only for reasoners in a nonceiling situation who trust the observations presented in phase 2 but doubt those in phase 1. To create an experimental procedure that allows the power PC theory to make different predictions for a ceiling and a nonceiling situation, the instructions encouraged participants in both groups of both experiments to doubt the observations in phase 1 if they perceived conflicting information in the two phases. At the beginning of phase 2, every participant was told that there may or may not be some inaccurate diagnoses of patients whose records they have just seen, but that the diagnoses of the patients whose records they were going to see were certainly accurate.

The power PC theory makes the following predictions. First, if participants in phase 1 of the Experimental group of the Nonceiling experiment perceived R and S as independent causes, then their estimated proportion of patients with hypertension given the (unseen) combination of R and S should be higher than estimates for each of these endomins alone. This follows because R and S should each be perceived to produce the disease at a nonceiling level. In contrast, other groups should not give a higher estimate for this combination than for the individual endomins. This follows because in the Control group of the Nonceiling experiment, R should be perceived to be noncausal; and for the Ceiling experiment, the R and S combination would not be expected to produce the effect beyond the ceiling level, regardless of whether both R and S were perceived to be causal (in the Experimental group), or only S was (in the Control group). Measuring the estimate for the unseen combination in phase 1 allows us to confirm that any observed reduction in the participants' estimates of the individual stimuli in phase 2 is indeed due to their overexpectation of the frequency for this combination. Second, endomin S should lose perceived causal power in phase 2 for the Experimental group (but not the Control group) of the Nonceiling experiment, because there should be overexpectation of the disease only in the former group. Finally, because participants in both groups of the Ceiling experiment should perceive no conflict in estimated causal power across the two phases, the power PC theory predicts that these participants should not reduce their estimates in phase 2.

A prerequisite for this theory's predictions is that the probability of the disease given the presence of each of the critical factors is perceived to be below ceiling in the Nonceiling experiment, but at ceiling for the Ceiling experiment. Our results confirmed this prerequisite: In phase 1 of the Nonceiling experiment, the mean estimated proportion of patients with endomin T who have hypertension (.90 in the Experimental group and .92 in the Control group) was reliably higher than that for either R (.76 in the Experimental group and .01 in the Control group) or S (.78 in the Experimental group and .74 in the Control group); in the Ceiling experiment, however, the estimates for the stimuli that were paired with the disease all ranged from .99 to 1.0.

The results of both phases of the two experiments were in accord with the predictions of the power PC theory. In phase 1, for the Experimental group in the Nonceiling experiment, the estimated proportion for the unseen R and S combination (.90) was reliably higher than that for R and S individually and for the estimated proportion for their subsequently presented combination (.70), confirming that participants in this group were overexpecting the disease. In contrast, participants in the Control group did not overexpect the disease. Neither did either group in the Ceiling experiment: the estimated proportion for the unseen combination was 1.0 for both groups, the same as the estimates for the individual stimuli that were paired with the disease and the estimates for the subsequently presented combination in both groups.

The pattern of estimated proportions for S obtained after phase 2 in the two experiments was consistent with the pattern of overexpectation observed in phase 1: A reduction in the estimate for S was observed after this phase only when there was overexpectation of the effect for the R and S compound in phase 1. On one hand, in the Experimental group of the Nonceiling experiment, the estimate for the critical endomin S decreased by .10 across the two phases. This reduction in the estimate for S in the Experimental condition was reliably greater than the corresponding decline of .02 observed in the Control group, which was not reliable. On the other hand, in the Ceiling experiment, the estimates for S were virtually unchanged across phases (ranging from .99 to 1.0) in both the Experimental and Control groups.

The number of participants who showed or did not show a reduction in their estimate for S in phase 2 indicated the same pattern of results. On one hand, in the Nonceiling experiment, most participants in the Experimental group (15) showed a decline in their estimate for S from phase 1 to phase 2; few did not (4 gave equal estimates in the two phases and 1 showed an increase). In contrast, few participants (5) in the Control group showed such a decline, and most did not (10 gave equal estimates and 5 showed an increase). These distributions differed reliably between groups. On the other hand, there was no corresponding difference between groups in the Ceiling experiment: None of the participants in either the Experimental or the Control group showed a decline in their estimate for S from phase 1 to phase 2 (11 participants in each group gave equal estimates across phases, and, respectively, 1 and 2 participants in the Experimental and Control groups showed an increase). In sum, as predicted by the power PC theory, but no other current theories, results from the two phases provide converging evidence that participants in the Experimental group of the Nonceiling experiment overexpected the outcome for the R and S combination, whereas those in the corresponding group of the Ceiling experiment did not.

4. Implications for the Probabilistic Contrast Model and Other Models

The results obtained by Park and Cheng (1995) provide strong support for the interpretation of contrasts as estimates of causal power. The power PC theory accurately predicts a boundary condition on the phenomenon of "overexpectation" for human causal induction with events that are naturally encoded in terms of probabilities. When each of two individual cues *sometimes* produced the effect (Nonceiling experiment), the estimated causal power of each of them was reduced after the two were presented in combination with the same probability of the effect as had been observed for each cue alone. However, when each cue alone *always* produced the effect (Ceiling experiment), the same design yielded no change in estimated causal power after the combination had been presented. The Rescorla–Wagner model and its variants cannot account for the absence of overexpectation in the Ceiling experiment. Without an interpretation in terms of causal power, no model of covariation is able to account for the difference in overexpectation across the two experiments.

B. A BOUNDARY CONDITION ON THE INTERPRETATION OF INHIBITORY CAUSES

1. The Paradigm of Conditioned Inhibition

Whereas the overexpectation paradigm permits a test of the boundary condition for inferring facilitatory causes predicted by the power PC theory, a causal analogue of another conditioning paradigm permits a test of the corresponding boundary condition for inferring preventive causes predicted by this theory: the *extinction of conditioned inhibition* (or in causal terms, the reduction in perceived power of a preventive cause). The initial *acquisition* of conditioned inhibition (Rescorla, 1969) can be readily explained by both the Rescorla–Wagner model and the power PC theory. First described by Pavlov (1927), this phenomenon occurs when some stimulus, A, which predicts the presence of some outcome (A+), is paired with a second stimulus, X, with the AX compound being followed by the absence of the outcome (AX−). Exposure to these events leads to X being perceived as inhibiting the outcome. This perception can be behaviorally tested using a transfer task, known as summation. Pavlov (1927) showed that when X is later paired with some excitatory transfer stimulus B, the response that had been previously evoked by B is attenuated. Summation indicates that the learner possesses a generalized inhibitory representation of X independent of the stimulus with which it was originally paired. (See Williams, this volume, Ch. 3, for a detailed discussion of conditioned inhibition).

Both the Rescorla–Wagner model and the power PC theory predict that people will judge X to be inhibitory in this negative contingency paradigm, consistent with Pavlov's (1927) and Rescorla's (1969) findings using animal participants. The Rescorla–Wagner model predicts the conditioned inhibition of stimulus X because there is a discrepancy between the actual outcome given the compound AX (outcome absent) and the expected outcome based on previous trials with stimulus A alone (outcome present). This discrepancy leads to a reduction in the strength of X, which must become negative to offset the positive strength of A.

According to the power PC theory, the optimal focal set for assessing the inhibitory power of X is that in which a known excitor, A, is constantly present [see Equation (6) above]. This theory predicts the conditioned inhibition of X due to the fact that the contrast for X conditional on the presence of A [i.e., $P(e|X\ A) - P(e|\overline{X}\ A)$] is negative.

2. Predictions for the Extinction of Conditioned Inhibition

Although both models account for the acquisition of conditioned inhibition, they make radically different predictions regarding the *extinction* of conditioned inhibition. The extinction of a conditioned inhibiting stimulus (such as X described above) occurs when new information leads to X no longer being perceived as preventive. The Rescorla–Wagner model predicts that conditioned inhibition will be extinguished by a "direct" procedure, in which a conditioned inhibiting stimulus, X, is later presented alone with the outcome absent (X−). In this situation the inhibitory strength of the stimulus will become less negative (approaching an asymptotic strength of zero), because the learning rule in this model revises the associative strength of a stimulus that is present to reduce the discrepancy between the actual and expected outcomes. Thus, this model predicts that X will be extinguished as an inhibitor in the direct procedure.

In contrast, the power PC theory predicts that the inhibitory strength of X will remain unchanged under the direct procedure, because the intervening experience with X in the absence of excitatory cause A yields the contrast, $P(e|X\overline{A}) - P(\overline{X}\,\overline{A})$, which is uninterpretable as an estimate of the inhibitory power of X. For this contrast, $P(a) \cdot p_a$ in Equation (6) equals 0. The new information therefore does not conflict with the estimate for X obtained in the earlier phase. Accordingly, the power PC theory predicts that this intervening experience will not alter the previous estimate, and the direct procedure will not lead to the extinction of X.[3] Experiments using this design with animals have supported the predictions of the power PC theory and contradicted those of the Rescorla–Wagner model: the direct procedure fails to extinguish conditioned inhibition. Zimmer-Hart and Rescorla (1974) found that when a conditioned inhibitory stimulus (a light flash) was presented alone with no outcome, it retained its inhibitory strength in later summation trials when paired with a novel excitatory stimulus (a tone).

Note that the above prediction of the power PC theory is the inhibitory analogue of the theory's prediction of lack of overexpectation due to combining facilitatory causes that produce the effect at a ceiling level. Recall that in phase 2 of that paradigm, information regarding the critical candidate in the presence of an alternative excitatory cause yields a contrast that is uninterpretable as an estimate of the candidate's facilitatory power according to Equation (4), as the effect always occurs in the presence of the alternative cause. The power PC theory therefore predicts (correctly) that this contrast will be ignored in favor of an available contrast that is interpretable. Analogously, in the extinction phase of the conditioned inhibition paradigm, experience with X in the absence of excitatory cause A yields a contrast that is uninterpretable as an estimate of the inhibitory power of X according to Equation (6), as the effect never occurs in the absence of A.

The predictions of the power PC and Rescorla–Wagner models are reversed for an "indirect" extinction procedure in which a previously excitatory stimulus A, which had been inhibited by a preventive stimulus X (i.e., A+, AX−), is at a later time no longer paired with the presence of

---

[3] As Spellman (this volume, Ch. 5) notes, the unconditional contrast for X is also unaffected by the direct extinction procedure. However, the power PC theory predicts that it is the relevant conditional contrast that is crucial. The overexpectation observed in Park and Cheng's (1995) Nonceiling experiment cannot be explained in terms of unconditional contrasts, which did not change across phases. Neither can such contrasts explain why subjects rated S similarly in phase 1 across conditions for both of Park and Cheng's experiments, despite the difference in unconditional contrast for this stimulus between conditions (also see Fratianne & Cheng, 1995, Experiment 3; Spellman, this volume, Ch. 5).

the outcome (i.e., the excitatory power of A is extinguished). Given this information, the Rescorla–Wagner model predicts that the inhibitory strength of X will remain unchanged, as this model does not update stimuli that are not present, and X is never present during the interval in which the excitor A is extinguished.

In contrast, according to the power PC theory, the optimal focal set available for X predicts that the inhibitory value of X will be attenuated using the indirect extinction procedure. The relevant conditional contrast, $P(e|X\,A) - P(e|\overline{X}\,A)$, which had been negative when A was excitatory, will approach 0 given the subsequent events (the value of the first term remains at 0, while the value of the second shifts from 1 toward 0). Several studies of animal conditioning, extinguishing either the conditioning context or some previously excitatory stimulus (Best, Dunn, Batson, Meachum, & Nash, 1985; Hallam, Matzel, Sloat, & Miller, 1990; Kaplan & Hearst, 1985; Kasprow, Schachtman, & Miller, 1987; Lysle & Fowler, 1985; Miller & Schachtman, 1985), have yielded results consistent with the predictions of the power PC theory, and contradicting those of the Rescorla–Wagner model: conditioned inhibition was extinguished using the indirect "retro-spective" procedure.

With respect to the extinction of conditioned inhibition, just as with overexpectation, it thus appears that the power PC theory provides a more accurate model of Pavlovian conditioning than does the Rescorla–Wagner model. The former model is more congruent with the results of several major animal conditioning studies. To continue to evaluate these alternative models as explanations of causal inference, however, we investigated the acquisition and extinction of conditioned inhibition by humans who are presented with the task of assessing causal relations (see Williams, this volume, Ch. 3). Moreover, previous studies have not compared the impact of the direct and indirect procedures on extinction of conditioned inhibition within the same experiment.

3.   An Experimental Test of Extinction of an Inhibitory Cause: Comparing Two Extinction Procedures

Yarlas, Cheng, and Holyoak (1995) performed an experiment designed to test these two procedures for "extinguishing" an inhibitory cause using college studies as participants. Participants were given a cover story that was a slight modification of the one introduced by Park and Cheng (1995). They were told that an outcome (a disease called DSE) was either caused, prevented, or not affected by each of five endomins, proteins that are sometimes produced by the body. These five candidates were labeled P, Q, R, S, and T; but the actual causal values can be represented more mnemonically by E_1, E_2, E_3, I, and U, where E indicates an excitatory cause, I an inhibitor, and U a candidate unrelated to the outcome. These candidates were associated with the outcome in specific covariational relationships, which were to be induced by participants through trial-and-error learning. We assume that under the context of the experiment, participants were willing to assume that candidate causes of DSE were limited to those presented. It follows that candidates E_1, E_2, and E_3 were all causes of the disease according to Equation (4), because when each of these candidates was present with all alternative candidates absent, the disease was always present, as opposed to the baseline of the disease being absent when all candidates were absent. Candidate I was an inhibitory cause according to Equation (6), in that when it was presented in tandem with either cause E_1 or E_2, the disease was no longer present, whereas the disease was always present when E_1 or E_2 occurred alone. (Candidate I was paired with two different excitors so as to increase participants' tendency to view I as a general inhibitor, rather than as a component of an inhibitory interaction involving one particular excitor; see Williams, this volume, Ch. 3.) Candidate U was irrelevant to the disease, in that the disease was always absent (at its baseline) when U was present, just as when U was absent.

In the learning phase of this experiment, all participants were given a series of learning trials for which they were given feedback. Table II summarizes the nature and number of trials administered during the learning phase, which was identical for all participants. Participants were then tested

TABLE II

Trials Administered in Each Phase for Each Condition[a]

Learning phase (all groups)	Extinction phases	Test phases (all groups)	
$E_1 \rightarrow + (8)^b$	Direct group	$E_1 \rightarrow$	?
$E_2 \rightarrow + (8)$	$I \rightarrow 0 (6)$	$E_2 \rightarrow$	?
$E_3 \rightarrow + (8)$	$E_3 \rightarrow + (6)$	$E_3 \rightarrow$	?
$U \rightarrow 0 (8)$	$U \rightarrow 0 (12)$	$U \rightarrow$	?
$E_1 \& E_2 \rightarrow + (8)$	Indirect group	$E_1 \& E_2 \rightarrow$	?
$E_1 \& I \rightarrow 0 (8)$	$E_1 \rightarrow 0 (6)$	$E_1 \& I \rightarrow$	?
$E_2 \& I \rightarrow 0 (8)$	$E_2 \rightarrow 0 (6)$	$E_2 \& I \rightarrow$	?
None $\rightarrow 0 (8)$	$E_3 \rightarrow + (6)$	$E_3 \& I \rightarrow$	?
	$U \rightarrow 0 (6)$	$I \rightarrow$	?
	Control group		
	$E_3 \rightarrow + (18)$		
	$U \rightarrow 0 (6)$		

[a] Experimental design used by Yarlas, Cheng, and Holyoak (1995).

[b] + indicates disease present; 0 indicates disease absent; number of presentations is shown in parentheses.

for the learning of these causal relations using the stimulus patterns listed under the "Test phases" column in Table II. The same tests were used for all test phases for all participants.

In the extinction phase, which immediately followed, participants were divided into three groups. The extinction trials administered to each of these groups are also summarized in Table II. In the *control* group, all participants were given additional trials of information that had been presented in the initial learning phase; this information was irrelevant to the strength of the inhibitory cause (candidate I) according to both the power PC theory and the Rescorla–Wagner model. In the *direct extinction* group, participants were presented with new trials in which the previously inhibitory cause was now presented alone in the absence of the disease. In the *indirect extinction* group, participants received trials in which two previously excitatory causes (E_1 and E_2) were now separately paired with the absence of the disease. Candidate I was not presented during the indirect extinction phase. Participants were again tested on causal efficacy both in the middle (extinction 1) and at the end (extinction 2) of the extinction phase. The measurements were taken twice in this phase to determine whether participants had reached asymptote in their causal judgments. In all groups, estimates did not differ across the two extinction phases, indicating that participants' estimates after extinction were at asymptote. We therefore report only the average of the estimates obtained in the two phases.

We measured causal efficacy using a summation test that assessed participants' beliefs regarding the likelihood of the outcome occurring given the inhibitory stimulus in combination with an excitor with which it had never been paired (I combined with E_3). This measure was of the same type as that described earlier in connection with Park and Cheng's (1995) experiments: participants were asked to estimate how many patients out of 100 would get the disease given various patterns of endomins (see Table II). If I is perceived as an inhibitor, estimates for the E_3 and I combination should be lower than those for E_3 alone; if the perceived inhibitory value of I has been extinguished, estimates for the E_3 and I combination should not differ from those for E_3 alone.

Figure 1 presents the means of participants' estimates of the number of patients (out of 100) getting the disease given the compound E_3 and I for each group across phases. Estimates for E_3 alone (not plotted) were uniformly high and did not vary significantly across either groups or phases; the overall mean estimation was that 91 of 100 people would have the disease, confirming that E_3 alone was viewed as a strong facilitatory cause.

Given the nature of the experimental design, effects could be analyzed both within participant (whether judgments were different at the learning

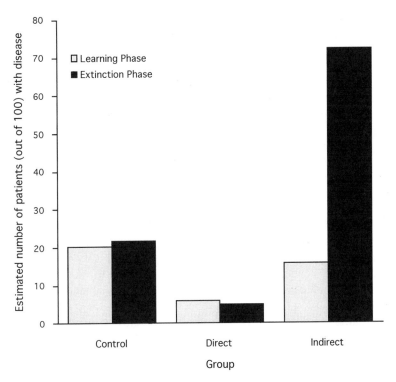

Fig. 1. Mean estimated number of patients (out of 100) who will get the disease given E_3 and I in combination, in learning and extinction phases of control group and two extinction groups (Yarlas et al., 1995).

and extinction phases) and between participants (whether judgments at the extinction phases for the direct and indirect groups differed from that of the control group). Both within- and between-participant analyses were consistent with the predictions of the power PC theory: extinction of the inhibitory cue was observed on the summation test for the indirect group, but not for the direct or control groups. For the direct and control groups on one hand, estimates for the E_3 and I combination were reliably lower than those for E_3 alone, indicating that I was perceived as inhibitory, and this difference remained unchanged across the learning phase and the extinction phase, indicating that the perceived inhibitory power of I was not extinguished. For the indirect group, on the other hand, while estimates for the combination were, as in the other groups, reliably lower than those for E_3 alone in the learning phase, this difference was significantly reduced at the extinction phase, providing evidence for the extinguishing of a perceived inhibitor.

In addition to the summation test, which provides an *implicit* assessment of participants' causal judgments, our test phases measured participants' verbal reports about the causal status of each individual candidate, including I. These reports provide an *explicit* assessment of participants' causal judgments. This measure required participants to indicate whether each individual endomin caused (coded as a value of 1), had no effect (coded as a value of 0), or prevented (coded as a value of −1) the disease. If I is perceived as an inhibitor, participants' judgments should approach −1; if I has been extinguished, judgments should approach 0. Results for the explicit measure converged with those for the implicit measure, supporting the power PC theory.

In sum, the results of both the direct and the indirect extinction procedures in Yarlas et al. (1995) strongly support the predictions of the power PC theory. Specifically, the effectiveness of these two procedures in extinguishing an inhibitory stimulus was in accord with the contrast of that stimulus in the optimal focal set for assessing an inhibitory cause according to the power PC theory—the contrast conditional on the constant presence of an excitatory cause. The failure of the direct procedure confirms the boundary condition for inhibitory causes predicted by the power PC theory. At the same time, the results for both the direct procedure and the indirect procedure are diametrically opposite to those predicted by the Rescorla–Wagner model.

There may, of course, be alternative associative theories that can accommodate the empirical findings concerning extinction of conditioned inhibition. For example, the configural theory of Pearce (1994; Pearce & Wilson, 1991) assumes that compound cues are treated as configural units, so that extinction of an elemental feature need not eliminate the inhibitory properties of the compound. This theory thus accounts for the failure to find extinction in the direct procedure; however, it does not offer a clear explanation of why extinction *is* produced by the indirect procedure (as both procedures involve extinction of one element of a configural compound). In contrast, the power PC theory offers a unified account of both results.

III.   Implications for the Rescorla–Wagner Model

We now consider further implications of our experimental findings for the Rescorla–Wagner model.

A.   A POWER ANALYSIS OF THE RESCORLA–WAGNER MODEL

A power analysis of a model requires as a prerequisite a mathematical function characterizing the model's asymptotic behavior. Connectionist models, which specify an algorithm and a representation, typically do not permit such characterizations. To make predictions for these models, researchers generally have to rely instead on computer or thought simulations of specific experiments. One of the attractions of the Rescorla–Wagner model is that it turns out to be an exception to this rule. Assuming that (1) λ (the parameter that the model associates with the unconditioned stimulus or the effect) equals 1 for trials on which the effect occurs, and 0 otherwise, and (2) the learning rates remain constant across trials on which the effect does and does not occur, Cheng (in press) derived that, for experimental designs that satisfy a condition she terms *nesting,* the Rescorla–Wagner model asymptotically computes conditional contrasts.[4] In a design with multiple stimuli, if there are no partially overlapping stimulus combinations unless for every pair of such combinations, all supersets of one combination (including itself) share the same intersection with the other combination, and this intersection occurs as a separate combination, then the design is nested. In other words, except for such partially overlapping combinations, every combination of stimuli in a nested design can be characterized as a proper superset of any combination that contains some but not all stimuli in it. For example, the design with stimulus patterns A, AB, and ABC is nested, whereas the design with stimulus patterns A, AB, and BC is not nested. For nested designs, the Rescorla–Wagner model asymptotically predicts that the sum of the associative strengths of the stimuli in each combination equals the relative frequency of the outcome given that combination. Because the strengths of the stimuli are additive in this model, it follows algebraically that *for any combination with multiple stimuli in a nested design, the strength of the stimuli in it that do not belong to the next proper subset is equal to the contrast for those stimuli (as a composite) conditional on the presence of the stimuli in the smaller combination (i.e., the rest of the stimuli in the larger combination).* When the design is not nested, the model does not, in general, compute conditional contrasts. Even when the design is nested, the contrast computed by the Rescorla–Wagner model may not be one that optimally reveals causal power among those available.

<hr />

[4] Although many researchers conduct simulations of the Rescorla–Wagner model with the assumption that the learning rate associated with the unconditioned stimulus differs between trials on which that stimulus is present and absent, most of the predictions of the Rescorla–Wagner model are in fact independent of that assumption (see Miller et al., 1995; also see the derivations of the model's predictions in Melz et al., 1993). If learning rates are assumed to vary depending on the presence or absence of the conditioned and unconditioned stimuli, the model will compute conditional contrasts in which the frequencies that estimate the components of contrast are weighted as a function of these parameter values. That is, variations in the learning rates yield weighted conditional contrasts without changing which conditional contrast is computed (unless assumptions about activation levels of candidate causes are also assumed to vary).

Cheng's (in press) result allows the Rescorla–Wagner model to be analyzed in terms of causal power. Armed with this result, let us derive the predictions of this model for the two studies reported earlier in terms of causal power. The model's prediction of overexpectation rests on a comparison between the two phases of the overexpectation paradigm. Recall that the design in phase 1 of Park and Cheng's (1995) experiments is : C−, AC+, and BC+ (where C is the context cue).[5] This design is nested because C, the intersection of the partially overlapping combinations, AC and BC, occurs by itself as a separate combination. According to Cheng's (in press) derivation, the model computes the contrasts for A or B in this design conditional on the presence of the context alone. As the context does not produce the effect [*i.e.*, $P(a) \cdot p_a$ equals 0], these contrasts closely estimate causal power according to Equation (4). The prediction of the Rescorla–Wagner model therefore coincides exactly with that of the power PC theory in this case. The prediction for the model in this phase is in accord with observed results.

In phase 2, the design is: C− and ABC+. Because ABC is a superset of C, this design is also nested. For this design, the model computes the contrast for AB as a composite conditional on the presence of the context alone. Because the effect occurs with equal probability in the presence of noncontext stimuli in this design, this composite contrast has the same value as that for the individual stimuli in phase 1. The additivity assumption of the Rescorla–Wagner model therefore yields the prediction that the strengths of the individual stimuli in phase 2 will asymptotically be reduced to half their previous strengths. For the Nonceiling experiment, this direction of change is consistent with that predicted by a hypothesized revision of observations in phase 1 to obtain a consistent estimate of causal power across phases. But with regard to the Ceiling experiment, as we explained earlier, the only contrast that reveals the causal power of A or B is that obtained in phase 1. Because the prediction of the Rescorla–Wagner model for phase 2 does not correspond to this contrast (instead, it predicts a value half the magnitude of this contrast), the power analysis predicts that the model should fail, as it did.

The design for conditioned inhibition in the acquisition phase of Yarlas et al. (1995) is: C−, CA+, and CAX−. Because every stimulus combination except the one with a single stimulus can be characterized as a superset of all combinations with fewer stimuli, this design is nested. For the inhibitory stimulus (X) in this design, the model computes its contrast conditional on

---

[5] Stimulus T in Park and Cheng's (1995) experiments was always presented by itself and will be dropped from our discussion because it does not affect the nesting of the rest of the design. The context cue, C, is included because it is a standard assumption made in applications of the Rescorla–Wagner model. The predicted contrast values in the designs discussed in this section do not depend on the assumption of such a cue.

the presence of a (composite) facilitatory cause that always produces the effect (the CA combination). This is the contrast that optimally reveals the causal power of an inhibitory cause [Equation (6)]. As contrast coincides with causal power, the Rescorla–Wagner model is accurate as an account of the acquisition phase of the conditioned-inhibition paradigm.

In the extinction phase of the paradigm for indirect extinction of conditioned inhibition, the Rescorla–Wagner model does not revise the strength of the inhibitory stimulus because it is absent. This stimulus therefore retains the value of its contrast from the acquisition phase, rather than changing to the updated value that is indicated by the extinction phase. As a result, the Rescorla–Wagner model fails to account for the observed extinction of inhibition for this stimulus.

For the extinction phase of the direct extinction of conditioned inhibition, the design is: C− and CX−, which is nested. For this design, the model computes the contrast for X conditional on the *absence* of all facilitatory causes (the context is noncausal in this design), rather than the available optimal contrast based on the presence of a facilitatory cause [Equation (6)]. The estimation of power thus explains why the prediction of the Rescorla–Wagner model fails for the indirect extinction paradigm.

A mathematical analysis of the Rescorla–Wagner model thus yields an understanding of what the associative strengths computed by the model actually represent. Cheng's (1995) analysis allows us to specify general conditions under which the model does and does not compute conditional contrasts, whether it computes a contrast that estimates causal power, and what it computes instead when it does not. Our analysis of the model's predictions for the two phases of the overexpectation paradigm, and for the acquisition and extinction phases of the conditioned inhibition paradigm, shows that the model is successful when it computes the conditional contrast among those available in the input that optimally reveals causal power; otherwise it fails, unless its prediction happens to coincide with that based on the estimation of causal power.

B. INTRODUCING EXPLICIT REPRESENTATION OF ABSENT STIMULI
    INTO THE RESCORLA–WAGNER MODEL

An implicit standard assumption in applications of the Rescorla–Wagner model (1972) is that α, the learning-rate parameter that is associated with the conditioned stimulus or cause, equals 1 for trials on which the cause occurs, and 0 otherwise. Contrary to Rescorla's and Wagner's specification, Van Hamme and Wasserman (1994) have suggested modifying the model by dropping this assumption. The goal of this modified model is to account for "retrospective" changes in associative strength in the indirect extinction and other similar paradigms, which involve apparent changes in the associative strength of unpresented stimuli. This modified model thus bears directly on the results obtained by Yarlas et al. (1995) that we discussed above, and more generally has been an influential theoretical development (see Miller et al., 1995; Shanks et al., this volume, Ch. 7; Wasserman et al., this volume, Ch. 6; Williams, this volume, Ch. 3). Accordingly, we will consider the adequacy of this modified version of the Rescorla–Wagner model.

The modification is to revise the strength of a stimulus that is absent on a trial by changing the value α, the learning-rate parameter associated with the stimulus, from a positive to a negative value on such trials. Although the stengths of absent stimuli are revised, such stimuli do not contribute to the expected outcome term $(\sum_k V_k)$. In order to avoid assuming that all absent cues have their strengths revised, Van Hamme and Wasserman added the qualification that the currently absent stimulus must be "relevant" for this modification to apply. They stipulated, "A cue would become relevant after acquiring some level of positive or negative association strength;" and that this can be accomplished by presenting it "at least once in the experimental context, either followed by reinforcement or presented together with a cue that had previously been reinforced" (1994, p. 132, Footnote 1). In effect, this modified model sometimes introduces explicit representations for absent stimuli.

Although Van Hamme and Wasserman's modifications can indeed account for extinction of conditioned inhibition in the indirect paradigm, and the retrospective aspect of results observed in other paradigms, this modification encounters both theoretical and empirical problems. On the theoretical side, the modification makes a number of assumptions that cause the Rescorla–Wagner model to lose its conceptual interpretation. First, it is logically impossible to learn at a rate slower than 0 (the lower bound), which is not learning at all. The modified parameter is therefore conceptually no longer a learning rate, or any kind of rate. Second, the Van Hamme and Wasserman model, unlike the Rescorla–Wagner model, is not interpretable as a connectionist model. Operations of current connectionist models are functions of two basic properties: the activation of nodes and the weight of connections between nodes. When revising weights Van Hamme and Wasserman's model implicitly treats absent cues as having an activation of 1 (the same value as present cues), so that when the actual outcome is smaller than the expected outcome (as in the indirect extinction of conditioned inhibition), the weight change for an absent cue is positive: the product of learning rate (negative), discrepancy (negative), and activation of i (positive). When summing strengths, however, this model implicitly treats an absent cue as having an activation level of 0, so that the product of its activation level and connection weight is 0, and does not influence the expected outcome. The model thus assumes that absent cues are represented by two activation levels on the same trial, one of which is the same as that for present cues. Representing present and absent cues the same way seems to require some justification, and having two simultaneous activation levels for a cue requires that there be some third property, beyond activation and weight, to represent the selection of these levels.

On the empirical side, the model does not suffice to avoid a variety of the other failures of the Rescorla–Wagner model. These include its failure to explain the observed asymmetries between facilitatory and preventive causes. For example, the modified model does not explain why an inhibitory stimulus cannot be directly extinguished by presenting the stimulus alone without reinforcement, whereas an excitatory stimulus can be directly extinguished by doing so (Yarlas et al., 1995; see Miller et al., 1995, for other cases of this asymmetry). In addition, the model does not explain why there was overexpectation in the Experimental group of the Nonceiling experiment by Park and Cheng (1995), but not in the corresponding group of their Ceiling experiment. In the direct extinction paradigm, the inhibitory stimulus is present during the extinction phase; a modification in the representation of absent stimuli is therefore irrelevant to its weight, which should revise downward toward 0 according to both the original Rescorla–Wagner model and this modification. In Park and Cheng's (1995) experiments, the stimulus patterns were identical across the Ceiling and Nonceiling experiments. A change in the representation of absent stimuli therefore cannot explain any observed difference between them.

In addition to failing to remedy known empirical failures of the Rescorla–Wagner model, Van Hamme and Wasserman's (1994) modification generates erroneous predictions that the original model avoids. For example, their modification predicts that while a candidate cause is paired with an effect, previously learned causes of that effect will lose strength. More specifically, when two facilitatory causes are being learned (e.g., by a mixture of A+ and B+ trials), the asymptotic associative strength of each candidate should be reduced (relative to a control in which only one candidate is causal). This prediction follows because each candidate, being presented in the experimental context and followed by reinforcement, will be "relevant" according to the Van Hamme and Wasserman criterion; hence each will be represented when it is absent. The model therefore predicts that each candidate will lose strength as a result of the negative learning rate on trials in which it is absent (since a mixture of A+ and B+ trials would in fact be represented as a mixture of $A\overline{B}+$ and $\overline{A}B+$ trials).

Phase 1 of Park and Cheng's (1995) experiments has exactly the above design (see Table I). In the Experimental group both stimuli R and S were paired with the effect, whereas in the Control group only S was. Van Hamme and Wasserman's (1994) model therefore predicts that S should attain lower strength in the Experimental group than in the Control group. Contrary to this prediction, Park and Cheng found absolutely no difference in the estimated strength of stimulus S between the Experimental and Control group in either the Ceiling experiment (.99 in both groups) or the Nonceiling experiment (.78 vs. .74, a trend in the wrong direction). These results thus contradict the prediction of Van Hamme and Wasserman's model.[6]

In sum, although a modification of the Rescorla–Wagner model that introduces explicit representation of absent stimuli can account for some of the retrospective changes in strengths observed in some paradigms, it cannot account for observed asymmetries between facilitatory and preventive causes. Moreover, the modified model has no clear conceptual interpretation and generates incorrect predictions that the original model avoids.

IV. Implications of the Power PC Theory

A. SOLUTIONS TO PROBLEMS OF THE COVARIATIONAL AND POWER VIEWS

To solve some of the fundamental problems afflicting the covariation and power approaches to causal induction, Cheng (in press) proposes that the relation between covariation and power is analogous to that between a scientist's model or law and his or her theory of it. Whereas models and laws concern observable entities, theories posit unobservable entities. This relation between model and theory, formalized in the power PC theory, implies that the acquisition of causal relations embodies an inherent interac-

---

[6] An alternative modification of the Rescorla–Wagner model that adjusts the weights of absent cues, but that does not have the theoretical problems of Van Hamme and Wasserman's (1994) modification, assumes an activation level of -1 and a positive learning rate for a cue that is absent. Like the Van Hamme and Wasserman variant, it predicts that if an alternative cause is producing the same effect, a candidate will have its strength reduced by merely being absent. In addition, the alternative modification predicts that the learning of a facilitatory cause will be blocked by the mere absence of an inhibitory cause (e.g., after the acquisition phase of the conditioned inhibition paradigm). The latter prediction follows because the product of the negative activation representing the absence of the inhibitory cause and the negative weight between the inhibitory cause and the effect may completely predict the presence of the effect.

tion between bottom-up information and abstract top-down knowledge. This relation makes it possible to pinpoint the conditions under which covariation implies causation. Moreover, it provides a justification for the leap from covariation to causation: under specific conditions covariation provides an estimate of the power of causes that either produce or prevent an effect. The general inequality between covariation and causation is a problem that confronts all covariation models of causality, associationist or statistical. Without a causal power theory, it is difficult to see how any covariation model can free itself of the chains that bind the interpretation of even formal statistical covariation.

At the same time, the power PC theory motivates an assumption typically made by covariation models: that causes are temporally prior to their effects (see Pearl, this volume, Ch. 10; Waldmann, this volume, Ch. 2). Covariation between two types of events has no inherent temporal order. It is possible, for example, to form an association from the effect to the cause. But if reasoners have the intuitive notion that causes produce (or prevent) the effect, it follows that the cause must precede the effect (even if only by an infinitesimal amount of time), as a cause must exist before it can produce any consequences. The cause should therefore precede the effect at least in theory, if not by measurable time. The power PC theory provides a coherent link between covariation and temporal priority.

The assumption that people have a causal-power theory of their covariation model not only solves the above problems afflicting the covariation view, it also solves the two problems afflicting the power view. Recall that this view previously has never presented a solution to the problem of causal induction. Specifically, it has never specified a mapping beween the input and the output of the causal induction process. Unlike previous variants of the power view, the power PC theory specifies how the output, which is an estimate of causal power, is computed from the input, which consists of the input to the covariation process. This input is purely restricted to observable events, such as the presence and absence of the candidate causes and of the effect. The power PC theory thereby honors Hume's indisputable point that causal relations are not explicit in our sensory input. Moreover, in specifying the function computed by the causal-induction process, it specifies the necessary a priori knowledge. Also recall that the power view has appeared to be circular, implying that people do not learn that a relation is causal unless they already understand it to be causal. The power PC theory removes the circularity in two ways. First, it specifies how the causal efficacy of a candidate cause can be assessed without prior knowledge about itself, or even the identity of alternative causes. All that is required is observable information sufficient to separate the causal power of the candidate from that of alternative causes. Second, it explicitly formulates how a *general* notion of causes producing or stopping an effect can yield a theory of covariation that allows *specific* causal powers to be inferred.

Cheng's (in press) approach has its roots in previous work. A number of researchers have specifically interpreted contrast in terms of causal power (Baker, Berbrier, & Vallée-Tourangeau, 1989; Cheng & Novick, 1992; Waldmann & Holyoak, 1992), or more generally interpreted covariation as the measurement of, or evidence for, causal power (Ahn et al., 1995; Cartwright, 1989; Cheng, 1993). The contributions of the power PC theory are (1) it is the first example of a formal theory of a psychological model, and (2) it solves some basic problems afflicting the covariation and power views.

B. PREDICTED INFLUENCE OF BASE RATE OF THE EFFECT ON ESTIMATING FACILITATORY AND PREVENTIVE CAUSAL POWER

Cheng's (in press) solution to the problems of the covariation and power views generates many testable predictions. One is that even untutored reasoners will be unwilling to conclude causality from covariation if they believe that alternative causes exist and do not occur independently of the candidate causes in their focal set. That is, people have an implicit understanding of possible confounding by alternative causes. If they erroneously infer causality from covariation, it is because they erroneously believe that alternative causes are either nonexistent or held constant. We are not aware of any experimental test of this prediction.

For situations in which reasoners believe that alternative causes occur independently of a candidate cause, the theory makes specific predictions regarding the interpretation of covariation. One prediction is that in cases in which contrast equals 0, different causal judgments may result depending on the base rate of the effect. A second prediction that interacts with the first is that the influence of this base rate on the interpretation of zero contrasts depends on whether one is concerned with the facilitatory or preventive nature of the candidate. Consider the following situations: (1) when an alternative cause is known to be present and is always producing the effect; (2) when an alternative cause is present but is producing the effect only sometimes; and (3) when no alternative cause is present, so the effect never occurs. When one is concerned with the facilitatory nature of a candidate cause, it is not possible to draw a firm conclusion about whether a candidate with a zero contrast produces the effect in situation (1), but one would infer that such a candidate is not a cause in situation (2) or (3). When one is concerned with the inhibitory nature of a candidate cause, however, the conclusions regarding situations (1) and (3) are exactly reversed: one would conclude that a candidate with a zero contrast is not an inhibitory cause in situation (1), whereas no firm conslusion can be drawn about such a candidate in situation (3). In situation (2), one would conclude that a candidate with a zero contrast is neither a facilitatory nor an inhibitory cause.

In the present chapter, we presented some evidence supporting these interactive predictions regarding the boundary conditions for interpreting facilitatory and preventive causes. Park and Cheng's (1995) experiments on overexpectation provide support for the boundary condition for facilitatory causes: whereas situation (2) falls within the predicted boundary, situation (1) falls outside it. Yarlas et al.'s (1995) experiment provides support for the boundary condition for inhibitory causes, in which case situation (1) falls within the predicted boundary, but situation (3) falls outside it.

Our experiments used causal analogues of paradigms in classical conditioning. Many cases of asymmetry between conditioned excitation and inhibition using other paradigms have been reported in the conditioning literature (see Miller et al., 1995, for a review). The power PC theory predicts that there should be causal analogues of these cases, as they reveal the same asymmetry that follows from the power analysis of facilitatory and preventive causes.

In addition to specifying boundary conditions for interpreting contrasts, the power PC theory also makes predictions about changes in the magnitude of causal estimates for positive and negative contrasts as the base rate of the effect approaches these two boundaries. For a positive ΔP_i of the same magnitude, as the base rate of the effect [i.e., $P(a) \cdot p_a$] increases, higher strengths will be inferred for candidate cause i; whereas for a negative ΔP_i of the same magnitude, as $P(a) \cdot p_a$ increases, lower strengths should be inferred for i. We are not aware of any study using discrete trials that systematically tests this prediction.

Two such experiments using rates, however, were reported by Wasserman, Elek, Chatlosh, and Baker (1993).[7] Participants in these experiments were asked to judge whether tapping a key had any effect on the occurrence of a white light. The light occurred with various probabilities at the end of 1-s sampling intervals. Seconds on a time scale are, clearly, not discrete entities. Thus, although the investigators represented their manipulations of the occurrence of the effect in terms of probabilities, they are more appropriately represented in terms of rates. As we mentioned, unlike probabilities, rates do not have an upper bound. For example, contrary to the maximum "probability" of one light flash every second set by Wasserman et al., the light could have flashed at a higher rate. Rates do have a lower bound, however: events cannot occur at a rate slower than not occurring

---

[7] Anderson and Sheu (1995) also tested the effects of covariation using rates. However, they did not report their results in a way that allows an evaluation of the predictions of the Rescorla–Wagner model and an analysis of causal power.

at all. Wasserman et al.'s light, for example, could not have flashed at a rate any slower than 0 times every second.

Wasserman et al.'s (1993) rate studies lie outside the domain of Cheng's (in press) analysis of probabilistic causal relations. If one were to apply an analogue of their analysis to events that occur with certain rates, however, the anlaysis would show consequences of a lower boundary condition for preventative causes, but no parallel of an upper boundary condition for facilitatory causes (unless one comes close to the limits of perception). For example, consider an observable difference of −.50 flash/s in rate when a candidate cause occurs and when it does not. If we compare a situation in which the context (i.e., alternative cause *a* in our analysis) is producing the flash at the rate of .75/s to a situation in which the context is producing it at the rate of 1.0/s, the candidate cause would need to have a power to reduce the rate, respectively, by 2/3 and 1/2, to yield the observable change of −.50 flash/s. Thus (analogous to the case for probabilities), for the same observable reduction in rate due to a candidate cause, as the base rate of the effect increases, a lower preventative power would be inferred for the candidate.

The pattern of results reported by Wasserman et al. (1993) supports this prediction regarding preventative power. Judged contingencies[8] were systematically less negative for the same objective negative contingency as the rate of the effect in the absence of tapping increased.

Whereas a preventive cause decreases the rate of the effect by some proportion of the distance to the lower bound of 0, the rates of the effect produced by facilitatory causes are additive. If we compare a situation in which the context is producing the flash at the rate of 0/s to a situation in which the context is producing it at the rate of .25/s, a candidate that has the power to produce the flash at a rate of .50/s would yield an observable difference of +.50 flash/s in rate in both cases. A power analysis thus predicts an asymmetry in the existence of a boundary condition between preventative and facilitatory causes of events coded as rates, with base rates of the effect influencing estimates of causal power only for inhibitory causes.

Wasserman et al. (1993) did not report separate analyses for positive and negative contingencies, but a visual inspection of the graphs of their results appears to confirm this predicted asymmetry between facilitatory and preventative causes: whereas the judged contingencies were less negative for the same observable *negative* contingency as the rate of the effect in the absence of tapping increased, the judged contingencies for the same observable *positive* contingency did not differ systematically as a function

---

[8] We use the term "contingency" to be consistent with Wasserman et al.'s (1993) report, in the sense of the analogue of contingency (which is defined in terms of probabilities) for cases involving effects that occur with certain rates.

of the rate of the effect in the absence of tapping, (see the right panels of Figures 1 and 3 in Wasserman et al., 1993). This pattern of results directly supports a causal-power analysis of events that occur with rates, and indirectly supports the analogous analysis of probabilistic events.

Cheng's (in press) analysis of the Rescorla–Wagner model shows that when the learning rate parameters in that model are held constant across trials, the model does not predict an influence of the base rate of the effect on the associative strengths of candidates wtih the same contingency. The conditional contrasts computed by this model when the design is nested are not adjusted by the base rate of the effect [$P(a) \cdot p_a$ in Equations (4) and (6)] to yield an estimation of causal power. To explain the empirically observed influence of the base rate of the effect, Wasserman et al. (1993; also Baker et al., this volume, Ch. 1) adopted two values for the learning-rate parameter associated with the effect (β) in the Rescorla–Wagner model), specifying that this rate is higher when the effect is present than when it is absent. Choosing values that give the best fit to the data, Wasserman et al. were able to explain the pattern of results for negative contingencies. Excitatory and inhibitory cues, however, are symmetric in the Rescorla–Wagner model. These parameter values for β predict a symmetrical influence of the base rate of the effect on positive contingencies, a prediction that according to the power PC theory should hold for neither rates nor probabilities. The predicted values for positive contingencies deviated systematically from the observed values in Wasserman et al.'s (1993) experiments (see their Figure 5).

C.   COMPUTATIONAL AND ALGORITHMIC LEVELS

Applications of the Rescorla–Wagner model often involved varying the values of its parameters and selecting those that provide a best fit to the data. These values are not justified independently of the fit, are not always kept consistent across experimental paradigms, and sometimes have no conceptual interpretation. We have seen cases in which the adoption of some particular set of parameter values explains some findings but fails to explain others, even at an ordinal level. For example, adopting both positive and negative values for α explains retrospective changes in associative strength; however, this assumption fails to explain the asymmetry between facilitatory and preventive causes, and it generates erroneous predictions for the learning of multiple versus single cues. Adopting a larger value for β when the effect occurs than when it does not explains the influence of the base rate of the effect on negative contingencies, but not that for positive contingencies. More importantly, in addition to these and other failures (see Cheng & Holyoak, 1995; Gallistel, 1990; Miller et al., 1995), parameter fitting will not enable the model to discriminate between situations in which people infer causation from covariation from those in which they do not, nor will it enable the model to justify this inference when it is made.

As we observed at the beginning of this chapter, the Rescorla–Wagner model is founded on an algorithm for discrepancy reduction on a trial-by-trial basis. Causal judgments are purely the output of this algorithm, requiring no a priori assumptions about the nature of causal relations in the world. Cheng's (in press) analysis of what this algorithm computes reveals that it often either yields contrasts that do not estimate causal power, or else does not compute contrasts at all. Even when it does compute a contrast that reveals causal power, the value of this contrast is directly reflected as associative strength, without the normative adjustment by the base rate of the effect. Although parameter adjustments can vary the weights given to the components of a contrast, they cannot vary which contrast is computed.

In contrast to the Rescorla–Wagner model, the power PC theory (Cheng, in press) has no parameters. This theory explains ordinal differences in causal judgments regarding single and multiple facilitatory and preventive candidate causes. These domains include such phenomena as the basic influence of contingency, the subtle influence of the base rate of the effect on the magnitude of causal judgments for a given contingency, interactive causes, the distinction between causes and enabling conditions, the distinction between a novel candidate and an irrelevant one, the boundary condition for interpreting facilitatory causes as manifested in overexpectation, the boundary condition for interpreting inhibitory causes as manifested in the extinction of conditioned inhibition, the asymmetry between these boundary conditions, and retrospective changes in causal judgments. The theory is motivated by the computational constraints of the problem of causal induction, rather than by any particular learning algorithm. It treats the following as self-evident facts: the environment contains such things as causes that either produce or stop an effect, causal relations are not explicit in our sensory input, and causes and effects can occur in the form of various types of variables (e.g., a discrete effect can occur in discrete entities or in continuous time). The goal of the process of causal induction is to uncover causal relations in the world given these constraints. To reach this goal, the theory postulates that reasoners adhere to a causal-power theory of their model of covariation, a theory that specifies and explains when one may infer causality from covariation. The ordinal predictions of the power PC theory follow not from parameter fitting, but from its solution to the constraints. The constraints and the theory's solution to them may guide the design of algorithmic models that match or surpass the power PC theory in parsimony and explanatory breath.

ACKNOWLEDGMENTS

Preparation of this paper was supported by National Science Foundation Grant DBS-9121298 to Patricia Cheng. This material is based in part on work supported under a National Science Foundation Graduate Research Fellowship to Aaron Yarlas. We thank Woo-Kyoung Ahn, Douglas Medin, David Shanks, Michael Waldmann, and Edward Wasserman for their valuable comments on an earlier draft. We also thank Barbara Spellman for stimulating discussions. Requests for reprints may be addressed to Patricia Cheng at the Department of Psychology, University of California, Los Angeles, California 90095-1563.

REFERENCES

Ahn, W., & Bailenson, J. (in press). Causal attribution as a search for underlying mechanisms: An explanation of the conjunction fallacy and the discounting principle. *Cognitive Psychology.*

Ahn, W., Kalish, C. W., Medin, D. L., & Gelman, S. A. (1995). The role of covariation versus mechanism information in causal attribution. *Cognition, 54,* 299–352.

Anderson, J. R., & Sheu, C.-F. (1995). Causal inferences as perceptual judgments. *Memory & Cognition, 23,* 510–524.

Baker, A. G., Berbrier, M. W., & Vallée-Tourangeau, F. (1989). Judgments of a 2×2 contingency table: Sequential processing and the learning curve. *Quarterly Journal of Experimental Psychology, 41B,* 65–97.

Best, M. R., Dunn, D. P., Batson, J. D., Meachum, C. L., & Nash, S. M. (1985). Extinguishing conditioned inhibition in flavor-aversion learning: Effects of repeated testing and extinction of the excitatory element. *Quarterly Journal of Experimental Psychology, 37B,* 359–378.

Bullock, M., Gelman, R., & Baillargeon, R. (1982). The development of causal reasoning. In W. J. Friedman (Ed.), *The developmental psychology of time* (pp. 209–254). New York: Academic Press.

Cartwright, N. (1989). *Nature's capacities and their measurement.* Oxford: Clarendon Press.

Cheng, P. W. (1993). Separating causal laws from casual facts: Pressing the limits of statistical relevance. In D. L. Medin (Ed.), *The psychology of learning and motivation* (Vol. 30, pp. 215–264). San Diego, CA: Academic Press.

Cheng, P. W. (in press). From covariation to causation: A causal power theory. *Psychological Review.*

Cheng, P. W., & Holyoak, K. J. (1995). Complex adaptive systems as intuitive statisticians: Causality, contingency, and prediction. In H. L. Roitblat & J.-A. Meyer (Eds.), *Comparative approaches to cognitive science* (pp. 271–302). Cambridge, MA: MIT Press.

Cheng, P. W., & Lien, Y. (1995). The role of coherence in differentiating genuine from spurious causes. In D. Sperber, D. Premack, & A. J. Premack (Eds.), *Causal cognition: A multidisciplinary debate* (pp. 463–490). Oxford: Clarendon Press.

Cheng, P. W., & Novick, L. R. (1990). A probabilistic contrast model of causal induction. *Journal of Personality and Social Psychology, 58,* 545–567.

Cheng, P. W., & Novick, L. R. (1991). Causes versus enabling conditions. *Cognition, 40,* 83–120.

Cheng, P. W., & Novick, L. R. (1992). Covariation in natural causal induction. *Psychological Review, 99,* 365–382.

Cheng, P. W., & Novick, L. R. (1995, September). *Explaining probabilistic contrasts as estimates of causal power.* Paper presented at the 1995 Joint EAESP/SESP Meeting, Washington, DC

Fratianne, A., & Cheng, P. W. (1995). *Assessing causal relations by dynamic hypothesis testing.* Unpublished manuscript. Los Angeles: University of California, Department of Psychology.

Gallistel, C. R. (1990). *The organization of learning.* Cambridge, MA: MIT Press.

Gluck, M., & Bower, G. H. (1988). From conditioning to category learning: An adaptive network model. *Journal of Experimental Psychology: General, 117,* 227–247.

Hallam, S. C., Matzel, L. D., Sloat, J. S., & Miller, R. R. (1990). Excitation and inhibition as a function of posttraining extinction of the excitatory cue used in Pavlovian inhibition training. *Learning and Motivation, 21,* 59–84.

Harré, R., & Madden, E. H. (1975). *Causal powers: A theory of natural necessity,* Totowa, NJ: Rowman & Littlefield.

Hume, D. (1987). *A treatise of human nature* (2nd ed.). Oxford: Clarendon Press. (Original work published 1739).

Jenkins, H., & Ward, W. (1965). Judgment of contingency between responses and outcomes. *Psychological Monographs, 7,* 1–17.

Kant, I. (1965). *Critique of pure reason.* London: Macmillan. (Original work published 1781)

Kaplan, P. S., & Hearst, E. (1985). Contextual control and excitatory versus inhibitory learning: Studies of extinction, reinstatement, and interference. In P. D. Balsam & A. Tomie (Eds.), *Context and learning* (pp. 195–224). Hillsdale, NJ: Erlbaum.

Kasprow, W. J., Schachtman, T. R., & Miller, R. R. (1987). The comparator hypothesis of conditioned response generation: Manifest conditioned excitation and inhibition as a function of differences in excitatory strength of CS and conditioning context at the time of testing. *Journal of Experimental Psychology: Animal Behavior Processes, 13,* 395–406.

Kelley, H. H. (1967). Attribution theory in social psychology. In D. Levine (Ed.), *Nebraska Symposium on Motivation* (Vol. 15, pp. 192–238). Lincoln: University of Nebraska Press.

Kremer, E. F. (1978). The Rescorla-Wagner model: Losses in associative strength in compound conditioned stimuli. *Journal of Experimental Psychology: Animal Behavior Processes, 4,* 22–36.

Lysle, D. T., & Fowler, H. (1985). Inhibition as a "slave" process: Deactivation of conditioned inhibition through extinction of conditioned excitation. *Journal of Experimental Psychology: Animal Behavior Processes, 11,* 71–94.

Marr, D. (1982). *Vision.* New York: Freeman.

Melz, E. R., Cheng, P. W., Holyoak, K. J., & Waldmann, M. R. (1993). Cue competition in human categorization: Contingency or the Rescorla-Wagner learning rule? Comments on Shanks (1991). *Journal of Experimental Psychology: Learning, Memory, and Cognition, 19,* 1398–1410.

Michotte, A. E. (1963). *The perception of causality.* New York: Basic Books. (Original work published 1946).

Miller, R. R., Barnet, R. C., & Grahame, N. J. (1995). Assessment of the Rescorla-Wagner model. *Psychological Bulletin, 117,* 363–386.

Miller, R. R., & Schachtman, T. R. (1985). Conditioning context as an associative baseline: Implications for response generation and the nature of conditioned inhibition. In R. R. Miller & N. E. Spear (Eds.), *Information processing in animals: Conditioned inhibition* (pp. 51–88). Hillsdale, NJ: Erlbaum.

Novick, L. R., Fratianne, A., & Cheng, P. W. (1992). Knowledge-based assumptions in causal attribution. *Social Cognition, 10,* 299–333.

Park, J., & Cheng, P. W. (1995). *Boundary conditions on "overexpectation" in causal learning with discrete trials: A test of the power PC theory.* Unpublished manuscript, Los Angeles: University of California, Department of Psychology.

Pavlov, I. P. (1927). *Conditioned reflexes.* New York: Dover.

Pearce, J. M. (1994). Similarity and discrimination: A selective review and a connectionist model. *Psychological Review, 101,* 587–607.

Pearce, J. M., & Wilson, P. N. (1991). Effects of extinction with a compound conditioned stimulus. *Journal of Experimental Psychology: Animal Behavior Processes, 17,* 151–162.

Rescorla, R. A. (1968). Probability of shock in the presence and absence of CS in fear conditioning. *Journal of Comparative and Physiological Psychology, 66,* 1–5.

Rescorla, R. A. (1969). Conditioned inhibition of fear resulting from CS-US contingencies. *Journal of Comparative and Physiological Psychology, 67,* 504–509.

Rescorla, R. A., & Wagner, A. R. (1972). A theory of Pavlovian conditioning: Variations in the effectiveness of reinforcement and non-reinforcement. In A. H. Black & W. F. Prokasy (Eds.), *Classical conditioning II. Current research and theory* (pp. 64–99). New York: Appleton-Century-Crofts.

Salmon, W. (1971). Statistical explanation. In W. Salmon (Ed.), *Statistical explanation and statistical relevance* (pp. 29–87). Pittsburgh: University of Pittsburgh Press.

Shanks, D. R. (1991). Categorization by a connectionist network. *Journal of Experimental Psychology: Learning, Memory, and Cognition, 17,* 433–443.

Shanks, D. R. (1993). Associative versus contingency accounts of category learning: Reply to Melz, Cheng, Holyoak, and Waldmann (1993). *Journal of Experimental Psychology: Learning, Memory, and Cognition, 19,* 1411–1423.

Shultz, T. R. (1982). Rules of causal attribution. *Monographs of the Society for Research in Child Development, 47* (Serial No. 1).

Taylor, R. (1967). Causation. In P. Edwards (Ed.), *The encyclopedia of philosophy* (Vol. 2, pp. 56–66). New York: Macmillan.

Van Hamme, L. J., & Wasserman, E. A. (1994). Cue competition in causality judgments: The role of nonpresentation of compound stimulus elements. *Learning and Motivation, 25,* 127–151.

Waldmann, M. R., & Holyoak, K. J. (1992). Predictive and diagnostic learning within causal models: Asymmetries in cue competition. *Journal of Experimental Psychology: General, 121,* 222–236.

Wasserman, E. A., Elek, S. M., Chatlosh, D. L., & Baker, A. G. (1993). Rating causal relations: Role of probability in judgments of response-outcome contingency. *Journal of Experimental Psychology: Learning, Memory, and Cognition, 19,* 174–188.

White, P. A. (1989). A theory of causal processing. *British Journal of Psychology, 80,* 431–454.

Yarlas, A. S., Cheng, P. W., & Holyoak, K. J. (1995). Alternative approaches to causal induction: The probabilistic contrast versus the Rescorla-Wagner model. In J. D. Moore & J. F. Lehman (Eds.), *Proceedings of the Seventeenth Annual Conference of the Cognitive Science Society* (pp. 431–436). Hillsdale, NJ: Erlbaum.

Zimmer-Hart, C. L., & Rescorla, R. A. (1974). Extinction of Pavlovian conditioned inhibition. *Journal of Comparative and Physiological Psychology, 86,* 837–845.

THE USE OF INTERVENING VARIABLES IN CAUSAL LEARNING

Jerome R. Busemeyer
Mark A. McDaniel
Eunhee Byun

Causal reasoning is a complex cognitive process that has been investigated from many different perspectives including philosophy (Bunge, 1959), science (Cook & Campbell, 1979, Ch. 1), artificial intelligence (see Pearl, this volume, Ch. 10), and psychology (the central theme of this volume). Within psychology, the field can be further broken down into two distinct areas of research: Deductive reasoning from a set of known causal relations (Einhorn & Horgarth, 1986) or inductive learning about new causal relations (Shanks & Dickinson, 1987). Furthermore, the latter topic has been investigated for over 30 years using several different paradigms that differ in terms of the complexity of the causal relations that have to be learned.

The simplest paradigm, called the contingency learning paradigm, started with the seminal work of Jenkins and Ward (1965). In this paradigm, individuals try to learn whether or not the presence or absence of antecedent events causes the presence or absence of a consequent event. The primary question is how do individuals learn the *contingencies* between the observed events.

The next most complex paradigm, called the function learning paradigm, originated with the incipient work of Carroll (1963). In this paradigm, individuals try to learn how continuous changes in antecedent variables cause continuous changes in a consequent variable. The primary question is how do individuals learn the *functional relationship* between the observed variables.

Finally, the most complex paradigm, called the multivariate learning paradigm, began with our own program of research (Busemeyer, McDaniel, & Byun, in press). In this paradigm, individuals try to learn how multiple antecedent variables are related to multiple consequent variables, when this relationship is mediated by an unobservable causal variable. The primary question is how do individuals learn the *intervening causal* relationship.

Intervening concepts are a familiar part of our natural as well as our scientific language (Miller, 1959). Much of our daily reasoning about causes is based on intervening concepts like hunger, thirst, fear, intelligence, self-esteem, ability, effort, intention, attitude, habit, gravity, genes, force, power, and the list could go on much longer.

The *fundamental hypothesis* of this chapter is that people spontaneously learn new intervening concepts whenever they encounter a new multivariate environment. Their purpose is to construct a *simpler yet accurate* representation of the new and complex environment. The intent of this chapter is to review our research and theory on the learning of intervening concepts. The first section reviews the basic evidence for the learning of intervening variables. The second section provides a general model of associative learning that includes category learning, contingency learning, function learning, and intervening concept learning. The third section presents results of a new test of this model that opens up fresh theoretical issues. The chapter concludes with an evaluation of various theoretical approaches to understanding causal learning.

I. Evidence for Intervening Concept Learning

It is helpful to begin with the concrete example shown in Fig. 1. The left panel depicts a hypothetical single-celled organism. Various organisms are constructed by varying the values of three cues: The first input cue is the cell wall thickness of the organism; the second input cue is the density of the cytoplasm within the cell body; and the third input cue is the size of the cell. If each cue has 5 cue values (magnitudes), then factorially combining the 5 values of 3 cues produces a total of $5 \times 5 \times 5 = 125$ different organisms as stimuli.

Subjects are also given information about the hypothetical chemical compounds produced by these organisms: A compound called stynophinapine may be present to various degrees; another compound called durialoktius may occur in various amounts; and a third compound called vituloris can be present at various values. The amounts of each compound (relative

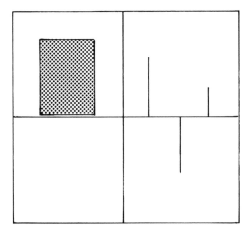

Fig. 1. Example input cue pattern on left-hand side and output values on right-hand side for studying intervening concept learning.

to a base level) are indicated by the positions of the vertical lines displayed on the right-hand side of Fig. 1.

On each trial, an organism is sampled, and subjects are first shown the input cue values for this organism (e.g., an organism with a thick wall, sparse cytoplasm, large size); then they draw lines indicating what they predict they will see as the output amounts of each compound, and finally they are given feedback showing the outcome values produced by this organism (e.g., lines indicating the correct amounts of stynophinapine, durialoktius, and vituloris). After training, subjects are given a transfer task in which they are asked to predict the outputs produced by various new combinations of cue values.

The results summarized later are based on work by Busemeyer et al. (in press). More specific details can be obtained from that paper. The results of the experiments all employed the basic procedure described previously but included some changes to increase the generality of findings. For instance, five input cues were used in some experiments instead of just three, four or three levels of cue values were used in some experiments instead of five, and a factory manufacturing system cover story was used in some experiments instead of a single-celled organism. The input cues were displayed as lines in a manner similar to the output amounts in some experiments. The number of training trials varied across experiments form 250 to 1000. Each experimental condition generally contained about 10 subjects, and subjects were paid depending on the accuracy of their predictions. The main conclusions remained the same across minor variations in procedure.

Three different types of manipulations and measures were used to obtain *converging* evidence for the spontaneous learning of intervening concepts in these multivariate environments (Garner, Hake, & Erikson, 1956). Each successive line of evidence provides a stronger and more direct test of the fundamental hypothesis.

A. PRINCIPLE COMPONENT ANALYSIS

Figure 2 illustrates two types of structures for generating multivariate causal systems. Figure 2A represents an input–output structure: Each input is linearly related to each output by a separate coefficient producing nine

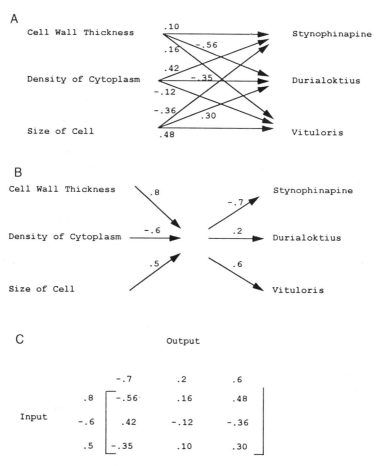

Fig. 2.   2.Input–output causal system (A); intervening factor causal system (B); and matrix used to determine input–output coefficients from intervening coefficients (C). For example, in (A), vituloris = (.16) thickness + (−.12) density + (.48) size.

linear relations and nine corresponding coefficients. A new input–output system of causal relations is generated by selecting a new set of nine coefficients for this same structure.

Figure 2B is called an intervening factor structure: The three inputs are linearly related to an intervening factor (using three coefficients), and this intervening factor is linearly related to the three outputs (using another three coefficients). A new intervening factor system of causal relations is generated by selecting a new set of six coefficients for this same structure.

In an attempt to equate overall learning difficulty across the two structures, the nine coefficients for each input–output system were computed from the six coefficients used to form the intervening factor system as follows (also see Figure 2C): each of the three input coefficients was multiplied times each of the three output coefficients to form nine cross-products, and then these nine cross-products were randomly rearranged to form the nine linear relations in the input–output system. In this way the same nine input–output coefficients are used in both structures. These nine can be factored into two sets of three for the intervening factor system, but the random rearrangement destroys the factorial structure for the input–output system.

One group of subjects received training with the input–output system, and a second group received training with the intervening factor system. Subjects were never informed about the possibility of an input–output or intervening factor structure. They observed only input–output values during training.

The training procedure for both groups was as follows. Within each experimental session, subjects were trained with a fixed multivariate system. At the beginning of each new session, a new set of coefficients was selected, creating a new system from the same structure, and subjects were informed about this change at the beginning of each session (specifically, they were told that they would have to learn all new relations between inputs and outputs at the beginning of each session). One group of subjects was trained with five different multivariate systems generated from an input–output structure (Figure 2A), and the other group was trained with five different multivariate systems generated from an intervening factor environment (Figure 2B). The only property that remained invariant across session was the type of structure (input–output or intervening factor). Intervening concept learning was measured as follows.

The subject's predictions for the three chemical compounds on the first 25 trials of each session provided the basis for the analysis. Predictions at the beginning of each session were used to capture transfer of learning about the causal structure before subjects had much opportunity to learn the specific coefficients for the current system.

The 25 (trial) × 3 (output prediction) data matrix produced by each subject and session was then analyzed by a principle component analysis. This was used to determine the percentage of variance in the three output predictions that could be reproduced by a single principle component.

If a subject generated output predictions based on a single intervening variable, then the percentage of variance reproduced by a single principle component would be near 100%. (It would not be exactly 100% because of trial-by-trial changes in the subject's estimates of the coefficients during learning.) If a subject generated output responses based on learning nine independent input–output relations, then the percentage of variance reproduced by the first principle component would be much lower (around 50%).

The results are plotted in Fig. 3. As training progressed across the five sessions, the two groups diverge. The intervening factor structure group approached the ideal of 100%, and the input-output group remained practically constant around 50%. These results are consistent with the hypothesis that subjects learned the intervening concept with the intervening factor environment, but not in the input–output environment.

B. EXTRAPOLATION TO A NEW OUTPUT

Suppose one individual has learned an intervening concept for an intervening factor system. This knowledge can be used to extrapolate to a new

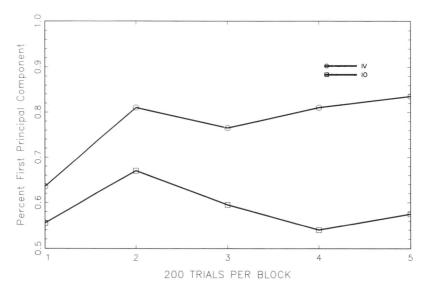

Fig. 3.   3.Percentage of variance reproduced by the first principle component (PC) as a function of training across different causal systems.

output because only one new coefficient (relating the intervening factor to the new fourth output) needs to be learned to make accurate predictions. The coefficients relating the three inputs to the intervening factor are the same and they do not need to be learned. The ability to extrapolate prior knowledge to the new output is one of the main advantages of forming an abstract intervening concept.

Suppose another individual has not learned an intervening concept. Then no knowledge is available for extrapolation to the new output. This subject would have to learn the linear relations between each of the three inputs and the new fourth output from scratch. Thus, it would take this individual longer to learn the new fourth output, compared to an individual who learned an intervening concept.

To test this hypothesis, we trained one group of subjects with an input–output system similar to that shown in Figure 2A, and another group of subjects with an intervening factor system similar to that shown in Figure 2B. Then, during a transfer phase, both groups were trained on the same new fourth output (using the same coefficients to relate the three inputs to the new output). Ignoring their previous training histories, both groups received identical input stimuli and output feedback to the new output during the transfer phase.

The basic measure of intervening concept learning was mean absolute error during the transfer test on the new fourth output. Table I shows the mean absolute errors for the two groups on the last session of training and on the transfer test. These errors are made with respect to a 200-point response scale.

The two groups did not differ significantly on the last session of training (the input–output group mean absolute error is slightly smaller). More important, the intervening factor training group produced a significantly smaller mean absolute error on the transfer test as compared to the input–output training group. According to our hypothesis, the intervening factor group learned the intervening concept, and these subjects were able to extrapolate this knowledge to facilitate learning the new output. The input–

TABLE I

MEAN ABSOLUTE ERROR

	Intervening group	Input–output group
Training	10.27	9.91
Transfer	15.9	20.28

output training group could not extrapolate to the new output, even though they received exactly the same learning problem in the transfer phase.

C. EXTRAPOLATION TO A NEW INPUT

The logic of the preceding test extends to inputs as well as outputs. Thus, one group was trained with an intervening factor system containing three inputs and four outputs. Another group was trained with an input-output system also containing three inputs and four outputs. Then, both groups were given a transfer test in which a new fourth input was added. The input stimuli were identical for both groups during transfer.

During the first part of the transfer test, all subjects were given additional training on only one of the four outputs. They were then tested on the remaining three output measures with no feedback. Note that an individual who has learned an intervening concept needs no further information. Once the input coefficient is learned from the feedback on the first output, this same coefficient can be applied to the remaining three outputs. However, an individual who has not learned an intervening concept would have no information about the coefficients relating the new input to the other three outputs.

One critical change in training procedure was made for this experiment. Subjects made predictions and observed feedback for only *one output at a time.* Furthermore, they never got feedback from different outputs on adjacent trials. For example, on one trial a subject saw an input pattern, made a prediction for one output (say Y1), and got feedback for Y1. Predictions and feedback for the same output, Y1, were used again on the next two trials. During the next three trials, a new output, say Y2, was used for predictions and feedback. During the next three trials, another new output was used, and this pattern was repeated throughout training. This procedure was designed to prevent subjects from learning the correlations among outputs across trials.

The basic measure of intervening concept learning was the mean absolute error on the last three outputs that did not receive any feedback during the transfer test. Table II shows the mean absolute errors for the two groups

TABLE II

MEAN ABSOLUTE ERROR DURING
TRANSFER FOR NEW INPUT CONDITION

	Output 1	Avg. for outputs 2,3,4
Intervening	10.9	28.2
Input–output	8.8	39.7

on (1) the first output that did receive feedback, and (2) the average of the three outputs that did not receive feedback. The two groups did not differ significantly on the trained output (output 1) during transfer. More important, the intervening factor training group produced significantly smaller mean absolute errors on the untrained outputs during transfer (outputs 2, 3, and 4), as compared to the input–output training group. Once again, according to our hypothesis, the intervening training group learned the intervening concept, and was able to extrapolate this knowledge to the new input. The input–output training group could not extrapolate to the new input, even though they received the same learning problem in the transfer phase.

D. CONCLUSIONS

All three lines of evidence converge toward the following conclusions. When subjects are confronted with a novel intervening factor causal system, they learn an intervening concept to simplify the relations between the inputs and outputs; but when subjects are confronted with a novel input–output causal system, they do not learn an intervening concept. Thus, intervening concepts are learned spontaneously in new multivariate environments, but only when the environment affords such learning.

Another important point is that subjects begin the learning process without any intervening concept, but later they form these concepts after experience with an intervening factor causal system. Subjects do not begin the learning process with an intervening concept, and either keep it if they encounter an intervening factor system, or drop it if it fails to fit an input–output system. Instead, they start out with an input–output type of conceptualization, and move toward an intervening concept with experience. A model of intervening concept learning that satisfies these properties is presented next. The key idea is to develop a learning system that trades off accuracy of prediction for parsimony of representation.

II. Intervening Concept Learning Model

The following is an extension of the connectionistic type of models discussed by Rumelhart and McClelland (1986). This model was chosen because it can be applied to all three paradigms (contingency learning, function learning, multivariate learning) in a straightforward manner with a common set of principles.

To facilitate the presentation, the model is developed in three stages. First, a simple model for contingency learning is presented; second, the model is extended to include function learning; and third, the complete model for multivariate learning is presented. Finally, simulation results that reproduce our basic findings concerning intervening concept learning are presented.

A. MODEL OF CONTINGENCY LEARNING

Consider the simple case in which there are only two binary cues and one binary outcome. For example, suppose that the organisms shown in Fig. 1 vary only in terms of two binary cues: X1 = cell wall thickness ($X1_1$ = thin, $X1_2$ = thick); and X2 = cytoplasm density ($X2_1$ = sparse, $X2_2$ = dense). Also suppose that there is only one binary valued outcome: stynophinapine (Y_1 = absent, Y_2 = present).

Table III illustrates the contingency between each binary cue and the binary outcome. The cell entries in the first two rows indicate a 2×2 contingency table relating the first cue, X1, and the outcome, Y. Similarly, the cell entries in the last two rows indicate a 2×2 contingency table relating the second cue, X2, and the outcome, Y. Of course it is possible to construct a table based on patterns of cue values in the rows, but the theory developed in the following text is based on use of separate cues.

Figure 4 outlines the network model for the case of two binary cues and one binary outcome. Actually, the model is not limited to two cues, and it is not limited to two levels of each cue. Two binary cues are used to make the example simple, while at the same time presenting all of the main ideas.

The network has four input nodes $\{A_{11,} A_{12}, A_{21}, A_{22}\}$ corresponding to the four rows of Table III. The input nodes are activated by the cue pattern $(X1_t, X2_t)$ presented on trial t. The activations of nodes A_{1i} for level i of cue X1 and A_{2j} for level j of cue X2 by the cue pattern $(X1_t, X2t)$ are given by Gaussian activation functions

$$a_{1i}(X1_t, X2_t) = \beta_1/\exp\{[(X1_t - X1_i)/\sigma_1]^2\} \qquad (1)$$
$$a_{2j}(X1_t, X2_t) = \beta_2/\exp\{[(X2_t - X2_j)/\sigma_2]^2\},$$

TABLE III

CONTINGENCY TABLE FOR TWO BINARY
CUES AND ONE BINARY OUTCOME

	Y_1	Y_2
$X1_1$	$f_{1,1,1}$	$f_{1,1,2}$
$X1_2$	$f_{1,2,1}$	$f_{1,2,2}$
$X2_1$	$f_{2,1,1}$	$f_{2,1,2}$
$X2_2$	$f_{2,2,1}$	$f_{2,2,2}$

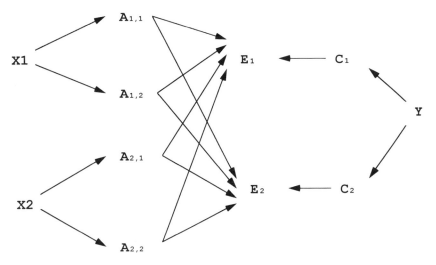

Fig. 4.   Connectionistic model for contingency learning. Input cue nodes (A) activated by cue values (X) appear on the far left, expectation nodes (E) appear in the middle, and consequence nodes (C) activated by outcome feedback (Y) appear on the far right.

where σ_j is a sensitivity parameter that determines the standard deviation of the activation distribution, and β_j is a normalizing constant used to guarantee that all the activations produced by a cue sum to unity.

The second layer in Fig 4 is a set of two expectation nodes, $\{E_1, E_2\}$, corresponding to the subject's anticipation of each outcome value given the cue pattern. The four input nodes are connected to the two expectation nodes by eight connections or associations. Each connection has a weight or association strength. The symbol $w_{ij,k}(t)$ represents the weight or strength of association between input node A_{ij} and expectation node E_k after experiencing a total of t pairs of observations.

The activation of expectation node E_k on trial t is symbolized e_k. Intuitively, this represents the subject's current estimate of the frequency that outcome value Y_k has occurred under the current cue pattern $(X1_t, X2_t)$. Activation is passed from antecedent nodes to expectation nodes by a linear transformation

$$e_k(X1_t, X2_t) = \Sigma_i \Sigma_j \, w_{ij,k}(t) \cdot a_{ij}(X1_t, X2_t). \qquad (2)$$

The subject's response on trial t, denoted $R(t)$, is a function of the activations of the expectation nodes. Specifically, the probability of choosing outcome Y_k when presented with cue pattern $(X1_t, X2_t)$ is given by the ratio rule:

$$\Pr[R(t) = Y_k \mid (X1_t, X2_t)] = e_k / (\Sigma_n e_n), \qquad (3)$$

where the summation in the denominator extends across all of the available outcome values of Y (two in this case of Table III). If subjects are asked to rate the strength of contingency between X1 and Y, holding X2 fixed at the first level, then they compute the contrast

$$CR(t) = \Pr[R(t) = Y_1 \mid (X1_1, X2_1)] - \Pr[R(t) = Y_1 \mid (X1_2, X2_1)],$$

where the probabilities in the above expression are defined by Equation (3). Essentially, the frequency estimates produced by the network are used to form the relevant contrasts for estimating contingency or influence (cf. Cheng & Novick, 1992). If only one cue is present (e.g., X1 only), the contrast reduces to a delta-p rule using estimated frequencies (see Busemeyer, 1991, p. 208, Equation 6).

Corresponding to the two outcome values, the network model employs two consequence nodes, $\{C_1, C_2\}$. The consequence nodes are activated by the outcome value, denoted Y_t, presented on trial t. The activation of node C_k on tiral t is also given by a Gaussian activation function

$$c_k(Y_t) = \beta_Y / \exp\{[Y_t - Y_k)/\sigma_Y]^2\}. \qquad (4)$$

Learning occurs by updating the connection weights as follows. The difference between the activations of the expectation and consequent nodes.

$$d_k(t) = [c_k(t) - e_k(t)],$$

represents the error signal for consequent node C_k. This error signal is used to update the connection weights according to the delta rule (Gluck & Bower, 1988; Sutton & Barton, 1981):

$$w_{ij,k}(t) = w_{ij,k}(t - 1) + \alpha \cdot a_{ij}(X1_t, X2_t) \cdot d_k(t). \qquad (5)$$

This error-driven learning rule is essentially the same as that used in previous associative models of contingency learning (Chapman & Robbins, 1991; Shanks & Dickinson, 1987; Van Hamme & Wasserman, 1994).

One final point needs to be addressed regarding the learning model Previously we argued for the incorporation of limited capacity attention into the learning algorithm shown in Equation (5) (Busemeyer, Myung, & McDaniel, 1993; see also Anderson, Reder, & Lebiere, in press). The basic idea is that the learner has a limited amount of attention to distribute to all of the associations. One way to formalize this idea is to assume that the learning rate, α is a decreasing function of the number of weights that are being updated to learn a causal relation.

B. MODEL OF FUNCTION LEARNING

Once again, consider the case in which there are two cues and one outcome variable or criterion, but suppose the cues and criterion vary continuously in values. For example, the organisms in Fig. 1 could have cell walls that vary across 20 equally spaced thickness levels, and the cytoplasm could vary across 20 equally spaced density levels. Subjects could be asked to predict the amount of stynophinapine on a 1 to 40 scale as a continuous function of thickness and density.

Table IV is an expanded version of Table III that shows part of the full set of 40 rows for the two sets of cue values, and 40 columns for the outcome values. Figure 5 outlines the network for this table. Now there are 20 input nodes for X1, 20 input nodes for X2, 40 expectation nodes, and 40 consequent nodes. The model is not limited to 2 cues, and it is not necessary to use 20 levels for each input cue, or 40 levels for the expectation nodes. These numbers were chosen to make the description concrete, while at the same time present all of the basic ideas.

A new layer is shown in Fig. 5, which is a layer of hidden nodes $\{H_1, H_2, \ldots H_{10}\}$ that intervene between the input nodes and expectation nodes. Each hidden node is a new subjective feature formed by a nonlinear transformation of the input activations. Without these nonlinear hidden nodes, the network would be limited to learning additive functional relations. The hidden nodes provide the network increased computational power to learn

TABLE IV

CONTINGENCY TABLE FOR MULTIPLE
CONTINUOUS CUES AND A SINGLE
CONTINUOUS CRITERION

	Y_1	$\ldots$	Y_{40}
$X1_1$	$f_{1,1,1}$		$f_{1,1,40}$
$X1_2$	$f_{1,2,1}$		$f_{1,2,40}$
$\vdots$			
$X1_{20}$	$f_{1,20,1}$		$f_{1,20,40}$
$X2_1$	$f_{2,1,1}$		$f_{1,20,40}$
$X2_2$	$f_{2,2,1}$		$f_{2,2,40}$
$\vdots$			
$X2_{20}$	$f_{2,20,1}$		$f_{2,20,40}$

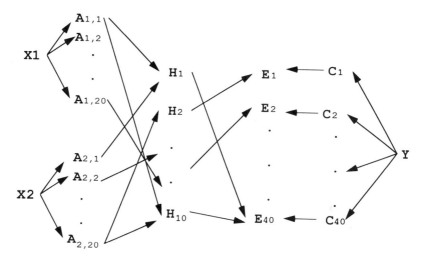

Fig. 5. Connectionistic model for function learning. Input cue nodes map activation into hidden nodes, which then map activation into expectation nodes, and finally the activation at the consequence nodes provides feedback for updating the connection weights.

nonadditive functional relations. This layer of hidden nodes can also be included in the contingency learning model to increase its computational power (e.g., to learn an XOR rule).

The 40 input nodes are activated according to the Gaussian activation function defined in Equation (1). The 40 input nodes are associated with each hidden node by a set of 40 connection weights. The weight, $w_{ij,k}(t)$, maps input node, A_{ij}, into hidden node, H_k, on trial t. The activation of hidden node, H_k, is denoted h_k. The hidden nodes are activated according to the following activation function (part b is omitted in linear networks):

$$s_k = \Sigma_i\Sigma_j \, w_{ij,k}(t) \cdot a_{ij}(X1_t, X2_t) \tag{6a}$$
$$h_k = 1/[1 + \exp(-\gamma \cdot s_k)]. \tag{6b}$$

The hidden nodes are connected to the expectation nodes by a set of connection weights. The weight connecting hidden node H_k to expectation node E_l is denoted $v_{kl}(t)$ on trial t. The activation of expectation node E_l is denoted e_l. Activation is passed from the hidden nodes to the expectation nodes by a linear transformation

$$e_l = \Sigma_k \, v_{kl}(t) \cdot h_k. \tag{7}$$

The probability that a subject will predict an amount of stynophinapine equal to Y_l, when presented with the cue pattern $(X1_t, X2_t)$, is given by

$$P_r[R(t) = Y_l|(X1_t, X2_t)] = r_l/\Sigma_n r_n,$$
$$r_l = \exp\{(Y_l - e_l)/\sigma_y]^2\} \tag{8}$$

where the summation in the denominator extends across all outcome values of Y (40 in the case of Table IV). The mean prediction, conditioned on the cue pattern $(X1_t, X2_t)$ equals

$$E[R(t)|(X1_t, X2_t)] = \Sigma_l (r_l \cdot Y_l) / (\Sigma_n r_n). \tag{9}$$

The 40 consequence nodes are activated by the outcome value, denoted Y_t, presented on trial t. The activation of the consequence nodes is determined by the Gaussian activation function shown in Equation (4).

Learning occurs by updating the connection weights on the basis of error signals as follows. The error signal for consequent node C_l is given by

$$d_l(t) = (c_l - r_l) \cdot (Y_l - e_l)$$

This error signal is used to update the connection weights from hidden nodes to expectation nodes according to the essentially the same delta rule as used before in Equation (5):

$$v_{kl}(t) = v_{kl}(t - 1) + \alpha \cdot h_k(t) \cdot d_l(t). \tag{10}$$

The error signal for hidden node H_k is obtained by the backpropogation rule

$$\delta_k(t) = \Sigma_l v_{kl} \cdot d_l(t). \tag{11}$$

This error signal is used to update the connection weights from the input nodes to hidden nodes according to the generalized delta learning rule:

$$w_{ij,k}(t) = w_{ij,k}(t - 1) + \alpha \cdot a_{ij} \cdot \delta_k(t) \cdot h_k \cdot (1 - h_k), \tag{12}$$

where $a_{ij} = a_{ij}(X1_t, X2_t)$ is the activation of input node A_{ij}.

This learning algorithm is based on the principle of learning a set of weights that will maximize predictive accuracy by minimizing the sum of squared prediction error. With a sufficient number of hidden nodes, this model can learn to closely approximate any continuous functional relation between cue patterns and outcome values (see Busemeyer et al., 1993, for more details).

C. MODEL OF INTERVENING CONCEPT LEARNING

Now consider the case where there are three continuous cues and three continuous criteria, such as that shown in Fig. 1. In terms of a contingency table, the multivariate task would entail three tables like Table IV, one table for each criterion variable. Figure 6 outlines the network for this multivariate learning task. Each cue is represented by a set of 20 input nodes, producing 60 input nodes for 3 cues. Each criterion is represented by 40 expectation nodes, producing a total of 120 expectation nodes for 3 criterion variables. Again, these numbers are used to make the example concrete, and the model is not restricted to these particular numbers.

The activation distribution across the 20 input nodes for each cue is determined by the Gaussian activation function described by Equation (1). The activation distribution across the 40 consequence nodes for each criterion is determined by the Gaussian activation function described by Equation (4).

The 3 activation distributions at the input nodes are transformed into activation at each of the 10 hidden nodes according to Equation (6). Finally, the activations of the 10 hidden nodes are transformed into activations of the expectation nodes for each criterion variable using Equation (7).

It is important to note in Fig. 6 that one set of connection weights is used to map the input nodes to the 10 hidden nodes. Furthermore, one common set of 10 hidden nodes intervenes between the input nodes and the expectation nodes. However, a new set of connection weights is employed to map the 10 hidden nodes to the 41 expectation nodes of each criterion variable.

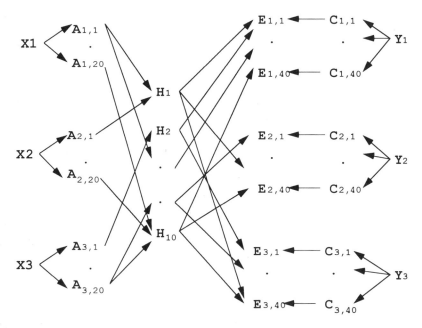

Fig. 6. Connectionistic model for intervening concept learning. Input nodes map into a common set of hidden nodes, and these are mapped into different sets of expectation nodes for each criterion variable.

The probability of choosing a value for a criterion variable is computed separately for each criterion variable using Equation (8). For example, the choice probabilities for Y2 are based on the 40 expectation nodes corresponding to Y2.

The learning algorithm described for the function learning model (Equations 10, 11, & 12) can be applied directly without any modification to this multivariate learning task. However, this learning model simply learns three separate criterion variables. This is equivalent to learning separate input–output relations (Figure 2A), and so at this point, the model has no mechanism for learning an intervening concept.

What is needed to learn an intervening concept is a mechanism for reducing the 10 hidden nodes down to a single hidden node. This can be achieved by changing the basic principles of the learning algorithm. Instead of using a single principle that only optimizes accuracy, we propose a dual principle that trades off accuracy for parsimony. In other words, the objective of the learning algorithm is to minimize both mean squared error and complexity.

To achieve this dual objective, we propose the following two measures of parsimony: the parsimony of the input-hidden layer, denoted S_1, is the negative of the sum of all the squared weights from the input nodes to the hidden nodes, excluding the weights to the first hidden node. The parsimony of the hidden-expectation layer, denoted S_2, is the negative of the sum of all the squared weights from the hidden nodes to the expectation nodes, excluding the weights from the first hidden node. The learning algorithm is modified by adding the negative gradient of S_1 to Equation (12), and adding the negative gradient of S_2 to Equation (10).

This modification produces the following learning algorithm for trading off accuracy and parsimony:
If k = 1 then use Equation (10), otherwise

$$v_{kl}(t) = v_{kl}(t-1) + \alpha_1 \cdot h_k(t) \cdot d_l(t) - \alpha_2 \cdot v_{kl}(t-1). \tag{13}$$

If k = 1 then use Equation (12), otherwise

$$w_{ij,k}(t) = w_{ij,k}(t-1) + \alpha_1 \cdot a_{ij} \cdot \delta_k(t) \cdot h_k \cdot (1 - h_k) - \alpha_2 \cdot w_{ij,k}. \tag{14}$$

The last term in each modified learning equation is the negative gradient of the parsimony indices. This modified learning algorithm was used in the simulations of the experimental results on intervening concepts described next.

III. Theoretical Results

The purpose of this section is to link the theoretical results derived from the model to the empirical evidence for intervening concept learning presented earlier in Section I. Simulations were calculated from the model when it was trained under an intervening factor causal system versus an input–output causal system. The model was trained for a total of 20 trial blocks with 64 trials per block. The learning rate parameter for accuracy (α_1) was set to the same value for both training conditions, and it was selected to approximate the same number of learning trials required by our subjects. The learning rate parameter for parsimony (α_2) also was set to the same value for both training conditions (see Appendix for more details about the simulation).

A. PRINCIPLE COMPONENT ANALYSIS

The first link is between the parsimony index and the principle component index. Recall that the percentage of variance in a subject's output predictions reproduced by the first principle component was used as an index of intervening concept learning. If a subject generates output predictions based on a single intervening variable, then the percentage of variance would be near 100%. In the Appendix, we prove the following proposition (for linear networks):

Proposition 1: If the parsimony index is maximized, then 100% of the variance in the model's expected output predictions can be reproduced by the first principle component.

Next we need to establish a link between the parsimony index and the type of causal structure presented during training. Recall that the percentage of variance reproduced by the first principle component was greater under the intervening factor structure as compared to the input–output structure. In the Appendix we prove the following proposition:

Proposition 2: If the model is trained under an intervening factor causal system, then both objectives, accuracy and parsimony, can be simultaneously maximized at asymptote. If the model is trained under an input–output environment, then both objectives cannot be simultaneously maximized at asymptote and one has to be sacrificed for the other.

First consider the simulation results produced when the learning rate for parsimony was set to zero (Figs. 7 and 8). In this case, only accuracy (negative of the mean absolute prediction errors) is being maximized.

Figure 7 shows the model results for accuracy plotted as a function of trial block with one curve representing the intervening factor training condition and the other curve representing the input–output training condi-

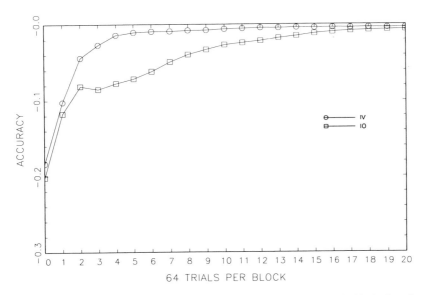

Fig. 7. Accuracy index as a function of training produced by the model with the learning rate for parsimony turned off.

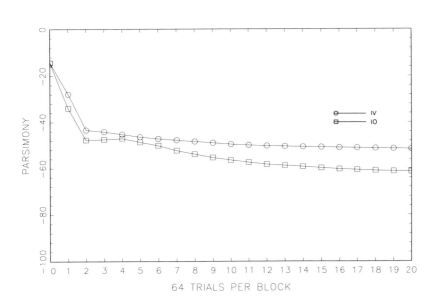

Fig. 8. Parsimony index as a function training produced by the model with the learning rate for parsimony turned off.

tion. The model produces a typical learning curve. Figure 8 shows the parsimony index plotted as a function of trial block separately for the intervening and input–output conditions. Note that when the parsimony learning rate is set to zero, the parsimony index naturally decreases with training for both conditions but more slowly for the intervening factor condition.

The next two figures show the effect of turning on the parsimony learning rate. Figure 9 shows the effect on the accuracy index, and one can see that turning on parsimony caused a small reduction in accuracy for the input–output condition. Little or no reduction in accuracy occurred for the intervening condition. Figure 10 shows the effect on the parsimony index, and one can see that turning on the parsimony learning rate produced an increase in the parsimony index, but only for the intervening factor condition. Parsimony did not increase for the input–output condition. These results are basically in accord with the principle component results presented in Fig. 3.

B. Extrapolation

Subjects who were trained with an intervening factor causal system were better able to extrapolate their knowledge to new input or output measures as compared to subjects trained with an input–output system. Table V

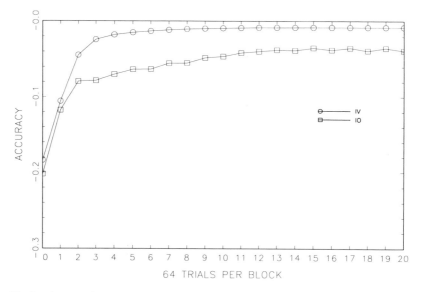

Fig. 9. Accuracy index as a function of training produced by the model with the learning rate for parsimony turned on.

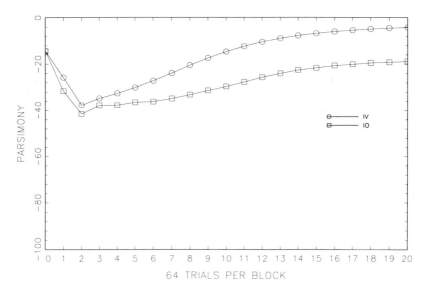

Fig. 10. Parsimony index as a function of training produced by the model with the learning rate for parsimony turned on.

shows the simulation results for extrapolation to a new output after being trained on either an intervening factor an an input–output causal system. The cell entries are the mean absolute errors accumulated during training on a new fourth output, following training on three inputs and three outputs.

The first column shows the results for the case when the parsimony learning rate was set to zero ($\alpha_2 = 0$), and in this case, there is little difference between the two learning conditions. The last two columns show the effects of increasing the parsimony learning rate. The intervening factor condition produces a mean absolute error that is half as large as that produced by the input–output condition. Again, these results are in basic accord with the empirical evidence.

TABLE V

SIMULATION RESULTS FOR EXTRAPOLATION: MEAN
ABSOLUTE ERROR TO LEARN NEW FOURTH OUTPUT

	$\alpha_2 = 0$	$\alpha_2 = .002$	$\alpha_2 = .005$
Intervening system	.10	.08	.07
Input–output system	.13	.12	.12

C. Prior Knowledge

So far, the model has been used to interpret past findings from our laboratory. In order to test predictions of the model in a new experiment (described later), we ran simulations to determine what the model predicted
regarding the effects of prior knowledge. In general, prior knowledge is
represented by the initial connection weights of the network. More specifically, prior knowledge about an intervening concept is produced in the
network by initially training the network on an intervening factor system
with one set of causal coefficients. The parsimony learning rate is fixed to
a sufficiently high value to generate a set of connection weights that maxi-
mizes the parsimony index. Then, this initial set of connection weights is
used in the model at the beginning of training with a new causal system
(defined by a new set of causal coefficients).

Two independent variables were factorially manipulated in the simulation. One was the prior weights of the network generated before training.
One set of initial weights was selected to represent prior knowledge of an
intervening concept (initial training with parsimony under an intervening
factor system), and another set of prior weights was selected to represent
prior knowledge of an input–output structure (initial training without parsimony under an input–output system). The second factor was the type of
subsequent training: One was a new intervening factor causal structure,
and the other was a new input–output causal structure. The connection
weights produced by the initial training were used to begin the learning of
the new causal systems during the subsequent training.

One important difference between the simulations for prior knowledge
and the previous simulations is the nature of the coefficients used to construct the causal systems. Notice that both positive and negative coefficients
are employed in the causal systems shown in Fig. 2. The negative coefficients
are important for maintaining a low percentage of variance for the first
principle component with the input–output system (around 50%). However,
the design of the next experiment with prior knowledge made it necessary
to restrict the coefficients to positive values. In this case, the percentage
of variance for the first principle component with the input–output system
is much higher (around 70%). The principle component accounts for about
100% of the variance in the intervening factor condition, whether or not
negative coefficients are used. The point is that it is more difficult to discriminate an intervening factor structure from an input–output structure when
only positive coefficients are employed.

First, consider the predictions computed for the set of prior weights
representing an intervening concept. The model essentially predicted that
the parsimony index started and remained at maximum throughout training,
whether or not the training condition was under an intervening or an

input–output structure. In other words, the model was insensitive to the training environment, at least when strictly positive coefficients are used to construct the causal systems (making it difficult to discriminate the presence or absence of an intervening factor).

Next, consider the predictions computed for the set of prior weights representing an input–output conceptualization. The predictions for the parsimony index are shown in Fig. 11. Note that the parsimony indices for the two training conditions diverge. Parsimony increases with training under the intervening factor training condition, but the input–output condition produces no increase in parsimony.

In sum, the model predicts an interaction effect between prior knowledge and training. A large training effect is predicted when prior knowledge is biased toward an input–output concept, but training corresponds to an intervening factor structure. No training effect is predicted when prior knowledge is biased toward an intervening concept, but training corresponds to an input–output causal structure. These predictions were tested in the following experiment.

IV. Prior Knowledge: New Experimental Work

Prior knowledge refers to either extensive previous experience with the inputs and outputs of some causal system or direct instruction about the

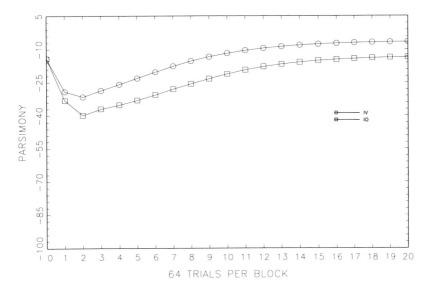

Fig. 11. Parsimony index as a function of training produced by the model under the no-prior-knowledge condition.

causal relations. In the present experiment, subjects in the prior-knowledge condition were informed that the three inputs represent the father's IQ, the mother's IQ, and environmental enrichment; and the outputs represent the verbal SAT, math SAT, and GPA. This cover story was chosen because college students (especially psychology majors, who comprise the majority of our subjects) have extensive knowledge about these causal relations, both through instruction (textbook presentations of general theories of intelligence) and personal experience. Therefore, it is assumed that the subjects had some concept of general intelligence that mediates between the inputs and outputs. Subjects in a no-prior knowledge condition were not provided with any such cover story during the course of the experiment. From almost any point of view, one might expect that such prior knowledge would facilitate acquisition of the intervening concept.

Using the model described earlier, the issue can be more precisely delineated. Prior knowledge is incorporated into the model by the initial connection weights prior to training (as described previously). According to the model, the IQ cover story should elicit prior knowledge of an intervening concept (general intelligence). Furthermore, the group given the cover story is predicted to show no effect of training if they later encounter an input–output environment (measured by the principle component analysis). Also according to the model, the group not provided with this cover story should start with an input–output conceptualization. However, if this group later encounters an intervening factor structure, they they are predicted to produce a large training effect (measured by the principle component analysis).

Having demonstrated that humans can spontaneously abstract intervening concepts, our most recent experimental efforts have focused on a better understanding of the acquisition of the component information that reflects an intervening concept. Our general analysis is that the learner must acquire two fundamental kinds of information. He or she must acquire knowledge about the structural features of the complex system. That is, the learner has to learn about the associative structure (which includes the intervening construct) that relates the inputs and outputs. In our paradigm this is reflected by the amount of variance in the predictions accounted for by the first principle component. Second, the learner needs to acquire information about the values of the weights and how these values are combined in producing particular output magnitudes. We gauge learning of this information by measure of prediction accuracy.

Thus far, we have not applied the model to predict how prior knowledge will affect learning of the weight values (as assessed by prediction accuracy). Our concern is that the instantiation of prior knowledge in the model may not be rich enough to provide a representative account of prior-knowledge effects on learning weight values. Some general considerations suggest that several experimental outcomes could be expected. On one hand, the prior knowledge is probably too general and unrelated to the experimental systems to allow closely accurate selection of the weight values. Accordingly, prior knowledge may not benefit acquisition of the weight values of any particular system.

On the other hand, there are a number of reasons why prior knowledge might facilitate learning the weight values, learning that would be expected regardless of the kind of system structure being encountered. Appropriate prior knowledge would probably include information about the direction of the relations between inputs and intervening factor and between intervening factor and outputs (or directly between inputs and outputs). Such information would presumably restrict the ranges of the values sampled, thereby enhancing learning. Prior knowledge could as well guide the learner toward appropriate combination of the input weights (in this case a weighted additive function). (Our previous work has suggested that without prior knowledge at least some learners assume that a single input is linked to a single output.) If prior knowledge exerted such effects, then its effects on weight learning would hold even after the learner has had direct experience with a number of systems. Though such experience (as discussed earlier in the chapter) can produce appropriate generalization of the structure of the target systems, it does not provide appropriate information on the weight values (in experiments where the values for each system are randomly determined).

Prior knowledge could also facilitate learning the weight values by reducing the cognitive demands on the learner and focusing his or her resources. The idea here is that prior knowledge reduces the learner's task to learning the weight values, allowing more effective acquisition of those values. If this were an accurate characterization, then any facilitation of prior knowledge should be primarily obtained on the initial systems (because by later systems, all subjects will be tuned to the structure of the input–output relations), and on the intervening-factor systems (because the prior knowledge would actually mislead subjects about the structure of the input–output systems).

With this analysis we can begin to explore in a more refined way how various other factors will influence intervening concept learning. Another factor that is expected to play a major role in the acquisition of an intervening concept is the sequence in which the environmental pairings (of inputs and outputs) are experienced by the learner. For example, a systematic sequence may facilitate hypothesis testing as compared to a random sequence. Thus, the sequence of training trials is another major new factor that we examined in this experiment. Some subjects received the trials in a systematic order that held the values of two inputs constant, while varying the values of the third input. Other subjects received the training trials in a randomly determined order. Unlike prior knowledge, the predicted effects of training sequence are more disputable. From the perspective of an adaptive-network model (connectionistic), it would seem that training sequence should have little impact, or perhaps random training would allow faster convergence on the actual weight matrix. To verify this impression, we performed simulations using parameters corresponding to a preliminary experiment similar to the one reported later that focused only on training sequence. The simulations verified that prediction accuracy was higher for random training than for systematic training. Thus, on this class of learning model, systematic training would not be expected to facilitate learning relative to random training.

Alternatively, on the notion that systematic training would serve as a memory aid and also perhaps enable more analytic learning strategies, we would expect systematic sequences of training trials to promote learning over those with random sequences. Bower (1994) has recently reported such a finding with another kind of complex concept learning task, and our preliminary experiment on this issue with intervening concepts demonstrated a similar effect. Within our analysis, the benefit of systematic training would be expected for acquisition of the weight values but not necessarily for acquisition of the system structure.

A. METHOD

To test these ideas, we factorially manipulated prior knowledge, system structure (intervening or input–output system), and presentation order for the trials. Half of the subjects (48 Purdue University undergraduate and graduate students participated) were given a cover story that described what the inputs and outputs represented (prior-knowledge group). Specifically, they were informed that the first input represented father's IQ, the second input represented mother's IQ, and the third input represented environmental enrichment. They were also told that the first output represented SAT Verbal, the second output represented SAT Math, and the third output represented GPA (Grade Point Average) of the first year of college. In contrast, the other half was not given a cover story that would activate detailed prior knowledge about inputs and outputs (no-prior-knowledge group). This group was told that there was a factory system where three input materials produced three output materials; the first input represented the first material, the second input represented the second material, and the third represented the third material. For the outputs, the first output represented the first product, the second output represented the second product, and the third output represented the third product.

The second factor was the structure of input–output systems. Half of the subjects (the intervening variable group) received multiple input–output systems, where the inputs were associated with the outputs via a "hidden" intervening factor. The other half (the input–output group) received multiple input–output systems where every input was connected with every output without an intervening variable.

The third factor was the presentation order. Half of the subjects were given a systematic sequence of training trials. The systematic presentation orders during training phase were constructed as follows. The values for one input would vary across two trials, while the values for the other two inputs would remain fixed. The other half of the subjects received a random training sequence. For the random presentation order, the same sets of input–output pairs as the systematic presentation order were used, but they were presented randomly.

The 48 training trials for each intervening variable system were constructed as follows. For the training stimuli, four equally spaced input values were used (0–3). Each of three input weights linking an input to the intervening factor was randomly sampled from uniform [0, 1] distribution. The same set of three input weights was used for all 48 trials of a given system, and a different set of three input weights was sampled for each new system. Similarly, the same set of three output weights connecting the intervening variable to the three outputs was used for all 48 trials of a given system, and a different set of three output weights was sampled for each new system. The value of the intervening variable was computed by summing the three products formed by multiplying each input value by the corresponding input weight. Each of the three output values was generated by multiplying the value of the intervening variable by one of the three output weights.

The 48 training trials for each input–output system were constructed from the weights and input values of a corresponding intervening-variable system as follows. Using the weights from one of the intervening systems, each of the 3 input weights was multiplied by each of the 3 output weights to form $3 \times 3 = 9$ input–output weights. Then each of these 9 input–output weights was randomly assigned to one of the 9 input–output relations to form an input–output system. For each trial, the three input values sampled for the intervening variable system were used as the input values for the corresponding input–output system. Finally, each of the three outputs for the input–output system was calculated by summing the three products formed by multiplying each input value by the corresponding input–output weight for a particular output.

Following each of three training systems, a transfer task consisting of 12 trials was given. During transfer, new sets of inputs that were not given during the training phase were given. For half of new input sets, each input had values within the learned input values (0–3) (e.g., 1 1 2), whereas the other half of new input sets included the new input value (4) for one or more inputs (e.g., 0 4 3). The presentation order for the systematic condition was constructed the same as it was during the training phase. Also, in transfer there was no feedback regarding the accuracy of the subject's predictions.

At the beginning of the experiment, the no-prior-knowledge subjects were asked to imagine that they were learning how to operate the controls of an industrial factory system in which there were three raw materials (three inputs) that yielded three different products (three outputs). The prior-knowledge subjects were told that they were learning how to predict each student's SAT Verbal, SAT Math, and GPA scores from IQ scores of one's father and mother and the degree of environmental enrichment. Subjects were told that on each trial the amounts of the three different inputs would be displayed as vertical bars on a video screen. They were informed that each vertical bar would represent one input, and that the height of each bar would represent the amount of the input. Subjects were instructed that they would have to try to predict the amount of the three outputs on the basis of the displayed inputs.

B. Results

We consider first the training data, followed by the transfer data. As in our previous experiments, the first principle component was computed using each subject's predicted output responses during the first 24 trials of training. The percentage of variance in the subject's output responses reproduced by the first principle component is used to indicate the extent of intervening concept learning. Table VI shows the percentage of variance reproduced by the first principle component, averaged across subjects, for each new causal system (rows), broken down by prior-knowledge group and causal structure training condition (columns).

Contrary to the predictions of our model, prior knowledge alone was not sufficient to completely abstract an intervening factor structure. Experience with an intervening factor environment was also needed to produce a high percentage of variance reproduced by the first principle component. This is indicated in two different ways in Table VI. First, there was an increase in the percentages across systems for the prior-knowledge group trained with an intervening factor system (from .73 to .91). Second, there is a difference between the intervening training condition as compared to input–output training condition for the prior-knowledge group at the end of training (.91 vs .83).

TABLE VI

PERCENTAGE VARIANCE ACCOUNTED
REPRODUCED BY THE FIRST PRINCIPAL
COMPONENT DURING TRAINING

System	Training condition	
	Intervening	Input–output
Prior knowledge		
1	.73	.77
2	.79	.75
3	.91	.83
No prior knowledge		
1	.56	.56
2	.70	.64
3	.90	.74

There was a significant interaction between prior knowledge and system, $F(2, 80) = 6.76$, $p < .002$, which was in the general direction predicted by the model. The model predicted a bigger training effect for the no-prior-knowledge cover story subjects trained under an intervening factor condition as compared to the prior-knowledge cover story subjects trained under an input–output structure condition, which is observed in Table VI. However, the pattern of this interaction was not entirely consistent with that predicted by the model. Based on the model, there should be no effect of training system for the prior-knowledge condition, but there should be an effect of training system for the no-prior-knowledge condition. Examination of Table VI shows that across systems both groups increased their use of an intervening factor, but the increase was less pronounced for the prior-knowledge group.

As anticipated, the trial sequence had no effect (either main effect or interactions) on the amount of variance accounted for by the first principle component. This result implies reasonably enough that abstraction of the system structure is not influenced robustly by the sequence in which input–output pairings are experienced. The kind of system structure that learners abstract is influenced, however, by prior knowledge. As shown in Table VI (which gives the percentage of variance in the predictions collapsed over the sequence factor), regardless of the actual structure of the target system, prior knowledge that suggests the existence of an intervening factor causes learners to more readily adopt such a structure ($F[1, 40] = 17.65$, $p < .0001$, for the main effect of prior knowledge).

Turning to learning of the weight values, the accuracy scores (in terms of the mean squared deviation of the subjects' predicted values from the target values) indicated that training sequence now did make an impact, though not an overly robust one. In general, systematic sequences facilitated more accurate performance early in training, but as training proceeded the particular sequence appeared to exert little effect. In particular, for the first half of the training trials (of each system), sequential training produced more accurate predictions than did random training (427 vs 510, respectively), but this advantage was eliminated (404 vs 379) for the second half of the training trials; $F(1, 40) = 9.16$, $p < .004$. The same tendency held for early versus later systems. As can be seen in Table VII, for the first training system, systematic training was generally better than random training, but by the third system this advantage was not evident.

Perhaps more interesting was the finding that prior knowledge significantly aided learning of the weight values ($M = 337$ for prior knowledge and 523 for no prior knowledge; $F[1, 40] = 9.27$, $p < .004$). Table VII shows that this advantage held even after direct experience with several systems (e.g., note the results for System 3) and that the advantage was obtained regardless of whether the system had an intervening-factor structure or an input–output structure. These findings are consistent with the postulated mechanisms outlined earlier: prior knowledge could help constrain the range of weights considered and might also alert the learner to how the weights are combined in influencing the outputs.

The transfer task showed somewhat different patterns. Recall that transfer was tested after training on each system by requiring subjects to predict outputs from a new constellation of inputs that sometimes included in-

TABLE VII

SUBJECTS' PREDICTION ACCURACY (MEAN SQUARED
ERROR) DURING TRAINING

System	Intervening		Input–output	
	Systematic	Random	Systematic	Random
Prior knowledge				
1	352.11	472.87	555.20	295.02
2	298.31	380.76	411.75	277.14
3	205.25	211.10	343.27	239.38
No prior knowledge				
1	523.77	721.89	531.98	655.13
2	460.59	453.18	552.26	626.19
3	334.45	299.75	420.70	700.32

put values not seen in training. The principle component analysis showed that the influence of prior knowledge extended from training to transfer. Prior-knowledge subjects showed signficantly more reliance on a single factor (intervening factor) in predicting output values than did no-prior-knowledge subjects (.84 vs .75, $F[1, 40] = 6.88$, $p < .01$). As expected, the same held true for subjects with direct experience on intervening factor systems relative to subjects given input–output systems (.87 vs .73; $F[1, 40] = 17.02$, $p < .0002$).

More interesting were the results of prediction accuracy. The greater accuracy produced by prior knowledge persisted into the transfer trials (538 vs 828 for no-prior-knowledge group; $F[1, 40] = 7.59$, $p < .01$). The intriguing finding was that the presentation sequence interacted with the system structure ($F[1, 40] = 8.70$, $p < .01$), such that a systematic order tended to produce more accurate responding than a random order (414 vs 837) for the intervening systems but not for the input–output systems (839 vs 642). This pattern held for all three systems. This result is reinforced by an analysis of the correlations between predicted outputs and correct outputs. This measure gives an indication of the degree to which the predictions accurately capture the topography of the set of outputs. Again, presentation sequence interacted with system structure ($F[1, 40] = 15.55$, $p < .0003$), with the systematic order supporting more accurate responding than the random order (.70 vs .34, respectively) for the intervening systems but not for the input–output systems (.62 vs .69).

The locus of these order effects is uncertain. It could be that the order in which the transfer trials are presented somehow influences how well subjects can retrieve appropriate information, from the acquisition phase, with the retrieval process being more variable for intervening systems. The more exciting interpretation is that the effect reflects influences of training order on what is learned. For instance, one possibility is that with an intervening structure there are fewer weights to learn, and systematic training allows a more analytic (e.g., hypothesis testing) learning process for the weights. Such a learning process might be more difficult to implement with random training trials or when there are many input–output weights to acquire. Further, an analytic learning process might better support transfer outside the range of training (transfer that was reflected in some of the present trials) than a more associative learning process (cf. DeLosh, Busemeyer, & McDaniel, in press). These ideas are clearly quite speculative, and require more work to disentangle.

C. SUMMARY

The most important finding was that the use of a highly familiar cover story suggesting an intervening concept was not sufficient to induce the use of an

intervening concept. Training with an intervening factor causal environment
was still necessary to develop the use of an intervening concept. According
to the predictions of the model that we developed, the extensive past
experience with the causal relations involved in the cover story should
have been sufficient to produce an intervening concept at the beginning of
training, and the use of this intervening concept should have persisted
throughout training regardless of the type of training environment.

There are at least three reasons why the prediction of the model failed.
First, perhaps our subjects were not sufficiently experienced with the cover
story to have previously formed an intervening concept for these causal
relations. This seems unlikely given the widespread use of the concept of
general intelligence in everyday conversations. Another possibility is that
subjects have formed an intervening concept of general intelligence, but
some training was needed to learn how to apply this previously formed
concept to the new laboratory environment. The third possibility is that
prior knowledge is not represented by the initial connection weights. Perhaps prior knowledge influences the learning process (e.g., eliciting hypothesis testing behavior) rather than influencing the initial connection weights.
Some evidence for this last explanation was obtained by the finding that
systematic input sequences (as opposed to random input sequence) facilitated prediction accuracy during transfer for subjects who received training
with an intervening factor environment.

V. Conclusions

This chapter demonstrated the links between our program of research on
intervening concept learning with other lines of research on causal learning.
More importantly, we showed how the model that we developed for intervening causal learning is a direct extension of previous models of category
learning, contingency learning, and function learning. The learning of intervening concepts is a fairly complex process, but many of the basic assumptions are the same as those used in simpler models.

One new and important assumption that we found necessary for explaining intervening concept learning was the idea of a dual objective for learning
(an idea also suggested by Rumelhart, 1988). Learners generally attempt
to trade off accuracy for simplicity or parsimony.

The model of intervening concept learning that we developed is far from
complete. The predictions of the model concerning the effects of prior
knowledge were not well supported. For instance, subjects given prior
knowledge about an intervening variable were nevertheless highly sensitive
to the experienced causal relations in the environment. The model predicted

that prior knowledge would cause the learner to persist in maintaining an inappropriate representation of the environment for two reasons. One is the difficulty discriminating the presence or absence of an intervening factor in an environment that contains all positive relations. Second, the parsimony component of the learning rule persists in keeping the weights tied to the initial intervening concept representation.

ACKNOWLEDGMENTS

This work was funded by NIMH Grant MH47126. Correspondence should be sent to Jerome R. Busemeyer, Department of Psychology, Purdue University, W. Lafayette, Indiana, 47907-1364, or to jbuse@psych.purdue.edu.

Appendix

Simulation:
Figures 7–10 were generated by training the model with either the intervening causal system or the input–output causal system shown in Fig. 2 (using the coefficients shown in the figure). Figure 11 was generated using an input–output structure with only positive coefficients. The inputs were selected from a $5 \times 5 \times 5$ factorial design with five equally spaced levels (.2, .4, .6, .8, 1.0).

The number of nodes used in the network is the same as that shown in Fig. 6. The predictions were generated from the model using Equations (1), (2), (3), (4), (6), (7), (9), (11), (13), and (14). The parameters were set as follows: $\beta_j = 1$, $\sigma_j = .05$, $\alpha_1 = .70$, $\alpha_2 = .004$, (Linear network was used). All of the simulations, except for one case described later, were conducted using random initial weights.

The one exception is the simulation for the prior knowledge of an intervening concept. In this case, the initial weights were selected by training the network to produce outputs according to an intervening factor system with positive weights using a single hidden node. Following this initial training, the network was retrained on a new causal system, either a new input–output system or another new intervening factor causal system with different coefficients.

Proof of Proposition 1 (for linear networks):
Define **W** as a $p \times m$ weight matrix with elements $w_{ij,k}$ connecting input node A_{ij} to hidden node H_k. Define **A** as a $m \times 1$ vector containing the activations, a_{ij}, of all the input nodes as elements. The activation of the hidden nodes (for linear networks) is then described by

$$\mathbf{H} = \mathbf{W} \cdot \mathbf{A}.$$

Define $\mathbf{V}$ as an $n \times p$ weight matrix with elements v_{kl} connecting the hidden nodes to the expectation nodes. Then the activation of the expectation nodes is described by

$$\mathbf{E} = \mathbf{V} \cdot \mathbf{H} = \mathbf{V} \cdot \mathbf{W} \cdot \mathbf{A}.$$

Define $\mathbf{C}$ as a $q \times n$ matrix containing all of the possible outcome values for the q criterion variables. The model response is described by

$$\mathbf{R} = \mathbf{CE} = \mathbf{CVH} = \mathbf{CVWA}.$$

The variance-covariance matrix of the model responses is described by (where $\mathbf{X}'$ denotes transpose of $\mathbf{X}$)

$$\mathbf{E[RR']} = \mathbf{E[CVWAA'\ W'\ V'\ C']} = \mathbf{CVWE[AA']W'\ V'\ C'},$$

with

$$\mathbf{E[AA']} = \sigma^2\mathbf{I}$$
$$\mathbf{E[RR']} = \sigma^2\mathbf{C(VW)(VW)'C'}.$$

If the parsimony index is maximized, the $\mathbf{V}$ has one column and $\mathbf{W}$ has one row, so that $\mathbf{VW}$ has rank of one. This implies that there is only one nonzero eigenvalue associated with $\mathbf{E[RR']}$, and finally, this implies that a single principle component can reproduce all of the variance of $\mathbf{R}$.

Proof of Proposition 2:

At asymptote, Equation (13) yields

$$v_{kl}(t) - v_{kl}(t - 1) = \alpha_1 \cdot h_k(t) \cdot d_l(t) - \alpha_2 \cdot v_{kl}(t - 1) = 0,$$

which implies

$$\alpha_1 \cdot h_k(t) \cdot d_l(t) = \alpha_2 \cdot v_{kl}(t - 1).$$

If the accuracy index is maximized, then the error signal is driven to zero so that $d_l(t) = 0$, and this implies $v_{kl} = 0$ for all $k > 1$. A similar argument holds for Equation (14) so that $w_{ij,k} = 0$ for all $k > 1$. This implies that the output responses produced by the model can be reproduced by a single principle component. In addition, the fact that the error signal is zero implies that the output responses produced by the model can perfectly reproduce the criterion values. Thus, the criterion values must also be reproduced by a single principle component.

REFERENCES

Anderson, J. R., Reder, L. M., & Lebiere, C. (in press). Working memory: Activation limitations on retrieval. *Cognitive Psychology.*

Bower, G. H. (1994, August). *Category discovery in unsupervised environments.* Paper presented at the Practical Aspects of Memory Conference, College Park, MD.

Bunge, M. (1959). *Causality* Cambridge, MA: Harvard University Press.

Busemeyer, J. R. (1991). Intuitive statistical estimation. In N. H. Anderson (Ed.), *Contributions to information integration theory: Vol. 1. Cognition* (Chap. 5, pp. 186–215). Erlbaum.

Busemeyer, J. R., Myung, I. J., & McDaniel, M. A. (1993). Cue competition effects: Theoretical implications for adaptive network models. *Psychological Science, 4,* 196–202.

Busemeyer, J. R., McDaniel, M. A., & Byun, E. (in press). Multiple input-output causal environments. *Cognitive Psychology.*

Carroll, J. D. (1963). *Function learning: The learning of continuous functional maps relating stimulus and response continuum* (ETS RB 63-6). Princeton, NJ: Educational Testing Service.

Chapman, G. B., & Robbins, S. J. (1991). Cue interaction in human contingency judgment. *Memory & Cognition, 18,* 537–545.

Cheng, P. W., & Novick, L. R. (1992). Covariation in natural causal induction. *Psychological Review, 99,* 365–382.

Cook, T. D., & Campbell, D. T. (1979). *Quasi-experimentation.* Dallas, TX: Houghton Mifflin.

DeLosh, E. L., Busemeyer, J. R., & McDaniel, M. A. (in press). Extrapolation: The sine qua non of abstraction. *Journal of Experimental Psychology: Learning, Memory, and Cognition.*

Einhorn, H. J., & Horgarth, R. M. (1986). Judging probable cause. *Psychological Bulletin, 99,* 3–19.

Garner, W. R., Hake, H. W., & Erikson, C. W. (1956). Operationism and the concept of perception. *Psychological Review, 63,* 149–159.

Gluck, M. A., & Bower, G. H. (1988). From conditioning to category learning: An adaptive network model. *Journal of Experimental Psychology: General, 117,* 227–247.

Jenkins, H., & and Ward, W. (1965). Judgment of contingency between responses and outcomes. Psychological Monographs, 7, 1–17.

Miller, N. E. (1959). Liberalization of basic S-R concepts: Extensions to conflict behavior, motivation, and social learning. In S. Koch (Ed.), *Psychology: A study of science* (Vol. 2, pp. 196–292). New York: McGraw-Hill.

Rumelhart, D. E. (1988). *Brain style computation.* Paper presented at the 21st annual meeting of the Society for Mathematical Psychology, Northwestern University, Evanston, IL.

Rumelhart, D. E., & McClelland, J. L. (1986). *Parallel distributed processing: Explorations in the micro structure of Cognition: Vol. 1. Foundations.* Cambridge, MA: MIT Press.

Shanks, D. R., & Dickinson, A. (1987). Associative accounts of causality judgment. In G. H. Bower (Ed.), *The psychology of learning and motivation* (Vol. 21, pp. 229–261). San Diego, CA: Academic Press.

Sutton, R. S., & Barto, A. G. (1981). Toward a modern theory of adaptive networks: Expectation and prediction. *Psychological Review, 88,* 135–170.

Van Hamme, L., & Wasserman, E. A. (1994). Cue competition in causality judgments: The role of nonpresentation of compound stimulus elements. *Learning and Motivation 25,* 127–151.

STRUCTURAL AND PROBABILISTIC CAUSALITY

Judea Pearl

I. Introduction

The central aim of many empirical studies in the physical, behavioral, social, and biological sciences is the elucidation of cause–effect relationships among variables. It is through cause–effect relationships that we obtain a sense of a "deep understanding" of a given phenomenon, and it is through such relationships that we obtain a sense of being "in control," namely, that we are able to shape the course of events by deliberate actions or policies. It is for these two reasons, understanding and control, that causal thinking is so pervasive, popping up in everything from everyday activities to high-level decision making: a car owner wonders why an engine will not start; a cigarette smoker would like to know, given his/her specific characteristics, to what degree his/her health would be affected by refraining from further smoking; a policymaker would like to know to what degree antismoking advertising would reduce health care costs; and so on. Although a plethora of data has been collected on cars and on smoking and health, the appropriate methodology for extracting answers to such questions of causality have not been given fully satisfactory answers.

The two fundamental questions of causality are:

1. What empirical evidence is required for legitimate inference of cause–effect relationships?
2. Given that we are willing to accept causal information about a certain phenomenon, what inferences can we draw from such information, and how?

393

The primary difficulty is that we do not have a clear empirical semantics for causality; statistics teaches us that causation cannot be defined in terms of statistical associations, while any philosophical analysis of causation in terms of deliberate control quickly reaches metaphysical dead ends over the meaning of free will. Indeed, Bertrand Russell (1913) noted that causation plays no role in physics proper and offered to purge the word from the language of science. Karl Pearson (1911) advocated such a purge from statistics, which, regretfully, has been more successful than that envisioned by Russell.

Philosophical difficulties notwithstanding, scientific disciplines that must depend on causal thinking have developed paradigms and methodologies that successfully bypass the unsettled questions of causation and that provide acceptable answers to pressing problems of experimentation and inference. Social scientists, for example, have adopted path analysis and structural equation models, and programs such as LISREL have become common tools in social science research. Econometricians, likewise, have settled for stochastic simultaneous equations models as carriers of causal information and have focused most of their efforts on developing statistical techniques for estimating the parameters of these models. Statisticians, in contrast, have adopted Fisher's randomized experiment as the ruling paradigm for causal inference, with occasional excursions into its precursor, the Neyman–Rubin model of potential response (Neyman, 1923; Rubin, 1974).

None of these paradigms and methodologies can serve as an adequate substitute for a comprehensive theory of causation, one suitable for explaining the ways people infer and process causal relationships. The structural equations model is based largely on informal modeling assumptions and has hardly been applied beyond the boundaries of linear equations with Gaussian noise. The statisticians' paradigm of randomized experiments is too restrictive in natural, prescientific learning environment, and it does not allow for the integration of statistical data with the rich body of (previously acquired) causal knowledge that is available in ordinary discourse. And philosophers have essentially abandoned the quest for the empirical basis of causation. Early attempts to reduce causality to probabilities got entangled in circular definitions (see Section IIB) and recent theories, based on processes (Salmon, 1994) or capacities (Cartwright, 1989, Chapter 4), though conceptually appealing, have not been formalized with sufficient precision to describe how people learn, represent, and use causality in ordinary practice.

A new perspective on the problem of causation has recently emerged from a rather unexpected direction—artificial intelligence (AI). When encoding and processing causal relationships on digital machines became necessary, the problems and assumptions that other disciplines could keep dormant and implicit had to be explicated in great detail, so as to meet the levels of precision necessary in programming.

Explicating cause–effect relationships has become a concern central to several areas of AI: natural language processing, automated diagnosis, robot planning, qualitative physics, and database updates. In the area of robotics, for example, the two fundamental problems of causation were translated into concrete, practical questions:

1. How should a robot acquire causal information through interaction with its environment?
2. How should a robot process the causal information it receives from its creator-programmer?

Attempts to gloss over difficulties with causation quickly result in a programmer's nightmare. For example, when given the information "If the grass is wet, then the sprinkler must have been on" and "If I break this bottle, the grass will get wet," the computer will conclude "If I break this bottle, the sprinkler must have been on." The swiftness and concreteness with which such bugs surface has forced computer scientists to pinpoint loosely stated assumptions and then assemble new and more coherent theories of actions, causation, and change.

The purpose of this paper is to summarize recent advances in causal reasoning, to show how they clarify, unify, and enrich previous approaches in philosophy, economics, and statistics, and to relate these advances to two models of causal judgment that have been proposed in the psychological, literature: the statistical contingency model (Cheng, 1992; Jenkins & Ward, 1965) and the power-based model (Shultz, 1982). The statistical contingency model and its variants are grounded in the philosophical literature of probabilistic causality, to be described and assessed in Secion II. Related advancements in probabilistic causal discovery, based on the language of graphs (Pearl & Verma, 1991; Spirtes, Glymour, & Schienes, 1993) are described in Section III. It is shown that graphs offer a powerful language for formulating and resolving some of the fundamental problems in probabilistic causality and, in addition, that graphs offer techniques of extracting causal relationships from intricate patterns of probabilistic dependencies, including distinct patterns created by unobserved factors. The power-based model takes after the structural equations models used in econometrics, in which causal relationships are defined in terms of hypothetical manipulative experiments. A general, nonparametric formulation of structural equations models is given in Section IV, and is shown to support a wide variety of causal relationships, including predictive, abductive, manipulative, and counterfactual modes of reasoning.

Integrated models, in which causal judgment is shaped by both statistical data and preconceived notions of power (Cheng, Park, Yarlas, & Holyoak, this volume, Ch. 8), are more closely related to an action calculus formulated in Pearl (1994b). In this formulation, prior causal knowledge is encoded qualitatively in the form of a graph containing both observed and unobserved variables, and the magnitudes of causal forces in the domain are inferred from both the probability of the observed variables and the topological features of the graph. The calculus (described in Section IVD) admits two types of conditioning operators: ordinary Bayes conditioning, $P(y|X = x)$, which represents the observation $X = x$, and causal conditioning, $P[y|do(X = x)]$, read: the probability of $Y = y$ conditioned on holding X constant (at x) by deliberate action. Given a mixture of such observational and causal sentences, together with the topology of the causal graph, the calculus derives new conditional probabilities of both types, thus enabling one to quantify the effects of actions and observations, to specify conditions under which manipulative experiments are not necessary, and to suggest additional observations or auxiliary experiments from which the desired inferences can be obtained.

I propose this formalism as a basis for theories of causal learning and, in particular, how humans integrate information from diverse sources— passive observation, manipulative experimentation, and linguistic instruction—to synthesize a coherent causal picture of the environment.

II. Probabilistic Causality

Probabilistic causality is a branch of philosophy that attempts to explicate causal relationships in terms of probabilistic relationships. This attempt is motivated by several ideas and expectations. First and foremost, probabilistic causality promises a solution to the centuries-old puzzle of causal discovery, that is, how humans discover genuine causal relationships from bare empirical observations, free of any causal preconceptions. Given the Humean dictum that causal knowledge originates with human experience and the (less compelling but currently fashionable) assumption that human experience is encoded in the form of a probability function, it is natural to expect that causal utterances might be reducible to a set of relationships in some probability distribution that is defined over the variables of interest. Second, in contrast to deterministic accounts of causation, probabilistic causality offers substantial cognitive economy. Physical states and physical laws need not be specified in minute detail because instead they can be summarized in the form of probabilistic relationships among macrostates so as to match the granularity of natural discourse. Third, probabilistic causality is equipped to deal with the modern (i.e., quantum theoretical) conception of uncertainty, according to which determinism is merely an epistemic fiction, and nondeterminism is the fundamental feature of physical reality.

The formal program of probabilistic causality owes its inception to Reichenbach (1956) and Good (1961) and has subsequently been pursued by Suppes (1970), Skyrms (1980), Otte (1981), Spohn (1980), Salmon (1984), Cartwright (1989), and Eells (1991). The current state of this program is rather disappointing considering its original aspirations. Salmon has abandoned the effort altogether, concluding that "causal relations are not appropriately analyzable in terms of statistical relevance relations" (Salmon, 1984, p. 185); instead, he has proposed an analysis in which "causal processes" are the basic building blocks. More recent accounts by Cartwright and Eells have resolved some of the difficulties encountered by Salmon, but at the price of, on one hand, complicating the theory beyond recognition and, on the other, compromising its original goals. The following is a brief account of the major achievements and difficulties of probabilistic causality, as elaborated in Cartwright (1989) and Eells (1991).

A. TEMPORAL ORDERING

Standard probabilistic accounts of causality assume that, in addition to a probability function P, we are also given the temporal order of the variables in the analysis. This is understandable, considering that causality is an asymmetric relation, while statistical relevance is symmetric. Lacking temporal information, it would be impossible, for example, to decide which of two dependent variables is the cause and which the effect, since every joint distribution $P(x,y)$ induced by a model in which X is a cause of Y can also be induced by a model in which Y is the cause of X. Thus, any method of inferring that X is a cause of Y must also infer, by symmetry, that Y is a cause of X. By imposing the constraint that an effect never precede its cause, the symmetry is broken and causal inference can commence.

The reliance on temporal information has its price though, as it excludes a priori the analysis of cases in which the temporal order is not well defined, either because processes overlap in time or because they (appear to) occur instantaneously. For example, one must give up the prospect of determining (by uncontrolled methods) whether sustained physical exercise contributes to low cholesterol levels or, the other way around, low cholesterol levels enhance the urge to engage in physical exercise. Likewise, the philosophical theory of probabilistic causality would not attempt to distinguish between the claims "tall flag poles cause long shadows" and "long shadows cause tall flag poles," in which, for all practical purposes, the putative causes and effects occur simultaneously.

We shall see when we discuss graphical methods that some determination of causal directionality can be made from atemporal statistical information, albeit with a weakened set of guarantees.

B. CIRCULARITY

Despite the reliance on temporal precedence, the criteria that philosophers have devised for identifying causal relations suffer from glaring circularity: In order to determine whether an event C is a cause of event E, one must know in advance how other factors are causally related to C and E. Such circularity emerges from the need to define the "background context" under which a causal relation is evaluated, since the intuitive idea that causes should increse the probability of their effects must be qualified by the condition that other things are assumed equal. For example, striking a match increases the chance of fire, but only when oxygen is present, when the match is dry, and so on. Thus, it seems natural to define

Definition 1 C is causally relevant to E if there is at least one condition F in some background context K such that $P(E|C,F) > P(E|\neg C,F)$.

But what kind of conditions should we include in the background context? On one hand, insisting on a complete description of the physical environment would reduce probabilistic causality to deterministic physics (barring quantum-level considerations). On the other hand, ignoring background factors altogether, or describing them too coarsely, would introduce spurious correlations and other confounding effects. A natural compromise is to require that the background context itself be "causally relevant" to the variables in question, a move that is the source of circularity in the definition of statistical causality.

The dangers of describing the background too coarsely will be illustrated via two examples, one using the celebrated Simpson's paradox, the other the issue of interactive factors.

Simpson's paradox (Simpson, 1951), first encountered by Pearson in 1899 (Aldrich, 1994), refers to the phenomenon whereby an event C seems to increase the probability of E in a given population P and, at the same time, decrease the probability of E in every subpopulaton of P. In other words, if F and $\neg F$ are two complementary events describing two subpopulations, we might well encounter the inequalities

$$P(E|C) > P(E|\neg C), \tag{1}$$

$$P(E|C, F) < P(E|\neg C, F), \tag{2}$$

$$P(E|C, \neg F) < P(E|\neg C, \neg F). \tag{3}$$

While such order reversal might not surprise students of probability, it becomes paradoxical when given a causal interpretation. For example, if we associated C with taking a certain drug, E with recovery, and F with being a female, under the causal interpretation of Equations (1)–(3) the drug would be harmful to both males and females and beneficial to the population as a whole. Intuition deems such a result impossible, and correctly so.

The explanation for Simpson's paradox is that the inequality

$$P(E|C) > P(E|\neg C)$$

is interpreted erroneously. It is not a statement about C being a positive causal factor for E because the inequality may be due to spurious confounding factors that may cause both C and E. In our example, for instance, the drug may appear beneficial on the average because the women, who recover (with or without the drug) more often than the men, are also more likely than the men to use the drug.

The standard method for dealing with potential confounders of this kind is to "hold them fixed,"[1] namely, to condition the probabilities on any factor that might cause both C and E. In our example, if being a female (F) is perceived to be a cause for both recovery (E) and drug usage (C), then the effect of the drug needs to be evaluated separately for men and women, as in Equations (2)–(3), and averaged accordingly.

Here we see the emergence of circularity: in order to determine the causal role of C relative to E (e.g., the effect of the drug on recovery), we must first determine the causal role of every factor F (e.g., gender) relative to C and E. More crucial, we must make sure that C is not causally relevant to F, or else no C would ever qualify as a cause of E, because we can always find factors F that are intermediaries between C and E that screen off E from C.[2]

Factors affecting both C and E can be rescued from circularity by conditioning on *all* factors preceding C but, unfortunately, other factors that cannot be identified through temporal ordering alone must also be weighed. Consider the following example. I must bet heads or tails on the outcome of a fair coin toss; I win if I guess correctly, lose if I do not. Naturally, once the coin is tossed (and while the outcome is still unknown), the bet is deemed causally relevant to winning, even though the probability of winning

---

[1] The phrases "hold F fixed" or "control for F," used by both philosophers (e.g., Eells, 1991) and statisticians (e.g., Pratt & Schlaifer, 1988), connote external interventions and may, therefore, be misleading (see later sections on acting vs seeing). In standard probability language, all one can do is to simulate "holding F fixed" by considering cases with equal values of F, namely, "conditioning" on F and $\neg F$, an operation I will call "adjusting for F."

[2] F "screens off" E from C if C and E are conditionally independent, given both F and $\neg F$; equivalently, if equalities hold in Equations (2) and (3).

is the same whether I bet heads or tails. To reveal the causal relevance of the bet (C), we must include the outcome of the coin (F) in the background context, even though F does not meet the common-cause criterion—it does not affect my bet (C) nor is it causally relevant to winning (E) (unless we first proclaim the bet relevant to winning). Worse yet, we cannot justify including F in the background context by virtue of its occurring earlier than C because whether the coin is tossed before or after my bet is totally irrelevant to the problem at hand. We conclude that temporal precedence alone is insufficient for identifying the background context, and we must refine the definition of the background context to include what Eells (1991) calls "interacting causes," namely (simplified) factors F that (1) are not affected causally by C and (2) jointly with C (or $\neg C$) increase the probability of E.

Due to the circularity inherent in all definitions of causal relevance, probabilistic causality cannot be regarded as a program for extracting causal relations from temporal-probabilistic information but, rather, as a program for validating whether a proposed set of causal relationships is consistent with the available temporal-probabilistic information. More formally, suppose someone gives us a probability distribution P and a temporal order O on a (complete) set of variables V. Furthermore, any pair of variable sets, X and Y, in V is annotated by a symbol R or I, where R stands for "causally relevant" and I for "causally irrelevant." Probabilistic causality deals with testing whether the proposed R and I labels are consistent with the pair $\langle P, O \rangle$ and the requirement that cause should both precede and increase the probability of effect.

Currently, the most advanced consistency test is the one based on Eells's criterion of relevance (Eells, 1991), which translates into:

Consistency test   For each pair of variables labeled $R(X, Y)$, test whether

(i) X precedes Y in O, and
(ii) there exist x, x', y such that $P(y|x, z) > P(y|x', z)$ for some z in Z, where Z is a set of variables in the background context K, such that $I(X, Z)$ and $R(Z, Y)$.

This now raises additional questions:

1. Is there a consistent label for every pair $\langle P, O \rangle$?
2. When is the label unique?
3. Is there a procedure for finding a consistent label when it exists?

While some insights into these questions are provided by the graphical methods to be discussed in Secion III, the point to notice is that, due to circularity, the mission of probabilistic causality has been altered: from discovery to that of consistency testing.

C. The Closed-World Assumption

By far the most critical and least defensible paradigm underlying probabilistic causality rests on the assumption that a probability function exists on all variables relevant to a given domain of discourse. This assumption absolves the analyst from worrying about unmeasured spurious causes, which might (physically) affect several variables in the analysis and still remain obscure to the analyst. It is well known that the presence of such "confounders" may reverse or negate any causal conclusion that might be drawn from probabilities. For example, observers might conclude that "bad air" is the cause of malaria if they are not aware of the role of mosquitoes, or that falling barometers are the cause of rain, or that speeding to work is the cause of being late to work, and so on. Because they are unmeasured, or even unsuspected, the confounding factors in such examples cannot be neutralized by conditioning or by "holding them fixed." Thus, taking Hume's program of extracting causal information from raw data seriously entails coping with the problem that the validity of any such information is predicated on the untestable assumption that all relevant factors have been accounted for.

Similar problems affect psychological theories that use statistical relevance to explain how children extract causal information from experience. The proponents of such theories cannot ignore the fact that the child never operates in a closed, isolated environment. Unnoticed external conditions govern the operation of every learning environment, and these conditions often have the potential to confound cause and effect in unexpected and clandestine ways.

Fortunately, that children do not grow in closed, sterile environments like those in statistical textbooks has its advantages too. Aside from passive observations, a child possesses two valuable sources of causal information that are not available to the ordinary statistician: manipulative experimentation and linguistic advice. Manipulation subjugates the putative causal event to the sole influence of a known mechanism, thus overruling the influence of uncontrolled factors that might also produce the putative effect. "The beauty of independent manipulation is, of course, that other factors can be kept constant without their being identified" (Cheng, 1992). The independence is accomplished by subjecting the object of interest to the whims of one's volition, to ensure that the manipulation is not influenced by any environmental factor likely to produce the putative effect. Thus, for example, a child can infer that shaking a toy can produce a rattling sound, because it is the child's hand, governed solely by the child's volition, that brings about the shaking of the toy and the subsequent rattling sound. The whimsical nature of free manipulation replaces the statistical notion of randomized experimentation and serves to filter sounds produced by the child's actions from those produced by uncontrolled environmental factors.

But manipulative experimentation cannot explain all of the causal knowledge that humans acquire and possess, simply because most variables in our environment are not subject to direct manipulation. The second valuable source of causal knowledge is linguistic advice, namely, explicit causal sentences about the working of things, which we obtain from parents, friends, teachers, and books, and which encodes manipulative experience of past generations. As obvious and uninteresting as this source of causal information might appear, it probably accounts for the bulk of our causal knowledge, and understanding how this transference of knowledge works is far from trivial. In order to comprehend and absorb causal sentences such as "The glass broke because you pushed it," the child must already possess a causal schema within which such inputs make sense. To further infer that pushing the glass will make someone angry at you and not at your brother, even though he was responsible for all previous breakage, requires a truly sophisticated inferential machinery. In most children, this machinery is probably innate.

Note, however, that linguistic input is by and large qualitative; we rarely hear parents explaining to children that placing the glass at the edge of the table increases the probability of breakage by a factor of 2. Yet, quantitative assessments of the effects of one's actions must be made in any decision-making situation, and the question arises: How does one combine quantitative empirical data with qualitative causal relations to deduce quantitative causal assessments? The problem is especially critical in situations in which empirical data is available on only a small part of the causal field, while the bulk of that field is represented as rudimentary statements of what affects what in the domain. By analogy, this resembles the task of figuring out how to fix a TV set when given only a general understanding of the principles of television electronics combined with empirical data on five knobs and one screen. This problem will be dealt with in Section IV.

D.   SINGULAR VERSUS GENERAL CAUSES

Wayne A. Davis (1988, p. 145) summarizes the distinction between singular and general causes as follows:

> A *general causal statement,* like "Drinking hemlock causes death," asserts that one general event causes another. A *singular causal statement,* like "Socrates' drinking hemlock caused his death," asserts that one singular event caused another. The relationship between singular and general causation is not simple. From the fact that being poisoned causes death, we cannot infer that Alan's being poisoned caused his death

(he might have died of a bullet wound first). And even though Jim Fixx's last run caused his death, it is too strong to say that going for a run causes death.

The account of probabilistic causality provided so far (Sections IIA–IIC) addresses only general causal statements. Whether probabilistic information suffices for asserting singular causal statements, and where knowledge about singular causes comes from if it does not, further exacerbates the problems of probabilistic causality.[3] The next example demonstrates that singular causes require knowledge in the form of counterfactual or functional relationships. Such knowledge is not needed for general causes, nor can it be extracted from bare statistical data even under controlled experimentation. It requires a higher level of inductive generalization, one capable of extracting temporal invariants.

My son Danny feeds the dog whenever I ask him to, with a few exceptions. Ten percent of the time he feeds the dog even when I do not ask him to, and 10% of the time he does not feed the dog even when asked to. Today I asked Danny to feed the dog, which he did, and I wonder, Did he do it *because* I asked him to or was he about to do it anyway?

Let C and E stand for "asking" and "feeding," respectively. The story above can be summarized by two conditional probability statements,

$$P(E|C) = .90, \qquad P(\neg E|\neg C) = .90, \qquad (4)$$

which, together with the prior probability $P(C)$, fully specify the joint probability on the variables in question. Moreover, we can safely assume that C is the only relevant cause of E in the story, and that C and E are not confounded by any hidden common cause, so the same probabilities would prevail if C (vs. $\neg C$) were chosen by randomized experiment, hence the outcome associated with interventions or decisions is likewise determined by Equation (4). For example, the probability that Danny will feed the dog tomorrow if I decide to ask him to is unequivocally .90.

Still, whether today's request was the *actual cause* for today's feeding is difficult, in fact impossible, to determine, given the information at hand. The difficulty stems from the ambiguity concerning the *mechanism* underlying Danny's occasionally abnormal behavior. We will show two alternative mechanisms, both compatible with the probabilistic behavior of Equation (4), yet each giving a different answer to the singular causal query, "Was my asking the *actual cause* of today's feeding? (equivalently: "Would E have been true had C been false?").

---

[3] Eells's (1991, Chapter 6) analysis of token-level causation and Cartwright's (1989, Chapter 3) argument for "singular causes first" (rejected by Eells) both presuppose knowledge of how the occurrence of one singular event raises the probability of another, and thus only beg the question of where that extra knowledge comes from and how it is encoded in the mind.

Consider two competing models:

A. 20% of the time, Danny is in an absent-minded trance; he would feed the dog at random with 50% probability, regardless of whether he was asked to.
B. 10% of the time, Danny is in a rebellious mood; he would feed the dog if he were not asked to, and would not feed the dog if he were asked to do so.

It is easy to see that Models A and B are both compatible with the probabilistic information given in Equation (4), while they differ on the counterfactual query. In Model B, Danny's feeding the dog today rules out the possibility that he is in a rebellious mood; hence, he would not have fed the dog if not asked, and we can rest assured that my asking was the *actual cause* of today's feeding. In Model A, however, today's feeding still leaves uncertain whether Danny is in an alert state of mind or in one of those absent-minded trances (giving a 8:1 chance to each possibility). If alert, Danny would not have fed the dog had I not asked him to; if in a trance, he would still have fed the dog as he did. Thus, the probability that my asking *actually caused* today's feeding is 100% in Model B, and less than 100% (8/9) in Model A.

We see now that probabilistic information, even enriched with information about temporal ordering and causal relevance, is insufficient for answering counterfactual queries; the task requires the specification of the *functional* relationship between the putative cause and the putative effect.

This deficiency of the probabilistic account cannot be dismissed as metaphysical, that is, on the grounds that counterfactual sentences are, by definition, empirically untestable, hence meaningless. Counterfactual statements do, in fact, have an empirical content, but only when coupled with assumptions of persistence (perhaps this is what Hume meant by "regularity"). For example, assume that Danny's state of being in an abnormal mood persists for not one but several days. Our counterfactual query would then translate into a sharp empirical question of whether we can count on the dog being fed tomorrow. In fact, the ingredient that makes counterfactual probabilities hard to compute is not the counterfactual phrasing of the query but rather the fact that the query is accompanied with information that renders the event in question unique, unlike any other event summarized in the probability distribution P. Before we find out that Danny, in fact, fed the dog today, we have no problem answering the counterfactual query, "Would he feed the dog if he were not asked to?" The difficulty stems from observing Danny feeding the dog today, thus making this day singular, unlike any other day summarized in P. In other words, Danny was not (and can never be) observed under both conditions, being asked and not being asked, on the very same day. Thus, it is only when we observe the persistence of some mechanism (Danny's abnormality) for several successive observations that we can substantiate a counterfactual claim, and it is due to such persistence that counterfactual statements acquire their empirical content and their unique role in planning and knowledge communication. We shall see in Section IVE that counterfactual knowledge is essential for predicting the effect of actions when measurements are available about conditions that are likely to be affected by those actions.

Proponents of probabilistic causality may argue that by introducing new hypothetical variables into the analysis and stretching the notion of a "factor" to include counterfactual strategies, singular causes can still be treated in the probabilistic framework. For example, in the situation above, we could introduce Danny's "mood" or "mode of behavior" as a factor in the background context and, by conditioning the outcome E on this new factor, the correct answer would obtain using ordinary probabilistic computations. In general, accessing the degree to which an event C *actually causes* an observed event E involves considering as factors each of the four possible functions from $\{C, \neg C\}$ to $\{E, \neg E\}$, for which the term "mood" is merely indexical.[4] However, introducing these new factors seems like a roundabout way of squeezing metaprobabilistic causal and counterfactual information into the probabilistic vocabulary, and it is a far cry from Hume's program of inferring causes from probabilities, because there is no way to distinguish Model A from Model B solely on the basis of statistical observations without either going into a deeper analysis of Danny's state of mind or assuming that whatever mood Danny is in persists unaltered for at least a few trials. Such specification is accomplished more naturally in the structural equations framework, to be described in Section IV.

III. The Language of Causal Graphs

Causal graphs appear sporadically in the writings of Simon, Reichenbach, Cartwright, and Eells, where they are used primarily for mnemonic or display purposes. The use of graphs as a formal mathematical language for defining and processing causal relationships is relatively recent. We shall see that graphs offer a powerful language for expressing and resolving some fundamental questions in probabilistic causality, as well as a plausible hypothesis of how causal relationships are organized in the human mind.

A. DIRECT CAUSES AND BAYESIAN NETWORKS

A convenient starting point for introducing causal graphs is through the notion of *Markovian parents*.

---

[4] Many more functions need be considered in cases where C interacts with other factors of E (see Balke & Pearl, 1994).

Definition 2   Let $V = \{X_1, \ldots, X_n\}$ be an ordered set of variables, and let $P(v)$ be the joint probability distribution on these variables. A set of variables PA_j is said to be Markovian parents of X_j if PA_j is a minimal set of predecessors of X_j that renders X_j independent of all its other predecessors. In other words, PA_j is any subset of $\{X_1, \ldots, X_{j-1}\}$ satisfying

$$P(x_j|pa_j) = P(x_j|x_1, \ldots, x_{j-1}) \tag{5}$$

such that no proper subset of PA_j satisfies Equation (5).

Definition 2 assigns to each variable X_j a slect set of parent variable that are sufficient for determining the probability of X_j; knowing the values of other preceding variables is redundant once we know the values pa_j of the parent set PA_j. This assignment can be represented in a form of a directed acyclic graph (DAG) in which variables are represented by nodes and where arrows are drawn from each node of the parent set PA_j toward the child node X_j. Definition 2 also suggests a simple recursive method of constructing such a DAG: starting with the pair (X_1, X_2), we draw an arrow from X_1 to X_2 if the two variables are dependent. Continuing to X_3, we draw no arrow in case X_3 is independent of $\{X_1, X_2\}$; otherwise, we examine whether X_2 screens off X_3 from X_1 or X_1 screens off X_3 from X_2. In the first case, we draw an arrow from X_2 to X_3; in the second, we draw an arrow from X_1 to X_3. If no screening condition is found, we draw arrows to X_3 from both X_1 and X_2. In general, at the ith stage of the construction, we select any minimal set of X_i's predecessors that screen X_i from its other predecessors (as in Definition 2), call this set PA_i (connoting "parents"), and draw an arrow from each member in PA_i to X_i. The result is a directed acyclic graph, called a "Bayesian network" in Pearl (1988), in which an arrow from X_i to X_j assigns X_i as a Markovian parent of X_j, consistent with Definition 2.

Figure 1 illustrates a simple yet typical Bayesian network. It describes relationships among the season of the year (X_1), whether rain falls (X_2)

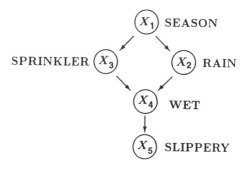

Fig. 1.   A Bayesian network representing causal influences among five variables.

during the season, whether the sprinkler is on (X_3) during that season, whether the pavement would get wet (X_4), and whether the pavement would be slippery (X_5). All variables in this figure are binary, taking a value of either true or false, except the root variable X_1, which can take one of four values: Spring, Summer, Fall, or Winter. The network was constructed in accordance with Definition 2, using intuition as guide. The absence of a direct link between X_1 and X_5, for example, captures our understanding that the influence of seasonal variations on the slipperiness of the pavement is mediated by other conditions (e.g., the wetness of the pavement). This intuition coincides with the independence condition of Equation (5), since knowing X_4 renders X_5 independent of $\{X_1, X_2, X_3\}$.

How do graphs enter our discussion of causality? To see the connection, we need to make three additional steps. First, we identify the ordering of the variables with their temporal order. Second, we make the closed-world assumption, namely, that $V = X_1, \ldots, X_n$ include *all* relevant variables for the phenomenon under study. Finally, we make a smooth transition from events to variables as the basic objects of causal relationships. This will enable us to say, for example, that force causes (or influences) acceleration, without specifying precisely what magnitude of force (an event) accounts for what level of acceleration (an event).[5]

With these provisions in mind, it is natural to identify the Markovian parents PA_i as "direct causes" of X_i; "causes," because they exhibit the temporal-probabilistic features of causal relevance described in Section II, and "direct" because they are not mediated (or screened off) by any other group of variables, especially when the parent set is unique.

Definition 3   (direct causes) Let $V = \{X_1, \ldots, X_n\}$ be a complete set of temporally ordered variables, and let $P(v)$ be the joint probability distribution on these variables. We say that X_i is a direct cause of X_j if X_i is a member of the parent set PA_j in a Bayesian network of $P(v)$ constructed along the temporal order.

Definition 3 provides a natural generalization of deterministic causality, in the spirit of Mulaik (1986). If deterministic causes are defined as a set of conditions sufficient for determining the value of X_j, regardless of other eventualities, then Definition 3 merely substitutes probability determination for value determination: once the direct causes of X_j are known, the probability of X_j is completely determined; no other event preceding X_j would modify this probability. In Section IIIB we will see that this invariance is in fact stronger; no other event except consequences of X_j would modify the probability of X_j. However, this invariance still falls short of the absolute

[5] Spohn (1980) and Mulaik (1986) are among the few who advocated this transition in the philosophical literature, though it has been used routinely in path analysis (Wright, 1921), economics (Simon, 1953), and artificial intelligence (Kim & Pearl, 1983).

invariance induced by deterministic causes, where the value of X_j remains determined against both past and future eventualities. A probabilistic version of such absolute invariance will be achieved through the manipulative and counterfactual accounts of causation, to be discussed in Section IV.

Definition 3 is also compatible with that of Eells (Section IIIB), which was based on causal relevance among events. A direct cause X_i of X_j must contain an event $X_i = x_i$ that is causally relevant to at least one event $X_j = x_j$ (i.e., $P(x_j|x_i, F) \neq P(x_j|x'_i, F)$ for at least two values, x_i and x'_i of X_i) because, otherwise, there would be some set of factors F that screens off X_j from X_i, thus violating the minimality of PA_j. Conversely, if any event $X_i = x_i$ is deemed causally relevant to event $X_j = x_j$, then X_i must be either a direct cause of X_j or causally relevant to some direct cause of X_j, because if X_i satisfies neither of these possibilities, it is not an ancestor of X_j in the graph; X_i would then be screened off from X_j by some of X_i's predecessors, and that would imply that X_i is not causally relevant to X_j after all.

However, the main advantage of commencing discussion of causality with the notion of direct causes is that the problem of circularity disappears (since each parent set is assigned independently of the others), the questions of consistency and uniqueness are resolved, and, not the least important, Definition 3 invites the language of graphs, with the help of which much harder questions of causality can be formulated and resolved.

Consider first the question of consistency. Assume we are given the pair $\langle p,O \rangle$ as before and we wish to find a consistent labeling (D) on pairs of variables, such that a pair (X_i,X_j) is labeled D iff "X_i is a direct cause of X_j" in accordance with Definition 3. It is a simple matter to find such a labeling by constructing a Bayesian network along O, and associating the labels with the links of the resulting DAG. Thus, the question of consistency is answered in the affirmative; every pair $\langle p,O \rangle$ has a labeling consistent with Definition 3, as given by the links of the constructed graph. The question of uniqueness also has a simple solution; if $P(v) > 0$ for every configuration v, then the parent sets PA_i are unique (Pearl, 1988, p. 119) and, hence, there will be a unique set of direct causes for every variable. Causal ambiguities emerge when some configurations obtain zero probability, representing deterministic constraints. For example, a chain $X_1 \rightarrow X_2 \rightarrow X_3$ of necessary and sufficient causes cannot be distinguished from a fork $X_2 \leftarrow X_1 \rightarrow X_3$ of necessary and sufficient causes, because $\{X_2\}$ and $\{X_1\}$ each is sufficient for determining $\{X_3\}$, hence, each can serve as a Markovian parent of X_3. This is precisely the ambiguity noticed in probabilistic causality (Otte, 1981): even given complete specifications of temporal ordering, probabilistic information fails to distinguish genuine from spurious causes when causal connections degenerate into deterministic, necessary and sufficient relationships.[6] Definition 3 confines the occurrence of such ambiguities to cases where deterministic constraints permit multiple minimal parent sets in the construction of the network.

An immediate beneficiary of graph language is the simplification and clarification of the notion of *background context* (sometimes called *causal field*) namely, the set K of variables that one should assume constant in assessing the causal relevance of one variable to another (see Definition 1). Section IIB summarizes the difficulties that philosophers have encountered in defining the appropriate background context for such assessment. The graphical concepts established by Definition 2 permit a constructive, noncircular definition of K, as follows:

Background context   In assessing the causal role of X relative to Y, the appropriate background context consists of all variables that are

1. direct parents of Y or of any intermediate variable between X and Y, and
2. nondescendants of X.

Since the notions of *parents, intermediate, and descendants* are defined unambiguously in the graph, and the graph is defined constructively from the pair $\langle p, O \rangle$, the background context, likewise, is well defined. Thus, one can now test systematically whether any event $X = x$ is a positive, negative, or a mixed cause of another event $Y = y$, by constructing the Bayesian network, identifying the variables in K, and, finally, comparing the probabilities $P(y|x, F)$ and $P(y|x', F)$ for each realization F of K.[7] For example, in assessing the causal role of having the sprinkler on ($X_3 = $ ON) on having a slippery pavement ($X_5 = $ true) in Fig. 1, the relevant background context consists of a single variable: Rain (X_2), and one needs to compare the quantities.

$$P(X_5 = \text{true}|X_3 = \text{ON}, X_2 = \text{true}) \text{ vs.}$$
$$P(X_5 = \text{true}|X_3 = \text{OFF}, X_2 = \text{true})$$

---

[6] We will argue later, in discussing the structural definition of causation, that neither causal chains nor causal forks can consist of strictly necessary and sufficient causes, because the meaning of the sentence "X_2 is a cause of X_3" rests in the claim that manipulating X_2, independently of events preceding X_2, would change X_3; the very existence of such manipulation rules out X_1 as being necessary and sufficient for X_2.

[7] If variable X is not an ancestor of variable Y then, clearly, event $X = x$ must be causally irrelevant to event $Y = y$. If X is an ancestor of Y, then $X = x$ may still be causally irrelevant to $Y = y$, since the causal relevance between X and Y shown in the graph may be due to other states of X and Y.

and

$$P(X_5 = \text{true}|X_3 = \text{ON}, X_2 = \text{false}) \text{ vs.}$$
$$P(X_5 = \text{true}|X_3 = \text{OFF}, X_2 = \text{false}).$$

Since inequality holds in the first pair and equality in the second, we conclude that Sprinkler = ON is a positive cause of Slippery. We need not (and, in fact, should not) adjust for X_4 because it is a descendant of X_3. There is no harm, however, in including additional variables (such as X_1) in K, as long as they are nondescendants of X_3.

We will see later (Section IV) that the variables in K possess a unique feature; it does not matter if we "hold K fixed" by external intervention or we "condition on K being constant." Although the two interpretations are generally not equivalent, they yield the same result for the relation between X and Y whenever K is selected by the graphical criterion above. This might explain why philosophers and statisticians, who generally ignore the distinction between "fixing" and "conditioning" (see footnote 1), often manage to escape the paradoxical consequences that such confusion may produce.

B. IMPLIED INDEPENDENCIES AND OBSERVATIONAL EQUIVALENCE

The construction implied by Definition 2 defines a Bayesian network as a carrier of conditional independence information relative to a specific temporal order O. Since temporal information is not always available (see Section IIA) and since variable ordering, in general, is a metaprobabilistic notion, one may ask whether the independence information conveyed by the graph can be communicated without making an explicit reference to the ordering O. This information would then impose constraints on the possible ordering of the variables, and would open the possibility of inferring, or ruling out, causal relations from P alone.

Assume that a Bayesian network G was constructed from a probability distribution P along ordering O. It is interesting to ask what features of P characterize all those distributions that are capable, under some ordering of the variables, to produce a Bayesian network identical to G. To answer this question, we recall that the essential property of P used in the construction of G was Equation (5), and that every distribution satisfying Equation (5) can be decomposed (using the chain rule of probability calculus) into the product

$$P(x_1, \ldots, x_n) = \prod_i P(x_i|pa_i), \tag{6}$$

where pa_i are the values of the parents (PA_i) of X_i in G. For example, the DAG in Fig. 1 induces the decomposition

$$P(x_1, x_2, x_3, x_4, x_5) = P(x_1) \, P(x_2|x_1) \, P(x_3|x_1) \, P(x_4|x_2, x_3) \, P(x_5|x_4). \quad (7)$$

The product decomposition in Equation (6) is no longer order specific, since, given P and G, we can test whether P decomposes into the product given by Equation (6) without making any reference to variable ordering. Moreover, for every distribution decomposed as Equation (6), one can find an ordering O that would produce G as a Bayesian network. We therefore conclude that a necessary and sufficient condition for a probability distribution P to induce a DAG G is that P admits the product decomposition dictated by G, as given in Equation (6). If P satisfies this condition, we say that G *represents* P.

A convenient way of characterizing the set of distributions represented by a DAG G is to list the set of (conditional) independencies that each such distribution must satisfy. These independencies can be read off the DAG by using a graphical criterion called d-separation (Pearl, 1988). To test whether X is independent of Y given Z in the distributions represented by G, we need to examine G and test whether the nodes corresponding to variables Z d-separate all paths from nodes in X to nodes in Y. By *path* we mean a sequence of consecutive edges (of any directionality) in the DAG.

Definition 4 (d-separation) A path p is said to be d-separated (or blocked) by a set of nodes Z iff:

(i) p contains a chain $i \to j \to k$ or a fork $i \leftarrow j \to k$ such that the middle node j is in Z, or,

(ii) p contains an inverted fork $i \to j \leftarrow k$ such that neither the middle node j nor any of its descendants (in G) are in Z.

If X, Y, and Z are three disjoint subsets of nodes in a DAG G, then Z is said to d-separate X from Y, denoted $(X \parallel Y|Z)_G$, iff Z d-separates every path from a node in X to a node in Y.

The intuition behind d-separation is simple: In chains $X \to Z \to Y$ and forks $X \leftarrow Z \to Y$, the two extreme variables are dependent (marginally) but become independent of each other (i.e., blocked) once we know the middle variable. Inverted forks $X \to Z \leftarrow Y$ act the opposite way; the two extreme variables are independent (marginally) and become dependent (i.e., unblocked) once the value of the middle variable (i.e., the common effect) or any of its descendants is known. For example, finding that the pavement is wet or slippery (see Fig. 1) renders Rain and Sprinkler dependent, because refuting one of these explanations increases the probability of the other.

In Fig. 1, for example, $X = \{X_2\}$ and $Y = \{X_3\}$ are d-separated by $Z = \{X_1\}$; the path $X_2 \leftarrow X_1 \to X_3$ is blocked by $X_1 \in Z$, while the path $X_2 \to$

$X_4 \leftarrow X_3$ is blocked because X_4 and all its descendants are outside Z. Thus $(X_2 \perp\!\!\!\perp X_3|X_1)_G$ holds in G. However, X and Y are not d-separated by $Z' = \overline{\{X_1, X_5\}}$, because the path $X_2 \rightarrow X_4 \leftarrow X_3$ is unblocked by virtue of X_5, a descendant of X_4, being in Z'. Consequently $(X_2 \perp\!\!\!\perp X_3|\{X_1, X_5\})_G$ does not hold; in words, learning the value of the consequence X_5 renders its causes X_2 and X_3 dependent, as if a pathway were opened along the arrows converging at X_4.

Theorem 1 For any three disjoint subsets of nodes (X, Y, Z) in a DAG G, if Z d-separates X from Y in G then X is independent of Y conditional on Z in every distribution represented by G (Geiger, Verma, & Pearl, 1990; Verma & Pearl, 1988).

The d-separation criterion can be tested in time linear in the number of edges in G. Thus, a DAG can be viewed as an efficient scheme for representing Markovian independence assumptions and for deducing and displaying all the logical consequences of such assumptions.

Note that the ordering with which the graph was constructed does not enter into the d-separation criterion; it is only the topology of the resulting graph that determines the set of independencies that the probability P must satisfy. Indeed, the following theorem can be proven (Pearl, 1988, p. 120).

Theorem 2 If a Bayesian network G is constructed recursively along some ordering O (as in Definition 2), then a construction along any ordering O' consistent with the direction of arrows in G would yield the same network. Consequently, any variable in a Bayesian network is independent of all its nondescendants, conditional on its parents.

An important property that follows from the d-separation characterization is a criterion for determining whether two given DAGs are observationally equivalent, that is, whether every probability distribution that is represented by one of the DAGs is also represented by the other.

Theorem 3 Two DAGs are observationally equivalent iff they have the same sets of edges and the same sets of v-structures, that is, two converging arrows whose tails are not connected by an arrow (Verma & Pearl, 1990).

Observational equivalence places a limit on our ability to infer causal directionality from probabilities alone. Two networks that are observationally equivalent cannot be distinguished without resorting to manipulative experimentation or temporal information. For example, reversing the direction of the arrow between X_1 and X_2 in Fig. 1 does not introduce any new v-structure. Therefore, this reversal yields an observationally equivalent network, and the directionality of the link $X_1 \rightarrow X_2$ cannot be determined from probabilistic information. The arrows $X_2 \rightarrow X_4$ and $X_4 \rightarrow X_5$, however, are of different nature; there is no way of reversing their directionality without creating a new v-structure. Thus, we see that some probability functions P (such as the one responsible for the construction of the Bayesian network in Fig. 1), unaccompanied by temporal information, can constrain the directionality of some arrows, and hence the directionality of the causal relationships among the corresponding variables. The precise meaning of such directionality constraints will be discussed in the next section.

Additional properties of DAGs and their applications to evidential reasoning are discussed in Geiger (1990), Lauritzen and Spiegelhalter (1988), Spiegelhalter, Lauritzen, Dawid, and Cowell (1993), Pearl (1988, 1993a, 1993b), and Pearl, Geiger, and Verma (1990).

C. CAUSAL DISCOVERY

The interpretation of DAGs as carriers of independence assumptions does not necessarily imply causation and will, in fact, be valid for any set of Markovian independencies along any ordering (not necessarily causal or chronological) of the variables. However, the patterns of independencies portrayed in a DAG are typical of causal organizations, and some of these patterns can only be given meaningful interpretation in terms of causation. Consider, for example, the following *intransitive* pattern of dependencies among three events: E_1 and E_3 are dependent, E_3 and E_2 are dependent, yet E_1 and E_2 are independent. If you ask a person to supply an example of three such events, the example will invariably portray E_1 and E_2 as two independent causes and E_3 as their common effect, namely, $E_1 \rightarrow E_3 \leftarrow E_2$. Fitting this dependence pattern by using E_3 as the cause and E_1 and E_2 as the effects, although mathematically feasible, is very unnatural indeed (the reader is encouraged to try this exercise).

Such thought experiments teach us that certain patterns of dependency, totally void of temporal information, are conceptually characteristic of certain causal directionalities and not others. Reichenbach (1956) has suggested that this temporal asymmetry is a characteristic of Nature, reflective of the second law of thermodynamics. Pearl and Verma (1991) have offered a more subjective explanation, attributing the asymmetry to choice of language and to certain assumptions (e.g., Occam's razor) prevalent in scientific induction. Regardless of the origins of this asymmetry, exploring whether it provides a significant source of causal information (or at least causal clues) in human learning is an interesting topic for research (Waldmann, Holyoak, & Fratiannea, 1995).

The distinction between transitive and intransitive dependencies has become the basis for algorithms aimed at extracting causal structures from raw statistical data. Several systems that systematically search and identify causal structures from empirical data have been developed (Pearl, 1988, p. 387–397; Pearl & Verma, 1991; Spirtes et al., 1993). Technically, because these algorithms rely solely on conditional independence relationships, the structures found are valid only if one is willing to accept forms of guarantees that are weaker than those obtained through controlled randomized experiments—namely, minimality and stability (Pearl & Verma, 1991). Minimality guarantees that any other structure compatible with the data is necessarily less specific, and hence less falsifiable and less trustworthy, than the one(s) inferred. Stability ensures that any alternative structure compatible with the data must be less stable than the one(s) inferred; in other words, slight fluctuations in experimental conditions will render the alternative structure incompatible with the data. With these forms of guarantees, the algorithms can provide criteria for identifying genuine and spurious causes, with or without temporal information.

Minimality can be easily illustrated in Fig. 1: if one draws all graphs that are observational equivalent to the one shown in the figure (there are exactly three such graphs) one finds that they all contain an arrow directed from X_2 to X_4. This still does not make X_2 a genuine cause of X_4, because the specific data at hand, summarized in P, could in fact be generated by another graph, say G', which is not observationally equivalent to G, and in which an arrow is directed the other way around, from X_4 to X_2. For example, one choice of G' would be a complete DAG (i.e., one containing a link between every pair of nodes) rooted at X_4; although G' contains an arrow from X_4 to X_2, it could be made (with the proper adjustment of parameters) to represent any probability distribution whatsoever, including P. Is there a rationale, then, for preferring G on G', given that both represent P precisely [in the sense of Equation (6)]? There is! Having the potential of fitting any data means that G' is empirically nonfalsifiable, that P is overfitted, hence, that G' is less trustworthy than G. This preference argument can be advanced not merely to complete DAGs but against any DAG G' that can be made to fit more experimental data (i.e., probability functions) than G. Indeed, it can be shown that the set of probabilities representable by any DAG G' that fits P and contains an arrow from X_4 to X_2 would necessarily be a superset of those represented by G.

The minimality argument above rests on the closed-world assumption, and would fail if hidden variables are permitted. For example, the DAG $X \leftarrow a \rightarrow Z \leftarrow b \rightarrow Y$ imposes the same set of independencies on the observed variables X,Y,Z as the v-structure $X \rightarrow Z \leftarrow Y$, yet the former does not present X as a cause of Z. The remarkable thing about minimality, however, is that it uniquely determines the directionality of some arrows even when we dispose of the closed-world assumption and allow for the presence of hidden variables. The arrow from X_4 to X_5 in Fig. 1 is an example of such occasion. Among all DAGs that fit P, including DAGs containing unobserved variables, those that do not include an arrow from

X_4 to X_5 are nonminimal, that is, each fits a superset of the probability distributions (on the observables) represented by G. It is this feature that encouraged Pearl and Verma (1991) to label certain links in the DAG "genuine causes," to be distinguished from "potential causes" and "spurious associations." The latter identifies certain associations as noncausal (i.e., no like exists between the corresponding nodes in all minimal DAGs that fit the data) implying that the observed association must be attributed to a hidden common cause between the corresponding variables. Criteria and algorithms for identifying genuine causes, potential causes, and spurious associations are described in Pearl and Verma (1991) and Spirtes et al. (1993).

Alternative methods of identifying causal structures in data assign prior probabilities to the parameters of the network and use Bayes's rule to score the degree to which a given network fits the data (Cooper & Herskovits, 1991; Heckerman, Geiger, & Chickering, 1994). These methods have the advantage of operating well under small-sample conditions, but they encounter difficulties in coping with hidden variables.

IV. Structural Causality

While Bayesian networks capture patterns of independencies that are characteristic of causal organizations, they still leave open the question of how these patterns relate to the more basic notions associated with causation, such as influence, manipulation, and control, which reside outside the province of probability theory. Manipulations are unquestionably central to the analysis of causal thinking. Even generative accounts of causality, according to which causal inquiries aim merely at gaining an "understanding" of how data are generated, are not totally divorced from notions of manipulation, albeit hypothetical. In the final analysis, the quest for understanding "how data is generated" or "how things work" is merely a quest for predictions of what could be expected if things were taken apart and reconfigured in various ways, that is, for expectations under various hypothetical manipulations.

An inspection of the Bayesian network depicted in Fig. 1 reveals that the network does, in fact, provide an effective representation for certain kinds of manipulations and changes of configuration. Any local reconfiguration of the mechanisms in the environment can be translated, with only minor modification, into an isomorphic reconfiguration of the network topology. For example, to represent a disabled sprinkler, we simply delete from the network all links incident to the node "Sprinkler"; to represent a pavement covered by a tent, we simply delete the link between "Rain" and "Wet." This flexibility is often cited as the ingredient that marks the division between deliberative and reactive agents, and that enables the former to manage novel situations instantaneously, without requiring training or adaptation. How then are these extraprobabilistic notions of reconfiguration and manipulation connected to the strictly probabilistic notion of conditional independence, which forms the standard basis for Bayesian networks and the entire study of probabilistic causality?

The connection is made through the structural account of causation, according to which probabilistic dependencies are but a surface phenomenon of more fundamental relationships—functional dependencies among stable, or autonomous, mechanisms. The roots of this account go back to path analysis in genetics (Wright, 1921) and structural equation models in econometrics (Haavelmo, 1943; Simon, 1953), and it can justly be regarded as the mathematical basis for the power models used in the psychological literature. The basic idea behind the structural account was extended in Pearl and Verma, (1991) for defining general probabilistic causal theories, as follows. Each child–parents family in a DAG G represents a deterministic function

$$X_i = f_i(pa_i, \, \varepsilon_i), \tag{8}$$

where pa_i are (values of) the parents of variable X_i in G, and where ε_i, $0 < i < n$, are mutually independent, arbitrarily distributed random disturbances. Characterizing each child–parent relationship as a deterministic function, instead of as the usual conditional probability $P(x_i \mid pa_i)$, imposes equivalent independence constraints on the resulting distributions and leads to the same recursive decomposition that characterizes DAG models [see Equation (6)]. However, the functional characterization $X_i = f_i(pa_i, \, \varepsilon_i)$ also specifies how the resulting distributions would change in response to external interventions, since each function is presumed to represent a stable mechanism in the domain and therefore remains constant unless specifically altered. Thus, once we know the identity of the mechanisms altered by an intervention and the nature of the alteration, the overall effect of an intervention can be predicted by modifying the appropriate equations in the model of Equation (8) and using the modified model to compute a new probability function of the observables.

The simplest type of external intervention is one in which a single variable, say X_i, is forced to take on some fixed value x_i'. Such *atomic* intervention amounts to replacing the old functional mechanism $X_i = f_i(pa_i, \, \varepsilon_i)$ with a new mechanism $X_i = x_i'$, which represents the external force that sets the value x_i'. If we imagine that each variable X_i could potentially be subject to the influence of such an external force, then we can view each Bayesian network as an efficient code for predicting the effects of atomic interventions and of myriad combinations of such interventions, without encoding these interventions explicitly. What is more remarkable yet is that it is possible, under certain conditions, to predict the effect of interventions without knowing the functions $\{f_i\}$; the topology of the graph combined with the probability of the observables suffice. This means that it is possible to infer and quantify causal influences, in the presence of unmeasured variables, from a combination of statistical data and qualitative linguistic assertions about the general workings of mechanisms. The following section presents these ideas in a formal setting.

A. CAUSAL THEORIES AND ACTIONS

Definition 5 A causal theory is a four-tuple

$$T = \langle V, U, P(u), \{f_i\}\rangle,$$

where

(i) $V = \{X_1, \ldots, X_n\}$ is a set of observed variables,

(ii) $U = \{U_1, \ldots, U_m\}$ is a set of exogenous (often unmeasured) variables that represent disturbances, abnormalities, or assumptions,

(iii) $P(u)$ is a distribution function over $U_1, \ldots, U_m$, and

(iv) $\{f_i\}$ is a set of n deterministic functions, each of the form

$$X_i = f_i(PA_i, u) \quad i = 1, \ldots, n, \tag{9}$$

where PA_i is a subset of variables in V not containing X_i.

We will assume that the set of equations in (iv) has a unique solution for $X_i, \ldots, X_n$, given any value of the disturbances $U_1, \ldots, U_m$. Therefore, the distribution $P(u)$ induces a unique distribution on the observables, which we denote by $P_T(v)$. The structural parent sets, PA_i, are again considered the direct causes of X_i and they define a directed graph G, which may, in general, be cyclic. However, unlike the Markovian parents defined in Section IIA. (see Definition 2), PA_i is selected from V by considering outcomes of manipulative experiments (according to Lemma 4 below), not by conditional independence considerations, as in probabilistic causality. The result of encoding this manipulative information in the equations will be a major relaxation of the small-world assumption (Section IIC); the analysis of actions will require only rudimentary, qualitative assumptions about the structure of the unmeasured U variables.

Consider the example depicted in Fig. 1. The corresponding theory consists of five functions, each representing an autonomous mechanism:

$$X_1 = U_1$$
$$X_2 = f_2(X_1, U_2)$$
$$X_3 = f_3(X_1, U_3)$$
$$X_4 = f_4(X_3, X_2, U_4)$$
$$X_5 = f_5(X_4, U_5) \tag{10}$$

The disturbances $U_1, \ldots, U_5$ are not shown explicitly in the graph of Fig. 1, but are understood to govern the uncertainties associated with the causal relationships. A typical specification of the functions $\{f_1, \ldots, f_5\}$ and the disturbance terms is given by the Boolean theory below:

$$x_2 = [(X_1 = \text{Winter}) \lor (X_1 = \text{Fall}) \lor ab_2] \land -ab_2'$$
$$x_3 = [(X_1 = \text{Summer}) \lor (X_1 = \text{Spring}) \lor ab_3] \land - ab_3'$$
$$x_4 = (x_2 \lor x_3 \lor ab_4) \land - ab_4'$$
$$x_5 = (x_4 \lor ab_5) \land - ab_5'), \tag{11}$$

where x_i stands for X_i = true, and ab_i and ab_i' stand, respectively, for triggering and inhibiting abnormalities.[8] For example, ab_4 stands for (unspecified) events that might cause the ground to get wet (x_4) when the sprinkler is off ($-x_2$) and it does not rain ($-x_3$), while $-ab_4'$ stands for events that will keep the ground dry despite the rain, the sprinkler and ab_4, say covering the ground with plastic sheet.

As stated in the introductory subsection, the main role of structural causal theories is to facilitate the analysis of actions. We will consider local concurrent actions of the form $do(X = x)$, where $X \subseteq V$ is a set of variables and x is a set of values from the domain of X. In other words, $do(X = x)$ represents a combination of direct actions that forces the variables in X to attain the values x.

Definition 6   (effect of actions) The effect of the action $do(X = x)$ on a causal theory T is given by a subtheory T_x of T, where T_x obtains by deleting from T all equations corresponding to variables in X and substituting the equations $X = x$ instead.

---

[8] Goldszmidt and Pearl (1992, 1995) describe a qualitative method of causal analysis based on attributing infinitesimal probabilities to the ab predicates.

For example, to represent the action "turning the sprinkler ON," $do(X_3 = \text{ON})$, we delete the equation $X_3 = f_3(X_1, U_3)$ from the theory of Equation (10), and replace it with $X_3 = \text{ON}$. The resulting subtheory, $T_{X_3=\text{ON}}$, contains all the information needed for computing the effect of the action on other variables. It is easy to see from this subtheory that the only variables affected by the action are X_4 and X_5, that is, the descendants of the manipulated variable X_3. This is to be expected, since nondescendants of X_3 (i.e., season and rain) are presumed to be causally irrelevant to X_3, yet it stands in marked contrast to the operation of probabilistic conditionalization (on X_3) which may potentially influence every variable in the network. The mathematics underlying these two operations, and the conditions that enable us to predict the effects of actions without specifying $\{f_i\}$, will be discussed in the next two sections.

Definition 6 should be taken as an integral part of Definition 5, because it assigns meaning to each individual equation in T. Specifically, it dictates what hypothetical experiments of the type $do(X = x)$ must be considered by the author of the structural equations in deciding which variables PA_i should enter into the r.h.s of each equation. By writing $X_4 = f_4(X_2, X_3, u)$, for example, the analyst defines X_2 and X_3 as the direct causes of X_4, which, according to Definition 6, means that holding X_2 and X_3 fixed determines the value of X_4 regardless of changes in the season (X_1) and regardless of any direct action we might take to make the ground slippery (X_5). In general, Definition 6 endows PA_i with the following meaning: PA_i is a set of variables that, if held fixed, would determine (for any u) the value of X_i regardless of any other action $do(Z = z)$ that one may perform, where Z is any set of variables not containing X_i or any member of PA_i. Moreover, no proper subset of PA_i possesses that quality.

Lemma 4 provides a succinct summary of this property, and can also be viewed as the structural definition of direct causes.

Lemma 4   Let $Y(x; u)$ stand for the solution of Y under subtheory T_x, as in Definition 6. The direct causes of variable X_i are the minimal set of variables PA_i that satisfy

$$X_i(pa_i, z; u) = X_i(pa_i; u) \qquad (12)$$

for every u and for every set Z not containing X_i or any member of PA_i.

Clearly, if a causal theory is given explicitly, as in Definition 5, then the direct causes PA_i can be identified syntactically, as the arguments of each f_i. However, if the theory is represented implicitly in a form of a function

F: Actions $\times U \to V$, (as is often assumed in decision theory (Heckerman & Shachter, 1995; Savage, 1954)); then Lemma 4 can be used to identify, given *F*, the unique set of direct causes for each variable X_i.[9]

We see that the distinctive characteristic of structural equations, which sets them apart from ordinary algebraic equations, is that meaning is attached to any subset of equations from *T*. Mathematically, this characteristic does not show up explicitly in the equations, but rather implicitly, in the understanding that *T* stands for not one but 2^n sets of equations. This restricts, of course, the type of algebraic transformations admissible on *T* to those that preserve the solution of not one but each of the 2^n sets.

The framework provided by Definitions 5 and 6 permits the coherent formalization of many nuances and subtle concepts found in causal conversation, including causal influence, causal effect, causal relevance, average causal effect, identifiability, counterfactuals, and exogeneity. Examples are:

- ***X* influences *Y* in context** *u* if there are two values of *X*, *x* and *x'*, such that $Y(x; u) \neq Y(x'; u)$. In other words, the solution for *Y* under $U = u$ and $do(X = x)$ is different from the solution under $U = u$ and $do(X = x')$.

  We say, for example, that the weather (X_2) influences the wetness of the pavement (X_4) in a context *u* where the pavement is uncovered, and the sprinkler controller is at off position, because a change in weather from not-rain to rain is accompanied by a change in pavement condition from dry to wet. This definition interprets causal influence as the transference of change from *X* to *Y* triggered by the local intervention $do(X = x)$. Although the word "influence" is sometimes used with no intervention in mind (as in the case of the weather), the hypothetical operator $do(X = x)$ ensures that the change in *Y* is attributable only to changes in *X*, and not to spurious side effects (e.g., strange people who set their sprinklers by the season.)

- ***X* can potentially influence** *Y* in context $U = u$ if there exists a subtheory T_z of *T* in which *X* influences *Y*.

  The difference between influence and potential influence is that the latter requires an additional intervention, $do(Z = z)$, to reveal the effect of *X* on *Y*. In our earlier example, we find it plausible to maintain that, although the weather does not influence wetness in a context (u) where the sprinkler controller is stuck at ON position, it nevertheless can potentially influence wetness, at *u*, as is revealed when the action

---

[9] Likewise, the local operator $do(X_i = x_i)$ can be identified from *F* as the unique action *A* for which the equality $F(A, u)_i = F(A \text{ and } B, u)_i$ holds for every action *B* compatible with *A*. In words, $do(X_i = x_i)$ is the only action that keeps the value of X_i invariant to any other action that can be implemented at the same time.

do(Sprinkler = OFF) is implemented, say, by manual intervention. Along the same vein, we may say that seasonal variations (X_1) have potential influence on wetness, even though their influence through rain may perfectly cancel their influence through sprinkler; this potential would surface when we hold Sprinkler fixed (at either ON or OFF position).[10]

- **Event $X = x$ is the (singular) cause of event** $Y = y$ if (1) $X = x$ and $Y = y$ are true and (2) in every context u compatible with $X = x$ and $Y = y$, and for all $x' \neq x$, we have $Y(x'; u) \neq y$.

This definition reflects the counterfactual explication of a singular cause: "$Y = y$ would be false if it were not for $X = x$," as used in Section IID. A separate analysis of counterfactuals will be given in Section IVE.

B. PROBABILISTIC CAUSAL EFFECTS AND IDENTIFIABILITY

The definitions above are deterministic. Probabilistic causality emerges when we define a probability distribution $P(u)$ for the U variables. Under the assumption that the set of equations $\{f_i\}$ and every subset thereof has a unique solution, $P(u)$ induces a unique distribution $P_{T_x}(v)$ on the endogenous variables for each combination of atomic interventions $do(X = x)$. This leads to a natural probabilistic definition of causal effects.

Definition 7 (causal effect) Given two disjoint subsets of variables, $X \subseteq V$ and $Y \subseteq V$, the causal effect of X on Y, denoted $P_T[y|do(x)]$ or $P_T(y|\hat{x})$, gives the distribution of Y induced by the action $do(X = x)$, that is,

$$P_T(y|\hat{x}) = P_{T_x}(y) \tag{13}$$

for each realization x of X.

The probabilistic notion of causal effect is much weaker than its deterministic counter-parts of causal influence and potential causal influence. For example (from Section IIB), if U is the outcome of a fair coin, X is my bet, and Y stands for winning a dollar iff $X = U$, then the causal effect of X on Y is nil, because $P[y|do(X = \text{Tail})] = P[y|do(X = \text{Head})] = 1/2$. At the same time, X will qualify as having an influence on Y in every possible context, $U = \text{Head}$ and $U = \text{Tail}$. Note that causal effects are defined relative to a given causal theory T, though the subscript T is often suppressed for brevity.

---

[10] The standard example in the philosophical literature (Cartwright, 1989) involves the potential positive influence of birth-control pills on thrombosis, which might be masked by its negative effect on pregnancy (another casue of thrombosis). Cartwright's proposal (rejected by Eells), that the influence of the pill be assessed by considering separately the population of women that would get pregnant (or remain nonpregnant) regardless of the pill, amounts to considering a subtheory T_z in which pregnancy (Z) is held fixed.

Definition 8   (identifiability) Let $Q(T)$ be any computable quantity of a theory T. Q is identifiable in a class M of theories if for any pairs of theories T_1 and T_2 from M, $Q(T_1) = Q(T_2)$ whenever $P_{T_1}(v) = P_{T_2}(v)$.

Identifiability is essential for integrating statistical data, summarized by $P(v)$, with incomplete prior causal knowledge of $\{f_i\}$, as it enables the reasoner to estimate quantities Q from P alone, without specifying the details of T, so that the general characteristics of the class M suffice.[11] For the purpose of our analysis, the quantity Q of interest is the causal effect $P_T(y|\hat{x})$, which is certainly computable from a given theory T, using Equation (13), but which we will now attempt to compute from incomplete specification of T, in the form of general characteristics such as the identities of the parent sets PA_i and the independencies embedded in $P(u)$. We will therefore consider a class M of theories, which have the following characteristics in common:

  (i) they share the same parent–child families (i.e., the same causal graph G),
  (ii) they share the same set of independencies in $P(u)$, and,
  (iii) they induce positive distributions on the endogenous variables,[12] that is, $P(v) > 0$.

Relative to such classes we now define:

Definition 9   (causal-effect identifiability) The causal effect of X on Y is said to be *identifiable* in M if the quantity $P(y|\hat{x})$ can be computed uniquely from the probabilities of the observed variables, that is, if for every pair of theories T_1 and T_2 in M such that $P_{T_1}(v) = P_{T_2}(v)$, we have $P_{T_1}(y|\hat{x}) = P_{T_2}(y|\hat{x})$.

The identifiability of $P(y|\hat{x})$ ensures that it is possible to infer the effect of action $do(X = x)$ on Y from two sources of information:

  (i) passive observations, as summarized by the probability function $P(v)$,
  (ii) the causal graph, G, which specifies, qualitatively, which variables make up the stable mechanisms in the domain or, alternatively,

---

[11] The notion of identifiability is central to much work in econometrics, where it has become synonymous to the identification of the functions $\{f_i\}$ or some of their parameters (Koopman & Reiersol, 1950), mostly under conditions of additive Gaussian noise. Definition 8, which does not assume any parametric representation of the functions $\{f_i\}$, extends the notion of identifiability to quantities Q that do not require the precision of parametric models. In particular, it permits one (see Definition 9) to dispose with the identification of functional parameters altogether, and deal directly with causal effects $P(y|\hat{x})$—the very purpsoe of identifying parameters in policy-analysis applications.

[12] This requirement ensures that the disturbances U are sufficiently rich to simulate a "natural experiment," that is, an experiment in which conditions change by natural phenomena rather than a human experimenter.

which variables participate in the determination of each variable in the domain.

Simple examples of identifiability will be discussed in the next section.

C. INFERRING CONSEQUENCES OF ACTIONS FROM PASSIVE OBSERVATIONS

The probabilistic analysis of actions becomes particularly simple when two conditions are satisfied:

1. The theory is recursive, that is, there exists an ordering of the variables $V = \{X_1, \ldots, X_n\}$ such that each X_i is a function of a subset PA_i of its predecessors

$$X_i = f_i(pa_i, U_i), \quad PA_i \subseteq \{X_1, \ldots, X_{i-1}\} \tag{14}$$

2. The disturbances $U_1, \ldots, U_n$ are mutually independent, which implies (from the exogeneity of the U_i's)

$$U_i \perp\!\!\!\perp \{X_1, \ldots, X_{i-1}\}. \tag{15}$$

These two conditions, also called Markovian, are the basis of the independencies embodied in Bayesian networks (Section IIIB), and they enable us to compute causal effects directly from the conditional probabilities $P(x_i|pa_i)$, without specifying either the functional form of the functions f_i or the distributions $P(u_i)$ of the disturbances (Pearl, 1993a, 1993b; Spirtes et al., 1993). This is seen immediately from the following observations: on one hand, the distribution induced by any Markovian theory T is given by the product in Equation (6),

$$P_T(x_1, \ldots, x_n) = \prod_i P(x_i|pa_i), \tag{16}$$

where pa_i are (values of) the parents of X_i in the diagram representing T. On the other hand, subtheory $T_{x'_j}$, representing the action $do(X_j = x'_j)$, is also Markovian; hence, it also induces a product-like distribution

$$P_{T_{x'_j}}(x_1, \ldots, x_n) = \begin{cases} \prod_{i \neq j} P(x_i|pa_i) = \frac{P(x_1,\ldots,x_n)}{P(x_j|pa_j)} & \text{if } x_j = x'_j \\ 0 & \text{if } x_j \neq x'_j \end{cases} \tag{17}$$

where the partial product reflects the surgical removal of the equation

$X_j = f_j(pa_j, U_j)$ from the theory of Equation (14). Thus, we see that both the preaction and the postaction distributions depend only on observed conditional probabilities, not on the particular functional form of $\{f_i\}$ and of the distributions $P(u)$ that generate those probabilities. This is the essence of identifiability as given in Definition 9, which stems from the Markovian assumptions (14) and (15). Section IVD will demonstrate that certain, though not all, causal effects are identifiable even when the Markovian property is destroyed by introducing dependencies among the disturbance terms.

In the example of Fig. 1, the preaction distribution is given by the product

$$P_T(x_1, x_2, x_3, x_4, x_5,) = P(x_1)P(x_2|x_1)P(x_3|x_1)P(x_4|x_2, x_3)P(x_5|x_4), \quad (18)$$

while the surgery corresponding to the action $do(X_3 = \text{ON})$ amounts to deleting the link $X_1 \rightarrow X_3$ from the graph and fixing the value of X_3 to ON, yielding the postaction distribution

$$P_T[x_1, x_2, x_3, x_4, x_5|do(X_3 = \text{ON})]$$
$$= P(x_1)\,P(x_2|x_1)\,P(x_4|x_2, X_3 = \text{ON})\,P(x_5|x_4). \quad (19)$$

Note the difference between the action $do(X_3 = \text{ON})$ and the observation $X_3 = \text{ON}$. The latter is encoded by ordinary Bayesian conditioning,

$$P_T(x_1, x_2, x_4, x_5|X_3 = \text{ON})$$
$$= \frac{P(x_1)\,P(x_2|x_1)\,P(x_3 = \text{ON}|x_1)P(x_4|x_2, X_3 = \text{ON})P(x_5|x_4)}{P(X_3 = \text{ON})}.$$

The former is obtained by conditioning a mutilated graph, with the link $X_1 \rightarrow X_3$ removed. This mirrors indeed the difference between seeing and doing: after observing that the sprinkler is ON, we wish to infer that the season is dry, that it probably did not rain, and so on; no such inferences should be drawn in evaluating the effects of the deliberate action "turning the sprinkler ON." The excision of $X_3 = f_3(X_1, U_3)$ from (10) ensures the suppression of any abductive inferences from the action, as well as from any of its consequences.

Generalization to multiple actions and conditional actions is straightforward. Multiple actions $do(X = x)$, where X is a compound variable, result in a distribution similar to (17), except that all factors corresponding to the variables in X are removed from the product in (16). Stochastic conditional strategies (Pearl, 1994b) of the form

$$do(X_j = x_j) \text{ with probability } P^*(x_j|pa_j^*), \quad (20)$$

where PA_j^* is the support set of the decision strategy, also result in a product decomposition similar to (16), except that each factor $P(x_j|pa_j)$ is *replaced* with $P^*(x_j|pa_j^*)$.

D. A CALCULUS OF ACTING AND SEEING

The identifiability of causal effects demonstrated in Section IVC relies critically on the Markovian assumptions given in (14) and (15). If a variable that has two descendants in the graph is unobserved, the disturbances in the two equations are no longer independent, the Markovian property (14) is violated, and identifiability may be destroyed. This can be seen easily from Equation (17); if any parent of the manipulated variable X_j is unobserved, one cannot estimate the conditional probability $P(x_j|pa_j)$, and the effect of the action $do(X_j = x_j)$ may not be predictable from the observed distribution $P(x_1, \ldots, x_n)$. Fortunately, certain causal effects are identifiable even in situations where members of pa_j are unobservable (Pearl, 1993a, 1993b; Spirtes et al., 1993). Moreover, polynomial tests are now available for deciding when $P(x_i|\hat{x}_j)$ is identifiable and for deriving closed-form expressions for $P(x_i|\hat{x}_j)$ in terms of observed quantities (Galles & Pearl, 1995).

These tests and derivations are based on a symbolic calculus (Pearl, 1994b, 1995), to be described in the sequel, in which interventions, side by side with observations, are given explicit notation and are permitted to transform probability expressions. The transformation rules of this calculus reflect the understanding that interventions perform "local surgeries" as described in Definition 6, namely, they overrule equations that tie the manipulated variables to their preintervention causes.

Let X, Y, and Z be arbitrary disjoint sets of nodes in a DAG G. Following Definition 4, we denote by $(X \perp\!\!\!\perp Y|Z)_G$, the condition that the set Z d-separates X from Y in G. We denote by $G_{\overline{X}}$ the graph obtained by deleting from G all arrows pointing to nodes in X. Likewise, we denote by $G_{\underline{X}}$ the graph obtained by deleting from G all arrows emerging from nodes in X. To represent the deletion of both incoming and outgoing arrows, we use the notation $G_{\overline{X}\underline{Z}}$. Finally, the expression $P(y|\hat{x}, z) \triangleq P(y, z|\hat{x})/P(z|\hat{x})$ stands for the probability of $Y = y$ given that $Z = z$ is observed and X is held constant at x.

Theorem 5 Let G be the DAG associated with a Markovian causal theory, and let $p(\cdot)$ stand for the probability distribution induced by that theory. For any disjoint subsets of variables X, Y, Z, and W we have:

Rule 1 Insertion/deletion of observations

$$P(y|\hat{x}, z, w) = P(y|\hat{x}, w) \text{ if } (Y \perp\!\!\!\perp Z|X, W)_{G_{\overline{X}}}. \tag{21}$$

Rule 2   Action/observation exchange

$$P(y|\hat{x}, \hat{z}, w) = P(y|\hat{x}, z, w) \text{ if } (Y \perp\!\!\!\perp Z|X, W)_{G_{\overline{X}\underline{Z}}}. \tag{22}$$

Rule 3   Insertion/deletion of actions

$$P(y|\hat{x}, \hat{z}, w) = P(y|\hat{x}, w) \text{ if } (Y \perp\!\!\!\perp Z|X, W)_{G_{\overline{X, Z(W)}}}, \tag{23}$$

where $Z(W)$ is the set of Z-nodes that are not ancestors of any W-node in $G_{\overline{X}}$.

Each of the inference rules above follows from the basic interpretation of the $\hat{x}$ operator as a replacement of the causal mechanism that connects X to its preaction parents by a new mechanism $X = x$ introduced by the intervening force.

Corollary 1   A causal effect Q: $P(y_1, \ldots, y_k | \hat{x}_1, \ldots, \hat{x}_m)$ is identifiable in a model characterized by a graph G if there exists a finite sequence of transformations, each conforming to one of the inference rules in Theorem 5, which reduces Q into a standard (i.e., hat-free) probability expression involving observed quantities.

Although Theorem 5 and Corollary 1 require the Markovian property, they can also be applied to non-Markovian, recursive theories, because such theories become Markovian if we consider the unobserved variables as part of the analysis and represent them as nodes in the graph. To illustrate: assume that variable X_1 in Fig. 1 is unobserved, rendering the disturbances U_3 and U_2 dependent, since these terms now include the common influence of X_1. Theorem 5 tells us that the causal effect $P(x_4|\hat{x}_3)$ is identifiable, because

$$P(x_4|\hat{x}_3) = \sum_{x_2} P(x_4|\hat{x}_3, x_2)P(x_2|\hat{x}_3). \tag{24}$$

Rule 3 permits the deletion

$$P(x_2|\hat{x}_3) = P(x_2) \tag{25}$$

because $(X_2 \perp\!\!\!\perp X_3)_{G_{\overline{X}_3}}$, while Rule 2 permits the exchange

$$P(x_4|\hat{x}_3, x_2) = P(x_4|x_3, x_2) \tag{26}$$

because $(X_4 \perp\!\!\!\perp X_3|X_2)_{G_{\underline{X}_3}}$. This gives

$$P(x_4|\hat{x}_3) = \sum_{x_2} P(x_4|x_3, x_2)P(x_2),\qquad(27)$$

which is a hat-free expression, involving only observed quantities.

The reader might recognize Equation (27) as the standard formula for covariate adjustment (also called "stratification"), which is used in experimental design both for improving precision and for minimizing confounding bias. However, a formal, general criterion for deciding whether a set of covariates Z (X_2 in our example) qualifies for adjustment has long been wanting (Shafer, 1996; Smith, 1957; Wainer, 1991).[13] Theorem 5 provides such a criterion (called the "back-door criterion" in Pearl, 1993a, 1993b) which reads:

Definition 10 Z is an admissible set of covariates relative to the effect of X on Y if:

  (i) no node in Z is a descendant of X, and
  (ii) Z d-separates X from Y along any path containing an arrow into X (equivalently, $(Y \perp\!\!\!\perp X|Z)_{G_{\underline{X}}}$).

We see, for instance, that X_2 and X_1 (or both) qualify as admissible covariates relative to the effect of X_3 on X_4, but X_5 will not qualify. The graphical definition of admissible covariates replaces statistical folklore with formal procedures, and should enable analysts to systematically select an optimal set of observations, namely, a set Z that minimizes measurement cose or sampling variability.

In general, it can be shown (Pearl, 1995) that:

1. The effect of interventions can often be identified (from nonexperimental data) without resorting to parametric models.
2. The conditions under which such nonparametric identification is possible can be determined by simple graphical criteria.
3. When the effect of interventions is not identifiable, the causal graph may suggest nontrivial experiments which, if performed, would render the effect identifiable.

While the ability to assess the effect of interventions from nonexperimental data has immediate applications in the medical and social sciences, such

---

[13] Most of the statistical literature is satisfied with informal warnings that "Z should be quite unaffected by X" (Cox, 1958, p. 48), which is necessary but not sufficient, or that X should not precede Z (Shafer, 1996, p. 326), which is neither necessary nor sufficient. In some academic circles, a criterion called "ignorability" is invoked (Rosenbaum & Rubin, 1983), which merely paraphrases the problem in the language of counterfactuals. Simplified, it reads: Z is an admissible covariate relative to the effect of X on Y if, for every x, the value that Y would obtain had X been x is conditionally independent of X, given Z.

assessments are also important in psychological learning theory: they explain how agents can predict the effect of the next action (e.g., turning the sprinkler on) on the basis of past experience, where that action has never been enacted out of free will, but only in response to environmental needs (e.g., dry season) or to other agents' requests.

E. PROCESSING COUNTERFACTUALS

A counterfactual sentence has the form

If A were true, then C would have been true, given o,

where A, the counterfactual antecedent, specifies an event that is contrary to one's real-world observations o, and C, the counterfactual consequent, specifies a result that is expected to hold in an alternative world where the antecedent is true. A typical example is "If Oswald were not to have shot Kennedy, then Kennedy would still be alive," which presumes the factual knowledge of Oswald's assassination of Kennedy, contrary to the antecedent of the sentence.

The majority of the philosophers who have examined the semantics of counterfactual sentences have resorted to some version of Lewis's "closest world" approach: "C if it were A" is true, if C is true in worlds that are "closest" to the real world yet consistent with the counterfactual antecedent A (Lewis, 1973). While the closest-world approach leaves the precise specification of the closeness measure almost unconstrained, causal knowledge imposes very specific preferences as to which worlds should be considered closest to any given world. For example, consider an array of domino tiles standing close to each other. The manifestly closest world consistent with the statement "tile i is tipped to the right" would be a world in which just tile i is tipped, while all the others remain erect. Yet, we all accept the counterfactual sentence "Had tile i been tipped to the right, tile $i + 1$ would be tipped as well" as plausible and valid. Thus, distances among worlds are not determined merely by surface similarities but require a distinction between explained and unexplained dissimilarities. The local surgery paradigm expounded in Section IVA offers a concrete explication of the closest-world approach that respects such causal considerations. A world w_1 is "closer" to w than a world w_2 is, if the set of atomic surgeries needed for transforming w into w_1 is a proper subset of those needed for transforming w into w_2. In the domino example, finding tile i tipped and $i + 1$ erect requires the alteration of two basic mechanisms (i.e., two unexplained actions or "miracles" [Lewis, 1973]), compared with one altered mechanism for the world in which all j tiles, $j > i$, are tipped. This paradigm conforms to our perception of causal influences and lends itself to economical machine representation.

The structural equations framework, coupled with the surgical operator $do(X = x)$, also offers the syntactic machinery for counterfactual analysis, while leaving the closest-world interpretation implicit. The basis for this analysis is the potential response function $Y(x; u)$ invoked in Lemma 4, which we take as the formal explication of the English phrase "the value that Y would obtain in context u, had X been x."

Definition 11 (potential response) Given a causal theory T the potential response of Y to X in a context u, denoted $Y(x; u)$ or $Y_x(u)$, is the solution for Y under $U = u$ in the subtheory T_x.[14]

Note that this definition allows for the context $U = u$ and the proposition $X = x$ to be incompatible in T. For example, if T describes a logic circuit with input U, it may well be reasonable to assert the counterfactual: "Given $U = u$, voltage Y would be high if current X were low," even though the input $U = u$ may preclude X from being low. It is for this reason that one must invoke some notion of intervention (alternatively, a theory change or a "mircale" [Lewis, 1973]) in the definition of counterfactuals. This is further attested by the suppression of abductive arguments in counterfactual reasoning; for example, the following sentence would be deemed unacceptable: "Had I done my homework, I would have felt miserable, because I always do my homework after my father beats me up." The reason we do not accept this argument is that it conflicts with the common understanding that the counterfactual antecedent "done my homework" should be considered an external willful act, totally free of normal inducements (e.g., beatings) as modeled by the surgical subtheory T_x.

Counterfactual sentences rarely specify a complete context u. Instead, they imply a partial description of u in the form of a set o of (often implicit) facts or observations. Thus, a general counterfactual sentence would have the format $x \rightarrow y|o$, read "Given factual knowledge o, Y would obtain the value y had X been x." For example, the sentence "If Oswald were not to have shot Kennedy, then Kennedy would still be alive" would be formulated:

$$\neg \text{Shot(Oswald, Kennedy)} \rightarrow \text{Alive(Kennedy)} | \text{Dead(Kennedy)},$$
$$\text{Shot(Oswald, Kennedy)}$$

[14] The term *unit* instead of *context* is often used in the statistical literature (Rubin, 1974), where it normally stands for the identity of a specific individual in a population, namely, the set of attributes u that characterize that individual. In general, u may include the time of day, the experimental conditions under study, and so on. Practitioners of the counterfactual notation do not explicitly mention the notions of "solution" or "intervention" in the defintion of $Y(x;u)$. Instead, the phrase "the value that Y would take in unit u, had X been x," viewed as basic, is posited as the definition of $Y(x;u)$.

The truth of such a sentence in a theory T can be defined in terms of the potential response $Y(x; u)$ as follows:

Definition 12 (counterfactual assertability) The sentence $x \rightarrow y|o$ is true in T if $Y(x; u) = y$ for every u compatible with o.

This definition parallels Lewis's closest-world approach, with u playing the role of a possible world. Note the difference between the treatments of o and x; the former insists on direct compatibility between u and o, while the latter tolerates a surgical face-lift whenever x and u are incompatible.

If U is treated as a random variable, then the value of the counterfactual $Y(x; u)$ becomes a random variable as well, denoted $Y(x)$ or Y_x. Moreover, the distribution of this random variable is easily seen to coincide with the causal effect $p(y|\hat{x})$:

$$P[Y(x) = y] = P(y|\hat{x})$$

Thus, the probability of a counterfactual conditional $x \rightarrow y|o$ may be evaluated by the following procedure:

- Use the observations o to update $P(u)$, thus forming a revised causal theory $T^o = \langle V, U, \{f_i\}, P(u|o)\rangle$
- Form the subtheory T^o_x (by deleting from T^o the equation corresponding to variables in X) and compute the probability $P_{T^o_x}(y|\hat{x})$ that T^o_x induces on Y.

In Section IID we have demonstrated that, unlike causal-effect queries, counterfactual queries may not be identifiable in Markovian theories, unless the functional form of $\{f_i\}$ is specified. However, the example also shows that the counterfactual probabilities computed under two different functional forms produced almost the same answer to a counterfactual query. This is no coincidence. In Balke and Pearl (1994), a method is devised for computing sharp bounds on counterfactual probabilities, and, under certain circumstances, those bounds may collapse to point estimates. This method has been applied to the evaluation of causal effects in studies involving noncompliance and to determination of legal liability.

Counterfactual reasoning is at the heart of many cognitive abilities, especially real-time planning. For example, when a planner discovers that the current state of affairs deviates from the one expected, a "plan repair" activity will be invoked to determine what went wrong and how the error can be rectified. This activity amounts to an exercise in counterfactual thinking, as it calls for rolling back the natural course of events and determining, based on the factual observations at hand, whether the culprit resides in previous decisions or in some unexpected, external eventualities. Moreover, in reasoning forward to determine whether things would have been different, a new model of the world must be consulted, one that embodies hypothetical changes in decisions or eventualities, hence, a breakdown of the old model or theory. The surgical semantics expounded in this section offers a formal account of such breakdown.

The capacity to mentally simulate theory breakdowns is required whenever one wishes to evaluate the merit of actions on the basis of the past performance. The odd statement: "Had I done my homework, I would have felt miserable, because I always do my homework after my father beats me up" demonstrates the consequences of failing to exercise this capacity. A person aware of the signals triggering the past actions, must devise a method for selectively ignoring the influence of those signals from the evaluation process. In fact, the very essence of *evaluation* is having the freedom to imagine and compare trajectories in various counterfactual worlds, where each world or trajectory is created by a hypothetical implementation of actions that are free of the very pressures that compelled the implementation of such actions in the past.

The task of inferring singular causes (Section IID), also requires counterfactual reasoning. Finding the probability that $X = x$ is the actual cause for effect E amounts to answering the counterfactual query: "Given effect E and observations O, find the probability that E would not have been realized, had X not been x." The technique developed in Balke and Pearl (1995) permits the evaluation of such queries in the framework of Definition 11.

F. HISTORICAL REMARKS

An explicit translation of interventions to "striking out" equations from linear econometric models was first proposed by Strotz and Wold (1960) and later used in Fisher (1970) and Sobel (1990). Extensions to action representation in nonmonotonic reasoning and statistical analysis were reported in Goldszmidt and Pearl (1992) and Pearl (1993a, 1993b). Graphical ramifications of this translation were explicated first in Spirtes et al. (1993) and later in Pearl (1993b). A related formulation of causal effects, based on event trees and counterfactual analysis, was developed by Robins (1986, pp. 1422–1425). Shafer (1996) offers a novel formulation of probabilistic causation, based also on event trees. Calculi for actions and counterfactuals based on surgery semantics are developed in Pearl (1994b) and Balke and Pearl (1994), respectively.

VI. Conclusions

Statistical contingency models of causal induction have had two major advantages over their power-based rivals. First, statistics-based models are grounded in direct experience and, hence, promise to explicate the evidence and the processes responsible for acquiring cause–effect relationships from raw data. Second, statistics-based models enjoy the symbolic machinery of probability calculus, which enables researchers to posit hypotheses, communicate ideas, and make predictions with mathematical precision. In comparison, as well as skirting the issue of causal induction by presuming the preexistence of a causal structure, power-based theories have lacked an adequate formal language in which to cast assumptions, claims, and predictions.

This chapter offers a formal setting, based on mechanisms, structures, and surgeries, which accommodates both the statistical and the power components of causal inference. It has shown how preexisting causal knowledge, cast qualitatively in the form of a graph, can combine with statistical data to produce new causal knowledge, that is both qualitative and quantitative in nature. It has also shown how the formal setting of structural causality provides not only a semantics for distinguishing subtle nuances in causal discourse, but also an inferential machinery for processing actions, observations, and counterfactuals.

Returning to the problem of induction, the question of how knowledge about mechanisms is acquired in the first place remains unanswered. Mechanisms, however, are nothing but ordinary physical laws, cast in the form of deterministic equations. Therefore, the acquisition of causal relationships is no different from the acquisition, using controlled experimentation, of physical laws such as Hooke's law of suspended springs or Newton's law of acceleration. The asymmetry associated with causal relations, which is normally absent from physical laws, is partly a by-product of the distinction we make between endogenous and exogenous variables, namely, between variables we choose to analyze within the system and those we prefer to take as given (see Simon, 1953), partly due to the distinction we perceive between manipulable and nonmanipulable variables, and partly due to inherent asymmetries induced when closed physical systems (described by symmetric equations) are placed in contact with powerful external influences, for example, wetting the ground does not make the sprinkler turn on, moving cars do not turn ignition keys, and so on.

The explication of causal relationships in terms of mechanisms and physical laws is not meant to imply that the induction of physical laws is a solved, trivial task. It implies, however, that the problem of causal induction, once freed of the mysteries and suspicions that normally surround discussions of causality, can be formulated as part of the more familiar problem of scientific induction.

ACKNOWLEDGMENTS

The research was partially supported by Air Force Grant No. F49620-94-1-0173, NSF Grant No. IRI-9420306, and Northrop/Rockwell Micro Grant No. 95-118.

REFERENCES

Aldrich, J. (1994, October). *Correlations genuine and spurious in Pearson and Yule.* (Tech. Rep.). Southampton, UK: University of Southampton, Department of Economics.

Balke, A., & Pearl, J. (1994). Counterfactual probabilities: Computational methods, bounds, and applications. In R. Lopez de Mantaras & D. Poole (Eds.), *Uncertainty in artificial intelligence,* (vol. 10, pp. 46–54). San Mateo, CA: Morgan Kaufmann.

Balke, A., & Pearl, J. (1995). Counterfactuals and policy analysis in structural models. In P. Besnard & S. Hanks (Eds.), *Uncertainty in artificial intelligence* (vol. 11, pp. 11–18). San Francisco: Morgan Kaufmann.

Cartwright, N. (1989). *Nature's capacities and their measurement.* Oxford: Clarendon Press.

Cheng, P. W. (1992). Separating causal laws from causal facts: Pressing the limits of statistical relevance. In D. L. Medin (Ed.), *The psychology of learning and motivation* (vol. 30, pp. 215–264). San Diego, CA: Academic Press.

Cooper, G. F., & Herskovits, E. (1991). A Bayesian method for constructing Bayesian belief networks from databases. In *Proceedings of the Seventh Conference on Uncertainty in Artificial Intelligence* (pp. 86–94). San Francisco: Morgan Kauffman.

Cox, D. R. (1958). *The planning of experiments.* New York: Wiley.

Davis, W. A. (1988). Probabilistic theories of causation. In J. H. Fetzer (Ed.), *Probability and causality* (pp. 133–160). Dordrecht, The Netherlands: D. Reidel.

Eells, E. (1991). *Probabilistic causality.* Cambridge, MA: Cambridge University Press.

Fisher, F. M. (1970). A correspondence principle for simultaneous equations models. *Econometrica, 38,* 73–92.

Galles, D., & Pearl, J. (1995). Testing identifiability of causal effects. In P. Besnard & S. Hanks (Eds.), *Uncertainty in artificial intelligence,* (vol. 11, pp. 185–195). San Francisco: Morgan Kaufmann.

Geiger, D. (1990). *Graphoids: A qualitative framework for probabilistic inference.* Doctoral thesis, University of California, Los Angeles.

Geiger, D., Verma, T. S., & Pearl, J. (1990). Identifying independence in Bayesian networks. *Networks, 20,* 507–534..

Goldszmidt, M., & Pearl, J. (1992). Default ranking: A practical framework for evidential reasoning, belief revision and update. In *Proceedings of the Third International Conference on Knowledge Representation and Reasoning* (pp. 661–672). San Mateo, CA: Morgan Kauffman.

Goldszmidt, M., & Pearl, J. (1996, July). Qualitative probabilities for default reasoning, belief revision, and causal modeling. *Artificial Intelligence.*

Good, I. J. (1961). A causal calculus. I-II. *British Journal for the Philosophy of Science, 11,* 305–318; *12,* 43–51; errata and corrigenda: *13,* 88. (Reprinted in *Good thinking,* by I. J. Good, 1983, Minneapolis: University of Minnesota Press).

Haavelmo, T. (1943). The statistical implications of a system of simultaneous equations. *Econometrica, 11,* 1–12.

Heckerman, D., Geiger, D., & Chickering, D. (1994). Learning Bayesian networks: The combination of knowledge and statistical data. In *Proceedings of the Tenth Conference on Uncertainty in Artificial Intelligence,* (pp. 293–301). San Mateo, CA: Morgan Kaufmann.

Heckerman, D., Shachter, R. (1995). A definition and graphical representation for causality. In *Proceedings of the 11th Conference on Uncertainty in Artificial Intelligence,* (pp. 262–273). San Mateo, CA: Morgan Kaufmann.

Jenkins, H., & Ward, W. (1965). Judgement of contingency between responses and outcomes. *Psychological Monographs, 7,* 1–17.

Kim, J. H., & Pearl, J. (1983). A computational model for combined causal and diagnostic reasoning in inference systems. In *Proceedings of the Eighth International Joint Conference on AI (IJCAI-83)* (pp. 190–193). Karlsruhe, Germany.

Koopman, T. C., & Reiersol, O. (1950). The identification of structural characteristics. *Annals of Mathematical Statistics, 21,* 165–181.

Lauritzen, S. L., & Spiegelhalter, D. J. (1988). Local computations with probabilities on graphical structures and their application to expert systems (with discussion). *Journal of the Royal Statistical Society, Series B, 50*(2), 157–224.

Lewis, D. (1973). *Counterfactuals.* Oxford: Basil Blackwell.

Mulaik, S. A. (1986, September). Toward a synthesis of deterministic and probabilistic formulations of causal relations by the functional relation concept. *Philosophy of Science, 53,* 313–332.

Neyman, J. (1923). On the application of probability theory to agricultural experiments. Essay on principles. Section 9. *Statistical Science, 5*(4), 465–480.

Otte, R. (1981). A critque of suppes' theory of probabilistic causality. *Synthese, 48,* 167–189.

Pearl, J. (1988). *Probabilistic reasoning in intelligence systems.* San Mateo, CA: Morgan Kaufmann. (Revised 2nd printing, 1992)

Pearl, J. (1993a). From Bayesian networks to causal networks. In *Proceedings of the Adaptive Computing and Information Processing Seminar* (pp. 25–27). London: Brunel Conference Centre. See also *Statistical Science, 8*(3), 266–269, 1993.

Pearl, J. (1993b). Graphical models, causality, and interventions. *Statistical Science, 8*(3), 266–269.

Pearl, J. (1994). A probabilistic calculus of actions. In R. Lopez de Mantaras & D. Poole (Eds.), *Uncertainty in artificial intelligence* (vol. 10, pp. 454–462). San Mateo, CA: Morgan Kaufmann.

Pearl, J. (1995). Causal diagrams for experimental research (with discussion). *Biometrika, 82,* 669–710.

Pearl, J., Geiger, D., & Verma, T. (1990). The logic of influence diagrams. In R. M. Oliver & J. Q. Smith (Eds.), *Influence diagrams, belief nets and decision analysis* (pp. 67–87). New York: Wiley.

Pearl, J., & Verma, T. (1991). A theory of inferred causation. In J. A. Allen, R. Fikes, & E. Sandewall (Eds.), *Principles of knowledge representation and reasoning: Proceedings of the Second International Conference* (pp. 441–452). San Mateo, CA: Morgan Kaufmann.

Pearson, K. (1911). *Grammar of science,* (3rd ed.). London: A. and C. Black.

Pratt, J. W., & Schlaifer, R. (1988). On the interpretation and observation of laws. *Journal of Econometrics, 39,* 23–52.

Reichenbach, H. (1956). *The direction of time.* Berkeley: University of California Press.

Robins, J. M. (1986). A new approach to causal inference in mortality studies with a sustained exposure period—applications to control of the healthy workers survivor effect. *Mathematical Modeling, 7,* 1393–1512.

Rosenbaum, P., & Rubin, D. (1983). The central role of propensity score in observational studies for causal effects. *Biometrika, 70,* 41–55.

Rubin, D. B. (1974). Estimating causal effects of treatments in randomized and nonrandomized studies. *Journal of Educational Psychology, 66,* 688–701.

Russell, B. (1913). On the notion of cause. *Proceedings of the Aristotelian Society, 13,* 1–26.

Salmon, W. C. (1984). *Scientific explanation and the causal structure of the world.* Princeton, NJ: Princeton University Press.

Salmon, W. C. (1994). Causality without counterfactuals. *Philosophy of Science Association, 61,* 297–312.

Savage, L. J. (1954). *The foundations of statistics.* New York: Wiley.

Shafer, G. (1996). *The art of causal conjecture.* Cambridge, MA: MIT Press. In press.

Shultz, T. R. (1982). Rules of causal attribution. *Monographs of the Society for Research in Child Development, 47*(1).

Simon, H. A. (1953). Causal ordering and identifiability. In W. C. Hood & T. C. Koopmans (Eds.), *Studies in econometric method* (pp. 49–74). New York: Wiley.

Simpson, E. H. (1951). The interpretation of interaction in contingency tables. *Journal of the Royal Statistical Society, Series B, 13,* 238–241.

Skyrms, B. (1980). *Causal necessity.* New Haven, CT: Yale University Press.

Smith, H. F. (1957). Interpretation of adjusted treatment means and regressions in analysis of covariates. *Biometrics, 13,* 282–308.

Sobel, M. (1990). Effect analysis and causation in linear structural equation models. *Psychometrika, 55*(3), 495–515.

Spiegelhalter, D. J., Lauritzen, S. L., Dawid, P. A., & Cowell, R. G. (1993). Bayesian analysis in expert systems. *Statistical Science, 8,* 219–247.

Spirtes, P., Glymour, C., & Schienes, R. (1993). *Causation, prediction, and search.* New York: Springer-Verlag.

Spohn, W. (1980). Stochastic independence, causal independence, and shieldability. *Journal of Philosophical Logic, 9,* 73–99.

Strotz, R. H., & Wold, H. O. A. (1960). Causal models in the social sciences. *Econometrica, 28,* 417–427.

Suppes, P. (1970). *A probabilistic theory of causation.* Amsterdam: North-Holland.

Verma, T., & Pearl, J. (1988, August). Causal networks: Semantics and expressiveness. *Proceedings of the 4th Workshop on Uncertainty in Artificial Intelligence,* Minneapolis, MN (pp. 352–359). Amsterdam: North-Holland.

Verma, T., & Pearl, J. (1990). Equivalence and synthesis of causal models. In *Proceedings, Sixth Workshop on Uncertainty in Artificial Intelligence,* July 27–29. (pp. 220–227.) Amsterdam: North-Holland.

Wainer, H. (1991). Adjusting for differential base-rates: Lord's paradox again. *Psychological Bulletin, 109,* 147–151.

Waldmann, M. R., Holyoak, K. J., & Fratiannea, A. (1995). Causal models and the acquisition of category structure. *Journal of Experimental Psychology, 124,* 181–206.

Wright, S. (1921). Correlation and causation. *Journal of Agricultural Research, 20,* 557–585.

INDEX

CONTENTS OF RECENT VOLUMES